STRATEGIC HUMAN RESOURCE DEVELOPMENT

John Walton

London Guildhall University

FINANCIAL TIMES
Prentice Hall
An imprint of Pearson Education

Harlow, England · London · New York · Reading, Massachusetts · San Francisco
Toronto · Don Mills, Ontario · Sydney · Tokyo · Singapore · Hong Kong · Seoul
Taipei · Cape Town · Madrid · Mexico City · Amsterdam · Munich · Paris · Milan

Pearson Education Limited
Edinburgh Gate
Harlow
Essex CM20 2JE
England

and Associated Companies
throughout the world

Visit us on the World Wide Web at:
http://www.pearsoneduc.com

First published in Great Britain in 1999

© Pearson Education Limited 1999

The right of John Walton to be identified as Author
of this Work has been asserted by him in accordance
with the Copyright, Designs and Patents Act 1988.

ISBN 0 273 62636 1

British Library Cataloguing in Publication Data
A CIP catalogue record for this book can be obtained
from the British Library

10 9 8 7 6 5 4 3
06 05 04 03 02

Typeset by Pantek Arts Ltd, Maidstone, Kent
Printed and bound in Great Britain by
Ashford Colour Press, Gosport, Hampshire

CONTENTS

Preface   ix

1 Introduction   1
Structure of the book   8

Part 1
GENERAL BACKGROUND

2 The strategic backcloth   13

Objectives   13
Introduction   13
Definitions   14
Strategy management   17
The systematic strategic analysis model   28
Stage 1 Setting the strategic context   30
Stage 2 Assessment and investigation   36
Stage 3 & 4 Reflection leading to strategy
   formulation   41
Stage 5 Strategy implementation
   and monitoring   44
Evaluation of strategy   46
Conclusion   49

3 The emerging concept of human resource
   development   51

Objectives   51
Introduction   51
Definitions   52
The rationale behind the term human resource
   development   56
Recent approaches to human resource
   development   66
The scope of human resource development   74
Conclusion: Is human resource development
   becoming too big?   78

4 Strategic human resource development versus
   human resource development strategies   81

Objectives   81
Introduction   81
Definitions   85
When does a human resource development
   strategy become 'strategic'?   87

What are piecemeal human resource
   development strategies?   88
When do training strategies contribute to
   strategic human resource development?   91
From 'training' to 'training and
   development' strategy   97
From 'training and development' to 'strategic
   human resource development'   99
How appropriate is the formal planning
   model for strategic human resource
   development?   105
Does linking strategic human resource
   planning and development help?   107
Practical examples of strategic human resource
   development   108
Do human resource development strategies
   have to be consistent to be strategic?   113
Creating a favourable organisational learning
   climate   114
Leveraging learning as a core competence   116
The integrated package   116
Conclusion   119

5 The human resource management versus
   personnel management debate and its
   implications for human resource development 121

Objectives   121
Introduction   121
Definitions   122
Human resource management versus
   personnel management   124
Claims for the distinctiveness of human
   resource management   126
Other perspectives on human resource
   management   135
Why did human resource management
   emerge when it did?   137
Human resource management versus
   personnel management in practice   139
The relationship between human resource
   management and human resource
   development   141
Conclusion   147

Part 2

EMERGING HUMAN RESOURCE DEVELOPMENT THEMES

6 Human resource development roles and relationships   153

Objectives   153
Introduction   153
Difference between task (functional) and process (interpretive) roles   154
Human resource development roles   155
Role players   164
New and emergent roles in the 1990s   165
Functional roles   166
Interpretive roles   175
Conclusion   179

7 The emerging role of managers and staff in strategic human resource development   181

Objectives   181
Introduction   181
The relationship between the human resource development function and the line   183
The increasing role of line management in the human resource development process   184
The emerging partnership   188
The role of top management   190
The role of line management   192
Mentoring   193
Coaching   196
The role of line managers in delivering learning   197
Appraisals and performance management   198
Advocacy   201
The role of staff in human resource development   201
The role of the human resource development specialist in the process   207
Conclusion   207

8 Career development in downsized organisations   210

Objectives   210
Introduction   210
Career development as a strategic theme   211
Career anchors   212
The traditional notion of a career   213
What is a career coming to mean?   216
What are the current trends?   221
Conclusion   227

9 Marketing the human resource development function   229

Objectives   229
Introduction   229
Market segmentation   231
Classifying learners by market segment   232
Customer analysis   236
The marketing mix   237
Product   238
Promotion   243
Price   248
Place   250
Marketing plan or marketing strategy?   251
Types of marketing strategy   252
Some problems with adopting a marketing perspective in human resource development   257
Does the marketing of learning require a supporting human resource development function?   258
Conclusion   258

10 The provision of learning support for non-employees   261

Objectives   261
Introduction   261
Non-employees   262
Non-employee stakeholder analysis   263
The value chain and vertical integration   265
The impact of outsourcing on non-employee learning needs   271
Non-employees operating within the organisation who contribute to the primary value chain   272
Non-employees operating within the organisation who contribute to the support value chain   273
Non-employee learning outside the value chain   274
The orchestration of learning processes for non-employees   275
The learning architects as non-employees   276
Conclusion   276

11 Outsourcing: What stays in and what goes out   279

Objectives   279
Introduction   279
The distinction between core and peripheral activities   280
Value chain analysis   281
Outsourcing versus insourcing   282

Outsourcing and out-tasking 284
The outsourcing–insourcing continuum 286
Other outsourcing issues 288
The relationship of outsourcing to core
  competences 289
Practical examples of outsourcing and
  out-tasking 290
Technical training, high-tech training and
  learning support 294
Developed insourcing–outsourcing
  continuum 297
Advantages of outsourcing for human resource
  development practitioners 298
Postscript: The 1997 US industry report of
  employer-sponsored training 298
Conclusion 299

**12 Benchmarking human resource
  development** 301

Objectives 301
Introduction 301
Defining benchmarking 303
The origins of benchmarking 304
Aspects of benchmarking 305
The benchmarking process 308
Benchmarking and human resource
  development 312
Practices and human resource development 316
Benchmarking and organisational learning 320
Global benchmarking and human resource
  development 320
Conclusion 322

**13 Small and medium-sized enterprises and
  human resource development** 324

Objectives 324
Introduction 324
Setting the context 326
Formal training in small and medium-sized
  enterprises 328
Informal and accidental human resource
  development processes in small and
  medium-sized enterprises and the
  development of tacit skills 330
Are more human resource development
  activities being undertaken than was
  hitherto recognised? 332
Differentiating between small and medium-
  sized enterprises for human resource
  development purposes 333

Developing structured human resource
  development initiatives in and for small
  and medium-sized enterprises 342
Conclusion 347

Part 3

ORGANISATION-WIDE LEARNING ISSUES

**14 Total Quality Management
  and human resource development** 355

Objectives 355
Introduction 355
Background to Total Quality Management 357
Deming 357
Juran 359
Crosby 361
Quality circles 363
Labelling the Total Quality Management effort 366
The Total Quality principles in the 1990s 366
Examples of organisational practice 368
Quality awards 374
Conclusion 379

15 The learning organisation 381

Objectives 381
Introduction 381
Can organisations learn? 384
Three levels of learning in organisations 387
Learning organisation frameworks 390
Company examples 401
The development perspective towards
  becoming a learning organisation 407
Implications for human resource development
  practitioners 407
Conclusion 409

**16 Human resource development and the
  corporate university** 412

Objectives 412
Introduction 412
From training schools to corporate
  universities 414
First-generation corporate universities 417
Second-generation corporate universities:
  The Motorola University 421
Vision and mission statements of corporate
  universities 425
The relationship between education and
  training 426
Corporate universities in the UK – towards
  the third-generation virtual university 429

Where do corporate universities fit into the overall strategic human resource development picture? 434
Conclusion 434

17 Managing transformational change from a human resource development perspective 438

Objectives 438
Introduction 438
Types of change: Developing a vocabulary 440
Transformational change 441
Transformational change versus transactional change 443
Transitional change 443
Incremental change 445
Metaphors for change 446
Plotting the scale, extent and style of proposed changes 447
Differentiating between organisational and individual dynamics in the change process 449
Handling the interplay of forces 452
The paradoxes of transformational change 453
The triggers for change 454
The levers of change 455
Stages in the management of transformational change from a human resource development perspective 457
Evaluation of transformational change 474
Conclusion 475

18 The role of human resource development in creating synergy among business units and sub-units 479

Objectives 479
Introduction 479
Creating synergies in existing organisations 482
The 'everything but' rule 486
Horizontal strategy 487
Synergy and diversification 488
Strategic alliances 495
Human resource development strategies to enhance synergy 496
Conclusion 501

19 Operating in a global environment 503

Objectives 503
Introduction 503

What is a 'global company'? 505
Four approaches to operating internationally 506
Where do the managers come from? 510
The global mindset 511
Target market for human resource development interventions 512
Cross-cultural issues 514
The human resource development contribution 519
Conclusion 533

20 Working in the virtual organisation 536

Objectives 536
Introduction 536
The virtual organisation as a network 537
The virtual organisation and electronic technology 543
Human resource development implications 549
Conclusion 556

Part 4

ORGANISATIONAL VALUES

21 The contribution of human resource development to the development of an organisational value base: commitment, business ethics, managing diversity and environmentalism 561

Objectives 561
Introduction 561
Objectives versus values 562
Definitions of organisational values 567
Types of organisational values 567
Whose values? 572
The value of 'commitment' in the literature 576
The values of human resource development practitioners 579
Manifestation of values in specific areas 581
Business ethics 582
Managing diversity 586
Environmental management 592
Conclusion 597

Author index 599
Subject index 605

PREFACE

This book is aimed at those who wish to become more familiar with strategic themes impacting upon the field of Human Resource Development. It is designed to appeal to both students undertaking higher level academic and professional qualifications and practitioners engaging in Continuing Professional Development (CPD). The objective is to provide avenues of thought and explanatory frameworks which will guide learning and enable people to reflect upon and develop practice. Accordingly, there is a conscious attempt throughout the text to incorporate a range of examples and arguments which balance theoretical and practical considerations.

Although it is designed to be broad in its coverage of strategic perspectives on HRD, the structure adopted is not that of a conventional textbook, and the purpose has not been to produce a compendium. Following a general introduction to strategic principles and to the emergent field of HRD, my approach has been to identify a set of strategic themes which are impacting on the world of work in general, and on the world of the HRD practitioner in particular, and to evaluate them in some detail. Although there are connecting references throughout the text, each chapter has been written as a self-contained topic in its own right. The process of selection in which I have engaged might mean that issues which some readers consider important have been omitted, and that others in which a given reader might be less interested included. Nevertheless, it has not been a capricious process, but is based upon a burgeoning body of practice drawn from both primary and secondary sources. The topics chosen have been discussed and analysed by my Masters students over the years and have proved relevant and valuable to them. The book is testimony to the debates in which we have engaged and to the insights these have provided.

Throughout the book a number of case study examples are provided in order to ground theoretical considerations. The majority have come from the UK and the USA, both because these have been the most frequently reported in the literature and because of my own limitations in accessing primary sources, but a number of examples from other countries have been included. Case studies provide a richness in terms of what is happening in the world at large and have a practical 'lived-in' feel to them. However, they can date remarkably quickly as organisational decision makers modify, adjust and sometimes overturn practices. Case studies should thus be treated as no more than examples – for purposes of illustration – from a given moment in time, and should not be relied upon as describing what an organisation is currently engaging in.

This book took three years to write. Even over such a short period things can change very quickly. In looking at some of the chapters written earlier, I notice how much my thinking has evolved. If I were starting the book today, there might be some different emphases, although its overall character would not be substantially different.

When I first undertook to write this book, I was aware neither of what a lonely undertaking it would be, nor how long it would take. My original proposal was for a work of 160 000 words – a daunting enough task in itself. My publisher 'talked it up' to 220 000 words and the final submission was some 240 000 words with two chapters 'in reserve'.

Writing a book of this size and nature has required some of the qualities of the Venerable Bede – tenacity and isolation. Because of the nature of the thought processes involved, I found myself switching off for long periods of time from the 'real world' – hard on the people 'out there' who are trying to communicate day-to-day concerns. And how could I have imagined the variety and ingenuity of displacement activities that can be engaged in to avoid having to sit in front of the word processor?

There have been a number of influences that have informed my thinking on the subject. For many years I have been a member of the Strategic Planning Society based in the UK, and have always felt that HRD interventions and processes in organisations should be subjected to an overriding strategic scrutiny. I am indebted to my Masters students and colleagues (and those from other centres with which I have been associated in my capacity as external examiner), who over the years have helped to develop my view of strategic approaches to HRD from an operational standpoint. I have attended a number of conferences in the United States run by both the American Society for Training and Development and by the Academy of Human Resource Development, and these have broadened my horizons from both a pragmatic and a research perspective. The overseas exchange visits co-ordinated by the EURESFORM network for my Masters students have provided a rich source of data on emergent practices in the Netherlands and France, and have contributed to my understanding on convergence versus divergence of approach across cultures.

During its gestation, the book has had many midwives. I have had the support of two editors. Penelope Woolf started me off, and I am very grateful for her comments on a number of my draft chapters as they came off the press. Sadie McClelland, who took over from her, has also been very supportive, gently steering me towards a deadline. I shall never forget hand-delivering the final manuscript to her late one Thursday afternoon in August 1998, after having worked on it non-stop for the previous two weeks with diminishing amounts of sleep. My Head of Department at London Guildhall University, Sue Proudfoot, has also been very understanding, trying to ensure that I was not unduly burdened with other commitments as the book moved towards completion. Last, and most important of all, I am particularly indebted to my wife Sue who gave me the time and space to stick at it over the three years.

Chapter 1

INTRODUCTION

This book is concerned with identifying and evaluating current and emergent themes about which professionals in the human resource development (HRD) field need to know in order to increase their strategic awareness and effectiveness. It is not designed to be a manual or a recipe book.

It is written for people who wish to become more familiar with organisation-wide learning and development processes. More particularly, it is about human resource development *strategies* which can contribute to the overall direction of organisations as well as benefiting individual learners.

As we shall see, HRD has been subjected to a number of definitions, interpretations and challenges since the term was first coined in the late 1960s. In its broadest sense it is about development and change through learning; about how, what and where individuals learn, and about what Lyon (1996) describes as 'encouraging people to develop and grow from dependency to independency to interdependency'. But this is too broad for the purposes of this text. We are not concerned with how individuals learn from cradle to grave, although notions of lifelong learning and continuous personal development are very current and pertinent. We pick up the story in the world of work, and focus on the skills, knowledge and abilities that people need in order to operate and co-operate effectively in a 'vocational' arena. Our concern is with approaches which facilitate and guide and co-ordinate work-related learning – recognising that the notion of what constitutes a 'workplace' is itself undergoing a transformation.

However, Lyon's definition of HRD draws attention to an ongoing tension associated with setting up HRD strategies in an organisational context. In such a situation there may be boundaries and possibly a purely instrumental value attached to what is permissible learning. HRD practitioners are often uncomfortable about seeing people just as a *work-force*; viewing them as such appears to limit the aim of learning to maximising *resource* potential. 'Work-force' implies something impersonal, 'large', co-ordinated and compliant. HRD is much more individualistic in conception. It can recognise and encourage individual aspirations. In its purest form it is neutral as to where skills/abilities are demonstrated so long as learning has taken place. If its goal is learning and personal growth, then its 'customers' need not be tied to an individual employer. In this sense it is fundamentally different to 'training' someone in a specific non-transferable skill.

Nevertheless many HRD practitioners operate within a given institutional context. They need to demonstrate that their activities add value to the organisation which is their paymaster. It is not sufficient to argue that their interventions and programmes are well received if the consequence is that people subsequently leave in droves to competitors. It is the basic dilemma, addressed many years ago by

Chris Argyris. How do we integrate the needs of individuals and organisations (Argyris, 1964)?

Swanson and Arnold (1997) consider that HRD in an organisational context has no meaning unless the connection is made to performance. They go even further and state that its basic purpose is to contribute directly to the organisation's goals through improving performance. They reach this position by concluding that the dependent variable of HRD is 'the measurable increase in performance which is the direct result of organisational development and/or personnel training and development' and not some other factor such as individual learning or participant satisfaction with a training intervention' – a position echoed by many. Speaking in advance of the UK Government's 1998 Green Paper, 'The Learning Age', Roy Harrison, policy adviser on education and training of the Institute of Personnel Development, adopted a similar instrumental orientation to HRD when he asked, 'Learning for what? No-one has defined it. An employer doesn't teach for the sake of learning ... What are the rewards?' (Welch, 1998).

This book, without focusing on individual learning as a desideratum in its own right, does not adopt such a hard-line utilitarian standpoint. It recognises that such a purpose may be true for most training-related activities – indeed methods such as just-in-time training are clearly concerned with cementing the connection with performance-in-task behaviours. But this does not reflect the broad scope of HRD notions prevalent today such as lifelong learning, continuous personal development, career self-reliance and the learning organisation.

Neither does it represent much of what is happening in the field. Indeed many organisations encourage broad educational and non-performance-specific development activities as a way of adding to their attractiveness as an employer. Companies such as Ford give each individual employee a sum of money to spend each year on a learning activity which may bear no relationship to workplace learning. This is part of a wider phenomenon whereby individuals increasingly see organisationally sponsored acquisition of transferable knowledge and skills as a reward – even an inducement – in its own right, a means to secure future employability. HRD thus becomes part of the organisation's reward structure irrespective of any contribution to its performance system. It is a measure of how times, and with them demands, have changed. The gradual removal of glass ceilings based on gender, race, class or educational background have further contributed to the greater perceived relevance to individuals of personal development.

It goes deeper than that. In the past it was assumed that a high percentage of people would stay with a given employer – there would be a career for some, job security for others. Commitment was associated with lifelong loyalty to 'the firm'. In today's world the received wisdom is that individuals can expect five or six career shifts in their lifetime. The legacy of the organisational downsizing of recent years is that the old psychological employment contract based on 'trust' is breaking down and the new 'knowledge workers' whose skills are at a premium will want guarantees of future employability wherever that might be. In a competitive marketplace for scarce intellectual resources commitment may still be the goal – but it has been reconfigured. The new challenge is to generate commitment for the duration of an individual's stay by offering the opportunity to acquire transferable skills. That is the new dependent variable of HRD. Organisational policy makers are being levered into providing learning and development activities which may have no direct bearing on the organisation's performance.

From the above it is apparent that much of the learning that this book on strategic HRD addresses takes place within or for organisations. But, as a result of global competitive pressures, IT breakthroughs and heightened customer expectations, the organisational landscape and architecture of today are not the same as those of twenty years ago. We have moved into what some term 'the post-industrial era' and what others describe as 'the Information Age'. In the developed world, large labour-intensive corporations with a high concentration of semi-skilled operatives are becoming a thing of the past. Technological developments have made possible the realisation of the location-independent virtual organisation. Business organisations are repositioning themselves in the global marketplace through strategic alliances, mergers and acquisitions, often across national boundaries. Pressures go well beyond resolving the efficiency, quality and customer service concerns which dominated the 1980s. What is significant today is not only the impact of IT on organisational forms and boundaries, but also the importance of an ecological awareness, new perspectives on business ethics – perhaps a move away from unbridled competition if resources are to be sustained.

Major organisation-wide initiatives such as Total Quality Management (TQM) and Business Process Reengineering have been undertaken to enhance the response capability of organisations. Other changes in structure and process are being introduced across the organisational spectrum to support creativity and innovation. Many organisations are in transition as the implications of such forces work their way through the system.

In such an environment, it is held, people are the only truly sustainable resource providing long-term competitive and customer advantage. Any organisation can quickly access the elements of new technology, reverse-engineer products; what is scarcer are the distinctive skills or competences which individuals bring to, and acquire during their stay with, a given enterprise. Waterman (1994) and Garfield (1992) are just two of a stream of influential American authors who argue that these competences can best be generated in the context of collaborative partnerships and team working. Others refer to the creation of learning organisations and corporate universities, and to the era of the 'knowledge worker', seen as a key source of 'intellectual capital', who can be empowered and trusted to take decisions and come up with innovative solutions without automatic reference to a higher authority. Throughout this book, examples will be provided to show that these notions with their accompanying rhetoric are filtering into organisational vocabulary and usage.

A number of writers have forcefully argued that the organisations of today need to go through a paradigm shift and be reinvented to accommodate these global, competitive and societal influences. Kuhn (1970) defines paradigm as 'a constellation of concepts, values, perceptions, and practices shared by a community which forms a particular vision of reality that is the basis of the way a community organises itself'. A community can be a nation state, a work organisation, or members of a specific discipline/professional body.

A paradigm is thus a set of beliefs or 'taken for granted' assumptions we make about our world, which in time become unchallenged and unchallengeable. By virtue of associating with other people we come to share a particular way of perceiving this world and this determines the range of acceptable explanations and courses of action we feel able to draw upon.

Another way of thinking about a paradigm is to treat it as an interpretive device invented in order to provide us with a practical route map for making our way in the world. The map enables us to sort out complexity, to comprehend, evaluate, categorise and filter the information that comes to us rapidly and incessantly from all directions.

In the sphere of work organisations our mental map – what we hold to be 'true' about the world and its workings – dictates, among many other things: which ethical standards we accept; how we organise the workplace; how we organise ourselves as managers and colleagues; how we treat new and experienced employees; which people we select and promote; how much of our resources we devote to training and development; how we treat customers; how we respond to competition and how we are involved with the community outside the workplace.

Garfield (op. cit.) generates another image, that of stories, to explain the notion of a paradigm and how it might be applied to the business world (*see* Fig. 1.1.).

Figure 1.1 A new organisational paradigm?

Garfield contends that most of us are not conscious of the stories by which we operate, but they dictate our behaviour nevertheless. He suggests that past behaviour in business organisations in the United States in particular, and in Western companies in general, has been underpinned by four main stories.

- the story of the organisation as a finely tuned machine;
- the story of progress as unlimited growth;
- the story of the pyramid as the primary structure of the organisation;
- the story of the lone pioneer, the rugged individualist, as the hero of the business world.

These stories have all outlived their usefulness and need to be replaced by a new story that has greater explanatory and functional power in the current economic and social environment. This is what Kuhn (op. cit.) termed a 'paradigm shift'.

He contends that creating a new story is not the same as pushing old stories to the limit. He quotes Pascale (1991) who stated at the end of the 1980s that: 'The trouble is, 99% of managerial attention today is devoted to the techniques that squeeze more out of the existing paradigm – and it's killing us. Tools, techniques, and 'how-to' recipes won't do the job without a higher order . . . concept of management.'

He feels that the 1980s witnessed the failure of many such how-to recipes. During that decade, most attempts to deal with a changing business landscape were partial ones. Senior management 'hopscotched' from one campaign to another – from organisational excellence to quality improvement, to customer service, to employee participation – in attempts to find the secret that would spark a 'management revolution' and make for greater competitiveness in the new global economy.

By and large, these attempts represented, not a paradigm shift, not a fundamentally changed view of the world and the corporation, but a revival of tired old strategies that were rendered ineffective because the old perceptions remained.

▶▶

▶▶ Figure 1.1 continued

Employee participation campaigns were thwarted by rigid hierarchies and by managers accustomed to command and control. Quality improvement campaigns were undermined by conflicting emphases on short-term deadlines and maximising profits. Campaigns to 'achieve excellence' fell flat in organisations that had been systematically demoralised by failed management promises, massive layoffs and generally poor treatment.

These attempts represented not so much creative responses to change as predictable reactions to it, desperate attempts to *stave off change*. They failed because they were based on stories that made sense in the industrial era but are ill suited to today's realities.

What is needed is a more powerful, more appropriate story to guide us into the next millennium. While the details need to be explored, the following features seem to be emerging. An upheaval is taking place at every level, and in every department of the corporation, as businesses transform themselves to cope with changing economic and social realities. IT is shifting the balance of power from the executive suite to the factory floor. Rigid, authoritarian styles of management are being discarded in favour of greater employee participation in decision making. Less hierarchical, more fluid organisational forms are being tried. Unions and management are being transformed from adversaries into allies. Command-and-control managers are becoming coaches and counsellors. The central theme of these changes is **partnership**. The effect is a paradigm shift. A 'partnership' paradigm entails a different set of skills and competences for organisational members. It also means 'unlearning' old ways of operating.

Source: Based on Garfield (1992).

There is a considerable body of evidence that Garfield's prognosis of a partnership model is manifesting itself in organisational practice. There is a growing trend to refer to employees as 'partners' or 'associates' (e.g. Rolls-Royce) or 'company members' (e.g. Toyota) to reflect the nature of an emerging 'commitment' contract. Throughout the book examples from organisational literature will be drawn upon to reflect a 'partners in performance and development' perspective. However, it would be a mistake to assume that a partnership ethos is going to become a ubiquitous organisational paradigm of the future. It is also a mistake to assume that there is a single 'partnership' concept based on a strengthening of the employer–employee relationship. A number of organisations have developed strategic partnerships with providers as part of an outsourcing philosophy.

If we accept that the old organisational paradigm is changing, then this should be reflected in a change in the prevailing HRD paradigm. One of the objects of this book is to explore whether, in the HRD world, there is a paradigm shift concerning:

■ the parameters of our discipline;

■ the core generalisations on the functioning of that world;

■ the key problems confronting us;

■ acceptable solutions to the problems;

- methods to be employed to study the field and carry out experiments;
- definitions of examples regarded as typical of the phenomena being dealt with;
- whether this world is different to that of HRM or other disciplines for which 'people issues' are their primary concern: and if so, how.

This in turn entails identifying previous HRD traditions and established boundaries to provide a basis for comparison.

One continuing theme of this book is that current organisational strategic thinking puts a high premium on learning – individual, team and organisational – as a way of helping people within an organisation to:

- recognise and interpret the relationship between its internal capability, external environment forces and strategic intent;
- set in train processes which have the potential to revolutionise its dynamics and transform its operating characteristics;
- generate 'intellectual capital' through individual and collective knowledge.

The era of the self-reliant knowledge worker can also become the era of the HRD professional – the learning architects of organisations and of learning itself – if only such learning architects themselves have the skills, vision and power base to see things through. This book is addressed to those who wish to become better and more effective learning architects – who have the patience and resilience to work through the sometimes contradictory remedies and suggestions available and to properly equip themselves to operate in the twenty-first century. They will need to work in partnership with other key players, with other HR specialists, line managers, government agencies, career guidance professionals. They will need to demonstrate familiarity with strategic concepts, change management approaches, group facilitation processes and individual counselling techniques as well as to exercise sophisticated negotiation skills and handle the subtleties of power dynamics. They will need to recognise that each case is different and that recipes recommended by others might reveal some insights but that the realities of the situation will dictate ways forward.

In this emerging world it is no longer adequate to see HRD as an exclusively organisation-centred practice. If lifelong learning has any meaning it has a truly individual orientation and is not tied to learning for a given organisation. Because organisations no longer guarantee lifelong employment, individuals must take a far greater responsibility than in the past for their careers and employability. Because highly skilled and motivated knowledge workers are at a premium, employers cannot afford to neglect their role in this employability.

In the past HRD careers in organisations have been largely locked into a functional arena which has deemed its core activity to be training provision. There is increasing evidence of new thinking and practice concerning the role of the HRD professionals as architects of learning. For instance a split is becoming apparent between the delivery side of training and the provision of courses etc. on the one hand, and an internal consultancy role on the other. A good example is the following job advertisement (*see* Fig.1.2):

Figure 1.2	Job advertisement placed by Pearl Assurance

INTERNAL TRAINING AND DEVELOPMENT CONSULTANT

Training delivery is not the priority. The role is to work very closely with line management in a specified line of business to identify how performance can be improved. This may involve training – it may not . . . you will have influencing skills, bottom line orientation and a passion for performance. Knowledge of a wide range of learning solutions is a must.

Source: *People Management*, 11 January 1996.

There is an abiding impression from the literature and from organisational practice that much of what now is seen to constitute HRD does not emanate from, nor in some instances does it involve, the career professional. New insights on HRD are as likely to be developed in the pages of the *Harvard Business Review* and *Long Range Planning*, as in the journals of the HR profession. The driving forces for HRD today are often chief executives and senior management, familiar with mainstream strategy literature and thinking, and who are reconsidering how to prepare and position human resources in the competitive marketplace. It may be a matter of indifference to them whether HR professionals are involved in the process of development. Indeed, writers from the Harvard Business School have influenced thinking, with the result that some feel that HR practitioners are far too operationally oriented and restricted in their thinking about their job role to be trusted with strategic decision-making processes (e.g. Beer and Spector, 1985). Ulrich (1998) even goes so far as to warn HR practitioners about the 'value sapping' way in which many of their activities are seen.

A consequence is that many of the more exciting HRD roles are being undertaken by individuals with operational management experience and no prior involvement in HRD. In many instances they are the 'champions' and sponsors of learning. Throughout this book, reference is made to organisation-wide macro-learning initiatives and inward investments into learning and development which seem to be independent of any HR involvement.

In the broader context this might seem not to matter. Yet many learning-based change initiatives run the risk of collapsing because those responsible for them have insufficient understanding of how individuals learn. In terms of career progression routes for HR staff, it is very important to demonstrate the value of ensuring that properly equipped seasoned professionals drive the learning process.

Accordingly the book consists of an extended analysis based on a series of propositions and assumptions.

1 The object of HRD strategy is individual and collective *learning* and the desired outcome is *development* of thinking and practice.

2 How individual and team learning are embedded in an organisation can become a distinctive and valued competence for that organisation and a source of differentiation from what takes place in other organisations.

3 Learning in organisations is not automatically, or even primarily, restricted to training interventions. Learning and development occur in a range of

intentional situations and accidental circumstances, which collectively add to the skills and knowledge base that people draw upon in the exercise in their organisational roles.

4 Human resource development gains in meaning and significance when its contribution to enhancing the strategic capability and intellectual capital of an organisation is clearly spelled out and understood across the spectrum of the membership.

5 For learning and development to take place effectively, have strategic focus and become a distinctive organisational competence, supporting processes are required, steered and guided by appropriately positioned specialists.

6 This will not happen if the tendency to accord low status to those specialists responsible for the accomplishment of HRD in an organisational context persists.

7 In turn, individual practitioners will need to acquire a strategic vocabulary and awareness, and demonstrate their fitness for purpose.

8 The likelihood of learning becoming a distinctive organisational competence will be greater when the HRD effort moves beyond an introspective performance-in-task orientation and takes into account the learning needs of individuals seeking to secure future employability. This necessitates a supportive learning climate that will foster development as an end in itself.

Some of these propositions are capable of being tested. For example throughout the text evidence will be provided to support the contention that HRD gains in significance when its contribution to strategic direction is spelled out. Some are based on theoretical modelling undertaken to underpin the text; in other words, my view of what strategic HRD entails determines the chapter headings and the content of chapters. What is excluded can often be as informative as what is included! In some ways I am also making predictions. In environmental scanning terms I am identifying what for some might be seen as weak signals in the environment and judging that they will become sources of interest and concern.

STRUCTURE OF THE BOOK

The book is organised into four parts and has the structure shown in Fig. 1.3.

Part 1 provides a general overview. Chapter 2 contains a strategic backcloth in which HRD strategies can be contextualised. Current perspectives on HRD are addressed in Chapter 3 in preparation for an analysis in Chapter 4 of approaches to strategic HRD. Chapter 5 explores the relationship between HRD and Human Resource Management (HRM).

Part 2 looks in more detail at some specific themes arising from the general overview. Chapter 6 addresses the emergence of new HRD roles. Chapter 7 considers the role of management and staff in an overall partnership in development. Chapter 8 looks at some of the current trends in career development and their implications for learners and learning. Chapter 9 subjects HRD and the HRD function to a marketing appraisal. Non-employee learning issues are considered in Chapter 10. Chapter 11 deals with the current interest in outsourcing and considers a range of HRD outsourcing – and insourcing – positions. Chapter 12 evaluates benchmarking from an HRD standpoint. Finally in this part, Chapter 13 focuses upon HRD issues for small and medium-sized enterprises (SMEs).

Figure 1.3 Structure of the book: chapter sequence

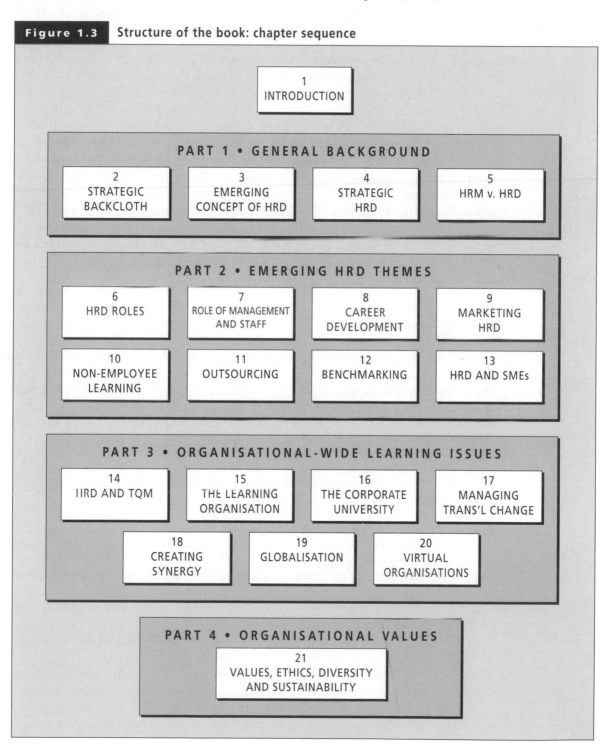

Part 3 considers broad-based organisation-wide learning issues. Chapter 14 by way of introduction demonstrates the impact that Total Quality Management (TQM) initiatives have had upon learning and upon providing the basis for a strategic learning philosophy. That theme is then pursued in Chapter 15 on the 'Learning Organisation'. Chapter 16 looks at the growth of corporate universities and evaluates whether they operate from a traditional training and development perspective or whether they represent an overarching philosophy of organisational learning. Chapter 17 then tackles the topic of managing transformational change from an HRD perspective. Many examples of transformational change occur because of strategic alliances and mergers; Chapter 18 provides a framework for an HRD contribution towards creating synergy between business units and sub-units. This leads on to considering in Chapter 19 the implications for HRD of the global corporation. Chapter 20 looks at the emergence of new organisational forms associated with the virtual organisation and how HRD perspectives can contribute to enhancing learning.

Part 4 consists of Chapter 21 which discusses the current interest in propagating organisational values, and the part HRD plays in the process. Following a general overview of values, this chapter addresses specific HRD issues which are associated with organisational approaches to business ethics, managing diversity and sustainability.

REFERENCES

Argyris, C. (1964) *Integrating the Individual and the Organisation*. New York: Wiley.

Beer, M. and Spector, B. (1985) 'Corporate Transformations in Human Resource Management' in R. E. Walton and P. R. Lawrence (eds) *HRM Trends and Challenges*. Cambridge, MA: Harvard Business School Press.

Garfield, C. (1992) *Second to None – The Productive Power of Putting People First*. Chicago: Business One Irwin.

Kuhn, T. S. (1970) *The Structure of Scientific Revolutions*. Chicago: University of Chicago Press.

Lyon, U. (1996) 'Influence, Communication and Neuro-Linguistic Programming in Practice', pp. 221–39, in J. Stewart and J. McGoldrick (eds) *Human Resource Development – Perspectives, Strategies and Practice*. London: Pitman.

Pascale, R. T. (1991) *Managing on the Edge*. Harmondsworth: Penguin.

Swanson, R. A. and Arnold, D. E. (1997) 'The Purpose of Human Resource Development is to Improve Performance'. Paper presented to the Academy of Human Resource Development Conference, Atlanta, 6–9 March.

Ulrich, D. (1998) 'A New Mandate for Human Resources', *Harvard Business Review*, January–February.

Waterman, R. (1994) *The Frontiers of Excellence – Learning from Companies that Put People First*. London: Nicholas Brealey.

Welch, J. (1998) 'Woolly thinking hampers view of a learning society', *People Management*, 8 January.

Part 1

GENERAL BACKGROUND

THE STRATEGIC BACKCLOTH

INTRODUCTION

In order to gain a full understanding of strategic approaches to HRD and of the contribution that HRD can make to the formulation and implementation of corporate strategy it is necessary to appreciate the nature of the strategic management process engaged in by corporate decision makers. How do they perceive strategy? What language do they use to refer to strategic issues? Without such an understanding members of the HRD profession are confronted with a communication chasm, a lack of credibility and a glass ceiling.

The chapter addresses a number of perspectives on strategy and provides a general scheme around core themes. It will not go into the level of detail found in specialised texts on strategic management. The chapter emphasises the significance in strategic thinking of the notions of 'strategic intent', 'core competences' and 'strategic capability'. It touches upon the increasing reference to 'learning' and 'people development' as sources of strategic concern contributing to competitive advantage. It also presents criticisms of adopting a formalised planning process as a means to strategy formulation.

DEFINITIONS

Definitio

The term   nilitary associations. It is
defined in   alship, or the art of conducting a   ciated terms of military
origin are   e presence of the enemy',
stratagem   advantage' and *logistics*,
'the art o   of the practical detail of
any large   War of the early 1990s
Schwarzk   eputed to have said that
strategy i   ess in achieving military
objective   btained about the intentions and   an be extended in terms
of condu   ggressor in an offensive
campaign   defender will be trying
to preser   create barriers to entry.
Accordin   ing a status quo. Both
aggressor   ort.

I am a   s in the conduct of this
game. In   y differentiated. Strategy
is the app   ion of your pieces on the
chess boa   uid position, others for a
closed po   ot, however, a matter of
free choic   pproach adopted by your
opponen   mpts to destabilise one's
opponen   hrusts. Note that in chess
the objec   Sometimes you may wish
simply n

It is no surprise that the above terms have been imported into the non-military yet intensely competitive world of business organisations which are jockeying for position in the marketplace, nor that they still retain some of their original connotations. The 'enemy' is now the 'competition'. 'Strategy' in commercial terms is often associated with *deployment* of resources, *outflanking* the competition, establishing *beachheads* in the global marketplace, creating *strategic alliances*. Manoeuvrability, availability of resources, flexibility of thinking and 'surprise' become integral features to the effective conduct of the resultant 'campaign'. *Surprise* is Janus faced; one aspect is to generate unpleasant surprises for the competition, the other aspect is to avoid unpleasant surprises from them. Military strategists from the past are still quoted for their insights into the strategic process. Hinterhuber and Popp (1992) devote a whole article in an issue of the *Harvard Business Review* to drawing business lessons from the writings of Helmuth von Moltke, Chief of the Prussian General Staff at the time of the unification of Germany in the nineteenth century. For him strategy was 'the evolution of the original guiding idea according to continually changing circumstances'.

Strategic intent

Hamel and Prahalad (1989), in an article which is littered with military analogies, use the term 'strategic intent' to capture a similar meaning. For them strategic intent envisages a desired leadership position (Moltke's 'original guiding idea') *vis-à-vis* the competition, and establishes a simple and focused criterion by which the organisation will chart progress towards its achievement. This approach, they contend, was adopted in the 1970s and 1980s by Japanese companies which were trying to take on far larger American rivals in the global marketplace. Thus Komatsu set out to 'Encircle Caterpillar' and Canon aimed to 'Beat Xerox'. They emphasise that strategic intent captures the strategic essence of winning and is also stable over time. As they put it, 'In battles for global leadership, one of the most critical tasks is to lengthen the organisation's attention span. Strategic intent provides consistency to short-term action, while leaving room for reinterpretation as new opportunities emerge.' In other words, be prepared for a long campaign and don't be deflected from your original purpose.

The hierarchy of strategic intent

The concept of strategy is not dependent upon such a single-minded and expansionist view of where one is going. If strategic intent, so interpreted, is a defining characteristic of strategy then many organisations are not engaging in strategy at all, and would not wish to. Nevertheless, it is clearly helpful to have some sense of what you are trying to achieve over the long term that will direct your actions. One way of conceiving this is to differentiate analytically between very broad-based objectives of intention and direction (such as 'vision' and 'mission'), and more specific and measurable objectives of result. Miller and Dess (1996) use the term 'hierarchy of strategic intentions' to capture this distinction. Their proposed conceptual hierarchy for seeking and setting direction adopts the following sequence:

1 A broad *vision* of what the organisation should be.

2 The organisation's *mission*.

3 Specific *goals*. These are operationalised as:

4 Strategic *objectives*.

Xerox is an example of an organisation that follows this broad outline. Andrew Smith, Quality Director of Xerox Document Company Ltd, referred to its practical application in terms of *policy deployment*, which he defined as the process of turning strategic intent into an annual operating plan (*see* Fig. 2.1).

It is noticeable that in this formulation, strategy is 'downstream' from 'vision'. Strategy becomes the process adopted for getting the organisation 'from here to there' (Wickens, 1987). It does not explicitly incorporate 'core values' which many organisations spell out in addition to their vision and mission. Argenti (1980) calls these 'ethological objectives' and they constitute a general statement of how the organisation wishes to conduct its transactions and be perceived by its various constituent stakeholders and publics.

Figure 2.1 Policy deployment

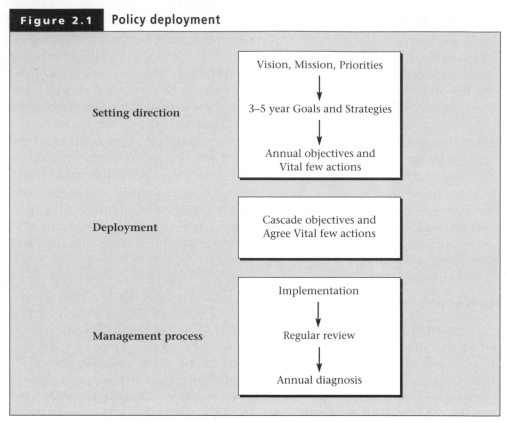

Source: Presentation by Andrew Smith, Quality Director, Xerox Ltd, Café Royale, London, March 1998.

Definitions of organisation strategy

There are a number of definitions of organisational strategy in the literature which are somewhat less prescriptive than that given by Hamel and Prahabad (op. cit.), of which the two given below are typical.

> A decision or series of decisions made by or on behalf of an organisation or organisational sub-unit which determines its medium to long term objectives, priorities and overall direction; and which repositions the organisation in relation to its changing external environment, including competitive pressures and the availability of key resources (Open Business School, 1991).

> Strategy can be seen as a key link between what the organisation wants to achieve – its objectives – and the policies adopted to guide its activities (Bowman and Asch, 1987).

These definitions emphasise:

- decisions
- change
- policies and objectives
- medium- to long-term perspective
- environment

- positioning
- competitive pressures
- managing resources.

They are designed to underpin approaches to strategy management.

STRATEGY MANAGEMENT

The literature on strategy management on the whole contends that strategic issues can be handled systematically and 'managed'. Strategy management is held to consist of three logical and sequential stages: preparatory fact-finding analysis; option generation and choice; and implementation.

Burnes (1992), from a survey of definitions of strategic management argues that the following basic features stand out. These are that strategic management is primarily concerned with:

- the full scope of an organisation's activities, including corporate objectives and organisational boundaries;
- matching the activities of an organisation to the environment in which it operates;
- ensuring that the internal structures, practices and procedures enable the organisation to achieve its objectives;
- matching the activities of an organisation to its resource capability, assessing the extent to which sufficient resources can be provided to take advantage of opportunities or avoid threats in the organisation's environment;
- the acquisition, divestment and reallocation of resources;
- translating the complex and dynamic set of external and internal variables which an organisation faces, into a structured set of clear future objectives which can then be implemented on a day-to-day basis.

Note that Burnes does not make explicit reference to the identification and subsequent development of strategies for the handling of key internal and external stakeholders.

From all the above it is relatively straightforward to develop a definition of strategic management.

> Strategic management is the process of making and implementing strategic decisions ... [It] is about the process of strategic change. [It is] the match an organisation makes between its own resources and the threats or risks and opportunities created by the external environment in which it operates (Bowman and Asch, 1987).

Hamel and Prahalad (op. cit.) advise caution against relying on notions such as 'strategic fit' which are implied by the matching process. For them, 'the application of concepts such as "strategic fit" [between resources and opportunities] ... have often abetted the process of competitive decline'.

According to Stewart and Ranson (1988), strategic management in the public sector also expresses values determined through the political process in response to a changing environment. They ask whether it is meaningful in the public sector to think of competitive pressures. Can public sector organisations pull out of products/markets if the environment seems unfavourable? Is there not an in-built imperative to respond to community needs, however expressed?

Does the strategic management process have to be planned?

It is often assumed that the concept of strategic management is taken to imply that the strategic process is planned. However Mintzberg (1988) argues that the notion of strategy as a plan is only one of a number of connotations.

1 *Strategy as a plan*: a consciously intended course of action, usually directed towards a goal.

2 *Strategy as a pattern*: a stream of actions – consistency in behaviour – which, whether intended or not, cause outsiders to infer that there was a chosen strategy.

3 *Strategy as a position*: a means of identifying where an organisation is located in its environment. Strategy becomes the mediating force between the organisation and its environment, for example, the way in which an organisation seeks to maintain an advantage over its competitors.

4 *Strategy as a perspective*: inward looking – an ingrained way of perceiving the world and the organisation's position within the world. The culture, ideology and character of the organisation influence the way the members view the world.

Emergent strategies

Mintzberg elsewhere (Mintzberg and Waters, 1985) distinguishes between a deliberate, intended and realised strategy and an unplanned, emergent strategy. Emergent 'sub-strategies' can collectively create the impression of an overall pattern or position or perspective.

Idenburg (1993) argues that the proponents of an emergent strategy perspective hold that one cannot develop a view of the future and formulate explicit objectives in an unpredictable environment. Instead, it is necessary to react in a flexible, opportunistic and accidental manner to new, unpredictable developments, and 'muddle through'. Organisations are regularly confronted with unexpected events; strategic objectives then have to be adjusted. Previous learning experiences may not be relevant to the new situation, and the learning process cannot be guided if an immediate reaction is required. In its extreme formulation it becomes a recipe of despair. Developments are motivated by external events which overshadow long-term trends and structured changes. There are no techniques, tools or programmes at the manager's disposal. Vision becomes hallucination, the issue of business definition becomes: 'What business are we in this year' (ibid.).

Logical incrementalism

Quinn (1980) has introduced the idea of 'logical incrementalism' to demonstrate how emergent strategic interventions might operate in practice in a managed way. It entails step-by-step movement towards ends which initially are broadly conceived, but which then are constantly refined and reshaped as new information is obtained. It involves giving conscious thought to what sort of resistance might be encountered at various stages in the process and how this might be handled.

Logical incrementalism recognises that the planned implementation of a strategy from A to Z is an illusion but that there is still the need for an overall goal orientation with a supporting process (Idenburg, op. cit.). The process develops in phases but each following phase builds on the previous phase and has its own internal logic. On the way from A to B to C to D it becomes apparent that there are many alternative routes. Some are blocked off, others are dead ends, but a number of steps can be taken in the desired direction as one moves from one observation point to the next.

In steering the process, decision makers also need to recognise that the players in the organisation have their own objectives and are products of their own personal learning experiences. Strategic management is not a simple question of rational decision making but also of understanding emotions, doubts, worries, intuition and stress. Power politics may turn productive and constructive communication on common objectives into destructive processes on the basis of open or hidden personal agendas and mental models. It is not sufficiently recognised that implementation problems in strategic plans not only are the outcome of defective learning processes but also result from the fact that a policy is seldom neutral but always contains elements of power politics and internal negotiation (Idenburg, ibid.).

Levels of strategy

Strategic interventions and considerations can apply to a number of organisational levels.

Grand strategy

Grand strategy in the private sector is the responsibility of the corporate chief executive officer and the corporate management team or board of directors. For public sector local authorities in the UK the equivalent to the board of directors is the political committee structure of councillors. The grand strategies adopted reflect the overall character of the corporation, the way in which it responds to its environment, and in general terms the sorts of issues on which resources are to be deployed. A rational approach to grand strategy would be to tie it in with all other sub-strategies (such as HRD) so that they do not work at cross purposes. However such integration rarely happens in practice.

Commercial concerns have a particular concern with how they position their resources in the external marketplace and this will condition the range of grand strategies they will adopt. Public sector concerns will be more constrained by political issues, but in recent years have been particularly concerned with how they reach their customers. There are a number of possible grand strategies, but in general they can be narrowed down to three; those concerned with achieving growth, stability or retrenchment (*see* Fig. 2.2).

| Figure 2.2 | Porter's generic strategies |

Michael Porter (1985) argued that there are three fundamental ways in which firms can achieve sustainable competitive advantage, that is, growth. For him, this would influence the choice of grand strategies.

1 A *cost leadership strategy*, where 'a firm sets out to become the low-cost producer in its industry ... a low-cost producer must find and exploit all sources of cost advantage. Low-cost producers typically sell a standard, or no-frills, product and place considerable emphasis on reaping scale or absolute cost advantages from all sources ... If a firm can achieve and sustain overall cost leadership, then it will be an above-average performer in its industry provided it can command prices at or near the industry average.'

2 A *differentiation strategy*, which Porter defines as seeking 'to be unique in its industry along some dimensions that are widely valued by buyers ... It is rewarded for its uniqueness with a premium price ... A firm that can achieve and sustain differentiation will be an above-average performer in its industry if its price premium exceeds the extra costs incurred in being unique ... The logic of the differentiation strategy requires that a firm chooses attributes in which to differentiate itself that are different from its rivals.'

3 A *focus strategy* based on 'the choice of a narrow competitive scope within an industry. The focuser selects a segment or group of segments in the industry and tailors its strategy to serving them to the exclusion of others.' There are two variants here. 'In *cost focus* a firm seeks a cost advantage in its target segment, while in *differentiation focus* a firm seeks differentiation in its target segment.' In other words, the organisation adopts a form of niche marketing, focusing on either cost leadership or differentiation in a narrow segment of the market.

Porter suggests that organisations should concentrate on one of the above strategies and avoid being 'stuck in the middle' by failing to concentrate their resources on one or other strategic option and thus failing to compete on favourable terms.

Critiques of Porter have pointed out that there is little empirical evidence to suggest that organisations do regard the generic strategies as mutually exclusive. Reservations have also been expressed about whether companies in practice compete primarily on price or on costs, as Porter suggests that they should. Issues such as market share, and differentiation on service, quality and product types seem to be equally important.

Source: Porter (1985).

Grand strategies can be external, market driven, or internal. External grand strategies reflect how the organisation *positions* itself in relation to its external environment. Internal grand strategies relate to the *posture* it adopts in relation to its internal operations. The measure of the success of the strategies undertaken is seen in its overall *performance* (*see* Fig. 2.3).

| Figure 2.3 | Aspects of strategy |

Position

The position of an organisation refers to such matters as:

- market share in particular segments;
- customer image;
- competence in relation to competitors;
- relative importance to suppliers.

Position shows how an organisation relates to the people that are its environment. The position is what you see when you stand at the organisational boundary and look outwards.

Posture

The posture of an organisation refers to matters such as:

- the composition of its activities in terms of product lines and services undertaken;
- the technologies on which those activities are based;
- the manner in which the organisation is structured and controlled;
- the predominant shared behaviours or culture of the people in the organisation.

In other words, the posture of an organisation is a picture of what it looks like, its shape and its capabilities. The posture of an organisation is what you see when you stand at the organisational boundary and look inwards.

Performance

The posture and the position of the organisation are the result of the strategy, the pattern in actions, it has pursued. That posture and position determine the performance at the time and performance refers to:

- financial dimensions such as cost levels, return on capital, profit growth;
- operational dimensions such as quality and service levels.

Analysing position, posture and performance is a form of static analysis. That is, it portrays a situation and its determinants at a moment in time.

Source: Stacey (1993).

External grand strategies

External grand strategies include:

1 *Market extension*: identifying new markets for existing products and services. It involves targeting new and different customer and or client groups.
2 *Market penetration*: attempting to maximise market share with existing products and services in existing markets. This is a very focused strategy dependent upon

maintaining competitive advantage in a particular market niche. It is often linked to cost leadership strategies (efficiency, economy, effectiveness). It is also associated with attempts to create barriers to entry for possible new competitors.

3 *Product development*: developing new products or services for existing markets.

4 *Product diversification*: developing new products or services for new markets.

5 *Backward vertical integration*: purchasing businesses which have previously been suppliers of essential raw materials and/or services. This strategy secures sources of supply.

6 *Forward vertical integration*: purchasing businesses which have been buyers or distributors of your organisation's goods or services.

7 *Conglomerate diversification*: purchasing another business because it is seen to be a good investment, not because it is at all related to the business of the purchaser. This is sometimes called unrelated diversification.

8 *Concentric diversification*: purchasing or merging with another business with markets, technology or products related to those of the purchasing firm.

9 *Joint ventures*: pooling resources with one or more other organisations to compete in a given market.

10 *Divestment*: selling part or all of the business as a going concern. This is sometimes referred to as harvesting.

11 *Liquidation*: selling off the assets of the business.

12 *Retrenchment or corporate turnaround*: Short- or medium-term survival strategies. This is associated with asset parsimony, that is, a squeeze on resources.

Internal grand strategies

Internal grand strategies include:

1 *Cost reduction*: a series of policies and actions designed to increase the efficiency of the organisation and the competitiveness of its products and services by reducing the overall outgoings.

2 *Quality enhancement*: a series of policies and practices designed to increase the responsiveness of the organisation to its customers and reduce the overall error and complaint level. The policy drive is often represented by Total Quality Management (TQM) and associated customer care initiatives.

3 *Corporate restructuring*: reconfiguring the overall 'architecture' of the organisation through major initiatives such as Business Process Reengineering.

4 *Innovation*: encouraging entirely new approaches which are still compatible with the organisation's business philosophy.

5 *Speed of response capability*: developing an organisational capability to respond quickly to external pressures, surprises and competitive moves.

Enterprise or business unit strategies

Enterprise strategy is the approach adopted for a single business within the corporation. An enterprise is often called a *strategic business unit* (SBU) to emphasise its relative autonomy. A diversified, divisionalised organisation is, by definition, engaged in various businesses. At the level of the SBU, decision makers focus on specific environments or markets or product/service ranges. One of the features of recent years has been the decentralisation of decision-making powers to operational sub-units, the establishment of profit centres and the *de facto* creation of SBUs within organisations.

In large organisations that have engaged in concentric or conglomerate diversification, the result has been a network of relatively autonomous businesses with their own products or services and markets. Each often has its own CEO and adopts a relatively independent set of external and internal strategies. There has also been a growing trend since the early 1980s for organisations to be reconfigured through the creation of market-driven SBUs, with devolved budgetary responsibility. Many public sector local authorities have adopted this approach as a way of delivering services such as housing and education to the community they serve. Britsh Telecom is an example of an organisation that has created internal trading units to support 'front office' external customer facing functions.

Functional strategies

Functional strategies are those adopted by specific functional support areas within the organisation such as finance, marketing and personnel/human resources.

Any major department is also a function. In an organisation adopting a rational planning system the strategies should dovetail and demonstrate coherence in the way they collectively contribute to the overall organisation effort. The process is rarely as clear cut as this statement implies. For example, it has been known for some functional areas to engage in survival strategies because the rest of the organisation is not convinced of the value of the service they provide. One of the tensions in organisations is in respect of the need to co-ordinate the whole while at the same time benefiting from the greater responsiveness to customers and environments resulting from the creation of effective SBUs.

This can entail the need for a *horizontal strategy* that is, a series of policies which seek to strengthen the interrelationship between operational business units for the benefit of the overall business. It is an attempt to ensure a strategic fit, a pulling together in the same direction.

Hamel and Prahalad (op. cit.) refer to organisational decision makers generating corporate challenges to invigorate the internal and external strategic process (*see* Fig. 2.4).

Figure 2.4	Corporate challenges

In a number of organisations, top managers have presented their organisation with a series of corporate challenges, each specifying the next hill in the race to achieve strategic intent. One year the challenge might be quality, the next total customer care, the next entry into new markets, the next a rejuvenated product line. As these examples indicate, corporate challenges are a way of staging the acquisition of new competitive advantages, a way to identify the focal point for employees' efforts in the near to medium term.

▶▶

▶▶ Figure 2.4 continued

Corporate challenges come from analysing competitors as well as from the foreseeable pattern of industry evolution. Together these reveal potential competitive openings and identify the new skills the organisation will need to take the initiative from better positioned players.

For a challenge to be effective, individuals and teams throughout the organisation must understand it and see its implications for their own jobs. Companies that have set corporate challenges to create new competitive advantages (as Ford and IBM did with quality improvement) quickly discover that engaging the entire organisation requires top management to achieve the following.

1 *Create a sense of urgency*, or quasi-crisis, by amplifying weak signals in the environment that point to the need to improve, instead of allowing inaction to precipitate a real crisis.

2 *Develop a competitor focus at every level through widespread use of competitive intelligence*. Every employee should be able to benchmark his or her efforts against best-in-class competitors so that the challenge becomes personal. (For example, Ford showed production-line workers videotapes of operations at Mazda's most efficient plant.)

3 *Provide employees with the skills they need to work effectively*: training in statistical tools, problem solving, value engineering, and team building for example.

4 *Give the organisation time to digest one challenge before launching another*. When competing initiatives overload the organisation, middle managers try to protect their people from the effect of shifting priorities. But this 'wait and see if they're serious this time' attitude ultimately destroys the credibility of corporate challenges.

Source: Hamel and Prahalad (1989).

Core competences and strategic capabilities

Prahalad and Hamel (1990) argue that strategic success is dependent upon the development of a limited number of *core competences* which are resources which provide the organisation with a distinctive and sustainable competitive advantage.

Barney (1991) proposes four criteria for deciding whether a resource can be perceived as a core competence:

■ value creation for the customer;

■ rarity compared to the competition;

■ non-imitability;

■ non-substitutability (such as substitutability of materials to compete with existing products, or availability of an external supplier who can provide a service more cheaply).

A number of authorities argue that for many organisations the only true source of sustainable competitive advantage that meets the above criteria is the people who work in the organisation, with their knowledge and skills.

A *core competence* can operate at business unit or functional level. For any given function it is worth asking questions such as:

■ What are we providing that is distinctive?

■ What are we doing that cannot readily be provided elsewhere?

Strategic capability is a related concept that specifically applies to the ability of an organisation to be an effective competitor by levering its resources and core competences speedily and effectively to where they are needed. The possession of, or access to, distribution networks which achieve high-quality service levels is an example.

Strategic types

In practice one can identify a number of different approaches that are adopted in organisations for handling strategic issues. Various attempts have been made to classify them. Miles and Snow (1978) provide a well-known four-fold classification of proposed organisational strategic types. It is very generalised and somewhat simplistic, but provides a useful diagnostic framework for looking at an organisation. Following Mintzberg (op. cit.), the four types can be used as 'coat hooks' for understanding patterns in action that seem to indicate a strategic preference.

Defenders

Characteristics of defenders include the following:

■ they seek stability;

■ they attempt to seal off a portion of the market;

■ they adopt a niche strategy, that is, a limited set of products aimed at a narrow segment of the total market;

■ they aim for production of goods or services as efficiently as possible;

■ they adopt strict organisation control to ensure efficiency.

Prospectors

Characteristics of prospectors include the following:

■ they find or exploit new product and market opportunities;

■ their domain is usually broad and in a continuous state of development;

■ they are constantly scanning the environment for opportunities;

■ they adopt flexible technological and administrative systems;

■ they adopt organic structures with top management expertise in marketing and R&D.

Analysers

Characteristics of analysers include the following:

■ they seek to incorporate the benefits of defenders and prospectors;

■ they seek or exploit new opportunities while maintaining their core business;

- they adopt a strategy of imitation;
- they adopt matrix structures to accommodate dynamic and stable areas.

Reactors

Characteristics of reactors include:

- the lack of a set of response mechanisms which can be consistently put into effect when faced with a changing environment.

Another well-known classification system is that developed by Goold and Campbell (1988), based on empirical work into 16 large UK-based business concerns. Their three-fold categorisation is as follows.

Financial-control organisations

Characteristics of financial-control organisations include:

- strategy creation is delegated to business unit managers within agreed financial constraints;
- budgets and targets are viewed as critical control mechanisms;
- a small residual head office operates as a 'controller' of results through close scrutiny of financial returns;
- each business is treated relatively autonomously and is rewarded and or punished on the basis of its results. Poor results can lead to divestment;
- there is little evidence of a horizontal strategy designed to create synergies.

Strategic-planning organisations

Characteristics of strategic-planning organisations include:

- strategy creation is based on strategic plans which are jointly developed by a head office and business unit managers. Planning is centralised with head office having the final say;
- head office orchestrates strategy development by setting and co-ordinating organisation-wide priorities;
- there is a prevailing mindset that a long-term perspective is realistic but requires central co-ordination and control;
- efforts are made centrally to create cross-business synergies;
- the tight central control can lead to an excess of bureaucracy and lack of ownership of strategy implementation at local level.

Strategic-control organisations

Characteristics of strategic-control organisations include:

- strategy creation involves two elements – decentralisation to business unit managers in the context of an overall corporate strategy;

- head office reviews business unit plans and approves strategic objectives and targets, recognising that they may need to be adjusted locally because of unforeseen competitive pressures;

- there is scope for strategy creation and budgetary control to be separated, thus permitting more flexible performance measurement.

Goold and Campbell (op. cit.) concluded that each style had its advantages and demerits and was dependent upon the context in which the organisation operated. For example, they held that where the external environment is turbulent and very competitive, the financial-planning approach is less appropriate because it restricts opportunities for adaptive strategic change.

Many writers reflect on the importance of planning in strategy. Following the military analogy, whereas strategy is the overall art of conducting a campaign, the 'plan of campaign' articulates specific objectives within an overall directional framework.

Giles (1991) derives the following four strategic styles from comparing approaches to planning on two dimensions. The first dimension is the degree of *planning sophistication*. The second dimension is the degree of *ownership* of key stakeholders in the process.

Cavaliers: low ownership and weak strategy

For cavaliers, planning has become an annual ritual to satisfy senior management. The plan is often thick and glossy, full of internal budgets and lengthy to-do lists that demonstrate frenetic activity on behalf of its originators. The whole process may have been delegated to a junior member of staff and rubber-stamped by senior management later. Despite the volume of documentation, there is little to indicate strategic intent or direction.

Pundits: good planning but low ownership

In the pundit situation specialist planning departments are recruited to do the job that belongs to operational management. Plans are made by a limited number of specialists and not shared with those who have responsibility for implementing them. The plan appears to have little relevance to the true situation.

Missionaries: ownership high and strategy improving

Where missionaries are involved, the organisation has a sense of shared direction and implementation issues have been addressed. However missionaries are at a transient stage and often seek greater sophistication in the planning process without impairing implementation. Missionaries are only a short leap from leaders (*see* below) but few organisations reach the last stage. Their preoccupation with improving the sophistication of the process leads them inexorably towards the ivory tower of the pundits.

Leaders: strategy sophisticated and ownership right

The leadership style is where all organisations would like to believe they are positioned. In reality, very few are. These organisations are typified by sustainable, competitive strategies that are well understood by the implementors who have, in their turn, played a part in fashioning them. Departmental and functional barriers have broken down and there is a coherent horizontal strategy. People work together in inter-departmental teams that focus firmly on the customer for the good of the entire organisation. There is no duplication or internal competition as the rewards of effective implementation are shared by all. These organisations exert significant influence on their customers and competitors.

Giles (op. cit.) thus adopts a normative stance in that, the closer the organisation is to the 'leader' position, the more effective it will become.

THE SYSTEMATIC STRATEGIC ANALYSIS MODEL

Many organisations purport to follow a rational planning route to strategy formulation and implementation. Idenburg (op. cit.) holds that models of rational planning are based on iterative strategy development. This assumes that there is a logical and sequential set of stages that need to be undertaken in order to encompass what happens before, during and after the making of strategic decisions. These are usually taken to be: strategy context setting; strategy analysis; strategy formulation or choice; and strategy implementation. The mission and basic objectives of the organisation are determined, after which a choice is made between alternative strategies. Implementation plans are made on the basis of an assessment of the opportunities and threats in the external environment, strengths (competitive advantage, core competences) and weaknesses in the internal environment.

Rational planning implies a deep involvement by top management in the formulation of strategies and action plans. This view of strategy development is founded on the assumption of a more or less predictable world in which the future position of the organisation can be determined in terms of quantifiable objectives. Minds and hands are separate, plan formulation is distinct from implementation.

The Xerox model referred to earlier (*see* Fig. 2.1) is a good example of a systematic approach to strategy management. As we shall see, there have been a number of criticisms relating to whether decision makers follow these stages in practice or, if they do, whether doing so contributes to organisational effectiveness. Nevertheless, for our purposes these stages form a useful framework for setting out and explaining the strategy management process. Note that the separation of these stages for analytical purposes does not require the existence of a formal corporate planning process, although they are often linked.

Figure 2.5 outlines the stages of the systematic strategy analysis process.

In essence the approach entails the establishment of organisation goals for some future time period and then the development of operational plans and targets for organisational sub-units which will contribute to the overall organisation objectives.

Hofer and Schendel (1978) give the following reasons for a systematic approach to strategy formulation:

- to aid in the formulation of organisational goals and objectives;
- to aid in the identification of major strategic issues;
- to assist in the allocation of discretionary strategic resources;

| Figure 2.5 | The systematic strategy analysis process |

Strategic context setting	Clarify/restate organisation • vision • mission • core values
Assessment and investigation	• External environmental appraisal • Internal audit of key result areas • Evaluation of expectations of key stakeholders
Reflection leading to	• Gap identification • Establishment of targets and critical success factors • Evaluation of alternative courses of action
Formulation	• Long-range strategic plan • Establishment of supporting business plans
Implementation and monitoring	• Action plan v. activity • Environmental scanning

■ to guide and integrate the diverse administrative and operating activities of the organisation;

■ to assist in the development and training of future general managers.

Langley (1988) further argues that there are four roles for strategic planning:

1 *Public relations*: to impress or influence outsiders. This leads to risk of producing merely impressive documents.

2 *Information*: to provide input for strategic visions. This avoids the ritualistic collection of information and the premature making of foreclosure or judgements.

3 *Group therapy*: communication of strategy visions and participation in them by people at all levels. This involves developing a vision and then selling to the rest of the organisation.

4 *Direction and control*: extending planning into implementation.

The process as recommended typically entails the following stages:

1 A strategic context-setting stage involving a clarification and, where appropriate, a restatement of the organisation's vision, mission and core values.

2 An assessment/investigation stage consisting of:

- an external environmental appraisal to identify any threats that might confront the organisation and any opportunities that might lead to the establishment of new markets and/or new products or services;

- an internal audit of key result areas across the 'value chain' to determine strengths and weaknesses associated with existing resources;

- an assessment of the expectations of key stakeholders, both internal and external. Stakeholders in this context represent the various groupings which have a vested interest in how the organisation carries out its operations.

3 From this analysis stage should come a reflection stage leading to the following outcomes:

- an identification of any gap between what the organisation policy makers wish to achieve and what is actually happening;

- the establishment of organisational targets or critical success factors for a time scale typically of five years' duration;

- an evaluation of alternative courses of action to achieve targets.

4 The fourth stage, which is based on and incorporates insights from the above, entails:

- the formulation of a long-range strategic plan for the whole organisation;

- the establishment of supporting business plans for SBUs and functional areas which are consistent with the overall organisational strategy.

5 The final stage entails:

- implementation of plan or strategy;

- monitoring of results against targets;

- monitoring of annual budgets and departmental plans in the context of the overall organisational strategic direction;

- ongoing environmental scanning in order to detect any environmental signals which might necessitate any modification to the plan or overall strategy;

- the reformulation of the strategy or plan as required.

Any written plan underpinning the strategy should be seen as a flexible document which provides the organisation with some sense of purpose and overall direction.

STAGE 1 SETTING THE STRATEGIC CONTEXT

What constitutes a corporate vision?

A number of enterprises have found it helpful to generate a 'corporate vision', which functions as a sort of directional map for their sphere of operations. According to El-Namaki (1992), *corporate vision* is a mental perception of the kind of future that individual decision makers aspire to create for the organisation over a broad time horizon, together with the underlying conditions for the actualisation of this perception. The vision defines the overall direction to be taken.

Why a vision?

El-Namaki suggests four reasons why decision makers in business concerns might seek to develop corporate visions.

1 *A desire to control an organisation's destiny*. The more quickly a chief executive officer can conceive a future vision wherein new products are positioned in emerging industry-market constructs, the greater is the ability of an organisation to influence its destiny.

2 *A need for creative strategies*. Trying to attain competitive advantage through analysing and reacting to rivals tends to be transparent and ultimately short lived. It is creative visions, and derived creative strategies, that provide a longer-term view of what consumers and end users really aspire to, and thus the key to success in the industries of tomorrow.

3 *Demands of turnaround and recovery*. One of the first requirements of recovery is the development of a sense of direction that will move the organisation away from the difficulties of the past. This can be facilitated by a visualisation of the kind of long-term organisation that people can aspire to and markets accommodate.

4 *A desire to change corporate culture*. A novel or innovative vision could set the parameters for a road to change. The vision could kick-start a re-evaluation of basic patterns of behaviour and provide a thematic justification of new behavioural patterns, leading to the mobilisation of the work-force around the new norms and the encouragement of new entrants whose norms and beliefs correspond to those advocated by the novel vision.

Each of the above reasons for adopting a corporate vision seems to reflect the concerns of the top echelons of the organisation and to be based upon their values; gaining commitment to it by those people who have a responsibility for its delivery can be quite a daunting task. Other authorities have emphasised the importance of a shared vision, something that individuals can buy into and perhaps have contributed to. Peter Senge (1990) encapsulates this perspective (*see* Fig. 2.6). He believes that a vision which is inconsistent with people's values not only will fail to inspire genuine enthusiasm, but often will foster outright cynicism. For him therefore, there is a real need to develop a shared vision.

What makes a good vision?

For a vision to provide a sound base for strategy formulation it should conform to the following conditions (El-Namaki, op. cit.):

■ be realistic and feasible, simple and clear;
■ provide a challenge for the whole organisation;
■ mirror the goals and aspirations of the constituents;
■ be far but close, in terms of time span and organisation commitment;
■ be able to focus the attention with respect to scope and time;
■ be translatable into goals and strategies;
■ be endorsed and frequently articulated by top management;
■ be derived from a sense of direction.

| Figure 2.6 | Organisation vision and 'governing ideas' |

Senge contends that building a shared vision is only one of the activities that contributes to an articulation of the 'governing ideas' for the enterprise. The others are its purpose or mission, and its core values. These governing ideas collectively answer the question: What do we believe in?

■ *Vision* is the *what* – the picture of the future we wish to create.

■ *Purpose* or *mission* is the *why* – the organisation's answer to the question 'Why do we exist?' For some organisations this demonstrates how they seek to contribute to the world in some unique way, to add a distinctive sense of value.

■ *Core values* are the *how* – how do we wish to act in a way that is consistent with our mission, along the path towards achieving our vision? An organisation's values might include integrity, openness, honesty, freedom, equal opportunities, leanness, merit and loyalty. These values characterise the organisation as it pursues the vision.

When Matsushita employees recite the company creed, 'To recognise our responsibilities as industrialists, to foster progress, to promote the general welfare of society, and to devote ourselves to the further development of world culture,' they are describing the company *purpose* or *mission*. When they sing the company song about 'sending our goods to the people of the world, endlessly and continuously, like water gushing from a fountain', they are proclaiming the corporate *vision*. And when they go to in-house training programmes that cover such topics as 'fairness', 'courtesy and humility', 'struggle for betterment', 'harmony and co-operation' and 'gratitude', the employees are learning the organisation's deliberately constructed *values* (what Matsushita calls its 'spiritual values').

It is important to distinguish between *positive* and *negative* visions. There are two fundamental sources of energy that can motivate organisations – *fear* and *aspiration*. The power of aspiration drives positive visions which relate to what we want. The power of fear underlies negative visions with their focus on what we want to avoid.

Negative visions are limiting, for the following reasons.

1 Energy that could build something new is diverted to preventing something we don't want to happen.

2 They carry a subtle yet unmistakeable message of powerlessness. We only pull together when there is sufficient threat.

3 They are inevitably short term. The organisation is motivated so long as the threat persists.

Source: Senge (1990).

Mission statements

A mission statement tries to express 'what we are in business for' or 'what is the purpose of us existing as an organisation at all'. Some authorities suggest that it is an attempt to make a vision more tangible by putting into words the beliefs and directions towards which a visionary leader wishes to direct the organisation. This may be true for some institutions. For many organisations the reality is much more prosaic: over the last few years mission statements have become almost *de rigueur* in both the public and private sectors, in most cases without the noticeable intervention of a visionary exemplar.

How organisations define their mission

David (1989) identifies from an empirical study the following features which organisations at that time considered putting in their mission statements:

■ customers

■ products or services

■ location

■ technology

■ concern for survival

■ philosophy

■ self-concept

■ concern for public image

■ concern for employees.

He goes on to argue that mission statements should:

■ define what the organisation is and what it aspires to be;

■ be limited enough to exclude some ventures and broad enough to allow for creative growth;

■ distinguish a given organisation from all others;

■ serve as a framework for evaluating both current and prospective activities;

■ be stated in terms sufficiently clear to be widely understood throughout the organisation.

He quotes earlier work by King and Cleland (1979) on the reasons given for organisations having mission statements:

■ to ensure unanimity of purpose within the organisation;

■ to provide a basis for allocating organisational resources;

■ to establish a general tone or organisational climate;

■ to serve as a focal point for individuals to identify with the organisation's purpose and direction; and to deter those who cannot, from participating further in the organisation's activities;

■ to facilitate the translation of objectives into a work structure involving the assignment of tasks to responsible elements in the organisation;

■ to specify organisational purposes and the translation of those purposes into objectives in such a way that cost, time and performance parameters can be assessed and controlled.

The Ford Motor Company provides a typical example of a mission statement:

Ford Motor Company is a worldwide leader in automative and automative-related products and services as well as in newer industries, such as aerospace, communications and financial services. Our mission is to improve continually our products and services to meet our customers' needs, allowing us to prosper as a business and to provide a reasonable return for our stockholders, the owners of our business (quoted in Miller and Dess, op. cit.).

Another example is that of Neville Russell Chartered Accountancy (*see* Fig. 2.7).

Figure 2.7	Neville Russell Chartered Accountancy

Neville Russell Chartered Accountancy was founded in 1890. The company offers a number of accountancy services, such as tax, audit and insolvency. In 1996 there were 20 practices and offices spread around the UK, employing approximately 800 people. The company has a mission statement called 'Going the Extra Mile' which comprises three elements with a distinctive HRD flavour.

Going the extra mile

- by exceeding our *clients*' expectations through the content, quality and integrity of our service delivered in a personal and professional manner;
- by developing the potential of our *people* through individual recognition, tailored training and constructive appraisal, leading to personal fulfilment, proper reward and enjoyment;
- by being a successful *firm* hallmarked through its national and international outlook, high ethical and technical standards, profitability, growth and corporate pride.

Source: Mission Statement, Neville Russell Chartered Accountancy.

Core values

Argenti (1980) coined the term 'ethological objectives', which describes what are now more commonly referred to as core values. His term is a neat composition, being redolent of both 'ethos' and 'ethics'. Many organisations have published core values, a good example being Morgan Stanley, a global financial services firm employing 45 000 employees, located in 409 offices in 22 countries.

In an October 1997 newspaper recruitment advertisement they expressed their core values as follows:

Since its founding in 1935, Morgan Stanley has demonstrated outstanding success through an ability to adapt to change while preserving what is central to its identity and culture of excellence. Morgan Stanley's success is firmly based on core values:

- Client focus
- Innovation
- Business diversity
- Commitment to employees
- Teamwork
- Dignity and respect.

Organisations that make public commitment to equal opportunities reflect their ethological objectives. The purpose behind them is two-fold:

■ to make a general statement to its various publics;

■ to act as organisational policy guidelines entailing operational constraints on what it is permissible to do.

Scepticism has been expressed by some about the translation into practice of a public articulation of values. Argyris and Schon (1978) distinguish between *espoused values* – public expressions of what the organisation holds dear – and *theory in use* – what actually happens behind the scenes. How often espoused values are converted into theory in use depends on the organisation's culture.

Figure 2.8 provides a further example of core values – those of Reuters.

| Figure 2.8 | Strategy at Reuters |

Reuters is a major world-wide provider of information, delivered electronically to 362 000 user access points. In 1997 it operated in 161 countries, had a staff of over 15 000, and an annual turnover of £2.9bn. The company's markets are changing rapidly, pushed principally by technological developments such as the Internet, and increasing demand for information of all types.

At the highest level the 'core values' were defined in 1997 as:

■ *Accuracy*: Reuters has an unparalleled reputation for the accuracy of its information and news stories.

■ *Speed*: in many cases, Reuters has been the first with the news. An example from history is the assassination of President Abraham Lincoln in 1865, Reuters being the first to publish the story in the UK.

■ *Think global/local*: Reuters is an international company that must face in a number of different directions at once.

■ *Innovation*: in both products and technology.

■ *Freedom from bias*: in order to preserve its reputation, Reuters must be seen as impartial.

■ *Focus on customers*: constantly asking what they want from the company.

■ *To be open and accountable*: this applies equally to customer and internal relations.

'Core values' are intended to be of long standing. Reuters supports them with the following 'Statement of Objectives'.

Reuters aims to be the number one supplier to the financial community in all countries and in all market segments in which we can sell our products profitably over time. The Reuter product line will be distinguished by its breadth and quality, and by the innovation it brings to all parts of the dealing process. Reuters will operate profitably as the leading source of international news for the world's media, and for the emerging new media reaching the home.

Reuters will build a third global business supplying information and related technology to managers and to professionals outside finance and the media. We shall rely for our success on proven values of speed, accuracy and freedom from bias, as laid out in our Trust principles.

▶▶

▶▶ Figure 2.8 continued

> Strategy in Reuters is implemented through what are termed 'Strategic Company Programmes'. These are organised around a core group of people who are responsible for each one. Each programme has a sponsor, chosen from the Board. Under each sponsor there is a 'programme leader', a senior manager. Goals and targets are applied to each programme.
>
> Reuters' Chairman, Peter Job, said in 1996 to an audience at the London Business School: 'Our strategy is to have no strategy.' He was trying to illustrate that Reuters must be ever watchful and flexible in the market it inhabits, and should not be tied to one course of action.

Source: Reuters.

Guiding principles

Hitachi has a set of guiding principles which serve as core values. Dore (1973) refers to the Hitachi 'Guiding Spirit', which sets out the company's key principles to its employees as 'sincerity of heart and mind, a spirit of forward looking positivism and a spirit of harmony'.

The Hitachi song goes:

> Over hill, over valley, each calls and each responds
>
> We are united and we have dreams
>
> We are Hitachi men, aroused and ready
>
> To promote the happiness of others
>
> Great is our pride in our home-produced products
>
> Polished and refined our skills.

STAGE 2 ASSESSMENT AND INVESTIGATION

Environmental appraisal

Environmental appraisal is usually undertaken to identify market opportunities and external threats. According to Fahey and Narayanan (1986) this process entails the following steps.

1 *Scanning*. This entails general surveillance of all environmental segments and their interactions in order to identify early signals of possible environmental change and to detect environmental change already under way. It can entail capacity to suspend beliefs, preconceptions and judgements.

2 *Monitoring*. This entails tracking of environmental trends, sequences of events or streams of activities and following signals or indicators unearthed during the

scanning phase. The object is to assemble sufficient data to discern whether certain trends and patterns are emerging.

3 *Forecasting.* This entails developing plausible projections of the direction, scope, speed and intensity of environmental change.

4 *Assessment.* This entails making judgements about the impact of the foregoing on the strategic management of the organisation.

It is worth noting that environmental appraisal can be effective in making judgements based on trends but will not pick up the unpredictable, one-off, unforeseeable events which can occur in a turbulent environment.

Kotler (1980) refers to an overall marketing environment which he defines as all the external forces and institutions that are potentially relevant to the organisation. He identifies four levels of environment, each of which can be independently scanned.

1 The *task* environment, which consists of the major participants in the performance of the organisation's task, such as suppliers and the end-users to whom you are offering your product or service.

2 The *competitive* environment, which consists of any organisations which compete with you for customers and scarce resources.

3 The *public* environment, which consists of institutions which watch or regulate the activities of the organisation.

4 The *macro* environment, which consists of the major societal forces that confront the organisation, namely, demography, economics, natural resources, technology, politics and culture.

The task environment

An analysis of the task environment would typically entail some form of market segmentation to classify existing and potential customers. One of the outcomes of an effective segmentation might be to identify potential customers not reached or services not offered.

The competitive environment

An analysis of the competitive environment usually entails an analysis of one's competitors and/or of other organisations offering a similar range of services. It is helpful to distinguish between the terms *competitor analysis* and *competitor intelligence.*

Competitor analysis is simply the analysis of one's competitors.

Competitor intelligence can be thought of as the entire process of systematic collection, collation, evaluation, presentation and use of information about one's competitors. Some of the results of the activity will lead to strategic decisions, but it is worth noting that many will be concerned with short-term operational issues.

Competitor intelligence is usually held to be important for reasons which include:

- to avoid surprise;
- to avoid takeover;
- to evaluate one's own performance;
- to exploit weaknesses detected in competitors;
- to respond quickly to actions by competitors;
- to gain and keep competitive advantage;
- to cope with shrinking markets.

Michael Porter (1980) has extended the notion of the competitive environment in an approach which he calls *industry analysis*. In essence he argues that five forces have an impact on any product/market area (industry) and determine how attractive that industry is to operate in. The more one can manipulate the forces in a direction favourable to oneself the more strategically effective one is. The five forces are:

- *supplier power*: the extent to which suppliers of resources are in a position to hold the organisation to ransom or to impose threats to its operation, survival or effectiveness;
- *buyer power*: the extent to which purchasers of services or products can switch loyalty or use their influence to demand higher quality and/or reduced price;
- *threat of entry*: the extent to which competitors can move in to markets that one has previously dominated. Porter argues that effective strategic management in this area should entail creating barriers to entry;
- *substitute products*: the extent to which there is a threat of new technology or product innovations making one's offer redundant;
- *jockeying for position*: the extent to which existing service providers complete with each other for market share by quality drives, price reductions, political lobbying, etc.

The public environment

The public environment is especially significant for today's organisations, which confront numerous statutory regulatory bodies and local community groups. At least seven publics can be identified:

- financial publics (banks, shareholders, investment houses);
- media publics (press, TV, radio, magazines, etc.);
- government publics (central, local, EEC);
- citizen action publics (conservation groups etc.);
- local publics (local residents, industry, commerce, etc.);
- general publics (general citizens);
- internal publics (trade unions etc.).

We will return to this area when we look at the expectations of stakeholders. It is important to remember that certain decisions taken in organisations can put one *in the spotlight* and lead to the emergence of pro and anti factions. There are many examples of problems that have occurred because of inadequate anticipation of the reactions from the public environment.

The macro environment

The macro environment can usefully be analysed in terms of the PESTLE acronym where:

P = Political environment
E = Economic environment
S = Social environment
T = Technological environment
L = Legal environment
E = Ecological environment.

Figure 2.9 presents five key strategy questions.

Figure 2.9   Five key strategy questions

Jack Welch, CEO of General Electric, formulated in the mid-1980s five key strategy questions for his business managers to answer in one page using 'compelling Churchillian prose'.

1 What are your market dynamics globally today, and where are you going over the next several years?
2 What actions have your competitors taken in the last three years to upset those global dynamics?
3 What have you done over the last three years to affect those dynamics?
4 What are the most dangerous things your competitors could do in the next three years to upset those dynamics?
5 What are the most effective things you could do to bring your desired impact on these dynamics?

Source: Quoted in Pascale (1991).

Internal appraisal

Internal appraisal typically involves an analysis of strengths and weaknesses associated with the primary and support activities of what Michael Porter (1985) calls the *value chain*.

Primary activities concern the day-to-day operational activities which need to be undertaken to get a product or service to the customer. Support activities refer to such functions as information systems, human resource management and development and financial services.

An analysis of key result areas could help an organisation's policy makers to identify its strengths or *distinctive (core) competences* in respect of its resources. These should be built upon. It could also identify certain weaknesses in respect of its resource management.

One current approach to reaching judgements in respect of strengths and weaknesses is associated with the idea of best practice benchmarking. Comparisons of a given set of practices in the value chain are made against other 'best in class' organisations.

Stevenson (1989) summarises the process of defining corporate strengths and weaknesses:

1 Recognise that the process of defining strengths and weaknesses is primarily an aid to the individual manager in the accomplishment of a task.

2 Develop lists of critical areas for examination which are tailored to the responsibility and authority of each individual manager.

3 Make the measures and the criteria to be used in evaluation of strengths and weaknesses explicit so that managers can make their evaluations against a common framework.

4 Recognise the important strategic role of defining attributes (organisation form, culture, etc.) as opposed to merely focusing on efficiency and effectiveness.

Expectations of stakeholders

The stakeholder model is a very effective explanatory model for identifying the various groups or 'publics' who directly or indirectly make or influence or should influence policy decisions, that is, those who have some impact on the 'government' of an organisation.

Each organisation has its own distinctive set of stakeholders. Thus one key group of stakeholders for a public sector local authority is its elected members. Their key role has led to such organisations being defined as *representative democracies*. That is, decisions are taken through elected members mandated to act on behalf of the electorate and who hold office for a specified period of time. The relationship between elected members and the management of the organisation has vital strategic implications. Of course, elected members do not constitute one cohesive block; the various interests of majority and minority parties need to be established.

A useful technique is to carry out a stakeholder analysis for each major strategic issue in order to establish likely support and resistance for a proposed course of action. Figure 2.10 is a grid which is a typical example of this approach. It is a version of a Force Field analysis.

Once the analysis has been completed it is necessary to develop strategies for handling the various anticipated positions.

| Figure 2.10 | Strategic issue analysis |

Strategic issue analysis

Anticipated degree of support

		Positive	*Negative*
Significance of reaction	*High*	Sponsors and advocates	Antagonists
	Low	Low-influence supporters	Low-influence detractors

STAGES 3 & 4 REFLECTION LEADING TO STRATEGY FORMULATION

In the systematic model, effective strategy formulation is seen as an outcome of the prior internal and external analyses. From one's knowledge of the competition, the expectations of stakeholders and one's own resource capability, and directed by the overall vision, mission and core values, one takes decisions on where and how to deploy one's efforts. Johnson and Scholes (1993) argue that evaluative criteria governing strategic choice fall into the following categories.

1 *Criteria of suitability*, which attempt to measure how far proposed strategies fit the situation identified in the strategic analysis. This would include techniques which help assess the strategic logic of proposals. Johnson and Scholes also consider that the cultural fit of options should be considered, by reviewing the option in the light of the organisation's political and cultural realities.

2 *Criteria of feasibility*, which assess how any strategy might work in practice. The issues addressed here include whether the strategy can be funded, whether the necessary market position can be achieved, the reaction of competitors, ensuring that the organisation has the required skills, and so on.

3 *Criteria of acceptability*, which assess whether the consequences of proceeding with a strategy are acceptable. Some of the issues here relate to the degree of risk, the impact on profitability, the effect on expectations in the organisation, the effect of the strategy on the organisation's environment, and so on.

The Johnson and Scholes approach centres on the problem of maintaining cultural fit while searching for inherently sustainable advantages. This can entail trimming ambitions to match available resources. In commercial terms it often implies seeking to reduce financial risk by building a balanced portfolio of cash-generating and cash-consuming businesses.

Hamel and Prahalad (1989) propose an alternative perspective with a significant difference in emphasis – that of taking decisions based on leveraging resources to reach seemingly unattainable goals. This approach emphasises the need to acceler-ate organisational learning to outpace competitors in building new advantages; it produces a quest for new competences and capabilities that can destabilise an entrenched competitor's advantages.

Figure 2.11 examines innovation, and in particular transilience.

Figure 2.11 Transilience mapping

In-house innovations can have a strong impact on strategy formulation so long as decision makers are receptive to them. Innovation is not a unitary phenomenon. Some innovations disrupt, destroy or make obsolete established organisational competences. Other innovations refine and improve them.

Transilience can be defined as the ability of an innovation to influence an organisation's existing resources, skills and knowledge.

The impact of an innovation can be mapped on two dimensions.

1 *Technology or production.* Does the innovation improve or extend or develop or does it disrupt an organisation's design capability, skills, knowledge and experi-ence base?

2 *Market or customer.* Does the innovation improve, extend or develop, or does it disrupt an organisation's market channels, service level or customer base?

Four categories of innovation can be identified in terms of their impact.

1 *Niche creation.* This applies to situations where an innovation disrupts existing markets but builds on existing competences. It entails careful sizing up of new market opportunities and developing a product package that exploits them.

2 *Regular mode.* This applies to situations where an innovation builds on existing markets and distinctive competences. It entails methodical planning and con-tinuous process development.

3 *Architectural.* This applies to situations where an innovation disrupts existing markets and existing competences. It entails attention to the management of creativity with keen insight into business risk. It also entails constant scanning for technological developments and unmet market needs.

4 *Revolutionary.* This applies to situations where an innovation disrupts existing competences but builds on existing markets. It implies a 'technology push' and a consensus about long-term goals through investments.

Source: Abernathy and Clark (1988).

Strategies for changing the internal dynamics to increase competitiveness

Much of the literature on strategy formulation has focused on the deployment of resources, products and services in the external environment. However in recent years there has been an increasing focus on internal grand strategies as sources of generating competitive advantage. For example it used to be argued that structure was downstream of strategy but structural change is now being treated as a strate-gic device in its own right. An instance of this is business process reengineering, a method which has been linked to (and often blamed for) the massive downsizings of large corporations during much of the 1990s (*see* Fig. 2.12).

Figure 2.12 | **Business process reengineering**

Business process reengineering is an approach designed to achieve radical improvements in customer service and business efficiency. The central challenge is to rethink and streamline the business process and supporting structural architecture through which the organisation creates and delivers value.

Traditional and functional boundaries are ignored. Instead, it places an emphasis on designing and implementing efficient cross-functional processes. Hence, reengineering offers the opportunity to re-examine the fundamentals of the business or key processes within it and then redesign from first principles.

Reengineering can bring substantial benefits – not only to the organisation but to its 'partners' in the broadest sense. The key internal benefits are:

- stronger alignment of core processes to business strategy;
- the creation of customer value becomes a driver for all business activity;
- the business architecture is optimised to efficient cross-functional performance;
- benchmarking is used to accelerate learning and provide a stimulus for change;
- enhanced capability and performance lead to increased ambition and conviction.

The concept was introduced in 1990 by Michael Hammer in an article in the *Harvard Business Review*. Hammer presents reengineering as a radical, IT-driven approach to improving business efficiency, focusing on the redesign of key business processes. He asserts that:

> At the heart of re-engineering is the notion of discontinuous thinking – recognising and breaking away from the outdated rules and fundamental assumptions that underlie operations. Unless we change these rules we are merely rearranging the deck chairs on the *Titanic*. We cannot achieve breakthroughs in performance by cutting fat or automating existing processes. Rather, we must challenge old assumptions and shed the old rules that made the business underperform in the first place.

In practice, 'breaking away' involves:

- examining how and why we add more or less value than our competitors;
- forcing a radical and continuous reappraisal of customer requirements and the trade-offs they make between price, functionality, quality and service;
- asking naïve and challenging questions such as, if we were starting again, what would we do differently?
- reappraising where and how we deliver service;
- eliminating unnecessary activities, and reducing the number of delays introduced by tasks such as reviews, authorisations, inspections and hand-offs between departments;
- minimising the delays between processing stages by automating workflows;
- increasing flexibility by creating a multiskilled work-force;

▶▶

▶▶ Figure 2.12 continued

- reducing duplication of effort and investment by forming stronger partnerships with customers and suppliers, sharing more key information and undertaking joint development activities;

- empowering staff with greater responsibility and decision-making authority;

- outsourcing activities which add no value but divert management time and energy.

From the basic concept, two major categories of reengineering initiatives have emerged. The first is *process reengineering*, which emphasises identifying one or more 'core processes', analysing them and then radically rethinking and redesigning their execution. An example of this core process-driven approach is that taken by the UK health insurer Western Provident Association. The company first applied the technique to reengineer the processing of new customer applications. The result was to shorten the process from one requiring seven people, performing 45 minutes of work over 28 days to an activity involving one case worker processing the entire application in four minutes.

Such processes work best when future objectives for the process are well known. This provides a clear target for those undertaking the redesign of the selected process. However, one of the key drawbacks of such an approach lies in managing the boundaries and 'interfaces' between the reengineered process and the unchanged areas of the business.

The second category is *business reengineering*. This approach involves a strategy-driven, top-down reappraisal and redesign of the entire business. The more wide ranging and fundamental the rethink, the greater the impact on cross-functional activities, working practices, management systems, organisation structures, motivation and reward systems, performance monitoring systems, and staff training and development. The approach builds on the premise that future competitive success will be based on a strong linkage between strategy, competence, core processes and architecture.

According to Talwar (1993), there are six key steps to the process:

1 Building the vision of the reengineered organisation.
2 Planning how the vision will be realised.
3 Analysing the current structure and processes.
4 Redesigning the 'business architecture'.
5 Implementing the redesigned organisation and processes.
6 Measuring the benefits and sharing the learning.

Source: Based on Talwar (1993).

STAGE 5 STRATEGY IMPLEMENTATION AND MONITORING

Strategy implementation is the process of converting ideas into practice and committing resources. If one is engaging in major strategic shifts, then to be truly effective one needs an understanding of the management of transformational change. This is addressed in more detail in Chapter 17, but the extract given in Fig. 2.13 provides a flavour of the issues involved.

Figure 2.13	Strategic change

Strategic change involves either a redefinition of organisational mission and purpose or a substantial shift in overall priorities and goals to reflect new emphases or directions. It is usually accompanied by significant changes in patterns of resource allocation and/or alterations in organisational structure and processes to meet changing environmental demands. It can be discussed in terms of changes in strategy *content* as well as transformations in strategy *process*. Changes in content typically involve alterations in competitive decisions in particular product or market domains such as price or quality. Change in terms of strategy-making processes involves shifts in organisational culture, formal management systems, and/or structures. Strategic change can capture both content and process dimensions. That is, an alteration of an organisation's alignment with its environment is accompanied by an attendant modification in processes to conform to the new alignment.

Some argue that this degree of change (i.e. simultaneous shifts of strategy, structures and processes) constitutes a pronounced discontinuity in the life of the organisation. Such a reorientation, as opposed to incremental changes that simply adjust an organisation's existing stance, requires top management to confront the difficult task of not only developing a vision of the intended reorientation, but also disseminating an 'abstract' of the transformed organisation to key stakeholders. Further, given that changes of this nature are seldom brought about by mandate, a process of negotiated social construction occurs. Such a process might include attempts to influence perceptions of the need for, or the nature of, strategic change through the use of symbols or symbolic actions. This perspective suggests that to understand and manage strategic change, it is necessary to examine symbolism and sensemaking, and to influence processes that serve to create and legitimate the meaning of the change.

When people are called upon to enact some change in their existing patterns of thinking and acting, the proposed change must make sense in a way that relates to previous understanding and experience. Symbols and metaphors are key to this process, partly because their inherent ambiguity provides a bridge between the familiar and the strange, thus fostering a sense of continuity while simultaneously facilitating change. In this sense symbols both conceal and reveal facets of change. They conceal threatening aspects within the camouflage of the known, yet reveal those aspects that emphasise difference: but differences are rendered in terms that echo the familiar. When a strategic change is proposed, different symbolic language is used to herald the change and to articulate its nature. A diagnostic focus could therefore be on the language used by organisational actors during the attempt to launch the strategic change process. Note how manipulating organisational symbols is emphasised in the recipes offered for managing change transitions.

Source: Based on Gioia *et al.* (1994).

Ansoff (1984) suggests that the practice and theory of strategic management has been hindered by three underlying assumptions about implementation.

1 That reasonable people will do reasonable things. If people are asked to plan and are given the relevant information and analytical tools, they will select the 'right strategy' and support its formulation and implementation.

2 That a correctly formulated strategic plan will be straightforward to implement, so the 'right' strategy will somehow be easier to implement than the 'wrong' one.

3 That strategy formulation and implementation are separate and sequential activities.

Peattie (1993) argues for a fourth assumption:

4 That written strategic plans are an accurate reflection of an organisation's strategic intent. In other words, we assume that what people want to do, and what they say they want to do, are much the same thing.

EVALUATION OF STRATEGY

Among the various techniques developed to evaluate strategy, that associated with the balanced score-card is becoming very fashionable.

The balanced score-card

The notion of a balanced score-card was introduced into the strategic arena through a series of articles written for the *Harvard Business Review*. Kaplan and Norton (1992, 1993, 1996) argue that strategy formulation and evaluation should be undertaken from four perspectives:

■ the financial perspective;

■ the customer perspective;

■ the internal business perspective;

■ the innovation and learning perspective.

These perspectives can give answers to the four fundamental questions set out in Table 2.1.

Table 2.1

Perspective	Question
Financial	What must we achieve to satisfy our shareholders?
Customer	What must we achieve to satisfy our customers?
Internal business	What processes must we excel at?
Innovation and learning	What must we do to ensure that we learn and grow?

Overall the approach is designed to provide management with a comprehensive framework within which to translate an organisation's strategic objectives into a coherent set of performance measures (*see* Fig. 2.14).

Figure 2.14 **The balanced score-card**

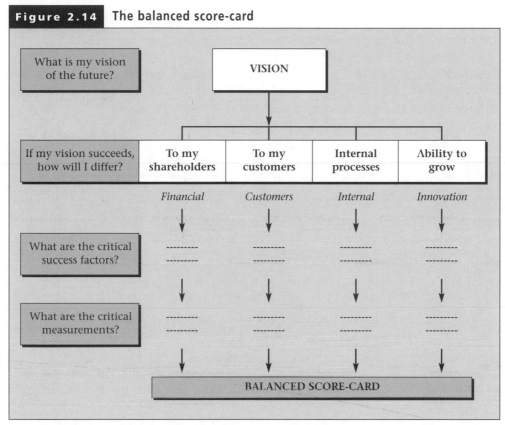

Source: Based on Kaplan and Norton (1992).

The balanced score-card approach is of particular interest to HRD practitioners because of the emphasis that is given to learning. Many organisations that have adopted this methodology have focused more on the 'innovation' component of learning and seen it in terms of new product generation. BT, on the other hand, has emphasised 'organisational learning' (*see* Fig. 2.15).

Figure 2.15 **British Telecom and the balanced score-card**

BT is one of a number of large organisations which has introduced the balanced score-card precepts into its practice. The following extracts are taken from an internal BT publication called 'Corporate Scorecard'.

▶▶

▶▶ Figure 2.15 continued

To remain a leader in a dynamic and unpredictable marketplace, BT needs to achieve excellence in four key areas of enterprise. We need to:

■ delight our customers;

■ maximise shareholder value;

■ install internal processes that help, not hinder, our people;

■ enable continuous learning and personal development.

We then need to ensure that our achievements in these areas feed off each other to form a 'virtuous circle' of continuous improvement, so that:

■ delighting our customers helps generate revenue and satisfactory returns for our investors;

■ increased revenue helps fund investments in processes and learning;

■ better processes and learning help our people to delight our customers.

BT has created objectives and measures against the following perspectives:

■ a shareholder/financial perspective;

■ a customer perspective;

■ a processes perspective;

■ an organisational learning perspective.

The organisational learning perspective has the framework set out in Table 2.2.

Table 2.2

Objectives	Measures
Leadership Demonstrate proactive leadership through visible actions and behaviours	■ percentage of people committed to BT Vision and Mission; ■ Aggregated Senior Executive Profile Score; ■ percentage personal objectives of Top 150 executives aligned with the Corporate Scorecard.
Capability management Enhance and develop the people capability required to achieve business success	■ percentage of agreed Personal Development Plans in place and being implemented; ■ percentage of required skills or competences to actual levels in critical areas; ■ percentage of line managers satisfied with development and training.
People Create and maintain an effective work-force of well-motivated and high-performance people	■ percentage of people feeling well managed and motivated; ■ percentage of people proud to work for BT.
Quality Create a quality culture through Group-wide European Quality Award Assessment	■ European Quality Award self-assessment score.

CONCLUSION

This chapter has provided a backcloth to the strategic environment in which HRD practitioners have to operate, and in which decisions about the development of people in and for organisations takes place. It provides an explanatory framework about strategic issues which underpins the rest of this book. It provides a context for understanding where HRD concerns fit into the overall strategic management of an organisation.

The chapter has demonstrated the military origins of the term strategy and shown how militaristic terminology has permeated the world of organisational decision making. It has distinguished between strategies designed to influence the positioning of the organisation in the external environment, and those intended to improve its internal functioning. Taken together, both should positively affect the overall performance.

It has been shown that strategies are not necessarily the outcome of a previously thought-out grand design, and can often be an emergent and opportunistic response to unexpected contingencies. However, a number of organisations have developed a corporate vision and mission, with supporting core values, in order to contextualise and set limits to their strategic approach.

A systematic approach to strategy formulation and implementation has been outlined, with the caveat that corporate decision makers rarely follow the precise steps of a rational planning model to make their major decisions.

The concepts of 'core competences' and 'strategic capability' have recently pervaded strategic thinking. People development and rapid response organisational learning processes are seen as significant contributors to enhancing an organisation's strategic capability. This theme will be developed in subsequent chapters.

REFERENCES

Abernathy, W. J. and Clark, K. B. (1988) 'Innovation – Mapping the Winds of Creative Destruction', in M. L. Tushman and W. L. Moore (eds) *Readings in the Management of Innovation*. New York: Ballinger Publishing Company.

Ansoff, I. (1984) *Implanting Strategic Management*. Englewood Cliffs, NJ: Prentice Hall.

Argenti, J. (1980) *Practical Corporate Planning*. London: Allen & Unwin.

Argyris, C. and Schon, D. A. (1978) *Organisational Learning: A Theory of Action Perspective*. Reading, MA: Addison-Wesley.

Barney, J. (1991) 'Types of competition and the theory of strategy: towards an integrative framework', *Academy of Management Review*, 11(4), pp. 791–800.

Bowman, C. and Asch, D. (1987) *Strategic Management*. Basingstoke: Macmillan.

Burnes, B. (1992) *Managing Change*. London: Pitman.

David, F. (1989) 'How organisations define their mission', *Long Range Planning*, 24(1).

Dore, R. (1973) *British Factory – Japanese Factory: The Origins of National Diversity in Industrial Relations*. London: Allen & Unwin.

El-Namaki (1992) 'Creating a Corporate Vision', *Long Range Planning*, 25(6), December.

Fahey, L. and Narayanan, V. K. (1986) *Macroenvironmental Analysis for Strategic Management*. West Publishing Co.

Giles, W. D. (1991) 'Making Strategy Work', *Long Range Planning*, 24(5), pp. 75–91.

Gioia, D. A., Thomas, J. B., Clark, S. M. and Chittipendi, K. (1994) 'Symbolism and Strategic Change in Academia', *Organisation Science*, 5(3).

Goold, M. and Campbell, A. (1988) *Strategies and Styles*. Oxford: Blackwell.

Hamel, G. and Prahalad, C. K. (1989) 'Strategic Intent', *Harvard Business Review*, May–June, pp. 63–76.

Hammer, M. (1990) 'Re-engineering work – Don't Automate, Obliterate', *Harvard Business Review*, July–August.

Hinterhuber, H. H. and Popp, W. (1992) 'Are You a Strategist or Just a Manager?' *Harvard Business Review*, January–February, pp. 105–13.

Hofer, C. W. and Schendel, D. (1978) *Strategy Formulation: Analytical Concepts*. West Publishing Company.

Idenburg, P. J. (1993) 'Four Styles of Strategy Development', *Long Range Planning*, 26(6), pp. 132–7.

Johnson, G. and Scholes, K. (1993) *Exploring Corporate Strategy* (3rd edn). Englewood Cliffs, NJ: Prentice Hall.

Kaplan, R. S. and Norton, D. R. (1992) 'The balanced scorecard – Measures that drive performance', *Harvard Business Review*, January–February.

Kaplan, R. S. and Norton, D. R. (1993) 'Putting the balanced scorecard to work', *Harvard Business Review*, September–October.

Kaplan, R. S. and Norton, D. R. (1996) 'Using the balanced scorecard as a strategic management system', *Harvard Business Review*, January–February.

King, W. R. and Cleland, D. I. (1979) *Strategic Planning and Policy*. New York: Van Nostrand Reinhold.

Kotler, P. (1980) *Marketing Management: Analysis, Planning and Control*. Englewood Cliffs, NJ: Prentice Hall.

Langley, A. (1988) 'The roles of formal strageic planning', *Long Range Planning*, 21(3), pp. 40–50.

Miles, R. E. and Snow, C. C. (1978) *Organisational Strategy, Structure and Process*. West Publishing Company.

Miller, A. and Dess, G. G. (1996) *Strategic Management* (2nd edn). New York: McGraw-Hill.

Mintzberg, H. (1988) 'Opening Up the Definition of Strategy', in J. B. Quinn, H. Mintzberg and R. M. James (eds) *The Strategy Process: Concepts, Contexts and Cases*. Englewood, Cliffs, NJ: Prentice Hall.

Mintzberg, H. and Waters, J. A. (1985) 'Of Strategies, Deliberate and Emergent', *Strategic Management Journal*, 6, pp. 257–72.

Open Business School (1991) 'Managing Public Services', B887 MBA Text. Milton Keynes: The Open University.

Pascale, R. T. (1991) *Managing on the Edge*. Harmonsdworth: Penguin.

Peattie, K. (1993) 'Strategic Planning: Its Role in Organisational Politics', *Long Range Planning*, 26(3) June.

Porter, M. E. (1980) *Competitive Strategy: Techniques for Analysing Industries and Competitors*. New York: Free Press.

Porter, M. E. (1985) *Competitive Advantage: Creating and Sustaining Superior Performance*. New York: Simon & Schuster.

Prahalad, C. K. and Hamel, K. (1990) 'The core competence of the corporation', *Harvard Business Review*, May–June.

Quinn, J. B. (1980) 'Managing Strategic Change', *Sloan Management Review*, Summer, pp. 3–20.

Senge, P. (1990) *The Fifth Discipline*. London: Century Business.

Stacey, R. (1993) *Strategic Management and Organisational Dynamics*. London: Pitman.

Stevenson, H. H. (1989) 'Defining Corporate Strengths and Weaknesses', in C. Bowman and D. Asch (eds) *Readings in Strategic Management*. Basingstoke: Macmillan.

Stewart, J. and Ranson, S. (1988) 'Management in the Public Domain', *Public Money and Management*, 8(1 and 2), Spring/Summer, pp. 13–19.

Talwar, R. (1993) 'Business Re-engineering – a Strategy-driven Approach', *Long Range Planning*, 26(6), December.

Tyson, S. (1995) *Human Resource Strategy*, London: Pitman.

Wickens, P. (1987) *The Road to Nissan*. Basingstoke: Macmillan.

Chapter 3

THE EMERGING CONCEPT OF HUMAN RESOURCE DEVELOPMENT

OBJECTIVES

By the end of this chapter you should be able to:

■ establish the basic functional elements of HRD;

■ differentiate between HRD and 'training and development';

■ describe broad and narrow perspectives to understanding HRD;

■ distinguish between societal, organisation-centred and individual learner approaches to HRD;

■ indicate influences on HRD that have led to an extension of the concept and its application in recent years.

INTRODUCTION

Before we can begin to understand *strategic* perspectives on HRD, the main theme of this book, we need first to gain a broad appreciation of what HRD has come to mean. What are held to be its defining characteristics? What differentiates it from other areas of study and of action? What are HRD exponents expected to know and do? This chapter will argue that HRD as an applied concept and as a discipline has historically been primarily seen in the context of securing an organisation's skill base. The literature has accordingly focused on that branch of adult vocational learning provision associated with the design, delivery and resourcing of learning interventions and opportunities within organisations in order to enhance the contribution of individuals employed. Attention has been concentrated on structuring training and development activities both on and off the job. Evidence will be presented to demonstrate that the arena is now being extended far beyond these original parameters to incorporate an array of approaches to individual, team, organisational and even societal learning.

One of the features of recent years has been a greater emphasis on the term 'learning' in organisational and indeed national vocabularies. Individuals are enjoined to engage in continuous lifelong learning. The UK Government in February 1998 produced a Green Paper entitled 'The Learning Age'. A number of organisations are referred to in their brochures and literature as 'Learning Organisations'. As a parallel trend there has been a shift in HRD terminology from *training* and development towards *learning* and development. The National Westminster Bank refers to its Learning and Development Services within a Learning Network, the Body Shop to its Learning and Development function. The swing towards learning has been followed by an interest in *knowledge* as a means of developing human and intellectual capital as a source of sustainable competitive advantage in a post-Industrial Revolution, Information Age. The changing perspectives on HRD are reflected in the changing roles of HRD exponents (*see* Chapter 6). This chapter touches upon some of the implications of the fashion for learning and knowledge for a profession that has always seen these themes as part of its *raison d'être*.

Human resource development can be seen purely in functional terms, as the provision of a set of activities that are undertaken to achieve desired individual and organisational outcomes. It can also be seen as a discipline with a philosophical and theoretical base on which to ground practice. This chapter draws attention to the interdisciplinary nature of the theory underpinning the practice of HRD. Weinberger (1998) makes the point that HRD now encompasses a vast spectrum of theory and practice. Blake (1995) contends further that the field keeps on growing. The chapter asks, in conclusion, whether – as more and more is brought into its potential sphere of coverage – there is a risk of making the domain too broad ranging and unbounded. Using the language of strategy, what is its core business?

DEFINITIONS

There is a risk, when defining any concept, of presenting it in such a way that it means exactly what you wish it to mean.

'I don't know what you mean by "glory",' Alice said . . .
    'When I use a word,' Humpty Dumpty said in rather a scornful tone, 'it means just what I choose it to mean – neither more nor less.'

There is also a risk of defining it in a way that is too complex or 'impenetrable'.

'Impenetrability! That's what I say!'
    'Would you tell me please,' said Alice, 'what that means?'
    'Now you talk like a reasonable child,' said Humpty Dumpty, looking very much pleased. 'I meant by "impenetrability" that we've had enough on that subject, and it would be just as well if you'd mention what you mean to do next, as I suppose you don't intend to stop here all the rest of your life.'
    'That's a great deal to make one word mean,' Alice said in a thoughtful tone.
    'When I make a word do a lot of work like that,' said Humpty Dumpty, 'I always pay it extra' (Lewis Carroll, 1871).

This problem of definition is particularly apparent in relation to HRD, where each authority on the subject seems to be taking a different stance. Megginson *et al.* (1993) refer to the 'fog factor' that has developed in the HRD world. 'Anyone new to the world of human resource development will quickly realise that one of the most important requirements for a speedy assimilation is to learn the language'. However, they go on to say, 'Don't assume that the people you are working with . . . share your understanding.' There are a number of reasons why this might be the case.

The first reason lies in the abstract nature of many of the concepts underpinning HRD, the meanings of which are deceptively difficult to capture in concrete words and phrases. 'Learning', 'development', 'change', 'knowledge', constructs that are central to an understanding of HRD, are complex and slippery enough in their own right. When they become attached to other equally complex and abstract constructs the complications and potential connotations seem to multiply exponentially. Yet 'learning organisation', 'development strategy', 'change agent skills', 'knowledge workers' are terms that HRD professionals wrestle with daily.

Another reason lies in the different routes people have taken to come to the topic. If much of your background has been as a training manager providing learning opportunities for employees in an organisational setting, your focus will inevitably be different from that of a government body responsible for developing national frameworks for post-school vocational skills development. If you are a chief executive officer evaluating the contribution that learning processes and the development of knowledge workers can make to the sustainable competitiveness and intellectual capital of your enterprise, your perceptions again are likely to be different.

Yet each of these represents a broad way of approaching HRD, contrasting traditions and strands that can lead to entirely different perspectives, which in turn will influence what words you use and what meaning you will give to them. It is important to recognise these variations and then perhaps to see whether they are capable of being integrated in a commonly understood language, or indeed whether that matters.

A third reason emanates from differences in who is seen as the prime beneficiary of HRD. Is it each individual citizen; is it the network of organisations that make up the global economy; is it the customers and stakeholders of these organisations; is it 'the State'; is it society at large?

Thus one approach is to see individual citizens as the prime beneficiaries, HRD being a process which helps them to achieve their potential throughout life and work. This was the position taken by Craig (1976) who argued that the central goal of HRD was 'developing human potential in every aspect of lifelong learning'. Another approach to understanding HRD is to see its roots and its *raison d'être* firmly embedded in an instrumental, work-oriented, employer-sponsored, performance-driven and organisation-centred perspective. Here HRD is often seen as either a synonym for or at best an extension of the functional area of 'training and development' and where the prime beneficiary is the employer.

An alternative and ambitious perspective is to see HRD as a 'holistic societal process of learning drawing upon a range of disciplines' (Stead and Lee, 1996). They suggest that there are two historical traditions for addressing HRD issues and are clearly more comfortable with the second.

1 Human resource development is an extension of Training and Development, with a specific orientation towards organisational learning interventions designed to improve skills, knowledge and understanding.

2 Human resource development has wider, more holistic origins, focusing on 'the interplay of global, national, organisational and individual needs'.

Without fully articulating their position – it is unclear, for example, how 'global needs' are to be identified and orchestrated – they argue that HRD encompasses national initiatives to improve the skills and knowledge base of a given society and is less 'instrumental' than organisation-centred training and learning interventions.

Even if one operates in an instrumental, work-oriented, organisation-centred perspective, there is no guarantee of a common understanding. The concepts used are reinterpreted in the context in which they are being applied and this will vary from organisation to organisation. Tyson (1995) argues that one of the functions of Human Resource Management (HRM) is concerned with interpreting symbols on behalf of organisation members. Although he does not pursue this point, I assume this is in order to generate individual and shared meanings around purpose and why *I* am here and *you* are here and *it* is here. Organisation symbols indicate to members and outsiders the value orientation of the institution and can range from frequently used expressions to dress codes, artefacts, space allocations, style of furnishings and who gets what. It can be argued even more powerfully that HRD practitioners have to undertake such an interpretive role as part of their *modus operandi*. However it is not just a question of interpretation. Teaching, presenting, coaching and counselling are just some of the HRD methods undertaken to make sense of such organisation symbols to stakeholders, to enable them to be learned. And what about the introduction of new symbols to indicate that an organisation is undergoing change and that things will be different in the future? This constant concern with meaning and learning and the subtleties of these concepts by those responsible for HRD can paradoxically be yet another reason why the language of HRD appears so jargon ridden and its meaning hidden. One is always asking – and being challenged about:

- *What are we doing?*
- *Why are we doing it?*
- *How are we being evaluated?*
- *How can we make sense of it all?*
- *How can we make sense of it to others?*

Words are used in the form of questions to express the ambiguities faced by those trying to translate the subtleties of meaning into learning frameworks and language that, it is hoped, capture all the nuances of actual experience and associated reflection, conceptualisation and experimentation. If care is not exercised it can lead to a paranoid profession!

A further reason for differences of meaning, and the topic of this chapter, lies in the emergent nature of HRD and a sense that people are finding their way to something new and creative. This sense of newness and expansion was expressed most forcibly by Robert Blake (the Blake of the Blake–Mouton Managerial Grid) (*see* Fig. 3.1).

| Figure 3.1 | Robert Blake's view |

'The field of human resource development defies definition and boundaries. It's difficult to put in a box. It has become so large, extensive, and inclusive that it's now greater than all outdoors.

And the field keeps growing. It continues to spread beyond where it was yesterday, not just domestically but worldwide. One of the few comparable examples, and even then on the physical side of things, is the microchip, which has spread in a few short years across borders and into every nook and cranny of human activity . . .

Whatever the specifics, the general category and focus of HRD seems to centre on human betterment, wherever and in whatever domain of life HRD is interested. The goal? As it may be judged in years ahead, at least in my 1995 view, the HRD field will be seen as crossing a great frontier, with the goal of bringing applications of the behavioural sciences into everyday use to better human activities in all of their shapes and forms.

When or where will its explanation ever stop? No one knows' (Blake, 1995).

This expansionist perspective, while undoubtedly somewhat extreme – even if it does come from one of the most respected names in the management literature – is not even touched on in the mainstream literature in the UK. On the whole UK writers have equated HRD with training and development and often, even more narrowly, with *employee* training and *employee* development, in each instance seeing its sphere of operation confined to a given organisation and often subsumed within an overall HRM framework.

The somewhat visionary nature of Blake's exposition has affinities in style if not in substance to the introductory – and exhortatory – address by Curtis Plott, the President of the American Society for Training and Development (ASTD), to the 1995 ASTD Conference in Dallas (Plott, 1995) (*see* Fig.3.2).

| Figure 3.2 | Plott's 'Wake-up call' |

Under an overall rallying cry of 'Wake-up call', Plott placed great emphasis on participating in the excitement of a profession whose time has come. The message was that HRD as a discipline in the US was in a period of transition. Whereas in the past it had focused on the classroom training and education of individual employees, its emerging rationale was now with workplace learning and the enhancement of performance. This in turn was leading to knowledge creation at a macro-organisational level and contributing to sustainable competitive advantage in a global marketplace.

As Plott put it, the HRD profession needed to recognise four truths.

1 As organisations have changed their systems and processes, so HRD professionals have to consider themselves as architects of that change.

2 No longer should HRD professionals consider their primary purpose to be the training of individuals, but rather to be operating at organisational level to create shared learning.

▶▶

▶▶ Figure 3.2 continued

3 Thinking in terms of an organisational world changes one's perspective: it is like operating from a different end of a telescope to thinking solely in terms of individual learning.

4 It is not just HRD professionals who are looking at learning from a different end of a telescope; line managers and other key organisational players are also thinking about learning issues from a new perspective.

Plott also made the following observations:

■ there is a ferment in the profession;

■ there is a new richness in the complexity of offerings;

■ HRD professionals occupy a pivotal role in orchestrating change;

■ learning and learning technology are not enough; the linkage between learning, performance and knowledge needs to be established.

The substantive conclusions related to workplace learning are unremarkable enough to a UK audience becoming accustomed to initiatives such as National Vocational Qualifications (NVQs) with their emphasis on performance and assessment in the workplace. NVQs, which were only introduced into the UK in 1986, also demonstrate that new disciplines, new ways of perceiving the world, can generate a technical vocabulary at remarkable speed:

> On the subject of terminology alone, as with all new areas, it is amazing how much 'vocabulary' can be generated over a relatively short period of time. Lead bodies, awarding bodies, assessment centres, D units (D31–36), elements, units, performance criteria, range statements, are just a few of the terms that players in the system have grown to know and love since 1986 when NVQs were first introduced. And for many of the terms there can be subtle shades of meaning and differences in interpretation . . . All this can be very frustrating for people who are trying to find their way through the labyrinth (Walton, 1996a).

The rest of this chapter is concerned with tracing some of the functional and intellectual roots of HRD, indicating emergent themes that are impacting on professional practice and redefining parameters within which the subject can be studied. Many of the themes have strategic implications which are developed more fully in subsequent chapters.

THE RATIONALE BEHIND THE TERM HUMAN RESOURCE DEVELOPMENT

An instructive debate on the sensitivities around HRD terminology and its symbolic connotations was enjoined in the pages of *Training and Development* (UK) in April 1992. The protagonists were Barry Oxtoby, then a Branch Chair of the former UK Institute of Training and Development (ITD) and Peter Coster, then Chairman of its Policy Committee (*see* Fig. 3.3).

Figure 3.3	The debate on HRD terminology

Oxtoby

'I hold the view that HRD should be eliminated from all official publications. The words "Human Resource" reduce people to the same level of importance as materials, money, machinery and methods – which are also resources. *People* need to be distinguished as the world's greatest asset. HRD is without feeling for people. Who can define what HRD is? Those outside our profession must be confused, when those inside it cannot describe it in a consistent way. HRD is a phrase of the verbose. It takes three words to describe a process when one word is quite sufficient. The bleak prospect for the term 'HRD' may be summarised as:

A fashionable flavour of the late 1980s and early 1990s which was promoted by those whose motives for the profession may have been reasonable – but which attempted to gain professional recognition and growth without an everyday feeling for people and their community: a lack of understanding that real growth comes from within the hearts and minds of ordinary people.'

Coster

'Words used in combination can and do have a distinct and separate meaning from their use individually – and that is what has been happening to "Human Resource Development". I do not think of HRD as a phrase which dehumanises people, but more optimistically as one which seeks to humanise and widen our thinking about resources and about who, and not just what, adds real value to an activity. "Developing human potential" is the meaning that HRD is acquiring. The ITD define HRD as "the process whereby people develop their full potential in life and work". It is no longer – and I don't think it ever was – about the use of human resources in a mechanical and heartless way, but about seeing people as a resource that constitutes the most important source of help to others.'

Human resource development as a technical term was coined by the American writer Leonard Nadler in the late 1960s and defined originally as 'a series of organised activities conducted within a specified time and designed to produce behavioural change' of organisational members (Nadler, 1970). It was conceived as a catch-all expression, specifically incorporating three types of vocational learning activity that would contribute to making individuals more effective at work:

■ training, focusing on immediate changes in job performance;

■ education, geared towards intermediate changes in individual capabilities;

■ development concerned with long-term improvement in the individual worker (Nadler, 1979).

This early formulation is broadly synonymous with what is commonly considered to be employer-sponsored 'training and development' and undertaken to achieve individual performance improvement. It does not have the breadth of connotations with which HRD is becoming associated today. Nadler himself has clearly wrestled with the concept over the years, and provided a series of expanded definitions as practice has changed, without moving his position substantially. His 1989 version was: 'HRD is organised learning experiences provided for employees within a specified period of time to bring about the possibility of performance improvement and/or personal growth' (Nadler and Nadler, 1989).

The practice of differentiating between training, education and development has become common practice in the HRD literature. The definition of training is conventional, representing the short-term acquisition of knowledge, skills and attitudes which individuals need to learn in order to be able to effectively undertake their job role. In the UK the literature has not distinguished between 'education' and 'development' in quite the same way as Nadler's formulation. On the whole, 'development' of the individual at the workplace has been associated with the realisation of potential, through activities and supporting processes which position people more effectively for medium- and longer-term opportunities. Education tends to have a greater spread of connotations, interpretations including:

■ exposure to planned learning activities which are intended to train the mind (Megginson *et al.*, 1993); or

■ a major contribution to the development process, affecting not only the formation of knowledge and abilities, but also of character, culture, aspirations and achievements (Harrison, 1992).

Since Nadler's original formulation numerous alternative, all-encompassing statements have endeavoured to capture the essence of the employee-focused concept of HRD. Weinberger (1998) provides a chronological list of such definitions from her in-depth literature research into US sources. The definition offered by Megginson *et al.* (1993) is one of many attempts from the UK. For them HRD is 'the term used to describe an integrated and holistic approach to changing work related behaviour, using a range of learning techniques and strategies'.

The work of Gilley and Egglund (1989) brings out the contradictions inherent in adopting a purely instrumental, employer and performance-driven position. They argue that calling people 'human resources' indicates an instrumental and asset-based orientation – with similar connotations to 'financial resources' and 'capital resources'. This leads them to conclude that HRD is about the utilisation of people *within* organisations and that performance improvement is the ultimate goal. When they look into the individual *development* connotations associated with the term and ask what is meant by the development of people they are faced with a difficulty in sustaining this conclusion. For them, 'development of people refers to the advancement of knowledge, skills and competencies, and the improved behaviour of people within the organisation for both their personal and professional use. This reflects a focus on the individual' (ibid., pp. 4–5). Although they do not make this point, it also implies that what people learn *within* organisations is transferable to a wider community. After all, unlike financial and capital resources, individuals have an independent existence.

The point can be demonstrated in diagrammatical form (*see* Fig. 3.4). An organisation can be perceived as a technical system to which financial, capital and human resources are inputs which contribute to value-adding processes resulting in customer-valued products and services.

| Figure 3.4 | The technical system |

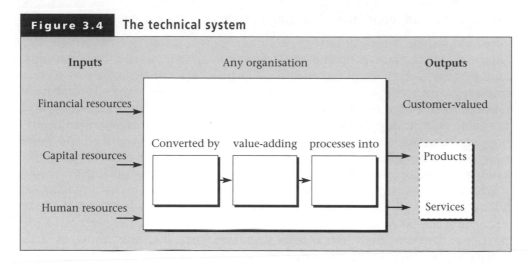

In the model shown in Fig. 3.4, the 'human resource' enters the system, but does not leave it. People are valued purely in instrumental terms for their asset value. But in practice they do leave the system. They do go home, find other sources of occupying themselves, draw upon learning in all its manifestations.

The sociotechnical model, on the other hand (*see* Fig. 3.5), captures the essence of the individual role. It was originally based on the proposition that one should jointly optimise individual and task needs when designing work processes. When viewed from an HRD perspective, it provides a theoretical model for demonstrating the distinctive nature of the human resource whose learning we are trying to enhance.

| Figure 3.5 | The sociotechnical system |

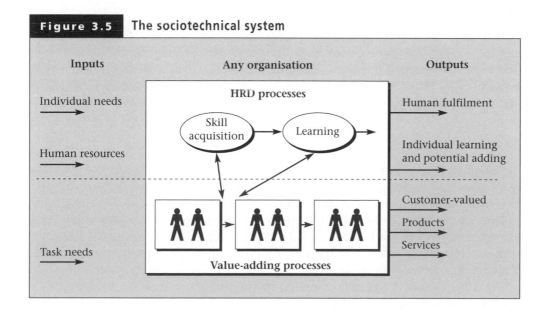

'Intentional' and 'accidental' learning in human resource development

Early (and some current) definitions of HRD emphasise a concern with intentional learning as opposed to 'incidental' or 'accidental' learning. Stewart (1998) differentiates between 'learning' and 'interventions', which he considers to be two distinct processes contributing to HRD. 'Learning,' he contends, 'can, will and does happen, irrespective of the wishes or actions of anyone.' It is as natural and inevitable as breathing. However, 'the practice of HRD is constituted by deliberate, purposive and active INTERVENTIONS in the natural process of learning. Such interventions can take many forms, most capable of categorising as education or training or development'. This is in large part a reflection of the instrumental way in which learning was perceived, and also because there was no methodology to capture 'accidental' processes for the benefit of the organisation. As we shall see throughout the book, there is a school of thought which argues not only that the practice of HRD can incorporate natural or 'accidental learning' and tacit skills acquisition but that it is also a matter of some importance to do so. The growing literature on knowledge management tries to address how learning in all its manifestations – accidental as well as intentional – can be captured and translated into organisational learning.

Hendry *et al.* (1991) connect accidental learning and learning climate in discussing two distinct meanings implicit in HRD, where HRD is seen as:

- a methodology for learning;
- a philosophy for investing in people.

They argue in the context of small and medium-sized enterprises (SMEs) that:

ultimately, HRD and effective learning depends on the 'philosophy' or attitude towards people which infuses the organisation. If that is positive, recruitment, job design, work organisation and the style of supervision/management will be of a kind to encourage individual learning and development, and the latter can be left more 'to chance'.

The extent to which learning can be left 'to chance', even in SMEs, is discussed in Chapter 13. One possible consequence of adopting this perspective is the risk that organisations will opt out of funding off-the-job learning opportunities that extend beyond basic skills acquisition. Much depends on the organisational learning climate and how a given organisation sees individual development.

Generic occupational or work-role training and development

Although the recipients of the HRD effort as originally conceived were individual employees, the approach to organising their learning has invariably been through generic occupational or work-role training and development.

Thus throughout the literature, as well as in in-house brochures describing HRD programmes, reference has been made to such activities as: operative training; apprentice training; sales training; staff training; supervisory training; staff development; management development and so on.

The 1997 'Industry Report', compiled by the magazine *Training*, incorporates a similar classification to report current employer-sponsored training-related activities in corporate America. Out of a total expenditure of $56.8 billion, 26 per cent was spent on professionals, 25 per cent on managers and 12 per cent on sales-people. The remaining 36 per cent was grouped together under the category 'All others' (*Training*, 1997).

'Human resource development' versus 'training and development'

In many quarters 'HRD' and 'training and development' are seen as interchangeable notions. There is also still a tendency in much of the literature to associate HRD merely with *employee* training and development and often with a particular focus on training. For example Holden (1995) identifies the following eight points as guidance for an HRD plan.

1 Discern the training and development requirements from the organisational strategy and business objectives.
2 Analyse the training requirements for effective work performance in organisational functions and jobs.
3 Analyse the existing qualities and training needs of current employees.
4 Devise an HRD plan which fills the gap between organisational requirements and the present skills and knowledge of employees.
5 Decide on the appropriate training and development methods to be used for individuals and groups.
6 Decide who is to have responsibility for the plan and its various parts.
7 Implement the plan and monitor and evaluate its progress.
8 Amend the HRD plan in the light of monitoring and evaluation and changes in business strategy.

It is indicative that this checklist was given in a chapter called 'Training'. It focuses on learning activities within the boundaries of a given organisation. It is a deficit model in that it focuses on what needs to be 'done' to individuals in order to bridge any gaps. It does not address 'learning' as a self-generated activity.

One of the first UK references to HRD as a distinctive functional area was made by Pettigrew *et al.* (1988) in a cross-sectoral review of 20 companies (*see* Fig. 3.6).

Figure 3.6   Human resource development versus 'training'

In their analysis of 20 companies, Pettigrew *et al.* (1988) distinguished between 'training and retraining' and 'HRD' as two of ten core personnel areas significantly influenced by internal and external change. Their overall categorisation system was somewhat unclear, partly because they did not define HRD, or other key terms such as personnel and HRM. The relationship between HRD and HRM/Personnel is addressed in Chapter 5.

Without formally defining HRD, they implicitly indicated what it meant for them by virtue of the following functions they included within its remit:

■ career management;
■ planned job experiences including secondment and job rotation;

▶▶

▶▶ Figure 3.6 continued

■ mentoring;

■ identification of individuals with development potential through use of appropriate recruitment and selection methods;

■ increased profiling of graduate recruitment, tiered recruitment (defined as placing new entrants into separate streams, each with their own set of employment conditions and commitment to career development), appraisal and assessment centres.

In essence, they differentiated 'employee training' and 'employee/career development' and reserved the term HRD for processes contributing to the latter.

Their observations on HRD were informative. Within their sample they found that most firms did not have an identified person or function specifically designated to carry out HRD. They found that HRD as a recognised term/activity tended to be the prerogative of the larger firms.

They also made the revealing observation that 'the real responsibility for carrying out many of these HRD activities lay in the hands of line management'.

The operational roots of human resource development – archetypes

To understand the current and likely future directions of HRD it is important to have some sense of what it has meant in the past.

The mainstream HRD tradition has its roots firmly planted in the world of training, in establishing methods whereby individuals can acquire the skills, knowledge and attitudes which will enable them to effectively carry out tasks in a work environment – usually in an organisation context. Although the point is not often made, training in employing organisations has been strongly influenced by approaches adopted in the Armed Services. Many training managers, particularly in commercial organisations, have been recruited from military personnel who were previously responsible for training in the Services. This is not too surprising, as in peace time the Armed Services function primarily as training institutions. Three major HRD historical archetypes can be identified.

Semi-skilled workers and scientific management

Much conceptual work on organisations in the early years of the twentieth century tended to characterise individuals entering the organisation as unskilled 'raw material' which needed to be 'trained up' to the standards required of a work-force. The traditional military drill stereotype exemplified this way of thinking. Individuals were seen, not as beings possessing, or needing to possess, distinctive characteristics or special learning needs, but as raw recruits to be modelled and fashioned in a particular way. Just as individual infantrymen were often seen as expendable – cannon fodder to achieve military ends – so too in machine-driven factories, as parodied in Chaplin's *Modern Times*, individuals were viewed as mere adjuncts to machines, to be substituted by machines when these became sufficiently cheap and sophisticated. In truth, many of the work functions were dull, repetitive, demeaning and deadening.

The scientific school of management, as epitomised by F. W. Taylor in the USA at the end of the nineteenth century and the beginning of the twentieth century, had militaristic overtones in the way people were trained to carry out a predetermined sequence of tasks in a predetermined way. The mechanistic view of people's roles meant that they were 'trained', not developed, much in the way that horses are trained to be compliant followers of orders. Taylor's world recognised no career progression. His approach – evocative of the drill – was a very good way of rapidly training large numbers of workers in narrowly defined tasks. It was particularly effective in the USA of the early twentieth century where a high percentage of the populace were non-indigenous and possessed a limited command of English, and, perhaps significantly, were not very effective in organising themselves into trade unions. Once the basic skills were acquired, this was sufficient. There was no scope for the development of advanced skills since jobs were so repetitive.

A number of writers have commented that the ethos of the machine model of organisation is still a dominant force in Western companies, at the expense of concerns for personal development. Bierama (1996) expresses it in the following forceful terms:

> HRD processes have embraced the machine mentality exemplified by rigid separation of work from life, quick-fix management gimmicks, reactive behaviours versus long-term planning, training unrelated to strategy, training for short-term performance gains, management ownership and control of development, over-reliance on formal training programmes, teacher-centred development programmes, incremental change, little or no support for personal development or needs assessment.

Bratton and Gold (1994) contend that subterranean barriers – based on the old ideology – to a progressive approach to HRD exist even within those organisations which espouse new forms of organisational learning.

One of the features of scientific management was a move away from learning on the job towards group-training methods that took place away from the workplace itself and into what could be described as a classroom environment. Current US thinking, however, is tending towards a reversal of this situation and to move learning – and HRD practitioners – back to the workplace. The ASTD currently presents one arm of its core business as facilitating workplace learning.

The craft worker tradition of training

The craft worker tradition of training emanated from the Guild system of the Middle Ages. Young adults registered as apprentices to experienced workers who trained them in somewhat leisurely fashion based on their own experience. Learning was very personal and the apprentice masters had no particular methodology in imparting their skills beyond those that they had learned from their masters. Much of early HRD work was associated with developing a technology for training of young people in a systematic way. Many manufacturing organisations established apprentice schools – some of which still exist – in close proximity to their factories. The development of such schools had the effect of taking HRD practitioners away from the workplace. Another feature of the growth of these schools was that they were often staffed by experienced workers in mid or late career as opposed to career professionals.

Career development of the professional cadre

Max Weber's model of bureaucracy, which drew together concepts originating from the last quarter of the eighteenth century, provided a tentative schema for the development of those individuals who were seen as having an organisational career route. He saw the need for a professional cadre, separate from the mass of subalterns operating at the lowest echelons of an organisational hierarchy. This cadre was selected on the basis of pre-eminent intellectual qualities, measured by success in open entrance examinations. Cadre members were then coached on how to interpret rules and procedures so as to be able to enact official decisions on behalf of the organisation and justify them to external clients. Subsequent skills and knowledge acquisition was accidental and experiential. Continued exposure to the rules and greater familiarity with how they might be 'correctly' interpreted were deemed sufficient learning to determine promotion, which in the absence of evidence disproving the validity of such an approach was based on experience measured by length of service.

Because of class divisions and the way society was perceived, there tended to be a hands-off approach to the officer cadre, or to supervisors and managers in the new commercial organisations of the mid-Industrial Revolution period. The implication was that they had the innate ability to develop themselves once put in a position of responsibility. In other words, whereas training has always been managed by others, historically development has been seen as more susceptible to self-management, something which happens by virtue of the individual's experience in, and exposure to, organisational contingencies. Management development, accordingly, has originated from a separate tradition to training and in some instances has not been orchestrated by the same functional area which takes responsibility for training interventions.

The interdisciplinary nature of human resource development

Figure 3.7 looks at the intellectual roots of HRD.

Figure 3.7   The intellectual roots of human resource development

Willis (1997) provides the following extended metaphor to describe the intellectual roots to HRD:

> The Mississippi River system began in many places including its own river source, and it is more than the sum of its tributaries. It is also distinctly different from any of them and different from what it once was. Metaphorically, HRD is like the Mississippi, downstream from its origins and its contributing disciplines. It is a whole new 'river'.
>
> To attempt a topological map or even a simple listing of root disciplines is hazardous, for HRD theorists and practitioners will dip from whatever disciplinary sources they need at any given time. Nevertheless there is considerable agreement that adult education, instructional design and performance technology, psychology, business and economics, sociology, cultural anthropology, organisation theory

▶▶

▶▶ Figure 3.7 continued

and communication, philosophy, axiology (the study of values), and human relations theories, principles and practices have all become a visible part of the HRD
milieu. On the river map, these are very large streams in their own right. Even this
should not be considered an exhaustive list of tributary disciplines.

She contends that it is difficult for those in HRD to maintain strong identifica-
tions with their root disciplines. Continuing in metaphorical vein, she suggests that
although they can travel overland or chug upstream to their roots, they are forever
changed by their trip downstream. She could equally have made the point that
whatever our destination we will have residual memories from the past, some of
which we cling on to and which forever influence our way of looking at the world.

Her comprehensive list contains for me some significant surprises. There is no
reference to the bodies of knowledge that constitute strategic management and
human resource management in particular, and management practice in general.

The development of the profession: The USA and the UK compared

In the USA the first professional association focusing exclusively on HRD issues
was founded in 1942 as the American Society of Training Directors. The first meeting, held in 1943, was attended by 15 training directors. In 1945 the association
published the first issue of *Industrial Training News*, renamed in 1947 the *Journal of
Industrial Training*. In the same year this journal produced one of the first definitions of training for the profession:

> It is suggested that training be defined as that tool of management which, through sound
> principles of teaching and learning, is utilised to raise the productive ability and to main-
> tain and improve the performance of all employees.

In 1964 the association changed its name to the American Society of Training
and Development (ASTD) and in 1966 it renamed its publication the *Training and
Development Journal*.

As already explained, HRD as a term was coined by Leonard Nadler in the late
1960s. However the ASTD has persisted with its 1964 designation.

In the UK the development of career professionals came somewhat later. It was
triggered by the Industrial Training Act 1964 which introduced a network of
Industrial Training Boards for designated industries, and a compulsory training
levy/training grant system for all but small organisations. It led in the same year to
the formation of the Institute of Training Officers which in the late 1970s was
renamed the Institute of Training and Development. As in the USA it sponsored its
own journal, entitled *Training and Development*.

Whereas in the USA the ASTD has maintained its separate identity, in the UK
in 1994 the Institute of Training and Development merged with the Institute of
Personnel Management to form the Institute of Personnel and Development. This
reflected the sense among members that although HRD practitioners might
follow different career paths to HRM professionals, there was a commonality of
interest that would be better served by coming together. Membership of the new

body is dependent upon becoming professionally qualified, which in turn requires a clear demonstration that core personnel and development issues are known and understood. The new body has full-time officers operating as policy advisers on HRD issues.

RECENT APPROACHES TO HUMAN RESOURCE DEVELOPMENT

Figure 3.8 explores the emerging concept of HRD.

Figure 3.8   The emerging concept of human resource development

The University Forum for HRD is a UK-based network of universities concerned with the development of professional qualification structures and research activities in the HRD field. In 1995 it adopted the following position statement on HRD. The statement implies that, although HRD as a concept and as a practical discipline owes many of its roots to employer-driven learning activities, it is beginning to encompass far more than traditional 'training and development'. It also reveals a concern to demonstrate appropriate structural and functional relationships with other areas of HR.

POSITION STATEMENT ON THE EMERGING CONCEPT OF HRD

The scope of HRD

Just as many authorities see Human Resource Management as a synonym for Personnel Management, so a number of people see Human Resource Development as a synonym for Training and Development. There is also a school of thought which further restricts the scope of Training and Development to the provision of learning opportunities for employees within a given organisation. These perspectives do not reflect current thinking or emerging practices on the subject. HRD as a process has been defined by Patricia McLagan of the American Society of Training and Development as 'the integrated use of training and development, organisation development and career development to improve individual, group and organisational effectiveness'. These three areas use development as their primary process. HRD as an emerging concept thus encompasses training and development but is not restricted to it.

The target for development opportunities has also been extended beyond the perimeters of a given organisation as activities are increasingly being outsourced and sub-contracted. Non-employee human resource development is concerned with enabling an organisation to influence its external environment through a planned process of learning so that the skills and knowledge of those outside its boundaries on whom it depends to a greater or lesser extent are enhanced.

Strategic HRD is an extension of the above. It puts particular emphasis on the development of comprehensive, co-ordinated and dynamic approaches for major learning initiatives within and outside an organisation in order to facilitate the achievement of corporate objectives in a competitive environment.

▶▶ Figure 3.8 continued

The emerging nature of theory and practice in this area is leading to much reflection on the future relationship between HRM and HRD. It is not helpful in this debate to think of HRD as a sub set of HRM, either in structural or functional terms. As the strategic significance of organisational learning as a source of competitive advantage gains recognition, a strategic need arises for appropriately positioned 'learning architects' with the distinctive competencies to orchestrate learning initiatives on behalf of organisations.

Source: University Forum for HRD.

The extension of the original rationale

From the late 1980s and extending throughout the 1990s a number of trends can be discerned in HRD practice and theory. These include the matters discussed in the following pages.

The connection to corporate strategy

Swanson and Arnold (1997) contend that:

it is difficult to find an article about HRD without at least some reference to linking HRD to the strategic goals of the organisation. It has become almost axiomatic that if HRD is to develop into a respected and useful player in organisations, then it will need to position itself as a strategically important partner. HRD will need to assume the same level of importance as the traditional core organisational processes: finance, production and marketing.

Garavan (1991) is typical of this line of thinking when he argues that HRD:

is best seen as the strategic management of training, development and of management/professional education interventions, so as to achieve the objectives of the organisation while at the same time ensuring the full utilisation of the knowledge in detail and skills of individual employees. It is concerned with the management of employee learning for the long-term, keeping in mind the explicit corporate and business strategies.

He summarises his literature review by arguing that 'when management at board level treat HRD as making an important contribution, the HRD function wields a higher profile'.

Figure 3.9 looks further at the connection between HRD and business strategy.

Figure 3.9 Human resource development and business strategy

Twigg and Albon (1992) also stress the connection with business strategy, and strengthen the link with other business processes. Their framework additionally incorporates a number of areas which are more conventionally associated with Human Resource Management. They suggest that HRD:

▶▶

▶▶ Figure 3.9 continued

> is a set of processes for developing people at work which should be linked to business strategy and integrated with other major business processes such as supplier management or purchasing.
>
> The processes involved in HRD are . . . training and development . . . performance management . . . resourcing.
>
> ■ *Training and development* comprises activities aimed at promoting learning from formal courses to informal counselling or advice.
>
> ■ *Performance management* refers to goal setting and appraisal processes, linked to reward through performance-related pay (PRP) and promotion.
>
> ■ *Resourcing* is the management of the 'stocks and flows' of the group including manpower planning, recruitment and career management.
>
> They emphasise the importance of an organisational climate where it is recognised that:
>
> ■ active learning starts at the top;
>
> ■ senior managers embrace an open, active approach rather than portraying HRD as an expensive 'treatment';
>
> ■ business and HRD managers are operating in partnership.
>
> They suggest three steps which they believe will contribute towards such an organisational climate:
>
> 1 Human resource development professionals decide jointly with senior management 'what we need to be good at'.
>
> 2 Refocus the training function – streamline it and encourage joint working with business managers, to ensure that trainers address business issues.
>
> 3 Increase the pace of learning – use innovative approaches to reduce the inertia usually associated with lengthy programmes of off-site courses.

Clarifying who benefits from learning

As we have noted, the relationship between learning which benefits the organisation and that which benefits the individual has always been an ongoing tension in the HRD arena. In recent years a number of organisations have tried to clarify this relationship, and to balance notions such as continuous personal learning and development, on the one hand, with planned training contributing towards performance enhancement, on the other. It has often been asked why organisations should provide individuals with transferable skills which will enhance their marketability to others. One of the current trends has been to recognise that competition for high-quality staff is high and that a given organisation needs to increase its attractiveness as a place to work. The promise to provide 'top of the range' development opportunities is a feature of many of the publicity packages sent to attract potential graduate trainees. The promise of ongoing development opportunities is not restricted to professional or managerial staff, although the evidence is that they gain the biggest slice of the cake. For example Motorola in the USA guarantee all employees a minimum of 40 hours off-the-job training per year.

Armstrong (1992) tries to establish a win-win relationship between these tensions when he contends that 'human resource development empowers members of the organisation to increase their contribution to its success while enabling them to build their skills and capacities simultaneously'. He believes this can be achieved through:

■ the use of systematic and planned training approaches;

■ adopting a policy of continuous development;

■ creating and maintaining a learning organisation;

■ ensuring that all training activities are performance related;

■ paying particular attention to management development and career planning.

This, of course, is a normative model for HRD – that is, it suggests the direction in which HRD should be going.

Individuals taking responsibility for their own learning

Individuals have always been the prime recipients of HRD. However since the early 1980s, perhaps influenced by the quality movement (*see* Chapter 14) there has been a gradual swing towards seeing the individual as a customer of the learning process as opposed to being a mere recipient. There has also been a swing towards seeing individuals taking greater responsibility for their own learning, and the development of partnership models with employers in which the shared nature of the responsibility is spelt out.

Vocational skills and knowledge acquisition is now often seen as part of a process of continuous personal development and lifelong learning which is no longer orchestrated – or indeed funded – in totality by the employer. Some of these needs will be met by an employing organisation, some by colleges and universities and independent training providers.

One of the core linked themes of recent years has been the growth of HRD perspectives which emphasise various approaches to non-classroom-based interventions such as self-directed and experiential learning.

The broadening of the human resource development constituency

The constituents of HRD are no longer held to be restricted to individuals operating as employees within a given organisation. Rothwell and Kazanas (1989) emphasised the significance of non-employee development as an area of theoretical and practical concern. Walton (1996b) further refined their concept, defining non-employees as 'those individuals or groups who have some relationship with an organisation but are not in an employer-employee relationship', and differentiating between non-employee training, education and development. This theme is developed in Chapter 10, where the extent of HRD investment in non-employee learning is highlighted.

The extension into team learning

In organisational practice there has been an increasing focus on team-building activities as well as individual-based learning events, the orchestration of which is seen as falling within the HRD purview. The range of team-building activities can be remarkably diverse, from facilitating self-managed teams on the factory floor, to outdoor training for the entire senior management team, to problem-solving groups such as quality circles.

Dumaine (1990) estimated that about half of America's large companies were experimenting with self-managing teams, which the magazine forecast 'may be the productivity breakthrough of the 1990's'. In the UK, a survey of lean organisations published by the University of Bath (Purcell 1996) found that team working was at the heart of modern production and service delivery methods. In the report Purcell contended that:

> teamworking is the fulcrum for responsiveness for most organisations, regardless of sector. As well as being a better way of working, providing improved decision making and response time, teams provide social cohesion, a focus for improving employee satisfaction and having fun, as well as cultural identity, the best means of building commitment and reinforcing identity with the firm.

Prentice (1996) points out the learning-time commitment associated with creating effective self-managed teams compared to more traditional ways of team working. This commitment has major implications for the extent and duration of the HRD effort.

The incorporation of organisation development

At the end of the 1980s an extension of the scope of HRD from its predominant focus on individuals started to emerge in the US literature. This was strongly influenced by the work of Patricia Mclagan for the ASTD. In 1983 the ASTD sponsored a study under the project management of McLagan entitled 'Models for Excellence'. An outcome of the study was the development of a Human Resource Wheel which included organisation development (OD) as one of nine separate but related HR areas. A 1987 extension of the study, again directed by McLagan, led to a revision of the wheel, with OD being incorporated as a mainstream component of HRD.

As an aside, the McLagan position is not strictly correct. Human resource development is not concerned with all aspects of organisational life that have development as their primary focus. It is not, for example, involved in research and development or product development. It would be more accurate to contend that HRD is concerned with those processes and practices which have individual and collective learning as their primary focus.

Although seeing OD as a constituent part of HRD is relatively recent, OD as a practical discipline has a tradition extending back to the 1960s. Warner Burke (1994) makes particular reference to the six-volume series of OD books published by Addison-Wesley in 1969 which he considers to be one of the first attempts to define the field. The quick growth of interest in the subject was demonstrated by a 1974 survey of OD practice carried out by Manab Thakar for the IPM which quoted no less than 50 separate definitions. The following three definitions of OD, taken, from the survey, highlight most of the underlying principles:

■ 'an effort, planned, organisation-wide, and managed from the top, to increase organisations' "processes" using behavioural science knowledge' (Beckhard, 1969);

■ 'a response to change – a complex educational strategy intended to change beliefs, attitudes, values and structures of organisations so that they can better adapt to new technologies, markets and challenges, and to the dizzying rate of change itself' (Bennis, 1969);

■ 'a total organisational effort to improve team effectiveness – decision making processes in particular – in collaboration with behavioural scientist consultants emphasising team and goal effectiveness' (French, 1971).

Extracting the key features from these and other definitions, we see that OD involves:

■ organisation-wide planned change to improve organisation effectiveness;

■ use of consultants with a behavioural science orientation as change agents or facilitators;

■ the active commitment and participation of the chief executive and the top management team;

■ acceptance by the organisation's management of deciding on a programme of action for improving the organisation's effectiveness.

On the whole OD has tended to be undertaken by external consultants supporting organisations in large-scale change efforts. This leads to a need to clarify the relationship between internal and external HRD contributions in the management of change.

The incorporation of career development

The 1987 'Models for Excellence' study also saw career development as a mainstream component of HRD. Thus HRD became defined as the 'integrated use of training and development, career development and organisational development to improve individual and organisational effectiveness' (McLagan, 1989). It was concerned with those aspects of organisation life which had development as their primary focus.

Human resource development thus came to be seen in the USA as a multifaceted discipline that employs well-qualified individuals who exercise instructing, advising/coaching, HRD designing, managing and consulting skills to integrate training and development, organisation development, and career development with the goal of improving individual, group, and organisational effectiveness (McLagan, 1989; Willis, 1990).

Career development used to be the preserve of the management and professional cadres in large organisations, and often associated with complex succession planning systems. As we shall see in Chapter 8, the trend towards individuals taking responsibility for their own learning has gone hand in hand with an expectation that careers will be more self managed and that the notion of a career for life within the same organisation is not a realistic assumption. Stewart (1997) quotes data showing that in the USA, one out of nine managers disappeared as a result of downsizing between 1983 and 1994, and that nearly half the drop had occurred since 1990. This in turn has led to a greater emphasis on vocational guidance. More significantly, perhaps, it has challenged the notion that HRD takes place within the boundaries of a given organisation for the sole benefit of that organisation. People are very conscious of the fact that organisations cannot offer a job for life and expect to be provided with transferable skills that makes then competitive in the marketplace.

The emphasis on internal consultancy

Organisational development as a technique emphasises the use of consultants, often external, with a behavioural science orientation. Recent thinking on HRD has led to a clarifying and strengthening of the role of internal consultant, particularly in terms of providing performance and facilitation support back at the workplace. For example Levi Strauss and Co. in the USA have specifically differentiated the in-house HRD organisation into two arms, one of which develops and administers training programmes in a traditional way, while the internal consultancy group work on a day-to-day basis with line managers and their work teams (Garfield, 1992).

One of the features of the internal consultancy role in the USA has been a focus on performance consulting. This will be addressed in more detail in Chapter 6 on HRD roles and relationships, but it must be queried how closely it connects to learning issues.

The focus on organisational learning

The concept of the Learning Organisation emerged around 1990, influenced by writers such as Pedler *et al.* (1991) in the UK, and Senge (1990) in the USA, who also set up a centre for Organisational Learning at the Massachusetts Institute of Technology. Chapter 15 is dedicated to the whole area of organisational learning and the learning organisation. One of the key implications of this trend is to focus more on processes contributing to learning as opposed to orchestrating specific interventions. To be effective at organisational level HRD needs to be in the context of an appropriate organisational learning climate which in turn will contribute to people's willingness to learn and transfer learning to the workplace.

The link to knowledge management and the intellectual capital of an enterprise

There has been a recent burgeoning of literature referring to the importance of knowledge management and developing an organisation's intellectual capital. This development has been mirrored by a parallel change in organisation practice, with a reconfiguration of job roles in some organisations. For example, at Price Waterhouse before its merger with Coopers & Lybrand, a Director of HRD and Intellectual Capital was appointed.

The focus on intellectual capital and concern with knowledge workers is leading to what some call the knowledge theory of the firm (e.g. Grant, 1997). This theory recognises the significance of tacit skills development by individuals. It holds the following:

1 Knowledge is the key sustainable source of value added in an organisation and central to the development of strategic advantage.

2 A key distinction is between explicit knowledge, which is manifest and capable of being documented and presented in a form that can be presented to others; and tacit knowledge which is manifest only in its application and not readily amenable to transfer.

3 Individuals are the primary agents of knowledge acquisition and in the case of tacit knowledge – learned by them in an *ad hoc*, indeterminate way – are its principal repositories.

4 Organisations need to tap into this tacit knowledge, identify ways in which it can be made public and transferable and capture it so that it becomes part of the 'structural capital' of the organisation, available to others when knowledge workers have gone home for the evening or, indeed, left permanently.

According to Grant the key to knowledge management as a source of competitive advantage is achieving internal replication while avoiding external replication.

Some companies such as Dow Chemical, Andersen Consulting, Polaroid, Skandia and ICL are developing corporate-wide systems to track, exploit and create 'explicit' organisation knowledge, typically under the leadership of a director or vice-president of 'knowledge' or 'intellectual capital'. Human resource development practitioners should have a significant role to play in such development, given that their *raison d'être* is to facilitate knowledge and skills acquisition, either through direct training or through development processes.

There is a sense in which 'the knowledge theory of the firm', with its concomitant value set of seeing the individual as only a source of net worth, has such an instrumental orientation that it fails to pick up how and why individuals learn. From an HRD perspective one would be encouraging the provision of development processes whereby individuals can gain experiences and thereby generate new ideas rather than invest all one's time and effort in somehow making individual experiences from the past accessible to future generations.

Figure 3.10	**Emergence of strategic human resource development in the UK employment department (group)**

The Employment Department in the UK merged in 1995 with another government department to form the Department for Employment and Education. Before its merger three phases in the Department's approach to HRD can be identified, which typify trends in the UK in the late 1980s and early 1990s, and which provide an instructive example of the shift from training to strategic HRD in a public sector organisation over a six-year period.

1 Pre-1985: Traditional job training

■ concentration of training effort on induction or change of job;

■ not a concern of top management;

■ very little senior management training or development, other than in the early stages of employment;

■ personal development accorded very low priority;

■ no connection made between training effort and achievement of *organisation objectives* as opposed to *job-specific* requirements.

▶▶

▶▶ Figure 3.10 continued

---

2 1985–1991: Personal development

- growing interest in training and development by top management;

- training increasingly linked with the idea of continuing professional development and lifelong learning;

- focus changes to emphasise personal development;

- rapid growth of training and development for senior and middle management;

- introduction of individual development plans;

- production of HRD plans at branch and division level, annual review of plans by top management.

3 1991: Strategic human resource development

- link established between HRD and delivery of business objectives;

- emphasis shifts from *personal* development to training/development for *organisational* goals;

- HRD planning begins to be integrated with operational planning;

- efforts to raise awareness and/or understanding of organisation's mission and contribution of individual branches to it;

- emergence of service-level agreements between internal and external customers;

- delegation of training and development budgets to line management;

- more customised training and development offered;

- active promotion of competence-based programmes (NVQs) for Employment Department (Group) staff.

THE SCOPE OF HUMAN RESOURCE DEVELOPMENT

Not only has the breadth of coverage of HRD expanded from its original focus on training and development within an organisation context; its scope has also been extended. The concept can additionally be understood at societal, national and transnational levels.

Human resource development at societal level

According to Horwitz *et al.* (1995) HRD is concerned with the processes whereby the citizens of a nation acquire the knowledge and skills necessary to perform both specific occupational tasks and other social, cultural, intellectual and political roles in a society. Organisationally, they contend, this requires an integrated approach which considers HRD as:

- overcoming labour market segregation through addressing past inequalities based on race, gender and class;
- linked to human resource objectives which are, in turn, a function of an organisational strategy;
- an investment, not a cost.

It is significant that they are writing from a South African context, which accounts for the specific emphasis they give to overcoming labour market segregation. They go on to argue that there is a national need for an HRD strategy which identifies skilled, managerial and professional needs for career entry, with co-ordinated, national, industry and organised strategies to give effect to the immediate and longer-term needs for institution building. In this formulation HRD strongly emphasises the significance of national approaches to HR planning and forecasting. They also contend that affirmative action is an important component of HRD in the South African context. Nationally, the effective implementation of affirmative action requires a 'robust strategy with a planned and holistic set of objectives to enhance skills capacity and provide real job responsibility'. They quote Hofstede and others whose work supports a perspective that individual potential cannot be optimised unless cultural differences are understood and managed.

National-level human resource development

National-level HRD is often expressed as National Vocational Education and Training (NVET). Key issues are broad-based initiatives:

- to resource learning;
- to provide learning frameworks;
- to encourage learning by individuals acting independently and on their own initiative, or through the auspices of employers;

in order to provide a knowledge and skill base that will meet the competitive demands impacting on the economy. In recent years attention in the UK has increasingly turned to the needs of small and medium-sized employers (SMEs) whose contribution to the overall economy has grown.

Rosemary Harrison (1992) defines NVET for the UK in the following way:

> NVET seeks to reconcile the educational and training needs of the individual, the employer and the economy in such a way as to increase the competitiveness of organisations and of British industry as a whole, while at the same time ensuring that individuals can develop in ways that will enable them to lead meaningful satisfying lives.

The salience of this definition is reflected in the objectives of the UK Department for Education and Employment. These include (1996):

- to encourage *lifetime learning* so that people can use their skills and knowledge to compete effectively in a changing labour market;
- to provide a framework to encourage *employers* to invest in the skills needed for competitive business.

It should be noted that the Department's objectives are not identical to the four national (UK) strategic priorities for vocational education and training originally specified in the 1993 government publication 'Prosperity through Skills' (Department of Employment, 1993):

National Training Priorities

Priority 1: employers, the self-employed, and individual people in the workforce, investing effectively in the skills needed for business creation and growth, and for individual success.

Priority 2: people who are out of work or at a disadvantage in the labour market acquiring and maintaining relevant skills and obtaining appropriate support to enable them to compete better for employment or self-employment and to contribute more effectively to the economy.

Priority 3: encouraging and enabling young people to gain the skills and enterprising attitudes needed for entry to the workforce and to prepare them to realise their full potential throughout working life, and in particular to progress to NVQ/SVQ level 3 and beyond if they are able.

Priority 4: making the market for vocational education and training work better so that it responds to the changing needs of employers and individuals quickly and cost-effectively.

Transnational human resource development

National vocational training and eduction in the UK (and in France, Germany, The Netherlands and other countries) should increasingly be seen in a European context. Harrison's 1992 definition could equally apply to European Vocational Education and Training (EVET). Take, for example, the following quotation from the 1995 European Commission White Paper on Education and Training:

The future of Europe and its place in the world depend on its ability to give as much room for the personal fulfilment of its citizens, men and women alike, as it has up to now given to economic and monetary issues.

To this end the European Union Council of Ministers adopted, on 6 December 1994, a Decision 'establishing an action programme for the implementation of an EC vocational training policy' (Decision 94/819/EC). This programme is entitled LEONARDO da Vinci. The programme comprises a set of transnational Community measures which came into force on 1 January 1995 and will last until 31 December 1999. The Community measures are implemented on the basis of a 'Common Framework of Objectives for Community Action' (*see* Fig. 3.11), which is set out in the December 1994 Decision. It is worth noting that Member States retain responsibility for the content and organisation of their own vocational training systems.

| Figure 3.11 | LEONARDO da Vinci programme: common framework of objectives for community action |

Common framework of objectives:

a Improving the quality and innovation capacity of Member States' vocational training systems and arrangements;

b developing the European dimension in vocational training and vocational guidance;

c promoting lifelong learning training so as to encourage ongoing adaptation of skills to meet the needs of workers and undertakings, contribute to reducing unemployment and facilitate personal development;

d giving all young people in the Community who so wish the possibility of one or, if possible, two or more years of initial vocational training after their full-time compulsory education, leading to a vocational qualification recognized by the competent authorities in the Member State in which it is obtained;

e encouraging specific vocational training measures for adults without adequate vocational qualifications, in particular adults without adequate education;

f enhancing the status and attractiveness of vocational education and training and promoting parity of esteem for academic diplomas and vocational qualifications;

g promoting vocational training for young people and preparing young people for adult and working life, taking account of the requirements of society and technological change;

h encouraging specific vocational training measures for disadvantaged young people without adequate training and, in particular, young people who leave the education system without adequate training;

i promoting equality of access to initial and continuing training for persons disadvantaged by socio-economic, geographical or ethnic factors or by physical or mental disabilities; special attention must be given to persons affected by several risk factors likely to cause their social and economic exclusion;

j supporting vocational training policies in such a way that all workers in the Community have access to continuing vocational training throughout their working life without any discrimination;

k promoting equality of opportunity as regards access for men and women to vocational training and their effective participation therein, in particular so as to open up new areas of work to them and encourage them to return to work after a career break;

l promoting equality of opportunity as regards access for migrant workers and their children and the handicapped to vocational training and their effective participation therein;

m promoting cooperation on skill requirements and training needs, and encouraging the acquisition and transparency of qualifications and an understanding of the key skills relevant to technological development and the functioning of the internal market, including the free movement of goods, services, persons and capital, the competitiveness of undertakings and the requirements of the labour market;

n promoting vocational training in the light of the results of technological research and development programmes, particularly by means of cooperation between universities and undertakings in the sphere of training in technologies, their application and their transfer;

o promoting the gradual development of an open European vocational training and vocational qualifications area, particularly through the exchange of information and experience on obstacles to application of the free provision of services by training bodies;

p supporting activities aimed at developing linguistic skills as part of vocational training measures;

q promoting the development of vocational guidance facilities with a view to providing every individual with the opportunity to have lifelong high-quality vocational guidance;

r fostering the development of methods of self-training at the workplace and of open and distance learning and training, in particular to facilitate access to continuing vocational training;

s encouraging the development and integration of key skills in vocational training measures, with the aim of promoting the acquisition of flexible qualifications and personal skills necessary to worker mobility and the needs of undertakings.

Source: Decision 94/819 EC – OJ L340/8 (1994), European Community, Brussels.

The Common Framework of Objectives is more individual focused than employer focused. Note, for example, point (c). Also of interest in terms of establishing the parameters of HRD is point (q).

There is a need for an integrative HRD framework which clearly demonstrates the relationship between individual vocational learning, the needs of employers, and NVET. Harrison (1992, 1997), although she deals very thoroughly with UK NVET, seems to treat HRD as a separate activity. She thus does not provide an overarching schema which effectively establishes a relationship between NVET activities and organisation-centred HRD activities.

CONCLUSION: IS HUMAN RESOURCE DEVELOPMENT BECOMING TOO BIG?

At the beginning of the chapter it was suggested that HRD might be becoming too big, and extending too far beyond its traditional boundaries. Some writers have suggested that as a consequence it is defying definition. Others have maintained a very focused perception of the field. The problem is that 'learning' and 'knowledge' and 'development' are big themes, not easily contained, influenced by and in turn influencing equally big themes such as globalisation and the Information Age which are influencing organisations and societies in new ways.

Irrespective of where one stands on this issue, this chapter has produced evidence that human resource development is a much more inclusive concept than has often been recognised by the organisation-focused literature. It respects the primacy of claims by the individual to be a person worth developing in his or own right. It thus addresses issues associated with the principles of lifelong learning, recognising the career paths of individuals as they weave in and out of particular organisations. An HRD practitioner is not necessarily a servant of a particular organisation, seeking to plug a perceived gap between competitive organisational needs and what individual employees and other involved stakeholders have to offer. Thus an HRD practitioner could be operating as a career counsellor or as a provider of vocational programmes in a university, college or adult education environment.

Human resource development is concerned with learning and with how it might be managed. It is concerned with interventions that might facilitate learning. It is concerned with change – of behaviour, as reflected in the demonstration of new or enhanced skills, new knowledge and understanding and new attitudes. It is concerned with both intentional and accidental learning. It has a vocational aspect to it. Thus its focus is vocational learning. It is not concerned with general education and many HRD practitioners have expressed discomfort over the years at attempts to label them as 'adult educators' (Gilley and Egglund, op. cit.), although some organisations do provide general educational opportunities.

Human resource development entails a clear differentiation between 'training' and 'learning'. Training implies instrumental interventions to achieve specific pre-determined outcomes. Someone is having something done to them by an outside agency. 'Learning', as such, is neutral in terms of interventions. It can, and does, often happen by chance. The proof of learning in the most general sense, is no more than an articulation of what we know and a demonstration of what we can do – HRD is concerned with ways of achieving that, be it at individual, organisational, societal, national or transnational level.

REFERENCES

Armstrong, M. (1992) *Human Resource Management – Strategy and Action*. London: Kogan Page.

Beckhard, R. (1969) *Organisation Development: Strategies and Models*. Reading, MA: Addison-Wesley.

Bennis, W. G. (1969) *Organisation Development: Its Nature, Origins, and Prospects*. Reading, MA: Addison Wesley.

Bierama, L. L. (1996) 'Development of the Individual Leads to More Productive Workplaces', *New Directions for Adult and Continuing Education*, 72, Winter, pp. 21–8.

Blake, R. R. (1995) 'Memories of HRD', *Training and Development*, March.

Bratton, J. and Gold, J. (1994) *Human Resource Management: Theory and Practice*. Basingstoke: Macmillan.

Burke, Warner W. (1994) *Organisation Development – A Process of Learning and Changing*. Reading, MA: Addison-Wesley.

Carroll, Lewis (1871) *Through the Looking Glass and what Alice Found There*. London: Macmillan.

Craig, R. (ed.) (1976) *Training and Development Handbook* (2nd edn). McGraw-Hill.

Department of Employment (1993) *Prosperity Through Skills*. December.

Dumaine, B. (1990) 'Who Needs a Boss', *Fortune*, 7 May, p. 52.

European Commission (1995) *White Paper on Education and Training – 'Teaching and Learning: Towards the Learning Society*. Brussels: EC.

Fredericks, J. and Stewart, J. (1996) 'The Strategy–HRD Connection', in J. Stewart and J. McGoldrick (eds) *Human Resource Development – Perspectives, Strategies and Practice'*. London: Pitman.

French, W. L. (1969) 'Organisation Development: Objectives, Assumptions and Strategies', *California Management Review*, 12, pp. 23–34.

Garavan, T. N. (1991) 'Strategic human resource development', *Journal of European Industrial Training*, 15(1), pp. 17–30.

Garfield, C. (1992) *Second to None – The Productive Power of Putting People First*. Chicago: Business One Irwin.

Gilley, J. W. and Egglund, S. A. (1989) *Principles of Human Resource Development*. Reading, MA: Addison-Wesley.

Grant, R. M. (1997) 'Strategy at the Leading Edge – The Knowledge-based View of the Firm: Implications for Management Practice', *Long Range Planning*, 30(3), June.

Harrison, R. (1992) *Employee Development*, London: IPM.

Harrison, R. (1997) *Employee Development*, London: IPD.

Hendry, C., Jones, A., Arthur, M. and Pettigrew, A. (1991) 'HRD in Small to Medium Sized Enterprises', *Employment Department Research Paper*, No. 88.

Holden, L. (1995) 'Training', in I. Beardwell and L. Holden (eds) *Human Resource Management – A Contemporary Perspective*. London: Pitman.

Horwitz, F. M., Bowmaker-Falconer, A. and Searll, P. (1995) 'Employment equity, human resource development and institution building in South Africa', *International Journal of Human Resource Management*, 6(3), pp. 671–85.

McGoldrick, J. and Stewart, J. (1996) 'The HRM-HRD nexus', in J. Stewart and J. McGoldrick (eds) *Human Resource Development – Perspectives, Strategies and Practice*. London: Pitman.

McLagan, P. (1989) *Models of HRD Practice*. ASTD Press.

Megginson, D., Joy-Matthews J. and Banfield, P. (1993) *Human Resource Development*. London: Kogan Page.

Nadler, L. (1970) *Developing Human Resources*. Gulf.

Nadler, L. (1979) *Developing Human Resources* (2nd edn). Austin, TX: Learning Concepts.

Nadler, L. and Nadler, Z. (1989) *Developing Human Resources: Concepts and a Model* (3rd edn). San Francisco: Jossey-Bass.

Oxtoby, B. and Coster, C. (1992) 'HRD – A Sticky Label', *Training and Development*, April.

Pedler, M., Burgoyne, J. and Boydell, T. (1991) *The Learning Company*. New York: McGraw-Hill.

Pettigrew, A., Hendry, C. and Sparrow, P. (1988) 'Changing Patterns of Human Resource Management', *Personnel Management*, November.

Plott, Curtis (1995). Introductory address to Conference of American Society for Training and Development, Dallas.

Prentice, G. (1996). Unpublished Masters Dissertation. London Guildhall University.

Purcell, J. (1996) 'People Management Implications of Leaner Ways of Working'. IPD Working Paper No. 15.

Rothwell, W. and Kazanas, H. C. (1989) *Strategic HRD*. Englewood Cliffs, NJ: Prentice Hall.

Senge, P. H. (1990) *The Fifth Discipline – The Art and Practice of the Learning Organisation*. New York: Doubleday.

Stead, V. and Lee, M. (1996) 'Intercultural perspectives on HRD', in J. Stewart and M. McGoldrick (eds) *Human Resource Development – Perspectives, Strategies and Practice*. London: Pitman.

Stewart, J. (1998) 'Intervention and Assessment: the ethics of HRD', *Human Resource Development International*, 1(1), March, pp. 9–12.

Stewart, T. A. (1997) *Intellectual Capital – the New Wealth of Organisations*. London: Nicholas Brealey.

Swanson, R. A. and Arnold, D. E. (1997) 'The Purpose of HRD is to Improve Performance'. Proceedings of the Academy of Human Resource Development, Atlanta.

Thakur, M. (1974) *OD: A Survey*. London: IPM.

Training (1997) 'Industry Report', October.

Twigg, G. and Albon, P. (1992) 'Human Resource Development and Business Strategy', in M. Armstrong (ed.) *Strategies for Human Resource Management – A Total Business Approach*. London: Kogan Page.

Tyson, S. (1996) *Human Resource Strategies*, London: Pitman.

University Forum for HRD (1995) 'Emerging Concept of HRD – A Position Statement'.

Walton, J. (1996a) *NVQ Handbook – Practical Guidelines for Assessors*. Oxford: Butterworth-Heinemann.

Walton, J. (1996b) 'The Provision of Learning Support for Non-Employees', in J. Stewart and J. McGoldrick (eds) *Human Resource Development – Perspectives, Strategies and Practice*. London: Pitman.

Waterman, R. (1994) *The Frontiers of Excellence*. London: Nicholas Brealey.

Weinberger, L. A. (1998) 'Commonly held theories of human resource development', *Human Resource Development International*, 1(1), March.

Willis, V. J. (1990) 'Looking ahead in HRD professional practice', in R. Jacobs (ed.) *Organisational Issues and Human Resource Development Research Questions*. Ohio State University.

Willis, V. J. (1997) 'HRD as Evolutionary System; From Pyramid-Building to Space-Walking and Beyond'. Proceedings of the Academy of Human Resource Development, Atlanta.

Chapter 4

STRATEGIC HUMAN RESOURCE DEVELOPMENT VERSUS HUMAN RESOURCE DEVELOPMENT STRATEGIES

OBJECTIVES

By the end of this chapter you should be able to:

- Identify the basic components of a strategic approach to HRD;

- differentiate between piecemeal HRD strategies and strategic HRD (SHRD);

- establish different methodologies for measuring whether an SHRD approach is being undertaken;

- clarify the difference between a strategic approach to training and development and a strategic approach to HRD;

- distinguish between managing an HRD function strategically and conducting a strategic approach to HRD;

- critique the formal planned model for achieving SHRD;

- describe an integrated SHRD model which shows how HRD processes can contribute to strategic intent.

INTRODUCTION

This chapter is concerned with trying to establish what is meant by a strategic approach to HRD. It will differentiate this from piecemeal HRD strategies or ways of doing things which collectively might contribute to the SHRD effort but fall short of an holistic approach. The position adopted is that a strategic approach entails the search for, and intention to implement, a coherent set of subsidiary strategies in accordance with a set of guiding principles that will contribute to an overall organisational 'grand design' or sense of direction. The sequence followed serves to illustrate different degrees of sophistication towards that end by distinguishing on a linear scale between piecemeal approaches to training, coherent training strategies, training and development strategies and SHRD (*see* Fig. 4.1).

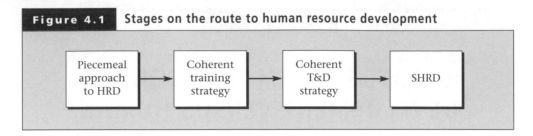

Figure 4.1 Stages on the route to human resource development

The position taken is that strategic human resource development (SHRD) is an extension of HRD, with a distinctive focus on the holistic orchestration of learning within organisations. It is based on the supposition that learning must be treated by organisational policy makers as a deliberate business process rather than an 'accident' (Mayo and Lank, 1994). It entails giving conscious and systematic attention both to the processes which support and encourage people's learning in a given organisation and to the organisation-wide factors which are operating as barriers to learning taking place. For SHRD to be accomplished, responsibilities for HRD at all levels need to be clarified. One outcome of SHRD should be a coherent set of policies and practices which collectively serve to ensure that learning is embedded in the fabric of the organisation to the benefit of all stakeholders.

Strategic human resource development involves introducing, eliminating, modifying, directing and guiding processes and responsibilities in such a way that all individuals and teams are equipped with the skills, knowledge and competences they require to undertake current and future tasks required by the organisation. It needs to be seen as part of the strategy management process of a given organisation, since the organisation is dependent on effectively utilising and enhancing all of its resources to cope with current and future contingencies. For the same reason it also needs to encompass the performance and reward management processes of the organisation, and ensure that how these are applied and interpreted enables and encourages learning and development to take place.

But SHRD goes beyond being merely driven by performance in task. Strategic significance is increasingly being attached to inculcating and embedding collective learning processes that enable people to be more customer responsive, team oriented, creative, innovative, business focused and strategically aware. Opportunities for and guarantees of personal growth and development are being sought by newcomers to the employment market, who are only too aware of the downsizing of the last decade and the personal risks of becoming too emotionally associated with jobs and skills that have an inbuilt obsolescence attached to them. Accomplishment of these various objectives is seen by many to be a source of competitive advantage. The measure of successful SHRD is that people development and the supporting learning processes should be considered to be one of the strategic capabilities and distinctive competences of those organisations that effectively undertake them.

It is alleged that we are in an era of hypercompetition, subject to an avalanche of technological breakthroughs and diverse global players, with traditional organisational forms and job roles breaking down. Many of the semi-skilled jobs associated with the labour-intensive industries of the past are disappearing because of automation, or are being relocated to developing economies where labour costs are cheaper. Many high-tech jobs are not dependent on location, being supported by globally integrated communication networks. It is impossible now to predict with any degree of precision the type and range of tasks and demands that people will be expected to undertake over the next few years. Yet it is vital that as new tasks and technologies emerge, people can be found who have the capability to rapidly acquire the associated skills, knowledge and competences. The emphasis in advanced economies is on developing knowledge workers capable of making rapid skills transitions and attitude adjustments in response to unforeseen and unforeseeable contingencies.

In addition to demonstrating high level job-specific skills, individuals are increasingly being expected to possess as a minimum set of capabilities:

- a general readiness and capacity to engage in personal development and growth contributing to lifelong learning;
- flexibility in what they undertake;
- responsiveness in the face of often conflicting demands.

Those responsible for SHRD must work alongside other strategic thinkers if these skills and competences are to be generated in a coherent fashion. They have a responsibility to ensure that, included among the innovative and dynamic approaches which are being generated to enable organisations to more effectively impact upon their environment, will be those that enhance learning at all levels.

However, SHRD rooted in HR planning or even business planning is insufficient to satisfy these demands. Traditional long-range business planning, even when supported by sophisticated forecasting models, is being superseded by a more dynamic and responsive approach to strategic management. Yet, as we shall see, theoretical perspectives on SHRD have largely adopted a rational-structuralist approach. They have focused on the contribution that planned learning can make to an organisation and on cementing the link with what is nowadays being deemed as old-style business and human resource planning.

One of the challenges of SHRD is to incorporate accidental learning processes into its purview. Human resource development will take place in any organisation irrespective of whether there is any deliberate intention to facilitate it. This is because individuals learn by virtue of the experiences they undergo. Indeed much has been made recently (Nonaka and Takeuchi, 1995) of the tacit knowledge that emanates from such accidental learning. However, for it to begin to be considered 'strategic', there needs to be some conscious endeavour within an organisation to translate these accidental learning experiences into an explicit experiential learning philosophy and framework that will contribute to meeting present and future knowledge and skills requirements.

At the same time, the mere existence of an explicit philosophy of learning within an organisation may have no strategic connotations whatsoever. The same may equally hold true even where it supports a tradition and willingness to invest resources on, for example, self-directed personal development planning and/or formal training programmes. This is because, for an approach to be strategic, certain conditions need to be met. Indeed, organisations that have concentrated on in-house training provision have, over the years, often been severely criticised for the absence of many of these conditions, such as a forward-looking, proactive focus, which clearly demonstrate how the activities in question contribute to taking the business forward.

Learning initiatives carried out by a functional HRD department are, in themselves, no more than instances of piecemeal strategies towards encouraging people development. Taken in isolation they represent only one possible and partial response towards achieving SHRD. In a number of instances they are carried out without any strategic intent whatsoever and without the commitment and involvement of those people who are supposed to benefit from them. It is worth remembering also that some organisations have a philosophy of learning, explicitly incorporated into their direction-setting guiding principles, which is not dependent on the existence of a department dedicated to internal training and development or the like. Their approach to HRD could still be strategic. Some of the exhortations for a learning organisation argue that its ultimate objective is the achievement of totally self-sustaining learning processes.

Nevertheless it is difficult to visualise a totally self-managed approach to SHRD. I believe it should be guided and overseen. Effective stewardship needs to be exercised. Harrison (1997) argues that, for SHRD to happen in practice, it needs to be driven by accomplished high-status career professionals. She also emphasises the importance of establishing strategic partnerships across the organisational spectrum.

> If in any organisation there is a lack of expertise, awareness and articulacy among HRD professionals, insufficient collaboration between HRD and other personnel practitioners in the business, or failure to build a strategic partnership between HRD and line managers in the business, then it will not be surprising if the strategic development of human resources is virtually non-existent. On the other hand, if there is a credible, high-status, expert and business-focused HRD presence in the organisation, then there is a real opportunity for HRD's strategic potential to be fulfilled (ibid.).

Garavan (1991), making a similar point, views it as a matter of perception. He summarises his literature review by arguing 'that when management at board level treat HRD as making an important contribution, the HRD function wields a higher profile'.

While I may agree with their assertions, I do not necessarily envisage that the HRD professionals of the future will emerge from training and development departments, or have a personnel or HRM background. The challenge for existing HRD practitioners is to make the jump to seeing themselves as responsible for something more than designing and delivering training and development programmes, or as passive providers and guardians of systems and processes that others have devised. In career terms, the challenge is to demonstrate that coming from a training and development background actually equips them to take responsibility for HRD in its broader manifestations. There is much evidence of the failure of organisation-wide initiatives with an HRD flavour because of a lack of understanding, by those who have introduced them, about people and how they learn. This is because changes are often being orchestrated by those whose prime concern is not people issues. Practitioners of HRD need to be able to articulate in a strategically based language, understood by chief executives and senior management, the contribution that development processes and learning in the round can make to enhancing the core capabilities and strategic responsiveness of a given organisation.

DEFINITIONS

There are remarkably few references in the literature on what is held to constitute SHRD. The earliest I have been able to trace date from the 1980s. They tend to reflect the perspective of the author/s and also, even though we are talking about a very short time span, the period when they were written. Most have concentrated on the importance of devising and pulling together, in a coherent framework, planned learning initiatives which contribute to the enhancement of the business performance of a sponsoring organisation. On the whole this 'planned learning' is seen as the responsibility of a training and developmental functional area. Rothwell and Kazanas (1989) take this position although they advise some caution. They make the point that the practitioner's chief responsibility is not 'to manage the HRD department strategically' but rather 'to lead efforts to formulate and implement a unified plan to guide the direction of learning in an organisation'. Strategic HRD is an organisation-wide holistic approach and encompasses what takes place within a designated HRD functional area only in so far as the activities of the function contribute to the overall development process. The function has to demonstrate that it is fit for a strategic purpose.

Most authors make the further point that SHRD as they define it does not seem to occur in practice. Harrison (1997) feels that, 'despite the hype that surrounds a number of organisations where the planned development of people *has* made a notable contribution to the achievement of business goals ... research has failed to reveal any significant connection between HRD and business strategy across UK organisations at large'. There is some measure of surprise in this. As Zemke (1981, quoted in Rothwell and Kazanas, op. cit.) expresses it, although HRD is the one area of human resource practice most amenable to supporting business plans, it is also the one area of HR practice least often used for this purpose by top managers.

The 1990s have seen a re-evaluation at top management level of the importance of HRD issues in terms of their making a strategic contribution. Human resource development is now at the top of the strategic agenda. This is because of an emergent awareness of the contribution that highly skilled, accomplished people can make to the long-term sustainability of an enterprise. As one moves away from a commercial environment dominated by labour-intensive, low-tech industries with a preponderance of semi-skilled operatives, to high-tech industries reliant on highly skilled knowledge workers in relatively short supply, individuals are becoming seen as the single most significant source of sustainable competitive advantage. At the beginning of the decade the strategic attention was focused on self-managed learning, continuous personal development, learning organisation and the people development messages associated with Total Quality Management (TQM).

At the time of writing one detects a top management concern with the contribution that HRD can make to the intellectual capital of the organisation through knowledge management and development and helping to translate human capital

– defined as the knowledge and skills and insights possessed by individuals – into structural capital.

Whatever form SHRD takes it should demonstrably contribute to the strategic management process. Let us recall what the notion of 'strategic' management is held to entail (*see* Fig. 4.2).

Figure 4.2 Strategic context – being purposeful

Strategic management needs to be undertaken in the context of the following.

1 An overall sense of mission and direction, an appreciation in general terms of where the organisation is going and why. This may include the articulation of core values, distinctive competences and corporate vision.

2 Some measure of coherence in what is being undertaken. Ongoing activities and new initiatives collectively seem to contribute to an overall sense of direction; this is not the same as saying that each activity undertaken has to be planned in detail and authorised before it can be undertaken.

3 Encompassing the full scope of an organisation's activities, both within and outside its boundaries. What is 'in' and what 'outside' can be reconfigured as a result of strategic action such as takeovers.

4 A concern with the long-term acquisition, deployment, reallocation and divestment of resources.

5 Matching the resources of an organisation to the environment in which it currently operates and intends to operate. This could entail cutting back on activities or markets where the organisation identifies a gap between its resource capability and the products and services it offers. Alternatively, an organisation's strategic response could be to consciously try to lever up its resource capability.

6 Ensuring that internal structures, practices, procedures and decision-making processes enable the organisation to achieve its objectives.

7 Enhancing an organisation's response capability, assessing how sufficient resources can be deployed to take advantage of opportunities or avoid threats in the organisation's environment. This will include identifying and selecting processes whereby customers are reached and competitors are kept at bay.

8 Translating the complex and dynamic set of external and internal variables which an organisation faces, into a future-oriented framework which can then be implemented on a day-to-day basis. As Helmuth von Moltke, chief of the Prussian and German general staffs from 1858 to 1888 noted, strategy is 'the evolution of the original guiding idea according to continually changing circumstances'.

9 Identifying and handling key internal and external stakeholders whose attitudes, perceptions and actions can influence the furtherance of organisational goals.

WHEN DOES A HUMAN RESOURCE DEVELOPMENT STRATEGY BECOME 'STRATEGIC'?

At first sight this might seem an odd question to ask. Surely the very existence of a thought-through, consciously designed HRD strategy means exactly the same as having a strategic approach to HRD. But this is by no means the case. Take, for example, a conscious decision to outsource the whole of your organisation's course-based training provision, and focus the efforts of your remaining HRD practitioners on providing a consultancy service to line managers on matters pertaining to individual and group learning. This could be construed as an HRD strategy. It may contribute to a strategic approach to HRD. It may prove to be a valuable way to reconfigure the HRD function within a given organisation, and enable practitioners to get closer to the customer. It has long-term implications in terms of resource allocations and deployments. But as such it is not 'strategic'. It is not of itself a holistic effort to meet the learning needs of a given organisation or a conscious effort to lever the competences of individuals so that they demonstrate greater strategic awareness.

For an HRD strategy to become 'strategic' it has to be undertaken with full strategic intent, with an understanding how the initiative being undertaken adds to the coherence of the SHRD effort, congruent with an explicit learning philosophy incorporated into the overall organisation mission.

Generalised measures of the strategic sophistication of human resource development

In diagnostic terms, one can establish a set of generalised criteria to help establish the degree of strategic sophistication for particular areas in a given organisation. The criteria need have no 'substantive' content. In other words, in themselves, they tell us nothing about the subject area. They could equally apply to a number of disciplines. Criteria typically adopted include:

■ degree of internal integration or coherence of processes that are held to be part of the functional area in question;

■ degree of alignment with other functional activities which are held to be related to the functional area in question;

■ degree of involvement of functional role holders in decision making on corporate-wide issues;

■ extent to which functional activities are seen as contributing to corporate strategy.

Of the number of helpful diagnostics of this type in existence which can be applied to SHRD, that produced by Burgoyne (1988) is the most well known.

The Burgoyne typology

Burgoyne's typology (1988) was originally intended to evaluate management development, but has been similarly used for SHRD. It provides some substantive indications on HRD practices. The link he makes to HR planning and forecasting is typical of thinking in the late 1980s.

■ *Level 1: no systematic HRD development.* No systematic or deliberate development is undertaken. There is a total reliance on natural, *laissez-faire* processes of HRD.

■ *Level 2: isolated tactical HRD.* There are isolated and *ad hoc* tactical development activities, of either structural or developmental kinds, or both, in response to local problems, crises or sporadically identified general problems.

■ *Level 3: integrated and co-ordinated structural and development tactics.* The specific HRD tactics which impinge directly on the individual – career structure management and assisted learning – are integrated and co-ordinated.

■ *Level 4: an HRD strategy to implement corporate policy.* Human resource development strategy plays its part in implementing corporate policies through HR planning and providing a strategic direction and framework for the tactics of career structure management and of learning, education and training.

■ *Level 5: HRD strategy input to corporate policy formation.* Human resource development processes feed information into corporate policy decision-making processes on the organisation's human assets, strengths, weaknesses and potential. They also contribute to the forecasting and analysis of the manageability of proposed projects, ventures and changes.

■ *Level 6: strategic development of the management of corporate policy.* Human resource development processes enhance the nature and quality of corporate policy-forming processes which they also inform and help implement.

I would add an additional level to the Burrgoyne list to reflect more recent developments:

■ *Level 7: strategic leverage of learning and development processes to enhance the core competences of the organisation.*

Burgoyne also makes the following points.

1 A strategic approach has to be conscious and reflective; unplanned, interpersonal and functional experiences cannot be classified as strategic in organisational terms unless *explicitly* linked to implementation of corporate policy.

2 The model infers incremental levels of maturity such that an organisation's approach to SHRD is likely to grow in sophistication.

3 In his opinion HRD needs to be linked to 'hard systems' of HRM on the one hand (such as HR planning, recruitment and selection strategies) and collaborative career planning on the other.

WHAT ARE PIECEMEAL HUMAN RESOURCE DEVELOPMENT STRATEGIES?

Piecemeal HRD strategies operate at Burgoyne's Levels 1 and 2. Figure 4.3 presents a range of human resource development strategies that could contribute to the overall picture but in isolation represent a piecemeal approach. They are apparent when:

■ new learning-oriented initiatives are introduced without any consideration being given to how they relate to existing processes;

■ existing HRD systems and processes seem to have no apparent coherence and operate independently of and without reference to each other;

Figure 4.3 Range of human resource development strategies that could contribute to the overall picture

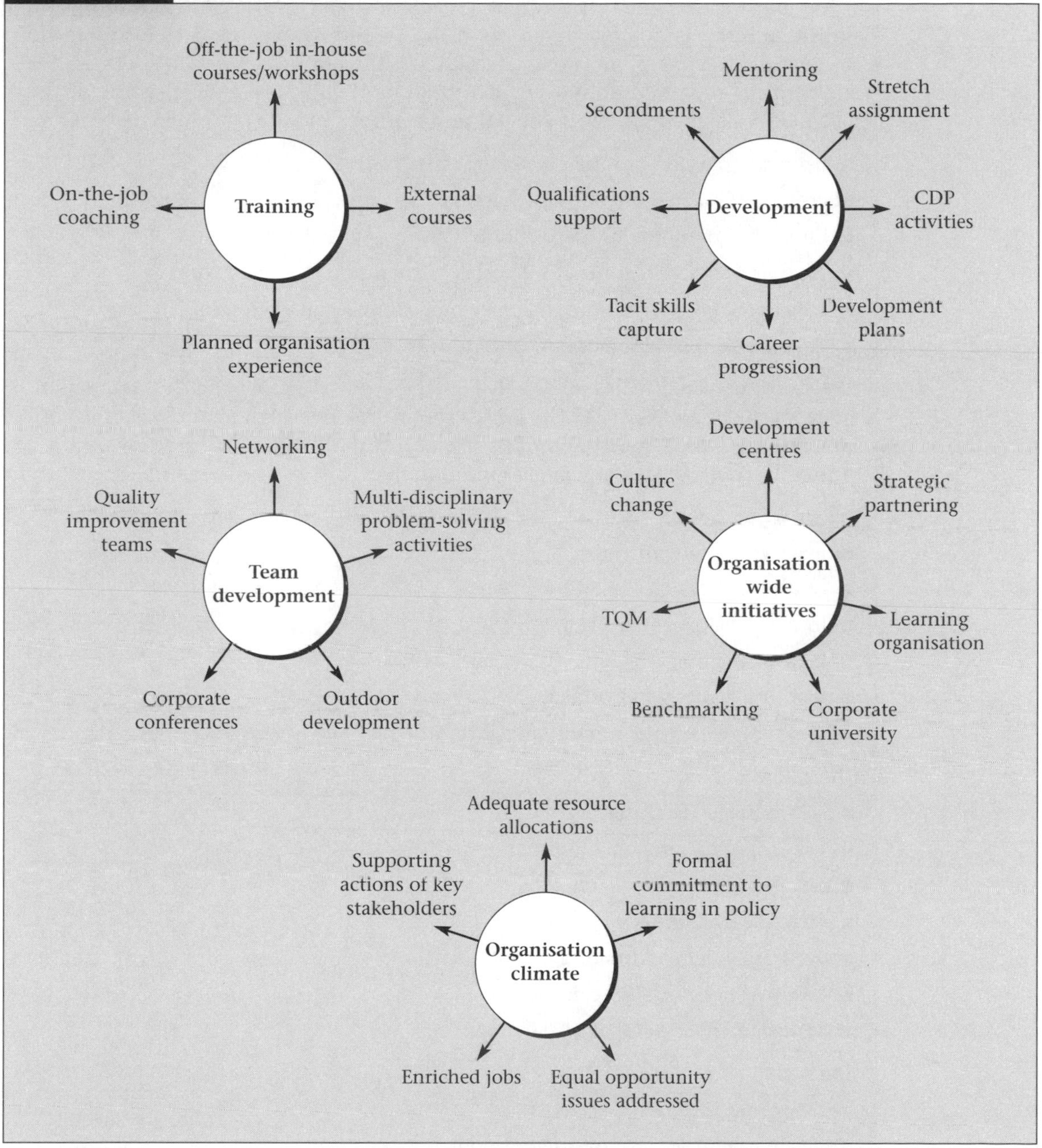

- activities such as training, staff development, organisational-wide change initiatives and performance review emanate from different functional areas with different agendas.

Figure 4.4 provides an example of an explicit people development philosophy and supporting strategy.

| Figure 4.4 | Moving from a piecemeal to a more sophisticated approach |

The following example is taken from a medium-sized UK enterprise, operating as a subsidiary of a large holding group in the steel industry. Until 1996 it had no coherent HRD strategy, nor were its links with the business direction specified. Six elements of the philosophy were identified in 1996 by a team consisting of the people development manager, the training manager and the personnel manager:

- bring people closer to their business;
- create a standards-driven organisation;
- build the commitment to exceptional levels of excellence;
- create an environment that supports collaboration and teamwork;
- educate employees for the challenge of a changing marketplace;
- encourage confidence, daring and innovation.

The training manager also made a deliberate decision to move the HRD effort from a reactive Burgoyne Level 1/2 to a more sophisticated level of maturity, through an incremental step-by-step approach. He contrasted 'Where we are now' with a future 'learning and development' vision.

Where we are now
- reactive training manager;
- sporadic best practice interventions;
- low line manager involvement;
- little evaluation;
- learning perceived as courses;
- emphasis on off-the-job training with little planned organisational experience.

The vision
- self-managed learning;
- towards a learning organisation;
- developing manager's role;
- effective evaluation;
- accurately defined training needs;
- best practice in training delivery;
- achievement of benchmark targets.

The steps
These would include:
- development of training and development policy;
- coaching skills development;
- mentoring;
- enhanced personal development reports;
- managers as developers.

WHEN DO TRAINING STRATEGIES CONTRIBUTE TO STRATEGIC HUMAN RESOURCE DEVELOPMENT?

'Training' is a sub-set of HRD, contributing to the overall learning and development effort. Kenney and Reid (1988) use the term 'training interventions' to include any event which is deliberately planned by those responsible for training, to assist learning to take place. These encompass a wide range of activities which they refer to as *strategies* and group under five main headings:

■ training on the job;

■ planned organisation experience;

■ in-house courses;

■ planned experiences outside the organisation;

■ external courses.

Some of their suggested interventions such as secondments go beyond what I would call 'training' and seem to relate more appropriately to 'development opportunities'.

They do not offer 'strategies' as such. What they provide is a range of options from which choices can be made. Their choices are not mutually exclusive. Each of the five could be undertaken. Figure 4.5 sets out Kenney and Reid's training strategies.

Figure 4.5 **Kenney and Reid's five training strategies**

Training on the job

Training on the job is traditionally associated with 'sitting with Nellie'. In a management development context, this may take the form of coaching and advice from immediate superiors and colleagues.

Planned organisation experience

Planned organisation experience can be designed within existing organisational processes and wherever possible as an integral part of mainstream developments. It can include planned experience in other departments within the same department, the assignment of special responsibilities, problem solving discussion groups and special projects.

In-house courses

There is likely to be better transfer of learning from internal rather than external courses, particularly if senior management are involved in some of the sessions. If the training can be directed at real organisational problems this is likely to increase the face validity of the training, and its chances of effectiveness. Courses are useful when many members of staff need similar training at one time. A variation is open access in-house training. Advances in information technology (IT) have enabled the provision of computer-based training programmes that include the use of interactive video.

▶▶

▶▶ Figure 4.5 continued

Planned experiences outside the organisation

Planned experiences outside the organisation include secondments to other organisations which supply services to the organisation or are customer organisations, in order to obtain external views of the organisation's products and services. Staff may also be encouraged to undertake self-developmental activities to enhance their career prospects.

According to Finn (1995), community secondments were once regarded as a way of easing people into retirement or giving them a taste of the outside world when their 'job for life' had prematurely come to an end through redundancy.

In the 1990s secondment programmes have been given a fresh image, new champions – and an astute change of title, often being referred to as 'development assignments'. At Coopers & Lybrand they are funded and administered by the human resources department under the heading of community affairs. Secondments no longer signal the end of the working road; they are increasingly seen by HR specialists as an innovative management development tool which can enhance the CV of mid-career high-flyers. Secondments can be a valuable way to keep graduates who might otherwise look outside for career opportunities.

'Development assignments' aim to accomplish the standard management development qualities of leadership, team building, communication skills and project management skills enhancement through hands-on exposure.

External courses

There are broadly two kinds of external course: the shorter, full-time variety, run by consultants, colleges and universities, and longer (usually part-time) courses, often leading to a qualification. Learning transfer is often not high. For example, a 1985 survey conducted by the Marks Group on the effectiveness of management training found that nearly a quarter of the participants had made no attempt to apply anything they had learned from their courses to their own organisation.

Kenney and Reid argue that there are four decision criteria to use in determining the appropriate training strategy:

- compatability with objectives arising from training needs analysis;
- estimated likelihood of transfer of learning to the workplace;
- available resources (including time);
- trainee-related factors such as family commitments.

Questions

1 *What are your views on the above as a comprehensive list of training strategies?*

2 *Are they the same list you would generate if asked about HRD strategies?*

3 *How do they relate to 'strategic HRD'?*

Source: Based on Kenney and Reid (1988).

In my opinion Kenney and Reid have developed a useful set of approaches to facilitating learning and equipping people with skills and knowledge that could help them in their current job. Each could contribute to a cohesive and integrated package to take the organisation forward. But the overall array is too restricted to encompass an overall approach to SHRD, which, to be fair to the authors, they are not purporting to provide.

The provision of learning through in-house courses and formal development programmes is, of course, a possible contributor to SHRD. However it is not a necessary or sufficient condition. 'Training' is but one strategic option among a number through which SHRD can be achieved. All organisations are reliant on the knowledge, skills, accomplishments and sensitivities of the individuals who are drawn upon to conduct their affairs. Where and how those skills and accomplishments are acquired is a strategic choice that is not necessarily dependent upon engaging in training-related activities. It is possible to have a strategic approach to HRD without engaging in any in-house training.

Training strategies in practice

A good example of the development of a training strategy which is consonant with the Kenney and Reid thinking is provided by the Eastman Chemical Company based in the USA (*see* Fig. 4.6).

| Figure 4.6 | Training strategy at Eastman Chemical Company |

The US Eastman Chemical Company, which produces industrial chemicals, fibres and plastics, is based in Tennessee, and employs some 18 000 people through its world-wide network of manufacturing locations and sales offices. In 1991 it moved from a function-oriented structure to a market-driven company focused on product lines. Over time all employees became involved in implementing the reorganisation under the auspices of a company-wide policy entitled, 'Education and Training: Encourage Learning and Personal Growth for Everyone Throughout Their Careers'.

The training department was asked by senior management to create a training plan for the restructured organisation. The following steps were followed.

1. A cross-functional project team was established, including trainers, sales staff and employees from the business units. Its remit was to create new, value-added training. It had strong top management support, and throughout the subsequent development process provided managers with regular progress reports. At the outset it was agreed that line managers would handle announcements once the team was ready for implementation.

2. A mission was created. The associated goals were to think of new methods of training delivery, to determine job competences, to establish training options for each competence and to create a system for monitoring and continuously improving training.

3. Teams of employees who would be affected by the reorganisation were also formed in order to get input from them on the content of their jobs.

4. From their input, jobs were clustered into 'job groups' of similar responsibilities. The next task was to establish core competences, defined as the essential knowledge and skills, for each group of jobs.

▶▶

▶▶ Figure 4.6 continued

5 The core competences for each job group were based on the competences possessed by individual job holders. The supporting methods to establish these included one-to-one interviews, employee focus groups and analysing written job descriptions. The original list was reduced to a number of critical competences, using an approach based on the Pareto 80–20 principle.

6 Various training options were then developed for each of the resultant core competences. Employees and their team leaders were involved in the process of determining which competences they wished to improve. The training options fell into four categories:
   ■ in-house training sessions;
   ■ self-directed courses;
   ■ literature other than internal training materials;
   ■ outside courses, seminars and conferences.

7 All of the learning options incorporated the following:
   ■ a description of each job competence that the training addresses;
   ■ the name of someone in the training department to provide help;
   ■ information about the courses offered at the main training facility in Tennessee;
   ■ information on courses offered at other locations;
   ■ a list of self-directed courses;
   ■ a list of relevant reading materials;
   ■ a data base that included outside courses, seminars and conferences, including ones in foreign languages;
   ■ the names of employees who have taken outside courses.

8 Employees were encouraged to choose the topics and learning methods that best suited them, relating these to their availability for training. Not everyone, for example, was able to attend classroom courses at the main training facility in Tennessee.

9 The new training process was launched by a project-team member and a senior manager explaining it initially to other senior managers and then to employees at all levels. Videotapes, audiotapes, overhead transparencies and an instruction book were developed to support the presentation. These materials proved to be essential at distant locations.

10 All employees were given copies of the *Training Process Manual*, which included a letter from the CEO which emphasised the importance of learning and linked the new process to the reorganisation.

11 Ongoing monitoring is conducted by a training-process improvement team, comprising seven representatives from the major business units and the training department. The team conducts periodic surveys on the process, and suggests improvements to management.

A survey conducted four months into the process showed that 70 per cent of respondents had used the new process, mostly for career planning purposes and that 95 per cent felt that the competences for their own jobs were accurately described.

A goal yet to be met is the provision of training for employees at all locations, in the employees' first language and reflecting their culture.

Source: Based on Keith and Smith Payton (1995).

The literature is full of examples of the application of training strategies. On the whole, they refer to ways in which resources and the T&D effort are deployed. There are overtones of being 'cost effective' in some instances, and/or of demonstrating flexibility in others. The more interesting are those where there seems to be a conscious attempt to shift resources and approaches from one direction to another. As I have pointed out above, just because one has changed direction doesn't make the approach 'strategic'.

A common move has been to turn to outside providers for all or a proportion of the training programmes that were undertaken in house. I have devoted a whole chapter (*see* Chapter 11) to evaluating outsourcing as a T&D strategy, because of the impact it is having upon traditional T&D departments.

Another shift has been to move from course provision at a designated training centre to the use of open learning methodologies which bring training closer to the workplace. Drewitt (1994) mentions that between 1990 and 1994 Lloyds Bank, before it merged with the Trustee Savings Bank, increased its number of multimedia open learning centres by 560 per cent, from 20 to 132. This was a conscious move by the Bank's Training Development Group, which in 1994 employed around 40 staff, including project managers, analysts and designers, with a remit for designing, developing, distributing, maintaining and supporting training throughout UK retail banking.

Another trend has been the move away from time-constrained, course-driven, off-the-job management development towards work-located experiential approaches.

An interesting US case study of getting top management backing and line management support for a new training strategy with a clear business focus is afforded by Pacific Bell. There is some evidence of the fit-split dilemma referred to in more detail later in the chapter. Within an umbrella company policy directive, individual business unit heads are interpreting the overarching guidelines in their own way and at their own speed (*see* Fig. 4.7).

| **Figure 4.7** | **Pacific Bell and 'Capability 97'** |

Pacific Bell is an American regional telephone operating company that serves California and Nevada, and is an offshoot of the original Bell Telephone Company. The whole telecommunications industry is subjected to fierce competition, including incursions from long-distance operators, and rapidly changing technology. Pacific Bell has, for example, modernised its network during the 1990s by switching from analog to digital transmission processes. It has also converted from copper to fibre optics, and has been building a statewide network to carry voice, data and video transmission simultaneously. One of the consequences of the new technology is that by the year 2000 the company intends to reduce its overall work-force by 10 000 people from that prevailing in 1995.

The chief executive was concerned that the company would be adopting new technology using employees whose skills were developed in the 1980s. He also felt that in the competitive environment of the future Pacific Bell would have the same switches and fibre as the competition. It needed to differentiate itself through its people and their capabilities. The company accordingly introduced in 1994 a major training initiative called 'Capability 97', designed to put employees' skills shoulder-to-shoulder with the new technology platform.

▶▶

▶▶ Figure 4.7 continued

The key steps and features are as follows.

1 A transition team that included the Executive Director for Education and Training evaluated the training done in the past. It established that more money was being spent on the training of staff personnel than on line personnel. Additionally, a disproportionate amount of money was being spent on high-level managers and general subjects, at the expense of first-line supervisors, technicians and technical skills training.

2 Following a formal presentation to the top management team in January 1994 by the Executive Director for Training and Development, the business-unit heads agreed to address capability building more formally. They appointed Capability 97 stewards to help develop and implement the capability plans.

3 A number of 'countermeasures' have been adopted by the business units in order to overcome past barriers or root causes to achieving an integrated approach to capability building. These include:
■ more on-the-job training;
■ specific, targeted education initiatives with nearby universities;
■ a training track, called the Data University, for Los Angeles marketing staff;
■ new partnerships with the central education and training unit;
■ policies requiring all employees to have their own training plans;
■ a strategy to focus training on fewer job titles.

4 The central training unit in turn has established a series of 'countermeasures'. These include:
■ helping business units to develop their own training/capability plan;
■ defining key job titles and skills;
■ developing curricula integrated with technology and product initiatives;
■ providing key job-title training courses and training tracks;
■ increasing access to alternative modes and anytime/anywhere delivery;
■ conducting benchmarking and demonstrating Return on Investment (ROI) improvements.

As might be expected, business unit heads have responded differently. One of the original prime movers for more training was the General Manager for Network Services, which tests new technology from an operational standpoint. He strongly contended that training was a strategic imperative, a real differentiator in the market place. He tackled the training gap by:

■ gathering a group of subject matter experts to look at every job classification and establish what should be the basis of core courses;

■ establishing gaps between core courses and a person's actual training history. The gaps were prioritised and people were 'sent to school';

■ establishing a training council, chaired by the unit's Head of Human Resources and made up of managers from each department in the unit;

■ ensuring that each individual has a personal development plan and a training plan. Employees can eliminate certain training if they can show competence based on experience.

Source: Based on Galagan and Tunis (1995).

FROM 'TRAINING' TO 'TRAINING AND DEVELOPMENT' STRATEGY

On the whole 'training' strategies tend to concentrate on performance-in-task skills and capability enhancement. 'Training and development' strategies are broader in focus, incorporating a range of approaches for preparing individuals for roles they might be called on to play in the future.

Many of the literature examples and theoretical models treat training and development strategy as though it were a synonym for an HRD strategy. A typical instance is the approach adopted by Mabey and Salaman (1995) who use the terms 'HRD' and 'training and development' interchangeably. They contend that there are six conditions which need to be met to demonstrate a rational and strategic approach to training and development.

1 *Alignment with organisation objectives*: T&D is demonstrably linked to business priorities.

2 *Senior management support*: senior managers promote learning. Training and development aligns with culture.

3 *Involvement of line managers*: active involvement in diagnosis planning, coaching and monitoring.

4 *Quality of programme design and delivery*: programmes and processes (courses, events and assignments) match learning objectives.

5 *Motivation of trainees*: shared diagnosis of training needs and relevance of T&D activities undertaken.

6 *Integration with HRM policy*: T&D has continuity with and is mutually reinforced by other HRM policies. These include recruitment and selection, appraisal and assessment, reward and recognition and career development.

The focus of their model is on the training and development activities undertaken. The strategic aspects are centred around the need to establish outward- and inward-facing conditions if the activities are to be of ongoing value. The need to establish clearly defined relationships with business priorities and HRM strategy is an outward-facing condition. The need to secure senior management support, involvement of line managers and motivation of trainees is an inward-facing condition (*see* Fig. 4.8).

As Mabey and Salaman (op. cit.) put it:

What the overall model highlights is the pivotal link that training and development activities *can* provide between business and human resource strategy. A strategic approach to training and development can be depicted as one where all those involved are engaged in a connected, explicit and developmental purpose which helps to simultaneously fulfil an individual's learning goals and the organisation's mission'. They are at pains to point out that this rarely happens in practice.

In strategic terms the model is incomplete. There is no sense, for example, of *how* the activities undertaken will contribute to the enhancement of the organisation's strategic response capability. It is a self-confessed training and development model, as opposed to a model for capturing SHRD in the broader sense of the present book. For them, 'the actual training and development activities as exper-

| Figure 4.8 | Interpretation of Mabey and Salaman |

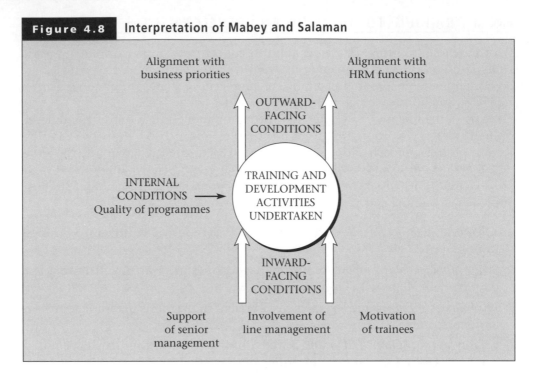

ienced by trainees (perhaps a training course or a set of workshops, or on-the-job assignments or other developmental initiatives) are central to the model' (ibid.). They do not purport to present an integrated philosophy of learning which provides an overarching rationale for supporting and sustaining ongoing developmental opportunities.

Investors in People

The UK Investors in People (IiP) standards framework affords an alternative generic model for measuring a strategic approach to training and development.

There are four broad criteria, each with supporting indicators, to achieving an IiP award.

1 *An IiP makes a public commitment from the top to develop all employees to achieve its business objectives.*
   a Every employee should have a written but flexible plan which sets out business goals and targets, considers how employees will contribute to achieving the plan and specifies how development needs in particular will be assessed and met.
   b Management should develop and communicate to all employees a vision of where the organisation is going and the contribution employees will make to its success, involving employee representatives as appropriate.

2 *An IiP regularly reviews the training and development needs of all its employees.*
   a The resources for training and developing employees should be clearly identified in the business plan.

   b Managers should be responsible for regularly agreeing training and development needs with each employee in the context of business objectives, setting
   targets and standards linked, where appropriate, to the achievement of NVQs
   (or relevant units).

3 *An IiP takes action to train and develop individuals on recruitment and throughout
their employment.*
   a Action should focus on the training needs of all new recruits and continually
   developing and improving the skills of existing employees.
   b All employees should be encouraged to contribute to identifying and meeting
   their own job-related development needs.

4 *An IiP evaluates the investment in training and development to assess achievement
and improve future effectiveness.*
   a The investment, the competence and the commitment of employees, and the
   use made of skills learned, should be reviewed at all levels against business
   goals and targets.
   b The effectiveness of training and development should be reviewed at the top
   level and lead to renewed commitment and target setting.

IiP can be a very powerful lever for the promotion of learning in an organisation. It has been influential in encouraging UK organisations to develop an explicit
commitment towards training and development and an implicit commitment to
learning. It is a useful stepping-stone towards a SHRD approach. However its focus
is on achieving learning by means of planned training and development in the
context of a formalised business planning process. In other words, training and
development is seen as being downstream of strategy and is conducted to help
achieve a predetermined plan. It is not seen as a source of competitive advantage
in its own right. Note that the achievement of IiP status by an organisation does
not necessitate the presence of a functional HRD department. It restricts its
purview to individual employees. It is silent on the relationship between HRD and
other HR activities. It does, however, emphasise the importance of a public commitment to learning from the top.

FROM 'TRAINING AND DEVELOPMENT' TO 'STRATEGIC HUMAN RESOURCE DEVELOPMENT'

How can we build upon the above analysis to establish an integrated SHRD
approach that extends beyond a coherent training and development strategy?
What additional features would we expect to see? What aspects should we be critical of? The following represent some of the issues.

Presence of an overall organisation vision emphasising learning

One of the measures of an overall strategic approach to HRD is the presence of
published statements at corporate level about the importance of learning and
development and how they contribute to the overall corporate vision and mission.
   There are a number of examples where organisations have incorporated HRD
perspectives in their organisational guiding principles. For example:

Levi Strauss:

'Educate managers and employees about "Aspirations" and give them the skills, programs, and policies support to operate in the new environment' (quoted in Walker, 1992);

Morgan Stanley:

'Commitment to personal development has created a truly global team with a unique vision. As a result, Morgan Stanley is a leading global investment bank achieving impressive results across all of its business areas . . . Central to supporting our core values is investment in training and development of individuals along with the seeking of diverse perspectives.'

Extract from the Cardiff-based Allied Steel and Wire Ltd Group (ASW) Ethos statement:

– to know of and aim at matching the World's Best Standards;

– to realise that matching World's Best Standards means the development of people so that they can accept more and more responsibility individually and in groups and remove all inertia.

The existence of such statements does not demonstrate a strategic approach. Take this example from the London Fire and Civil Defence Authority: 'To develop the authority as an organisation where staff are given the opportunity to learn and develop in a supportive organisational environment where initiative is encouraged.'

The statement does not indicate how this supportive learning environment contributes to the strategic imperatives facing the organisation.

Making the human resource development function more strategic

As mentioned in the introduction to this chapter, there is a tendency and a temptation for established training and development functions to endeavour to make their function more strategic. This can contribute to the overall SHRD effort so long as: (a) it is not seen as an alternative to adopting an organisation-wide strategic approach to HRD; and (b) the outcome is a demonstration that the HRD function has a key role in strategy development.

There are a variety of ways in which this can be attempted. It can, for example, be manifested through the adoption of a customer-benefit driven approach to organising one's HRD strategies. This is particularly significant if one is responsible for an HRD department or training centre in an organisation.

In essence a customer-benefit approach works as follows.

1 Endeavour to get an HRD perspective incorporated in the overall organisational vision and reinforced in its core values or guiding principles. A reliance on a separate functional perspective implies that HRD is not seen as part of the business imperative.

2 Clarify unit HRD mission.

3 Detail supporting HRD strategies from the perspective of major stakeholders.

4 Generate strategic keys to translate those strategies into practical guidelines.

The approach developed by a leading institution based in the City of London may be taken as an example. In practical terms, this might map out as follows.

Unit mission statement

A unit mission statement could take the following form.

> As a Leading Human Resource Development Unit our Mission is to support the business by providing consistent and fully comprehensive solutions to its requirements.

The elements of the mission statement are presented in Table 4.1.

Table 4.1 Defining the elements of a mission statement

Mission	Defined by
'Leading'	■ Used as a benchmarking exemplar ■ Highly respected service provision ■ Range of product and service solutions ■ Highly valued place to work
'Consistent'	■ Delivery of solutions (praised by line managers) ■ Quality standards
'Fully comprehensive'	■ Range of products and services ■ Consultancy advisory approach
'Solutions to requirements'	■ Meet individual customer demand through innovative and creative approaches
'Support the business'	■ Understanding customers' business so that their success can be supported

To achieve the mission customer-benefit strategic areas have been identified to define the relationships with key stakeholder groupings, as defined by the executive management team (*see* Table 4.2).

The strategic keys for each strategy could be expertise, range of solutions, defined quality, accessibility, proactive and creative.

Table 4.2 Customer-benefit strategic areas

Strategic area	Relationship with stakeholders
Customer strategy	It benefits our *customers* to use HRD services by . . .
Opinion leader strategy	It benefits *decision makers* to build relationships with HRD services by . . .
Supplier strategy	It benefits our *suppliers* to develop partnerships with HRD services by . . .
Shareholder strategy	It benefits our *shareholders* to own HRD services by . . .

Thus *expertise* as a strategic key in the shareholder strategy could be defined as follows:

> *Expertise* in the management of the unit will deliver expected outcomes and return on investment.

What one is doing is developing a strategy as though the functional area were a business in its own right. This can be helpful where training and development, for example, is seen as a semi-autonomous functional activity. In essence, it entails the basic strategic management processes of 'looking out' and 'looking in'; and establishing a relationship between the products and services offered 'out there' and the resources and capabilities available 'in here'. The next step involves deciding how to deploy one's resources over time. 'Out there', we have to navigate around competitors to reach customers. For a functional area, 'out there' can be other parts of the host organisation.

A good example of this sort of approach to strategy was adopted by SunU (*see* Fig. 4.9). 'U' indicates that the training and development activity has been rebadged as a corporate university.

Figure 4.9	Reinventing SunU

SunU is the training and development arm of Sun Microsystems, a manufacturer of computer workstations and computer-network software based in California. SunU provides training to 13 000 employees and a growing number of suppliers and sales partners.

In late 1992 it found it needed to 'reinvent' its way of operating. Increasingly customers had less time for classroom training. They needed training solutions that could be developed quickly (time-to-market) and that could train a lot of people quickly (time-to-volume). Also there was a need to adopt new perspectives on maintaining the competence of knowledge workers and on developing a learning organisation. Finally there was a need to do more – or at least the same – with fewer resources. In early 1993 SunU was reduced from 60 to 45 employees.

SunU started its reinvention with a 'white paper' on its own 'training business' generated as part of the annual planning process. The paper gave answers to the questions:

- Who are our customers?
- Who are our competitors?
- Why will customers buy from us?
- What must we do to make that happen?
- Do we have the necessary resources?
- Do we have the necessary skills and abilities?
- Where are our interdependencies (including those with such external partners as vendors and educational organisations)?

After the downsizing, a consultant in reinvention methods was hired. One approach that came out of workshops and team-planning sessions was the use of '*stands*' as a way of articulating how an organisation wants to operate in the future. A *stand* is a sort of stake in the ground that maps out a future position that drives action, goal setting and resource allocation.

The SunU team developed stands for each of the seven elements of a model developed during the team-planning sessions. The model, entitled the SunU

▶▶

▶▶ Figure 4.9 continued

system model, also shows the linkages between these different elements of SunU's operating system. Customers, the most important element, are in the centre.

In the complete model, each element has three to five stands which are responses to questions relating to the element. In the following example only one question and resulting stand per element is given.

1 **Customers:** *Who are our customers and how do we work with them?*
'We are fully knowledgeable about Sun Microsystem's business and are the first source of products and services that meet the skills, knowledge, and information needs that result from our customers' business plans and strategies.'

2 **Organisation:** *What is the nature of SunU's organisational practices required to fulfil our charter and stands?*
'Our internal and external partners are the keys to our success. They are fully cognisant of our directions, plans, and related requirements. We continually review our mix of partners and their contributions.'

3 **Products and services:** *How do we ensure that all of our products and services meet specific strategic requirements?*
'We provide products and services that are clearly related to strategic and role competences; that are required by business plans and strategies; that are supportive of fast time to volume; that are wide ranging in their delivery methods; that are easy to access and use; and that are price and performance competitive.'

4 **Research and development:** *How do we stay current in and optimise our knowledge of all fields related to fulfilling our charter and stands?*
'SunU identifies, acquires, and implements research findings and third-party products – specifically in the areas of information delivery and training and development.'

5 **Business systems:** *What are the processes, procedures and tools required to achieve our product, service and organisational goals?*
'Pricing, registration, charge-back and financial-management processes are critical to SunU's success. They are understood by all of SunU's staff and aligned with our product and customer requirements.'

6 **Continuous learning:** *How do we recognise that learning at Sun Microsystems is continuous, conscious and obtained from many sources?*
'Sun Microsystem's capability to learn faster than its competitors is a key to competitive advantage. Its expertise in learning processes enables it to achieve and sustain competitive advantage at all levels – individual, team and organisational.'

7 **Results:** *How do we actively pursue successful results on our customers' terms?*
'We demonstrate the return on investment in planned or actual training to our customers, using their performance measures.'

SunU also adopted the concept of inventions. When team members can say, 'We need an invention to . . .', they are less likely to select only known solutions to problems. They are also more willing to admit that they do not yet know the solution. Invention issues included: 'We need a competencey model and an assessment process that are easily adapted to different functional groups'; and 'We need a method of communicating training's return on investment that increases customers' perceptions of the positive effect of training.'

Source: Based on Smith (1994).

Figure 4.10   The elements and stands of a human resource development strategy

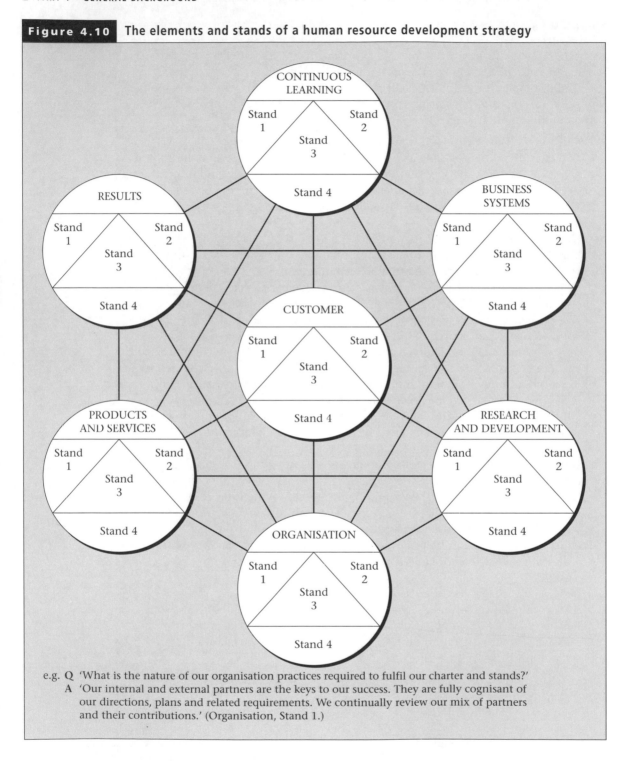

e.g. **Q** 'What is the nature of our organisation practices required to fulfil our charter and stands?'
    A 'Our internal and external partners are the keys to our success. They are fully cognisant of our directions, plans and related requirements. We continually review our mix of partners and their contributions.' (Organisation, Stand 1.)

Mapping perceptions of human resource development and its contribution to strategy

Another way of mapping the strategic contribution of an area is as follows:

■ From: *Not important enough to have a strategy in its own right.*

■ To: *Too important to have a strategy in its own right.*

Although apparently paradoxical, this latter position emerged in a 1995 Cabinet Office consortium project into establishing ways of developing approaches to SHRD. A number of members of the consortium felt that it was inappropriate to be looking for an independent HR strategy, but that HRD should be incorporated into the overall business ethos.

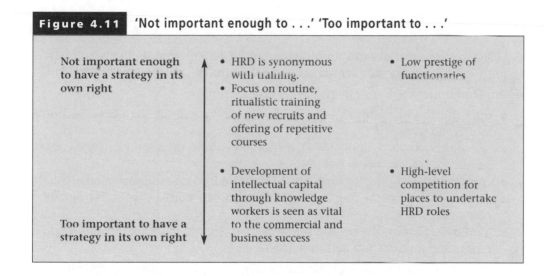

Figure 4.11 'Not important enough to . . .' 'Too important to . . .'

Not important enough to have a strategy in its own right
- HRD is synonymous with training.
- Focus on routine, ritualistic training of new recruits and offering of repetitive courses
- Low prestige of functionaries

Too important to have a strategy in its own right
- Development of intellectual capital through knowledge workers is seen as vital to the commercial and business success
- High-level competition for places to undertake HRD roles

HOW APPROPRIATE IS THE FORMAL PLANNING MODEL FOR STRATEGIC HUMAN RESOURCE DEVELOPMENT?

The most commonly recommended model for achieving SHRD is through formal planning. There are a number of frameworks which emanate from strategic planning ideology. They are based on the proposition that for an approach to be strategic it needs to be planned in accordance with predetermined criteria following a detailed internal and external organisational analysis. Rothwell and Kazanas (1989) adopt this position.

They define SHRD as 'the process of changing an organisation, stakeholders outside it, groups inside it, and people employed by it through planned learning so they possess the knowledge and skills needed in the future'. To achieve this there needs to be 'an Organisational Strategy for the HRD Effort which guides, unifies, and provides direction to planned learning sponsored by an organisation. In SHRD, the focus of planning centres around roles and responsibilities of everyone – HRD practitioners, line managers and participants'. They amplify their position:

Organisation strategy for HRD positions the HRD effort, it supports strategic business plans, work unit plans, individual career plans and effective job performance. It prioritises HRD activities, concentrating initiatives where they are most likely to be useful; it encourages long-term thinking among learners, and it exerts pressure on top managers to consider linkages between long-term 'Strategic Business Plans and shorter-term HR decisions.

Their recommended process for developing the organisation strategy for HRD is akin to that undertaken in conventional strategic business and HR planning. Their proposed steps are:

1 Clarify the purpose of the HRD effort.

2 Assess the present strengths and weaknesses of the organisation's skill base.

3 Scan the external environment for threats and opportunities that are likely to influence human performance.

4 Compare strengths and weaknesses to future threats and opportunities.

5 Select a long-term organisational strategy for HRD which is likely to prepare both individuals and the organisation for the future.

6 Implement the chosen strategy, paying attention to:

- organisation development (what should be done to change organisational and group norms?);
- non-employee development (what should be done to meet learning needs of people external to the organisation?);
- employee development (what should be done to create long-term talent?);
- employee education (what should be done to help people realise career objectives?);
- employee training (what should be done to help people master job requirements and improve job performance?).

(*See* Chapter 9 on Marketing HRD for further discussion of these terms.)

7 Evaluate HRD.

The above process embodies some key assumptions for it to be effectively managed:

a There should be an overall purpose or mission statement for the corporation, and the HRD effort should be related to it.

b Every major plan of the corporation should be weighed in terms of the human skills available to implement it and alternative ways of obtaining those skills.

c People at all levels in the organisation's chain of command should share responsibility and accountability for HRD.

d There should be a formal, systematic and holistic planning process for the corporation, personnel department and HRD.

Although superficially very attractive because of its structured and disciplined approach, this process places great reliance on analysis and planning as the best way to make decisions about the future. It founders when there is:

- no formal, systematic process for the corporation as a whole; or
- a need for responsiveness and flexibility, in order to 'adjust to continually changing circumstances', using Von Moltke's terminology.

DOES LINKING STRATEGIC HUMAN RESOURCE PLANNING AND DEVELOPMENT HELP?

It has been suggested that the formal SHRD planning model can be strengthened by linking the process specifically to human resource planning. Burgoyne (op. cit.) takes this position. It is seen as a way of bringing together the 'soft' aspects of 'learning' with the 'hard' requirements of ensuring the current and future existence of a clearly defined skill base by means of prescribed techniques of needs forecasting.

A recent example is provided by Grundy (1997), who specifically refers to Strategic Human Resource Planning and Development (SHRPD). He considers 'development' to be an integral part of a broader HR planning process, as opposed to being something worth pursuing in its own right. SHRPD, as he describes it, 'entails the close integration of thinking about *future* HR needs with thinking about competitive strategy, organisational strategy and the business environment'. He contrasts this to traditional 'manpower planning' where the effective deployment of human resources is a side issue, the emphasis being on establishing the *quantity* of resources required as opposed to their *quality*.

One of the objectives of his SHRPD process is to achieve 'human advantage', which he defines as 'the contribution which human resources makes towards adding value to customers, towards managing cost, through accelerating operational and management processes, and in challenging the status quo through innovation and change'. 'Human advantage' is an essential ingredient in what he calls an organisation's 'competitive software', which can be contrasted to its more tangible 'competitive hardware'. As I understand it, the 'competitive software' is another way of referring to 'intellectual capital' as described earlier.

Grundy describes how SPHRD is carried out at Amersham International Life Sciences, a major technology marketing, distribution and manufacturing business, based in the UK, but serving markets world-wide. The process is a fairly conventional approach to succession planning incorporating a prior identification of the management roles and competences required to take the business forward, and then establishing a pool of talent to meet expected future requirements. In the context of this book, it is a particular, albeit somewhat restricted, approach to achieving SHRD.

This attempt to link SHRD with HR planning is subject to the same criticisms as those levied at clarifying the link with business planning. HR planning itself is, of course, dependent upon the prior existence of a formal planning framework. It is not concerned with broader issues of developing learning within organisations as a strategic feature in its own right. However, if one is in an organisation that has a strong planning orientation, the relationship between SHRD and HRP should, of course, be clarified.

PRACTICAL EXAMPLES OF STRATEGIC HUMAN RESOURCE DEVELOPMENT

Whereas the literature is full of practical examples of 'training', and 'training and development' strategies, there are fewer references to broader SHRD. This is partly because of the relative newness of the concept, and partly because of the difficulties associated with forging links between the various drivers of the process. There are a number of 'learning organisation' case studies that meet some of the criteria that I would be looking for. These are the subject of Chapter 15. Others that have a distinct SHRD sense to them are still referred to by the authors as instances of 'training and development' strategy. The example from Trustee Savings Bank presented in Fig. 4.12 is a case in point.

Figure 4.12	Trustee Savings Bank

TSB Retail Banking and Insurance was started in 1810 in Scotland by the Reverend Henry Duncan as a vehicle for the working classes to save and thus be more able to support themselves in times of hardship rather than applying to the Parish for financial assistance. Over the next 150 years a number of regional savings banks emerged, based on the original concept; these amalgamating in the 1960s and 1970s. In 1986 the organisation was floated on the Stock Exchange as a public company. By 1990 it consisted of a network of 1400 branches, and some 24 000 staff were involved in insurance, bank card, mortgage and finance-house operations. Executive and support functions were based at the Head Office in Birmingham, UK. In 1996 it merged with Lloyds Bank.

In the latter part of 1990 TSB Retail Banking and Insurance attempted to generate a learning culture that would be an integral part of both its training and development and its business strategy. Until then personal development was not valued, with employees lacking the skill and understanding to develop themselves or their staff effectively, and not recognising the potential for learning from work itself. It was 'training' that was talked about – something which either was provided for you, or you did to others, or was done to you, and which largely entailed course attendance.

In 1990 TQM was introduced into the organisation as part of the overall corporate strategy. This emphasised continuous improvement of workplace processes using a process analysis approach. This helped managers to grasp the concept of continuous learning which TSB defined as: 'An approach which recognises the individual's responsibility and control of life-long learning. It encourages everyone to view learning as an everyday experience and actively use opportunities available for personal development.' A TSB project team, drawn from representatives across the business, worked from this perspective in an endeavour to make continuous self-managed learning an everyday experience and thereby to achieve a shift from dependence to independence, from passive to proactive learning approaches.

The main objective of the strategy is to achieve competitive advantage through managers being absolutely clear about their roles, and being equipped and motivated to assume responsibility for their own learning and the development of others. It was also hoped that competitive advantage would be demonstrated through:

▶▶

▶▶ Figure 4.12 continued

- staff 'working smarter' by means of planning, executing and reviewing both work and learning;
- achieving greater role clarity, by focusing on core activities and outputs;
- more frequent use of local learning resources to achieve cost-effective, sustained performance improvement;
- the adoption by individuals of learning activities appropriate to their learning styles, thereby shortening the learning curve;
- applying learning back in the workplace;
- creating a learning and improving climate;
- developing an understanding of the consistency and integration of the various corporate strategies, including TQM.

It was also intended that the TSB strategy would enhance the performance management system introduced in 1987. From the outset, this system promoted the use of personal development plans as an integral part of the continuing improvement process. The new approach was designed to provide them with a development or learning focus and rationale and thereby to overcome the initial resistance to their use.

There is evidence of tension between the 'rhetoric' and the practical application of the philosophy. The TSB approach, as described by Taylor (1992), consciously focused on 'learning' becoming a future core competence of the business. It was 'a longer-term generic approach to achieving the transition from training to learning, changing values and ideals along the way', and providing signposts and resources to guide managers in their new role. It eschewed 'developing people as a core competence', partly because of the associations of this concept, however paradoxical, with interpreting that objective into 'running training courses for managers'.

However, in 1992, the TSB Group Executive Board made a decision to invest the sum of £11 million in training in support of its policy and associated HRD strategies. As a result four projects were set up:

- personal learning records;
- a customer care programme;
- learning resource centres;
- a management skills programme.

This latter programme attracted the bulk of the resources allocated, some £8 million in total. The programme, which was contracted out, centred around the development of a range of 21 competences. Some had an operational focus and centred around 'team effectiveness' and 'planning and reviewing'; some had a customer focus, centring around 'business solutions' and 'customer service'; and some related to 'personal drive'.

To support its strategy TSB produced the following policy statement.

The aim of TSB's Training and Development policy is to support the achievement of the organisation's strategic goals through the culture of continuous development and shared

▶▶

▶▶ Figure 4.12 continued

learning which enables TSB to respond flexibly and quickly to a rapidly changing business environment. All training and development activity will be driven by business needs and will support the establishment of TSB's values throughout the organisation.

Our policy therefore is that all staff should have access to training and development to improve their competence in their current job role or to prepare them for future or changing roles. Anyone with responsibility for managing people must support the development of staff and must regard training and development as a fundamental part of their role. All managers and staff must take responsibility for improving their capabilities by using the learning programmes and packages available to them and by ensuring that learning and work are integrated to provide opportunities for continuous development through work.

The overall policy statement is amplified in supporting policy guidelines. These include:

- training and development activities will have clear objectives and learning outcomes, which are measured in business terms and the achievement of specified standards and qualifications;
- training will be designed to meet the identified needs of staff, will be accessible and will accommodate the needs of the job;
- opportunities will be provided to staff where appropriate to enable them to acquire relevant transferable skills and qualifications in support of their development and personal.

Source: Taylor (1992) and the author's own sources.

Figure 4.13 describes the continuous development approach adopted by Nissan UK.

Figure 4.13   Continuous development at Nissan

To what extent does the approach adopted in the following example from Nissan UK provide evidence of an integrated SHRD strategy?

1 Instead of asking, 'What does the individual need?' the question asked is, 'What does the company require of its people to ensure that they can properly undertake their responsibilities?'

2 When this question was initially asked of operational directors, it led to 250 topics.

3 When training staff asked individuals at departmental level, the list was expanded to 1200 topics.

4 Individualised continuous development programmes resulted. These comprised:

  a *Company core curriculum*: topics which everyone needs to know, such as basic induction material, understanding of the roles of other departments and introduction to the concepts of Kaizen, TQM and problem-solving techniques.

  b *Occupational skills*: topics that are common to an occupational level in the company, irrespective of the department in which staff work. Thus all

▶▶

▶▶ Figure 4.13 continued

administrative assistants need to have clearly defined levels of skill or knowledge in, for example, written communications, telephone techniques, word processing and purchase requisition systems.

c *Professional programme*: applies to everyone. This relates to the particular skills needed to do a particular job.

d *Personal development plan*: this is specific to the individual and includes, for example, time management, stress management and assertiveness.

5 Every manager has seen every other manager's list. This has led to managers adding to topics for their own department – cross-fertilisation of ideas and knowledge.

6 The whole process means that departmental managers and supervisors are fully involved in the identification of the T&D needs of their staff and in many topics are responsible for the individual inputs.

7 Continuous development combines with succession planning, external recruitment, assessment of internal candidates for promotion and the evaluation and validation of training and manpower planning to become part of a fully integrated and comprehensive strategy.

8 The whole 'compound' must fit closely with the business needs and objectives as defined at board level and must be securely fastened to the needs and demand of individual line managers and supervisors. This is no easy task.

Source: Wickens (1991).

An attempt to develop a composited HRD strategy, sustained by a number of contributory initiatives, and reinforced from the findings of a benchmarking study has been undertaken by English Nature (*see* Fig. 4.14).

Figure 4.14 Approach to human resource development strategy at English Nature

English Nature is the UK government's adviser on nature and conservation. It has over the years run 'respected and well managed training courses', but the organisation has more recently become aware of problems associated with high costs, slow speed of delivery, relevance of the training, transfer of learning and exchanging skills with colleagues. The training budget, excluding staff costs, is about 3 per cent of running costs and 4.5 per cent of salary costs. This allowed for 4000 training days to be provided per annum for the 725 staff. In attempting to transform itself into a 'learning organisation' it has developed a number of new approaches.

First, it identified a number of organisational imperatives which it was felt could be met through the learning process:

▶▶

▶▶ Figure 4.14 continued

1 A more flexible work-force was required to enable change to be handled more effectively.
2 Managers were being asked to become leaders rather than controllers, and some needed to acquire a different range of skills to achieve this change.
3 Morale was fairly low, and it was decided that quality learning and improved skills could ameliorate the worst effects.
4 Ways to improve performance needed to be found without increasing training costs.

A small project team was set up to provide views from across the organisation and to spread the workload of implementation. The team compiled a list of more than 30 learning options available within English Nature aimed at encouraging people to consider ways of learning other than training courses. This became known as the 'learning passport' and included desk training, external attachments and secondments, fellowships, bursaries, job rotation and shadowing.

A 'dating agency' was also set up to encourage mentoring and coaching. Generally steps were taken to persuade everyone to take a broader view of learning.

The existing open learning centre, which provided a range of learning materials, was updated and promoted.

Part of the training budget was delegated to local teams to increase line management responsibility for, and involvement in, training and to give everyone an appreciation of the costs involved in formal training.

The performance agreement constituting part of the staff appraisal system included a requirement to identify at least one personal development objective each year. A learning and development plan was included as part of the process and managing learning was one of the core competences.

Rules on funding private study were reviewed. Managers should now encourage anyone who wants to acquire a new skill, even if it has little or no immediate relevance to their current job.

Support has been given to focus groups – meetings of people who would not normally get together – so that a diverse range of people co-operate to solve problems. This will help to break down hierarchical boundaries and encourage networking with outsiders.

Benchmarking visits were made to 12 organisations which had adopted innovative approaches to learning and business development. A common feature was the warm welcome received and the friendly atmosphere of the organisations. It confirmed why Rank Xerox describe benchmarking as 'industrial tourism'.

Most of the organisations visited found the theory of the 'learning organisation' of limited use. It did help to pull together a series of related training issues, but was a hindrance in explaining and selling the changes to senior managers and staff.

A number of common approaches were identified in the organisations visited which can be generally applied.

1 Get the support of relevant senior staff, particularly for changes concerned with the wider issues of organisational management. They will need to be involved in learning reviews and networking arrangements.

▶▶

▶▶ Figure 4.14 continued

2 Such senior staff will need to act as role models for the rest of the organisation. This role modelling should demonstrate an open, available, supportive and visible management style, where mistakes can be admitted.

3 Introduce systems of working that bring action, review and application of learning so closely together that it is difficult to distinguish their boundaries.

4 Introduce working practices that allow staff to network freely, move between jobs as required and have ready access to senior staff.

5 Get senior staff to network outside the organisation and report back on a regular basis.

6 Support as much learning as possible, so that staff get the learning habit and begin to question existing systems.

7 Introduce new ways of learning, so that a wide range of learning options are available to meet individual preferences and needs.

8 Co-operate with partners and colleagues in other organisations by holding joint events, sharing resources and swapping ideas.

Source: Based on Dolan (1995).

DO HUMAN RESOURCE DEVELOPMENT STRATEGIES HAVE TO BE CONSISTENT TO BE STRATEGIC?

The conventional wisdom is that there needs to be a structural and systemic coherence of the various constituent elements of HR for an organisation to demonstrate a strategic approach to HR. First, it is held, human resource strategies should be integrated with organisational 'business' strategy to demonstrate evidence of their being mutually supportive and reinforcing. Second, there should be evidence that the elements of HR are internally consistent and mutually reinforcing. Yet, as Andrew Mayo (1995) points out, this could be in conflict with one of today's structural imperatives – that organisations should move from a structure based on centralised co-ordination to one centred around autonomous business sub-units.

Mayo puts a new perspective on one of the 'escalating and seemingly possible demands' that Rosabeth Moss Kanter considers that corporations of today have to contend with, namely:

> Decentralise to delegate profit and planning responsibilities to small, autonomous business units. But centralise to capture efficiencies and combine resources in innovative ways (Kanter, 1989).

Mayo suggests that one resolution of the structural shift is to substitute universal processes in functional areas such as HR with a common policy umbrella which permits diverse ways of implementation. Flexibility and adaptability to the conditions of the particular unit must, he contends, be in principle beneficial. Specialists at HQ may despair at seeing what they regard as reinvented wheels, unprofessional choices, units changing established processes 'for the sake of it' and so on. But they must live with these. The task for HQ, his experience indicates, is to determine the *frameworks* of best practice which will enable diverse and locally owned implementation, and to provide consultant help built round the local need.

A second, related, consequence entails dispensing with consistency in HR systems, such as approach to staff development, and allowing individual units discretion in dealing with these. For a long time HR systems have been managed on the principle of cross-company equitability. Mayo believes that in tomorrow's world we must recognise diversity and individual contribution and adopt an approach that is more market facing.

Nevertheless, systems divergence has its risks, which may become apparent when it is necessary to redesign the boundaries of the devolved units and one is faced with all the problems of a 'merger' of incompatible systems and commitments. In moving away from what Michael Porter (1980) calls a 'horizontal strategy' there is a loss of economies in systems design; and knowledge, experience and 'best practice' become more difficult to share. Internal tensions may develop as people are treated differently depending on where they work. A new set of processes may be needed to ensure knowledge sharing across the new boundaries. These, Mayo feels, will be both IT based and people to people based, and without them there is the risk of immense invisible costs throughout the organisation.

Keith Sisson (1995) sees the situation in a somewhat different light. He suggests that the widespread adoption of divisionalisation, devolved budgeting and internal markets pose serious questions about the ability of organisations to develop a strategic response to HR, for the HR function is itself being crucially affected by the new developments. Superficially, the devolution of the specialist function from HQ to divisions and the passing of responsibilities for HR to line managers are to be welcomed if they encourage greater local ownership. There are inherent dangers, nevertheless. The rundown of HR specialists at HQ potentially denies the organisation strategic capacity. *In theory* specialists at local level can do what is required in close co-operation with supportive line managers. *In practice* it is debatable whether local managers will have the time or expertise to develop the kind of integrated approach to HR that is needed.

If there is to be an overall policy umbrella, as Mayo suggests, it is worth considering what sort of things would be covered. In SHRD terms, one would hope there would be a series of framework 'directives' setting the context for an overall 'learning climate', and how individuals and their contributions are to be valued and sustained.

CREATING A FAVOURABLE ORGANISATIONAL LEARNING CLIMATE

Successful SHRD depends on the existence of a favourable learning climate. Learning climate can be defined as the prevailing set of attitudes – ranging from positive to indifference to negative – that individuals hold towards learning opportunities and personal growth.

Honey and Mumford (1989) generated a 11-point checklist for measuring the learning climate, viewing it in large part from the perspective of a manager. They suggested that a positive climate exists when the following conditions are fulfilled.

1 Individuals receive a regular review of performance and learning.

2 Individuals receive timely feedback on both performance and achieved learning.

3 Managers are encouraged to identify their own learning needs.

4 Managers are encouraged to set challenging learning goals for themselves.

5 Managers receive guidance in their performance in helping to develop others.

6 Managers are assisted in seeing learning opportunities on the job. (By inference, jobs need to be constructed in such a way that they provide opportunities for challenge and for adding to an existing repertoire of skills.)

7 Managers seek to provide new experiences from which others can learn.

8 Opportunities are afforded for off-the-job training (and, by implication, barriers are not placed in the way of individuals who wish to attend learning events off the job).

9 Managers are encouraged to take risks so long as they try to learn from their mistakes.

10 Managers are encouraged to review, conclude and plan learning activities.

11 Managers are encouraged to challenge the traditional way of doing things.

Their perspective excluded a number of structural and symbolic factors which have a marked impact on people's attitude to learning.

1 *Job design features*: jobs are constructed in such a way that they provide opportunities for challenge and for adding to an existing repertoire of skills.

2 *Stretch assignments*: opportunities are afforded for individuals to engage in stretching activities, with an understanding that they will not be punished for mistakes.

3 Senior managers demonstrate by personal involvement their commitment to learning. Jack Welch of GEC is one example of a CEO who has been known to personally deliver training to groups of staff at the GEC corporate training centre.

4 A commitment to learning is expressed in corporate policy statements and staff handbooks – intentions such as becoming a 'learning organisation' or a 'corporate university'. Evidence that espoused commitments are translated into actual commitments.

5 *Resource adequacy*: HRD-related activities are appropriately resourced, not just in terms of financial allocations such as a percentage of payroll, but in terms of generosity of time of key executives.

6 *Even-handedness*: all groups are given equal opportunity to access development opportunities.

7 Absence of change initiative overload, whereby barriers to learning are created because of a sense of never touching the ground and being able to get involved in change processes that could be rapidly overturned.

8 *A sense of trust*: that learning is not going to be overtaken by corporate downsizing and delayering.

Bartram *et al.* (1993) developed a 70-item questionnaire to test respondents' feelings about the prevailing learning climate. The Learning Climate Questionnaire comprises the following seven broad categories.

1 *Management style*: measures the extent to which respondents consider their manager to be supportive and stimulating.

2 *Time*: measures the time pressure employees experience in their work.

3 *Autonomy*: measures the degree to which employees are able to perform their work autonomously.

4 *Team style*: measures the degree to which employees consider their colleagues as supportive and encouraging.

5 *Opportunities to develop*: measures the degree to which employees feel they have opportunities to contribute to the policy of their department and the opportunities employees experience to perform tasks that are unrelated to their work.

6 *Guidelines*: measures the availability of written guidelines in the workplace.

7 *Satisfaction*: measures the atmosphere of the department.

In the context of the organisation-wide learning we are discussing in this book, this questionnaire seems very narrow in focus. It also reflects the values of the authors. For example, there is a presumption that written guidelines in the workplace will contribute to a positive learning climate.

LEVERAGING LEARNING AS A CORE COMPETENCE

There is one key factor above all others which differentiates the SHRD perspective developed in this text from approaches discussed so far in this chapter. This factor is that, whatever the details of the approach adopted, the aim should be to achieve a position whereby learning and development processes and outcomes become a core competence of the organisation, contributing to its strategic intent.

The development of this argument recurs throughout the book. For example, it will be a theme when we analyse the current interest in the learning organisation (*see* Chapter 15). It will emerge when we look at some of the more advanced ways of perceiving a corporate university (*see* Chapter 16). It will be presented as a major contribution that HRD can make to the development of nationally dispersed subsidiaries in a global corporation (*see* Chapter 19).

It was stated in the introduction to this chapter that SHRD rarely happens in practice. It is hypothesised that SHRD requires people in key roles who can meet the following criteria:

1 They are able to intellectually link:
   ■ structural processes and systems;
   ■ learning initiatives; and
   ■ strategy issues.

2 They are appropriately positioned in an organisation to steer SHRD through.

3 They are able to communicate their understanding to others and gain commitment.

4 They are able to focus on these key relationships and see them through (i.e. they have strategic time).

THE INTEGRATED PACKAGE

The model presented in Fig. 4.15 is as a framework for a strategic approach to learning and development that I believe has the potential to be embedded in the corporate business ideology. It endeavours to capture the range of approaches that are held to represent good practice in the field.

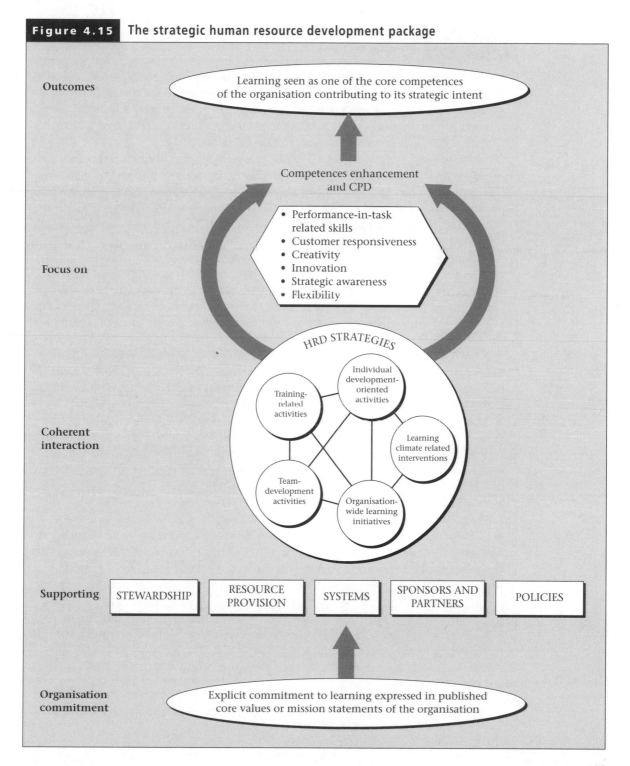

Figure 4.15 The strategic human resource development package

Figure 4.16 is a case example of an initiative which forms part of an overall business strategy. What features exist which give it an SHRD flavour?

| Figure 4.16 | Texas Instruments Defence Systems and Electronics Group's internal strategy |

By the end of the 1980s Texas Instruments Defence Systems and Electronics Group (DSEG) identified *customer focus*, *employee involvement*, and *continuous improvement* as the cornerstones of its internal business strategy. Top management championed the use of criteria from the US Malcolm Baldrige National Quality Award (*see* Chapter 14) as self-assessment tools and internal benchmarks.

Early successes with self-directed teams at one plant contributed to the decision in 1991 to form a support group called the High-Performing Organisations Development Unit. The unit was championed by the HR manager and by DSEG's president. Its mandate was to promote the development of empowered teams in other parts of the organisation and to create a unified team and empowerment strategy that would guide the company through the 1990s.

Earlier, management had responded to the promises of TQM by pushing for the creation of teams. Teams had been created with little understanding of the other changes that would be needed – for example, in job definitions and support systems – before the new teams would have a chance of success. Without supervision, adequate training, clear objectives or understanding of customer needs, many of the earlier teams had been ineffectual.

Now DSEG realised that creating teams was not enough; the entire organisation had to be aligned with the strategy. Within six months the new approach realised dramatic results, including a 50 per cent reduction in cycle time, a 60 per cent reduction in scrap and a 30 per cent improvement in productivity.

The plan included job enrichment and expansion, cross-functional and integrated product-development teams, and extensive cross-training for employees.

The most important factor influencing the pace of empowered-team development was the level of trust established within business units. Empowerment developed rapidly in units that had open and co-operative relations between managers and employees. Where relations lacked trust, empowerment stalled.

From its earlier failure with teams, DSEG learned that empowered teams require major changes in nearly all the company's systems, policies and practices. It redesigned its performance appraisal system to reward individual performance in the context of a team environment. In the new flatter organisation, 'criteria for success' replace the old career paths. Management layers have shrunk and total employment is down. Managers have new roles as coaches and change agents in the transfer of knowledge and skills to teams. Use of the Baldrige Award criteria has focused management on removing obstacles to team development rather than on tracking day-to-day financial indicators.

Source: Wellins *et al.* (1994).

CONCLUSION

Strategic HRD is concerned with introducing, directing and guiding learning activities undertaken by individuals during the time they are associated with the organisation in such a way that they will more effectively contribute to the achievement of organisational goals. In today's terminology, it is concerned with providing opportunities for the furtherance of learning that will enhance the 'human and structural capital' (Edvinsson, 1997) of the organisation.

Strategic HRD is concerned with ensuring that individuals are equipped – not just now but also in the future – with the skills and knowledge to offer the goods and services which the organisation's customers need, at a quality which they expect. But it is not just a matter of enabling individuals to respond to market conditions. It is concerned with providing them with a range of competences which will increase their strategic awareness and the particular contribution they can make individually and collectively in the overall growth of the business. It is concerned with demonstrating that the development of skills and knowledge is a strategic imperative for the organisation.

It is concerned with: ensuring that there are processes in the organisation which facilitate learning; ensuring that appropriate stewardship is exercised over the learning processes; and providing direction to ensure that core competences of organisations are enhanced through learning. It is further concerned with ensuring that sufficient information is available about learning practices exercised elsewhere to inform practices within the organisation.

Mintzberg (1988) contends that one can infer an organisation's strategy from patterns in action – inferring the strategic imperatives from what actually happens. However, strategy management and strategic HRD are based on the principle that there should be some conscious intent in what is being undertaken. Again, this is not the same as saying that there has to be a predetermined strategic plan. As many people have pointed out such a plan can be a fantasy, in no way representing what takes place in practice.

REFERENCES

Bartram, D., Foster, J., Lindley, P. A., Brown, A. J. and Nixon, S. (1993) *The Learning Climate Questionnaire*. Employment Service and Newland Park Associates Ltd.

Burgoyne, J. (1988) 'Management Development for the Individual and the Organisation', *Personnel Management*, June, pp. 40–4.

Dolan, S. (1995) 'A Different Use of Natural Resources', *Personnel Management*, 5 October.

Drewitt, T. (1994) 'Secrets of the Black Horse', *Training and Development* (UK), November, p. 17.

Edvinsson, L. (1997) 'Developing Intellectual Capital at Skandia', *Long Range Planning*, 30(3), pp. 366–73.

Finn, W. (1995) 'Born again secondment', *Human Resources*, March/April.

Galagan, P. A. and Tunis, C. J. (1995) 'Building Capability at Pacific Bell', *Training and Development* (US), February, pp. 24–31.

Garavan, T. N. (1991) 'Strategic human resource development', *Journal of European Industrial Training*, 15(1), pp. 17–30.

Grundy, T. (1997) 'Human Resource Management – A Strategic Approach', *Long Range Planning*, 30(4), August.

Harrison, R. (1997) *Employee Development*. London: IPD.

Honey, P. and Mumford, A. (1989) *Manual of Learning Opportunities*. Peter Honey.

Kanter, R. M. (1989) *When Giants Learn to Dance*. New York: Simon & Schuster.

Keith, J. and Smith Payton, E. (1995) 'The New Face of Training', *Training and Development* (US), February.

Kenney, J. and Reid, M. A. (1988) *Training Interventions*. London: IPM.

Mabey, C. and Salaman, G. (1995) 'Training and Development Strategies', in *Strategic Human Resource Management*. Oxford: Blackwell.

Mayo, A. (1995) 'The pain and gain of devolution and empowerment'; *Organisations and People*, 2(4), pp. 14–18.

Mayo, A. and Lank, E. (1994) *The Power of Learning*. London: IPD.

Mintzberg, H. (1988) 'Opening Up the Definition of Strategy', in J. B. Quinn, H. Mintzberg and R. M. James (eds) *The Strategy Process: Concepts, Contexts and Cases*. Englewood Cliffs, NJ: Prentice Hall.

Nonaka, L. and Takeuchi, H. (1995) *The Knowledge-Creating Company*. Oxford: Oxford University Press.

Porter, M. E. (1980) *Competitive Advantage*. New York: Free Press.

Rothwell, W. J. and Kazanas, H. C. (1989) *Strategic Human Resource Development*. Englewood Cliffs, NJ: Prentice Hall.

Sisson, K. (1995) 'Organisation Structure', in S. Tyson (ed.) *Strategic Prospects for HRM*. London: IPD.

Smith, P. A. (1994) 'Reinventing SunU', *Training and Development* (US), July.

Taylor, S. (1992) 'Managing a Learning Environment', *Personnel Management*, October, pp. 54–7.

Walker, J. W. (1992) *Human Resource Strategy*. McGraw-Hill.

Wellins, R. S., Byham, W. C. and Dixon, G. R. (1994) *Inside Teams*. San Francisco: Jossey-Bass.

Wickens, P. (1991) 'Innovation in Training Creates a Competitive Edge', quoted in J. Stevens and R. Mackay (eds) *Training and Competitiveness*. London: Kogan Page.

Zemke, R. (1981) 'Curriculum Development as Strategic Planning', *Training*, 18(4).

Chapter 5

THE HUMAN RESOURCE MANAGEMENT VERSUS PERSONNEL MANAGEMENT DEBATE AND ITS IMPLICATIONS FOR HUMAN RESOURCE DEVELOPMENT

OBJECTIVES

By the end of this chapter you should be able to:

- distinguish between HRM and personnel management;

- describe and evaluate a range of theoretical positions on the relationship between HRM and personnel management;

- describe the Harvard and the contingency models of HRM and how these have influenced theory and practice;

- establish where writers on HRM and personnel management see HRD;

- establish various approaches to understanding where the emerging concept of HRD fits into the HRM v. Personnel Management debate;

- judge whether HRD strategies have an integrity in their own right or are contained in an overall HRM purview;

- indicate practical implications of the above for developing a strategic approach to HRD.

INTRODUCTION

As we saw in Chapter 4, it has frequently been emphasised that it is of strategic importance that HR practices and policies be mutually reinforcing and aligned (*see*, e.g. Mabey and Salaman, 1995). Harrison (1997) further draws attention to the need for collaboration and, by implication, partnership between HRD and other HR practitioners if this is to occur.

It should almost go without saying that, from both a strategic and operational perspective, HR professionals working in the same organisation benefit from having a common understanding on 'people and development' issues. It is not very helpful for a personnel or HR director, say, to contend that 'they do things differently there' when talking of the corporate learning centre to other corporate decision makers. Nor does it instil a great deal of confidence for training and development (T&D) staff, or organisation development (OD) consultants, to profess total or near-total ignorance of personnel activities and strategies.

It is a basic contention of this book that knowledge of mainstream people management is important for HRD practitioners, just as an understanding of HRD is important for other HR practitioners in circumstances when the roles are separated. This is quite apart from the fact that a number of managers have a functional responsibility which encompasses a whole gamut of people and development activities. Any approach to HRD which does not incorporate a perspective on other branches of HR is accordingly held to be impoverished. Of course, the reverse is equally valid. It is not just a matter of having a knowledge base. It is how this knowledge base informs one's actions and how much time is devoted to each area in practice.

To comprehend how HRD relates in a theoretical and practical sense to other areas which see people issues as their primary concern demands an awareness of what the terms 'HRM' and 'personnel management' mean. However, as with 'HRD', they are not precise constructs but represent complex, abstract and fluid concepts whose interpretation depends on the backgrounds and experiences of the users and on 'where they are coming from'. How they are understood can determine HR reporting and power relationships, career structures, functional divisions and job roles. More importantly, they can establish parameters for dealing with those very people who constitute their *raison d'être*. Establishing current views on their similarities and differences is the subject of this chapter. In conclusion the question will be asked whether a different mindset is entailed when adopting an HRM focus as compared to an HRD focus and what the implications might be.

DEFINITIONS

Changes in terminology

In the 1970s the term HRM was hardly ever used to describe mainstream people management. The received terminology, reflected both in theory and organisational practice, was 'personnel management' or, in the USA, 'personnel administration'. This has changed. One of the features of the last few years has been a steady stream of books, articles and jobs either with HRM in their title, or focusing explicitly on HRM as an issue.

Today there are very few new books with 'Personnel' in the title. Based upon current titles, one might draw the logical inference that 'old-style' personnel managers are being replaced by 'new-style' HRM managers. It is not so clear, however, that 'personnel' as a concept or as a term has been replaced in practitioner or professional circles. It is certainly not reflected in the nomenclature of the merged UK professional 'Institute of Personnel and Development', created in 1994 out of the two previous institutes – of 'Personnel Management' and 'Training and Development'. It also is not reflected in job titles as represented in advertisements. A survey I conducted in Autumn 1995 of recruitment advertise-ments in professional HR journals in the UK showed a 50–50 split between jobs that had HR in the title and jobs that had 'personnel'. A similar survey in Spring 1998 showed a 60–40 split.

In the burgeoning literature HRM is interpreted in a variety of ways dependent on the position the authors present in an ongoing debate, initiated in the USA in the early 1980s, as to whether HRM is just a new term for the supposedly 'old' con-cept of 'personnel' or whether it embodies something substantially different. At an early stage in the debate a number of writers argued that HRM was no more than 'new wine in the old personnel bottle'. This view is more than understandable if one sees HRM as no more than a change of terminology to keep up with fashion. However, one of the implications of adopting this perspective is to contend that the problems, issues and functions that professionals in the field have to undertake today are not substantially different to those of their counterparts of twenty years ago. This runs counter to the prevailing wisdom that the 1980s and 1990s have heralded a real shift in organisational thinking and practice. It is accordingly becoming less common nowadays to see HRM used merely as a synonym, albeit a more up-to-date term, for traditional 'personnel management'. On the whole, in theoretical terms, it is felt to herald something new.

It is more fashionable to argue that HRM as a concept reflects a 'paradigm shift' which over the last two decades has influenced the way people are expected to act in organisations and the way the employer–employee relationship is acted out. There are strong parallels here to a view expressed in this book that new perspec-tives on HRD might reflect a paradigm shift from 'training and development'. This is not to say that it has happened overnight or that everything has changed. As Shaun Tyson (1995a) points out, we have not moved from one steady state called 'personnel' to another steady state called 'HRM'.

Karen Legge (1989), in a much quoted article, looked at the background under-pinning the change in terminology from personnel to HRM. She argued that as organisations, most noticeably in the USA and the UK, attempted to cope with new competitive pressures and environmental forces, 'so the vocabulary for man-aging their workforces has tended to change'. As a consequence, 'Human Resource Management', or even 'Strategic Human Resource Management' was beginning to replace 'Personnel Management' as the received terminology for the profession. She was reflecting an earlier American academic position, expressed most forcibly in a 1982 article by Fombrun, Tichy and Devanna.

> The long-run competitiveness of American industry will require considerably more sophisticated approaches to the human resource input that deal with its strategic role in organisational performance . . . and the strategic human resource concepts and tools needed are fundamentally different from the stock in trade of the traditional personnel administrator (Tichy *et al.*, 1982).

In the intervening years since this was written, the trend towards 'human resource management' has continued. The question remains, however, whether given these new competitive pressures and environmental forces, there has been an associated change in practice. Or is the debate merely an academic discussion?

HUMAN RESOURCE MANAGEMENT VERSUS PERSONNEL MANAGEMENT

The first task is to establish whether there is a difference between personnel management and HRM. We will look at the traditional approach to defining personnel management, and identify the range of functions that are normally considered to fall under its purview. This will then form the basis for a comparison with current views on HRM:

What is traditional personnel management?

Definitions abound on what constitutes personnel management.
Most UK writers on the subject start with the following 1963 definition developed by the IPM.

> Personnel management is a responsibility of all those who manage people, as well as being a description of the work of those who are employed as specialists. It is that part of management which is concerned with people at work and their relationships within an enterprise. Personnel management aims to achieve both efficiency and justice, neither of which can be pursued successfully without the other. It seeks to bring together and develop in an effective organisation the men and women who make up an enterprise, enabling each to make his own best contribution to its success both as an individual and as a member of a working group. It seeks to provide fair terms and conditions of employment, and satisfying work for those employed (IPM, 1963).

From this definition of over thirty years ago some clear strands are discernible which both date it and create some problematic issues.

1 The assumption is that personnel management is concerned with people's relationships *within* an enterprise. Many personnel specialists now operate as independent consultants. Many personnel-related activities (alongside other activities such as IT) are now quite likely to be outsourced.

2 It is concerned with individuals who are in a contractual *employment* relationship with an employer. Such relationships are representing a smaller and smaller percentage of the working population – witness the growth of casualisation of employment and of the demand for agencies such as Manpower.

3 The definition attempts to bring out the key role of *line management* in managing people. The importance of line managers in the process undoubtedly needs to be stated, and in many ways their role is being strengthened in current organisational practice – but because of this, the definition does not draw out the distinctive contribution that personnel professionals bring to the process. This is surprising in that the Institute of Personnel Management – and its successor the Institute of Personnel and Development – has always drawn the bulk of its membership from specialist practitioners.

4 Following on from the above, the definition is so broad and generalised that it does not reflect specific functions that individuals hoping to pursue personnel as a career would be expected to carry out. It is more in the form of a mission statement.

Later IPM statements have attempted to amplify the original 1963 definition and looked at personnel management more from a specialist practitioner standpoint. Take, for example, the following statement extracted from the 1994 guidance notes on the IPM Professional Education Scheme:

> Ultimately, personnel managers are concerned with the efficiency of the organisation. To be successful, organisations must satisfy their customers, provide value for money, be efficient and cost effective. These objectives can only be met if the organisation employs the correct number of people with the right skills and ensures that these skills are updated to keep pace with the changing demands and conditions which affect an organisation.
>
> Personnel professionals must therefore understand the nature of their organisation and ensure that the workforce is sufficiently well trained and motivated to meet company objectives. To achieve this, personnel managers must work closely with line managers to ascertain their human resource requirements, to ensure that the right people are employed, developed and maintained by the company (IPM, 1994).

Nevertheless, the emphasis is still on effectively managing operations within the confines of a given organisation. The restricted reference to 'company' is surprising since many HR practitioners are working in non-commercial environments such as local authorities and the voluntary sector.

Functional areas of personnel

Most studies into the practice of personnel management have adopted a functional perspective. Definitions have emphasised the role of personnel managers in the development and application of policies governing, in particular:

- HR planning, recruitment and selection, placement and termination;
- employee training and development, career management;
- terms and conditions of employment, employment contract rights and obligations;
- performance management, staff appraisal;
- reward systems, payment and benefits, job evaluation;
- job design, employee motivation;
- managing diversity;
- employee relations, to include industrial relations and negotiations with trade unions;
- health and safety, and staff welfare.

The Tyson and Fell model of personnel

Tyson and Fell (1986), on the basis of research which they conducted to uncover any general principles governing personnel work, came up with three explanatory models.

1 *'The Clerk of Works'*. This is a basic administrative model, where personnel provides a basic administrative service to line managers. It is this model which is often contrasted with the new HRM, especially in the US literature.

2 *'The Contracts manager'*. This is a sophisticated, industrial relations-oriented model where personnel seek to maintain the industrial relations systems and procedures in order to sustain or create harmony.

3 *'The Architect'*. This is a business-oriented, strategically aware function, where personnel design the employment relationship. It is this 'architect' perspective which critics allege is missing from the traditional personnel approach.

They also argued that there are four main traditions underpinning personnel, based on how fundamental problems in managing the employment relationship are addressed. These they defined as:

■ the welfare tradition;

■ the industrial relations tradition;

■ the employment management tradition;

■ the professional tradition.

There is no explicit reference to a development tradition underpinning personnel. This, in my opinion, is because their concept of personnel is with *managing* the employment relationship and not with how people learn and grow during their time with a given employer. This way of perceiving the world is a theme to which we shall return when evaluating the relationship with HRD.

Strategy and the traditional approach to personnel

A number of observers have argued that the traditional approach to personnel did not encompass any involvement of personnel practitioners in 'strategy'. The validity of this assertion has been hotly contested but nevertheless strategic considerations do not leap out at one from the personnel management literature. 'Manpower planning' or 'HR planning' has been held in some quarters to provide the link between personnel practices and business strategy. However, as Hendry (1995) points out, 'manpower planning falls short of delivering what HRM aspires to . . . distinctive cultures geared to long-term business strategies'. In practice, those organisations that purported to follow manpower planning precepts concentrated on developing detailed information systems on labour turnover, retention levels, forthcoming retirements and absenteeism as the basis of labour supply and demand forecasting.

The IPM also recognised that strategy was only covered tangentially in its Professional Education Scheme. In 1992, the IPM produced a specialist module entitled 'Strategic *Human Resource Management*' (my italics) specifically in order to encourage the development of strategic thinking for people who had already qualified in personnel management. This was to be seen as part of a Continuing Professional Development (CPD) approach.

CLAIMS FOR THE DISTINCTIVENESS OF HUMAN RESOURCE MANAGEMENT

There have been a variety of contributions suggesting that there is an approach to people management which is significantly different to 'personnel' and which can be labelled 'human resource management'. There are some common threads to these perspectives which I will attempt to pull together, but also some differences in emphasis which I will equally attempt to draw out. The arguments in favour of a distinctive HRM ideology have been heavily influenced by two separate, albeit linked and mutually reinforcing, perspectives emanating from the USA in the early 1980s.

The Harvard school and human resource management as a management-led philosophy

Beer *et al.* (1984) have provided a highly influential conceptual framework which they used to underpin the Harvard Business School course in HRM launched in 1981 (*see* Fig. 5.1).

General managers are at the heart of the Harvard model, with management taking the decisions affecting people day in, day out. 'Human resource management involves all management decisions that affect the nature of the relationship between the organisation and its employees – its human resources. General management make decisions daily that affect this relationship' (ibid.).

As we have seen, earlier definitions of personnel emphasised the importance of line managers in the people management process, but not to the downgrading of the role of the specialist professional. In the Harvard model, the role of a discrete personnel function is, to say the least, downplayed. Thus Beer and Spector (1985) contended in polemical fashion that conventional personnel practice is:

> All too frequently a hodge-podge of policies based on little more than outmoded habits, current fads, patched-up responses to former crises and pet ideas of specialists. HRM practice urgently needs to be reformed from the perspective of general management. HRM issues are much too important to be left largely to specialists.

The Harvard philosophy emphasises the management of work relations around the value of commitment. It requires the creation of high trust relations, which in turn mean employees being able to exercise influence. The creation of this commitment is dependent upon 'mutuality'. The notion of mutuality of course has strong affinities with the notion of 'partnership' which, as we have seen, is so current today:

> The new HRM model is composed of policies that promote mutuality – mutual goals, mutual respect, mutual rewards, mutual responsibility. The theory is that policies of mutuality will elicit commitment which in turn will yield both better economic performance and greater human development (Walton, 1985).

Beer *at al.* (1984) state that the following questions are important ones when considering whether HR policy enhances the performance of the organisation, the well being of employees, or the well-being of society, each of which is deemed to be of importance in the people management equation.

1 *Commitment*. To what extent do HRM policies enhance the commitment of people to their work and their organisation? Increased commitment can result not only in more loyalty and better performance for the organisation, but also in self-worth, dignity, psychological involvement, and identity for the individual.

127

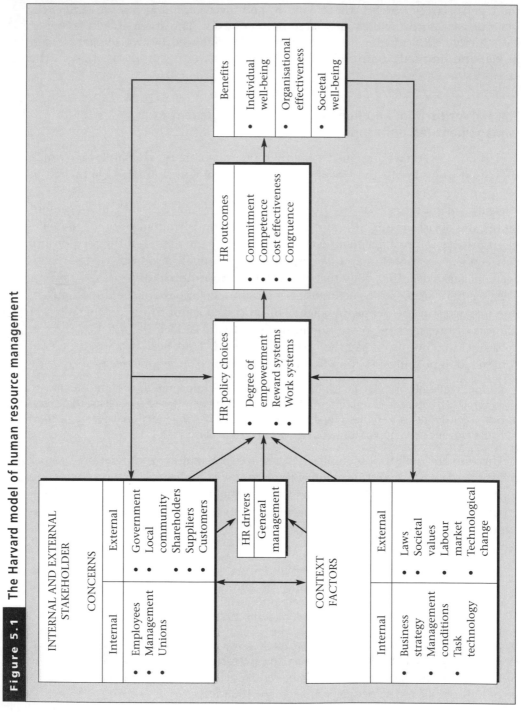

Figure 5.1 The Harvard model of human resource management

Source: Based on Beer *et al.* (1984).

2 *Competence*. To what extent do HRM policies attract, keep, and/or develop people with skills and knowledge needed by the organisation and society, now and in the future? When needed skills and knowledge are available at the right time, the organisation benefits and its employees experience an increased sense of self-worth and economic well-being.

3 *Cost effectiveness*. What is the cost effectiveness of a given policy in terms of wages, benefits, turnover, absenteeism, strikes, and so on? Such costs can be considered for organisations, individuals, and society as a whole.

4 *Congruence*. What levels of congruence do HRM policies and practices generate or sustain between management and employees, different employee groups, the organisation and community, employees and their families, and within the individual? The lack of such congruence can be costly to management in terms of time, money, and energy, because of the resulting low levels of trust and common purpose, and in terms of stress and other psychological problems it can create.

As Hendry (1995) points out, the Harvard connotation presents HRM as having a distinctive philosophy underpinning it, not just any set of values:

> This philosophy emphasises securing employee commitment and motivation in organisations characterised by high-trust relations, with scope for employees to exercise influence. Management style and organisational culture then become an important focus for action in their own right. It is not enough that employment practices cohere, nor even that they should express the values of the organisation. These values are of a particular kind.

Hendry also emphasises the perception of HR professionals contained in the Harvard way of thinking:

> The Harvard perspective on HRM tackles head on the issue of the personnel (HR) manager's status and role in organisations. Personnel managers cannot be expected to display a strategic approach since they are frequently shut out from business decision making. One obvious consequence is that general managers who do make strategy, should take direct responsibility for people-related decisions. The Harvard writers, therefore, explicitly direct their arguments at 'general management', and as a core module in the Harvard MBA, HRM is taken by future *general managers* (ibid.).

Walker (1992) adopts a similar perspective in terms of the primacy of the managerial role, although eschewing the term 'HRM', preferring to focus on 'human resource strategy'. He argues that the process of developing and implementing this strategy is inherently a line management responsibility. In the final resort, organisations do not need human resource specialists; managers can be self-sufficient. However he does provide some crumbs of comfort for HR practitioners by going on to say that, in practice:

> the human resource staff provide the guidance and support that managers need to understand and apply the process. Human resource staff play a vital role on the management team – to ensure that people-related business issues are effectively addressed by management.

Hollinshead and Leat (1995) suggest that many subsequent notions of HRM draw upon the fundamental tenets of the original Harvard model, and that the following ideas are now commonplace:

- the need for HR policies to be integrated, to feed into corporate strategy, to promote organisational adaptability to rapid external change;

- the need to obtain employees' commitment to change, through their empowerment;

- the importance of a 'strong culture' of shared beliefs and norms across the organisation;

- the need for longer-term planning to anticipate labour market changes;

- the need for the HR function to show a clear contribution to the achievement of organisational goals and in particular to meet line management's needs;

- the need for flexible working practices;

- the need to measure the success of change more rigorously through performance appraisal, attitude surveys, etc.

Their summary incorporates a number of elements from the following contingency perspective.

Aligning employment practices to business strategy – the contingency approach

The classic HR statement adopting this perspective was developed by Fombrun, Tichy and Devanna (1982, 1984). Whereas with the Harvard school the emphasis is on the day-to-day responsibilities of managers for people, here the emphasis is on systems. In essence, they are arguing that there should be a vertical alignment between HR systems and business strategies, and a horizontal alignment between the various HR systems. The desired outcome from such alignment will be increased individual and organisational performance:

> Just as firms will be faced with inefficiencies when they try to implement new strategies with outmoded structures, so they will also face problems of implemention when they attempt to effect new strategies with inappropriate HR systems. The critical managerial task is to align the formal structure and the HR systems so that they drive the strategic objectives of the organisation.

The key HR systems for them were selection, appraisal, development (including training) and rewards. These were the main levers available to organisations for channelling individual behaviour towards specific performance goals, if they were properly aligned with one another. In an extension of their position, they emphasised the importance of organisational culture, which they termed the 'dominant value', as the crucial intervening variable between HR practices and behavioural outcomes. This can be viewed as an archetypal 'contingency' model – any HR practices introduced need to reflect and should be conditioned by the specific business concerns facing a given organisation.

Their 'contingency' approach is exemplified through the following dimensions which they contend that senior management (not senior HR management) might want to consider in the design of their human resource systems. They present these dimensions in the form of bipolar scales.

Nature of the employment contract

At one end of the spectrum employers emphasise 'a fair day's pay for a fair day's work' and focus on short-term performance and extrinsic rewards. At the other end the psychological contract stresses that challenging meaningful work will be provided in return for loyal committed service.

Degree of participation in decision making

Organisations can be ranked on a top-down/bottom-up continuum identifying the extent to which senior managers are willing to share decision making and power. In a top-down decision-making situation, the HR system centralises all key selection, appraisal, reward and development decisions. A bottom-up system enables widespread participation in these activities.

Internal versus external labour markets (recruitment)

Organisations can also be classified on the extent to which they promote from within or rely on external recruitment. They make the interesting point, to which we shall return later in the book, that organisations with a strong 'promote from within' orientation will stress development of staff as a key HR tool. Organisations operating from the other end of the spectrum will demonstrate a relatively weak development function.

Group versus individual performance

Human resource systems can be geared towards collective, group-based performance or towards individual performance or towards some mixture of the two. Sometimes such choices are dictated by the nature of the technology used, with group-based performance systems being adopted where it is difficult – even impossible – to evaluate the distinctive contribution of individuals to the overall effort. For some organisations the choice might be dictated by a cultural preference for a co-operative as opposed to a competitive climate.

As presented, the formulation is not value driven in the same way as the Harvard model. It does not demand a specific set of universal behaviours from individuals irrespective of the organisational environment in which they operate.

It is not entirely clear what they consider to be the role of the HR function in this process. Note that this is essentially an 'empirical-rationalist' approach to structuring HRM activities. They suggest that there should be a logical coherence between reward strategies, performance management approaches, recruitment and selection practices and so on. This coherence can be derived from and contribute to a given business strategy.

It is informative to reflect on the words typically used to describe an empirical-rational based contingency approach to HRM:

- align
- integrate
- fit
- cohere.

Elsewhere in the book we address the implications of an alternative 'split' model for strategy development and HRD (*see* Chapter 18).

Extensions of the contingency perspective

There have been various extensions to, and modifications of the contingency model since the original 1984 formulation. An interesting example is afforded by the approach adopted by Ackerman (1986) who, like Walker (op. cit.), has substituted for 'HRM' a more broad-based notion of HR strategy. He defined HR strategy as 'a pattern in a constant stream of human resource management decisions'.

Based on responses to a questionnaire circulated to a number of business concerns, he identified four HR policy-making 'patterns' or strategies. These were:

- *development strategy*: emphasises training, long-term planning, internal hiring;
- *control strategy*: emphasises performance appraisal, performance-based rewards; no job evaluation;
- *administrative strategy*: short-term manpower planning, external hiring, low level HR;
- *scanning strategy*: emphasis on labour market scanning, attitude surveys, money incentives.

He then used a carefully constructed contingency model to test the proposition that there are five influencing determinants on human resource strategies, namely:

- business strategies (defender, prospector, analyser, reactor, hybrid);
- environment (in terms of dynamism, heterogeneity, challenge);
- organisation structure;
- company size;
- availability of resources.

He concluded that HR strategies follow business strategies, that they tend to be independent of environmental pressures up to the point when the challenge forces a change and that they are independent of company size and resource availability (except the development strategy); but that they do vary with organisation structures.

The notion of a development orientation to HR strategy helps indicate how HRD may be introduced into a given organisation, although the specific features of the development strategy that Ackerman articulates are much narrower and restrictive than the position adopted in this book.

Soft contracting versus hard contracting

The distinction that is often made between 'soft contracting' and 'hard contracting' sits firmly within the contingency framework.

Tyson (1995b) defines HRM as 'a set of practices, activities and philosophies to manage the employment relationship'. He also draws attention to the contractual aspect of this employment relationship, differentiating between hard and soft contracting. Drawing upon Williamson and Ouchi (1983) he contends that: 'Soft contracting implies an elaborate internal labour market, managed by a sophisticated HR function, with strong HR policies to govern relationships, pay, promotions, appraisal and development.'

Organisations which favour 'soft contracts' are held to embody the following features:

- emphasis on vision and values of the organisation;
- 'clan culture' supported;
- long-term socialisation is normal;
- experience and length of service are rewarded;
- employee and management development policies are sophisticated, with an emphasis on careers and appraisal;
- employee commitment is expected as part of the psychological contract.

Tyson (1995a) writes of 'hard contracting' that it 'implies a link back into the wider labour markets, with a more legalistic and instrumental attachment to work as the norm for the effort-reward bargain'

Organisations which favour 'hard contracts' are held to demonstrate the following features:

- emphasis on transaction costs;
- service agreements between departments inside the organisation;
- non-employee options are openly canvassed;
- 'Taylorism' (i.e. an emphasis on extrinsic rewards in return for specific performance outcomes) in reward policies is accepted;
- people are employed in jobs not careers.

Another way of viewing 'hard' and 'soft' contracting is to see 'hard' contracting as representing a 'compliance' orientation to HR strategy and 'soft' contracting as representing a 'commitment' orientation, akin to the values espoused by the Harvard school.

Composite versions of the Harvard and the contingency schools

Over the last few years, a number of composite versions of the Harvard and contingency models have been propounded, incorporating core features of each. On the whole, they tend to be quite idealistic (*see* Fig. 5.2).

| Figure 5.2 | Managing people: the changing frontiers |

In October 1993 the IPD issued a consultative document entitled 'Managing People – the Changing Frontiers'. It argued that as a result of significant economic and social trends impacting upon organisations, new thinking about people management practices and strategies would be needed to secure long-term organisational success. Those who responded to the consultation, including a number of

▶▶

chief executives, felt that a turning-point had been reached in recognising that people management theories which emphasised the contribution that people play in the survival and growth of organisations needed to be translated into reality. Note the subtle shift from 'personnel management' to 'people management' as well as the avoidance of the term 'HRM'.

The follow-up 1994 paper from the IPD, entitled 'People make the Difference', suggested that:

people management practices are changing irreversibly. For more and more organisations the success of people management practices now depends on the ability to stimulate and focus:

- initiative
- creativity
- motivation
- judgement
- capability

- adaptability
- business orientation
- responsibility
- willing contribution

The approach can be seen as an updated extension of the basic Harvard ideology. There are echoes in the paper of the American Society for Training and Development plea, expressed at its 1994 Annual Convention, that 'we need to reinvent our profession'. The whole tone is different from the detailed analytic attempts of some writers to argue against a paradigm shift in the people management field.

The paper goes on to argue that:

the following characteristics can be seen time and again in organisations which have a reputation for transforming their approach to people management:

- interdependence between the various parts of the business, extensive team working and strong individual contributions;
- performance management to identify results, measure attainment and continuously improve;
- motivational systems to underpin achievement in outputs, behaviour and competence development;
- training and development geared to operational needs, longer-term adaptability and personal growth;
- conscious efforts to make sure these changes are understood and supported by the culture of the organisation.

The contention is then made that these characteristics, on their own, are not enough. There needs to be an understanding by those who attempt to adopt them that business has to be:

- *strategic* – aiming at customer-related objectives;
- *integrative* – ensuring that values, management actions, information and support systems are mutually reinforcing.

Human resource management versus personnel perspectives: the Storey model

Storey (1992a) provides a continuum of possible meanings for HRM to reflect the range of perspectives being provided.

- Starting with *HRM as a synonym for personnel management*;
- he moves to *HRM as an integrated set of techniques*;
- on to *HRM as a business-oriented approach*;
- and ends with *HRM as all of these plus a set of policies aimed at obtaining employee commitment to explicit organisational values*.

He recognises in developing this typology that one could be 'contrasting an idealised version of HRM with a practical, lived-in account of the messy reality of personnel management' (op. cit., p. 33). His continuum also does not reflect the view of some that HRM, as opposed to personnel management, is primarily the province of line management. This is the position taken by Sadler (1995):

> Human resource management should be seen as that part of overall managerial responsibilities dealing with the people dimension. Personnel on the other hand is the title to be given to the specific professional function which makes a distinctive contribution to management in this field.

Figure 5.3 provides a relationship between line management involvement and the range of positions on the HRM – Personnel scale.

OTHER PERSPECTIVES ON HUMAN RESOURCE MANAGEMENT

Managing human resources for their asset value

Chris Hendry (1995) offers as a separate perspective the view, or governing principle, that 'people are our most important asset'. This, of course, is implicit in the title of the mainstream text from the Harvard school, *Managing Human Assets* (Beer *et al.*, 1984). It is also a concept familiar to HRD in the context of the contribution of learning processes to generating 'intellectual capital'.

I think that, by introducing it as a separate category, Hendry means that 'Human Resource Management' can be restated as 'the management of people as a resource or tangible asset'. In the Harvard formulation the asset is only realised if people are appropriately treated, recognised and rewarded – an extension of the old paternalistic welfare approach to personnel but with a specific business-oriented focus. This is in sharp contrast to the view that people are a cost to be minimised. This is often indicated by those organisations which adopt a 'control and command', compliance-oriented, hard-contracting perspective to managing people.

Hendry contends that the idea of people as a valuable organisational asset has a sound pedigree in the economist's theory of human capital. He omits to mention that practical attempts to introduce 'human asset accounting' into organisations' financial processes have never been noticeably successful. This could, of course, be due to the fact that the administration of such attempts is undertaken by accountants.

Figure 5.3 Personnel versus human resource management perspectives

	Specialist function taking all HR decisions and carrying out HR operations	Some HR operational issues delegated to line management	Partnership relationship	Line management taking all HR decisions
Integrated operational and strategic approach with adoption of specific values such as 'commitment'				
Business-oriented and integrated strategic approach				
HRM as a integrated set of techniques				
HRM as a synonym for personnel management				

Ideology continuum

Role of line management continuum

Assets mean something specific, that is, in principle, measurable. So, for example, human capital can be enhanced by the further investment in education and training, just as the physical capital of a factory can be by modernisation. Equally, both can deteriorate through ageing, obsolescence and neglect.

The idea of seeing people as 'assets' or 'resources' has led to some seeing human resources as nothing more than the readily manipulable footsoldiers of organisations. Morris (1974) contrasted approaches to managing people where they are viewed as 'human resources' to approaches where they are viewed as 'resourceful humans' or people who initiate.

Hendry does not quote the commonly stated view which we have already encountered (in, for example, the IPD 1994 paper, 'People make the Difference'), that people can be seen as the 'primary sustainable source of competitive advantage'. However, in many respects it is that point of view that has led to such interest in HR issues by senior management. One of my Masters students, Helen Duguid, in 1996 described the key difference between HRM and personnel management in her organisation, Microsoft, as follows:

> In essence our employees are now overtly regarded as a valuable resource. No longer are they viewed as a cost to be minimised but as a resource which, if effectively managed, rather than administered, can from a strategic point of view contribute significantly to organisational effectiveness, thus confirming themselves to be a source of competitive advantage in an increasingly competitive industry.

WHY DID HUMAN RESOURCE MANAGEMENT EMERGE WHEN IT DID?

Beaumont (1992) identified a series of factors which led to the emergence of HRM as a concept in the early to mid-1980s and significantly, in the USA:

- the increasingly competitive, integrated characteristics of the product market environment;
- the 'positive lessons' of the Japanese system and the high performance of individual US companies which accord HRM a relatively high priority;
- the declining levels of work-force unionisation, particularly in the private sector, in the USA;
- the relative growth of the service, white collar sector of employment;
- the relatively limited power and status of the personnel management function in individual organisations due to its inability to demonstrate a distinctive contribution to individual organisational performance.

Singh (1992) has commented on the suitability of some of the features in the UK environment to adopt HRM perspectives despite their origin in the USA:

- increasing international competition, with old models for the management of labour seeming not to be working effectively in a rapidly changing environment;
- new technology, notably in manufacturing and office computerisation, facilitating moves towards flexible working arrangements and new reward systems;

- the diminishing power of trade unions coupled with a strong trend towards individual achievement encouraged by government policy. This was alongside a loss in the traditional membership reservoir, as a result of decline in the coal, steel and manufacturing industries;

- demographic changes, including an increasing proportion of women, part-timers and young people in the work-force. Singh noted that companies which are associated with HRM approaches such as Toshiba and Marks & Spencer employ a high proportion of women. He suggested that women have historically been more compliant with management initiatives of which moves towards HRM are an instance;

- Japanese companies establishing plants in greenfield sites providing the opportunity for the introduction of new initiatives in the management of labour.

Summary of differences held to exist between human resource management and personnel

Those who argue that HRM is different from personnel management make the following points in support of their claim.

1 Human resource management makes explicit the relationship between HR policies, practices and procedures and business strategy. There should be a clear fit between these HR practices and the business; it should be absolutely clear as to how they contribute.

2 Human resource management emphasises the need for coherence between the various HR policies and practices that are adopted. It should be apparent how they fit together and collectively contribute to the achievement of business objectives.

3 Human resource management is much more concerned with orchestrating change than is personnel management. In so doing, it has a greater role in creating and sustaining new organisational values and symbols and explaining these to employees.

4 Human resource management is much more focused on an underpinning philosophy and set of values governing employment strategy and how people can be seen as a source of sustainable competitive advantage.

As customers increasingly make choices on the basis of how people perform rather than how products perform, the management of human resources becomes a primary source of differentiation (Reif, 1991, quoted in Walker, 1992).

5 Human resource management entails a specific ongoing commitment from line management in establishing and delivering HR strategies. General managers become the driving force in initiating and pushing through HR policies and practices.

6 In conceptual terms HRM subsumes 'personnel management'. Traditional functions still need to be carried out, but other perspectives are now seen to be required of practitioners. This is especially the case at more senior levels. Much

has to do with changing organisational thinking on what leads to competitive advantage and of the role of the HR function in providing, retaining and developing committed individuals throughout the system who can contribute to the strategic effort.

Many of the definitions of HRM which we have encountered so far, make the introduction of the word 'strategic' redundant. This is because one of the defining characteristics of the new HR approach emanating from the USA in the early 1980s is its integration into organisational strategy. Nevertheless, there are a substantial number of organisations which use HRM as a synonym for traditional personnel management. Other organisations accept the strategic connotations of HRM but do not accept some of the value-driven aspects of the term which were part of the original US schema. We are thus left with quite different connotations associated with HRM, leading to much potential confusion.

It is accordingly helpful to use 'strategic HRM' to denote those organisational approaches which specifically endeavour to align their HR systems and associated practices to a definite business strategy and philosophy, without being tied to an overarching set of predetermined values.

HUMAN RESOURCE MANAGEMENT VERSUS PERSONNEL MANAGEMENT IN PRACTICE

Evidence from job advertisements

Recruitment advertisements in professional and trade journals provide useful insights into how job roles are perceived. The following are typical examples from the UK and show a range of perspectives.

Examples of director-level HR appointments

DIRECTOR OF HUMAN RESOURCES
for Health Care Trust

■ Lead professional Human Resource team. Support board, report to Chief Executive. Deliver Investors in People accreditation.

■ Strategic and operational control of organisational development. Drive significant change, cultivating multiskilled workforce with progressive training and development activities.

■ Proactively manage Employee Relations issues. Ensure cohesive employee communication, resourcing and reward policy and practice.

This advertisement very much reflects the new HR 'paradigm' with its emphasis on strategic as well as operational issues, its concern with organisational development and change and its identification of communication and cohesiveness of approach as an organisational imperative.

How would you position the advertisements on the next page on the HRM–Personnel continuum?

DIRECTOR OF HUMAN RESOURCES
for Housing Association

■ Overall responsibility for developing and maintaining Human Resources Strategy.

■ Closely involved in the overall strategic management of the business.

■ Major role in the support and development of staff – a key resource.

■ Working with line managers and other key players in taking on the challenges of the future.

■ Helping in re-engineering the way services and objectives are approached so that better services and value for money to tenants are achieved.

Examples of HR manager-level appointments

HUMAN RESOURCE OFFICER
for market leader in the field of business information

■ Key competencies include recruitment, employee relations and performance management.

■ Above all, capable of establishing personal and professional credibility quickly and easily, dealing with Directors and Executives on a regular basis.

HR MANAGER
for the integrated UK distribution and service division of an international commercial undertaking

■ Reporting to the Director of HR.

■ Challenge is to support the implementation of major organisational and cultural change, designed to improve both the quality of customer service and operational performance.

■ Responsible for all aspects of employee relations and resourcing.

HR MANAGER
for commercial concern specialising in the provision of consumer products and services

■ Reporting to the MD.

■ Redesign and restructuring of the business to enable it to maximise its customer focus.

■ Upgrade the quality and contribution of the people to take best advantage of the strong market position.

■ Define and introduce HR policies and practices relevant to a growing, field based sales and service operation.

Evidence from human resources and personnel strategy documents

According to Shaun Tyson (1995b), a survey of human resource strategy documents from different organisations shows certain similarities.

1 A review of external influences. These include political (e.g. what will be the effect of a government change, or of new European institutional arrangements); economic (impact of inflation, interest rates, unemployment, pay prospects); social (demographic, marital, crime and other trends); technical (the impact of new technology on work, communications, etc.) and legal (any specific legislative trends or changes anticipated).

2 An examination of the main business trends as they are likely to affect human resources in particular – expansion, contraction and any collaborative arrangements.

3 The examination in turn of each main policy area, in order to analyse the impact of external and business change on, for example:

■ employee resourcing;
■ employee relations;
■ rewards;
■ health and safety;
■ training and development;
■ performance management.

4 A description of the prospects for the type of service from the specialist HR function. Relationships with line management, the expertise required in the function and the way the function should operate in the future are dealt with here.

There can be considerable variation in emphasis on each of these topics according, for example, to the degree of trade union recognition, the effects of legislation on any specific industry and the organisation's stance on such issues as equal opportunities. Tyson (1995b) also identifies an overall 'flavour' to the strategy emanating from an organisation's philosophy of management:

> Espoused values can generate particular emphasis on such policy areas as rewards, seen for example in a move towards single status; and employee relations, through, for example, methods of employee involvement. Human resource strategy documents often explicitly state what the values are, and how the management process should reflect these values.

Thus the HR strategy documents often seek to reinterpret business strategy into HR policies, while maintaining a coherent management philosophy. Tyson goes on to point out that the process of creating a strategy, entailing the need to reconcile various pressures, is met with varying degrees of success.

What conclusions are to be drawn from this? The approach to strategy described seems to be based on providing an HR element to a corporate business plan. The HR plan seems to be based on identifying each of the mainstream personnel areas and demonstrating for each what contribution they can make. It also appears very reactive. One is responding to environmental forces, or perhaps trying to anticipate them, rather than experimenting with homespun innovative and creative measures. It comes from traditional personnel roots using corporate planning methodology. There is not a great deal of evidence of a learning and development orientation.

THE RELATIONSHIP BETWEEN HUMAN RESOURCE MANAGEMENT AND HUMAN RESOURCE DEVELOPMENT

Sambrook and Stewart (1998) suggest that the apparent shift since the mid-1980s from a functional and operational *personnel* orientation to a more strategic and integrated *HRM* focus has parallels with the swing from seeing HRD purely in narrowly defined, T&D, functional terms and towards having a strategic significance in its own right. They argue that whereas personnel and T&D strategies concentrate on technical issues, such as planning current manpower or training requirements, HRM and HRD address broader organisational issues. This perspective leads them to the following conclusion: 'It seems that "old-style" training and development and personnel management can be conceived as old relations (perhaps brother and sister). In the new generation of organisational theories, HRD has been born to accompany HRM.'

Another way of capturing the relationship is to think of 'personnel management' and 'training and development' as representing the East and West points on a compass, and HRM and HRD as reflecting a North–South direction (*see* Fig. 5.4).

Figure 5.4	The human resource compass

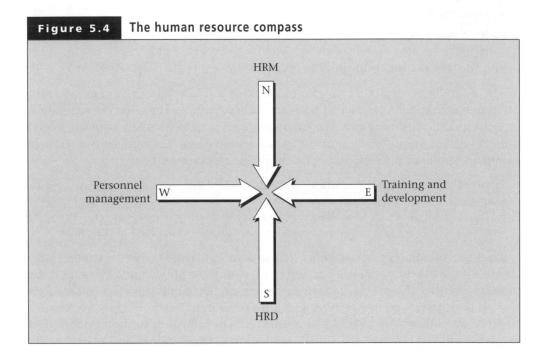

Common strategic concerns

Organisational strategic concerns in the HR arena certainly incorporate HRD dimensions. Indeed, on the evidence of the 1994 Cranfield study into HR practices, these could be said to predominate.

The Cranfield study

Tyson (1995a) refers to a joint Cranfield School of Management and 'P-E International' survey, conducted into HR practices in 1994. This focused on those organisations which were held to represent, in some respect, 'best practice' and which would thus be more appropriate for benchmarking than merely for identifying general trends. The survey restricted itself to commercial concerns. It found that all the companies in the sample regarded the following three main HR policy areas as the major contributors to business strategy:

- employee development (with a particular focus on management development, Tyson's respondents seeing management quality as constituting a significant source of competitive advantage);

- organisation development (used by Tyson as a catch-all term to categorise organisation-wide change programmes);

- employee relations (the management of employee relations being seen as a strategic matter regardless of whether the organisation in question recognised and negotiated with trade unions).

The first two of these policy areas represent core HRD issues.

How do personnel and human resource management texts discuss human resource development?

In many of the personnel and HRM texts, the term HRD is not even mentioned. This might be expected in traditional personnel-oriented publications which tend to restrict their HRD purview to 'training and development' or 'employee development'. It is rather more surprising in more recent publications. There is no reference to HRD, for example, in Shaun Tyson's 1995 publication, *Human Resource Strategy – towards a general theory of Human Resource Management* (1995a). Chris Hendry in 470 pages of *Human Resource Management – a Strategic Approach to Employment* (1995) provides only one fleeting reference to HRD as a term. The reverse is also true. There is no guarantee that texts on HRD make any reference to other areas of HR. Rothwell and Kazanas (1989), in their substantial text, *Strategic Human Resource Development*, are totally silent on the subject.

This is not to say that mainstream HRD concerns are not addressed in these texts. Organisation development and management development, for example, are both given coverage and their importance for today's organisations is emphasised. But they are subsumed within an overarching HR management framework.

Human resource development is often seen as a subset of HRM. Take the perspective presented in Fig. 5.5.

Figure 5.5 Definitions and objectives of human resource development

Human resource development is concerned with the recruitment and retention of high quality people who are best fitted to fulfil the organisation's objectives, defining and measuring levels of performance and providing continuous opportunities for training and development. Human resource development as part of HRM involves:

- recruiting and inducting high quality people and deploying them effectively;

- identifying and improving the skills and motivation of existing and longer-serving employees;

- regularly analysing job content in relation to organisation objectives and individual skills;

- reviewing the use of technology and its use in replacing routine tasks;

- focusing on people's skills and general intelligence rather than on educational attainment;

▶▶

▶▶ Figure 5.5 continued

- identifying training needs;
- providing training to improve current performance and to enhance individual careers;
- providing opportunities for individual self-development and personal growth;
- helping employees to manage their own careers;
- encouraging employees to accept change as an organisational 'norm' and an opportunity.

Both HRM and HRD need to be fully embedded in the overall policy and strategy of the organisation if they are going to be effective.

By definition, all HRD activities and programmes imply change, whether at an individual, workgroup or organisational level. A number of different objectives for HRD can be identified:

1 To use it as a *tool* in pursuit of quality, cost reduction and some form of enhanced performance.

2 To use it to gain competitive edge, both through the content of activities and the way in which they are delivered. More and more organisations are using HRD as a way of integrating their business planning processes with wider organisation development and HR activities.

3 To use it to create a general climate of *learning* in the organisation. The focus here is on the learning needs of individuals, hopefully in accordance with organisational goals. The belief behind it is that in each member of staff is a vast creative potential waiting to be unleashed.

4 To use it as a key device in engineering organisational change and, in particular, as a way of managing change.

Given this range of very ambitious objectives, it is unclear why HRD should be seen as part of HRM.

Source: Based on Thomson and Mabey (1994).

McGoldrick and Stewart (1996) adopt a different perspective. They contend that neither HRM nor HRD is a sub-set of the other but rather that each has its distinctive, albeit problematical, space in the analysis of the human aspects of contemporary organisations. Viewing HRM and HRD as separate yet complementary processes, is, for them, vital.

Conceptualising HRD as being in a subordinate and enclosed relationship to HRM is an issue in the USA just as in the UK. Willis (1997) comments that 'despite the trend toward more complex and systemic definitions of the field, a mind-set remains that HRD is part of, though peripheral to, HRM'. She considers that much modelling of the past shows HRD as marginalised by the organisation maintenance tasks of HRM and believes that if the motif of learning is the heart of HRD then it needs to be demonstrated in the models used to define the field. She draws our attention to the Human Resource Wheel which shows HRD outside HRM, although recognising that it is still bound up in issues of the status quo and not an HRD model in its own right.

The HR wheel

As we saw in Chapter 4, Patricia McLagan (1989) uses the notion of the HR wheel
to differentiate between HRD and other HR functional activities, *see* Fig. 5.6.

Figure 5.6	The human resource wheel

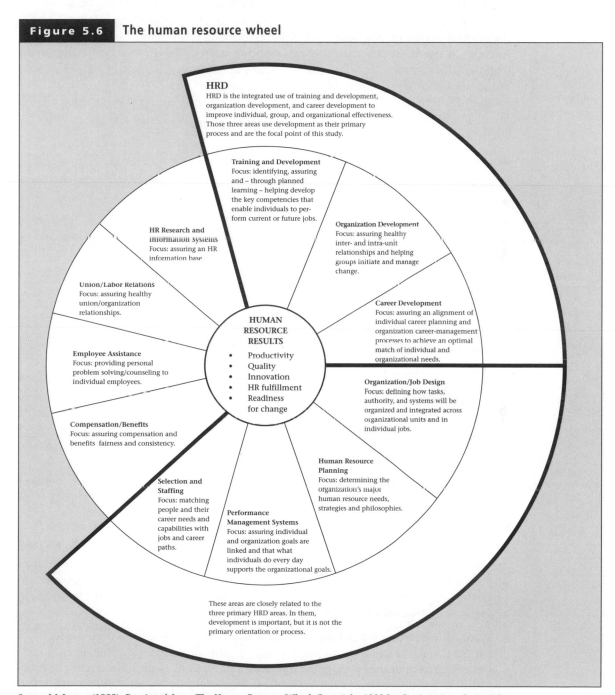

McLagan argues that HRD is concerned with 'development' issues – 'training and development', 'organisation' development and 'career' development. Her perspective is helpful in that it does not see HRD as a sub-set of HRM but as a major area in its own right. It also looks at HR through an HRD telescope as opposed to the HRM telescope of the other authorities we have looked at so far.

The wheel attempts to show direct and indirect relationships with other HR functional activities. She looks at these relationships in analytical, not structural-functional terms. In other words, she does not address the question whether, in an organisational context, all of the activities contained within the wheel should come under an overarching HR director or equivalent.

She identifies four HR areas as being closely aligned to the three primary HRD areas. Development has an important place in them but is not the primary focus. These areas are:

- selection and staffing;
- performance management systems;
- human resource planning;
- organisation/job design.

Other HR areas are outside the HRD ambit in terms of having no development associations. These she classifies as:

- human resource research and information systems;
- union/labour relations;
- employee assistance/individual counselling;
- compensation/benefits.

All areas are linked as a set of processes for achieving a set of HR results:

- productivity;
- quality;
- innovation;
- human resource fulfilment;
- readiness for change.

Does the relationship matter?

At one level the debate about the relationship between HRD and HRM can be seen as a purely academic and rather empty discussion about establishing boundaries and parameters based on analytical constructs. In a 1995 summary of a consortium project co-ordinated by the Cabinet Office on behalf of a number of government agencies and departments it was reported that:

> The usual definitions of HRM and HRD often seek to put boundaries between the two . . . . But the theoretical and practical perimeters are extremely blurred. For example, most HRM systems (eg performance management) include a strong HRD element. In practice, it is not particularly useful to try to maintain artificial distinctions. Indeed, it could be argued that the whole system of ideas embodied in an HR approach argues for a single, integrated set of policies covering all aspects of people management (Cabinet Office, 1995).

At another level it can turn into a significant political discussion on who reports to whom and where priorities lie. I recall some years ago asking a group of HRD managers from British Rail what would be the effect of HRD subsuming HRM and was greeted with the view that this would be treated as heresy. Sambrook and Stewart (op. cit.) refer to problems of ownership, identification, perceived loss of status and staff resistance when a previously autonomous training and development function whithin a UK Hospital trust was relocated and 'integrated' in the HR function. It is *not* the purpose of this book to make suggestions about organisational reporting relationships. It *is* the contention of this book that learning and development issues need to be orchestrated in a way that reflects their unique contribution to an organisation's strategic capability: and that this can only be undertaken effectively by people with a learning and development perspective.

CONCLUSION

Given the above analysis what is the relationship between HRD and HRM in people's *thinking*? Is this perceived relationship appropriate to sustain and enhance learning and development given the competitive and customer pressures, environ mental demands, individual expectations and organisational processes of the turn of the century? We are asking the same question the Harvard school asked of the personnel profession in the early 1980s but from a different, *developmental as opposed to managerial* perspective.

In essence it can be argued that although HRM and 'personnel management' represent different approaches to managing people, they are nevertheless both concerned with *managing* people and in particular 'employees' or those in a contractual employment relationship with a given organisation. Their sphere of operations is located firmly within an organisation context. The concern is with what you can get out of people *however* undertaken. As Armstrong (1992) pointedly puts it, 'the essence of HRM is that employees are valued assets'.

This is unlike HRD, which can be seen as an outcome of learning *wherever* undertaken. Even organisation-centred HRD addresses issues such as the development of non-employees in a way that is not within the purview of HRM as conventionally understood. None of the literature sources on HRM summarised in this chapter make any reference to non-employment issues.

Human resource management versus human resource development worldview

Bolman and Deal (1991), among others, have used the analogy of the 'frame' for explaining how our understanding of the world is conditioned. Frames, they contend, are both windows on the world and lenses that bring the world into focus. Through them we filter out some things while allowing others to pass through easily. Gareth Morgan (1993) makes the further point that frames of reference can act as different lenses, enabling us to see what otherwise might not be seen.

Each of us uses a personal frame or image of reality to gather information, make judgements and decide upon courses of action. Using another analogy, what you point your telescope at determines what you see. And what you point your telescope at demonstrates what you deem to be important.

The evidence is that looking at the world through an HRD frame or with an HRD-focused telescope provides a different perspective to looking at it through an HRM frame or with an HRM telescope. Human resource development practitioners tend to look through the telescope for ways to achieve 'lifelong learning' and 'development'. It is these concerns which help frame their worldview. Human resource management practitioners are more likely to look through the telescope for ways to measure and enhance the effective contribution of individuals in an organisational contractual framework.

But even in mainstream people management there is not one overriding worldview. The examples presented in the chapter demonstrate that for many people the concept of HRM is fundamentally different to the meanings they attach to 'personnel'. This, of course, is implicit in the notion of 'paradigm shift'. The argument is also presented that the emerging concept of HRD fits more comfortably with new-style 'HRM' than with old-style 'personnel'.

REFERENCES

Ackerman, K-F. (1986) 'A contingency model of HRM strategy. Empirical research findings reconsidered', *Management Forum*, 6, pp. 65–83.

Armstrong, M. (1992) *HRM – Strategy and Action*. London: Kogan Page.

Beaumont, P. (1992) 'The US Human Resource Management Literature – an overview', in G. Salaman (ed.) *Human Resource Strategies*. Beverly Hills, CA: Sage.

Beer, M. and Spector, B. (1985) 'Corporate transformations in human resource management', in R. E. Walton and P. R. Lawrence (eds) *HRM Trends and Challenges*. Cambridge, MA: Harvard Business School Press.

Beer, M., Spector, B., Lawrence, P. R., Mills, Q. N. and Walton, R. E. (1984) *Managing Human Assets*. New York: Free Press.

Bolman, L. G. and Deal, T. E. (1991) *Reframing Organisations – Artistry, Choice, and Leadership*. San Francisco: Jossey-Bass.

Cabinet Office, Office of Public Service and Science (1995) *A Strategic Approach to People Management*. London: Personnel Publications Ltd.

Fombrun, C. J., Tichy, N. M. and Devanna, M. A. (1982) 'Strategic Human Resource Management', *Sloan Management Review*, Winter.

Fombrum, C. J., Tichy N. M. and Devanna, M. A. (1984) 'Strategic Human Resource Management. New York: Wiley.

Harrison, R. (1997) *Employee Development*. London: IPD.

Hendry, C. (1995) *Human Resource Management – a Strategic Approach to Employment*. Oxford: Butterworth-Heinemann.

Hollinshead, G. and Leat, M. (1995) *Human Resource Management – An International and Comparative Perspective*. London: Pitman.

IPD (1993) *Managing people – the Changing Frontiers*. London: IPD.

IPD (1994) *People make the difference*. London: IPD.

IPM (1963) 'Statement on Personnel Management and Personnel Policies', *Personnel Management*, March.

IPM (1994) *Professional Education Scheme – Study Routes*. London: IPM.

Legge, K. (1989) 'Human Resource Management: a critical analysis', in J. Storey (ed.) *New Perspectives on Human Resource Management*. London: Routledge.

Mabey, C. and Salaman, G. (1995) 'Training and Development Strategies', in *Strategic Human Resource Management*. Oxford: Blackwell.

McGoldrick, J. and Stewart, J. (1996) 'The HRM–HRD nexus', in J. Stewart and J. McGoldrick (eds) *Human Resource Development – Perspectives, Strategies and Practice*. London: Pitman.

McLagan, P. (1989) *Models of HRD Practice*. ASTD Press.

Morgan, G. (1993) *Imaginisation*. Beverly Hills, CA: Sage.

Morris, J. (1974) 'Developing Resourceful Managers', in B. Taylor and G. Lippitt (eds) *Management Development and Training Handbook*. New York: McGraw-Hill.

Rothwell, W. J. and Kazanes, H. C. (1989) *Strategic Human Resource Development*. Englewood Cliffs, NJ: Prentice Hall.

Sadler, T. (1995) *Human Resource Management – Developing a Strategic Approach*. London: Kogan Page.

Sambrook, S. and Stewart, J. (1988) 'No I didn't want to be part of HR', *Human Resource Development International*, 1(2), pp. 171–87.

Singh, R.(1992) 'Human Resource Management: a Sceptical Look', in B. Towers (ed.) *A Handbook of Human Resource Management*. Oxford: Blackwell.

Storey, J. (1992a) *Developments in the Management of Human Resources*. Oxford: Blackwell.

Storey, J. (1992b) 'Human Resource Management in the Public Sector', in G. Salaman (ed.) *Human Resource Strategies*. Beverly Hills, CA: Sage.

Swanson, R. A. and Arnold, D. E. (1997) 'The Purpose of Human Resource Development is to Improve Performance'. Proceedings of Academy of Human Resource Development Conference, Atlanta, 6–9 March.

Thomson, R. and Mabey, C. (1994) *Developing Human Resources*. Oxford: Heinemann.

Tyson, S. (1995a) *Human Resource Strategy – Towards a General Theory of Human Resource Management*. London: Pitman.

Tyson, S. (1995b) 'Human Resource and Business Strategy', in *Strategic Prospects for HRM*. London: IPD.

Tyson, S. and Fell, A. (1986) *Evaluating the Personnel Function*. London: Hutchinson.

Walker, J. W. (1992) *Human Resource Strategy*. New York: McGraw-Hill.

Walton, R. E. (1985) 'Towards a strategy of eliciting employee commitment based on policies of mutuality', in R. E. Walton and P. R. Lawrence (eds) *HRM Trends and Challenges*. Cambridge, MA: Harvard Business School Press.

Williamson, O. E. and Ouchi, W. G. (1983) 'The markets and hierarchies programme of research: origins, implications and prospects', in A. Francis, J. Turk and P. Willman (eds) *Power, Efficiency and Institutions*. Oxford: Heinemann.

Willis, V. J. (1997) 'HRD as Evolutionary System: From Pyramid-Building to Space-Walking and Beyond'. Proceedings of the AHRD Conference, Atlanta.

Part 2

EMERGING HUMAN RESOURCE DEVELOPMENT THEMES

HUMAN RESOURCE DEVELOPMENT ROLES AND RELATIONSHIPS

OBJECTIVES

By the end of this chapter you should be able to:

■ differentiate between task-based roles and interpretive roles;

■ distinguish between trainer-oriented roles, training and development roles, and HRD-driven roles;

■ establish whether emergent HRD roles are an extension of conventional training management roles or are emanating from a different source and tradition;

■ establish which roles are most likely to contribute to a strategic perspective.

INTRODUCTION

A number of studies over the years have sought to determine what constitute *training* roles, and in operational terms a broad consensus has been reached. Training and *development* roles, on the other hand, have been less clearly defined. Harrison (1992), for example, believes that a major problem with the UK Training and Development NVQ standards is a failure to recognise the difference between *training* and *development*, therefore treating them as part of the same process.

However, in recent years there has been a move away in organisational practice from thinking about HRD merely in terms of either trainer roles on their own, or training and development roles together. As the architecture of organisations is changing to reflect the transformations and new strategic imperatives of the so-called post-industrial era, so too is a new approach towards organisational learning emerging, and with it a new set of associated HRD work roles.

This chapter is concerned with presenting the emerging new roles that can be expected of HRD professionals if they are to contribute to the emergent strategy-driven HRD practices of today's organisations. Many of these roles are already being carried out in leading edge organisations, but they are not necessarily being carried out by career professionals with a training and development background. This book draws upon a considerable body of evidence to show that they are often being undertaken by 'imports' from other areas of the business. It is very refreshing to see so many people being introduced to facilitation, needs analysis and guiding learning processes as a full-time occupation. It is nevertheless a potentially worrying feature for those who have chosen training and development and learning support as a full-time career, if they see themselves being excluded from some of the more strategically oriented roles.

The chapter analyses the functional roles that were held to be significant up to the late 1980s and how they were interpreted. It compares and contrasts them with those that seem to be important in today's environment. Many of the previous roles will continue to exist. However it is less clear that they will all contribute to the core competences of the organisation or that they will be undertaken under the protective umbrella of a vertically integrated host organisation.

Those involved in learning processes have become much more conscious of the role of line managers and staff members in the equation. Their roles are touched upon in this chapter and dealt with more thoroughly subsequently.

DIFFERENCE BETWEEN TASK (FUNCTIONAL) AND PROCESS (INTERPRETIVE) ROLES

In looking at HRD roles (indeed, looking at roles in general) it is helpful to differentiate between task-orientated, functional roles and process-oriented, interpretive roles. In functional terms, a role can be defined as the collection of task-specific behaviours, attitudes and values expected of a person occupying a given position in an organisation or carrying out a service on behalf of a client. These may be formally laid down in terms of duties and responsibilities, terms and conditions of employment or other contractual arrangements. They may be more subtly inferred in terms of informal norms, codes of practice and sanctions governing membership of the 'club'. It is thus more than the 'job', if the job is taken to consist merely of formal activities and relationships.

In interpretive terms, a role is more associated with how people 'read' and then 'play' their part; how they project their persona; what distinctive qualities they bring to bear. The more open ended and flexible the formal role requirements, the more scope and need for interpretation. Managerial positions, for which there are rarely detailed job descriptions, afford opportunities for substantial interpretation. Consultancy roles fall into the same category.

An example of an interpretive classification system is that developed by Mintzberg (1973) for managerial roles (*see* Fig. 6.1). This was based on what managers said they did (i.e. how they interpreted their role) as opposed to the formal content of their title and job definition.

Figure 6.1 Mintzberg's classification of managerial roles

1 **Interpersonal roles**

   a *Figurehead role*: carrying out duties of a ceremonial nature – for example, giving gold watches to retiring employees, taking clients to lunch.

   b *Leader role*: for example, functioning as 'gatekeeper' – protecting staff from pressure from above, providing or withholding access to opportunities and visibility outside the functional area.

   c *Liaison role*: making contacts outside of the vertical chain of command.

▶▶

▶▶ Figure 6.1 continued

2 Information roles

a *Monitor (information scavenger)*: managers perpetually scan their environment for information. This entails interrogating liaison contacts and subordinates; receiving unsolicited information often as a result of a network of personal contacts. Much will be gossip, hearsay, speculation.

b *Disseminator*: this involves passing some of the privileged information gleaned directly to subordinates who would otherwise have no access to it.

c *Spokesperson*: this involves informing and satisfying the influential people who control the organisational decision-making processes.

3 Decisional roles

a *Entrepreneur*: seeking to improve the unit, to adapt it to environmental change.

b *Disturbance handler*: this entails responding to and dealing with crisis management issues.

c *Resource allocator*: this entails deciding who gets what, how scarce resources are to be distributed among staff members.

d *Negotiator*: this entails fighting one's corner for resources for the maintenance

Source: Mintzberg (1973).

Mintzberg indicates that all of these roles fall into the overall spread of activities carried out by an individual purporting to be a manager. He does not say that we can subdivide the managerial job so that one person carries out a decisional role and another carries out an informational role. In other words, he provides a role-set based on how, in practice, managers interpret what they should do.

With HRD practitioners, the production of such an interpretive role-set is extremely problematical because of the emergent and still contentious nature of the boundaries and parameters associated with the area.

HUMAN RESOURCE DEVELOPMENT ROLES

The US perspective in the 1970s and 1980s

One of the first attempts at an HRD categorisation was generated by Nadler (1970) in the USA. He identified three primary roles, each with several sub-roles. The 'learning specialist' and 'administrator' roles are functional, the 'consultant' role is interpretive. The typology, listed below, has been extremely influential in subsequent classification systems, not just in the USA.

- *Learning specialist*
  - facilitator of learning
  - curriculum builder
  - instructional strategist

- *Administrator*
  - developer of personnel
  - supervisor of ongoing programmes
  - arranger: facilities, finance
- *Consultant*
  - advocate
  - expert
  - stimulator
  - change agent

Walton (1973) developed an interpretive typology which differentiated between the trainer as:

- voyeur
- conscientious objector
- therapist
- catalyst
- skilled craftsperson
- missionary
- entrepreneur.

He looked at these roles in the context of potential conflicts between the values of the trainer and those of the organisational 'client'. This issue is looked at in more detail in the final chapter of this book.

ASTD roles

In 1983, the American Society of Training and Development (ASTD) identified the following fifteen key roles for HRD practitioners. On the whole these are primarily functionally oriented with a significant emphasis on programme delivery:

1 *Evaluator*: identifying the extent of impact of a programme, service or product.

2 *Group facilitator*: managing group discussions and processes so that individuals learn and group members consider that the experience has been positive.

3 *Individual development counsellor*: helping an individual assess personal competences, values and goals, and to identify and plan development and career actions.

4 *Instructional writer*: preparing written learning and instructional materials.

5 *Instructor*: presenting information and directing structured learning experiences in such a way that individuals learn.

6 *Manager of training and development*: planning, organising, staffing and controlling training and development operations or training and development projects, and linking training and development operations with other organisation units.

7 *Marketer*: selling training and development viewpoints, learning packages, programmes and services to target audiences outside one's own work unit.

8 *Media specialist*: producing software for, and using audio, visual, computer and other hardware-based technologies for training and development.

9 *Needs analyst*: defining gaps between ideal and actual performance and specifying the cause of the gaps.

10 *Programme administrator*: ensuring that the facilities, equipment, materials, participants and other components of a learning event are present and that programme logistics run smoothly.

11 *Programme designer*: preparing objectives, defining content and selecting and sequencing activities for a specific programme.

12 *Strategist*: developing long-range plans for what the training and development structure, organisation, direction, policies, programmes, services and practices will be in order to accomplish the training and development mission.

13 *Task analyst*: identifying activities, tasks, sub-tasks, human resource and support requirements necessary to accomplish specific results in a job or organisation.

14 *Theoretician*: developing and testing theories of learning, training and development.

15 *Transfer agent*: helping individuals apply learning after the learning experience.

For each of these roles a number of critical outputs were identified, in some ways similar to the performance criteria attached to NVQ elements in the UK. Thus, to give an example:

Group facilitator – critical outputs

1 Group discussions in which issues and needs are constructively assessed.

2 Group decisions where individuals all feel committed to action.

3 Cohesive teams.

4 Enhanced awareness of group process, self and others.

Figure 6.2	Singapore Competency Study in Training and Development

In 1986 the Singapore Competency Study in Training and Development was undertaken to identify roles and responsibilities of training professionals based on the ASTD classification.

The following primary roles of trainers were identified:

■ Instructor

■ Group facilitator

■ Training administrator

■ Programme designer

■ Needs analyst.

▶▶

▶▶ Figure 6.2 continued

The following were identified as secondary roles:

■ Manager
■ Transfer agent
■ Instructional writer
■ Marketer
■ Resource finder/Selector/Co-ordinator
■ Policy maker
■ Media production specialist
■ Quality circle facilitator/trainer
■ Evaluator
■ Facilities manager.

Other peripheral roles identified were:

■ Productivity manager
■ Task analyser
■ Career development counsellor
■ Research.

The competency study found that there were many job titles for trainers in Singapore, including management trainers, customer trainers, training consultants, training officers, training co-ordinators, on-the-job trainers and simply 'trainers'. These job titles were grouped into five major types of trainers, as follows:

1 *Technical instructor*: one who instructs others in operational skills or manual skills or teaches others to perform the technical parts of their job.
2 *Management/Supervisory instructor*: one who instructs others in supervisory or managerial skills such as decision making, problem solving or communication.
3 *Training administrator/Training officer*: one who is responsible for the physical and administrative aspects of training, such as arranging for training facilities, equipment and trainers, and carrying out administrative tasks such as updating training records.
4 *Training manager/Director/Consultant*: classified as having the highest position in the training function, these persons are responsible for the planning, organising, directing and controlling of the physical, human and financial resources allocated to the training function to meet corporate objectives. Usually they are also responsible for marketing training both internally within the organisation as well as externally. Key tasks may also include performing needs analysis, policy formulation and evaluation as well as acting as an internal consultant.
5 *Manager/Supervisor with training responsibilities*: one of the key responsibilities of any manager or supervisor is the training of subordinates. Many managers and supervisors provide various kinds of training like orientation training, on-the-job training, coaching and counselling.

It was also found that the following were generally considered to be part of training and development in Singapore:

▶▶

▶▶ Figure 6.2 continued

- education and training;
- career development;
- orientation and induction;
- productivity and performance improvement;
- organisation development.

It is not immediately apparent how the job titles in common use reflected the organisation development or the career development component, and it is no surprise that the survey saw career development as a peripheral role. Nevertheless, 66 per cent of an 'expert' panel set up to identify emergent roles mentioned that of career development counsellor.

The UK perspective in the 1970s and 1980s

In the UK a typical early classification of HRD roles was developed under the auspices of a government body, the Manpower Services Commission (MSC), which included within its remit the development of good training practice nationally. In 1978 the Training of Trainers Committee set up by the MSC reported that there were four 'role elements' in the trainer's job. These were:

- direct training;
- planning and organising;
- determining and managing;
- consulting and advising.

Spoor and Bennett (1984), in a report co-sponsored by the MSC and the Institute of Training and Development, suggested that trainers were involved in three key activities:

- direct training entailing face-to-face contact;
- planning, preparing and developing courses, and doing background research work;
- needs identification and analysis and translating demonstrated needs into learning objectives.

Other activities were: involvement in educational technology, keeping informed, administration, management, interaction with individuals, evaluation, contact with outside agencies, advising, development, meetings, finance and liaison.

They looked at interpretive roles as well as task roles. These were:

- caretaker
- evangelist
- educator
- innovator.

Carrying out these more open-ended interpretive roles has always created problems for trainers in the past for the following reasons.

1 The trainer has typically had a low-level position in the organisational hierarchy and has lacked ascribed status. This has frequently meant a lack of credibility in terms of operating as evangelist or innovator in anything beyond showing enthusiasm for one's subject and being imaginative in terms of the way that course materials and syllabi are designed and delivered.

2 There are issues associated with imposing one's own values on a group in a training situation and moving outside the boundaries expected by the participants and sponsors. Vocational training is not often seen as a forum for creating an educational experience in which one engages in a challenging academic dialogue.

In broader HRD terms, however, we may well be looking for people who can demonstrate comfort with some of the interpretive roles articulated in the literature. They could become champions and sponsors of learning who can enthuse about such issues at board and divisional or departmental level and be credible, either because of the respect in which they are held, or because their hierarchical level gives them political clout.

One of the best known UK classifications was generated by Pettigrew *et al.* (1982) as a result of a survey into activities conducted by training officers in the chemical industry in the UK. Both functional and interpretive elements can be found.

Figure 6.3 **Trainer roles**

The provider

The provider role is perceived as being a steady state and maintenance one. The provider is not concerned with changing the organisation in any major way, but is offering training services and systems with the principal objective of maintaining and improving organisational performance.

The provider has a generally accepted though limited role in offering training expertise geared towards the maintenance and development of the organisational performance but not with organisational change.

The training manager

The focus of the training manager role is on planning, organising, directing and controlling the training and development effort in a given organisation. The training manager concentrates effort on the management and performance of training staff and on the development of the function. The training manager sees him/herself as a manager, not a trainer, and is likely to be concerned with policy development and co-ordination issues.

The change agent

The change agent is concerned with the definition of organisational problems and helping others to resolve these problems through changing the organisational culture. This role is concerned with helping with the implementation of organisation-wide culture change, and helping individuals unfreeze values and

▶▶

▶▶ Figure 6.3 continued

assumptions about current ways of operating. They saw this as an emergent role, forecasting, in 1982, that it would become increasingly significant.

The passive provider

The passive provider, although having some similarities with the provider described above, tends to operate at a very low level of activity and influence within the organisation. This is partly because of inexperience and temperament, partly because of restrictions within the job description, partly because of a lack of expertise in putting across a more proactive perception of the role to others. Like the provider, this person is concerned with maintenance and development of the organisation. However the passive provider tends not to take initiatives, has low self-esteem and is not 'politically' skilled in securing support. This person is not good at putting across a clear image of role and/or in articulating what distinctive services can be offered to potential clients.

The role in transition

Where the role is in transition, the role occupant is in the process of moving from being a provider to being a change agent or adviser. This person may not have a clear understanding of what the new role entails and there may be very considerable opposition to such a move from within the organisation.

Source: Based on Pettigrew *et al.* (1982).

Pettigrew *et al.* go on to argue that successful training activities depend on the training officer's personal effectiveness, which itself is a function of the degree of 'fit' or 'congruence' between the organisation culture, the personality and style of the training officer and the role assumed. A training officer therefore needs to recognise that there may be a choice of roles that can be played, to select what seems to be the most appropriate one given the particular context, and then be able to meet the expectations of the role. Sloman (1994) makes the additional point that a number of practitioners feel more comfortable with the passive provider role.

Phillips and Shaw (1989) agreed that trainer roles were in transition, contending that the move was from training to consulting. Within the consulting role, they identified the following three career paths for trainers:

■ training consultant

■ learning consultant

■ organisation change consultant.

Of course it could be argued that the HRD role is inevitably in a state of transition because organisations are in a state of transition, from the industrial to the post-industrial era.

Trainer task inventory

An interesting framework for describing and portraying trainer roles is the trainer task inventory. This was developed by staff working initially at the UK Air Transport and Travel Industry Training Board and, after its abolition in the early 1980s, at the Manpower Services Commission (Morgan and Costello, 1984). Their preparatory literature review revealed a lack of consensus in respect of the meaning of 'trainer roles'. It quickly became clear that these words had very different connotations for different writers. Nevertheless from their research they were able to identify a number of existing and emergent task-oriented roles which they presented pictorially in the form of a model representing 'spheres of activity' (*see* Fig. 6.4).

Figure 6.4   **Trainer task inventory**

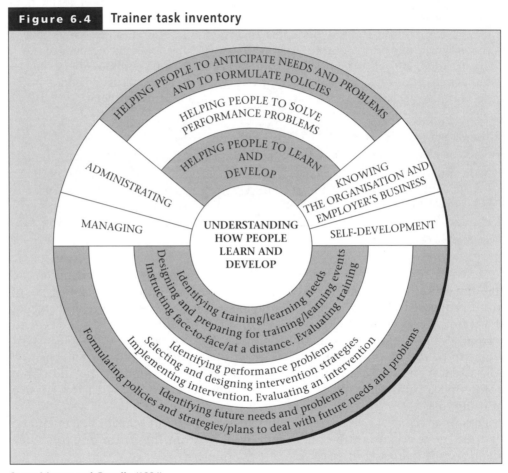

Source: Morgan and Costello (1984).

Although the model is referred to as a 'trainer task inventory', it goes beyond a simple focus on direct-trainer related activities, and considers issues of learning and development in a broader context than classroom or workshop provision.

The innermost circle represents the most central and underpinning competence, a *sine qua non* if one is to operate effectively in the profession. Each outer circle or sphere is intended to represent an increasing order of complexity, and a higher order of skill. It is thus a developmental model. As a practitioner one can engage in the activities represented in the outer spheres once one can show that competence has been acquired and demonstrated in the activities in the immediately preceding inner circle.

The model portrays roles in three categories:

■ helping roles

■ diagnostic roles

■ functional roles.

The helping and diagnostic roles are linked.

The most basic sphere of activity is 'Helping people to learn and develop'. Broadly, this refers to direct training.

The second sphere of activity, 'Helping people to solve performance problems', is much more of a consultancy role. The outcome may well be training activities, but this is by no means certain.

The third sphere of activity – 'Helping people to anticipate needs and problems and to formulate policies' – strongly reflects the extension of the consultancy role. The whole ethos of this model is to suggest a career and competence progression for training and development professionals, away from direct training towards broad-based internal consultancy and facilitation. It is a joint problem-identification, problem-solving and facilitating framework.

Cutting across the spheres of activity are four general 'functions', each of which is different in kind. Two represent skills, one is knowledge based, and self-development is a personal learning goal:

■ administrating

■ managing

■ knowing the organisation and employer's business

■ self-development.

The term *'trainer* task inventory' is a somewhat distorting title, since it clearly extends beyond the conventional notion of a trainer's role. *'Developer's* task inventory' would be more appropriate. Also, 'task inventory' gives it a more mechanistic feeling than the subtlety of the model warrants.

Training and development roles

In 1992, the Training and Development Lead Body (TDLB) in the UK, set up as part of the national process of developing and accrediting standards in training and development, identified the following four training and development roles, which have a very strong functional task orientation:

■ managing human resource development strategy;

■ managing training operations;

■ meeting training needs in general;

■ meeting specialised training needs.

The TDLB also identified five associated functional areas of competence, which were more normative, 'ought-to' roles:

■ identifying training and development needs;

■ designing training and development strategies and plans;

- providing learning opportunities, resources and support;
- evaluating the effectiveness of training and development;
- supporting training and development advances and practices.

Pilot studies in advance of the launch of the standards established that many individuals in a training and development role did not cover all these areas of competence. Few were involved in needs identification and even fewer were involved in evaluation activities. There was considerable pressure at the time to remove evaluation from the standards since it did not reflect actual practice in the workplace. It reinforces the 'passive provider' orientation to much of training and development in the UK, and also the rather narrow way in which roles had been developed in practice, reinforcing the low level of HRD.

ROLE PLAYERS

Most of the classification systems on HRD roles seem to infer that HRD activities are going to be undertaken by full-time HRD practitioners. The emphasis in this chapter is on HRD from a professional practitioner's perspective operating within a given organisation. Nevertheless, key players include:

- HRD professionals
- line managers
- chief executive officers

| Figure 6.5 | Human resource development role players |

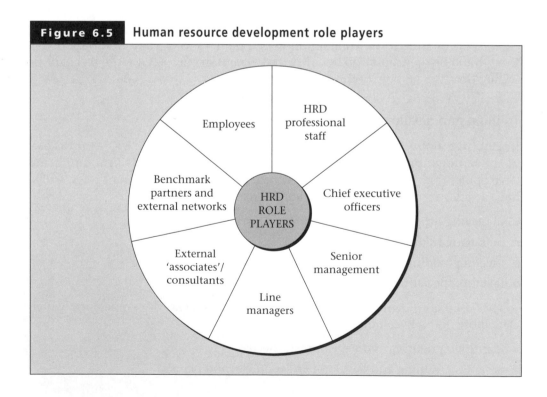

■ external 'associates'/consultants
■ staff
■ external benchmark and network partners.

NEW AND EMERGENT ROLES IN THE 1990s

As we have seen, HRD is in a state of substantial reorientation as new ways of thinking about individual and collective learning have started to impact. This in turn has influenced the way HRD roles are perceived. New and emergent roles include:

■ *Functional*
  – learning and development manager
  – contract/partnership manager
  – facilitator at the corporate university
  – internal consultant
  – performance or business consultant
    organisation (OD) consultant
  – knowledge manager
■ *Interpretive*
  – co-learner
  – change facilitator
  – learning architect

Table 6.1 Comparison of emergent and traditional human resource development roles

OLD		EMERGENT	
Functional roles	*Interpretive roles*	*Functional roles*	*Interpretive roles*
Direct trainer	Passive provider	Learning and development manager	Co-learner
Training administrator	Provider	Contract/partnership manager	Change facilitator
Technical instructor	Caretaker	Facilitator at corporate university	Learning architect
Needs analyst	Evangelist	Internal consultant	Orchestrator of learning processes
Programme designer	Innovator	Performance consultant	Intrapreneur
Transfer agent	Educator	Organisation (OD) consultant	Facilitator of strategic processes
	Change agent	Knowledge manager/ intellectual asset controller	

- orchestrator of learning processes – as opposed to provider of training services
- intrapreneur
- facilitator of strategic processes

We shall look into each of these in turn. They are not necessarily mutually consistent, and depend often on the distinctive organisational ethos. They raise issues that are looked at in more detail at different points within the book.

FUNCTIONAL ROLES

Learning and development manager

There is an increasing tendency in a number of organisations to move away from the term 'training' and to replace it with 'learning'. Anita Roddick, founder of the Body Shop, commented in this connection that 'training' was something they did to animals. 'Training' is also felt to have connotations associated with encouraging passive participation as opposed to recognising the active contribution of the learner. The change of designation is more than just a symbolic gesture: it reflects concerns to encourage continuous learning at both individual and organisational level, and moves to demonstrate commitment to the ethos of a 'learning organisation'.

To carry out this role means having the creativity to satisfy learning needs as they emerge, the ability to sell and market development throughout the organisation, and a degree of global strategic understanding that will make one a welcome adviser at every organisational level.

Watkins and Marsick (1993) emphasise the move away from a traditional training ideology towards a learning focus. They provide an example of how the new role has begun to manifest itself in practice from Manulife Financial, an American based life insurance company. Manulife Financial has developed a continuous learning centre with the following aims:

1 Be managed by leaders who create an environment conducive to learning and supporting to personal and professional employee growth.

2 Operate with a continuous improvement mindset, compelling employees to learn to do things differently, to constantly challenge why and how they do specific work activities.

3 Create an effective and valued open-communication culture that encourages the flow of information and ideas between management and support staff.

4 Recognise that learning is an ongoing process that applies to all staff at all levels and requires a collaborative effort to balance values and needs of the organisation and the employees (op. cit., p. 53).

Contract/partnership manager

With the growing emphasis on outsourcing, there is an increasing need for people to undertake a contract or partnership manager role. The nature of that role varies, depending on whether the contract is of short duration and not seen as of strategic significance to the organisation, or whether there is an attempt to engage in a strategic partnership relationship.

If the latter, the partnership manager would need to oversee and manage the partnership from a strategic perspective, to be involved in handling day-to-day issues affecting the partnership and to operate as a troubleshooter as and when problems occur. The role entails building an effective learning loop between the client and the supplier. For example, there will be a requirement to evaluate the quality of service delivery, feed this back to the supplier and work with the supplier towards future improvements.

Facilitator at corporate university

One of the features of recent years has been the growing tendency to establish corporate universities to take overall responsibility for the learning and development effort. Some of these are no more than traditional training and development departments under a new guise. Some, however, have a holistic and strategic feel to them, with every member of the organisation being attached to a 'faculty', and with senior managers operating as 'Deans' of these faculties. In these latter instances HRD staff are there to facilitate the underpinning learning ethos.

Internal consultant

There has been a swing in some organisations towards developing an internal consultancy role. However there are a number of interpretations as to what it might mean in practice for HRD.

Levi Strauss interpreted this role in the following way:

> What we have found is that just to ship people off to a class-room and provide training for them, and then let them go back to their work environment and not provide any follow-up support is not a cost-effective strategy. Consequently, what we now call the human resource development organisation has two arms. One arm develops and administers training programmes. The other is an internal consulting group. The role of the consultants is to work with managers and their work groups, to integrate the skills learned in a training session into their work environment and use their skills on the job (Sue Thompson, Director of Human Resource Development, Levi Strauss & Co, quoted in Garfield, 1992).

Thompson defines the new role as downstream from training. Formal classroom learning comes first, followed by support from the internal consultancy arm to ensure that learning is appropriately transferred to the workplace. It is akin to the 'transfer agent' role of the 1985 ASTD classification.

This is a different interpretation of the internal consultancy role, whereby support is provided to a departmental, divisional or organisational clientele in developing a full needs assessment of learning which may or may not entail formal classroom events. Lippitt and Lippitt (1986) provide a helpful framework for perceiving this role. They argue that when functioning as a trainer or educator, the consultant must be able to:

- assess the training needs related to the problem involved;
- develop and state measurable objectives for learning experiences;
- understand the learning and change process;

- design a learning experience;
- plan and design educational events;
- go beyond traditional learning and use heuristic laboratory methods;
- employ multiple learning stimuli, including various kinds of media;
- serve as a group teacher or trainer; and
- help others learn how to learn.

The role of trainer or educator may be part of a continuing consulting relationship with various parts of the business. In fact in structural terms the role of internal consultant becomes more significant with the decentralisation and devolution of responsibilities to line managers. One consequence of this is that they are less likely to be railroaded down one avenue of learning provision offered by a centralised HRD function in support of holistic policy requirements.

The role of internal consultant is tied to personal and professional relationships, so the credibility of the service offered hinges on skills and direct personal relationships, not on any structure (Prete and Boschetti, 1990). We examine the interpretive nature of the internal consultancy role when we look at the 'change facilitator' role.

Trainers as business or performance consultants

One of the most significant trends in the USA in recent years has been the incorporation of performance consulting into the remit of the HRD practitioner. In many respects performance consulting reflects a trend away from the focus on 'learning' which has been central to the HRD field. I do not get a sense either from the literature or from reports on practical examples of a focus on improving and developing learning processes.

The essence of performance consulting is described in Robinson and Robinson (1995, 1998). They define the role as 'partnering with clients for purposes of enhancing human performance in support of business needs and goals. The outputs from this role are strong relationships with clients, identification of potential opportunities for working together, and achievement of human performance improvement' (Robinson and Robinson, 1998). They present it as a business consultancy role, whereby trainers operate as troubleshooters rather than functioning as mere deliverers of training packages. Trainers who have conventionally been involved in a classroom, course-delivery environment often need to be retrained and reoriented to get out into the businesses and address performance problems where they happen. The basic idea follows a well-trodden path – before looking for a training solution to a performance problem, see whether, by engaging in a root cause analysis, there are more fundamental and appropriate remedies. Thus organisational systems, absence of incentives, inappropriate tools with which to carry out the job, factors in the physical environment, all may need to be addressed in preference to training.

Ives and Torrey (1998) describe a typical model developed by the Performance Design and Development Competency Leadership team in Andersen Consulting. It purports to look at both individual and organisational factors that affect performance, focusing on obtaining measurable outcomes that benefit the organisation and the individual. In the business context, they ask: What is the business mission and strategy? Is it understood? Are tasks aligned to it? They list the factors as:

■ *Organisation performance factors*:
  – *Processes*: What are they supposed to do?
  – *Culture*: What social and political factors affect performance?
  – *Physical environment*: Where do people perform?

■ *Individual performance factors*:
  – *Direction*: What direction do people receive?
  – *Measurement*: How are they measured?
  – *Means*: Do they have the tools to enable performance?
  – *Ability*: Do they have the skills and knowledge to perform?
  – *Motivation*: Will they perform?

Welch (1997) reports a move in Barclays Bank in the UK towards recruiting a number of erstwhile line managers to become such 'consultant-trainers'. As well as having a direct training responsibility, they will be expected to carry out business output analyses on functional units, including reviewing staffing levels and workloads, as part of a drive towards achieving greater workplace productivity. *Inter alia*, it is hoped that the status of training will be enhanced within the company because the business units will believe they are dealing with professional banking staff who possess consultancy expertise. It is not intended that this new group of 'managers with training skills' will replace career trainers. As I understand the new role, it is a merging of training with old-style 'organisation and methods'. This latter discipline entails specialist investigators engaging in critical scrutinies of business systems, procedures and operating processes in order to identify opportunities to increase efficiency and effectiveness.

The organisational consultant

McLagan (1989) has argued that HRD consists of all those activities within organisations that have development as their primary function. This includes organisation development (OD). Her incorporation of OD into core HRD is based upon a longstanding tradition. The US Organisation Development Network, which was formed in 1964 and had nearly 2500 members in 1997, is seen as one of the mainstream HRD professional groupings in North America. The larger American Society for Training and Development (ASTD) has for many years contained a specialist OD subgroup.

The OD role is usually held to involve internal and external consultants operating under an overall action research framework in order to achieve change in a client system. Burke (1992) contends that for change in an organisation to correspond to the OD ethos it must:

■ reflect an actual or perceived need on the part of a client;

■ involve the client in the planning and implementation stages of the change process;

■ lead to change in the organisation's culture.

According to Burke (1992) organisational consultants today must be highly knowledgeable and skilled about such matters as:

- the psychological consequences of 'downsizing' – layoffs – on both employees who are let go and those who remain;

- downsizing with the least amount of psychological pain;

- designing and managing flatter organisational structures. The old maxim that an optimum span of control is seven, eight or nine is just that – old. Organisation consultants today must know how to help managers deal with 15, 20 or even 50 direct reports, not a mere seven subordinates. This means, for example, that they must be knowledgeable about semi-autonomous and self-managed work groups;

- defining core competences required to execute a corporation's core businesses. This requires:
  - knowledge about the business;
  - the ability to determine (by means of interview, observational, and analytical skills) whether individual organisational members possess the requisite competences;

- the particular nature of the client's business itself, the larger industry in which the business is a player and the primary factors that cause fluctuations in that industry, such as seasonal differences, changing government regulations and changing technology. A CEO told me recently that the principal value of his human resources chief was the fact that he knows, studies and cares about the business.

It is interesting to compare Burke's list with the consultancy contexts offered by Lippitt and Lippitt (1986):

- the downsizing situation, in which the client needs help with the challenges and requirements of cutback (doing more with less);

- the expansion, rapid-growth situation, in which the client is facing the complexities and heady challenges of expansion of enterprise;

- the decentralisation situation, in which major shifts are occurring in the client's accountability and communication structure;

- the merger situation, in which two or more systems are facing the challenges and requirements of combining structures and functions;

- the quality-improvement situation, in which a decision has been made to focus on the quality of the product and the production process;

- the demonstration and dissemination situation, in which an innovation or a new personnel practice is being tried in one part of the system, with the intention of disseminating the learning and model to all relevant parts of the system; and

- the entropy-prevention system, in which the focus is on maintaining the charge and preventing the loss of momentum that develops in most major change situations.

The work of Lippitt and Lippitt (1986) has been very influential over the years in helping to form our understanding of consultancy competencies. The extract presented in Fig. 6.6 is based on their insights.

Figure 6.6	Consultancy competencies

One of the difficulties in developing a taxonomy of competencies and skills is the nature of the consultative process as a personal relationship between people who are trying to solve a problem. The degree to which a consultant is able to influence this relationship is affected by four factors:

a The consultant's behavioural competency.

b The consultant's communication of helpful concepts and ideas.

c The client's acceptance of the consultant.

d The client's legitimisation of the consultant's role.

No matter how competent or creative the consultant, the last two factors – the client's acceptance and the extent to which the client legitimises the consultant's role – are essential both to the consultant's opportunity to contribute toward the problem-solving effort and to the actual contribution. In this context the professional behaviour of the consultant is of prime importance. In the search for competency, the following questions may be useful for evaluating the consultant.

1 Does the consultant form sound interpersonal relations with the client?

2 Does the consultant's behaviour build the client's independence rather than dependence on the consultant's resources?

3 Does the consultant focus on the problem?

4 Is the consultant non-judgemental and tolerant toward other consultants and resource disciplines?

5 Does the consultant respect the confidences of his or her clients?

6 Is the consultant clear about contractual arrangements?

7 Does the consultant appropriately achieve influence in the organisation?

8 Does the consultant truthfully represent the skills he or she possesses that are relevant to the client's problem?

9 Does the consultant clearly inform the client concerning the consultant's role and contribution?

10 Does the consultant express willingness to have his or her services evaluated?

11 Does the consultant participate in a professional association, discipline, or educational process to maintain competency?

Source: Lippitt and Lippitt (1986).

In 1983, the Organisation Development Division of the ASTD created an 'Organisation Development Practitioner Self-Assessment Guide' that incorporated a list of competencies within an overall action research framework. At the 1997 Conference of the USA-based Academy of Human Resource Development (AHRD) in Atlanta, Georgia, a list of 171 competencies, grouped under the conventional phases of the action research model plus a number of core personal competencies, was presented by Gary McLean of the University of Minnesota, for further refinement. Examples of some of the proposed competencies are given in Fig. 6.7.

Figure 6.7	Extracts from OD Practitioner Self-assessment Guide

Phase 1: Entry (Marketing Phase)
- identify potential client organisations that are presently undergoing crises or accelerated change or growth;
- assess the possibility of a match between the potential client organisation's needs and the consultant's capabilities.

Phase 1: Entry (Initial Contact Phase)
- use the language of the client system;
- determine the client's perception of the problem.

Phase 2: Start-up
- help clients reflect on their motivations for change;
- develop relationships at all organisational levels.

Phase 3: Assessment and Feedback
- use an appropriate mix of data gathering methods;
- design the assessment to incorporate diverse perspectives.

Phase 4: Action/Intervention Planning
- help participants co-create a clear vision of the future;
- help the client evolve the process for managing the transition.

Phase 5: Intervention
- help the client deal with barriers and resistance as they surface during the change process;
- use appropriate group and intergroup facilitation skills.

Phase 6: Evaluation
- choose an appropriate evaluation method;
- establish a feedback system to monitor the change effort continuously.

Phase 7: Adoption
- link the ongoing change process to both the organisation structure and daily operations;
- mobilise internal resources for ongoing self-direction, self-learning and self-renewal.

Phase 8: Separation
- gradually wean the client organisation away from dependence on the consultant;
- manage own post-separation emotions.

Core competencies
- clarify personal values;
- clarify personal boundaries;
- collaborate with internal/external OD professionals.

Expert versus process consultant

Irrespective of whether you are operating as an internal or external consultant, there are a range of consultancy styles that can be adopted. They are often portrayed as being on a range from expert to process consultant.

Edgar Schein (1988) summarises the main assumptions of the process consultation philosophy as follows.

1 Clients or managers often do not know what is wrong and need special help in diagnosing their problems.

2 Clients or managers often do not know what kinds of help consultants can give to them and which consultant can provide the kind of help that may be needed; they need to be helped to know what kinds of help to seek.

3 Most clients or managers have a constructive intent to improve things, but they need help in identifying what to improve and how to improve it. However, for process consulation to work the client needs to be motivated by goals and values that the consultant can accept, and to have some capacity to enter into a helping relationship.

4 Most organisations can be more effective if they learn to diagnose and manage their own strengths and weaknesses. No organisational form is perfect; hence every form of organisation will have some weaknesses for which compensatory mechanisms must be found.

5 The client is ultimately the only one who knows what forms of intervention will work in the situation. A consultant probably cannot, without exhaustive and time-consuming study or actual participation in the client organisation, learn enough about the culture of the organisation to suggest reliable new courses of action. Therefore, unless remedies are worked out jointly with members of the organisation who do know what will and will not work in their culture, such remedies are likely either to be wrong or to be resisted because they come from an outsider.

6 The nature of the problem is such that the client not only needs help in identifying what is wrong but would benefit from participation in the process of making a diagnosis. Unless the client or manager learns to see the problem for him or herself and thinks through the remedy, he or she will not be willing or able to implement the solution and, more important, will not learn how to fix such problems should they recur. The process consultant can provide alternatives, but decision making about such alternatives must remain in the hands of the client.

7 The essential function of process consultation is to pass on the skills of how to diagnose and fix organisational problems so that the client is more able to continue on his own to improve the organisation. This requires that the client is capable of learning how to diagnose and solve his own organisational problems.

With these assumptions in mind process consultation can be defined as:

a set of activities on the part of the consultant that help the client to perceive, understand, and act upon the process events that occur in the client's environment.

The process consultant seeks to give the client insight into what is going on around and, within the client, and between the client and other people. Based on such insight, the consultant then helps the client to work out what to do about the situation. But the core of the model is that the client must be helped to remain 'proactive', in the sense of retaining both the diagnostic and remedial initiative.

Intellectual asset controller and knowledge manager

Some companies such as Dow Chemical, Andersen Consulting, Polaroid, Skandia and ICL are developing corporate-wide systems to track all sources of individual and collective knowledge available to them and exploit them by creating 'explicit' organisation knowledge. This is typically under the leadership of a director or vice-president of 'knowledge' or 'intellectual capital'.

Lank (1997), who at the time of writing occupied the role of Programme Director, Knowledge Management at ICL, suggests that there are four main responsibilities for a 'Chief Knowledge Officer':

1 Identifying the tacit and explicit knowledge assets currently owned or accessible by the organisation.

2 Developing appropriate mechanisms to create repositories, sharing mechanisms and maintenance processes for this knowledge base.

3 Identifying knowledge gaps and mechanisms for filling them.

4 Managing the investment in processes, information technology and roles to move knowledge and expertise around the organisation and establishing measures to determine the return on that investment.

She contends that the effective operation of the role requires a blend of personal qualities and professional background. Personal qualities include those of a change agent and a systems thinker and business awareness. Professional background includes exposure to OD, business process development, consultancy, project management and IT expertise.

According to Grant (1997) key to knowledge management as a source of competitive advantage is achieving internal replication while avoiding external replication. A significant role in this should be played by HRD practioners. After all, their *raison d'être* is to facilitate knowledge and skills aquisition, either through direct training or through development processes. Their role is to provide the 'knowledge workers' of the future, to ensure that the learning of these from the past is not lost to the generation of the future. There is a sense in which the knowledge theory of the firm, with its concomitant value sets of seeing the individual as only a source of utility value, has such an instrumental orientation that it fails to pick up how and why individuals learn. Perhaps it is better to provide development processes whereby individuals can gain experiences and generate new ideas rather than somehow make individual experiences from the past explicit to the future. As presented, the concept is in conflict with notions of self-managed learning which feature so strongly in learning philosophy.

There is evidence that knowledge management is becoming increasingly IT focused and moving away from the individual learning arena.

INTERPRETIVE ROLES

Co-learner

It is axiomatic to this book that a core role is that of the lifelong learner. But what does this mean in respect of our exchanges with other members of our own or a client's work-force learning community? Perhaps more important than anything is the willingness and capacity to learn from others, whoever they are and whatever the situation. Whatever our formal role – training provider, internal or external consultant, change agent, or a composite of these – we should above all see ourselves as co-learners. We need to get into the discipline of asking ourselves the following questions:

- What am I learning from this experience?
- What am I learning from you?
- What can I offer you?
- What can you offer me?

This habit should be built into the psychological commitment contract. It takes seriously the notion of dialogue, which Senge (1990) sees as part of team learning.

Self-reflective learning records provide a framework for capturing the nature of the learning experience, but the keeping of such records may be too ritualistic for the learning style of some individuals. It is an attitude of mind.

Change agent or change facilitator

The internal HRD consultant role has often been seen as that of a change agent (*see* Fig. 6.8).

Figure 6.8	Principles of being a successful change agent

Hunsaker (1982) lists ten principles that he considers make a successful inside change agent:

1 Know yourself, and be aware of your own needs, values and objectives as a basis for determining what you need to be happy in your own organisation.

2 Fully understand the organisation. Knowledge of values, norms, key people, subsystems, cliques and alliances is a prerequisite for assessing the situation and planning realistic change efforts.

3 To make informed decisions, keep lines of communication open. Cutting off communication with adversaries can create one of the most devastating obstacles to change efforts. It can affirm negative stereotypes and block the possibility of of receiving new, disconfirming information that could shed light on the situation.

4 Establish how others feel about the situation. If no one else agrees with your assessment of the situation, another self-assessment may be called for. On the other hand, if you can identify potential allies who share your beliefs and

▶▶

▶▶ Figure 6.8 continued

desires, they can contribute to an effective team effort with a higher probability of success.

5 Analyse the situation from the many points of view of all the parties involved. Assessing the perceptions of a proposed change from your adversaries' point of view may reveal that they have overlooked an important point that would change their minds. On the other hand, it might demonstrate something that convinces you to change your own position.

6 Have a thorough understanding of all dimensions of the proposed change. The innovator must be the 'expert' on the change to maintain his or her own credibility and to help others understand where the goal is. This knowledge should include all strengths, weaknesses, evaluations and possible objections.

7 Successful changes are not usually accomplished without continued effort. The innovator must be persistent in making inroads whenever opportunities to do so present themselves.

8 Have a sense of timing, which is as important as the strategy employed. Waiting for the opportune moment, as opposed to reacting spontaneously, can make a key difference in the success of a change effort.

9 Share credit with others to create enthusiasm about a desired change. People support and feel committed to ideas they feel part of.

10 Avoid win-lose strategies and seek changes in which everybody wins, in order to avoid stand-offs in which everyone loses what they want, directly or indirectly, because of hard feelings.

Hunsaker quotes Ronald Havelock of the University of Michigan Institute for Social Research, who identified the four following ways in which the internal change agent role can be tackled.

■ *Catalyst*: needed to overcome inertia, to energise the problem-solving process.

■ *Solution giver*: to have any ideas accepted, one should know how and when to offer them, and how others in the organisation can adapt them to their needs.

■ *Process helper*: this involves helping organisation members to: (1) recognise and define their needs; (2) diagnose problems and set objectives; (3) acquire relevant resources; (4) select or create solutions; (5) adapt and carry out solutions and (6) evaluate solutions.

■ *Resource linker*: brings people and resources together to be applied to the problem.

Havelock also suggested the following advantages of operating from within, as opposed to being an external consultant:

1 Knowledge of the system – where the power is, who the opinion leaders are, where the strategic leverage points are.

2 An understanding of, and ability to speak, the organisation's language – the particular ways in which members refer to things, the tone and style of discussing things.

3 A familiarity with the norms and codes of behaviour existing in the organisation.

4 Being known to the members of the organisation, and not representing a threat as an outside figure.

The advantages of working from within, suggested by Havelock, would seem to apply in particular to organisation members who have been with the organisation for some time and who have had considerable exposure to operational practices. They can help to explain the propensity to recruit people with an operational background into the HRD arena. Their knowledge of the business, and of the personalities involved, gives them credibility with the line managers from whose ranks they have come.

It is misleading to assume that, because someone has been with a given organisation for some time, they are aware of the culture of its different operating departments, each of which can have its own very distinctive ethos. It is a basic requirement for any internal or external consultant to go through the basic steps of establishing trust with a client, and gaining entry into the client system.

Not everyone has been happy with the term 'change agent' and the connotations associated with it. Steinburg (1992) voices a number of concerns and perspectives expressed by practitioners who feel that the role should more approximate to that of 'change facilitator':

> As long as we think of ourselves as change agents, it implies that we are doing something to the system.
>
> [The change agent] is going for the end goal. A change facilitator is someone who is looking not for closings but for openings.

A third practitioner refers to the change facilitating role as one of 'conduit'. This entails coaching, counselling and generally supporting and facilitating line managers and peer groups in the changes they are making.

What seems to be emerging is a clear differentiation between the notion of a 'change agent' who attempts to control change and 'stay in charge'; and that of 'change facilitator' who is more concerned with guiding the flow of change. The assumptions underlying this role are those of facilitating the flow of change as it emerges; of bringing forward different interpretations of change; of providing frameworks for exploring change and the context for change from individual, group and organisational perspectives.

Learning architect

A learning architect has some features in common with the 'architect' role proposed by Tyson and Fell (1986) as one of three generic personnel roles. For them, the 'architect' role reflected a business-oriented, strategically aware perspective. In an HRD context, the architect is responsible for designing learning processes that meet the development needs of individuals and groups, and ensures that the organisation's business imperatives are met and hopefully exceeded. The outcome of these processes would be a demonstration of an organisation-wide strategic approach to HRD.

Learning orchestrator

'Architect' implies a design role. An orchestrator is an interpreter of the processes, in the same way as a conductor interprets the music of a composer, and translates it into practice. The musical analogy is helpful in that a conductor has a responsibility for ensuring that the whole is greater than the sum of the parts in performance. It captures the essence of team learning and working together.

Intrapreneur

The concept of intrapreneuring was coined and popularised by Pinchot (1986). Gilley (1987) suggested that providing instruction on intrapreneuring was at the beginning of its life cycle in the mid-1980s. It is an attractive interpretive role from an HRD perspective because it draws attention to facilitating innovation and operating flexibly and moving away from being a passive provider.

Figure 6.9	**The intrapreneur's ten commandments**

1. Come to work each day willing to be fired.
2. Circumvent any orders aimed at stopping your dream.
3. Do any job needed to make your project work, regardless of your job description.
4. Find people to help you.
5. Follow your intuition about the people you choose, and work only with the best.
6. Work underground as long as you can – publicity triggers the corporate immune mechanism.
7. Never bet on a race unless you are running in it.
8. Remember it is easier to ask for forgiveness than for permission.
9. Be true to your goals, but be realistic about the ways to achieve them.
10. Honour your sponsors.

Source: Pinchot (1986).

Garfield (1992) advises some measure of caution in operating entirely from an intrapreneurial perspective, which he considers focuses on overcoming the environment in which one operates. His position is that one needs to work with, rather than against, the grain for maximum effect. Nevertheless, as noted in Chapter 17, if HRD practitioners are to play a positive role as change facilitators, then a degree of working beneath the surface is entailed.

Strategic facilitator

Human resource development specialists may contribute to the strategic process by facilitating senior management decision-making forums. In so doing they would need to draw upon a range of group process skills as well as demonstrating business awareness. However, this can be done by external consultants as readily as by internal exponents.

Sloman (1994) refers to another connotation of the strategic facilitator role. This relates to an individual who is clearly positioned in the mainstream of the organisation, and thereby enabled to develop a close relationship with key stakeholders who influence strategic direction. Sloman discusses the role from the viewpoint of a training professional rather than someone with a broader learning responsibility. This limitation creates problems for him, since training methodology has so often been restricted to operating within the 'training cycle'. As he puts it, the training cycle 'defines training objectives narrowly, ignoring the link with development and the other human resource benefits that can be captured by a proactive training function'. He goes on to say: 'If the training manager is to focus his or her activities to maximum effect, a more comprehensive perspective on the role of training is required.' If we extend his analysis beyond training into a more fully fledged HRD framework, we find that the associated skills are:

- strategic awareness;
- diagnostic capability: the ability to offer specialist guidance in methods of skill enhancement and learning processes;
- influencing skills: the ability to exert an influence within the organisation to manage the learning culture.

CONCLUSION

This chapter has looked at a number of current and emerging roles for HRD practitioners that differentiate the professionals of today from their counterparts of the past. That analysis has been further informed by a differentiation of functional and interpretive roles.

Some of the roles identified have a strong learning focus to them; they reflect a general swing from thinking about development in terms of 'training' and to thinking about it in a more holistic way. This is reflected in functional roles such as 'learning and development manager' and 'organisational consultant'; and in supporting interpretive roles such as 'learning architect' and 'learning orchestrator'.

However, the connection with learning is less clear in other cases. This is particularly so for the 'performance consulting' which has in recent years become so fashionable. The focus seems to be on performance improvement in the context of modifying organisational systems and processes, and not on learning as a desired outcome. At best we are talking about organisational single-loop learning (Argyris and Schon, 1978). The ASTD has emphasised the need to reinvent the profession and now see its core business as supporting workplace learning and performance. Where is the individual as a responsible learner in all this? The same argument can be applied to the trend towards creating knowledge managers and intellectual asset controllers.

REFERENCES

American Society for Training and Development (1983) *Models for Excellence.* ASTD.

Argyris, C. and Schon, D. (1978) *Organisational Learning: A Theory of Action Perspective.* Reading, MA: Addison-Wesley.

Burke W. W. (1992) *Organisation Development – A Process of Learning and Changing* (2nd edn). Reading, MA: Addison-Wesley.

Garfield, C. (1992) *Second to None: The Productive Power of Putting People First*. Chicago: Business One Irwin.

Gilley, J. W. (1987) *Lifelong Learning: An Omnibus for Research and Practice*. American Society for Adult and Continuing Education.

Grant, R. M. (1997) 'The Knowledge-based View of the Firm: Implications for Management Practice', *Long Range Planning*, 30(3), June, pp. 450–4.

Harrison, R. (1992) *Employee development*. London: IPD.

Hunsaker, P. L. (1982) 'Strategies for Organisational Change – The Role of the Inside Change Agent', *Personnel*, September–October.

Ives, W. and Torrey, B. (1998) 'Supporting Knowledge Sharing', *Knowledge Management*, April/May, 5(1), pp. 17–25.

Lank, E. (1997) 'Leveraging Invisible Assets: the Human Factor', *Long Range Planning*, 30(3) June.

Lippitt, G. and Lippitt, R. (1986) *The Consulting Process in Action* (2nd edn). Pfeiffer & Co.

McLagan, P. (1989) *Models for HRD Practice*. American Society for Training and Development.

Mintzberg, H. (1973) *The Nature of Managerial Work*. New York: Harper & Row.

Morgan, K. M. and Costello, M. (1984) 'Trainer Task Inventory'. London: Manpower Services Commission.

Nadler, L. (1970) *Developing Human Resources*. Reading, MA: Addison-Wesley.

Pettigrew, A. M., Jones, G. R. and Reason, P. W. (1982) 'Training and Development Roles in Their Organisational Setting'. London: Manpower Services Commission.

Phillips, K. and Shaw, P. (1989) *A Consultancy Approach for Trainers*. Aldershot: Gower.

Pinchot, G. III (1986) 'The intrapreneur's ten commandments', *Intrapreneuring*. New York: Harper & Row.

Prete, M. and Boschetti, C. (1990) 'The Corporate Planner as Consultant', *Long Range Planning*, 27, December, pp. 23–30.

Robinson, D. G. and Robinson, J. C. (1995) *Performance Consulting: Moving Beyond Training*. Berrett-Koehler.

Robinson, D. G. and Robinson, J. C. (eds) (1998) *Moving from Training to Performance – A Practical Guidebook*. Berrett-Koehler.

Schein, E. (1988) *Process Consultation (Vol 1): Its Role in Organisation Development* (2nd edn). Addison-Wesley.

Senge, P. M. (1990) *The Fifth Discipline – The Art and Practice of the Learning Organisation*. New York: Doubleday.

Sloman, M. (1994) 'Coming in from the Cold: A New Role for Trainers', *Personnel Management*, January, pp. 24–7.

Spoor, J. and Bennett, R. (1984) 'Guide to Trainer Effectiveness'. London: Manpower Services Commission.

Steinburg, C. (1992) 'Taking Charge of Change', *Training and Development* (US), March.

Tyson, S. and Fell, A. (1986) *Evaluating the Personnel Function*. London: Hutchinson.

Walton, R. E. (1973) 'Ethical issues in the practice of organisational development', *Harvard Graduate School of Business Administration Working Paper* No. 1840, May.

Watkins, K. E. and Marsick, V. J. (1993) *Sculpting the Learning Organisation – Lessons in the Art and Science of Systemic Change*. San Francisco: Jossey-Bass.

Welch, J. (1997) 'Bank trainers take on a troubleshooter's role', *People Management*, 23 January, p. 7.

Chapter 7

THE EMERGING ROLE OF MANAGERS AND STAFF IN STRATEGIC HUMAN RESOURCE DEVELOPMENT

OBJECTIVES

By the end of this chapter you should be able to:

- describe the emerging role of senior management and line managers in SHRD;

- identify a framework for achieving a successful partnership between HRD specialists and their organisational stakeholders;

- describe in general terms the role of a mentor;

- establish the contribution of line managers to the HRD dimensions of the performance management process;

- describe current trends towards self-managed learning;

- indicate the significance of these for individual employees;

- establish particular ways in which individual staff members can contribute towards the HRD effort.

INTRODUCTION

With some notable exceptions, the senior management of organisations has not, until recent years, given a great deal of attention to HRD issues. They have not been seen as strategically significant. A variety of factors has led to a change in this position, most particularly a more general acceptance of the frequently voiced proposition that people are the only sustainable source of competitive advantage for today's organisations. This new consciousness has led to senior management taking a greater interest than hitherto in the development of HRD-oriented strategies designed to move the business forward. Orchestrating 'organisational learning' is now fashionable.

Line managers, on the other hand, have always played a key part in the development of their staff. The exercise of this responsibility has varied from organisation to organisation and from manager to manager, and has been dependent upon the prevailing learning climate and their own perceptions of their role. Using an image first generated by Kurt Lewin in the 1930s, they can be seen as holding a gatekeeper role in respect of the provision of learning opportunities.

181

Either they can open the gate and keep it open to allow individuals access to developmental opportunities; or they can keep the gate closed. How they carry out their gatekeeping role is an operational issue of great importance to the conduct of HRD in any organisational setting.

They also have 'a pivotal role in integrating the overarching strategic objectives of their organisation with its people development policies and practices' (Mabey and Salaman, 1995). It is this strategic role which is the subject of this chapter. It needs to be set in context. In recent years there has been considerable emphasis in organisational theory and practice on delegating to line managers responsibilities that were previously undertaken centrally, or by specialist support departments. The focus has ranged from devolving budgets and marketing operations to devolving responsibilities for HR functions and processes. This entails a significant strategic shift in the positioning and allocation of decision making and resources. Over the same time period there has been a trend towards organisational delayering which has cut out significant numbers of middle managers.

What are the implications of these strategic shifts for those involved in fashioning HRD policies and processes? This question can in turn be broken down into a series of sub-categories:

■ What are the implications for senior managers given their greater interest in HRD issues? What does it mean in terms of commitment and obligations and time spent?

■ What are the implications for line managers? What new expectations arise as a result of new responsibilities?

■ What are the implications for those within the HRD function? How can they play a part in any emerging interplay of forces? Is it possible that non-HRD functional areas will take on all responsibility for major learning initiatives within organisations? To some extent such a shift has been signalled by the Quality Movement, with its heavy investment over the years in training and development related activities, where in many instances responsibility for learning has been conducted by individuals without a conventional HRD background and without any direct involvement in the HRD function.

If one is an HRD specialist responsible for corporate HRD within an organisation what activities should one engage in to protect and sustain one's operation? This issue will be taken up in Chapter 9. In terms of this chapter there are two common approaches to the provision of HRD support to the line.

The first relies heavily on giving managers the skills and knowledge to manage HRD activities and systems without subsequent recourse to specialist advice and support. The second places more emphasis on the development of an ongoing client-customer relationship between the HRD function and line managers. How these two approaches develop will probably determine the future of the HRD function.

Harrison (1992) sets the issue in a broad-ranging context. She considers that line managers have a fundamental responsibility for ensuring that their staff are enabled to perform their jobs effectively and efficiently. She also believes that the responsibility goes beyond this and that staff should be able to enjoy continuous learning opportunities through which their abilities and potential can be developed. She concludes that, with or without the support of specialist HRD staff, there is an imperative to:

■ create a work environment, with associated policies and systems that encourage and support the acquisition of the skills, knowledge and attitudes people need in order to perform well in their jobs;

■ regularly review work targets, appraise performance and assess potential in order to help people to improve in their jobs and develop in ways that will be beneficial to the organisation as well as motivating to themselves;

■ regularly monitor and evaluate the results of formal and informal learning in the workplace.

This chapter contends that these are very worthy, but very demanding, tasks to carry out systematically without external guidance and co-ordination.

THE RELATIONSHIP BETWEEN THE HUMAN RESOURCE DEVELOPMENT FUNCTION AND THE LINE

Megginson *et al.* (1993) contend that the trend in recent years has been towards decentralisation, which may or may not involve the retention of some form of HRD strategy-making and co-ordinating function.

Bevan and Hayday (1994), operating from an HRM perspective, identify a series of issues that might be considered if one is thinking of devolving HR responsibilities to the line. Their list has been modified to give it more of an HRD slant. One problem with their approach is that it assumes that the HR function in some way has a say in how this devolution happens, as opposed to the line or senior management taking the initiative into their own hands.

1 Be clear what HRD roles line managers want and what skills they need to perform them.

2 Define what 'ownership' really means – distinguish it from 'dumping'.

3 Clarify the training and support available to the line and on what basis it can be discussed.

4 Move from rule books and procedures to standards and values.

5 Review the state of HRD in the organisation. How well equipped are the line managers to cope with increased pressure from staff?

6 Keep the communication channels open both ways.

Figure 7.1 presents one way of capturing the relationships which can exist between the HRD function and line departments in different organisational settings. On the whole there is a swing away from corporatist central control of learning and recipe-driven courses towards strategic internal consultancy and action learning.

| Figure 7.1 | The tensions of human resource development and line management |

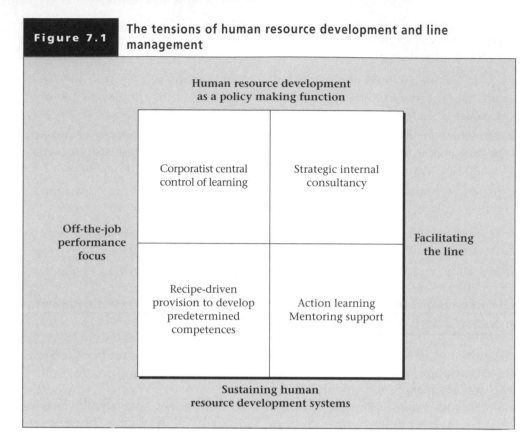

THE INCREASING ROLE OF LINE MANAGEMENT IN THE HUMAN RESOURCE DEVELOPMENT PROCESS

The literature is full of examples of the increasing role of line management in the HRD process. Walker (1992) argued that the 'Leadership Through Quality' movement which permeated Xerox from 1983 led to a substantial redefinition of the role of the manager, with a new focus on HRD-related competences. The switch is illustrated in Table 7.1.

Table 7.1 Changing human resource development role of line management at Xerox

From	To
One-to-one supervision	Team leader
Telling	Teacher
Planning	Facilitator
Controlling	Workers assume responsibility
	Trained to function as a work group

Training at Marks & Spencer in the 1980s took place off the job and away from people's place of work. Management of the learning process was also seen as the responsibility of a specialist function. In common with many other organisations they amended their approach in an attempt to more effectively involve line managers in a co-operative ongoing learning dialogue with individual staff members. A key feature of their revised training and development policy was that every manager must support the development of their staff; this was an integral part of their job on which they were assessed. This reinforced their training and development mission that training and development would be driven by the individual and their line manager (quoted in Harrison, 1992).

Mabey and Salaman (1995), drawing upon Ashton *et al.* (1975) and an analysis of HRD in diverse organisations, identify three levels of apparent commitment by line managers to HRD.

The first 'intermittent' pattern represents a situation where there is little or no genuine commitment to HRD by most line managers. It is reflected by little visible training and development. The second 'institutionalised' pattern is manifested through considerable evidence of visible training and development activity. However, just because there is considerable investment in training activities does not necessarily demonstrate a commitment to HRD *per se*. It may possibly reflect pressure from above to record training activity, for example when there is a policy commitment to spend a certain percentage of turnover on training. The third pattern they classify as 'internalised'. This occurs when HRD has become a natural and ongoing part of normal work activities, but is less visible to an external observer. It could reflect a situation where line managers are highly skilled in coaching their staff, and adept at creating learning opportunities, and 'where the prevailing ethos of people development militates against departmental talent hoarding' (Mabey and Salaman, op. cit.).

Problems of delegating human resource development to line managers

Even the best motivated line managers cannot give the strategic attention to HRD issues that a specialist function would offer. There are problems of co-ordination, even of sharing learning between business sub-units in a systematic way. Also, there is a likelihood that line managers will interpret learning issues in a way that is particular to their own specialism or operational interest. An interesting example of this is provided by the approach adopted by the project team working towards the production of a *balanced score-card* at Rexam Custom Europe (*see* Fig. 7.2).

Figure 7.2   Rexam Custom Europe

Rexam Custom Europe (RCE) is a precision coater, laminator and converter of flexible materials to customers' special orders.

One of the four key segments of a balanced score-card as originally proposed by Kaplan and Norton (1992) is 'Innovation and learning perspective'. At RCE the goals for this segment on their first run-through or pilot were 'extraordinary growth' and 'reduction in development cycle time'. The measures included: 'percentage of sales from new products' and 'average product cycle time': not the sort of goals and

▶▶

▶▶ Figure 7.2 continued

measures that one would anticipate from an HRD perspective on learning. On the second run-through, 'it became apparent to all the participants in the process that Kaplan and Norton's "four perspectives" model was not the most appropriate model for RCE's culture'. Instead, three perspectives only were adopted, namely:

■ shareholders' (or financial) perspective;

■ extraordinary growth perspective;

■ continuous improvement perspective.

Learning, as a term, disappeared. Part of the reason for this was that people development issues were not seen as part of the strategic drive of the organisation even though they were central to the principles that RCE espoused. Their People Principle is:

We believe that people make the difference. We insist on integrity and respect for personal values. Our success depends on incorporating different cultures and people who make learning a lifelong experience. We develop world class people through training and education.

The measures developed for this are: 'Employee satisfaction index' and 'training hours per employee'.

The key issue here is that the design team for the balanced score-card were essentially project-management driven, with external support from project engineers, accountancy and financial specialists. They clearly found it very difficult to perceive the strategic significance of learning, which accordingly influenced the range of measures incorporated in the balanced score-card, which in turn affected the balance as initially conceived by Kaplan and Norton.

In terms of the data collection methods, 13 senior managers covering the functional areas of Operations, Finance and Human Resource Management were circulated with an information pack about the balanced score-card and then each was interviewed individually. There is no evidence from the published findings of any major contribution from an HRD perspective.

Line managers' approach to human resource development – self-report questionnaires

A number of self-report questionnaires have been devised to help line managers establish their approach to HRD. Megginson *et al.* (op. cit.) have developed a 24-item questionnaire based on eight 'leading ideas' which include: line manager's role in the learning process; linking learning and work; focus on company learning; and link to strategy.

The basis of the questionnaire is to get managers to judge the extent to which, for example, they:

■ allow staff to prepare personal development plans;

■ actively engage with staff in planning their development;

■ use staff's needs and aspirations at work as a starting-point for planning learning;

- involve staff in the formulation of policies and strategies;
- encourage staff to spend their own time on learning activities;
- focus on what the individual wants as well as what the organisation needs;
- review learning and development in terms of its contribution to organisation strategy.

Exclusion of the human resource development function from the learning process

Focused organisation-wide learning activities do not necessarily need the involvement of HRD intermediaries. Activities that are HRD related can be carried out without any role in the process for an HRD function and in some quarters this has been strongly argued for.

Thus, as we saw in Chapter 5, the Harvard model developed by Beer *et al.* (1984) emphasised the importance of line managers in the people *management* process, with a concomitant downgrading of the role of the specialist professional. The same argument could be presented *against* HRD. Thus, if we substituted 'HRD' for 'HRM' in the quotation from Beer and Spector (1985) provided in Chapter 5, the contention would be that conventional HRD practice is:

> All too frequently a hodge-podge of policies based on little more than outmoded habits, current fads, patched-up responses to former crises and pet ideas of specialists. HRD practice urgently needs to be reformed from the perspective of general management. HRD issues are much too important to be left largely to specialists.

A case in point, where HRD specialists have no involvement in the process, is the Ove Arup Partnership (*see* Fig. 7.3).

Figure 7.3   Ove Arup Partnership

The Ove Arup Partnership is a firm of consulting engineers based in the UK. It has set up a series of occupation-based skills networks to promote the development of skills in the various disciplines represented in the partnership. Each reports to its respective strategy committee. Skills leaders are appointed by the operational boards to be responsible for co-ordination and leadership of the skills across the groups within their division. For some skills it is anticipated that there will be an active involvement in assisting the operational boards with project resourcing.

Some skills networks have skills champions appointed by the policy board to be responsible for co-ordinating skill leadership across the whole partnership. Co-ordination and development across the partnership of other skills networks are the responsibility of overall skills network leaders appointed by the respective strategy committees.

Each skills network has the following responsibilities:

- to set the standards for the practice of the skill;
- to keep under review the development needs of the skills areas in its remit;
- to propose and prioritise development projects and the investment needed;
- to arrange events and activities associated with skill development.

▶▶

▶▶ Figure 7.3 continued

Skills leaders have the following responsibilities:

■ to lead the practice of skills within their operational division;

■ to be responsible for steering the successful execution of technical developments within their remit;

■ to collaborate with other skills leaders, skills champions and overall skills network leaders, where appropriate, on firm-wide issues;

■ to report on the network's activities to their operational board;

■ to identify and develop future skills leaders;

■ in conjunction with group leaders, to review the skill development of staff in a way that encourages them to achieve their potential;

■ to advise on recruitment and training policies.

Skills champions and overall skills network leaders have the following responsibilities:

■ to lead the skill network for the whole partnership;

■ to ensure that the skill network functions satisfactorily;

■ in conjunction with the skills leaders, to take such steps as are necessary to maintain Arup skills at the leading edge;

■ to report to their respective strategy committees and, in the case of skills champions, to the policy board, as requested.

Skills networks report to strategy committees acting on behalf of the Ove Arup Partnership and are funded as follows:

■ skills champions, overall skills network leaders and skills leaders by their respective strategy committees through budgets agreed by the policy board;

■ Other members of skills networks by their respective groups.

There is no HRD function within the Ove Arup partnership. This is entirely a senior management and line-driven activity.

THE EMERGING PARTNERSHIP

Megginson *et al.* (1993) suggest the creation of a policy framework which clearly differentiates between the responsibilities and obligations of four key stakeholder groupings – senior managers; line managers; employees; and training specialists. In this proposed framework:

■ senior managers have the responsibility for its overall establishment, linking HRD with other aspects of HRM in ways which clearly support current and future organisational requirements;

■ line managers need to ensure that the policy framework and detailed proposals reflect operational requirements. Within the policy guidelines they should actively support subordinate learning with particular emphasis to its application and utilisation;

- employees should commit themselves to their own continuing development and support management's attempts to relate this to enhanced organisational effectiveness;

- training specialists (HRD specialists) need to work with senior managers in establishing the policy framework and designing and implementing detailed proposals for learning against specified objectives.

Significantly, their guidelines do not address the nature of any ongoing relationship between the HRD specialist and the line managers. The way they explain the process seems to imply that HRD specialists maintain a hands-off stance in terms of day-to-day relationships with the line. It is a basic contention of this chapter that such an approach is to their detriment. Yet it is not unusual for the connection to be absent. This chapter provides a number of real-life examples where there is no relationship of HRD *vis-à-vis* the line.

Figure 7.4   Partners in development

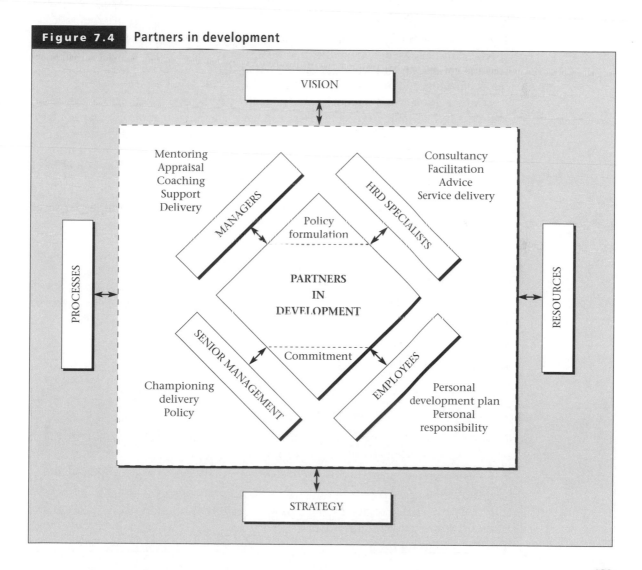

Figure 7.4 builds on their suggestions and proposes a 'Partners in development' framework. The word 'development' is deliberately chosen. 'Partners in *learning*' was rejected on the grounds that it seemed too encompassing. 'Partners in *performance*' was considered but seemed too prescriptive. Note that policy formulation is not felt to be the prerogative of one or two of the stakeholders if there is to be a true partnership.

THE ROLE OF TOP MANAGEMENT

Top management has a vital role in championing the HRD process. What they say and do will in large part create the learning climate for their organisation. A clear example of the sort of positive messages that can be provided comes from the Chairman, Chief Executive and founder of the Gensler Group which offers world-wide architecture, design and planning services. Take the following quotations from the 1996 annual report:

> Bringing people and performance in line with the demands facing our customers requires special skills, knowledge, flexibility and diversity. We must move toward a firm-wide learning culture, which encourages gaining knowledge from our customers, our partners, our competitors, and from our own mistakes.
>
> Learning goes beyond training, where proficiency is the goal. Learning is active; training is passive. We want our people to learn and to share things that may or may not have an immediate or obvious return – a client's business operation, emerging technologies, teamwork skills. Every Gensler person is personally responsible for driving his or her own learning process. I learned more in 1995 than in any previous year, but not as much as I will in this coming year (M. Arthur Gensler Jr., Chairman and CEO).

The Gensler attitude to learning has echoes of the transformational leader summarised by Bennis and Nanus (1985) – *see* Fig. 7.5.

Figure 7.5	Leaders – the strategies for taking charge

Bennis and Nanus (1985) argue that the new leader is one who:

■ commits people to action;

■ converts followers into leaders;

■ may convert leaders into agents of change.

The associated leadership style they call 'transformative leadership'.

There are three aspects to the leadership context:

1 *Commitment* – bridging the 'commitment gap' because leaders have failed to instil vision, meaning and trust in their followers.

2 *Complexity* – turbulent environments are not susceptible to linear thinking and incremental strategies.

3 *Credibility* – leaders have to be credible to external watchdog authorities and others who challenge authority.

▶▶

▶▶ Figure 7.5 continued

They identify four leadership strategies, based on the skills exercised by 90 senior executives, one-third of them from the public sector.

Strategy 1: Attention through vision

This entails creating a focus, having an agenda and magnetism towards the vision, together with paying attention and listening.

Strategy 2: Meaning through communication

This entails capturing imaginations, the ability to organise meaning for the members and creating a 'commonwealth of learning'.

Strategy 3: Trust through positioning

This entails appropriate positioning in the marketplace; congruence of direction and structure. Positioning is the niche as opposed to the vision. Positioning also means staying the course, 'courageous patience'. The leader must be the epitome of constancy or reliability (trust).

Strategy 4: The deployment of self

This entails, first, positive self-regard – recognising one's strengths and compensating for weaknesses; nurturing of skills with discipline (i.e. working on or developing talents); the capacity to discern the fit between one's perceived skills and what the job requires.

Second, it entails awareness of the Wallenda factor – being on the tightrope is living; everything else is waiting. This requires the ability to integrate learning with failure and maintain optimism about a desired outcome.

Wiggenhorn of Motorola reinforces this perspective, on the basis of his experience of working with a committed chief executive officer when developing the Motorola Corporate University: 'There has to be a senior manager around for a while . . . Someone who believes that education and training will help him or her make this a better institution in new products, new market possibilities, or what have you' (W. Wiggenhorn, Senior Vice President of Motorola, quoted in Garfield, 1992).

Another committed CEO has been Jack Welch of General Electric in the USA. He had a personal involvement since the mid-1980s in the GE Management Development Institute located at Crotonville, New York, where up to 10 000 GE managers receive training each year. To demonstrate his personal commitment he has even taken some of the classes. Another example is Lawrence Bossidy, CEO of the US-based Allied Signals Inc., who said in a *Harvard Business Review* interview in 1995: 'The only way to bridge the gap between where we are and where we want to be is education. We put every one of our 80 000 employees through total quality training within 2 years. All our business leaders including me go through the training' (Tichy and Charan, 1995).

At Ericsson Telecommunication, a company which in 1997 employed 3300 people in the UK and 94 000 people world-wide, the UK chief executive does a quarterly roadshow where he reviews the business, including HR aspects, and reinforces messages about the importance of learning and development. One of the things he emphasises is that the company is operating in a changing and dynamic environment and that people in the organisation need to change and be dynamic also in order to compete. This requires flexible employees – and to ensure flexible employees, there must be a corresponding investment in HRD (Hartley, 1997).

However, this degree of commitment is not a universal norm! A different set of messages emerge from the findings of a UK Cabinet Office (1993) project. The objective of the project was to identify ways of achieving successful delegation of responsibilities for HRD matters to line management in ten government departments and agencies. A key finding was that line managers generally wanted top management to signal commitment to the HRD effort in a tangible way: 'It would make a difference if, just once, we were questioned at "morning prayers" about what use we had made of our delegated training budgets' (Cabinet Office, 1993).

The report argued that it is very easy for top managers to underestimate the effect they have as role models for the rest of the organisation. It also emphasised the importance of senior management demonstrating, by example, an appropriate set of knowledge, skills and attributes if an organisation is to achieve its business goals. Consulting line managers, it concluded, is not an optional extra. Ownership of the HRD strategy is as important as its degree of sophistication, and top management needs to invest as much time and commitment to communicating the strategy and to obtaining such ownership as in developing the strategy.

It is implied that senior management should first develop the HRD strategy and then engage in steps to gain commitment to it from the lower echelons of the organisation. Many organisations would argue for a more participative, two-way approach and this is suggested in the 'Partners in Development' model. We will address the issue of the management of change in Chapter 17.

The White Paper 'Continuity and Change', which deals with the career paths of civil servants in the UK, reinforces the messages about the reluctance of top management in the civil service to get involved in driving HRD. It speaks of achieving developmental experience through 'a close partnership between individuals, their line managers and the relevant specialist functions'.

Nevertheless, as Harrington (1987) observes, one can be very dependent upon the attitude of the chief executive and the senior management team, and this can be capricious. 'The process starts with top management, will progress at a rate reflecting management's demonstrated commitment, and will stop soon after managers lose interest in the process.'

An essential criterion for gaining commitment is that senior management should act consistently and publicly in accord with the ethos of the vision and supporting policies. If the policy guidelines state that all managers and staff will have personal development plans, then that should mean *all*.

THE ROLE OF LINE MANAGEMENT

There are a range of possible roles for line managers in the HRD process, from provision of general support for learning and development to direct interventions. They include:

■ championing HRD – through chairing committees, resourcing HRD, etc.;

■ delivering HRD learning activities – as direct trainers;

- acting as a central link in the process – e.g. in performance management and appraisal-related activities;
- providing a supportive learning climate;
- mentoring;
- coaching.

Megginson *et al.* (1993), in a publication targeted at line managers, contend that 'the objective is not to turn managers into training specialists but to show them that they have so many ways of helping people to learn in the context of their existing jobs and responsibilities'. They anticipate resistance, and go on to say: 'The secret – if there is one – for achieving this lies in changing their perceptions of what managing people involves.' It is not just a matter of changing perceptions relating to HRD – it is intrinsic to the future competitiveness of the organisation. Nor is it a matter of choice: 'It is no longer a tenable idea that managers are free to choose whether or not to commit themselves to new HRD activities. Whether they like it or not, the implication of decentralisation and the increasing tendency for CEO's and MD's to commit themselves to major change initiatives . . . is that managers at all levels will be required to respond.'

We now explore some of the operational activities for managers that emerge from the 'Partners in Development' model.

MENTORING

One of the key support roles for implementing a comprehensive HRD strategy is that of mentoring. In Homer's *Odyssey*, reference is made to Mentor, the faithful retainer of Ulysses, to whom was entrusted the care of his young son Telemachus, until the wanderer returned from the Trojan Wars. The word 'mentor' has been imported into organisational practice to refer to experienced and often senior employees who support and advise less experienced and often younger colleagues through their personal and career development. It is not usually recommended that the mentor should be in a direct reporting relationship with a protégé, because issues that may come up for discussion could have been caused by interactions with the line manager.

Scope of the mentoring role

There is a general consensus on the following elements of the role of mentor:

- the basis of the mentor–protégé relationship;
- the core skills a mentor should possess;
- activities that a mentor should undertake.

The basis of the mentor–protégé relationship

Collin (1994) considers that the relationship should be based on mutual trust and should have the capacity to develop over time, possibly into full friendship.

Geiger, Dumond and Boyle (1995) argue that successful mentoring relationships do not just happen. Even if an organisation has a workable mentoring system, the relationship will not be a productive one unless the mentor and mentoree both understand their role. They go on to offer the following mentor guidelines.

■ meet on a regular basis, at least once a month. A good mentoring relationship cannot be developed if the parties do not get to know each other;

■ be a good listener;

■ do not betray confidences;

■ discuss strengths and development needs with protégés and provide guidance in developing these areas. Provide feedback on technical and interpersonal competence as perceived by customers and influential decision makers.

The mentoring process typically starts with the protégé and his or her mentor holding a personal development discussion that covers the protégé's strengths, development needs, specific skills to work on to develop for the future and a development plan. Time commitment and joint expectations also need to be discussed. It is difficult for either party to be clear on what is expected unless such matters have been discussed.

There could well be a formal agreement between the protégé and the mentor. Such an agreement could take the form of a document with headings such as those in Fig. 7.6.

Figure 7.6	Headings in a mentoring agreement

MENTORING AGREEMENT

Area of agreement   *Substance of agreement*

■ **Confidentiality**

■ **Duration of relationship**

■ **Frequency of meetings**

■ **Specific role of mentor**

■ **Specific role of protégé**

■ **Desired outcomes**

Sometimes HRD advisers interview prospective mentors, together with their protégés, in order to facilitate mutual understanding and establish guarantees of sustained support throughout the development process. It is also worth considering a tripartite agreement between the HRD adviser, the protégé and the mentor on such matters as the development plan. However this can often be no more than a paper exercise unless the HRD adviser maintains some contact with mentors.

Arrangements should be made for getting mentors together so that they can compare experiences and develop a network. In such a situation there could well be a mentor co-ordinator, who could also monitor the effectiveness of the mentor–protégé relationship.

Although some organisations give careful attention to the selection of mentors there is a school of thought that the relationship should be a voluntary one and be initiated by the protégé. This is congruent with the current perspective that individual members of staff should be responsible for their own learning and development.

The core skills of a mentor

According to the publication jointly issued by the Business and Technician Education Council and the Council for National Academic Awards (BTEC/CNAA, 1990), good mentors are, in general:

- confident of and clear about their own position in the organisation and not threatened by, or resentful of, their protégé's opportunities;
- sufficiently senior to be well informed about the organisation and able to facilitate the protégé's opportunities;
- knowledgeable about the protégé's area of interest, thus complementing the more general role of the tutor;
- supportive of the objective of learning, and perceptive of, and committed to their own responsibilities to the protégé;
- easily accessible to the protégé and willing to negotiate a planned timetable;
- already in a positive professional relationship with the protégé;
- able to treat their mentoring role as an integral part of their own job responsibilities, not an add-on.

It is unwise for one individual to take on too many protégé's. Geiger, Dumond and Boyle (1995) recommend two as a maximum.

Roles for mentors

Kram (1985) differentiates between the vocational and the psychosocial functions of mentoring. The vocational function serves to aid a protégé's career development. The psychosocial function assists in the development of self-concepts such as self-identity and self-esteem.

Leibowitz and Schlossberg (1981) develop some of the mentor roles.

Communicator

A communicator:

- encourages two-way exchange of information;
- acts as a sounding-board for ideas and concerns;
- schedules uninterrupted time to meet with the protégé.

Counsellor

A counsellor helps the protégé plan strategies to achieve mutually agreed upon personal goals.

Coach

A coach:

- helps to clarify performance goals and development needs;
- reinforces effective on-the-job performance;
- recommends specific behaviours in which the protégé needs improvement;
- serves as a role model to demonstrate successful professional behaviour.

Adviser

An adviser:

- recommends training opportunities from which the protégé could benefit;
- reviews the protégé's development plan on a regular basis.

Broker

A broker:

- helps the protégé identify resources;
- expands the protégé's network of professional contacts;
- helps link protégés with appropriate employment opportunities.

Referral agent

A referral agent:

- identifies resources to help the protégé with specific problems;
- follows up to ensure that the referred resources were useful.

Advocate

An advocate intervenes on the protégé's behalf, representing his or her concerns to higher-level management for redress on specific issues.

COACHING

References to coaching as a development technique are experiencing something of a resurgence in the literature, partly because of its associations with mentoring. However, there are substantial differences between them. Megginson and Clutterbuck (1996) argue that mentors focus on the individual learner developing through his or her career or life. By contrast the coach shifts attention to the results of the job, exploring specific problems with learners and setting out opportunities for learners to try out new skills. Megginson and Boydell (1979) define coaching as 'a process in which a manager, through direct discussion and guided activity, helps a colleague to solve a problem or to do a task better than would otherwise have been the case'. Mumford (1993) has suggested that sometimes coaching is carried out not because the individual recipient wishes it but because it is in the interest of the manager.

Coaching skills that have been identified include:

- listening and understanding;
- observing;
- giving feedback;
- understanding people;
- communication – written and verbal;
- influencing.

Figure 7.7 sets out ten characteristics of a coach, drawn from the answers of several hundred ARCO Corporation employees based in Los Angeles. How managers carry out the coaching role provides major insights into the attitude towards learning within a given organisation.

Figure 7.7	Ten characteristics of a coach

1 Took time to listen to me.

2 Saw me as a person not just an employee.

3 Cared about me personally and helped if I had personal problems.

4 Set a good example.

5 Let me know I could do more than I thought I was capable of – stretched me.

6 Encouraged me.

7 Never pulled rank: rolled up his or her sleeves and pitched in.

8 Didn't keep me in the dark: let me know what was going on.

9 Praised me for a job well done.

10 Let me know in a straightforward manner when I didn't do a job well.

Source: Quoted in Zemke (1996).

THE ROLE OF LINE MANAGERS IN DELIVERING LEARNING

Line managers have had a long association with in-house training programmes, although their involvement may not be particularly strategic. They have, for example, provided specialist input on technical topics, or provided insights into organisational structure and culture for new recruits. However, in recent years, increasing attention has been given to providing a more strategic thrust to their contribution. Of particular interest has been the development of corporate universities (discussed in greater detail in Chapter 16) where senior managers often have a direct responsibility for delivering significant parts of the programme. At the AXA Corporate University, all graduates of their TELEMAQUE programme for high-potential managers are, for example, asked to run an AXA MANAGER seminar at one of the university sites.

APPRAISALS AND PERFORMANCE MANAGEMENT

In many organisations, the most significant involvement of line managers in the HRD process over the years has been through a staff Performance and Potential Review process. This is often encapsulated in an annual interview between manager and staff member, the determination of action plans and the completion of associated documentation. The review process typically entails an evaluation of past performance and the identification of future development needs. The documentation and the received terminology for the process may change over the years. Nevertheless, as expressed by the Gensler group (referred to earlier in this chapter), if the process is to have a developmental as opposed to a performance management orientation, certain features should be manifest.

> No matter how many times we change the 'Review' form, the focus will still be on the need to communicate with staff about their future in the Firm. The new name is Professional Development Plan! (Gensler Group, January 1997).

Typical guidance to managers for the development discussion, as it is sometimes termed, is as follows:

> Development needs may be identified for a range of reasons. They may be identified as a result of shortfalls in performance, but may also relate to achieving higher levels of performance in the current position or to develop for future career progression. It is important to recognise, however, that development should not just be considered once a year, but should be considered on a regular basis.
>
> The purpose of the development discussion is to review job knowledge, skills and competencies in order to identify areas of strength and development need. Also it is to anticipate likely future job demands, so that specific training and development can be planned.
>
> In the Development Discussion the appraiser is expected to act as a **Coach** and **Mentor** to the appraisee. This is a different role to that in the Performance Review where the appraiser is expected, in consultation with the appraisee, to form judgments of the appraisee's past work contribution.

The outcome of the discussion should result in an agreed Development Plan for the staff member in question. One large UK-based organisation divides development needs into two sections. The first focuses on formal off-the-job training requirements. The second is concerned with on-the-job experience requirements.

In looking at development needs, the following points must be established:

1 The objective or need to be met: there should be a clear definition of the need, ideally in the form of a development objective, that is, what is it, in precise terms, that the appraisee should be able to do differently as a result of development. These should be divided into Priority Training Needs or needs which could be fulfilled by the numerous other development options available, for example, project work or on-the-job coaching.

2 Where the appraiser and appraisee are unsure about what development action is appropriate, they may need to seek assistance after the development discussion.

3 Responsibilities: it should be agreed who is doing what. For example, the appraiser may agree to arrange some coaching or it may be agreed that the appraisee arranges a fact-finding visit.

4 Timescale: there should always be a timescale set for development actions to enable both parties to monitor progress. Timescales must be realistic.

5 Monitoring and reviewing: the appraiser and appraisee should agree how development against agreed development objectives is to be monitored and reviewed.

Appraisers and appraisees may, if they wish, use a separate sheet for the development plan with the headings Objective, Action, Responsibility, Timescale and Monitor and Review Process and attach it to the appraisal document.

It is significant that is it stated in the above scheme that specialist advice on appropriate development opportunities might need to be sought. It is not realistic to expect each line manager to keep abreast of the range of learning opportunities that might be available, be they work-based secondments or special projects in the organisation or specialist courses. The same situation would apply if individual staff members are made responsible for identifying their own personal learning needs and implementing their own personal development plans.

Appraisal schemes or performance and potential review schemes, under whatever in-house name is used, are increasingly been seen as part of an integrated performance management system. Hendry *et al.* (1997) define performance management as 'a systematic approach to improving individual and team performance in order to achieve organisational goals'. Performance management goes beyond HRD issues. It is an attempt to integrate a series of HR components including rewards.

One organisation based in the City of London calls its performance management system 'Partners in Performance'. Figure 7.8 presents extracts from its resource guide.

Figure 7.8	Partners in Performance

As Partners in Performance, each of us has a responsibility to participate actively in managing performance. This resource guide will help clarify your role as a manager or an employee within each component of the Performance Management Process. But the Resource Guide's overall objective is to help foster philosophies and actions that lead to effective performance management.

Employees

■ Take a personal responsibility and initiative for performance and results.

■ Work with their manager to establish a meaningful set of objectives that support the company's vision and the goals and strategies of the business unit.

■ Maintain a thorough understanding of job responsibilities.

■ Seek ongoing feedback about performance to determine whether or not objectives are being met.

■ Initiate Update Discussions if manager does not do so first.

■ Develop skills that enhance performance, and explore innovative approaches to the job.

■ Assume responsibility for personal skills development.

Managers

■ Provide continuous, ongoing performance feedback to employees.

■ Actively participate in each component of the Performance Management Process and guide employees towards meeting their objectives.

▶▶

▶▶ Figure 7.8 continued

- Establish an environment that promotes communication, quality, innovation, teamwork and results.
- Promote joint management of performance, making it a shared responsibility between managers and employees.
- Recognise and encourage employee achievement.
- Understand the company's vision and business strategy and their role in the company's success.
- Act as a resource for skills development discussions.

Next level managers

- Establish an environment that promotes communication, quality, innovation, teamwork and results.
- Ensure each component of the Performance Management Process is completed for each employee.
- Act as a resource for skills development.

Interestingly, there is no reference to HRD (or HRM or indeed personnel) as participating in the partnership.

The Performance Management Process is comprised of four components which are to be completed during the performance period:

STEP ONE: Performance Management Plan

At the beginning of the performance period, the manager and employee agree upon a schedule for completion of each component of the process. Each of them completes the Performance Management Plan, filling in the dates and assigning responsibilities.

STEP TWO: Setting Objectives

The manager and employee develop a list of objectives for the employee to achieve during the performance period. These objectives should be results oriented and include individual skill building goals. Objectives should be prioritised, and accompanied by specific measurement criteria.

STEP THREE: Update Discussion

To foster an atmosphere of ongoing communication, the manager and employee meet for a formal Update Discussion during the performance period. However, we encourage managers and employees to discuss objectives and progress on performance as often as needed.

STEP FOUR: Performance Summary Discussion

This is an opportunity to discuss progress in performance since the Update Discussion, to review skills development needs, and to determine an overall assessment of employee performance. The result of the Performance Summary Discussion is the Annual Performance Summary Form, which documents the overall assessment of employee performance and serves as input for merit reviews.

One of the most significant public initiatives in the UK in recent years has been the introduction of Investors in People (IiP). This provides a clear link between business strategy and HRD. It also provides a very clear set of responsibilities for senior and line managers in the performance review process. The guidelines state that managers should be responsible for regularly agreeing training and development needs with each employee in the context of business objectives, setting targets and standards linked, where appropriate, to the achievement of NVQs.

ADVOCACY

We have seen the importance of senior managers acting as advocates for a holistic approach to learning. This cannot be achieved merely through the adoption of piecemeal organisational strategies such as mentoring, coaching and counselling. Dibella and Nevis (1998) make particular reference to the existence of line managers operating as advocates as well. They emphasise Motorola's singling out of 300 advocates from line management to support the learning associated with their quality programme. Another fruitful source of advocacy can be erstwhile line managers being transferred to HRD on a temporary or permanent basis. This can also be a source of reinvigoration for some of the individuals concerned, as they learn to see the world from a different perspective. When conducting my research on the corporate university I was struck, first, by the number of former line managers involved and, second, by their enthusiasm for the learning entailed.

THE ROLE OF STAFF IN HUMAN RESOURCE DEVELOPMENT

We are in an environment where the mutuality and reciprocity of the employment relationship is constantly being emphasised. Garfield (1992) captures the views of many when he contends that 'competing in an era that demands continuous innovation requires us to harness the brainpower of *every* individual in the organisation . . . The model employee in the new story of business . . . must be the *fully participating partner'*. Organisations such as Rolls-Royce and Rover have reinforced the new nature of their expectations by redesignating 'employees' as 'associates'. Along with this new move to partnership has come new expectations of the erstwhile employee in terms of whose responsibility learning is. In the past, new recruits and established employees would often be expected to undergo a structured development programme and attend predetermined training events. The new model imposes an obligation on employees to identify their own learning needs, and take advantage of training opportunities provided.

This shift has extended to career development also. There is an ongoing tension between self-managed and structured learning leading to career enhancement. Individuals are being expected to provide for their own ongoing employability as opposed to expecting the organisation to secure this for them.

This is echoed in the IPD position statement, 'People make the difference' (IPD, 1994) which contends that one of the challenges facing 'the flexible organisation of tomorrow' is to develop strategies to help individual employees take on greater responsibility for their own development and growth. Included in its summary of key points associated with the new ethos are statements such as:

■ 'People need to participate fully in the identification of their own development needs. Those closest to the job are best able to define development objectives so long as they are fully aware of what is expected or needed for the future.'

■ 'Individual responsibility for planning work-based and longer-term career-based training and development is growing.'

The move towards personal development has a number of positive features, not least the sense that individuals can feel that what they are learning is based on personal choice. However, an over-emphasis on individuals taking responsibility for their own learning can lead to others within the organisation abdicating any commitment. From the individual's perspective the process can become directionless. The notion of partnership assumes a shared responsibility. But where should the boundaries be drawn? For example BP identified personal development planning as a crucial process in individual career development. However they found that individuals needed considerable assistance, which was not present in the devolved structure that replaced a previous centralist model. Some parts of the company were particularly slow in supporting those individuals who were endeavouring to take responsibility for their own development. BP has subsequently turned to a 'partnership' approach in which responsibilities are more clearly to be shared between individuals and company (Hirsch and Jackson, 1996).

Taking responsibility for one's own learning

Tom Peters has long argued that people need to behave as if they were self-employed in order to sustain their employability. It is even more incumbent on those who are self-employed to develop their own 'career development' programme.

The commitment orientation

Organisations such as Neville Russell (*see* Fig. 2.7) have developed joint commitment statements emphasising the mutuality of the employment relationship. Obligations imposed on employees include ensuring that they gain the most out of the training and development opportunities provided.

The training policy statement of TSB includes clauses such as:

Members of staff will identify opportunities for personal growth and agree with their line manager how they will achieve these.

Members of staff are responsible for meeting their own learning needs by using the programmes, packages and facilities available in order to achieve competence in their job and to contribute to corporate objectives.

The aim of TSB's policy statement is to support the achievement of the organisation's strategic goals through a culture of continuous development and shared learning which enables TSB to respond flexibly and quickly to a rapidly changing business environment.

At Rover every employee (today termed an 'associate') is responsible for her or his own learning. Using Rover's terminology, it is part of an attempt to get learning seen 'as a way of putting the future in your hands' as opposed to 'something that you had done to yourself'. The concept of associate ownership of personal development and learning has been intensely promoted within the Group. It remains

Rover's firm belief that people who are given a genuine responsibility for their own development will in turn build a deeper commitment to the company.

In their learning activities Rover associates are expected to seek to accomplish three goals:

■ enhance job skills;

■ acquire knowledge of new technologies;

■ expand both personal and corporate vision.

These goals are supported by the following principles of learning:

1 *Active participation*. Learners should be involved in the design of their own training and its future application. Pre-briefing of learners before a training event is essential.

2 *Knowledge of results*. Learners should know how they are doing during and after training. Feedback mechanisms must be in place to ensure that this happens.

3 *Learning transfer*. Where learning is off the job, opportunities need to be created to transfer the learning to job applications.

4 *Reinforcement of appropriate behaviour*. Learners who demonstrate changes in behaviours should be actively recognised and given feedback as well as encouragement.

5 *Motivation of learners*. Individuals must recognise the need to learn something: and managers need to utilise the learner's own drive and purposes.

6 *Willingness to change*. Visible support from the manager is most likely to encourage the learner to change.

7 *Practice and repetition*. It is necessary to provide opportunities to practice on real-work situations without fear of failure.

8 *Time for reflection*. All learners need time and space to assimilate learning by talking to others and having questions answered – thinking and planning are real work.

A foundation-stone of the ownership concept is the personal development file. Each associate summarises in their file the learning and skills gained through experience and formal education. This underpins the subsequent personal development plan, created jointly by the individual and manager to meet the aspirations of the individual and the business needs of the company.

The National Partnerships Division of Guardian Insurance refers to the provision of learning solutions that enable people to take control of their own development while deriving clear benefits for other stakeholders such as the customer. The approach embodied in the Division's training policy guidelines incorporates the following features:

1 Everyone should know how to organise their own development and the options available for learning.

2 Learning should take place through everyday work experiences as well as formal training. People should aim to make the most of opportunities for new skills acquisition. These opportunities may occur through job swaps, work shadowing, coaching, projects, partner involvement and other flexible team play.

3 Everyone should actively seek to share knowledge and skills with others.

As at Rover, the approach at Guardian Insurance is not entirely self managed and entails shared responsibilities. For example, it is emphasised that the services of the training team should be used whenever solutions are unknown, and for structuring learning in respect of commonly encountered situations in order to achieve a consistent and quality approach. The training team is thus responsible for giving all new entrants structured initial job training which aims to be appropriate to their current degree of knowledge and skills and to ensure rapid quality performance of key tasks.

Such an ethos is mirrored in the USA. Thompson (quoted in Garfield, 1992) describes the approach adopted by Levi Strauss in the following terms:

> With increasing use of technology as new data processing systems are implemented, jobs are changing significantly. We are trying to encourage employees to take responsibility for their own training and development, to contract with their managers or supervisors, and then to be aggressive in making sure that they are developing skills that will prepare them for the future.

This trend is dependent upon jobs and/or team-based working which provide opportunities for 'learning' and development.

Self-development

Self-development is a term for a 'growing family of approaches which give the learner ownership and some measure of control over, the processes and tasks leading to his or her own development' (Pedler, 1994). Self-development methods stress that it is the learner who takes primary responsibility for diagnosing needs and identifying goals; selecting the methods, means, times and places for learning; and evaluating the results. The emphasis is on empowering the learner to act autonomously rather than expecting a third party such as a trainer to direct and prescribe.

Pedler (op. cit.) breaks the concept down even further. It involves:

- 'self', meaning 'by self' in that the learner initiates and manages the development process, and 'of self' in that the learner develops the ability and willingness to develop;
- 'development', which embraces the relationship between inner growth and outward capability;
- 'self-development', involving facilitators working to the learner's agenda rather than 'training' to meet their own or the organisation's goals.

Self-development is part of the ethos of the learning organisation and is one of the 11 defining characteristics of a 'learning company' presented by Pedler *et al.* (1991), manifested by everyone being encouraged to take responsibility for their own learning and development. Pedler *et al.* also make the point that, for the learning company conditions to be met, the organisation must provide supporting resources, facilities and enablers such as coaching, mentoring and opportunities for feedback.

Continuous development

Continuous development is yet another articulation of the self-development philosophy. It has been suggested (Wood, 1988) that it is a practical approach to management as opposed to a theoretical concept, understood through the following 'laws' from which individuals must construct their own definition:

- the integration of learning with work and the responsibility of the individual;

- being concerned with 'self-directed learning', with individuals being responsible for what they need to learn and how;

- a process not a technique, relevant to all workers including the self-employed;

- an attitude, a way of tackling work that promotes learner responsibility and self-reliance;

- being concerned with 'the simultaneous improvement in the performance of employees and the organisation'.

Reid *et al.* (1992) build on these principles and describe continuous development as the 'ultimate intervention in that it allows and encourages all other training interventions. as an attitude of mind, an approach, a philosophy, which attempts to promote endless learning, and designs environments to that end'.

The Work in America Institute generated a continuous learning model in the 1980s that Watkins and Marsick (1993) believe fits the changing learning norms of today's workplace. Its precepts are:

- Learning becomes an everyday part of the job and is built into routine tasks.

- Employees are expected to learn not only skills related to their own jobs but also the skills of others in their work unit and how their work unit relates to the operation and goals of the business.

- Employees are expected to teach, as well as learn from, their co-workers. In short, the entire work environment is geared toward and supports the learning of new skills (Watkins and Marsick, 1993, p. 26).

Continuing professional development

Self-managed learning is increasingly being seen in the context of how one plans and manages one's entire working life. Terms in current usage include lifelong learning, continuing personal development and continuing professional development (CPD). A number of professional bodies in the UK have introduced CPD as a condition of continuing membership.

IPD guidelines

The IPD guidelines define CPD as systematic, ongoing, self-directed learning. It is an approach or process that many authorities maintain should be a normal part of how professional staff plan and manage their working life. Development should be owned and managed by the individual learner. Learning objectives should be clear, though they may be complex, and wherever possible they should serve organisational as well as individual goals. Continuing professional development is:

- *continuing* because learning never ceases, regardless of age or seniority;
- *professional* because it focuses on personal competence in a professional role;
- concerned with *development* because its goal is to improve personal performance and enhance career progression.

The IPD argues that reasons for CPD include:

- ensuring that professionals remain up to date in a changing world. Professional expertise demands on-going appreciation of new concepts, values, laws, technology, skills, organisational forms and the appreciation of many other new influences;
- encouraging professionals to aspire to improved performance;
- ensuring that professionals are committed to learning as an integral part of work, and can devise and manage learning methods which are appropriate to the needs of their own work-related circumstances.

The CPD emphasis on *systematic* development and the comprehensive identification of learning needs provides a framework within which formal and informal, planned as well as accidental and opportunistic learning activities can be set. Definitions include:

> The systematic maintenance, improvement and broadening of knowledge and skill and the development of personal qualities necessary for the execution of professional and technical duties throughout the practitioner's working life ('Continuing Professional Development, Perspectives on CPD in Practice', Sandra Clyne Construction Industry, CPD group).

Individual staff members as trainers and facilitators

The emphasis on provision of learning in corporate mission statements can be seen as part of a social responsibility ethos, that is, in terms of valuing employees.

In 1993, Corning, the USA-based glass and ceramic manufacturing firm, began training specially selected employees to facilitate the work of self-directed work teams. The initial intervention was to train two employees from one of the factories on how to facilitate team learning. These two individuals would then become site facilitators, working with established teams to enable them to manage their own interventions. This programme is akin to the training of employees to facilitate TQM programmes.

The London Borough of Hackney has adopted a similar approach as part of its 'Transforming Hackney' change programme. It set up a 'Quality Leaders Programme' for 50 internal facilitators taken from the ranks of middle management. They were trained in group facilitation techniques, mentoring skills and facilitation of action learning sets. Their responsibility is to spend a period of approximately two weeks facilitating cultural change, with particular emphasis on management style, attitudes and behaviours, devolution and empowerment and managing/living with change.

THE ROLE OF THE HUMAN RESOURCE DEVELOPMENT SPECIALIST IN THE PROCESS

As signalled in earlier chapters, there is a need to reconfigure the traditional training and development role to encompass the new strategic imperative and the heightened expectations of employees. This needs to be done in parallel with the extended role of line managers. The move towards an internal consultancy, facilitation and manager of change role will facilitate this, linked to a more closely articulated customer service and delivery orientation.

CONCLUSION

Some of the key points that emerge from the preceding analysis are as follows:

1 Top management are taking a more proactive and interventionist stance towards learning and development issues.

2 This interest has come increasingly to the fore as it is seen as a source of substantial competitive advantage to meet the current and anticipated learning needs of individuals in organisations.

3 Driven from the top, a number of organisations now emphasise the central role of line managers in the learning process. In some instances there is a concomitant risk that the HRD function will be squeezed out of the process.

4 Line managers have always had a key gatekeeping role in determining access to learning and development opportunities for individual staff members.

5 In the past, the conduct of this role has often been focused on coaching and the annual performance and potential review process. In recent years much attention has been given to the use, as mentors, of senior staff in the organisation

6 In strategic terms, it is important, if not vital, that processes are in place that will demonstrate the contribution that line managers can make to the development of their staff. However, there is a need for co-ordination of these processes, for specialist advice. Even more importantly, line managers will not see learning and knowledge enhancement in the same way as an HRD specialist. They will not be able to provide the strategic and directive overview that will keep a given organisation on its learning journey.

7 There has also been an increased focus on the responsibility of the individual in the learning process as part of an ethos of mutuality and joint commitment that is pervading many organisations.

8 This individual responsibility is reinforced by trends in the direction of self-managed learning and continuous personal development.

9 It is suggested that one way of ensuring a 'balanced score-card' to development is through a policy formulation and implementation process based on a model or framework such as the 'Partners in Development' proposed in this chapter.

REFERENCES

Ashton, D., Easterby-Smith, M. and Irvine, C. (1975) *Management Development: Theory and Practice*. Bradford: MCB University Press.

Bennis, W. and Nanus, B. (1985) *Leaders – The Strategies for Taking Charge*. New York: Harper & Row.

Bevan, S. and Hayday, S. (1994) 'Towing the line; Helping managers to manage people', Institute of Manpower Studies, No. 254.

BTEC/CNAA (1990) *The Assessment of Management Competencies*.

Cabinet Office (Office of Public Service and Science, Development Division) (1993) 'Encouraging and Supporting the Delegation of Human Resource Development Responsibilities to Line Managers'.

Collin, A. (1994) 'Learning and Development', in I. Beardwell and L. Holden (eds) *Human Resource Management – A Contemporary Perspective*. London: Pitman.

Dibella, A. J. and Nevis, E. C. (1998) *How Organisations Learn – An Integrated Strategy for Building Learning Capability*. San Francisco: Jossey-Bass.

Garfield, C. (1992) *Second to None – The Productive Power of Putting People First*. Chicago: Business One Irwin.

Geiger-Dumond, A. H. and Boyle, S. K. (1995) 'Mentoring: A Practicioner's Guide', *Training and Development,* March.

Harrington, H. J. (1987) *The Improvement Process*. McGraw-Hill.

Harrison, R. (1992) *Employee Development*. London: IPM.

Hartley, R. (1997) 'The Learning Company – Fashion or Necessity'. Unpublished dissertation, Portsmouth Business School.

Hendry, C., Bradley, P. and Perkins, S. (1997) 'Missed Motivator', *People Management,* 15 May, pp. 20–5.

Hirsch, W. and Jackson, C. (1996) 'Ticket to Ride or no Place to go?', *People Management,* 27 June, pp. 20–5.

IPD (1994) *People Make the Difference*. London: IPD.

Kaplan, R. S. and Norton, D. P. (1992) 'The Balanced Scorecard – Measures That Drive Performance', *Harvard Business Review,* January–February.

Kram, K. E. (1985) *Mentoring at Work: Developmental Relationships in Organisational Life,* Scott Foresam, p. 416.

Leibowitz, Z. B. and Schlossberg, N. K. (1981) 'Training Managers for their Role in a Career Development System', *Training and Development,* 35(7) July.

Mabey, C. and Salaman, G. (1995) 'Training and Development Strategies', in Mabey and Salaman, *Strategic Human Resource Management'*. Oxford: Blackwell.

Megginson, D. and Boydell, T. (1979) *A Manager's Guide to Coaching*. London: BACIE.

Megginson, D. and Clutterbuck, D. (1996) *Mentoring in Action – A Practical Guide for Managers*. London: Kogan Page.

Megginson, D., Joy-Matthews, J. and Banfield, P. (1993) *Human Resource Development,* London: Kogan Page.

Mumford, A. (1993) *Management Development: Strategies for Action* (2nd edn). London: IPM.

Pedler M (1994) 'Applying Self Development in Organisations', in C. Mabey and P. Iles (eds) *Managing Learning*. London: Routledge.

Pedler, M., Burgoyne, J. and Boydell, T. (1991) *The Learning Company*. New York: McGraw-Hill.

Reid, M. A., Barrington, H. and Kenney, J. (1992) *Training Intervention: Managing Employee Development,* 3rd edition. London: IPM.

Tichy, N. M. and Charan, R. (1995) 'The CEO as Coach: an Interview with Allied Signal's Lawrence A. Bossidy'. *Harvard Business Review,* March–April.

Walker, R. (1992) 'Rank Xerox – Management Revolution', *Long Range Planning,* 25(1), pp. 9–21.

Watkins, K. E. and Marsick, V. J. (1993) *Sculpting the Learning Organisation – Lessons in the Art and Science of Systemic Change.* San Francisco: Jossey-Bass.

Wood, S. (ed.) (1988) *Continuous Development.* London: IPM.

Zemke, R. (1996) 'The corporate coach', *Training,* December.

Chapter 8

CAREER DEVELOPMENT IN DOWNSIZED ORGANISATIONS

OBJECTIVES

By the end of this chapter you should be able to:

■ identify the traditional approach to career development in large bureaucratic organisations;

■ evaluate its appropriateness for organisations operating in the modern arena;

■ establish the relationship between individual and employer responsibility for career planning;

■ establish a relationship between lifespan planning and career planning;

■ evaluate the likely course of career paths for today's knowledge workers;

■ establish the extent to which career paths are available for previously excluded groups such as semi-skilled workers.

INTRODUCTION

Career development is included by Patricia McLagan (1989) as one of the core themes of HRD. She sees it as one of the three mainstream activities impacting upon organisations that have development as their primary process. She describes its focus as assuring an alignment of individual career planning and organisation career-management processes to achieve an optimal match of individual and organisation needs'. We must ask to what extent this proposed alignment is realistic in a world of post-downsized organisations, where:

■ traditional vertical progression routes are less available because of delayering;

■ a higher percentage of people are working in small and micro organisations;

■ organisations no longer operate on the job-for-life model;

■ organisations are becoming reliant on a more highly skilled work-force;

■ individuals are being exhorted to take responsibility for their own career development and told to anticipate a number of career shifts in their working lifetime.

Concerns such as this have contributed to a changing perception of what constitutes a career, who careers are for, and who should be responsible for career development. This chapter will address these issues and establish a number of strategic implications for HRD.

CAREER DEVELOPMENT AS A STRATEGIC THEME

Career development has come to the fore as a strategic theme in recent years for a variety of reasons.

The first is that, in order to maintain their competitive advantage organisations will, it is held, become more and more dependent on highly qualified and adaptive 'knowledge workers' who will contribute to the 'intellectual capital' of the enterprise, and who will be in relatively short supply. As organisations have moved to flatter, leaner and decentralised structures, one of the key sources of attractiveness for working with a given employer, that of promotion opportunities, has diminished. How can the notion of a career be represented to these employees of the future in the absence of traditional career progression? Figure 8.1 examines the characteristics of knowledge workers.

Figure 8.1 What distinguishes the knowledge worker?

Reich (1991) forecasts that the future for unskilled labour seems bleak in first world economies. He suggests that there are three work-force categories which in global terms, and excluding the agricultural and public sectors, encompass 75 per cent of the labour force.

1 Routine production services

These are semi-skilled activities which can be performed anywhere and everywhere. This group does not fit into the conventional notion of enjoying a career, and until recently any attempt to provide a career path for them would have been laughed at. In many respects they can be seen as a neglected resource. Efforts are being made in a number of manufacturing organisations, where semi-skilled work has been endemic, to broaden the range of skills involved, and to create opportunities for career development through lateral moves.

2 In-person services

These consist of basically simple and repetitive tasks that require relatively little training. Once skills are acquired, there is little prospect of learning and development. They consist of the provision of services direct to the consumer, so the job holder has to be present at the consumer location. Some are under threat from computerisation. For example, cash dispensers and other IT innovations are replacing face-to-face service in banks. Here too, the conventional notion of a career seems inappropriate.

3 Symbolic analytic services

These require a range of skills in problem identification and problem solving. Post holders will benefit most from prosperity, since they bring added value to the 'production' process. These are the so-called knowledge workers on whom the distinctive competences of first world economies will rely.

The second reason that career development has emerged as a strategic issue has been the change in attitude among many highly skilled workers towards employers – from one of loyalty to a perception of themselves as free agents. The change has emanated from the shock-waves of the labour shake-out of recent years operating in parallel with a boom in some western economies. In the USA a 1997 survey conducted by the Society for Human Resource Management revealed that 40 per cent of employers were offering 'signing-on bonuses' plus loyalty awards for staying with them for periods of, in some instances, as little as 90 days. According to E. R. Greenburg, Director of Management Studies for the American Management Association, 'There's a delicious irony at work . . . Companies have spent the last decade automating their businesses to cut costs only to find a shortage in technical expertise to run the new systems' (quoted in Lee, 1997).

A third reason relates to the perceived need to tap the potential of the whole work-force. In the past many organisations have operated as large bureaucracies in which careers have only been for the chosen few. In labour-intensive manufacturing concerns, for example, the majority of employees have been a neglected and forgotten resource in developmental terms, semi-skilled operatives locked into a timeless and unchanging set of routine activities. The speed of access to global distribution channels, together with the relative cheapness of workers, has meant that organisations in many industries no longer need to rely on a location-specific work-force. Semi-skilled workers in developed economies become an expensive luxury compared to their cheaper counterparts in the developing world. All workers need to demonstrate they offer something distinctive if they are to secure their future employment. In turn employers need to draw out their untapped potential. Can the notion of a career be reconfigured as part of an educational process to encourage flexibility and responsiveness? And can it help lever semi-skilled workers towards becoming more akin to knowledge workers?

CAREER ANCHORS

Schein (1978) suggests that individuals' careers and career choices are guided, constrained, stabilised and integrated by a set of 'career anchors'. Functioning as self-perceived talents and abilities, motives and needs and attitudes and values, these are:

- *technical functional competence*: the career is organised around a set of functional skills which can often be used in a range of organisations;
- *managerial competence* (analytical, interpersonal and emotional): the career is built upon the ascent of a ladder of increasingly senior managerial positions;
- *security and stability*: the point of the career is to provide stability and security for the individual and her/his family;
- *creativity*: the purpose of the career is to create new things, be they products, businesses or services;
- *autonomy and independence*: the career is organised around the search for an occupation such as lecturing, writing or consulting which allows the individual to determine work hours and life style.

He further differentiated between these 'internal' career anchors which predispose people towards certain occupational choices during their lifetime, and 'external' careers which are the career paths or developmental routes established within organisations.

Miller and Rice (1967) contended that organisations' career structures did not recognise these individual predispositions. Career development was postulated on the assumption that the most successful individuals in an organisation would be directed towards a managerial career, which would embody the highest salary and status differentials. Commenting specifically on the career paths of sales representatives, they remarked that the promotion structure meant that 'the representative who seeks a higher status and a more certain future has to try to get promotion out of selling'. They have to leave jobs at which they are specialists and take one in which the skills that have earned them the promotion will probably turn out to be a disadvantage rather than an advantage. 'Even worse, those who fail to get promotion are often made to feel ashamed that they are still representatives. They find it difficult to admit, even to themselves, that they do not want to "get on".' Their example could be extended across a whole range of occupational types. In teaching it is exemplified by the 'Mr Chips' archetype.

Tournament notion of a career

Rosenbaum (1984) points out that a number of organisations seem to practice a 'tournament' model of career development for people who seek management progression as their career anchor, in which early success in the tournament is seen as a predictor of later progress. In effect, an employee needs to win in the early stages in order to remain in the game. This system has been held to reflect practices in Japanese companies such as Nissan, where entry to the cadre of potential managers is ruthlessly elitist and dependent upon a qualification from one of the top Japanese universities. There follows a number of years of training, job rotation and general socialisation until individuals reach their early thirties. Then, those individuals deemed to have high potential are promoted more quickly than the rest of their peers, who may be encouraged to leave.

The notion of a tournament is a powerful metaphor even if it is not associated with such a specifically defined approach. Where promotion opportunities are few – as for example in delayered and downsized organisations – competition can become intense as people jockey for position. This assumes, of course, that vertical progression and hierarchical position are still seen as goals to be aimed for, an assumption embedded in the traditional notion of a career.

THE TRADITIONAL NOTION OF A CAREER

In the past clear differences were made between manual workers and shop-floor workers who were perceived to have a job but not a career; and management and professional trainees, often graduates, who had access to specialist career-related training and fast-track progression routes. Much of career development was linked to processes designed to secure promotion for a select few through managerial grades. It was assumed that so long as the selected élite wanted to stay, there would be a career for them. Figure 8.2 presents the traditional pyramid notion of career development.

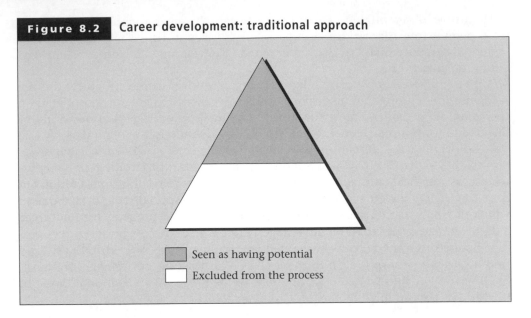

Figure 8.2 Career development: traditional approach

Seen as having potential

Excluded from the process

Traditionally, many organisations had well-established career progression routes for those seen as having potential, predicated on continuing lifelong service within the organisation. In organisations such as Shell, it was not unusual for a graduate recruit to spend 30 years before reaching his or her projected level in the organisation.

Much of the traditional approach to career planning also seems to be predicated on the assumption that one works in a large organisation. It is in that context that one can identify predetermined career routes or career paths. It also seems predicated on the notion that there are job hierarchies and categories which allow for skill progression and developmental opportunities.

A number of distinctive features have been associated with the traditional approach to career development.

Succession planning

Succession planning is a process whereby organisations fill management openings with individuals identified and prepared as candidates in advance of the vacancy occurring. Such planning is not particularly common. Companies in the USA have reported that fewer than half of all management appointments involve individuals named as candidates in succession and development plans (Walker, 1992). (Note that succession planning is more difficult in the USA than in the UK because of legislation in the USA enabling individuals to continue working until *they* choose to retire.)

Targeted development

Walker (1992) further differentiates between succession planning and targeted development:

> Through targeted development, companies fill openings with employees who have been prepared for possible future assignments, as a result of development planning focused on

career path steps. Through succession planning companies fill management openings with individuals identified and prepared as candidates for one or more specific management positions.

Career path analysis

Walker (op. cit.) contends that everyone has a career path. As he puts it, 'employees move through patterned sequences of positions or roles, usually related to work content, during their working lives. This is the essence of a career path . . . Everyone has one'. As mentioned previously I am not convinced that assembly workers on the factory floor or other semi-skilled operatives have in the past moved 'through patterned sequences of positions or roles'. Indeed there used to be a clear dividing line between individuals who had a 'job' and those who perceived themselves to have a 'career'. Reward systems implicitly had built into them notions of 'deferred gratification' for those individuals with career advancement aspirations – that is, the sacrifice of short-term material gain while one was undergoing extended training or education for the likelihood or promise of longer-term benefits in terms of status and wealth.

Walker (op. cit.) believes that career paths should be formally defined and documented by means of *career path analysis*. The traditional approach to career path analysis is to restrict the coverage to what takes place within the confines of a given organisation and to further assume that, in the main, the range of career options open to an individual is constrained by organisational guidelines. A career path can accordingly be defined as an 'explicit description of possible alternative sequences of jobs that an individual may hold in an organisational career' (Walker, 1980).

Rothwell and Kazanas (1989) go on to suggest that there are two types of such organisationally constructed career paths:

- *formal*: made explicit by the organisation;
- *informal*: made explicit by examining historical movements of employees.

Career path analysis in the first formulation is literally the process of working out progression routes available to individuals during their stay with the organisation, given the posts they occupy when they join. Its purpose it to define a basis for replacement planning based on internal promotions. There are two different but related approaches:

- *prescriptive*: detailing logical relationships between jobs and logically related knowledge and skills necessary to qualify for movement from one job to the next;
- *descriptive*: detailing historical employment experiences of individuals who have moved through the ranks over time. The actual career paths that seem to be available in practice to people in a given organisation is sometimes called the 'manpower system'.

To develop a prescriptive career path framework Walker (1980) proposes a number of systematic techniques:

1 Collect data about activities involved in each job, how important these activities are, and how much time is devoted to them.

2 Infer from job information what knowledge and skills are necessary for incumbents to perform each activity.

3 Group jobs together in 'families' or 'clusters' based on common knowledge and skills.

4 Pinpoint logical patterns of movement between jobs, based on similarities in knowledge and skills required.

5 Assemble results of all such analyses for the entire organisation.

Rothwell and Kazanas (op. cit.) argue that the informal descriptive approach to career path analysis can be derived from employees' work perceptions. 'Analysts ask experienced people to describe their past jobs and other matters that they feel have contributed to their career progress. This can help determine whether there are common historical patterns in career paths and then enable reflection on whether they are still relevant.' This whole approach depends on a relatively stable organisational environment in which jobs, associated skills and hierarchical levels do not change significantly over time. It also implies a strong degree of central control to monitor the process.

However, it must be asked whether there is still a place for structured career planning for individuals in today's downsized and delayered organisations.

WHAT IS A CAREER COMING TO MEAN?

Does career development today extend to more than just the chosen few? If so, is that a consequence of the new knowledge workers in the high-tech industries and the multiskilled operatives on the factory floor and elsewhere?

A career has conventionally been associated with moving upwards in one's chosen line of work, and thereby achieving a higher salary and greater responsibility, status and prestige. The exception would be people in privileged occupations who had a choice as to whether, for example, they wished to stay in a professional role or move into a managerial role. Such a perspective restricts the notion of a career to a relatively small proportion of the world's population. It excludes, for example, manual workers or semi-skilled operatives for whom there is little opportunity for advancement. It also excludes the impact of non-work life and roles.

A more broad-based concept, albeit still work focused, is to see a career as the individually perceived sequence of attitudes and behaviours associated with work-related experiences and activities over the span of the person's life (Hall, 1986). By virtue of working each individual automatically has a 'career' but it is up to the individual to interpret it in a way that is meaningful to him or her. Such an interpretation is essentially autobiographical and retrospective in its connotations. The definition gains its meaning through individuals looking back and reflecting on where they have been and how they have progressed. It is quite possible, of course, that a number of individuals do not identify with such a broad-ranging concept, and would not consider that the collection of work-related experiences and activities adds up to a career.

Relationship to lifespan development

More and more individuals are now, of necessity, being forced to determine their own career development. This is partly because fewer organisations offer a job for life, and even where they purport to do so, downsizing and delayering in the 1980s and 1990s have reduced employees' confidence in such prospects. It is also partly associated with the increasing emphasis being put on people taking more responsibility for their own learning and development.

Figure 8.3 looks at the idea of partnership in career development.

Figure 8.3 **Partnerships in career development**

Walker (1992) cites the USA-based company Johnson Wax where the partnership concept is made explicit in company documentation dating back to 1989:

> Effective career development requires that the organisation, the manager and the employee accept their responsibilities . . .

The employee must:

■ take responsibility for career development

■ obtain and use feedback on career options and realistic potential . . .

■ communicate career interests and discuss developmental needs with manager.

The manager must:

■ support employees in their career development responsibilities . . .

■ provide organisational career information and realistic feedback on employee career aspirations . . .

■ encourage and support implementation of the employee's developmental plans.

The organisation must:

■ communicate business mission, objectives and strategies so that realistic development can occur . . .

■ provide employees with the resources necessary for development, to include on-the-job experiences, training and education . . .

■ evaluate and recognise managers for their role/success in employee career development.

Managers are trained specifically in coaching and counselling skills to support the initiative through a two-day programme called 'Partners in Career Management'.

Individuals have always had to take some responsibility for their own learning – despite the existence of cosy paternalistic umbrella protection succession planning systems in a number of organisations. The reduced level of organisational support for career development that is now apparent has been paralleled by an interest in executive life planning models (*see* Fig. 8.4)

| Figure 8.4 | Life planning |

The simplest dictionary definition of a career is 'advancement through life'. Some have been attracted to trying to map out parameters affecting this advancement through engaging in a process of *life planning*. According to Tame (1993) life planning is a process without an end, with its subject being the growing, changing, developing individual. Although she sees a certain falsity in the attempt to define end-points in life and plan their accomplishment, without this attempt she believes our decisions are reactive rather than proactive, and our lifespan is a mere series of events rather than a meaningful whole. Thus life planning is the attempt to impose order and purpose on the chaos of life's experiences, situations and opportunities.

Tame defines the major concepts in life planning as: values, life goals, mission or purpose, objectives, strategy. The terms she uses are much the same as those used by corporate strategists, contextualised at the individual level.

Values are those situations, sensations, experiences, activities, principles and motives that are important to the individual. We may not be aware of them but they are implicit in the choices we make. We may find that clarification of this area will uncover a discrepancy between real values (i.e. manifest in action) and stated values.

A personal mission statement/purpose derives from an analysis of past experience and current values, and is a statement of what the individual has to contribute to the team, the job, to people in general or to life.

Life goal is a desired long-term outcome of major significance to the individual, reflecting his or her most important values, and mission or purpose, which provides a focus for all major activities and decisions in life. Here we have the paradox of life planning because even highly successful people will probably agree that there is no 'arrival point' in life. Yet it helps to behave as if there is. A life goal provides a focus and a compass bearing so that we have a means of discriminating between the many options available in modern life. Knowing specifically where we want to be, we can judge each career move, each life possibility, according to whether it takes us closer or further away from our life goal.

Objectives provide defined medium-term operational ends which mark one's progress in life towards the goal. The attainment of the life goal may require action in a number of different functional areas – for example, objectives for health and fitness will probably figure in most life plans, because, whatever the life goal its accomplishment will be easier if one is in good health.

Strategy is the sum of all intentional actions directed towards the accomplishment of the life goal via medium-term objectives, and constituting a life plan. Intentional means that the individual consciously chooses his or her situation, rather than falling into it by default.

Framing goals and objectives

Tame goes on to generate some basic rules for formulating life goals and objectives which have strong echoes from corporate objective setting. They should be:

■ written down

■ expressed in simple, not complex words

■ as brief as possible

▶▶ Figure 8.4 continued

- highly specific
- attainable (avoid grandiose statements)
- emotive.

Objectives should be:

- measurable, and
- time limited.

Above all, life goals and objectives should be genuine. They should be personal rather than conventional, and express the true self rather than project an image.

Reasons for the current interest in life planning

Macnulty (1985) reported on research that indicated that the British population could be divided into three major categories.

1 *Sustenance-driven people* are motivated by the need for security. Their major concern, whether rich or poor, is survival. They are fearful and cautious, and if they are comfortably off, to them survival means clinging on to an existing life style. They are very resistant to change.

2 *Outer-directed people* are motivated by the search for esteem and status. The criteria by which they measure their success are external to themselves. They are competitive and very concerned about the impression they make on others (the 'right' car, the 'right' area).

3 *Inner-directed people* hold criteria of success and standards of behaviour within themselves. They are far less concerned with the opinions of others and 'keeping up with the Jones's'; thus they are self-motivated.

In 1984 it was found that about one-third of the UK population was inner directed and that this proportion was increasing.

Christine Macnulty, Managing Director of Applied Futures, referring to follow up research conducted in 1990, predicted that: 'As the population's values change, to become more self-motivated, self-determined and concerned about responsibility and freedom, so we will see a more balanced pattern of life, work and leisure.' Within this context, the central role of life planning should be clear. Its philosophy of self-motivation and self-direction is based on the values of a substantial and growing segment of the population. Macnulty's comments should also be seen in the context of the end, in all but a few cases, of the principle of lifelong employment with a given institution.

Career resiliency

Waterman *et al.* (1994) argued that we are seeing the demise of the lifetime employment covenant and described an emergent new relationship in which 'the employer and employee share responsibility for maintaining – even enhancing –

the individual's employability inside and outside the company'. They termed the consequence of this relationship for the employee, 'career resiliency'. One of Waterman's co-authors, and Director of the California-based Career Action Centre, has subsequently referred to 'career self-reliance' which she defines as 'the ability to actively manage one's work life in a rapidly changing environment – the attitude of being self-employed whether inside or outside an organisation'. What the notion means is that companies help employees assess and update their skills and interests so that they can adapt speedily to changing business needs – or readily find work elsewhere. In return, employers get renewed loyalty from employees as well as the increased productivity that arises from individuals operating at the intersection of personal fulfilment and corporate need. Figure 8.5 presents a model of a career development map, which represents a possible progression for the individual, between organisations and an outsourced support unit.

| Figure 8.5 | Career development: a possible progression |

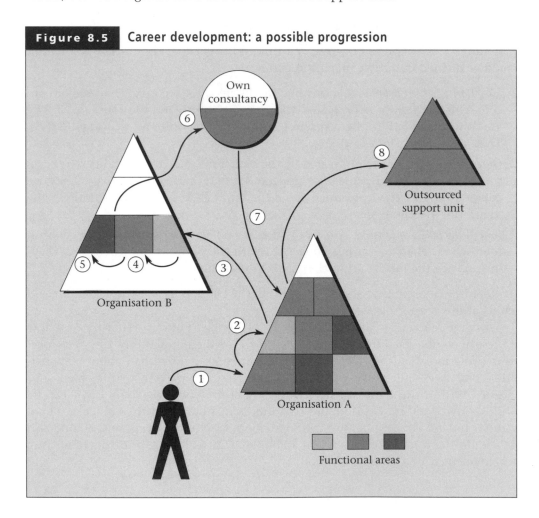

WHAT ARE THE CURRENT TRENDS?

The end of jobs for life?

David Blunkett, the UK Minister for Education, when announcing the publication of the long-awaited Green Paper on the Learning Age, commented on the end of lifelong job tenure and on the likelihood that the generation now coming to the employment market for the first time could expect to go through five to six career shifts in their lifetime.

This, of course, is a forecast that remains to be tested. Underpinning it has been the dramatic shake-out of labour in the late 1980s and throughout the 1990s as organisations have engaged in downsizing to achieve efficiency in the competitive global environment. However there is little tangible evidence of a substantial decline in job tenure in the deregulated labour markets of the USA and the UK.

Newmark *et al.* (1997) suggest that job tenure in the USA has not altered to any appreciable extent since the 1980s. Their findings were that workers are slightly more likely than before to be with the same employer after four years, but marginally less so after eight years. The eight-year retention rate fell from 36.8 per cent in 1983–91 to 34.7 per cent in 1987–95. They also found a slight increase in the percentage of workers still in the same job over an eight-year period. Whereas only 17.4 per cent of workers with less than two years in the job in 1983 were still doing the same job in 1991, the figure for the 1987–95 period had increased to 20.5 per cent.

Smith (1997) has provided comparable findings for the UK. Average job tenure in 1977 was six years; by 1997 it had declined slightly to five-and-a-half years.

Burgess *et al.* (1997) compared length of service in the UK with that in Italy which has a regulated job tenure model. Contrary to expectations, the findings were that the British were no less secure in their jobs than their continental counterparts. For example, they found that 59 per cent of British male workers over the age of 25 had been with the same company for more than five years, whereas only 52.3 per cent of Italian men had.

Some Japanese organisations still operate on a 'job for life' model. Canon employs more than 72 000 people world-wide yet has never in its history asked any employee to take early retirement. To manage through times of slow growth it transfers its employees within the company or reduces the numbers of new recruits. Overseas the situation has been slightly different because employees in some countries have been less ready to accept job transfers (or reduced pay) than their Japanese counterparts (Kaku, 1997).

The findings quoted above do not necessarily mean that fears about job security are groundless. It could be that the figures mask an increase in the numbers of employees being laid off because the survivors are less willing to move. There is as yet little evidence to support this contention. Burgess also contends that the fear of job loss might be encouraging employees either to work harder or to moderate their wage claims, thus allowing organisations to cut costs and become more flexible without reducing job tenure.

In respect of management jobs, however, studies from the American Management Association show that in the USA management and supervisory jobs are being eliminated nearly twice as fast as they are being created (Stewart, 1997). Stewart also quotes figures from the *Wall Street Journal* (27 November 1995) showing that there were 12.5 managers per 100 employees in 1983, and 11.2 in 1994. In other words, in just over a decade one out of nine managers in the USA disappeared. The figures also revealed that half the drop occurred in the early 1990s.

Jobs for life or jobs for now

Hirsch and Jackson (1996) have developed a helpful career development continuum to summarise the findings of their empirical study into the career development practices of 15 large UK-based organisations which included BP, Norwich Union and Rolls-Royce. Most have engaged in substantial downsizing and restructuring. They found that, in the main, the old corporate processes for supporting career development were played down, but did not disappear, in the late 1980s and early 1990s. New emphasis was placed on interventions aimed at getting employees to take responsibility for their own career development. This supported an earlier contention by Hirsh (1992) that there is a move away from formal succession planning systems: 'The current approach to succession centres on the consequences of a serious shift towards *employee self-development*. Some organisations now believe that the most robust approach towards succession rests on developing all employees to the limits of their potential.'

Approaches adopted included personal development plans, career workshops, development centres and learning resource centres. The approach differed from that adopted previously in three key respects.

1 They were designed to inform and support the individual rather than contribute specifically to organisational succession planning.
2 They were seen to apply to the whole work-force rather than being restricted to selected groups.
3 They were often designed and implemented at business unit level rather than centrally.

The evaluation of these initiatives by Hirsh and Jackson, which drew on interview data with line managers and researchers, produced a number of surprises.

1 The HR function was heavily criticised for constant tinkering with the processes. Nothing lasted long enough to be understood and used properly.
2 Small, fragmented HR functions located in the business units did not sustain their support. They were accused of breezing in, 'rolling out' initiatives and then disappearing in a cloud of dust.
3 Many of the interventions helped individuals to think about their careers, but few processes were set up for facilitating lateral job moves.
4 Line managers did not have the time, the information or the skills to offer career advice or to facilitate career moves.

5 A number of processes such as performance-related pay concentrate on short-term business objectives and accordingly do not encourage people to take individual career development seriously.

Their continuum postulated an ongoing pendulum swing between a centrally controlled organisation career structure and an individually focused do-it-yourself self-reliant model.

In some of the large consultancy and law firms graduate trainees, during their training for their professional exams, do not have to think for themselves. They are closely monitored, with the firm organising their working lives, so that they will have a higher chance of success in the examinations. They are what Hirsh and Jackson (1996) call 'first class ticket holders on the corporate train', with career moves largely planned by the organisation and employment guaranteed in the medium term.

Career plateauing

Walker (1992) believes that shrinking opportunities for promotion have resulted from the downsizing and delayering of large organisations. The consequence is that more and more employees 'are finding that their career is stagnating or "plateauing" at increasingly early ages. There is more competition for a diminishing number of higher-level positions for managers' (ibid.). He suggests a number of ways by which management can ameliorate the effects of fewer advancement opportunities. These include keeping job duties and responsibilities in a constant state of flux and hence more challenging and interesting.

Mid-career rustout

Leider and Buchholz (1995) have coined the term 'rustout' to refer to what happens when people's lives deteriorate through the disuse of their potential and they feel that they have plateaued. They contrast it to burnout which they define as 'overdoing'. Rustout is 'underbeing'. In their scenario rustout occurs when individuals feel they are not using their gifts and talents in support of something they believe in. Life lacks purpose, relationships lack commitment, work lacks promise, routine has stifled growth. They contend that the rustout syndrome is an endemic ailment in organisations, with a twofold impact. From the organisation's perspective rustout means less productivity and less ability to respond to emerging challenges. From a personal perspective rustout means that employees feel passive and unwilling to grow and change.

Career development for manual workers and semi-skilled operatives

Figure 8.6 examines one example of moves to introduce career development for manual workers and the semi-skilled.

| Figure 8.6 | Career workshops at Eli Lilly & Co Ltd |

The pharmaceutical company Eli Lilly has introduced a series of career decision-making workshops at its UK manufacturing site in Basingstoke which are available to any employee who wishes to attend. They focus on the individuals' taking control of their careers. Employees at Lilly manufacturing, some of whom have only single skills, are encouraged to think about how they can develop a wider range of skills. The workshops form part of a broader employability initiative which is aiming to make employees more employable in the marketplace as well as in the company. The objective from the company's point of view is to achieve continued competitiveness through a multi-skilled and flexible workforce.

The programme consists of three stages.

1 *Preparation* involves employees working through a workbook to identify personal values for work and home life; what gives them satisfaction at work; personal skills about which they seek feedback from two people whose opinion they value.

2 *A one-day workshop* involves participants in identifying a profile of their 'ideal' job based on personal skills and values; a comparison of the 'ideal' with jobs available in the company; the identification of possible target jobs and learning how to find out more about them.

3 *Follow-up* involves individuals taking responsibility for finding out more about the target jobs and identifying associated development needs.

There is no obligation for employees to share the outcomes of the programme with the line manager, although in practice most people do.

The workshops had such an enthusiastic take-up that within six months of the launch a quarter of all employees on the site had attended. Subsequently so many sought advice on what to do next from senior staff that Eli Lilly has introduced a training programme in counselling skills for managers.

From the perspective of the individual the benefits are seen as:

1 Identify personal skills, values and satisfaction drivers, and on the basis of that information assess whether a given job or area of work is suitable.

2 Develop a greater sense of personal control over career destination and responsibility for skill development.

3 Benefit from the opportunity to think about and discuss the range of career development alternatives.

From the perspective of the employer the benefits are seen as:

1 Encourage people to consider their progression and development in terms that are satisfactory to them (and beneficial to the business through greater motivation and productivity).

2 Create a work-force which is more flexible, adaptable and prepared to develop new skills.

3 Facilitate a move to multiskilling and employability in an increasingly competitive business environment.

Source: Based on King and Harrison (1998).

Lateral moves/cross careering

King and Harrison (op. cit.) make the point that in flatter organisational structures a number of traditional career options are no longer available. As an alternative, consideration could be given to lateral and cross-functional moves at the same organisational level. For this to be effectively undertaken, employees need to accept that this is a realistic form of career development. Those who are more likely to accept this are workers who have in the past been excluded from the career arena and from development opportunities in general. For such groups, however, career development is probably no more than a synonym for employee development. For those with managerial aspirations the situation is more problematic. Herriot *et al.* (1993) cite evidence that existing managers judge their future career aspirations on the basis of their career history and believe they are behind their career timetable if they do not continue to progress upwards as rapidly as they have done in the past.

Oral-B Laboratories Ireland is a manufacturing plant and the European distribution hub for the company's oral-care products, employing some 300 people and exporting to more than 40 countries. Its flat organisational structure provides limited opportunities for moving up the organisational ladder. Career development has accordingly been structured to incorporate horizontal as well as vertical moves. The lateral 'cross-careering' element has been implemented to broaden the skills base and to provide outlets for individuals who need to further their understanding of the business (Ryan, 1995).

One of the consequences of the focus on lateral moves as part of career development is that there is a blurring of the traditional distinction between 'employee development' and 'career development'.

Career routes for knowledge workers

Stewart (op. cit.) proposes a career model for knowledge workers based in project-oriented organisations such as specialist consultancies or computer houses operating at the forefront of the information age. He cites Frank Walker, the president of GTW Corporation, a USA-based enterprise selling project-management consulting services, software (in an alliance with Microsoft) and construction management services. Walker contends that project-oriented organisations have four basic levels. These are shown in Fig. 8.7.

- Level one – the *top management team,* operating at the strategy apex.
- Level two – the *resource providers,* responsible for developing and supplying talent, money and other resources. These include HR managers and finance officers as well as heads of traditional functional departments such as engineering and outsourced agencies.
- Level three – the *project managers,* who buy or lease resources from the resource providers by negotiating a budget and getting people assigned to a project.
- Level four – the *talent,* the specialist knowledge workers with in-depth occupational skills.

Figure 8.7 The four levels of the project organisation

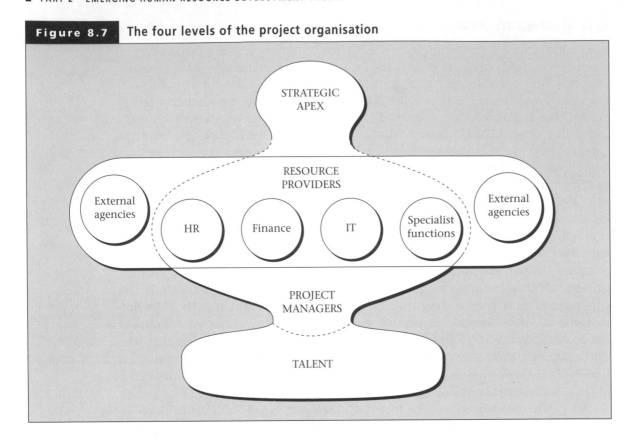

Figure 8.8 looks at the existence of these levels in a consultancy organisation.

Figure 8.8 The four-level career model in practice

Andersen Consulting is an organisation where some 80 per cent of employees are each engaged on one or more consulting assignments that can last from a few weeks to several years. Newcomers to the firm (*talent*) are attached to a regional office where an HR group (*a resource provider*) is responsible for overseeing the trainee consultant's development. The process entails liaising with lead consultants (*project managers*) in order to find appropriate assignments, co-ordinating feedback and helping to develop the analytical, technical and communication skills against which progress is measured.

The next posting is to an industry group, such as financial services or telecommunications, where consultancy assignments have a specific focus. Each of these has an HR team which act as resource provider and career developer.

With the acquisition of industry-specific knowledge, those who aspire to do so can move to the next stage, operating as a project manager, leading teams of *talent* in assignments of varying importance and complexity.

Andersen has a set of formal hierarchical levels consisting of 'consultant', 'manager', 'experienced manager' and 'partner' and these levels determine pay. However, according to Carol Meyers, the firm's world-wide head of human resources in 1997,

▶▶

▶▶ Figure 8.8 continued

> hierarchical decisions are not the key consideration in career development terms: 'Demand comes into the pipeline when someone makes a deal with a client and says "I need twenty-five people to do X on such-and-such a date". Supply comes in as people free up. Your career happens as we match supply and demand.'

Source: Stewart (1997, p. 205).

Thinking of careers in relation to projects leads Stewart to propose a number of ways in which choices and paths are affected.

1 *A career is a series of gigs driven by project management, not a series of steps driven by hierarchy.* The key determinant of success is the value and complexity of projects worked on. This can be contrasted to the situation in conventional hierarchical organisations in which being assigned a special project has often been considered to be the kiss of death.

2 *In a project-driven organisation, it follows that power flows from expertise, not from position.* The value and complexity of projects worked on is governed by the range of skills a worker is perceived to possess as indicated by feedback from previous projects worked on.

3 *Most roles in an organisation can be performed by outsiders as effectively as by insiders.* Thus, strategy setters as well as resource providers, project managers and talent, can be outsiders.

4 *Careers are made in markets, not hierarchies.* It helps workers to conceive of themselves as self-employed sub-contractors operating in a competitive market for work.

5 *The fundamental career choice is made, not between one company and another, but between specialising and generalising.* Many years ago Gouldner (1954) differentiated between 'cosmopolitans' whose primary allegiance was to their professional area and 'locals', who attached themselves to a given organisation. Stewart is suggesting that 'locals' are out of place in today's project-driven arena.

CONCLUSION

Much of the recent literature on career development has emphasised that in today's organisations there is no longer a guarantee of a career for life in a single institution and that individuals who were previously cosseted need to take greater responsibility for their own career development. Traditional approaches to career path analysis and targeted development are breaking down. This trend is borne out by empirical studies into a number of large corporations. These developments are taking place in parallel with moves towards creating horizontal development opportunities and inventing the notion of a lateral career as a way of compensating for reduced vertical progression opportunities. An outcome of this is that the boundaries between what constitutes career development and what constitutes employee development are becoming blurred. Every development activity can be seen as a career experience. In strategic terms there is an ongoing tension between employers expecting individuals to take responsiblity for their own career development; and yet using the existence of career development opportunities as an inducement and distinctive competence to attract the knowledge workers they are becoming dependent upon.

REFERENCES

Burgess, S., Rees, H. and Pacelli, L. (1997) 'Job Tenure and Labour Market Regulation: a Comparison of Britain and Italy using Micro Data'. CEPR discussion paper, October.

Cabinet Office (1994) 'Efficiency Unit Report'. London: Cabinet Office.

Finn, W. (1995) 'Born again Secondments', *Human Resources,* March/April.

Gouldner, A. W. (1954) *Patterns of Industrial Bureaucracy.* New York: Free Press.

Hall, D. T. (ed.) (1986) *Career Development in Organisations.* San Francisco: Jossey-Bass.

Herriot, P., Gibson, G., Pemberton, C. and Pinder, R. (1993) 'Dashed Hopes: Organisational Determinants and Personal Perceptions of Managerial Careers', *Journal of Occupational and Organisational Psychology,* 66, pp. 115–23.

Hirsh, W. (1992) Succession Planning: Current Practice and Future Issues', *Human Resource Management International Digest,* pp. 22–6.

Hirsh, W. and Jackson, C. (1996) 'Strategies for Career Development: Promise, Practice and Pretence', Institute of Employment Studies, Report No. 305.

Kaku, R. (1997) 'The path of Kyosei', *Harvard Business Review,* July–August, pp. 55–63.

King, Z. and Harrison, R. (1998) *The IPD Guide on Career Management in Organisations.* London: IPD.

Lee, C. (1997) 'The Hunt for Skilled Workers', *Training,* December.

Leider, R. and Buchholz, S. (1995) 'The rustout syndrome', *Training and Development* (US), March, pp. 7–9.

McLagan, P. (1989) *Models of HRD Practice.* ASTD Press.

Macnulty, W. K. (1985) 'UK change through a wide-angle lens', *Futures,* August.

Miller, E. J. and Rice, A. K. (1967) *Systems of Organisation – The Control of Task and Sentient Boundaries.* London: Tavistock.

Newmark, D., Polsky, D. and Hansen, D. (1997) 'Has job stability declined yet? New evidence for the 1990s'. NBER Working Paper, December.

Reich, R. B. (1991) *The Work of Nations Preparing Ourselves for Twenty-First Century Capitalism.* New York: Alfred A. Knopf.

Rosenbaum, R. E. (1984) *Career Mobility in a Corporate Bureaucracy.* New York: Academic Press.

Rothwell, W. and Kazanas, H. C. (1989) *Strategic HRD.* Englewood Cliffs, NJ: Prentice Hall.

Ryan, J. (1995) 'Giving people the chance to sparkle', *People Management,* 29 June.

Schein, E. H. (1978) *Career Dynamics: Matching individual and organisational needs.* Reading, MA: Addison-Wesley.

Smith, D. (1997) *Job Insecurity vs Labour Market Flexibility.* London: Social Market Foundation.

Stewart, T. A. (1997) *Intellectual Capital.* London: Nicholas Brealey.

Tame, J. (1993) 'Life Planning for Executives', *Long Range Planning,* 26(5).

Walker, J. W. (1980) *Human Resource Planning.* New York: McGraw-Hill.

Walker, J. W. (1992) *Human Resource Strategy.* New York: McGraw-Hill.

Waterman, R. H., Waterman, J. A. and Collard, B. A. (1994) 'Towards a Career Resilient Workforce', *Harvard Business Review,* July–August.

Chapter 9

MARKETING THE HUMAN RESOURCE DEVELOPMENT FUNCTION

OBJECTIVES

By the end of this chapter you should be able to:

- describe the basic principles of a marketing orientation to HRD;

- provide reasons why a marketing orientation could be appropriate in an HRD context;

- develop a marketing strategy for an HRD function.

INTRODUCTION

Over the years the HRD function has proved to be one of the most vulnerable areas to being downsized or dispensed with when an organisation is in a crisis or is looking for efficiency savings. One reason is that in financial terms, the provision of training and related activities has frequently been treated as one of the out-goings which can be foregone without the basic products or services of the organisation being sacrificed. Training, other than basic skills training, has often been seen as a luxury, and it has proved extremely difficult to establish any tangible relationship between the costs incurred and the benefits gained, especially in terms of the 'bottom line'. Those HRD departments which concentrate on course delivery, based at specialist in-house training centres, have been particularly affected because of the committed fixed costs involved.

The current emphasis on a skilled work-force being the only sustainable source of competitive advantage to an organisation should act as a powerful boost to protecting and promoting the function. National initiatives such as Investors in People (IiP) in the UK, and the increasing familiarity of senior managers with terms such as the Learning Organisation strengthen the case for HRD. Nevertheless, on the whole, HRD staff within organisations have proved themselves to be remarkably unable to promote their service. This has proved particularly true for departments which have concentrated on the provision of a predetermined, menu-driven set of in-house courses. They have fallen victim to a variety of internal and external pressures and threats against which they have had great difficulty in protecting themselves. These have ranged from competition from external providers, to cynicism from line managers about the value of in-house programmes, to a reluctance of staff to attend courses which for them have little status or esteem. Indeed, many exponents of the

Learning Organisation contrast its ethos and value orientation with that of a course-driven approach.

In some organisations HRD has the backing of the Chief Executive Officer, everyone talks about the Learning Organisation, the philosophy of learning seems embedded in the fabric and culture of the organisation. It is almost as if HRD markets itself. Even in such a situation it is not wise to be unduly sanguine. We are all subject to environmental and other forces which can rapidly change the situation. And even if HRD has a high profile, this is not to say that the HRD function is seen as being a necessary driver of learning.

This chapter is not just concerned with marketing HRD in large organisations which have the resources to sustain a training and development function. It offers a marketing perspective to all individuals with an HRD remit irrespective of organisation size. Let us take training in small and medium-sized enterprises (SMEs) as an instance of the difficulties in sustaining an HRD effort. Some training is of course vital. Operatives in a workshop, for example, must know the basic requirements of what they have to do. Sales staff must possess requisite product knowledge in order to deal with customers. Clerical staff need to know the operating systems and procedures which govern their activities. But as Hendry *et al.* (1988) pointed out in their analysis of SMEs the emphasis on training often lessens as soon as it is felt that staff possess the basic skills.

A marketing orientation will encourage HRD managers and others to think of their activities in terms of the relationship between the products or services they offer and the clientele or customers they are trying to reach. It will also help HRD practitioners to think about how and from whom they might gain support for the HRD effort. It is based on the proposition that HRD practitioners must 'convince the organisation that their products and services should be utilised; they [HRD practitioners] must see themselves as selling a specific set of products and services to the organisation' (Zemke, 1981).

The chapter follows a conventional path for thinking about marketing. What is less familiar is placing it in the context of learning terms. Whereas much marketing literature talks about products and achieving sales, in HRD terms we talk about identifying and satisfying learning needs. The chapter first addresses issues of market/customer segmentation. It will then try to establish ways of establishing a relationship between the HRD customer and the products and services offered. It will also address how HRD as an organisational function in its own right might be promoted.

The chapter will encourage HRD practitioners to think about their services in a broad way. For example, the provision of consultancy and mentoring services and conduct of training needs analyses should be considered as avenues for reaching and satisfying customers and meeting learning needs. It should cause readers to reflect on a consequence that faces HRD exponents who see HRD as a synonym for training. They are putting self-imposed restrictions on what they are marketing and may be concentrating their efforts on products and services that in marketing terms could be defined as 'dogs'.

The chapter will end by addressing a dilemma that confronts HRD. Is the marketing of learning the same as marketing the HRD function or marketing HRD programmes? Can learning be effectively orchestrated and enhanced and marketed without any need for a supporting function? This reiterates a point made in Chapter 4 where we address the nature of SHRD. Developing an organisational strategy for HRD is not the same as strategically managing an HRD function.

MARKET SEGMENTATION

A market is often perceived as an identifiable group of people from which customers for products and services can be drawn. A market segment is a subgroup which has 'special needs and preferences and which represents sufficient pockets of demand to justify separate marketing strategies' (Buell, 1984). According to Ohmae (1982) the aim of market segmentation is to understand whether different subgroups are in fact pursuing objectives that are different enough to warrant corporations (or competitors) offering differentiated products or services.

Obvious differences in age, race, gender, profession etc. may be the basis of segmentation. These constitute convenient statistical classes for helping to decide where the marketing effort should be directed. Life-style differences constitute another common basis for segmentation.

Effective segmentation can influence strategic decisions by virtue of careful analysis of the value each customer group perceives in the product or service – which will of course differ in accordance with their professed needs and wants and actual or desired life style.

Ohmae (op. cit.) argues that there are two basic modes of market segmentation.

Segmentation by customer objectives

Segmentation by customer objectives focuses on trying to identify the different motives of customers for using the product or service as a basis for determining how to reach them. Taking coffee as an example, some people drink it to wake up or keep alert, whereas others view it as a way to relax or socialise (coffee breaks). What effect should such knowledge have upon the marketing strategy?

In HRD terms, it is extremely useful to establish why people access (or not) learning opportunities. What is it that our customers deem to be valuable? Over the years I have run many in-house training courses for clients. Frequently I have experienced entirely different group attitudes to the same basic programme. For example one group consisting of low-grade manual workers was highly motivated because this was the first time that the organisation had invested in them; they felt special. Another group of more senior staff attending an identical programme were initially disaffected because they felt the course was beneath them.

It is worth emphasising that the *needs* arising out of *training needs analysis* are not 'needs' as understood in this marketing context. Training needs analysis (TNA), as conventionally undertaken, may establish the motives and attitudes of individuals towards work, but not to learning *per se*. This is because TNA is functionally oriented, concerned primarily with resolving performance issues and skills gaps at the workplace; the individual is accordingly not seen as an autonomous customer but as a functionary. Even on end-of-course evaluations, questions such as the following are rarely asked:

- 'Why did you come on this course?'
- 'Were you looking forward to it?'

Segmentation by customer objectives challenges this narrow perspective.

Segmentation by customer coverage

Even when there is a large group or subgroup of customers with similar wants and needs, the provider's ability to serve them all may be constrained by factors such as limited resources and the cost of serving a fragmented market at a price acceptable to the customer. This type of market segmentation normally results in a trade-off of product/market costs versus market coverage. Product costs are the direct costs of providing goods and services. Marketing costs may include the costs of promotion to establish brand awareness, sales activities, a servicing network, inventories to provide adequate delivery, etc.

In HRD terms, this leads to some extremely salient questions. How can we effectively meet the learning needs of the maximum number of people given the resources at our disposal? Are there groups with priority learning needs? Are there alternative products to, say, course-based learning which can reach as wide a spectrum of individuals as possible at an acceptable cost? What is the value orientation of those undertaking the cost versus coverage trade-off? Is the basic product of HRD off-the-job 'training' events or 'learning' activities?

Resegmenting the market

In a fiercely competitive market, the provider and its head-on competitors are likely to be dissecting the market in similar ways. Over time, therefore, the effectiveness of a strategic segmentation will tend to decline. In such a situation, it often pays to pick a small group of key customers and re-examine what they are really looking for.

Furthermore, environmental forces such as threats of replacement from other types of products and services are constantly changing customers' likes/dislikes, and shifting their purchasing priorities.

In HRD terms, training and development departments have been under a range of pressures as customers' priorities have shifted, and the people responsible for commissioning services have changed. To give but one example, in recent years there has been significant devolution of budgetary autonomy to line managers. Alongside this has been increased discretion as to whether to use in-house functions for the provision of specialised services such as training and development. Even organisations which specify as a matter of HRD policy that each individual is entitled to a certain number of days training per year, may leave it to the discretion of individual managers (or the individuals themselves) whether this is undertaken in house or externally.

CLASSIFYING LEARNERS BY MARKET SEGMENT

According to Rothwell and Kazanas (1989), HRD practitioners have to assess learning needs and talents according to precise learner characteristics. They contend that there are at least four possible ways of segmenting the market for such an HRD effort:

- The job market;
- The individual or career market;
- The work group market;
- The external market.

For each of these markets they identify a distinctive generic HRD response – a form of linked market coverage or market needs segmentation. As we shall see, this is influenced by an unstated assumption that one is operating within a large and rather mechanistic organisational setting.

For the purposes of this text I have modified and added to the original Rothwell and Kazanas classification, partly to reflect usage more familiar to a UK readership and partly to give it a more up-to-date flavour (*see* Table 9.1).

Table 9.1 Revision of terms relating to human resource development market coverage and market needs segmentation

Walton	Rothwell and Kazanas	Market
Employee training	Employee training	Job market
Employee development	Employee education	Individual/ career market
Management development	–	Individual/career market
Team development	Employee development	Work group
Employee education	–	Individual
Non-employee training	Non-employee development	Job market
Non-employee development	Non-employee development	Individual/career market
Non employee education	Non employee development	Individual/ external groups

The job market

One way to classify learners is to group them by their formal role, consisting of job tasks and responsibilities. One then establishes the performance criteria expected of an experienced member of staff occupying such a role and then assesses learners in terms of knowledge, skills and attitude gaps. The HRD need is role-specific *employee training*, seen by Nadler (1979) as a short-term change effort, geared to producing immediate, observable results and to socialising individuals into an organisation. It includes induction training, but also encompasses identifying and remedying performance discrepancies for more established workers. Rothwell and Kazanas suggest as a possible classification system of the market:

1 Senior managers;

2 Middle managers;

3 First-line supervisors;

4 Professionals;

5 Administrative staff;

6 Clerical support;

7 Skilled production or service workers;

8 Semi-skilled production or service workers.

This is a somewhat hierarchical classification for today's delayered organisations and the method is not to everyone's taste, being seen as overly mechanistic in an environment where job boundaries are rapidly changing. Many would also challenge the proposition that specific performance gaps that are amenable to short-term training solutions are appropriate for senior managers.

The individual or career market

A second way to classify learners is on the basis of individual career development prospects in a given organisation. The need is 'employee development' to prepare an individual for movement to other jobs. It also upgrades skills and elicits new insights. It is related to performance appraisal and succession planning, continuous personal development and the development of transferable skills.

A particular form of employee development, to which Rothwell and Kazanas make no reference, is management development, which seems worthy of separate classification.

The work group or department market

A third way to classify learners is on the basis of work groups. Team development (as opposed to 'employee development', the term used by Rothwell and Kazanas) is geared to creating a collective mix of employee skills appropriate to the responsibilities of the work group or department. These authors restrict a work group to a supervisor and her/his immediate subordinates and emphasise the role of the supervisor. They suggest that to prepare a long-term plan for team development, each supervisor should examine:

■ the purpose of the work group;

■ the differences between how the group should be performing and how it is actually performing;

■ the human skills and knowledge which can narrow the gap between desired and actual results over time;

■ the methods of obtaining necessary skills and knowledge.

Their notion of 'work group' seems insufficiently developed and very narrowly defined given the range of permanent and semi-permanent team situations that one confronts in organisational settings. They also seem to be operating from a control and command perspective in the way they talk about the role of the supervisor in determining the learning needs of the group. Such a view fits uneasily with today's emphasis on team building and autonomous work groups. It also does not recognise the weight of empirical evidence suggesting that many team problems are caused by the leadership style of the manager or supervisor.

The external market

Employees should not be considered the only potential customers for planned learning activities. A number of external groups which have a relationship with the organisation may also have learning needs worth addressing. Rothwell and Kazanas refer to non-employee development, ranging from short-term to long-term instructional efforts geared to meeting the learning needs of people outside an organisation, as meeting the needs of this market. Benefits include the creation of:

> consumers who know how to use company products and services, suppliers who are aware of unique needs of an organisation with which they transact business, distributors who are familiar enough with organisation products or services to market them effectively to consumers, and members of the general public or community who understand the unique needs and problems of an employer (Rothwell and Kazanas, op. cit.).

Quite clearly, Rothwell and Kazanas are thinking in terms of markets from the perspective of how they relate to a given organisation. Their formulation excludes, for example, training for individuals who are unemployed. Yet, at national level, governments have sought to create learning opportunities which such individuals could access to equip them with the skills and abilities to apply for jobs in a given occupational area. Is this a different market segment?

| Figure 9.1 | Segmenting by learning need |

Another way of segmenting the market is more specifically in terms of categories of needs. This is the approach taken by Guardian Insurance National Partnerships Division in the UK. They aim to identify all learning needs of internal staff and external business partners at the earliest opportunity so that they can be addressed in a timely fashion. Their 1997 Training Policy Guidelines state:

Categories of Needs

Learning needs can occur for many different reasons but the challenge for the business is to recognise these quickly. It helps to think of learning needs as being driven by the following situations:

1 *New entrants* – learning for those who are newly recruited, changing jobs, changing responsibilities or being promoted.

▶▶

▶▶ Figure 9.1 continued

> **2** *Change* – learning for those whose jobs will be affected by changes to systems, procedures, products, services, legislation, etc. Ensuring we have correct skill sets to match the needs of prospective, new or existing Partners is crucial.
>
> **3** *Improvement* – learning to improve current work performance due either to required improvements in individual or operational performance.
>
> **4** *Long-term development* – development of people to meet the long-term requirements of National Partnerships Division and its Partners as well as individual aspirations.

CUSTOMER ANALYSIS

Customer analysis is an extension of market segmentation. Wilson *et al.* (1992) contend that for the majority of products or services, identifying the buyer is a relatively straightforward activity. Nevertheless the decision of what and whether to buy can involve several people occupying separate roles. They distinguish between:

- the *initiator* who first suggests buying the product or service;
- the *influencer* whose comments affect the decision made;
- the *decider* who ultimately makes all or part of the buying decision;
- the *buyer* who physically makes the purchase;
- the *users* who consume the product or service.

In HRD terms customer analysis can become quite complex. In the 1980s a number of organisations in the UK, particularly local authorities, decided that all members of staff involved in interviewing needed to attend an Equal Opportunity Recruitment and Selection programme. The *initiator* would be the majority political party. It would often draw on an Equal Opportunity Adviser who would *influence* the decision on where to look for suitable providers of the resultant interviewing courses. The *decision* on which provider to opt for could be made by a panel including personnel and training officers. The *buyer* often was the Central Training Manager. The *users* consisted of managers of organisational functions, attending whether they wanted to or not.

A customer orientation should not be particularly unfamiliar to HRD practitioners who have been associated with Total Quality Management (TQM) initiatives where the customer – internal or external – is seen as a primary focus.

Segmentation and loyalty

It is an interesting exercise for HRD departments to establish which departments take most advantage of their services. This is particularly significant in view of the tendency to decentralise decision making to autonomous business units and to afford divisional heads discretion as to whether they take advantage of in-house services or go to external providers. Table 9.2 provides an example of such an analysis.

Table 9.2 Analysis of loyalty patterns

Loyalty classification	Buying patterns							
Hard-core loyals	X	X	X	X	X	X		
Soft-core loyals	X	X	Y	X	Y	Y		
Shifting loyals	X	X	X	Y	Y	Y	Z	Z	Z
Switchers	X	Y	Z	X	Y	Z		

Key
X = Consistent use of in-house services
Y = Use of one alternative provider
Z = Use of another alternative provider

Source: Based on Wilson *et al.* (1992).

The analysis is undertaken in the context of an HRD operation which sees its rationale as being the provision of training programmes. A contrast would be provided by the view of HRD in a learning organisation such as Rover, where line managers are seen as instrumental in facilitating learning for individuals who are responsible for their own learning.

Thus the issue becomes: are learners, as conventionally defined, the real customers for an HRD function? They may be the end beneficiaries of an HRD effort, but those responsible for an HRD function have to be concerned with enlisting support and sponsorship. How one perceives one's customer base has enormous impact on how one promotes one's service.

THE MARKETING MIX

Marketing has a particular concern with identifying and meeting customer needs. Whereas market segmentation and customer analysis are concerned with establishing sources of current and potential customers, the next stage of marketing is concerned with strategies for effectively reaching the customer. What is the relationship between what the customer wants and what the provider can offer? How can one achieve successful matching of customer needs with a provider's abilities? A way of developing a coherent strategy for reaching customers is through devising an effective marketing mix. The main components of the marketing mix are:

■ product or service;
■ promotion;
■ price;
■ place.

Each of these components of the marketing mix will be looked at in terms of what they might mean in an HRD context.

PRODUCT

What does it mean to talk about a product in an HRD context? Let us take a course. Is it the course? Is it the location? Is it the tutors who deliver it? Is it all of these? Are there any attributes that specifically make a given course distinctive?

The term product can be used to refer to each of:

■ physical goods;

■ services; and

■ 'intangibles'.

In HRD terms a physical good could be a set of materials to support distance learning. A service could be the conduct of a training needs analysis or the provision of mentoring. An 'intangible' could be the ideas which are generated in a particular learning environment. A training course would consist of elements of all three.

For an HRD process consultant who is, for example, facilitating action learning for a client, the service is clear enough, but from the client's perspective the product includes the consultant who is providing the service. In marketing terms, it is as though the consultant becomes a 'physical good' with specific attributes.

Kotler (1988) suggests that three distinct elements need to be considered in determining the nature of a product. These are:

■ the product's attributes;

■ its benefits;

■ the nature of the support services.

Product attributes are associated with the core product and include such elements as brand name, packaging, size and colour variants.

Product benefits are the elements that consumers perceive as meeting their needs. These are sometimes referred to as the 'bundle of potential satisfactions' that the product represents. Included in this bundle are the product's performance and its image.

The *marketing support services* consist of all the elements that the organisation provides in addition to the core product. These typically include delivery, installation, after-sales service and reputation.

It is quite revealing to look at advertisements for specific products and to identify which of these aspects of a product are being emphasised.

It is a useful undertaking for HRD providers to reflect on the above attributes and benefits for a given product or service and establish:

■ their relative importance to the consumer; and

■ the consumer's perception of them.

To some extent this is done through course evaluation 'happiness' sheets. When one asks for delegates' views on individual trainers, what they felt about the location, whether the joining instructions were sufficiently clear, one is in effect asking for feedback on the product's performance.

An understanding of consumers' perceptions can enable modification of the product, for example:

- adding features (real repositioning);
- changing beliefs about it by giving greater emphasis to particular attributes (psychological repositioning);
- changing the relative importance of particular attributes.

It is worth emphasising that in marketing terms customers are often held to be more interested in the benefits they obtain from buying a particular product than in the product itself. This is particularly true for a number of HRD-oriented activities. Macdonald (1984) suggests a simple formula to ensure that this customer-oriented way of looking at things is adopted. Always use the phrase 'which means that' to link a feature to the benefit it brings. Thus:

- 'A course handbook has been produced *which means that* you are provided with a detailed synopsis of the programme together with learning philosophy adopted . . .'; or
- 'An HRD policy statement has been produced stating that all staff members are entitled to 40 hours off-the-job formal learning each year, *which means that* you have a clear picture of our commitment to your development.'

Macdonald also feels that one should undertake detailed analyses to identify the full range of benefits being offered to the customer, as a prelude to comparing these against the full range of benefits that customers actually want or will respond to.

Boston matrix

One way of thinking about the products and services that you offer is to engage in a portfolio analysis. The best known is the Boston Matrix, designed in the United States by the Boston Consulting Group (*see* BCG, 1971) to assess the 'cash flow dynamics' in a given portfolio of products. The Boston Matrix is a particularly effective way to think about training course provision but can be applied to other areas of the HRD effort such as the growth of internal consultancy provision.

The model recognises that for many organisations the products being evaluated are at different stages of their life cycle. In the original matrix products are classified according to two dimensions: *market share* relative to that of the largest competitor, and *market growth rate*.

Market share

The product's market share relative to its competitors indicates the extent to which it can generate cash.

Market growth rate

The market growth rate gives an indication of the extent to which the product will use cash. In a fast-growing market a product will be a high user of cash in order to support the development and usage of materials, high promotion costs, etc.

Product types

Products are then further classified into four cells against these two dimensions:

1 Dogs (low market share, low market growth)

Dogs are products that have a weak market share in a low-growth market. Typically they generate either a low profit or return a loss. If one holds a dog one must decide whether to hold on to it for strategic reasons or to phase it out. Dog products frequently take up more time than they can justify and divert resources and attention away from more attractive propositions. Many courses which once were popular can become dogs as fashions and requirements change. For example supervisory skills training was very common in the 1970s but less so in the down-sized 1990s. Often there is a temptation to hang on too long to courses which have reached the end of their life cycle, perhaps because of allegiance to the providers of the course, perhaps because the training manager has in the past personally identified with the programme.

2 Question marks or problem children (low market share, high market growth)

These are products which are operating in high-growth markets but with a relatively low market share. They generally require considerable sums of cash to sustain them because of the need to keep abreast of market developments. The term 'question mark' or 'problem child' is used because management has to decide whether to continue investing or to withdraw from the market. It is tempting for a training department, for example, to offer courses in an area which has become fashionable, or which is of considerable business value. However, perhaps for reasons of credibility (in-house staff offering strategy management programmes) or perhaps because the culture is not yet right (managing diversity programmes which other organisations are offering in house) potential customers either go to external providers or do not attend.

3 Stars (high market share, high market growth)

Stars are products which have moved into the position of leadership in a high-growth market. As stars also generate large amounts of cash, on balance there is unlikely to be any positive or negative cash flow until the rate of market growth declines and the product becomes a cash cow. In HRD terms stars are those courses which suddenly become the centre of attention. Equal Opportunity programmes fitted into this category for many public sector organisations in the 1980s. There was a surge of demand, which in the short term could not readily be met by training providers. The effect was to hoist the price.

4 Cash cows (high market share, low market growth)

When the rate of market growth declines, stars typically become cash cows. Such products can generate large sums of cash, but, because of the lower rate of growth, use relatively little. In HRD terms, we could be talking about courses for which there is a consistent high demand, and which are well established.

It can be a useful exercise to plot the current range of HRD provision on the Boston Grid style matrix shown in Fig. 9.2.

Figure 9.2	Human resource development portfolio matrix

	High demand	Low demand
High growth	STARS	QUESTION MARKS
Low growth	CASH COWS	DOGS

Product life cycle

An associated approach is to think where each course fits in terms of a product life cycle. The concept of the product life cycle suggests that any product moves through a sequence of identifiable stages, each of which is related to the passage of time and the generation of demand.

1 *Introductory phase.* Many products do not survive this stage. For example customers may not believe that the product will do what it promises. New skills will have to be learned, and there may still be competition with an older product. At first the new product may not compete well on cost and performance. There will be teething problems and there will be a need to invest a lot of time and energy in keeping an eye on things.

2 *Growth phase.* Product benefits by now have become accepted. More people want to avail themselves of the product and demand can grow quite rapidly, carried forward by a sort of bandwagon effect. The product can turn into a 'star'.

3 *Maturity phase.* No market is infinitely expandable. Demand peaks and stabilises. Product modifications and promotion ploys are used to sustain demand and to ensure that the benefits remain current. There is a tendency increasingly to look for untapped market segments.

4 *Saturation phase.* Similar products are now available from a variety of sources. In HRD terms there is a range of providers offering their services, and this tends to bring the price down. The number of providers outstrips the demand and some providers stop offering the product. It goes into decline.

5 *Decline/dying stage.* The product has come to the end of its profitable life cycle. It has become a 'dog' and should be allowed to die. Continuance of the product is associated with seriously declining demand and expensive or non-effective promotion. Continued production is sustained for reasons of sentiment not of logic.

It is held to be important to have products at different stages of the life cycle. For example, it is only at the later stages of the life cycle that products become net cash generators. They will help to fund emergent and developing products which will become future cash cows.

Figure 9.3 The stage reached by US human resource development programmes in the product life cycle, 1987

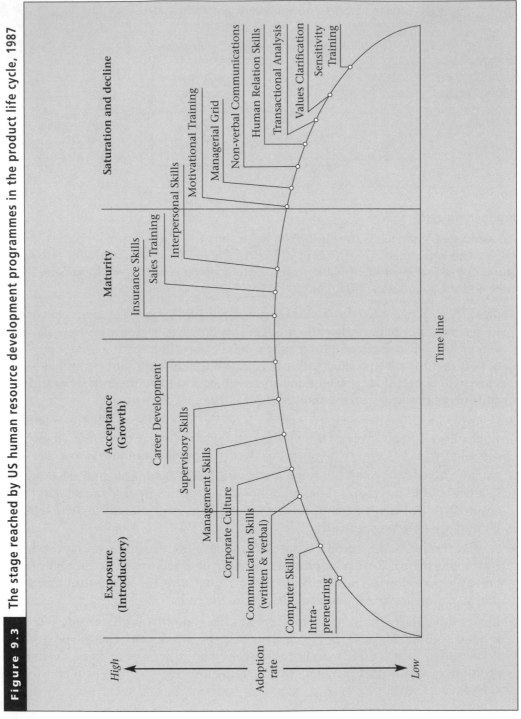

Source: Based on Gilley (1987).

It is important to think of HRD 'products' other than courses. For example, many large companies in the 1970s invested in large prestigious management training centres, often converting large country houses for this purpose. How many are still used for this purpose? Outdoor training has become a very competitive aspect of management development. Is there an overprovision of providers? NVQs and IiP did not exist in 1985. Where do they fit on the product life cycle model in UK organisations? What about 'corporate universities'?

Gilley (1987) asked a similar set of questions in respect of courses and other HRD-related initiatives in the USA in the mid-1980s. Figure 9.3 presents the findings in terms of the stage of these programmes in the product life cycle.

How accurate have Gilley's predictions been in the years since 1987?

PROMOTION

Promotion can be defined as the process of communicating effectively with the people or organisations who are existing or potential customers or clients. The basic purpose of such communication is to create a favourable image of one's own operation and its products or services. Successful promotion in traditional HRD terms should lead to maintaining or increasing the range of services provided, consistent support from key stakeholders and the existence of a positive climate for learning. Promotion of learning as a strategic tool can go substantially beyond this rather narrow perspective, as CEOs and divisional directors, through roadshows, international conferences and other devices, try to get staff to support transformational change efforts that redirect the energies of an entire corporation.

Promotional methods are often referred to as primary sources of communication since costs are under one's direct control. Of particular significance to HRD practitioners are personal selling and advertising.

Personal selling

Personal selling entails person-to-person contact either face to face or by telephone. Personal communication allows the approach to be tailored to each individual with whom contact is being made. It enables dialogue and feedback. Personal selling can be done through mechanisms such as visits, conferences or initiating or responding to enquiries by telephone. It is vital to use appropriate techniques for gaining entry to and establishing trust with a customer.

It is useful to reflect on the fact that whenever one endeavours to convey to a manager or member of staff the value of a given HRD based activity, one is at the same time sending messages about the value of learning and the importance of generally HRD.

Figure 9.4 looks at the question of trainer credibility.

> | Figure 9.4 | Trainer credibility |
>
> 'One of the biggest problems faced by any training department is ensuring that it remains in touch with what is really happening in the organisation.
>
> A training department must therefore develop a staffing policy that requires most of the trainers to have experience of the subject to be taught. This is rather a basic principle, but it is often ignored. When adhered to, it can begin to establish the elusive credibility that is essential for a good training department.
>
> Notice that I said *most* of the trainers. I disagree with the notion that the department must consist entirely of successful field personnel. A realistic combination of talents can keep a department from developing a 'tunnel vision' approach to ideas and techniques. Diversity breeds change and creativity, which are imperative in any department, especially a training department. One formula for an ideal department calls for 75 per cent of the training staff members to be from the field, teaching exactly the areas they previously worked in. The other 25 per cent of the training staff would have related experience.
>
> The next step a training department should take to build credibility is to develop a plan to keep the department relevant. In other words, it must make sure trainers know their stuff – not only when they are first hired, but throughout their tenure with the organisation. Some organisations think they are adhering to this policy simply by sending to training presenters copies of all literature, magazines, memos and correspondence that relate to their particular topics of expertise.
>
> I am not saying that such information is not important and that it should not be read. But the most successful approach to ensuring that relevance is maintained is to send the presenter out of the office regularly, and into the field where she or he belongs. One day of field observation or coaching is more valuable than a week of perusing literature and documentation of any type.
>
> Getting trainers out into the areas where the actual work is being performed is valuable in more ways than one. It makes a strong statement to those who question the credibility of the training department and who see it as 'out of touch'. It also boosts a presenter's confidence.'
>
> These opinions were expressed by Robert Jolles (1994) in an article in *Training and Development* entitled 'R-E-S-P-E-C-T'.
>
> *What are your views on them? Should prior subject-specific experience in the field and regular field exposure be a requirement for direct trainers? How effective as a promotional tool is drawing on people from the field?*

Advertising

Some advertising is designed to do no more than *inform* its audience about an organisation or operation and its products and services. Much of advertising, however, is designed to *persuade* an audience about specific product benefits and to give reasons why a particular product or service is superior to others. An effective persuasive advertisement should attract and sustain interest, create a desire to buy the product or service and encourage action to buy. Advertising which *reinforces* existing positive attitudes tells the customer that the provider is still able to offer the same degree of service and satisfaction as ever. As a general rule about advertising, it is important to stay *visible*.

Secondary sources of communication are those which are not under one's direct control and for which one does not have to pay. They include word of mouth and personal recommendation. In some ways, secondary sources of communication can be more influential than primary sources in determining the success or otherwise of the HRD effort – for example, what delegates say to their colleagues about a given course when they return to their workplace. Equally, an HRD practitioner operating as an internal consultant on, say, action learning facilitation is very dependent on getting favourable comments made by her or his client in respect of the level and type of support provided.

In a strategic sense, it is of crucial significance if one is operating in a particular organisation to promote the overall HRD effort in such a way as to obtain ongoing support from sponsors. In this respect it is important first to publish a statement of intent. A typical example is that produced by the Information Technology Services Agency (ITSA) which has operated since 1990 as an Executive Agency of the UK Department of Social Security:

> ITSA is investing in the continuous Development and Training of all our people to equip them with the necessary skills, knowledge and attitudes to make the maximum contribution to the business success. It is vital that such activities are undertaken as a partnership between individuals, their line managers and HR managers.

Another example is that produced by Rexam plc, a multinational organisation which until mid-1995 traded in the UK as Bowater plc. One of their core principles is:

> We believe that people make the difference. We insist on integrity and respect for personal values. Our success depends on incorporating different cultures and people who make learning a lifelong experience. We develop world class people through training and education (Butler, Letza and Neale, 1997).

Rothwell and Kazanas (op. cit.) suggest that a fruitful way to build support for an organisational strategy for HRD is to create a standing advisory committee. Such a committee should ideally include top management representation. The claimed advantages of a committee include that it:

■ makes HRD activities more visible;

■ underscores the responsiveness of hrd practitioners to meeting needs;

■ sets priorities while allowing for many perspectives and viewpoints;

■ settles jurisdictional issues;

■ co-ordinates activities when solutions are difficult to reach;

■ enhances the personal and professional development of members.

One American example from the public sector is the Human Resources Advisory Council of the Governor of the State of Illinois. As part of its operations it has developed a human resource model that is designed to support a human resource system based on skill matching and merit progression (State of Illinois, 1993, pp. 15, 59).

Rothwell and Kazanas go on to suggest that such a committee would work best in organisations with clearly defined departmental structures, although they do not provide supporting evidence for this. They contend that in establishing a committee one should take the following steps.

1 Clarify its purpose and objectives from the outset. For example there should be a basic purpose statement such as:

The purpose of the HRD Advisory Committee is to establish priorities and guidelines for the selection, scheduling, development and evaluation of all staff training, education and development. It shall provide the Director of HRD with advice on selection and scheduling of formal and informal learning experiences, and evaluate the effectiveness of the HRD effort.

2 Select members who are in sympathy with the committee's purpose.

3 Establish a way of maintaining some continuity on the committee while at the same time ensuring that there is a regular infusion of new members so that the group does not stagnate.

4 Find ways to feed back to the committee information for decisions and results of prior decisions or recommendations.

5 Build member involvement without burdening members with so many demands and so much information that they become unable or unwilling to participate in decision making. Involvement is increased if committees are chaired by a member, not by an HRD practitioner.

It is unwise to establish an advisory committee without first assessing how much top management support it will receive, and, once the idea is accepted, what 'training' members will require. It is unreasonable to expect managers or employees to advise on HRD issues which they know little about.

An organisation that went beyond the advisory committee is Motorola, which in 1980 set up an education service department to carry out an organisation-wide re-education and training programme. The Motorola Training and Education Centre (MTEC) had its own board of directors consisting of the CEO, two other top executives and senior managers from each of Motorola's operating units. That in turn was just a stepping-stone to the top management support provided for the corporate university (Wiggenhorn, 1990). In a number of organisations, the device of a corporate university is enabling divisional heads to sponsor learning in the capacity of Dean.

Figure 9.5   **The heart of human resource development partnerships**

Chip Bell, in the January 1995 edition of the American Society for Training and Development journal *Training and Development,* asks:

Why do some training departments grow and prosper while others get outsourced? According to management guru Peter Drucker, outsourcing is about quality, not cost. The decision to let external suppliers take over an internal unit isn't due to negative economics; it's due to a lack of perceived value in terms of cost, outcome, and service.

What makes internal customers rate a service experience highly enough so that they'll fight to keep it from being outsourced?

▶▶

▶▶ Figure 9.5 continued

He goes on:

> In the case of a training department, good service alone won't keep the wolves at bay. Most training departments give good service. But those that survive achieve more; they develop partnerships with their customers. When the words 'We're going to outsource the training department' are spoken on Mahogany Row, loyal customers say, 'No way. The internal training department is just too vital.'
>
> Long-term loyalty comes from partnerships between customers and service providers. People who feel as if they are partners and not just customers tend to be more committed, realistic, and mature in their expectations. They don't expect to be delighted with every encounter. They forgive mistakes and champion the service provider to others. And they give candid feedback for improved service.
>
> We trainers in our pursuit of credibility in boardrooms tend to wrap customer relationships in numbers. We talk about ROI and cost justification. But most decision makers base their judgments of the training unit on anecdotal evidence – what internal customers say. Those tales defy tallies.
>
> So what is the stuff of which partnerships are made? Pick up any 'cookbook' on partnerships and you'll find the ingredients: mutual goals, candid communication, and shared values. The recipe is to know where you're going and then to communicate along the way. But there are other essentials. If customers use training only because they need it, they won't hesitate to swing the axe at budget-cutting time. But when customers think training contributes to their work lives, they'll become 'apostles' – advocates who champion one's value to others.

Chip Bell goes on to contend that the heart of a partnership holds a passionate connection, undying faith and an attitude of abundance. The following list shows his approach to passionate connection.

Is it too culturally specific to be applicable outside of the US or are there any messages for an international audience?

Putting in the passion

Here are some actions you can take to passionately connect with your customers.

- Communicate in active language.
- Replace sombreness with joy in all of your correspondence.
- Approach customers with optimism and confidence.
- Send notes of appreciation to training team members for valued actions.
- Seek opportunities to compliment customers. Get fans by becoming a fan.
- Visit customers. Attend events that are important to them.
- Give customers resources on topics they're interested in. Include a note: 'Thought you might find this useful.'
- Conduct needs analyses in person, not with mail-in surveys.
- Listen to customers in ways that make them feel their inputs are valued and make a difference.
- Follow up, follow up, and follow up.

▶▶

▶▶ Figure 9.5 continued

> The Chip Bell perspective is interesting and contains some fascinating insights into his way of thinking. But he is seeing HRD in training terms. This provides a very limited array of activities for the HRD exponent to be involved in. Throughout this book the point is made that policy makers and strategists in leading-edge organisations see training as only one component of a holistic learning ideology. Interest is focused on notions such as continuous learning and the corporate university in which line managers play a substantial and critical part. To repeat the message from previous chapters: HRD professionals need to demonstrate that they have the strategic awareness to be trusted with the leverage of individual knowledge and the skills of team working into a mainstream platform leading to competitive survival and advantage. Just as Beer and his Harvard colleagues argued in the 1980s (Beer *et al.*, 1984) that HRM was too important to be left to HR professionals, so too there is a risk that the same argument will be applied to HRD.

PRICE

Price is becoming an issue for many in-house HRD providers, because of the increasing requirement that they charge users for their services as opposed to HRD-related activities being seen as a fixed overhead, controlled centrally. This requirement is associated with a trend in organisations towards responsibility accounting, with each individual department being responsible for its own budget and having to justify specific outgoings. Departmental heads in such a situation will look very carefully at the costs incurred in using an in-house HRD service, and will make comparisons against the price charged by external providers for similar services.

In price/cost terms, in-house providers are always at a disadvantage to compared external providers because of the fixed costs involved. A number of external suppliers market their consultancy services on the basis that they can allow organisations to move from a fixed to a variable cost regime.

Price sensitivity

In setting a price it is quite obviously necessary to have a clear understanding of the likely effect that a given price will have on levels and patterns of demand. Price sensitivity relates to the extent to which a potential customer's decision to buy is influenced by price. If customer demand is largely unaffected by price changes then it is said to be 'inelastic' to price. An 'elastic' market is very sensitive to price changes. Nagle (1987) has produced the following list of principal influencing factors on consumers.

1 The *unique value effect*: the more distinctive a product is, the less price sensitive buyers become.

2 The *substitute awareness effect*: the more aware consumers become of substitute products, the greater their price sensitivity.

3 The *difficult comparison effect*: the more difficult it is to make direct comparisons between products, the less price sensitive consumers are likely to be.

4 The *total expenditure effect*: the lower the expenditure is as a proportion of consumers' total income, the lower the degree of price sensitivity.

5 The *end-benefit effect*: as perceived benefit increases, so price sensitivity reduces.

6 The *sunk investment effect*: when the product is used in association with products bought previously, price sensitivity is reduced.

7 The *shared-cost effect*: price sensitivity is reduced when the costs are shared with one or more parties.

8 The *price–quality effect*: the greater the degree of perceived quality or exclusiveness, the lower the price sensitivity.

9 The *inventory effect*: when the product cannot be stored and consumption takes place immediately, price sensitivity again reduces.

Some HRD products are very price sensitive because of perceptions of what is on offer compared to what is available 'out there' in the external marketplace. It is very revealing to undertake, for in-house courses, an exercise establishing the relationship between price and 'product' positioning. 'Positioning' refers to how the courses are viewed by customers in comparison with similar courses. For example, are they viewed as quality or prestige products such as a Rolls-Royce, which has a cachet value? One must decide what position one wants the courses to hold in relation to customer perceptions. A central issue is to establish how the people delivering the courses are perceived and whether these perceptions can be changed. For example, can the marketing mix be changed by engaging in promotional activities which will influence product perceptions and thus price and usage?

A similar exercise could be undertaken in respect of the provision of internal consultancy services. Price may not be the key determinant. The question might well be whether the internal staff have the credibility or cachet value to compete with external consultants from high-profile organisations or those with a high reputation.

Figure 9.6 presents the principles of offensive pricing. These principles are of particular significance to external HRD consultants, as they reflect on the commercial aspects of their contract with a given client.

Figure 9.6 **The principles of offensive pricing**

1 Know the price dynamics

Pricing decisions must be based on a detailed understanding of the nature and degree of existing price sensitivity. In some markets, for example, overall demand may be generally inelastic whereas the demand for individual brands may be highly price responsive. Consider therefore:

■ the frequency of purchase: as a general rule of thumb, levels of price sensitivity increase with the frequency of purchase;

■ the degree of necessity: greater need means lower sensitivity;

■ unit price: high prices lead to greater price consciousness;

■ the degree of comparability: if easy, price awareness increases;

■ the degree of fashion or status: as this increases, the direct importance of price reduces.

▶▶

▶▶ Figure 9.6 continued

2 Strengthen pricing muscles

By placing a greater emphasis to non-price features such as higher quality, packaging, advertising and after-sales service, one can change the nature of the selling proposition in one's favour.

3 Choose price segments

In choosing segments of the market in which to operate, one needs to consider the implications for pricing and one's ability to operate effectively. In certain market sectors, for example, the prerequisite is not that one currently has a low cost base, but that one is capable of maintaining this cost base over time. One needs to consider the relative profitability of each segment; the fit between the segment and what one can offer; and competitors' intentions and capabilities.

4 Consider the alternatives

How might price be integrated most effectively with other elements of the marketing mix to reduce its direct significance?

5 Manage the ripples

In most competitive markets, different buyers pay different prices depending on their purchase volumes, delivery methods, servicing demands and negotiating skills. Because of the potential sensitivity of this, one needs to give emphasis to: a clearly communicated trading strategy; understanding the cost implications of altering the above variables; building long-term relationships so that the implications of problems arising from the above can be reduced.

6 Beware of profit cannibalisation

Marketing one product can significantly reduce the profit on another.

7 Rectify pricing mistakes quickly

If one makes a pricing mistake, admit it and remedy it fast.

8 Beware of markets with falling prices

One can only survive in markets with falling prices if one is confident that one has a competitive edge which can be maintained over competitors.

Source: Davidson (1987).

PLACE

Place is the final ingredient of the marketing mix. It relates to the locations or outlets from which customers can access the product or service. Issues addressed include logistical decisions about how the product or service reaches the customer and the associated distribution costs. In HRD terms, a decision about place has been made whenever classroom-based courses are replaced by a distance learning approach.

Effective logistics management is concerned with trying to ensure that a given product or service is available to customers when and where they want it. The resulting costs should be outweighed by the benefits which this level of service generates, in terms of increased demand or utilisation. In an attempt to reach learners more effectively, many organisations are setting up open learning drop-in centres. Some global organisations are experimenting with videoconferencing. However, to keep costs down – and also to be able to offer a greater choice of sites – attention is increasingly being given to working through centres shared with other organisations. This is particularly true of SMEs that cannot support their own centre.

MARKETING PLAN OR MARKETING STRATEGY?

Undertaking a marketing segmentation analysis and an evaluation of the marketing mix should contribute to an HRD marketing strategy. This often is presented as the final stage of a written marketing plan which spells out the supporting analysis. Gilley and Eggland (1989) suggest that a marketing plan for HRD *programmes* 'should consist of a mission statement, internal and external environmental analysis, goals and objectives, an identified target market or markets, an appropriate marketing mix, and an overall marketing strategy centred around the marketing concept'. Producing such a plan can be quite a time-consuming activity, and is subject to the same criticisms relating to strategic planning as those addressed in Chapter 2. A marketing plan is of most value when there is some measure of predictability about the future or when there is some specified need to write it down as a promotional activity in its own right. It would be more effective to subsume the outcomes of a marketing analysis – and the resultant marketing strategy – within an overall HR strategic framework. This is the approach adopted by SunU, the training and development arm of Sun Microsystems (*see* Chapter 4).

Wilson *et al.* (op. cit.) recommend the following questions be answered in putting together a marketing plan.

1 Where are we now?

2 Where do we want to be?

3 How might we get there?

4 What route do we want to follow?

5 How can we ensure arrival?

If one is adopting a true customer orientation a recommended corollary to Question 2 would be: Where do our customers want us to be?

The questions that SunU incorporate are:

■ Who are our customers?

■ Who are our competitors?

■ Why will customers buy from us?

■ What must we do to make that happen?

■ Do we have the necessary skills and abilities?

■ Where are our interdependencies?

TYPES OF MARKETING STRATEGY

Segmentation strategy

Wilson *et al.* (op. cit.) propose a classification system for establishing a relationship between the providers of products or services, and the customers they are trying to reach. In essence, they suggest a scale ranging from no attempt by the provider of products or services to segment markets, to undertaking customer segmentation on an individual by individual basis (*see* Table 9.3).

Table 9.3

No customer segmentation	*Market segmentation*	*Individualised segmentation*
Undifferentiated or mass marketing	Targeted marketing	Customised marketing

We examine each of these approaches in turn, providing examples of HRD applications.

Undifferentiated or mass marketing

Unidifferentiated or mass marketing emerges when a provider deliberately ignores any differences that exist in its markets and decides to focus on a feature that appears to be common or acceptable to a wide variety of buyers. Perhaps the most quoted example of this is Henry Ford's strategy with the Model T that buyers could have 'in any colour as long as it is black'. A more recent case is that of Black and Decker which, in order to counter Japanese competition in the late 1970s, moved away from a strategy of customising products for each market. It concentrated instead on making a smaller number of products that could be sold everywhere with the same marketing approach.

Human resource development equivalent

This is the sort of marketing approach followed by external providers of training programmes who offer standardised packages or products. Such programmes have been criticised for not being based on any prior organisational or individual analysis of training needs. It is for the buyer to determine whether the programme is suitable. Mole (1995) draws attention to the existence of what he calls 'genre training' courses on subjects such as team building and leadership, which fit into this category.

> [Their] presence is evidenced by the kilos of unsolicited mail which those responsible for management training can expect to receive each year from the many suppliers of these services. The descriptions . . . offered are highly homogeneous, displaying common characteristics about the training content and method of delivery . . . A . . . characteristic is that the delivery method is a short (typically between one and five day) training course, often residential and open to any individual regardless of organisation. There would not be time, in a few days, to treat the subject matter as anything other than material which

can be readily 'learned' in a cognitive sense, particularly if nothing is known beforehand about the history or needs of the individuals who attend, or their jobs, or their organisational contexts (Mole, op. cit., p. 19).

Mole is particularly scathing about the prescriptive tone of publicity materials which purport to offer absolute and comprehensive solutions to what are held to be universal problems. Why, he wonders, 'should so much pre-packaged short duration and unfocused training continue to be supplied to and demanded by, organisations'? (ibid.)

Another HRD example relates to some culture change initiatives, where individuals and groups from across the organisational spectrum are subjected to an identical set of messages and learning interventions.

A variant of the mass marketing approach is product-variety marketing, which can be seen as a strategy for offering existing buyers greater variety, as opposed to seeking new market segments. Coca-Cola, for example, for many years produced only one type of drink for the entire market in the expectation that it would have a mass market appeal. More recently, partly to cope with an increasingly competitive environment and partly to capitalise on different patterns of consumer demand, it modified its approach. This resulted in its product being packaged in a number of different sizes and types of container

In HRD terms, this approach is adopted when training providers introduce additional courses into their sales or publicity brochures, which are then circulated to the same people as previously.

Targeted marketing

Targeting marketing is a strategy based on market segmentation. Here the major market segments are identified, one or more of these segments are targeted, and programmes are developed and tailored to the specific demands of each segment. An example of its use is that of the Burton Group in the UK which during the 1980s paid specific attention to a variety of distinct customer groups by means of different types of retail outlet, each with its own distinct target market, image and customer appeal.

Targeted marketing and the human resource development function

Rothwell and Kazanas (op. cit.) see a targeted market-oriented perspective, which clearly demonstrates the contribution that HRD products and services make to the achievement of corporate strategy, as being an important way of embedding HRD into an organisation. As we saw earlier in this chapter, a key feature of their perspective is to segment the various categories of employees who might access training and development opportunities in a given organisation and establish their learning needs. They go on to argue that if the strategic connection is not made, a market-driven approach could lead to managers and employees alike identifying learning needs on the basis of past problems. Rothwell (1984) says HRD practitioners 'too often rely heavily on the examination of past deficiencies or past behaviours as a basis for planning instruction intended to equip learners for meeting future conditions'.

However, if they act like entrepreneurs, HRD practitioners can take the lead and identify learning needs before others are aware that they exist. According to Rothwell and Kazanas (op. cit.), HRD practitioners adopting the market-oriented approach should take the following steps:

1 Classify employees into distinct groups, such as job category.

2 Predict the future knowledge and skills that employees will need to perform in ways consistent with business strategy.

3 Assess the current knowledge or skills available in each employee group.

4 Identify gaps between present and future knowledge or skill requirements.

5 Plan training and development activities to close gaps over time in each group of employees.

6 Mount a promotional campaign to inform managers and employees about the relationship between organisational strategy and HR plans, implications of those plans for them and the value of HRD programmes in preparing for the future.

Although these authors do not make this point, the logic of their position is that a similar exercise could be conducted for non-employees who might be identified as customers who have learning needs that might have an impact on the achievement of the strategic plans.

In many ways what Rothwell and Kazanas present is a reformulation into marketing terms of systematic training needs analysis. What they suggest also seems to me to be a 'product-driven' model not a 'market-driven' model. By that I mean that they rely on an approach to analysing and meeting needs which presents the customer with a product (training or development) that they *must have*. They view 'the business' as the client, rather than the individuals who make up the business. What do the customers themselves want? In this model, they seem to be passive participants in the process.

Rothwell and Kazanas think in terms of HRD practitioners who operate as training managers or HR consultants in a given organisation and who have a functional obligation to meet the needs of targeted groups. Is their formulation a necessary and/or sufficient strategy to protect the HRD function from being 'downsized' and/or 'outsourced'? Will it generate sufficient support?

Note that a target market-oriented strategy, with its focus on trying to establish a coherent relationship between customers (current and prospective) and products and services (current and prospective) is concerned with intentional and planned learning. Strategic HRD is equally concerned with establishing a favourable and supportive learning climate and culture.

A more dynamic approach from the perspective of the HRD function would entail the following steps.

1 Work in partnership with key stakeholders to identify current and emerging needs.

2 Devise training and development products and services to meet the needs of individuals and corporate clients in the context of business philosophy and learning climate.

3 Anticipate and respond to changes in the environment.

4 Seek to identify new market segments.

5 Involve key stakeholders at every stage in the design and delivery of the marketing strategy.

Customised marketing

The ultimate expression of market segmentation occurs where the product or service is modified to match the specific demands of each buyer. This approach is very attractive in broader HRD terms, where each individual is seen as having a discrete set of learning and development needs. It is congruent with a whole range of initiatives relating to career development, life planning and portfolio-driven individual personal development planning.

From a consultancy perspective, it takes the position that each client, and each client's problems, are distinct and that one's approach to establishing the consultancy relationship should be tailored to the specific dynamics of the situation.

Product-market strategy

The product-market strategy of an organisation (or functional sub-unit) is dependent upon its approach to market segmentation. It sets out the goals and routes to those goals for each of its products in relation to the markets it has identified. There are often held to be four basic product-market strategies (Ansoff, 1957).

Market penetration

Market penetration involves either increasing sales or services to existing users or finding new customers in the same market. In HRD terms it is demonstrated when existing learning initiatives receive a greater take-up. Gilley and Eggland (1989) suggest it can happen when an organisation's leadership endorses a programme that previously other managers and employees have not endorsed.

Product development

Product development entails some form of modification of the product or service such as quality, style, performance and so on. One of the stated purposes of getting feedback about programmes of learning from mechanisms such as course reaction sheets and participant review sessions is to use it as the basis of making improvements for the future. It may be established, for example, that course starting times, the terminology adopted or examples used in a training environment are proving unacceptable to members of various groups and not meeting the requirements of a diversity policy.

Market extension

Market extension involves either finding new uses for the product or service, thereby accessing new markets, or taking the product into entirely new markets. For example, if a consultancy service has been exclusively offered in house, it would then be promoted to other organisations.

Diversification

Diversification involves both product development and market extension, that is, offering a new product in a new market. For example, rather than just offering courses for employees, one could also provide distance learning packages and access to new open learning centres for suppliers and distributors. Gilley and Eggland (op. cit.), contend that diversification can be risky because it exposes HRD staff to areas outside their areas of expertise. However, learning is about taking risks and about being exposed to the unfamiliar, and that is what HRD practitioners are asking their clients to do in any learning intervention.

Figure 9.7 presents an example of diversification in the HRD product at Levi Strauss – out of the classroom into the workplace.

Figure 9.7	Continuous learning at Levi Strauss

Levi Strauss & Co. is a USA-based organisation that has dedicated itself to continuous learning as a way to remain competitive. Sue Thompson, its Director of Human Resource Development, noted in 1992:

> The importance of training has grown significantly, and the recognition of the need for training is staggering. What we're finding is that as we give more and more training, it uncovers more need for other training. As so much changes in the workplace, employees now have a need for a multitude of skills.

The training emphasis has shifted from individuals to groups. She reflects:

> In the past, employees operated as individual contributors, but people are now working, in many cases, as groups or work teams. We are clearly seeing that in our home office, and even in our production facilities. Work groups are forming naturally. We are seeing the move to self-managing teams, which is requiring us to relook at our pay system, for one, and secondly, to provide extensive training on how to work together and how to collaborate and solve problems. The changes are astounding, and the need for training associated with those changes is extensive.

In order to ensure that the organisation truly learns as a result of corporate training, Levi Strauss integrates what is done on the job with what is taught in the classroom. Says Sue Thompson:

> Our goal and strategy are to try and make sure that the training is much more integrated into the way departments actually function. We do some team training, and then we work with the group in real time to try and help them integrate those concepts into the workplace.
>
> What we have found is that to just ship people off to a classroom and provide training for them, and then let them go back to their work environment and not provide any follow-up support, is not a cost-effective strategy. Consequently, what we now call the Human Resource development organisation has two arms. One arm develops and administers training programmes. The other is an internal consultancy group. The role of the consultants is to work with managers and their work groups, to integrate the skills learned in a training session into their work environment and use their skills on the job.
>
> The HRD group is heavily involved now in working with managers and their work teams to help them better understand what the vision of the company is, what the

▶▶

▶▶ Figure 9.7 continued

department manager's vision is for his or her organisation, and to help employees take a look at their own desired future for the company and for their department – how they need to be as a group, and what kind of changes they need to make as a group to help them get there.

With increasing use of technology as new data processing systems are implemented, jobs are changing significantly. We are trying to encourage employees to take responsibility for their own training and development, to contract with their managers or supervisors, and then to be aggressive in making sure that they are developing skills that will prepare them for the future.

In some cases we don't know what those skills are. We know that jobs are changing significantly. We are encouraging employees to become more computer literate, and to network with colleagues and scan the environment, and just stay on top of changes that are happening in the way we do business. We are trying to staff up the training and development organisation so that we can be one step ahead of the training needs as they unfold (reported in Garfield, 1992).

SOME PROBLEMS WITH ADOPTING A MARKETING PERSPECTIVE IN HUMAN RESOURCE DEVELOPMENT

Do the customers' needs and preferences always need to be taken into account?

One of the outcomes of adopting a marketing orientation could be to take the perspective that one always needs to meet the expressed needs of customers. This creates something of a dilemma when one is engaging in evaluation activities. There is always a temptation to modify programme features to satisfy customer preferences – what they like is enhanced, what they dislike is dropped. This is not necessarily the way forward. Learning is not always easy. There are, for example, circumstances when it might be desirable to identify sources of group conflict or indeed prejudice. Should HRD programmes always avoid areas of difficulty? At the same time, unfavourable reports from previous participants in a programme can deter potential participants. Much promotion is based on word of mouth communication. Deciding on the extent to which customer preferences should be comsidered is an ongoing dilemma.

Can learning interventions be seen in terms of a product/market mix? Where does process fit in?

The notion of a market with needs met by a product or a service tends to direct one towards something tangible. Gilley and Eggland (op. cit.) reflect this idea when they refer to the need for a marketing plan for HRD programmes. But what is the 'product' in today's HRD world? Increasingly, it is not a course. The product could be mentoring; secondments; career counselling; personal development plans; competency profiles; development centres; the orchestration of learning organisations and corporate universities. What about the creation of a positive learning climate?

Indeed the HRD product might be seen as an integrated approach to orchestrating learning which might not entail any formal activities at all. It is entirely process driven.

Should one take a retrospective as opposed to a forward-looking approach?

There is an argument that adopting a market-oriented perspective runs the risk of identifying historical rather than future-oriented learning needs. This is not entirely convincing. It might be so in terms of identifying the types of product or service that might be offered. However the very fact of thinking about identifying the potential target markets for HRD can lead to the identification of groups whose learning needs are not currently met beyond the acquisition of tacit skills. An analysis, if properly conducted by individuals who are sufficiently familiar with the business, its goals and its plans, can establish both current and future needs.

DOES THE MARKETING OF LEARNING REQUIRE A SUPPORTING HUMAN RESOURCE DEVELOPMENT FUNCTION?

At the beginning of this chapter it was asked whether one can market learning in organisations without an associated HRD function. The fact that the question needs to be asked at all reflects an odd paradox. The promotion of learning and HRD as an organisational desideratum is becoming increasingly commonplace. It is increasingly finding expression in organisational core values. Yet at the same time we are witnessing the demise of a number of well-established training and development departments. In part this is because these established departments do not see themselves as being in the learning business as broadly conceived, but in the programme provision business. And many programmes can be offered elsewhere, by external providers.

If learning is to be marketed in an organisation without an associated HRD function, what form might the marketing effort take? Where would the emphasis lie? Who would take responsibility for it? Elsewhere in this book it is argued that all parties can reap benefits when learning is orchestrated by a discrete functional unit. The corollary is that those responsible for learning need to operate from a mental set that is capable of balancing the tangible and intangible aspects of the learning process.

CONCLUSION

This chapter has subjected the HRD function in particular, and HRD activities in organisations in general, to a marketing perspective. It has shown how applying concepts such as market segmentation, customer analysis and the marketing mix can benefit HRD practitioners and provide a rich insight into the range of learning provision and how this reflects a broad set of needs. It has also shown that traditional approaches to marketing HRD have focused almost exclusively on the tangible aspects of course and programme provision.

Different approaches to developing a marketing strategy for HRD have been addressed, based on different approaches to market segmentation and interpreting a product and market mix. It has been argued that presenting an HRD marketing strategy in the form of a detailed marketing plan suffers from the same limitation as strategic plans – inflexibility in an unpredictable environment. It also serves to reinforce the programmatic aspects of HRD.

The chapter has finished by touching on the relationship between marketing the HRD function and marketing learning as something to be desired. It is held that all parties benefit from there being a discrete area with overall responsibility for learning issues. However, to take on this responsibility requires a mental set that can balance the tangible and less tangible aspects of the process.

REFERENCES

Ansoff, H. I. (1957) 'Strategies for Diversification', *Harvard Business Review*, 25(5), September–October, pp. 113–24.

Beer, M., Spector, B., Lawrence, P. R., Mills, Q. N. and Walton, R. E. (1984) *Managing Human Assets*. New York: Free Press.

Bell, C. (1995) 'The Heart of HRD Partnerships', *Training and Development* (ASTD), January

Boston Consulting Group (1971) *Perspectives on Experience*. Boston: Boston Consulting Group.

Buell, V. (1984) *Marketing Management: A Strategic Planning Approach*. New York: McGraw-Hill.

Butler, A., Letza, S. R. and Neale, B. (1997) 'Linking the Balanced Score Card to Strategy', *Long Range Planning*, 30(2), April, pp. 242–53.

Davidson, J. H. (1987) *Offensive Marketing or How To Make Your Competitors Followers* (2nd edn). Harmondsworth: Penguin.

Garfield, C. (1992) *Second to None – The Productive Power of Putting People First*. Chicago: Business One Irwin.

Gilley, J. W. (1987) 'Lifelong Learning: An Omnibus for Research and Practice', American Society for Adult and Continuing Education, reproduced in J. W. Gilley and S. A. Eggland (1989).

Gilley, J. W. and Eggland, S. A. (1989) *Principles of Human Resource Development*. Reading, MA: Addison-Wesley.

Hendry, C., Jones, A., Arthur, M. and Pettigrew, A. (1988) 'Human Resource Development in Small to Medium Sized Enterprises', *Employment Department Research Paper*, No. 88.

Jolles, R. (1994) 'R-E-S-P-E-C-T', *Training and Development* (ASTD), July.

Kotler, P. (1988) *Marketing Management: Analysis, Planning, Implementation and Control*. (6th edn). Englewood Cliffs, NJ: Prentice Hall.

Macdonald, M. (1984) *Marketing Plans: How to Prepare Them, How to Use Them*. London: Heinemann.

Mole, G. (1995) 'The Management Training Industry in the UK: An HRD Directors' Critique', *Human Resource Management Journal*, 6(1).

Nadler, L. (1979) *Developing Human Resources* (2nd edn) Austin, TX: Learning Concepts.

Nagle, T. (1987) *The Strategies and Tactics of Pricing*: Englewood Cliffs, NJ: Prentice Hall.

Ohmae K. (1982) *The Mind of the Strategist*. New York: McGraw-Hill.

Rothwell, W. (1984) 'Thinking Strategically: The Business of Career Decisions', *Training News*, May.

Rothwell, W. and Kazanas, H. C. (1989) *Strategic HRD*. Englewood Cliffs, NJ: Prentice Hall.

State of Illinois (1993) *Governor's human resources advisory council: Recommendations for change in Illinois. Final Report.*

Walton, J. (1996) 'The Provision of Learning Support for Non-Employees', in J. Stewart and J. McGoldrick (eds) *Human Resource Development – Perspectives, Strategies and Practice.* London: Pitman.

Wiggenhorn, W. (1990) 'Motorola U: When Training Becomes an Education', *Harvard Business Review*, July–August.

Wilson, Richard, M. S., Gilligan, C., with Pearson, D. J. (1992) *Strategic Marketing Management.* Oxford: Butterworth-Heinemann.

Zemke, R. (1981) 'Curriculum Development as Strategic Planning', *Training*, 18.

Chapter 10

THE PROVISION OF LEARNING SUPPORT FOR NON-EMPLOYEES

OBJECTIVES

By the end of the chapter you should be able to:

- distinguish between different categories of non-employee stakeholder and establish the distinctive contribution that they make to an organisation's operations;

- differentiate between non-employee training, non-employee education and non-employee development as providing different responses to learning needs;

- establish the significance to HRD practitioners and organisational decision makers of strategic initiatives such as outsourcing;

- establish circumstances under which the provision of learning opportunities for non-employees have been seen to be appropriate.

INTRODUCTION

For a number of years strategic management literature and practice have demonstrated the importance for organisations of operating outside their boundaries and establishing strategic relationships with external stakeholders such as suppliers and distributors. More recently much attention has been given to the growth of strategic alliances and joint ventures. Another trend has been the downsizing of organisations and the outsourcing of a range of functions which were previously considered to be an integral part of in-house operations. There has also been a move towards subcontracting of and franchising arrangements for in-house services. Furthermore many voluntary organisations are re-evaluating the use of volunteers for the provision of front-line services.

Thus, not only are institutions increasingly relying on and developing relationships with groups operating outside their boundaries, but also more and more organisation functions are being conducted by individuals who are not in a conventional employer–employee relationship.

The implications of this for HRD practitioners should be far reaching – in terms of establishing new market segments for HRD activities and indicating emerging organisational learning needs – but with few exceptions such a development has not been reflected in mainstream HRD literature and practice. Training managers have traditionally seen their constituents as operating in the organisation for which they themselves work. This focus can be narrowed down even further. In most organisations, the traditional target group where training and development needs are established, and for whom learning opportunities are provided has been employees.

This focus is also reflected in UK national initiatives such as Investors in People (IiP) which provides a set of criteria for organisations to meet, to achieve a national standard for effective investment in people. The core criteria are unashamedly employee based and include:

■ an Investor in People makes a public commitment from the top to develop all *employees* to achieve its business objectives;

■ an Investor in People regularly reviews the training and development needs of all *employees*;

■ an Investor in People takes action to train and develop individuals on recruitment and and throughout their *employment*.

No reference is made to the learning needs of non-employees.

This emphasis on employees may have been a valid approach in the past. But with new organisational forms and new approaches to the employer–employee relationship this way of thinking is rapidly becoming outmoded.

One way of addressing this matter is for training and development managers and others to identify the range of organisation stakeholders who are non-employees and to see the provision of services and programmes for such categories of learner as constituting a significant part of their portfolio.

This chapter is concerned with developing the notion of non-employee learning and providing a framework within which the strategic importance of providing learning opportunities for non-employee stakeholders can be fully understood.

NON-EMPLOYEES

Non-employees are those individuals or groups who have some relationship with an organisation but who are not in an employer–employee relationship. They could be employees of another organisation operating within the boundaries of the `home' organisation by providing services on a subcontracting basis. They could be employees working for suppliers of the raw materials on which the organisation depends, or for distributors of organisational products to customers. They could be self-employed or volunteers. They could be members of the general public who in some way or form use, or are affected by, organisational products or services. Thus they could be actual or potential customers, members of environmental pressure groups or even potential members of as yet unformed pressure groups. They could be governors of schools, members of watchdog authorities, prison visitors. The list is potentially endless because of the range of organisations operating in our society.

Who constitute relevant non-employee stakeholders for any given organisation depend on its particular activities. The learning needs of each group of non-employees identified depends on the actual and desired relationship with the organisation in question.

As we saw in Chapter 9, Rothwell and Kazanas (1989) propose a classification system which incorporates non-employees as a potential target group for an organisation's HRD activities, necessitating separately prepared objectives, policies and activities. The outcome is *non-employee development*, which they define as a long-term effort for improving relations between a 'business', the general public and external stakeholders. This reference to non-employee development as a planned and significant area for organisation involvement and HRD interventions is of particular interest and is groundbreaking so far as the HRD literature is concerned.

Rothwell and Kazanas (op. cit.) develop their position by arguing that HRD has traditionally focused on meeting learning needs *within* an organisation. They contend that the literature of the HRD field offers surprisingly little advice about identifying the learning needs of *external groups*.

They also argue that any strategic orientation to HRD should emphasise the importance of the external environment and entail a responsibility for scanning the learning needs of groups operating outside the organisation but having an impact on it. For example, consumers who do not know how to use a product will not buy it, suppliers who are unaware of an organisation's quality standards may not be complying with them.

Thus the purpose of non-employee development is to enable the organisation to influence its external environment through a planned process of learning, so that the skills and knowledge of those outside its boundaries on whom it depends to a greater or lesser extent are enhanced. This in turn will allow the organisation to work more effectively towards achieving its strategic goals. The process of non-employee development can be thought of as enabling organisations, groups and individuals external to the organisation to learn how to interact better with it.

The Rothwell and Kazanas typology as it stands is not complete. Logically, if one is talking about employee training, employee education and employee development then there should also be non-employee training, non-employee education and non-employee development. Indeed, much of what they describe as non-employee development could more suitably be described as non-employee training or non-employee education. Their classification is also limited, in that it appears not to cover the learning needs of non-employees operating within a given organisation such as subcontractors or volunteers carrying out a key operational activity.

The following definitions are offered to extend the Rothwell and Kazanas perspective.

Non-employee training can be defined as short-term efforts to ensure that individuals not in an employment relationship with a given organisation, but who are in some way responsible for providing services to it, have the skills necessary to carry out these services.

Non-employee education can be defined as efforts to ensure that individuals who have some current or potential relationship to the organisation are provided with knowledge and understanding about the organisation's products, services and values.

NON-EMPLOYEE STAKEHOLDER ANALYSIS

If training and development managers are to extend their repertoire to encompass non-employees, including learners operating outside the organisation, they need to develop a method for identifying target groups or market segments. One recommended approach is through non-employee stakeholder analysis.

Stakeholders can be defined as the various groupings which have an interest or stake in the organisation. Internal stakeholders are those groups which operate within the boundaries of an organisation, many – but not all – of whom engage in activities which contribute to the development of products or services to external customers. Exceptions include union representatives and subcontractors of, for example, the staff canteen, who provide services to internal customers.

External stakeholders are those groupings which operate outside the boundaries of an organisation but who engage in activities which can affect the operation and viability of an organisation. For a typical commercial enterprise they include suppliers, distributors, consumers or end users and shareholders.

Stakeholder analysis can become quite complicated as one reflects on the range of potential groupings that can have an impact on a given organisation. Outside the supplier–distributor–consumer chain of a commercial concern they could include environmental pressure groups, watchdog bodies, local and central government agencies, major debtors and creditors and so on.

Each organisational type, for example, manufacturing concern, local authority, bank, has its own discrete set of stakeholders. Even within an organisation, different stakeholder groupings impact on discrete areas of operation. Thus the stakeholders with an impact on a social services directorate of a local authority could be very different from those with an impact on an education directorate. Figure 10.1 presents a framework in the form of a stakeholder wheel for non-employees.

Figure 10.1 The stakeholder wheel for non-employees

Source: Stewart and McGoldrick (1996, p. 124).

A number of other frameworks have been developed for further classifying stakeholders. For example, Johnson and Scholes (1993) have developed a stakeholder mapping model based on the two dimensions of degree of interest and degree of power. From an HRD perspective two useful dimensions are: degree of organisational involvement and extent of learning needs (*see* Fig. 10.2).

| Figure 10.2 | Non-employee stakeholder matrix |

Organisational involvement

Low   High

Learning needs

Low

SHAREHOLDERS	TRAINED SUB-CONTRACTORS
ENVIRONMENTAL PRESSURE GROUP	UNTRAINED VOLUNTEERS

High

Source: Stewart and McGoldrick (1996, p. 125).

The linked typology developed in this chapter classifies the organisational involvement of non-employee stakeholders in terms of:

■ their involvement or otherwise in activities which are part of the organisation's value chain; and

■ whether they are operating within or outside the boundaries of the organisation;

and to use this categorisation to reflect on learning needs.

THE VALUE CHAIN AND VERTICAL INTEGRATION

One group of non-employee stakeholders who have in the past been identified as having significant learning needs are those who directly contribute to the value chain of an organisation. The Unipart Group of companies in their 1996 review categorically state that the mission of the corporate university is to increase utilisation of the value chain through learning that is shared with its key stakeholders, which it identifies as 'customers, employees, investors, suppliers and the communities in which it does business' (Unipart Review, 1996).

The notion of value chain is that a sequence of activities needs to be undertaken to translate raw materials and other inputs into a finished product or service that reaches an end-user; and that each activity should add value to the product. In commercial terms, value is the amount buyers are willing to pay for what a firm provides them with. Within a given value chain Michael Porter (1980) distinguishes between primary and support value activities, both of which are central to an organisation's success in getting its products or services to its customers.

Primary activities are those leading to the actual provision of a product or service. They entail, for a manufacturing concern, inbound logistics (receiving, storing, materials handling, etc.), operations (machining, packaging, assembly, etc.), outbound logistics (storing, distribution, etc.), marketing and sales (advertising, promotions, etc.) and service (installation, repair, parts supply, etc.).

Support activities assist the primary activities through purchasing functions, technology development, human resource management and an overall infrastructure that includes planning and finance (*see* Fig. 10.3).

Figure 10.3 The generic value chain

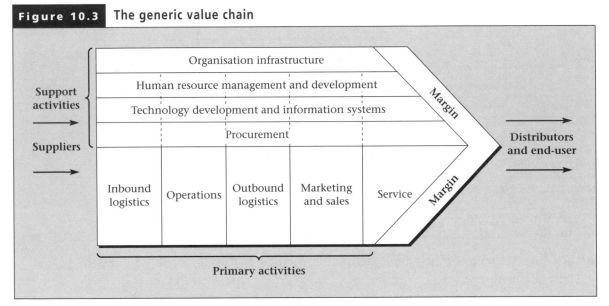

Source: Stewart and McGoldrick (1996, p. 126). Based on Porter (1980).

Porter's definition of value chain can be extended beyond the boundaries of a particular organisation, especially in so far as the primary activities are concerned. This extension becomes particularly helpful when linked to another strategic management term, that of vertical integration.

Taking a given organisation's products and services as the base, one looks at 'upstream' and 'downstream' value chain activities and establishes the degree of existing and desirable backward vertical integration and forward vertical integration respectively.

Backward vertical integration reflects the extent to which an organisation establishes control over 'upstream' activities, that is, the sources of supply of the raw materials for the organisation. Various strategies can be identified, including owning the sources of supply, investing heavily as shareholders in supplier organisations and demanding that intending suppliers achieve a quality certification.

Forward vertical integration reflects the degree of control and involvement that a given organisation has over 'downstream' activities, that is, the channels of distribution whereby a product reaches end-users. Thus some organisations not only operate as manufacturers but also own their retail outlets. Figure 10.4 presents a model of vertical integration.

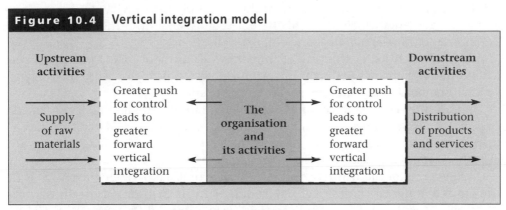

Figure 10.4 Vertical integration model

Source: Stewart and McGoldrick (1993, p. 127).

Non-employee stakeholders providing primary activities within the value chain and operating outside the organisation boundaries

Schuler and Macmillan (1985) argue that there are discrete targets or stakeholder groupings for HRD interventions outside the organisation yet which are part of its value chain. A modified version of their classification is presented in the following pages to describe some practical examples of how learning needs are being met.

The supplier as target

Some organisations have adopted as a strategy the establishment of quite stringent controls over their suppliers without actually owning them. They have introduced quality control inspectors to check the processes being undertaken, and have restricted the extent to which a supplier can supply competitors.

Organisations are, however, moving away from this type of control model in an endeavour to add value by shifting skills upstream, as the following examples show.

As part of its environmental policy, BT has developed a set of environmental procurement standards. These were considered important since minimising the risks at the procurement stage could provide long-term benefits with knock-on effects through the supply chain. BT considers that suppliers who run active environmental improvement programmes are more likely to deliver a quality product. BT has developed a number of different but complementary approaches to supplier communications, all of which are based on a process of working with suppliers to encourage continuous improvement (Tuppen, 1993).

Rosabeth Moss Kanter (1989) argues that, facing imperatives to cut costs and improve quality, leading American companies are creating closer relationships with their suppliers. They are moving away from the old 'adversarial' model which used to dominate purchasing in American corporations. Price was minimised by maintaining a large supplier base, with each provider being subject to short-term contracts and frequent rebidding. However such arm's-length arrangements do not motivate suppliers to invest in technology to improve quality or manage the complexities of just-in-time inventory. Kanter quotes Digital as a company that has developed partnership arrangements with suppliers which include integrated information systems, regular forums with key suppliers to review business plans and other activities which are virtually indistinguishable from these which a corporation might undertake with one of its own divisions.

A logical extension of this way of thinking is to introduce HRD initiatives and extend training and development opportunities to suppliers to ensure that organisational standards and requirements are being satisfied.

Thus an internal Digital team has organised a training programme for suppliers. Digital has also introduced a 'Vendor Performance Management System' – a performance appraisal system akin to that used for employees – in which suppliers are measured on quality, delivery, price and flexibility.

Cadillac, one of the winners of the 1990 Malcolm Baldrige Quality Awards in the United States, includes over 640 suppliers in its own quality-training programmes (Steeples, 1992). Suppliers are also members of 75 per cent of the 55 product development and improvement teams.

Xerox, a 1989 winner of the Baldrige Award, instituted a supplier certification process in the early 1980s that required suppliers to go through an ordered procedure to analyse their processes. Suppliers that met the requirements were awarded Certified Supplier status. Suppliers were invited to take part in the product delivery process, which allowed them to be significantly involved in product design and manufacturing. Xerox also began training suppliers in total quality, statistical process control, and just-in-time delivery.

A further extension of this way of thinking is to engage in joint ventures between HRD departments to provide a common understanding of issues and problems affecting both organisations. This is moving closer to the Japanese notion of strategic networks or *keiretsu*.

The distributor as target

Many organisations have invested heavily in providing learning support to distributors and dealers. Macmillan and Schuler (op. cit.) refer to the strategy adopted by Mercedes of training mechanics in their distributors' garages. This practice is quite common in the motor/engine manufacturing industry. Perkins Engines, as long ago as the 1960s, provided training courses at its UK factory in Peterborough for mechanics from dealers' organisations which serviced its engines.

A pure vertical integration strategy would entail the 'home' organisation having total responsibility for the process, with the dealer or distributor being in a dependency relationship. Increasingly, however, organisations are developing partnership arrangements with their distributors similar to those discussed above for suppliers.

In the past Cadillac tended to regard dealers as product distributors. Dealers often did not see the product until it was introduced to the public. In 1984, Cadillac implemented a Dealer Quality Improvement Process with its 1600 independent dealers. Suggestions from dealers about marketing strategies and current and future products are now encouraged. As part of the initiative, training is provided to support dealers in achieving customer service excellence.

In summer 1997 the Rover Group unveiled a new £3 million, purpose-built Technical Academy to train service technicians from Rover and Land Rover dealerships throughout the world. In the Academy's first full year of operations, 6000 training days are expected to be completed, with delegates working towards NVQ level 3 in a relevant discipline. The Rover Group Sales and Marketing Director said:

> The Technical Academy represents a substantial investment on the part of Rover Group, and has been built with two objectives in mind. Firstly, the expectations of Rover and Land Rover customers are rising all the time. We need to equip service technicians with the skills that they need to deal with vehicles that are becoming more and more technologically advanced. The microchip is as important today as the spanner was in the past, and the skills of the modern technician must be far beyond those of the traditional mechanic.
>
> Secondly we wish to demonstrate that Rover Group's commitment to life-time learning and continuous improvement does not just apply to our own associates within Rover Group but extends outwards to those who work within the dealership network.

In the insurance and pension industry the 'distributors' of products to individual clients are financial advisers – who are often non-employees. Such financial advisers are required by law to give best advice. It is clearly important that they have sufficient information on the range of products and benefits individual companies have on offer. Insurance companies are beginning to address the strategic importance of non-employee development for independent financial advisers.

The customer as target

In today's Total Quality Management (TQM) world, quality is seen from the perspective of the customer, and organisational cultures are being changed to embrace a focus on customer-driven quality and continuous improvement. The provision of learning support for external customers is an obvious aspect of continuous improvement. Customers can facilitate learning processes within the organisation by giving feedback on how their products and services are perceived. A focus on customers also helps to create barriers to entry to competitors by helping to develop customer loyalty and trust.

According to Madu and Kuei (1993), the traditional approach to TQM has focused on a team approach whereby employees have identified areas for continuous improvement. The emerging Strategic TQM approach is extending the team approach to incorporate external stakeholder groups in the team decision-making process.

The development of TQM as a concept has led to a 'customer comes first' perspective for a number of organisations, of which IBM is a good example.

For many years IBM adopted a technology-driven approach to strategy. Within this overall approach, one way in which it differentiated itself from competitors was by selecting and training programmers for customers, in an era when training in computer programming was not available at schools and colleges. IBM correctly reasoned that without computer programmers there would be no computer sales, so it was important to have as many programmers as possible who were trained on IBM equipment. Other manufacturers followed suit. For example, in the early

1970s I attended a one-month programming course run by Honeywell (now Bull). However, there was no involvement of customers in IBM's processes or operations.

More recently IBM has swung towards a Market-Driven Quality (MDQ) model. Launched in 1990 by its Chairman, John Akers, MDQ is grounded on four principles: 'Make the customer the final arbiter, understand our markets, commit to leadership in markets we choose to serve, and deliver excellence in execution across our enterprise.' IBM Rochester, located in Rochester, Minnesota, is a manufacturer of intermediate computer systems including IBM's flagship mid-range business computer, the Application System/400. The quality process at Rochester provides a continuous loop with the customer, from the product-planning process through production and on to delivery. Customers are involved in the development and manufacturing process through methods such as advisory councils, round tables, information systems and prototype trailing. In the case of the AS/400, its basic architecture was the result of customer input. To secure feedback after installation, the company conducts a quarterly marketing and customer satisfaction survey of approximately 2200 AS/400 customers.

Although perhaps not seen as a planned learning programme, this sort of initiative clearly has a major impact in creating an organisational awareness of IBM in its customers, as well as enhancing IBM's own understanding of how its products are perceived. The introduction of planned developmental programmes for customers and their employees is a logical extension.

Boeing has been training its customers since 1917. Today its training facility serves the needs of its airline customers from around the world. The customer-training organisation provides formal courses on maintenance, flight and ground operations; Boeing typically supplies the training as part of a new aircraft purchase. Most of Boeing's classes last for six to eight weeks. In many cases, instructors conduct the classes at airline facilities around the world. In 1992 and 1993, more than 150 instructors in the Boeing maintenance-training organisation trained a total of 7500 trainees in 706 classes. In most cases, airline employees receive training on a new aircraft before its delivery – sometimes several months before. The extra time allows airline instructors to take course materials presented by the aircraft manufacturer and use it to train local employees who cannot attend the manufacturer's training course.

Commercial aircraft are among the most complex and technically advanced products created by industry today. Large commercial jets have more than 30 major systems, and each system has many subsystems. The systems use multiple levels of computer processing. They communicate with each other on high-speed data buses that link operational systems with an integrated display system and an on-board maintenance system. To keep these planes flying reliably requires substantial investments in the training of airline employees. Airline employees receive training from their own employers. But they also receive training from commercial aircraft manufacturers such as Boeing. Such training partnerships constitute a key factor in the effective operation and maintenance of airline fleets (Cox, 1994).

Other organisations as targets

Rosabeth Moss Kanter (op. cit.) contends that the traditional approach to achieving control through vertical integration is breaking down and that new organisational forms based on strategic alliances are emerging. She suggests that organisations are moving from adversarial to partnership arrangements, with both stakeholders and erstwhile competitors on the supplier–distribution chain. She also contends that organisations can become better **PALs** by:

- Pooling resources;
- Allying to exploit an opportunity;
- Linking systems in a partnership.

The learning support mechanisms that would allow synergy to develop between strategic partners are both complex and difficult to develop. However, it is clearly significant that if partnerships are to work there should be some approach to shared learning that entails the pooling of HRD resources and the linking of HRD systems.

THE IMPACT OF OUTSOURCING ON NON-EMPLOYEE LEARNING NEEDS

Jarillo (1993) argues that vertical integration has been the dominant organisation form of the twentieth century. He cites organisations such as Ford in the early days of its operations as an exemplar of the philosophy that one should establish control over all activities that contribute to the value chain of a given product. However he suggests that this dominant organisational form is beginning to break down in favour of variants of subcontracting and strategic networks, which essentially constitute an alternative, market-based organisational form. When an organisation needs an input, he asks, why not go to the market and have it delivered by an external party rather than look to internal resources? In other words, proponents of the subcontracting approach will increasingly seek to outsource activities.

The adoption of this perspective has been indicated for some time by those influenced by the Institute of Manpower Studies 'flexible firm' model which distinguishes between core and peripheral activities (Atkinson, 1985 and IMS, 1985). In human resource terms the flexible firm consists of a 'core' group of employees surrounded by peripheral groups of workers who may not be employees. Among a number of options for achieving flexibility are so-called distancing strategies, which involve the displacement of employment relationships by commercial ones for peripheral workers. Thus only activities which are core to the organisation's operations are carried out 'in house'. Others are outsourced and subcontracted or franchised out – to non-employees.

Such an approach helps to explain the philosophy underpinning the recent trend to contract out and 'market test' central government activities. The UK Government *Next Steps Review* (1993) recommended a critical scrutiny (a Prior Options Test) of government functions to ascertain whether the function:

- needs to be carried out by government at all or whether it could be abolished;
- if it does need to be carried out, could be privatised;
- could be contracted out to private organisations as a whole;
- could be market-tested (i.e. unlike contracting out, its allocation to either civil service or private organisations would be decided competitively); .

■ was sufficiently large to be made into an agency (executive agencies are staffed by government employees but are given autonomy to carry out the executive functions of government within a policy and resources framework set by a government department).

The same philosophy also underpins compulsory competitive tendering (CCT) in the local authority sector. In this process, unless it can be demonstrated that value is added by preserving an activity within the public domain, then it is outsourced.

In strategic terms, outsourcing creates a major dilemma for senior management. Increasingly it is being argued that it is the knowledge and skills that individual knowledge workers possess that add value to organisations. A product, it is argued, is obsolete the moment it is produced in today's competitive environment; what cannot be replaced and replicated are the distinctive competences that highly qualified staff bring, operating in a culture that can be seen to encourage team learning. Thus the increasing creation of non-employee relationships entails considerable risks unless such distinctive competences can be learned and sustained outside an employment relationship.

NON-EMPLOYEES OPERATING WITHIN THE ORGANISATION WHO CONTRIBUTE TO THE PRIMARY VALUE CHAIN

An obvious example of this category of non-employee are volunteers working for voluntary organisations such as OXFAM or the Citizens Advice Bureau who are involved in front-line service delivery. In many ways their learning needs are similar to those of paid employees, and many voluntary organisations have well-established training and development departments which cater for these needs. The Citizens Advice Bureau, for example, has a national training network.

Changes in the employment market have caused a change in the profile of volunteers and their reasons for volunteering, which in turn have caused voluntary organisations to think differently about the volunteers they use. Many of these people are doing voluntary work rather than be unemployed. The changing external environment and increasing competitiveness combined with customer expectations about service delivery are causing voluntary organisations to examine the cost effectiveness of volunteer involvement and evaluate volunteer achievement. Volunteers themselves are more likely than in the past to see volunteering as a developmental activity and will be attracted to organisations that offer training. There is an increasing likelihood that volunteers will be recruited on the basis of their ability to do a given job and that they will receive training to carry out the work they do. The 1991 National Survey of Voluntary Activity in the UK revealed that 11 per cent of people volunteered in order to gain a new skill and that this motivation was more likely in the under-35 age group.

There has been an increasing trend over the last twenty years to use self-employed subcontractors to carry out core services and functions in lieu of employees. In the gas supply industry, for example, central heating installations are invariably carried out by contractors. The legality of such arrangements was tested as long ago as 1968 in a famous court case involving Readymix Concrete, which used self-employed subcontractors to drive their lorries. The case against Readymix was that they were trying to escape the contractual obligations of being an employer. The drivers were contractually restricted to using the lorries on Readymix business only; the lorries had the Readymix logo; the drivers wore the Readymix uniform and had to take instructions 'as though they were an employee'. Nevertheless the court held that they could be treated as non-employees on a 'contract for services' (self-employed) as opposed to a 'contract of service' (employment) since they 'owned the instrumentalities of the business' and had to invest their own capital in the leasing of the lorries – even though this was from a Readymix subsidiary!

Public perception of the performance of such front-line individuals is clearly central to the organisation's image and success in the marketplace, and considerable thought and attention should be given to their learning needs.

NON-EMPLOYEES OPERATING WITHIN THE ORGANISATION WHO CONTRIBUTE TO THE SUPPORT VALUE CHAIN

This area is most obviously associated with the use by organisations of external consultants to whom organisations have subcontracted specialist activities. These activities typically include:

- the introduction and development of IT and systems;
- auditing;
- recruitment and selection activities such as the development and administration of selection tests;
- the design and delivery of management development and other staff development programmes;
- organisation development activities, including the introduction of major culture change programmes.

The learning needs of such consultants depend upon the precise activities in which they are engaged, but could be quite substantial. For example, the development of information systems to meet specific organisational needs can require the consultant to spend considerable time in becoming familiar with existing organisation systems, procedures and practices.

Non-employees in this category also include representatives of organisations to whom in-house services are subcontracted on a franchise or equivalent basis. Examples include a whole range of office services such as cleaning and catering.

Health and safety legislation requires employers to ensure that contractors working on any of their sites comply with the law. Thus the Scottish Prison Service, for example, has special training courses for employees of contractor firms who work inside prisons, to ensure that they are able to work within prison regimes.

NON-EMPLOYEE LEARNING OUTSIDE THE VALUE CHAIN

In their classification of non-employees, Rothwell and Kazanas (op. cit.) differentiate between external stakeholders, the general public and the family of an employee. Neither the family nor the general public are part of the 'value chain' of the organisation as conventionally defined.

The inclusion of the general public within an HRD framework is interesting because of the overlap with public relations (PR) Many organisations invest substantially in PR. Groups are invited to visit factories to see how products are made; major campaigns can be launched to justify an activity or initiative which may have an impact on a local community. Representatives of organisations may spend vast sums on projecting, or in some instances attempting to transform, the organisation's image.

I am not aware of many organisations having established internal links between the training and development function and PR, nor even whether at strategic level a connection has been made. That is not to say that HRD practitioners should not participate in the PR area. If we define HRD as being about learning and interventions then clearly HRD practitioners should consider what the relationship with PR should be and perhaps contribute in a more proactive way than heretofore to policy developments in this area.

There are a number of instances where the education of specific groups from within the general public can be targeted as part of an organisation's planned learning activities. Doctors in general practice, for example, have been asked by the government to set up particular programmes, such as clinics for the overweight, screening clinics for cancer (breast and cervical) and awareness groups for young mothers and the elderly.

Much of the provision of learning activities for the general public can best be viewed as non-employee education. This is also the case for another of Rothwell and Kazanas's categories. They include representatives of an employee's family in their framework, arguing that they are silent partners in a 'business'. What happens in the organisation affects the well-being of the family and that of the family member employed by the organisation.

Thorn Lighting, located in the northeast of England, has been providing team building programmes for the unemployed, supported by funding from the Department for Education and Employment, with the intention of providing them with more marketable skills. In 1993, the first group of ten trainees attended a five-day workshop that covered job interview skills, occupational testing and a grounding in basic business principles, as well as techniques relevant to understanding modern-day manufacturing such as *Kaizen*. By August 1997, some 300 unemployed people had been trained, of whom nearly 100 had obtained employment with Thorn, the rest with other local employers. An additional initiative called Citizen 2000 has involved schoolchildren aged between 12 and 16. The initial voluntary seven-day learning programme was designed to explain to pupils the realities of working life and covered areas such as coping and resilience (*Kaizen*, lifetime learning); ethics and mutuality; lateral thinking; entrepreneurial skills; teamworking; tolerance and understanding; and decisiveness and persuasion (Hood, 1997). This latter initiative is presented as an altruistic activity, although the knock-on effect might be to make Thorn Lighting appear an attractive employer when the children leave school.

Organisations and T&D departments have not really addressed the learning needs of partners and other family members. One exception has been the provision of crosscultural and language training for families of employees being posted overseas. Barham and Oates (1991) conducted a survey of how organisations prepared their managers for international postings. Crosscultural training was included as one of the five most important activities for their organisation by 42 per cent of respondents; 23 per cent included language training for the family. Rhinesmith (1996) argues that such predeparture language and cultural training should be routine practice for accompanying family members of expatriates and should be reinforced by in-country training on arrival.

THE ORCHESTRATION OF LEARNING PROCESSES FOR NON-EMPLOYEES

The issue now is how to orchestrate appropriate learning processes as part of a coherent strategy for non-employee learning. Rothwell and Kazanas (op. cit.) provide a useful set of guidelines, given below. It is important to recognise that they are postulated on the assumption that most learning activities will be orchestrated from within an organisation that has an established in-house HRD function. They suggest the following steps that HRD practitioners and operating managers should take.

1 Classify external groups by their general interests or concerns.
2 Analyse existing relationships between the organisation and the various groups whose learning needs are to be met.
3 Establish what these relationships should be in the future.
4 Pinpoint discrepancies for both the present and the future between desired and actual learning relationships.
5 Separate HRD from non-HRD solutions.
6 Identify changes in relationships and design HRD activities to meet desired changes.
7 Select instructional content and delivery methods.
8 Follow up over time.

A straw poll of T&D managers responsible for organisational skills development in a range of institutions has indicated that few have analysed the issues. Thus Point 6 above becomes a major resource problem with no allocated budget. Accordingly, additions to the Rothwell and Kazanas guidelines would be:

9 Establish what percentage, if any, of the current resources invested in HRD activities is devoted to non-employee learning, and determine whether this percentage is appropriate for future needs.
10 Develop a negotiating strategy for bidding for additional resources should this prove necessary.

11 Building on Points 2 and 3 above, establish links with HRD departments of organisations with which one has a significant business relationship in order to consider the options of pooling resources and integrating learning systems.

12 In-house T&D managers should establish their organisation's current attitude to outsourcing, since this may reveal areas which could be future targets for outsourcing. These could well include the T&D function unless HRD practitioners can persuade organisational decision makers of the strategic relevance or economic benefit of its remaining in house.

THE LEARNING ARCHITECTS AS NON-EMPLOYEES

What the literature has significantly failed to touch on at all is the impact on organisation activities of outsourcing the T&D function. The assumption is made that learning processes will be orchestrated by people operating within and employed by the organisation. However, increasingly, many training departments are being outsourced and are not seen as part of the organisation's core services. Similarly, many HRD initiatives and training programmes are being developed and delivered by external consultants. In the public sector such programmes are subject to CCT or market testing. Thus the 'learning architects' themselves are becoming non-employees.

This is, perhaps, an inevitable consequence of the low status and lack of strategic role that has been afforded to HRD professionals in organisations. However, it is increasingly being argued that knowledge workers help provide the distinctive competences which differentiate one organisation from another in the perceived satisfaction of customers in the marketplace. It would accordingly seem vital to undertake an effective orchestration of the learning processes, which would lead to the retention and development of such knowledge workers. With the growth of strategic alliances and networks, it would seem even more essential to have people available in an organisation who have a strategic understanding of learning systems and an ability to apply them.

An alternative, but one that seems to be some way off, would be for outsourced T&D departments to help develop a strategic network of internal and external stakeholders of which they themselves are part, and to become PALs in the same way as other external contributors. This would be an extension of the idea of a 'corporate university'.

CONCLUSION

This chapter suggests that non-employees who directly or indirectly impact on an organisation's operations could be usefully classified in terms of:

■ those operating outside the organisation who contribute to the primary value chain, e.g. suppliers, dealers, customers;

■ those operating outside the organisation who contribute to the support value chain, e.g. outsourced HRD departments;

- those operating within the organisation who contribute to the primary value chain, e.g. volunteers, self-employed subcontactors;

- those operating within the organisation who contribute to the support value chain, e.g. consultants, franchisees;

- those operating outside the organisation who do not contribute to the value chain but who have an interest in its activities, e.g. environmental pressure groups, families of employees;

- those operating within the organisation who do not contribute to the value chain but who have an interest in its activities, e.g. union representatives, works convenors.

The schema in Figure 10.5 can be used as an enabling framework for classifying the learning needs of non-employee stakeholder groups contributing to the primary value chain.

Figure 10.5 Learning needs of non-employees contributing to the primary value chain

Non-employees contributing to the primary value chain		HRD strategies to meet learning needs		
Non-employee type	*Learning needs*	*Training*	*Education*	*Development*
Suppliers Dealers Consumers Volunteers	High priority Medium priority Low priority			

Source: Stewart and McGoldrick (1996, p. 136).

Similar tables can be developed for non-employee stakeholder groups contributing to the support value chain and for stakeholders impacting upon the organisation but operating outside the value chain.

Whatever approach is adopted it is important that those responsible for skills development and learning within the organisation develop a coherent and planned strategy for training, education, development and learning support for these non-employee stakeholders. This clearly becomes more difficult if the learning architects have themselves been outsourced; organisational decision makers should reflect on the implications of such a strategic decision for the continuous improvement and development of its human resources.

REFERENCES

Atkinson, J. S. (1985) 'Flexibility: planning for an uncertain future', *Manpower Policy and Practice*, 1, Summer.

Barham, K. and Oates, D. (1991) *The International Manager*. London: Economist Books.

Cox, C. R. (1994) 'Customer Training takes off at Boeing', *Training and Development* (US), December, pp. 39–42.

Hood, G. (1997) 'Teaming with ideas', *People Management*, 28 August.

Institute of Manpower Studies (1985) 'New Forms of Work Organisation', *IMS Manpower Commentary*, No. 30. London: IMS.

Jarillo, J. C. (1993) *Strategic Networks – Creating the Borderless Organisation*. Oxford: Butterworth-Heinemann.

Johnson, G. and Scholes, J. (1993) *Exploring Corporate Strategy*. Englewood Cliffs, NJ: Prentice Hall.

Kanter, R. M. (1989) *When Giants Learn To Dance*. New York: Simon & Schuster.

Madu, C. and Kuei, C. (1993) 'Introducing Strategic Quality Management', *Long Range Planning*, 26(6), December.

Next Steps Review (1993). London: HMSO, Cmnd. 2430.

Porter, M. (1980) *Competitive Advantage*. New York: Free Press.

Rhinesmith, S. H. (1996) *A Manager's Guide to Globalisation – Six Skills for Success in a Changing World* (2nd edn). Homewood, IL: Irwin.

Rothwell, W. and Kazanas, H. C. (1989) *Strategic Human Resource Development*. Englewood Cliffs, NJ: Prentice Hall.

Schuler, R. S. and Macmillan, I.C. (1985) 'Gaining a Competitive Edge through Human Resources', *Personnel*, April.

Steeples, Marion M. (1992) *The Corporate Guide to the Malcolm Baldrige National Quality Award*. ASQC Quality Press.

Stewart, J. and McGoldrick, J. (eds) (1996) *Human Resource Development – Perspectives, Strategies and Practice*. London: Pitman.

Tuppen, C. (1993) 'An Environmental Policy for British Telecommunications', *Long Range Planning*, 26(5), pp. 24–30.

Unipart (UGC) (1996) *Review*. London: UGC.

Chapter 11

OUTSOURCING: WHAT STAYS IN AND WHAT GOES OUT

OBJECTIVES

By the end of this chapter you should be able to:

■ account for the current interest in outsourcing as a strategic initiative;

■ establish advantages and disadvantages of outsourcing;

■ differentiate between outsourcing, out-tasking, insourcing and intasking;

■ reach informed judgements on what HRD functions and services should be out-sourced, and what kept or brought in-house.

INTRODUCTION

It is an apparent paradox that at a time when more and more attention is being given to the strategic significance of HRD and the importance of ensuring the 'intellectual capital' of an organisation, the HRD profession seems to be under threat. It goes beyond the frequent non-involvement of HRD practitioners in initiating or furthering major new learning initiatives within an organisation. The profession is increasingly finding that what was traditionally its core business – the provision of formal classroom or workshop training – is being seen as peripheral to the core business of the organisation, and being handled outside the organisation boundaries. In other words, it is being outsourced.

According to a 1994 survey of personnel professionals in the UK by the Brook Street Recruitment Agency and the Henley Research Centre, training is the function most likely to be outsourced or contracted out by organisations in the next decade (nominated by 24 per cent of those surveyed).

This opinion may of course be related to the way that many personnel professionals have distanced themselves from HRD issues over the years. A 1990 survey conducted by Millward *et al.* (1992) reported that only 24 per cent of designated HR managers claimed a responsibility for training and development compared to 82 per cent of non-HR managers.

Nevertheless, there is substantial current interest among organisational decision makers in outsourcing as a strategic option. They are reviewing the various constituent parts of their value chain and deciding what should be contracted out, what should be kept in and what should be brought in. The emphasis in recent years has been on contracting out rather than bringing in. This chapter looks in detail at the reported trend towards outsourcing of course-driven training and development (T&D) in the context of this broader trend. How pervasive is it? What are its implications for the profession? Should it be deemed an opportunity or a threat? What arguments should be brought to bear when the issue comes up for debate?

Note that to consider the outsourcing of training and development is not an all-or-nothing, either or situation. As we shall see, a number of organisational policy makers have been very selective about what goes out and what stays in. On the whole, outsourcing focuses on areas of major capital and revenue expenditure such as in-house training, operating from in-house training centres. It is in these areas that the organisation faces significant outgoings and senior management might consider that savings can be achieved and services more effectively provided by an outside provider. The outsourcing of training is, of course, not the same as outsourcing of all intentional learning and HRD. It does not necessarily mean that those responsible for HRD as a *process* have been outsourced. In many organisations there has been a considerable investment in the development of people. There should be real concern about the implications for the development of HRD processes in particular, and learning in general, if the architects of those processes are located outside the organisational boundaries.

Some outsourcing is now being challenged, leading to 'insourcing'! In fact there is an ongoing tension and movement between these two polar extremes in organisational practice. The chapter develops a simple continuum for analysing the outsourcing–insourcing debate. In particular, a clear distinction is made between outsourcing and out-tasking on one side of the scale, and intasking and insourcing on the other.

Outsourcing should not be confused with 'abdication'. This typically occurs when an organisation decides to close down all in-house T&D provision and associated support services. Opportunities for attending external courses might be offered as a substitute, but on an *ad hoc*, 'sheep dip' basis. In the situation just described there is no attempt to identify external partners or providers who can contribute in any structured way to the learning process for the benefit of the organisation.

THE DISTINCTION BETWEEN CORE AND PERIPHERAL ACTIVITIES

The distinction between core and periphery activities has a long pedigree, but gained most impetus in the UK following the publication of the influential report by the Institute of Manpower Studies in the mid-1980s entitled, 'New Forms of Work Organisation' (Atkinson, 1984). The report identified four types of flexibility which organisation policy makers should consider: numerical flexibility, functional flexibility, pay flexibility and distancing strategies.

1 *Numerical flexibility* means that organisations should be sufficiently flexible to adjust labour inputs to meet demand fluctuations. Options available include the use of part-time and temporary staff, short-term contracts and casual workers.

2 *Functional flexibility* relates to the versatility of employees and their working flexibility within and between jobs. For many well-established organisations with a strong trade union presence, it can mean developing approaches to break down traditional demarcation lines between jobs.

3 *Pay flexibility* enables the organisation to adjust its wage and salary outgoings in accordance with fluctuations in output. It puts increasing emphasis on merit pay and other forms of performance-related and output-driven reward.

4 *Distancing strategies* refer to subcontracting certain functions rather than reorganising internal staffing practices. The choice of whether to keep an activity within the boundaries of a given organisation would depend on the extent to which it was seen as being central (core) to the organisation's operations or ancillary (peripheral) to them.

The report was influential in the decision of the Government of Mrs Thatcher (as she then was) to legislate for compulsory competitive tendering (CCT) for a range of local authority activities. It also influenced a similar initiative to subject all Civil Service departments to 'market testing'. Activities were subjected to 'critical scrutiny' to see whether they should stay within the public domain.

Outsourcing is a form of 'distancing strategy' as defined by the Institute of Manpower Studies. But it goes beyond issues of flexibility. It relates also to economic judgements about transactions (exchange of goods and services) between partners and the transaction costs involved. What form of transaction creates the greatest value to the organisation, be it in terms of affording the most benefits and/or generating the least costs? The outsourcing argument holds that an organisation can possess a limited number of distinctive competences, and that a number of transactions currently taking place in-house would be more effectively accomplished by a specialist provider operating outside its boundaries. It is a particular aspect of the economic theory of the firm that the smaller the agent, the greater the potential for efficient transactions in terms of the real cost and benefits provided.

VALUE CHAIN ANALYSIS

It is helpful in this context to recall value chain analysis as developed by Michael Porter (1980). Underpinning the notion of 'value chain' is that a sequence of activities needs to be undertaken in order to translate raw materials and other inputs into a finished product or service that reaches an end-user; and that each one of these should add value to the product. In commercial terms, value is measured in terms of the amount buyers are willing to pay for what a firm provides them with. In a given value chain Porter distinguishes between primary and support value activities, each being integral to the success of an organisation in getting its products or services to its customers.

Primary activities are those that lead directly to the provision of a product or service to a customer. They vary according to the nature of the goods and services provided. Support activities assist the primary activities. They include IT, technology development, marketing research, finance and payroll, HRM and HRD and the overall organisational infrastructure, including policy making and its implementation.

Many organisations over the years have differentiated between primary and support activities by referring to them as *line* and *staff* functions respectively. Those responsible for line functions have often seen themselves as being at the 'sharp end' of the business as opposed to (as they see it) the more 'cushioned' existence of their colleagues in staff functions.

The outsourcing argument is that all activities contributing to the value chain need to be subjected to a critical scrutiny in order to establish whether greater value could be obtained by conducting the transactions through an external agent. The extreme version is that all transactions contributing to the value chain should be conducted by specialist agents, linked together in some form of holding and co-ordinating network – a particular interpretation of the virtual organisation looked at in Chapter 20.

OUTSOURCING VERSUS INSOURCING

The term 'insourcing' can be interpreted in a number of ways. One approach is to see 'insourcing' as a means of sharing internal services, whereby a number of organisational support functions such as T&D are combined and their services sold at cost to the various business units which make up a large decentralised corporation. The objective is to capture the economies of scale of centralisation, but with the customer focus and responsiveness desired by the business units. If the shared services unit cannot deliver the desired service better or more cheaply than an external provider, the business units are at liberty to go outside.

The Forum Corporation, a training and development consultancy based in Boston, Massachusetts, and with offices world-wide, including one in the UK, uses a different definition. One of its stated core areas of expertise is managing training as a business through *strategic insourcing* or unique partnerships with clients to manage all or some portion of the organisation's existing internal training. An aim of such partnerships is to convert fixed training costs into variable costs. The key element that differentiates this approach from outsourcing is that services by the external agent are provided in house, using a client's premises and facilities, but fixed costs are reduced by the replacement of existing full-time staff. In the context of the definitions used later in this chapter, the Forum model is a variant of *strategic partnering*.

The approach adopted in this book is to see insourcing as the reverse of outsourcing. Activities which were previously provided by an external agent are bought in. This could be done to secure sources of supply, or because it is felt that in other ways extra value could be added by running the function in house. Purchasing departments in manufacturing industries dealing with products that consist of a large number of component parts refer to such decisions as 'make or buy' considerations. In broader strategic terms the degree of insourcing determines the extent of *vertical integration*.

Taking a given organisation's operations as the base, one can look 'upstream' and 'downstream' in order to determine the degree of existing, and desirable, backward vertical integration and forward vertical integration respectively. Backward vertical integration reflects the extent to which an organisation establishes ownership and control over 'upstream' activities, that is, of the sources of supply of its raw materials. Forward vertical integration relates to 'downstream' activities, that is, the channels of distribution whereby a product reaches end-users. The greater the degree of vertical integration, the more an organisation has exercised ownership and control over its primary value chain and thus taken direct responsibility for the conduct of a greater spread of its operations.

In the past, functional operations associated with the support value chain have largely been excluded from the vertical integration debate and the related make or buy decision. It has been assumed that they will be automatically included within the organisation's sphere of direct responsibility. Much of previous theoretical discussion in the organisational literature has been concerned with the resultant relationship between specialist support functions such as Personnel on the one hand, and line managers involved in primary value chain activities on the other. This is not to say that in the past everything associated with the support value chain has been done in house. The functional areas have often 'out-tasked' a number of their subsidiary tasks – for example specialist agencies have often handled recruitment advertising. As the practice of outsourcing shows, the debate has now shifted (*see* Fig. 11.1).

Figure 11.1 The new regime

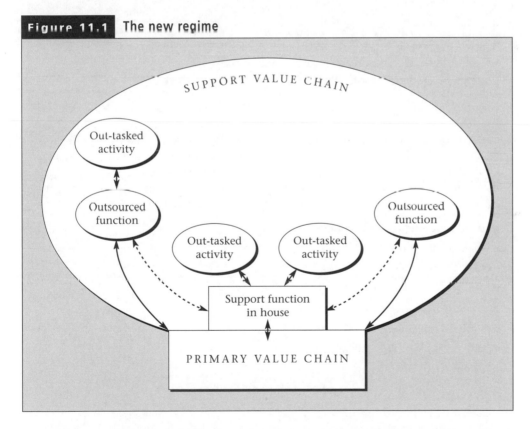

The relationship between outsourcing and insourcing is dynamic and quite fluid. In the area of recruitment, some organisations in recent years have relied on established external agencies. The Oracle Corporation is a US company which produces database software used to process sales orders and customer records and employs

32 000 people world-wide. The UK headquarters in Reading handles a large proportion of recruitment for Europe, the Middle East and Africa. In 1994, 80 per cent of this recruitment was handled by external agencies. As the jobs market for specialists in IT has become more active, Oracle has become less reliant on agencies and expanded its own recruitment function. Oracle now claims to have a team of recruiters that understands the business far better than any external supplier could.

| Figure 11.2 | Outsourcing and IT |

Since the early 1990s the in-house IT function has borne the brunt of much of the swing towards outsourcing. IBM, the UK's second largest outsourcer after Cap Gemini, claims to have signed more than £47.5bn worth of outsourcing contracts since 1991. A survey of 123 UK companies conducted by the KPMG managing consultancy group and published in September 1997 (KPMG, 1997) found that the following benefits were claimed for outsourcing:

- more cost-effective;
- greater expertise;
- reduces IT costs;
- enables company to concentrate on core business expertise;
- lack of in-house resources/resource constraints;
- lack of in-house expertise/access to specialist skills outside.

For 21 per cent of the survey, these expectations were exceeded, 14 per cent felt that they were not met, and just under half said their ability to concentrate on core businesses went beyond expected levels. In relation to contracts 59 per cent of respondents said that these were scheduled for renewal within the next two years. Only 29 per cent were intending to renew them with the same supplier.

A significant number of outsourcing problems were presented. Each of the following was mentioned by at least 30 per cent of the respondents:

- over-dependence on supplier;
- locked into supplier;
- lack of influence on the service levels of supplier;
- length of time in getting service right;
- limited/no control over supplier;
- more management time spent on dealing with supplier issues;
- loss of skills on IT applications;
- difficulty in reverting to in-house service;
- supplier does not understand the company's business.

OUTSOURCING AND OUT-TASKING

The USA-based company Corning make a helpful distinction between *outsourcing* and *out-tasking*.

In *outsourcing*, the entire responsibility for a service area or functional activity, which was previously undertaken in house, is transferred to an outside supplier. The work is still undertaken, but not by staff employed by the organisation.

In *out-tasking*, external providers are contracted to provide some services in house, because of their specific expertise in a particular area. This has long been a way of obtaining T&D services – especially for course delivery – from outside suppliers.

Walker (1992) also makes the point that as organisations seek to contain their staffing levels and costs, there is an increasing reliance on external consultants and suppliers for training design, curriculum and materials development and programme delivery. Many vendors will also adapt their programmes and materials to meet specific requirements. He refers to a practice adopted by Xerox, where much of the design and development work is contracted out. Actual instruction is undertaken by employees, who may not be training professionals, but employees brought in for a special assignment. It is not a simple decision of whether to outsource or insource; organisations will maintain involvement and control in the areas they feel are most important and cost effective to undertake in house, and contract work out as well. It becomes a very complex and fluid dynamic (*see* Fig. 11.3).

| Figure 11.3 | NALGO case study: an example of out-tasking |

NALGO, the trade union for white collar workers in the UK which became incorporated into UNISON in the early 1990s, had for many years a well-established training and development unit, consisting of two full-time members of staff located at the union's HQ in Central London. Their remit was to ensure that training needs analyses were carried out for new and existing members of staff, and that in-house courses were made available to help meet those needs. Many of the courses were carried out at a staff training centre on the banks of the River Clyde, south of Glasgow in Scotland. Others were conducted in a variety of London locations. However none of these courses was delivered by the members of the unit. All course providers were individual training consultants, separately contracted because of their expertise in a given area. In order to make the courses as meaningful as possible to delegates, some of the consultants undertook visits to various NALGO work centres to gain, at first hand, knowledge of the activities being undertaken and of the problems being faced by course delegates.

The role of the two full-time members of the unit was to find suitable consultants, to ensure that they were appropriately briefed and to provide them with ongoing support.

This situation is typical of that confronting many T&D departments. The full-time members of staff act as intermediaries between the employees needing the training, and the external providers who have the skills to offer it. It is particularly appropriate where there are not sufficient employees to justify full-time trainers to cover all of the subject/role specialisms, or where there are emergent areas affecting jobs or the way they are interpreted, and where there are no in-house competences. In the case of NALGO, as the organisation expanded, union officials were increasingly being asked to take on a staff management role without having any managerial background. Indeed, in the past, everything that smacked of management had been eschewed as alien to the culture of what NALGO was about.

Figure 11.4 presents another example of out-tasking, that of British Rail.

Figure 11.4 | **British Rail**

On a larger scale, British Rail before privatisation used external associates or training consultants to deliver many of the management development programmes run at their national training centre, a large country house called The Grove, near Watford, just north of London. It was felt that external facilitators, who were versed in BR issues and able to communicate ideas from a strong subject knowledge base, would provide a breadth of approach that internal staff would not be able to match.

There was a concern to demonstrate that the external associates were familiar with the railway business. The Grove's 1992 publicity booklet distributed to BR employees stated:

> We seek to ensure that The Grove is a centre for learning excellence by continually reviewing our associates' abilities to meet current needs. We have a collaborative process of reviewing performance involving programme managers, associate consultants and participants. All our associate consultants are regularly briefed on latest BR developments.
>
> Currently The Grove's associate network exceeds 80 consultants in various specialisms. With this large base we are ideally placed to advise, and assist business colleagues with resources.

The Grove also started to develop partnerships with academic institutions as well as individual consultants, especially in terms of building up a range of accredited programmes leading to externally recognised qualifications. On this the 1992 publicity booklet stated:

> We are currently in partnership with a number of educational institutions and accreditation agencies . . . It is our perception that these partnerships offer the best value-added products to meet needs. In addition, we are exploring the possibility of three-way partnerships between ourselves, BR businesses and academic institutions.

One of the features of the partnerships was that representatives from the associated academic institutions were involved in the delivery of programmes at the Grove. It was the responsibility of BR staff located at The Grove to oversee the programmes and maintain a support service for the external associates and partners. Following privatisation, BR disposed of The Grove as a dedicated training centre.

THE OUTSOURCING–INSOURCING CONTINUUM

Having defined *outsourcing* and *out-tasking*, it is now appropriate to differentiate between *insourcing* and *intasking*.

In *insourcing*, the entire responsibility for a service area or functional activity, which was previously undertaken by an external agent, is brought in house, and carried out by staff employed by the organisation. In some circumstances this might entail buying the entire business of an external agency.

In *intasking*, activities which were previously conducted externally are brought in-house either because the organisation considers it possesses the relevant expertise or because it is willing to buy it in.

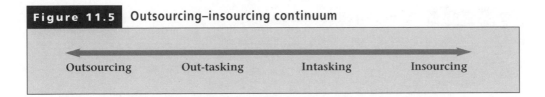

Figure 11.5 Outsourcing–insourcing continuum

Figure 11.5 shows the outsourcing – out-tasking – intasking – insourcing continuum. This continuum presents a range of options. A number of HRD units draw upon external consultants in the first instance because they lack the necessary expertise. Over a period of time, as they work in partnership with the consultant, they develop the relevant skills and expertise themselves. In development centres, a number of patented tests and exercises might be used by the consultant. The internal unit might be given permission to use them under licence and may eventually develop their own exercises and tests and run the whole programme in house.

There is often a relationship between organisation size and the decision whether to outsource or insource. Smaller organisations do not have the resources for large in-house specialist departments and staff. As they get larger, the traditional tendency has been to bring things in house. Out-tasking is often associated with buying in specific expertise. Storey (1992) refers to the range of consultants used by ICI Films who were involved in HRD activities to support its various change programmes in the 1980s. ICI Films is located in Dumfries in Scotland and manufactures 'Melinex', which is converted into photographic film and also into propafilm for computer tape and food packaging. For example the Coverdale organisation and Peter Honey, the independent consultant responsible with Alan Mumford for designing the well-known 'Learning Style Questionnaire, were drawn upon to help facilitate a consultant-led process contributing to improved group working. Line managers operating under licence from Crosby, the Quality Improvement Consultancy, were trained as facilitators for the mandatory Crosby Quality Improvement programme.

Outsourcing versus 'embedded outsourcing' or 'strategic partnering'

A differentiation can be made between outsourcing and 'embedded outsourcing' or 'strategic partnering'. The USA-based Corporate Leadership Council (1995) suggest that outsourcing contracts are typically short term (one to two years), and that the contractor manages the contract as it would any other. Because of its relatively short duration, the contract tends not to be tailored to the specific needs of the client.

Strategic partnering contracts are of longer duration (five to ten years). The outsourcer is represented on senior-level strategy committees, and can contribute specialist inputs to larger decision-making processes. The longer-term nature of the contract encourages the outsourcer to customise services for the benefit of the client. In other words, the outsourcer becomes increasingly 'embedded' in the fabric of the client organisation. The outsourcing–insourcing continuum may be expanded, with the inclusion of 'embedded outsourcing (*see* Fig. 11.6).

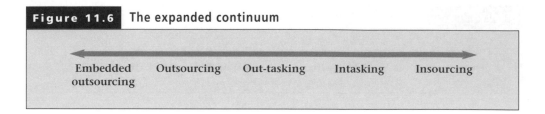

Figure 11.6 The expanded continuum

Embedded outsourcing — Outsourcing — Out-tasking — Intasking — Insourcing

OTHER OUTSOURCING ISSUES

Outsourcing should not be a simple matter of sloughing off non-core activities and then forgetting about them. There may be substantial costs for the organisation in managing the residual relationship. Just because something is perceived as peripheral to the core business does not mean that it is not important and that the service should not be carried out.

Specialist outside providers may have economies of scale compared to the larger organisation, but can be costly in some respects. The decision whether to outsource an activity is not just a simple make or buy consideration. External suppliers do not have detailed knowledge of all facets of the business of a potential client. As regards their facilities and approach, these sometimes are not behind the times. Wiggenhorn (1990) describes Motorola's search among local colleges for external partners to deliver some of its programmes and its discovery that their facilities were not up to modern industrial standards.

Without internal support, the external HRD provider will encounter problems in identifying in advance the learning needs of participants. It will need to ensure that training provision is up to date and continues to meet the needs of clients. It will need to develop a strategy for anticipating shifts in business direction (not that this is always done especially well by in-house HRD staff).

The real cost of 'buying' an output as opposed to making it includes the cost of identifying suitable providers, communicating needs to them, monitoring their progress and outputs, preventing them from engaging in predatory behaviour and so on (Alexander and Young, 1996). A further issue concerns value. An external provider may be able to run training courses far more cheaply than I (for example) could do, but will they retain all of the value that they create or pass some of it on to me? Value could go beyond a simple matter of saving costs on *their* operations: they could learn some extremely interesting things from course delegates about how I could improve the running of *my* operations. Additionally, if I do not have the ability to switch easily to alternative suppliers, will they exert their power to appropriate even more value from me, for example, by charging me more for the services provided?

Once an activity has been outsourced, both parties to the arrangement will endeavour to establish barriers to exit so long as the arrangement holds value for them. In other words, the purchasing organisation will try to secure its source of supply by trying to make it difficult or unattractive for the providing organisation to go elsewhere. One can expect that the terms of the outsourcing agreement will make it difficult for the outsourced unit to sever the links. The supplier, by providing a service of appropriate quality and cost, will try to ensure that the customer does not feel tempted to look elsewhere. As a protection against entrapment in unproductive partnerships, the vendor may be asked to take on a number of former in-house staff, on the condition that if the partnership does not work, the host organisation can rehire them (Corporate Leadership Council, 1995).

At the same time, the outsourced unit will try to impose 'barriers to entry' to outsiders moving in. In general terms, the more value that is attached to a contract with a given customer, the greater the efforts to create barriers to entry from outsiders and 'barriers to exit' for the 'customer'.

In addition to looking at cost reduction and quality enhancement, the host organisation will only contemplate outsourcing when it does not feel threatened by any prospect of losing ownership and control. This is either because the activity is not regarding as of great significance – in particular in terms of affording competitive advantage – and/or because it feels it can establish a partnership of trust with an external contractor.

Of course, outsourced entities can be treated as fiefdoms, with the supplier being allowed to 'trade' only with the client organisation. In such a situation the organisation gets the benefit of the external expertise and security of supply over 'imported goods', without the problems and costs of ownership. This seems to run counter to the notion of 'trust' that is often referred to in the establishment of long-term partnerships. Despite the much-vaunted benefits of 'partnership', it is still much easier (and cheaper) to untie the knot with external than with internal commitments. If 'trust' really existed, one would not expect the host organisation to restrict the freedom of action of its suppliers – especially if the larger host company was not manifestly restricting its own customer base and was endeavouring to preserve its own freedom of action in terms of its trading associations.

In HRD terms, the decision on whether to outsource is influenced by the scale of courses and programmes being contemplated and the identification of suppliers with the capacity to handle the range of activities being proposed. But 'trust' and 'partnership' are ongoing motifs.

THE RELATIONSHIP OF OUTSOURCING TO CORE COMPETENCES

Where so-called leading edge organisations like IBM and Corning have outsourced HRD activities, they have given careful thought to what to outsource and what to retain. Concern has been expressed that one does not want to lose something which imparts distinctive competences to the organisation, thereby adding to its sustainable competitive advantage and overall intellectual capital. The general arguments for outsourcing are well known, but there is much uncertainty as to what constitutes 'core competences'.

Building on the various attributes which are imputed to core competences by authorities such as Barney (1991) and Petts (1997), we see the following as significant to the outsourcing debate. It is more likely that an activity will be undertaken in-house if it meets these criteria.

1 *Deliverability.* There is a group of expert people in the organisation who demonstrate a capacity to use diverse technologies and approaches.

2 *Inimitability.* What is being undertaken cannot be copied or provided easily by outsiders.

3 *Durability.* The value added is not dependent on a current range of products and services. There is confidence that those responsible for the activity will be able to respond to future contingencies.

4 *Non-substitutability.* It cannot be replaced by an alternative competence.

5 *Superiority:* It is clearly better than other competences provided elsewhere.

6 *Source of envy.* Others, such as competitors, would dearly like to be able to provide the product or carry out the service but do not have the requisite skills. Its possession thus constitutes a considerable barrier to entry to competitors.

7 *Translatable into tangible customer benefits.* Its exercise is seen as being valuable by customers. Until it manifests itself in something tangible for the customer it remains impotent. This ability to effect the transference process is described by Petts (1997) as a *core capability*.

PRACTICAL EXAMPLES OF OUTSOURCING AND OUT-TASKING

Figures 11.7 to 11.10 provide case study examples of organisations that have undertaken varying degrees of outsourcing and out-tasking.

Figure 11.7 **IBM**

In 1991 IBM United Kingdom Ltd as part of its restructuring programme evaluated the added value of its in-house training functions in terms of whether they could be more effectively and economically delivered by an external source. The company is renowned for its commitment to training and had an extensive education department which delivered high quality programmes in several key areas: technical, marketing, personal and professional skills and management development.

The outcome of the IBM evaluation was that in November 1991, all interpersonal and professional skills training and all management development education were outsourced to Skillbase Ltd. Skillbase already existed as an IBM alliance company in which at the time IBM held a 40 per cent stake. Technical training was not outsourced since this was close to IBM's core business and linked closely to product development.

The objectives of the outsourcing were:

■ to have the same quantity and quality of training delivered at 30 per cent less cost;

■ to support IBM's programme of 'right sizing' the organisation by reducing its payroll by up to 50 people;

■ to encourage the development of new business opportunities by a specialist skills company in an area which would generate for IBM a royalty payment on external revenue.

IBM also saw an opportunity to extend the concept of a partnership approach with suppliers of services as a strategic way of operating in the future.

▶▶

▶▶ Figure 11.7 continued

The planning of the new arrangement was detailed. The programmes to be delivered were itemised and quantified. Development work was assessed and agreed. The management processes, including requirements planning, measurements, administration and accounting, were fixed. Legal and copyright issues were resolved. The relationships of Skillbase with IBM customers, agents, and third parties were established.

The most careful attention was paid to the people involved. After the transfer about 50 training jobs no longer existed in IBM. The resource required by Skillbase was calculated and it emerged that three types of professional would manage, develop, deliver and administer the programme. Some people would be hired directly by Skillbase as permanent employees. Some would become associate trainers paid on a daily basis as consultants but without guaranteed employment. A small number would remain with IBM but would be seconded to Skillbase for a specific period and would focus on the management development mission.

Figure 11.8 BT

In 1995 BT examined its personnel and training function to ascertain whether its services could best be delivered in house or be outsourced. After a year-long review BT concluded that most of the services were best kept in house for the time being. Some non-specialist training services were farmed out and some responsibility has been devolved to line managers.

Theoretically BT could have outsourced much of the HR function – such as health and safety matters – if such a move had been sensible in terms of cost and quality. The position may well change in the future as BT intends to carry out diluted versions of the review annually.

The review formed part of an analysis of all internal functions under the umbrella of BT's transformation project, Breakout. A task force with representatives from all divisions was set up to analyse some 17 separate personnel and training services, including executive recruitment and development, welfare, internal communications and health and safety. These were ranked in order of strategic importance and efficiency of delivery. According to the reorganisation project director services not deemed strategically important were clear candidates for outsourcing. Executive development and technical training were on the strategic list whereas others such as payroll and recruitment were not.

Again according to the project director, as the organisation becomes more customer and service oriented, so skills in marketing, technical development and sales become major differentiators between BT and its competitors. Assessing the need for these skills and then developing them is a strategic issue for the HR function in the future.

Significant amounts of training have, however, been outsourced – such as management development. Outsourcing training, it is argued, means that external providers, rather than the organisation, deal with the peaks and troughs. Training traditionally encounters fluctuations in demand.

▶▶

▶▶ Figure 11.8 continued

> BT feels that, despite all the talk of the move towards outsourcing, the industry is still very young, particularly in the personnel area. It is one thing to decide to outsource a particular function and another to find someone to do it. There are plenty of firms well placed to take on outsourced recruitment and payroll, but not so many able to undertake such functions as internal communications, management development and strategic thinking in the personnel area.

Source: *Personnel Today*, 23 May 1995.

Figure 11.9 Corning

Since 1987, the American multinational company Corning has outsourced the heart of its traditional training. Corning HQ is in New York State and the company has 39 000 employees, $4.8 billion sales and 60 000 different products including optical fibres and space shuttle technical support. It is a corporate requirement that each employee is expected to spend 5 per cent of his or her time on training-related activities.

Reasons for outsourcing included cost reduction and moving work peripheral to Corning to an organisation for whom training is its specialism. This enables Corning to focus on developing strategic competences which include innovation (how to get ideas from R&D to the marketplace more quickly), quality, partnership (including between management and union), dimensions of leadership (competences giving competitive advantage if leaders behaved that way) and diversity (allowing individuals to be themselves). Outsourcing traditional training also enables the residual Corning HRD function to focus in house on driving fundamental cultural change at organisational level and to be a change agent in the total system.

There are some 100 outsourced courses, providing training in technology, sales and marketing, individual skills, managerial skills and finance and control. The outsourcing went beyond training delivery, however. It included course advertising, delegate registration, programme scheduling, course content, facilities, course evaluation, programme development and finances, including payment of instructors.

When Corning first took this step, the word outsourcing had not been coined and the term partnership was used. Note that Corning differentiated between *outsourcing*, which is transferring responsibility for a service area – its objectives and activities, and *out-tasking* for example, getting a university to provide a course.

Corning paid great attention to choosing a partner for outsourcing. Factors included shared values – an organisation was needed that was flexible and could cope with change, reputation, quality, stability, experience of and expertise in training delivery, financial strength, recruiting capability (was the chosen partner capable of recruiting staff to replace any who might leave and still maintain quality?) and customer focus.

The partner Corning chose was an education and training centre operating as a non-profit organisation and focusing on adult training. Attention was given to contractual details but the basis of the partnership was and has continued to be

▶▶

▶▶ Figure 11.9 continued

> based on trust. There were also regular project meetings and every member of Corning's HRD staff had in their contract reference to key result areas to make the partnership work. It was regarded as important to make it seem that the partner organisation was part of Corning – it was included in the internal telephone directory, went on to e-mail/VAX and also was included in internal mail drops. It even had access to the mainframe computer.

There are some several aspects of Corning's philosophy that deserve comment. First, the provision of training is seen to be a non-core related activity. This is not the same as saying that Corning is not interested in achieving highly skilled employees out of the training, nor that as a company it is not interested in HRD. Its interest is implied by the number of days individuals are expected to spend on training related activities.

A second point relates to the reconfiguration of the HRD role in the company. There is a new emphasis on operating as a 'contract manager', and sustaining the relationship between the outside supplier and the internal customer. There is also a focus on residual HRD staff becoming involved as internal consultants in broader strategic and change issues.

Figure 11.10 Nuclear Electric

Nuclear Electric is one of the organisations that emerged when the Central Electricity Generating Board was split up in 1991. It inherited two out of the 15 management development tutors that had previously operated out of the Bricket Wood management training centre in Hertfordshire, located just a few miles north of The Grove centre referred to in Fig. 11.4. It did not, however, inherit the Bricket Wood site, which was allocated exclusively to National Power, another offshoot of the 1991 break-up.

Nuclear Electric, with 14 000 employees and operating 13 nuclear power stations in England and Wales, needed to ensure that its managers learned how to operate as a commercial business, capable of responding effectively to changing circumstances.

The solution adopted was to set up a network of associate tutors, originally eight and currently 20, whose role was to design and deliver management training and to support development projects. A training needs analysis identified three priorities: privatisation and culture change programmes, commercial and financial skills, and management skills.

The associate tutors operate as self-employed consultants on an annual contract, with 20 days' work at a fixed daily fee rate guaranteed each year. Opportunities are provided to attend corporate training events, to shadow other associates and to be trained as company observers for assessment and development programmes.

The associate tutor network is co-ordinated by four training programme co-ordinators, who also provide an advisory service, design and deliver some training, work on new projects and assist in policy formulation.

Nuclear Electric split in 1996 into two: Nuclear Electric Ltd which controls five gas-cooled reactors and one pressurised-water reactor; and Magnox Electric which

▶▶

▶▶ Figure 11.10 continued

> runs the six magnox-fuelled power stations. The associate consultant network services both organisations.
>
> Among the advantages claimed for the arrangement is the fact that although the external tutors increasingly become more familiar with the culture of the organisation and the ways that people work, they can still retain the objective stance of outsiders.

Source: Poulteney, 1997.

TECHNICAL TRAINING, HIGH-TECH TRAINING AND LEARNING SUPPORT

When we move into the technical and high-tech training arena, the situation becomes even more complex. Many organisations are understandably reluctant to outsource the technical, product-oriented area of their training provision, which is so closely and directly linked to their core business. However, as the training becomes increasingly high-tech, they may need to look for support to external providers.

An interesting example of the relationship between insourcing and outsourcing for the development of multi-skilling in a high-tech environment is afforded by SmithKline Beecham.

Figure 11.11　SmithKline Beecham

> The SmithKline Beecham factory in Irvine, Scotland, which was set up in 1971, produces semi-synthetic penicillins and other drugs. In the mid-1990s a dedicated training centre was built on the site at a cost of £400 000. One of its functions has been to equip factory floor operators with basic engineering skills as part of a plant-wide multiskilling drive. The training programme commences with four days initial training which combines theoretical training in the centre's two classrooms with practical exercises on the kind of equipment used in the factory's manufacturing areas, and then continues with one-to-one coaching on the shopfloor. Operators are not expected to carry out any engineering tasks until they feel comfortable about doing so – and have been fully accredited by trained assessors.
>
> Craftsmen have also been included in the cross-skilling initiative. The aim is not to turn electricians into fitters or fitters into electricians, but to enable each to carry out some of the activities previously exclusively undertaken by the other. Training in these new skills, which commenced in January 1995, takes longer to complete than the operator's training programme. Most of the work is conducted in the training centre, where rooms have been equipped to provide practical training in instrumentation, electrical testing and other specialist areas. The training centre staff have also developed a range of multimedia learning packages, making use of information gleaned from years of experience but not written in any training manual.
>
> In the development and the implementation of the programme there has been an element of out-tasking. For example, the local Training and Enterprise Council

▶▶ Figure 11.11 continued

> helped train 25 experienced shopfloor workers to act as trainers and assessors for the multiskilling programme. Some external training of the craftsmen is provided by Scotwest, a training organisation based in the area.

Source: Arkin, 1995.

In Fig. 11.11 above, reference is made to the production of in-house multimedia packages by training centre staff. Often, however, such packages are produced by external consultants because in-house staff do not have the technical skills or expertise required, or because production is too time-consuming or not cost effective.

Lloyds Bank has been using technology for training since 1968, when they started with audiotapes in an attempt to bring training as near as possible to the workplace.

Figure 11.12 Lloyds Bank

> In the 1980s Lloyds made a significant investment in interactive video systems for branch training and installed over 1500 units. These were largely used for procedural training on topics such as stocks and shares. At this time, the training material was produced in house, and gave the company experience in distance learning techniques. Computer-based training was also delivered, initially using interactive video 'trolleys' within the branches, and later through the bank's mainframe computer system.
>
> To save costs and also provide a faster response to training needs, the bank began to consider customising off-the-shelf products, rather than developing them from scratch. They changed their technology to accommodate generic materials produced by external suppliers by introducing a multimedia platform which included CD-Rom. They then customised generic CD-Rom programmes and the associated work books that had been developed by external training specialists. An example was 'Business Calls', chosen as part of a major initiative by the bank in the early 1990s to improve the quality of the telephone service it was offering to customers. The approach enabled the bank to train a large number of staff very quickly, at their own pace, in their own time and in their own workplace.

Source: Drewett, 1994.

Figure 11.13 presents the example of the Fire Service College training system.

Figure 11.13 Fire Service College

> In 1997 a training system for fire fighters was launched which combines artificial intelligence, virtual reality and multimedia techniques. The development has been jointly undertaken by the Fire Service College and a specialist Virtual Reality consultancy. The system, known as VECTOR, can be run from a desktop PC with a vast range of scenarios to ensure that no two exercises are the same. VECTOR puts the user in a virtual command centre, either on site or at a remote location. It is claimed that a wide range of skills must be used to analyse the situation, devise a strategy and react to unforeseeable and frequently changing events.

There are a number of industries, such as the aircraft manufacturing industry, whose products are of such complexity and sophistication that it would be inappropriate to outsource their core training activities. The manufacturer's responsibility goes beyond training for production. International regulatory agencies and airline procedures govern maintenance practices at the local level, so each aircraft manufacturer must design a basic training programme that satisfies its entire customer base.

To standardise course structure for the industry, members of the Air Transport Association's maintenance-training panel worked to create a specification that defines a high-level, task-oriented approach to course development. Airlines and aircraft manufacturers worked together on the panel, so the specification reflects a global response to their needs. Manufacturers such as Boeing provide training for maintenance employees using the overall parameters of the regulatory agencies. The training can be of great technical sophistication as Fig. 11.14 indicates.

Figure 11.14 **Boeing**

Boeing has used computer-based training (CBT) to supplement classroom teaching since the mid-1980s. In 1994 classes on the 777 were initiated for aircraft maintenance employees at the Boeing maintenance training centre in Seattle, Washington. Trainees attend classroom sessions covering more than 4000 pages of training manual material, involving 30 to 40 CBT lessons and six or seven aircraft simulator sessions in which fault isolation is practised. The 777 course for maintenance employees incorporates instructor-led sessions in which animated examples support other classroom material. The lessons, projected on a large screen, focus on descriptions of the more complex functions of an aircraft system.

Aircraft simulators are used to add realism. Specially configured maintenance- training simulators permit trainees to operate aircraft systems and practise fault isolation in an environment similar to their work setting. Many of the simulators have the ability to 'fly' but their primary purpose is for systems-oriented ground training.

Figure 11.15 looks at the training of air traffic controllers.

Figure 11.15 **National Air Traffic Services**

Welch (1996) reports on the training of about 800 air traffic controllers, employees of National Air Traffic Services, on the use of state-of-the-art technology that allows fewer opportunities for human error. This training is in preparation for working at the £350 million control centre in Hampshire that has been designed to handle all civilian and military flights in UK air space. The UK Civil Aviation Authority hopes that staff using its interactive monitors and error-spotting equipment will be able to cope with the predicted doubling of traffic by 2010.

The approach to training controllers had to be reinvented to keep up with technological advances. Virtual reality and computer modelling were developed to allow operators to familiarise themselves with the new workstations. Initial familiarisation training is computer based, providing multiple choice questions on interactive touch screens. Realistic simulations of emergency scenarios are played out by 'pseudo-pilots' linked to controllers' consoles. The programme was developed by an external aviation training provider.

DEVELOPED INSOURCING–OUTSOURCING CONTINUUM

On the basis of the preceding discussion it is useful to develop a vertical axis for the continuum model which will incorporate a range of HRD-related activities. Table 11.1 indicates what might be included. For each item the answer could be Yes or No or Perhaps for both the current situation and the future.

What has governed your choice? Who do you need to check it with?

Table 11.1 Developed insourcing–outsourcing continuum

HRD activities	Outsource	Out-task	Intask	Insource
Technical training (low-tech)				
Technical training (high-tech)				
Safety training				
Induction training				
Management development (course driven)				
Management development (continuous personal development)				
Development centres				
Team building				
Senior executive workshops				
Facilitating transformational change				
Learning organisation processes				

ADVANTAGES OF OUTSOURCING FOR HUMAN RESOURCE DEVELOPMENT PRACTITIONERS

As a broader HRD issue, individuals can gain substantially from being outsourced. Previously they may have belonged to a department that had low status and was perceived as a peripheral area. Perhaps regarded as being a low priority target for development in their original organisation, they are likely to become central to the core business of the new, outsourced enterprise. This could result in enhanced opportunities for building experience and developing careers. Andersen Consulting believes that, through significant attention to training, personal development and appraisal systems, it can dramatically improve the performance of those staff who were carrying out the same activities before they were outsourced (Alexander and Young, 1996).

There is nothing new in thinking about the benefits of operating outside the boundaries of a parent institution, and contrasting them with the frustrations of being locked into a larger establishment that does not seem to value one's contribution. Anthony Jay in *The Corporation Man* (1972) touched upon these ideas when referring to the need for autonomy and flexibility for BBC production teams of programmes such as 'Tonight'. As he put it:

> The answer came quite suddenly, and it came in the form of another question. Suppose *Tonight* and all the other production team programmes, were completely outside the BBC organisation? Suppose they simply contracted with the BBC to produce a certain number of programmes each year at a certain price? The prospect was Elysian, not just for the money I could save if it were my own, but for the simplicity it would bring to my life, the problems it would take out of the job, the freedom I would have to think about the programme. Instead of the endless internal negotiations, the cajolery and threats and memos and proposals and meetings . . .

One's response to outsourcing depends on one's attitude of mind. On the one hand it can be perceived as a threat by individuals who in the past have been 'protected' by the apparent security of tenure of operating as a salaried member of staff with a contract of employment. One can bemoan one's fate and see it as the end of learning within a given organisation (which of course it is not). On the other hand, as pointed out by Anthony Jay, it can be an opportunity, a loosening of the organisation bonds which restricted one's freedom of action.

One trend that is reportedly emerging in the USA is the tendency to consolidate small private training companies into one large holding which then goes public (Galagan, 1998). Building a large holding by acquiring a lot of small companies in an industry that is not dominated by a single supplier is called a 'roll-up'. A quite unexpected consequence of the outsourcing trend could be a reconfiguration of 'training' into a concentrated industry dominated by a number of large suppliers.

POSTSCRIPT: THE 1997 US INDUSTRY REPORT OF EMPLOYER-SPONSORED TRAINING

Each year the US magazine *Training* produces a detailed analysis of trends in the HRD area. The 1997 figures on outsourcing reveal that 38 per cent of training design and development is carried out by external contractors, compared to 32 per cent of programme delivery. The figures were higher for IT training where 45 per cent of the IT training budget went to external contractors. Of the organisations surveyed, 18 per cent indicated an increasing use of outsourcing. The survey did not differentiate between outsourcing and out-tasking.

CONCLUSION

This chapter has argued that the outsourcing of course-delivered 'generic' training and development can be seen as a logical extension of much of the thinking about whether activities are 'core' or 'periphery', which has been circulating since the mid-1980s. In HRD terms, it is in many cases no more than an extension of the out-tasking that has taken place over the years. The original motivation to outsource or out-task has its roots in some notion of value added, which can manifest itself in a variety of ways. If it is being seen as a cost-cutting exercise, the implication is that the original service was not sufficiently valued. However, for the arrangement to work effectively, the resultant relationship does require substantial time to be devoted to it. It brings to the fore the role of the 'contract manager' as a key HRD function.

As the Corning example (Fig. 11.9) shows, the effect of fully fledged outsourcing has been that rather than go to many small independent suppliers of training and learning services, organisations are developing a significant partnership with a single institutional supplier. An external supplier for whom T&D-related activities is part of its core business can provide a range of dedicated services and expertise that is often not possible for an internal department.

The Corning example also shows that outsourcing can enable HRD staff who remain in house to concentrate on providing specific consultancy services to the business, especially in relation to the management of change. There is emerging a major reconfiguration of the traditional HRD role. There may also be substantial benefits for the outsourced staff in terms of career opportunity and development.

Like all initiatives, outsourcing does have its disadvantages. These include the following:

1 Organisations that have not outsourced the HRD function but operate on an out-tasking basis have often benefited from 'cherry picking' individual training consultants for specified areas. This flexibility may no longer remain.

2 Providing training services in house can be used as an opportunity to draw in line managers and other staff members who have a detailed knowledge of the business.

3 Providing training services in house can be used as a development opportunity for members of staff who wish to develop skills as trainers.

It is a mistake to assume that organisations contemplating outsourcing will inevitably outsource all of their HRD activities. The tendency is to focus on those which do not manifestly add to the core competences of the organisation and which are relatively accessible externally. A number of examples have demonstrated a reluctance to outsource technical training associated with new product development. It is also worth recognising that intasking and insourcing instances continue to occur.

REFERENCES

Alexander, M. and Young, D. (1996) 'Outsourcing: Where's the value?', *Long Range Planning*, 29(5), pp. 728–30.

Arkin, A. (1995) 'Breaking down skills barriers', *People Management*, 9 February, pp. 34–5.

Atkinson, J. (1984) 'Manpower Strategies for Flexible Organisations', *Personnel Management*, August.

Barney, J. (1991) 'Types of competition and the theory of strategy: towards an integrative framework', *Academy of Management Review*, 11(4), pp. 791–800.

Corporate Leadership Council (1995) 'Vision of the Future: Role of Human Resources in the New Corporate Headquarters'. Advisory Board Company.

Drewett, T. (1994) 'Secrets of the Black Horse', *Training and Development (UK),* November, p. 17.

Galagan, P. A. (1998) 'Roll 'Em Up', *Training and Development*, May, pp. 26–31.

Jay, A. (1972) *The Corporation Man*. London: Jonathan Cape.

KPMG (1997) *The Maturing of Outsourcing*, London: KPMG.

Millward, N., Stevens, M., Smart, D., and Hawes, W. (1992) *Workplace Industrial Relations in Transition*. Dartmouth Press.

Petts, N. (1997) 'Building Growth on Core Competences – A Practical Approach', *Long Range Planning,* 30(4), August.

Porter, M. (1980) *Competitive Advantage*. New York: Free Press.

Poulteney, J. (1997) 'Rapid reaction', *People Management*, 23 January, pp. 38–40.

Storey, J. (1992) *Developments in the Management of Human Resources*. Oxford: Blackwell.

Walker, J. W. (1992) *Human Resource Strategy*. New York: McGraw-Hill.

Walton, J. (1996) 'The Provision of Learning Support for Non-Employees', in J. Stewart and J. McGoldrick (eds) *Human Resource Development – Perspectives, Strategies and Practices*. London: Pitman.

Welch, J. (1996) 'Air traffic controllers pilot paperless centre', *People Management*, 19 December, p. 10.

Wiggenhorn, W. (1990) 'Motorola U: When Training becomes an Education', *Harvard Business Review*, July-August.

Chapter 12

BENCHMARKING HUMAN RESOURCE DEVELOPMENT

OBJECTIVES

By the end of this chapter you should be able to:

- define benchmarking and distinguish between competitive and best practice approaches;
- differentiate between 'practices' and 'metrics' in the context of benchmarking;
- establish the significance of benchmarking for HRD;
- differentiate between the benchmarking of training and development and more holistic approaches to benchmarking HRD;
- describe the basic steps entailed in carrying out a benchmarking exercise.

INTRODUCTION

As we saw in Chapter 2, on the strategic backcloth to HRD, environmental analysis has long been used as a strategic management diagnostic tool. It is based on the view that if one is to make realistic and informed decisions about the future then one needs to look outside one's own organisational and operational reality in a systematic and focused way. This is a necessary part of the twin processes of anticipating threats to one's survival and growth, and discovering new ways of thinking and acting. A supporting technique is competitor analysis, where one pays particular attention to the activities of current and prospective players in the arena where one is operating. Benchmarking is associated with both environmental analysis, as broadly defined, and competitor analysis, with its more specific connotations.

Fowler (1997) reminds us that the dictionary meaning of benchmark is a short groove cut by a surveyor into the stone cornice of a building and marked by an arrow, the height of which above sea level has been accurately measured. It functions as a reference point when the heights of other locations in the vicinity are being measured. He considers that benchmarking in an organisational context is based on a similar principle. For him, it entails checking a given organisation's systems and processes and performance against those of others in order to assess whether its standards are higher or lower.

Benchmarking goes beyond merely seeking comparisons with other organisations, irrespective of where they might be found. The identity of those against which comparison is made is considered to be important. Thus benchmarking has been defined as 'the continuous process of measuring products, services, and practices against the toughest competitors or those companies recognised as industry leaders' (Kearns, 1990). This definition refers to the continuous nature of the process, although this is more symbolic than a reflection of actual practice. It serves to draw our attention to the importance of always being prepared to look outwards in order to inform our practices within. In reality, to do this 'continuously' is an ambitious aspiration unless the organisation has an Environmental Scanning Department or equivalent, and even then attention could not be realistically given to the whole range of an organisation's systems, procedures, processes and practices. Nevertheless, most authorities hold that benchmarking should not be an *ad hoc*, 'bolt-on', occasional activity, but a systematic and ongoing attempt to obtain comparative data on practices elsewhere.

The search for comparative performance data is the rationale behind benchmarking. However, benchmarking goes beyond monitoring standards and passively cross mapping others' activities with those of one's own organisation. It should enable lessons to be learned from the successes and mistakes of others. Benchmarking can also be used to identify practices that others are undertaking and which one should be pursuing or to which consideration should be given. The prime objective should thus be to draw upon such discoveries to influence one's own practice. This is captured in another definition which refers to 'the search for industry best practices that lead to superior performance' (Camp, 1989).

The process of benchmarking can be applied to virtually any area of an organisation's value chain – primary processes and functions such as manufacturing, sales, distribution as well as support processes and functions including HRD. This chapter is concerned with the importance and implications of benchmarking from a variety of HRD perspectives:

■ to establish the operational and strategic value to an organisation of benchmarking HRD activities;

■ to demonstrate that lessons can be learned from so doing which will contribute to the overall enhancement of HRD processes, practices and philosophies;

■ as a by-product, to show how comparison with other organisations can serve to strengthen the negotiating hand of those responsible for orchestrating learning activities in an HRD functional area. For example, it may be established that the investment in HRD is lower than that of 'best in class' organisations. It can of course have the opposite effect if it turns out that existing practices are dated and more costly than those of leading edge organisations;

■ to demonstrate that benchmarking, as an activity, can be a key contributor to organisational learning, and should be seen as an HRD process in its own right.

HRD practitioners should be no exception to the rule that substantial benefits can be obtained from conducting benchmarking exercises, and making comparisons with others. This chapter argues that benchmarking is an essential activity. It also suggests that the credibility of HRD is at stake if there is a lack of awareness of benchmarking. Benchmarking is increasingly seen, by those enterprises which are enthusiastically adopting it, as a major contributor to organisational learning (Williams and Ellis, 1995). Where are HRD professionals in all this?

DEFINING BENCHMARKING

Benchmarking is often seen as an important tool of strategy management. Drew (1997) makes the point that benchmarking is not, in itself, a strategy for achieving competitive advantage. He contends that it is 'a related set of activities which support and enhance strategies of imitation and/or collaboration leading to such advantage'.

Ellis and Williams (1995) conclude that:

benchmarking is a continuous search for and application of significantly better practices that lead to superior business performance. It has three key elements, namely:

■ the identification and selection of world class performance in respect of key business areas/functions;

■ an assessment of the processes that have generated the world class performance;

■ the task of seeking to apply such processes to the organisation itself.

Their emphasis on 'world class' encompasses a global perspective which is a helpful, albeit challenging, dimension. In today's global marketplace it is very restrictive to limit oneself to a narrow ethnocentric perspective. Their suggested focus on 'key business areas/functions' also requires comment. At the macro-strategic level, it may be important to focus on those 'processes that have generated the world class performance'. However this should not distract attention from the value of conducting benchmarking activities at all levels and for all functions, irrespective of the perceived contribution or added value of a given functional area. If the activity is not worth benchmarking, then why is it being undertaken?

Some people have considered that what underpins benchmarking is what Tom Peters calls 'creative swiping'. Thus Main (1992), in an article provocatively entitled 'How to steal the best ideas around', defines benchmarking as 'the art of finding out, in a perfectly legal and aboveboard way, how others do something better than you do – so you can imitate – and perhaps improve upon – their techniques'. Lawrence Bossidy, the chief executive of Allied Signal Inc., the $13bn industrial supplier of aerospace systems, automobile parts and chemical products based in New Jersey, USA, defined it as 'looking at specific practices, getting the benefit of expertise, bringing it back and having no inhibitions about adopting it and letting people know where it came from' (Tichy and Charan, 1995). But benchmarking should result in more than simple emulation or matching; it is a mechanism to search for and learn from best practices in order to improve strategic and operational performance. A reliance on emulation is unlikely to be successful, not least because organisations have different resources, technological expertise, distinctive competences and corporate culture.

Nevertheless, some organisations have relied excessively on comparative performance data as a key plank in their competitive strategy. This may help a company meet competitors' performance, but it is unlikely to reveal practices to beat them. For example an official of General Motors once summed up the car maker's strategy in the following terms: 'It was not necessary to lead in technical design or run the risk of untried experiments, provided that our cars were at least equal in design to the best of our competitors' (quoted in Shetty, 1993). This reactive competitive strategy failed to maintain General Motors' position in the marketplace. Japanese car manufacturers, on the other hand, who made great inroads into General Motors' market share in the 1980s, have consistently used benchmarking data in a proactive manner. They have systematically studied their competition in parallel with trying to understand what makes people buy cars. They then use the information to develop innovative products. Mazda Chairman Yamamoto calls this 'Kansei engineering', which he defines as 'absolute awareness of both reason and emotion' (Drew, 1997).

THE ORIGINS OF BENCHMARKING

Man has always shown curiosity about what is happening in the world around him, and today much of what is happening is taking place in an organisational context. Benchmarking can be viewed as a structured organisational approach to satisfying our thirst for curiosity. On the whole, people within organisations have been willing to satisfy the curiosity of those outside about the products and services they provide. For example, factory and site visits have long been encouraged for existing and potential customers and investors by public relations departments. Such 'industrial tourism' transcends national boundaries. I have taken groups of management and HR students for site visits to French, German and Dutch corporations, and have always been made to feel more than welcome. I have also been surprised at how often we have been shown publicity material and even videos of the organisations' operations – in English.

Benchmarking, as an integrated concept, is not an offshoot of such industrial tourism, although it can have public relations connotations and a site visit can be an invaluable source of benchmarking information. It has its origins in two other main areas:

- competitor analysis; and
- demonstrations of quality.

Competitor analysis involves finding out what one's competitors are doing through a range of legitimate, albeit covert, techniques.

One of the outcomes of the quality movement has been the opening up of a range of practices to external scrutiny, in order to demonstrate that one is 'best in class'. Much of the interest in benchmarking has been the result of the introduction of quality awards such as the Malcolm Baldrige National Quality Award in the USA.

Xerox (*see* Fig. 12.1) is usually quoted as the most influential original exponent of benchmarking, developing it into a systematic and coherent operating philosophy.

Figure 12.1   Xerox

Like General Motors in the car industry, Xerox was subjected throughout the 1980s to a concerted Japanese challenge to its dominance in the world-wide photocopier market. Initially it restricted itself to a competitive benchmarking analysis of manufacturing, concerned with establishing performance gaps between itself and its

▶▶

▶▶ Figure 12.1 continued

Japanese rivals. It soon appreciated that benchmarking could be applied to a wide range of processes across the entire value chain, improvements in which could collectively contribute to quality enhancement and organisational effectiveness. It also recognised that one did not need to restrict the approach to known competitors, and that excellent performance in key processes should be sought out irrespective of the industrial or occupational sector in which they were found. As part of its approach, Xerox piloted training and development programmes to ensure that all employees knew about benchmarking, and had the requisite skills to conduct benchmarking exercises.

ASPECTS OF BENCHMARKING

Practices and metrics

Benchmarking can generate both qualitative and quantitative data, often referred to as *practices* and *metrics* respectively. Qualitative data on practices are notes and observations about success factors or critical factors which have led to the achievement of superior performance elsewhere. Zairi (1994) views 'practices' as characteristics that describe internal and external business behaviours that tend to lead to the creation of a performance gap between one organisation and another. They could be related to such things as operating processes, organisational structures, management systems, human factors and strategic approaches. An example would be obtaining data about management development practices from an organisation that was held to be advanced in this area, and trying to pinpoint sources and causes of differences.

Quantitative data can provide a measure of comparative performance at a particular moment in time. They are typically presented in the form of 'metrics' or short-term measurements against chosen indicators that have to be continually calculated and reviewed. They can represent such things as percentage of days spent per head on off-the-job training per annum.

Benchmarking by means of metrics can help one to assess how a particular functional area matches up generally against industrial or national norms. This assessment can often be undertaken by tapping in to externally generated databases on such things as salary comparisons or average annual number of days spent on training and development per employee. In the HRM field, national salary surveys by specialist consultancies have for many years provided a helpful source of pay benchmarks. Such databases are especially useful for providing comparative data by industrial sector, organisation size and so on.

Spendolini (1992) advises against focusing on the measurement of operations or becoming fixated on numbers. He stresses the importance of concentrating on improvements in practices. He advocates maintaining a process (i.e. dynamic) rather than an object (i.e. static) focus.

Competitive and best practice benchmarking

There are two basic types of benchmarking, *competitive benchmarking* and *best practice benchmarking*.

Competitive benchmarking

Competitive benchmarking is concerned with assessing key parts of the organisation's processes, systems and procedures with those of designated competitors in the field. To gain a superior competitive position, it is often held that organisations must reduce costs, improve productivity, enhance quality, provide better customer service and become more innovative. Developing new products, introducing new technologies and more effective marketing strategies are all essential components of a successful competitive strategy. Benchmarking, if properly implemented, can identify competitors' strategies, strengths and weaknesses, determine the key factors of success and utilise this information to surpass the competition. Nowadays, it is increasingly being contended that learning processes and the development of 'intellectual capital' will underpin these strategic outcomes. Benchmarking learning processes and practices thus becomes a significant feature.

A variety of techniques are used for competitive benchmarking, dependent upon the purpose of the exercise. One well-known approach is reverse engineering. This involves getting hold of a competitor's product and breaking it down into its component parts in order to identify in what key respects it differs from one's own product. Some retail stores will check each morning the prices their competitors are charging locally and make adjustments accordingly. Some hotel chains will send staff or pay for privileged customers to stay in competitors' hotels and report back on the quality of service received. Typical comparators will be price, facilities, cleanliness, value for money, staff helpfulness, quality of product, redecoration and/or refurbishment.

Best practice benchmarking

Best practice benchmarking entails comparing a particular aspect of an organisation's product or service against organisations which are held to be 'best in class' in that particular area. They may or may not be competitors. Techniques tend to be more overt than competitive benchmarking and often include prearranged site visits in order to confirm by observation what one has been told. Williams and Ellis (1995) emphasise the *commitment* element of these visits: 'Through active participation in visits to other organisations' premises, managers can see superior operational practice at first hand and can convince themselves that the benchmarks which other companies achieve are valid and comparable.'

Types of comparison

The comparisons made in both competitive and best practice benchmarking can be broken down into the following types.

1 *Strategic benchmarking*, which involves the comparison of different business strategies to identify key elements in a successful overall strategy. Increasingly, HRD elements are being encompassed, such as how leading edge organisations set about identifying and developing strategic management competences in their staff.

2 *Process benchmarking*, which focuses on an evaluation of organisation systems, procedures and processes which cut across functional areas. Comparisons of systems underpinning performance management and staff development would fit into this category.

3 *Operational benchmarking*, which focuses on relative cost position or ways to increase product quality or improve service provision across functional areas. It can be seen as an external reinforcement of information gleaned from an internal strengths and weaknesses analysis. The activities to be benchmarked depend on the function analysed. For engineering functions, for example, analysis may concern design efficiency, for HRD functions, analysis may concern the cost of training per employee.

General and selective benchmarking

Fowler (1997) differentiates between 'general' and 'selective' benchmarking when deciding from which organisations to draw comparative data.

General benchmarking is used when one is trying to establish comparative data across an entire sector. Examples include the performance indicators produced by the Audit Commission in the UK for local authorities, and national salary surveys undertaken by specialist consultancies.

Selective benchmarking is more focused. It may arise from studying the evidence from general comparative data and concluding that competitors or other organisations have higher standards. It can lead to topic-based benchmarking, when one is focusing on a single issue.

Informal and formal benchmarking

Drew (1997) provides a useful differentiation between informal and formal approaches.

Formal benchmarking is seen as making a significant ongoing contribution to operational activities and processes. There are specific budgetary allocations and project control mechanisms to support the activity. It entails regular environmental scanning, data gathering and analysis activities. There are close linkages with organisation-wide systems such as strategic planning. Managers in the organisation can draw upon central sources of expertise.

Informal benchmarking is only sporadically linked to ongoing work activities. There is no special budget. It tends to be *ad hoc* and opportunistic, entailing occasional company visits, informal interviews and literature searches. It is likely to be topic based and conducted on a 'needs must' basis by individual line managers. Linkages with systems such as strategic planning, if they exist at all, will be minimal.

THE BENCHMARKING PROCESS

There are a number of suggestions from the literature on how the benchmarking process should be conducted. Fitz-ens (1993b) argues that they all revolve around four basic stages or phases, which he refers to as:

■ value planning;

■ data collection and management;

■ data analysis;

■ evaluation and action.

These recall the four steps to achieving quality recommended by J. Edwards Deming – plan, do, check and act.

Drew (1997) advocates a five-step model, which provides some more specific guidelines:

1 Determine what to benchmark.

2 Form a benchmarking team.

3 Identify benchmarking partners.

4 Collect and analyse information.

5 Act by transferring and integrating best practice.

Shetty (1993) proposes five basic steps which we shall broadly follow:

1 Identify the function and activity to be benchmarked.

2 Choose organisation for best practice benchmarking against.

3 Determine methods of data collection and analysis.

4 Familiarise organisation with findings and set performance goals.

5 Implement and measure.

Identify the function and activity to be benchmarked

It is necessary to identify the function and decide why benchmarking is necessary. One can then choose either to undertake a general benchmarking exercise of the entire area, to elicit across the range how it is being undertaken and resourced in other organisations, or to undertake a much more selective exercise focusing on a narrower spread of activities. In topic-based benchmarking one concentrates on a specific activity within the functional area (*see* Fig. 12.2).

Figure 12.2	Benchmarking decision matrix

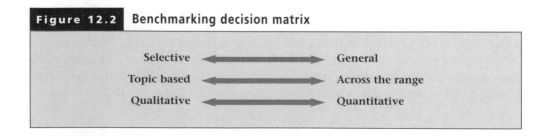

Every function of an organisation delivers some 'product', whether a physical good, an order or a service. Benchmarking can be applied to all these products. Xerox, for example, initiated benchmarking some years ago for its manufacturing operations and examined unit manufacturing costs. Selected products and operating capabilities were compared against those of competition, in terms of product quality and features. Xerox then looked at processes and compared transportation, warehousing and inventory management. Xerox found that managers initially tended to concentrate on comparative costs. As managers became more familiar with benchmarking, they emphasised practices, processes and methods, factors which determine whether the benchmark costs can be achieved.

Choose organisations to best practice benchmark against

Competitive benchmarking requires comparison, business to business, with direct product or service competitors. For best practice benchmarking one should compare with suitable partners regardless of industry or sector. The report of the UK Department of Trade and Industry (DTI, 1994) categorises four different types of organisation for benchmarking purposes:

■ internal benchmarking against other parts of your own organisation;

■ benchmarking against direct competitors;

■ parallel organisations. Local authorities, for example, have traditionally sought information from other local authorities;

■ companies in totally different industries.

In general, organisations should be identified that best perform the benchmarked function. This, however, is more easily said than done. Fitz-ens (1993a) contends that there is 'no magic list of best practice companies'. Nevertheless, having a clear idea of your own processes and what you want to know will help you in the selection process. He suggests the following sources to initiate the process:

■ publications: articles, reports, books;

■ experts: experienced people and consultants from your own industry;

■ contacts from meetings, conferences, trade and professional events;

■ associations: trade and professional contacts and data bases;

■ personal contacts: customers, suppliers, peers, etc.

Fitz-ens identifies a useful set of primary criteria for choosing benchmarking partners:

■ *Diversity*: develop a cross-section of different type of business, size of organisation and geographical location. Each benchmark partner will offer different perspectives on the topic and the diverse opinions and practices will help provide insight.

■ *Creativity*: seek organisations with different ideas on a given matter. This can help to add value to your own situation.

■ *Desire*: look for people who are anxious to do things well.

Finding 'world class' partners to benchmark against can present some difficulty. A 1994/5 IBM/London Business School study entitled *Made in Britain* concluded that only 2 per cent of UK manufacturing companies were worthy of the appellation. For HRD practices, winners of and strong contenders for national and/or international quality awards are an obvious source. However, relying solely on so-called best practice organisations can be limiting.

Determine methods of data collection and analysis

There are many ways to collect data. The approach adopted depends on the purpose of the benchmarking exercise and the openness or otherwise of the enquiry. Competitive benchmarking, by its very nature, tends to be covert. Typical sources include published reports and data obtained by own employees – from networking through professional and personal associations and so on. Analysis should be based on a full understanding of one's own organisation's current processes as well as those of benchmarked organisations. In general, qualitative data about processes and practices are more interesting and reliable than quantitative metrics. The qualitative approach requires the exercise of considerable interpretive skills in order to make sense of what is being obtained and how that can be compared to one's own organisation's practices.

A very effective way of gaining data is by means of a site visit. This should be seen as more than industrial tourism. It needs to be planned in advance so that one knows whom one will meet, and one has a clear idea of what to ask and what to see.

Organisations vary in their openness to site visits and the sharing of information about their practices. The more progressive club together in benchmarking forums to compare insights on best practice. Some also provide developmental projects, enabling staff from partner organisations to engage in problem solving activities for them. Benchmarking can also be facilitated through participation in cross-sectoral action learning sets. Others are more circumspect, even in the area of HRD. An American study (Holton *et al.*, 1997) reported difficulties in obtaining comparative data on HRD practices because these were seen as a source of competitive advantage by the proposed partners.

For site visits the international benchmarking code of practice should be adopted. This defines principles of legality, information exchange, confidentiality, use of information and preparation. Members of a UK Civil Service HR benchmarking project group generally sent this out to each comparator organisation in advance of a proposed visit, together with a written brief outlining the areas to be covered (Clulow, 1997).

Familiarise organisation with findings and set performance goals

Establishing operational goals for improvement involves careful planning to incorporate new processes and practices. One must expect some resistance if one is challenging established ways of doing things. The fact-finding stage of the benchmarking exercise might reveal problems faced by the partner organisation and how these were overcome. Findings must be clearly communicated to all organisational levels. One must allow sufficient time for employees to evaluate benchmark findings and to agree on the performance levels and the practices and processes to be used to reach these goals. Note that designing appropriate measures can be problematic, and a compromise may be required between what is practicable and what is desirable. Performance goals and the selection of best practices should be incorporated into functional, business and operating plans.

The Ford Motor Company in the UK used an interesting technique in the 1980s to get across the messages from benchmarking. They referred to the Nissan factory in Sunderland as the 'Trojan Horse' and made detailed business presentations across the company contrasting Ford's performance with that of Nissan (Storey, 1992).

Implement and measure

In competitive terms, benchmarking should be viewed as a means to improve performance to gain superiority. In best practice terms, it should be viewed as a means to doing things better, to more effectively meeting the needs of the various constituent groups for whom products, processes and services are provided. On the whole, improvements should result in significant leaps as opposed to small incremental changes, although the change process itself may be gradual and incremental. Implementation should involve periodic measurement and assessment of attempts to reach stated goals. One should take corrective action if performance does not reach goals. Note that a proactive strategy balances the focus between innovation, quality enhancement, cost effectiveness and customer responsiveness, reducing the risk of selective attention or simplification. Measurement may be seen as squaring the circle – regularly comparing activities undertaken against those of other organisations recognised as key players.

Implementation should be the outcome of a process. On a site visit, say, one will observe a range of practices. One's prime aim will be to obtain as much information on these practices as possible. Things that other organisations do differently can constitute the germs of a number of ideas. It is, however, quite easy to be seduced by new ideas. Subsidiary questions should be:

- Is this a good idea?
- Will it work in our organisation?
- How will it work?
- Who will drive its implementation?

Fitz-ens (1993a) lists what he considers to be the three essential factors to bear in mind when benchmarking.

1 *Be realistic*. Benchmarking is not a solution for all problems. It raises questions and points one in the direction of process improvement.

2 *Stay focused*. Massive problems cannot be solved at one time. If too large a problem is tackled, the quantity of data to be gathered and analysed will be commensurately large.

3 *Prepare carefully*. Organisations should pick strong teams with the skills, motivation and willingness to share and learn together. Benchmarking partners should also be chosen with care.

He also suggests that if benchmarking is kept focused on adding value for customers, then a great deal will be gained from the effort put into it.

The American Strategic Planning Council on Benchmarking has developed a code, the main points of which are:

- Don't go on a fishing expedition. Pick a specific area you want to improve and do your homework. Study your own procedures fully and choose an organisation or organisations to benchmark that handle the process well.
- Send out the people who will have to make the changes. They need to see for themselves. It won't help if senior executives or consultants do the benchmarking, then come back and tell the 'owners' of a process what to do. Keep visits short and teams small.
- Be prepared to exchange information. Be ready to answer any question you ask another organisation.
- Avoid legal problems. Don't expect to learn much about new products. Most benchmarking missions tend to focus on existing products, business practices, human resources and customer satisfaction.
- Respect the confidentiality of the data you obtain. Organisations that do not mind sharing with you may not want the information going to a competitor (quoted by Main, 1992).

BENCHMARKING AND HUMAN RESOURCE DEVELOPMENT

Benchmarking as a concept should create no problems for HRD practitioners. For a profession concerned with acquisition and provision of knowledge and insights, it can be construed as yet another facet of learning. There is a clear relationship between the discovery and fact-finding aspects of benchmarking, and the principles of learning which underpin the profession – we learn from and build on the ideas of others.

It is a reasonable hypothesis that 'creative swiping' of course design and course materials has been in existence since courses began! In some instances it is encouraged. How many of our course materials are truly original? To afford some measure of protection from abuse, boundaries are set up in relation to what it is legitimate to copy and what not. These are explicit in the term 'copyright'. But it is only in recent years that attention has been given to benchmarking as a systematic strategic tool for comparing standards and ways of working.

The scope of human resource development benchmarking

In HRD terms, it is important to think beyond the conventional notion of focusing on a functional area, and to consider benchmarking such features as organisation-wide learning processes or the learning climate. Hiltrop and Despres (1994), drawing upon Glanz and Daily (1992), argue that building a learning mentality has become an important goal for many organisations in recent years;

benchmarking can open minds and help to create a climate in which active learning is encouraged. It can be used as a tool for creating the motivation to change. A concentration on benchmarking HRD from a purely functional perspective would be unduly restrictive. As we shall see, where this has happened, it has led to a concentration on the *metrics* of T&D-related operational activities and associated resource allocations to the exclusion of *practices* which influence broader strategic considerations.

The benchmarking of HRD can be considered to operate at three levels (*see* Fig. 12.3).

Figure 12.3 **Three levels of benchmarking HRD**

1 **The level of organisational learning**
   - ∎ How have other organisations generated a learning climate?
   - ∎ How have other organisations generated a creative climate?

2 **The level of organisation-wide HRD processes**
   - ∎ How have other organisations identified and developed competences for staff?
   - ∎ How have other organisations balanced on- and off-the-job learning?

3 **The level of training and development activity and resource allocation**
   - ∎ How are other organisations handling the insourcing versus outsourcing debate?
   - ∎ What percentage of payroll is devoted to training and development in other organisations?

Metrics and human resource development

Much of the literature on benchmarking HRD has focused rather narrowly on quantitative comparisons of training provision and associated resource allocation. Typical of the areas singled out for comparison are those developed by Ford (1993). His set of metrics cover three broad areas which he says that most HRD practitioners consider essential.

1 *Measures of training activity.* These concern how much training and development occurs. The focus is on formalised, structured learning.
2 *Measures of training results.* These concern how well training and development achieves its goals.
3 *Measures of training efficiency.* These concern the extent to which training and development maximises resources in pursuit of its mission.

The metrics presented in Fig. 12.4 are based on Ford's approach.

Figure 12.4 Training metrics

Training activity

- Percentage of payroll spent on training _____
- Training amount (£ or $ or FFr.) spent per employee per annum _____
- Average number of training days per employee per annum _____
- Average number of training days per manager per annum _____
- Percentage of employees trained per year _____
- Percentage of managers trained per year _____
- HRD staff per 100 employees _____

Training results at reaction level

- Average percentage of positive course participant ratings (e.g satisfied/very satisfied) per year _____
- Average percentage of satisfied HRD customers based on customer rating of HRD services in annual survey _____

Training results at learning level

- Average percentage gain in learning per course based on difference between pre-course and post-course test results _____

Training results at behaviour level

- Average percentage of improvement in on-the-job performance after training per-course _____

Training results – bottom line

- Profits per employee per year _____
- Cost savings as a ratio of training expenses _____

Training efficiency

- Training cost per delegate hour _____

Ford carried out a pilot benchmarking study using his metrics on nine companies that won the US Malcolm Baldrige National Quality Award between 1988 and 1991. He had difficulties in getting responses to the questionnaire he sent out since most of the companies contacted were apparently unable to answer the questions. He found that training activity was easiest to measure, training results more difficult, and training efficiency virtually untracked. He also found that some of what were considered to be the best training organisations did not regularly track certain measures such as percentage of payroll spent on training, the percentage of the work-force trained, the average improvement in on-the-job performance, and the productivity and efficiency of the HRD staff.

Each year the Saratoga Institute, as part of its annual Human Resource Effectiveness Report, collects data from participating organisations on training and development. These relate only to total training costs and training hours:

■ training costs include design, delivery and administration of training, participants' pay and benefits, consultancy costs and accommodation and facility costs;

■ training hours, including how long the trainee was away from the workplace and how long their job was halted (Saratoga, 1995).

There are no 'qualitative' indicators in this analysis, and there is a risk that the Saratoga approach might encourage organisations to treat training as a cost, rather than an investment. Saratoga established their criteria by asking senior personnel professionals in Europe how they would measure personnel against business performance. This would seem to be a somewhat restrictive approach.

Broader human resource development benchmarking

If one follows a quantitative approach, one might include broader HRD metrics, such as percentages of:

■ employees completing personal development plans;

■ line managers acting as mentors;

■ employees undertaking developmental projects;

■ staff involved in benchmarking visits.

Nevertheless, there are certain problems in HRD terms associated with the quantitative measurement approach typically adopted. These include the following:

1 Emphasis on input-driven criteria such as number of days allocated to training does not indicate whether the training has been valuable.

2 Many of the measures relate to formal off-the-job training provision only. This is true of France, where there is a legal requirement that a certain percentage of payroll is allocated to formal training activities. The measures are unable to identify and include 'learning' through informal activities. There is a case for a 'balanced score-card' of measures.

3 The measures do not address innovative HRD processes that are being adopted by leading edge and other companies. Most of the real benefits of benchmarking are associated with investigative delving into practices that are adding value to a given organisation at a chosen location in the value chain.

On the other hand, formal measures and comparators can be very beneficial to HRD professionals trying to reinforce their position in an organisation. It can be invaluable to say that Xerox or IBM, say, are investing x per cent of their payroll on HRD-related activities, that nationally in the UK the average number of days managers spend on formal management training is 5.5.

Developing broad-based metrics can, however, be troublesome. In 1992, a Benchmarking Forum was established under the auspices of the American Society of Training and Development. The forum identified eight areas of training information in which to begin benchmarking. These were:

- organisation structure of training and development;
- financial models of internal education and training;
- design, development, delivery and publishing;
- measurement and evaluation;
- customer requirements;
- facilities;
- the training and certification of instructors;
- administration and logistics.

The members of the forum decided that the data collected with the 1994 instrument contained a number of problems and should not be published. Certainly, some of the headings seem unsuitable for generating 'metrics'.

PRACTICES AND HUMAN RESOURCE DEVELOPMENT

For HRD benchmarking, as elsewhere, one can decide to obtain data against a broad spread of practices or to engage in topic-based benchmarking. Ulrich *et al.* (1989) advise against attempting too much. They suggest that rather than try to do everything well and please everyone with limited resources, an HR manager can set directions and priorities by benchmarking, which will help them to focus on critical activities.

Fitz-ens (1993b) contends that before beginning the benchmarking exercise one should ask the following questions.

- Where is the greatest customer value to be found?
- Which HR processes are most directly linked to that value?
- Which HR processes offer the greatest room for improvement?
- Which HR processes might be the easiest to fix?

Table 12.1 Generic framework for HR benchmarking topics

HR competences/purposes	HR domains
Generating competence	Staffing Development
Reinforcing competence	Appraisal Reward
Sustaining competence	Organisation design Communication

Source: Based on Ulrich *et al.* (1989).

A number of off-the-shelf published frameworks have been developed as a basis for identifying HR benchmarking topics. Ulrich *et al.* (1989) developed for this purpose a complex network of three HR competences or purposes, six HR domains, 21 HR practices and 67 HR activities which can apply to either strategic or operational level activities (*see* Table 12.1).

They propose four activities for the development domain:

1 Offer training programmes.
2 Design development programmes to facilitate change.
3 Prepare talent through cross-functional moves.
4 Offer career-planning services.

As they stand, these activities are both too broad based and too prescriptive for conducting a benchmarking exercise. For instance, not all organisations would wish to 'prepare talent through cross-functional moves'. Assuming that this is something one's organisation currently undertakes, or wishes to explore, one can convert the overall activity into questions which one could ask of suitable benchmarking partners. For example:

- How important are cross-functional moves in your organisation?
- What levels of staff are involved?
- How many staff are involved?
- Are they short-term secondments or longer-term placements?
- How do you prepare staff for such moves?
- How do you prepare the receiving line managers?
- How do you identify suitable staff?
- What benefits do you expect to get from such moves?
- What skills do you expect staff to develop?
- How do you handle international placements?

Criteria underpinning Quality Awards such as the European Foundation for Quality Management (Business Excellence model) provide a framework for moving organisations away from metrics towards qualitative benchmarking. They also move away from the use of financial measures as criteria for performance in an endeavour to encourage managers to adopt a broad long-term view of organisational performance. The EFQM performance criteria for leadership and people management are listed below. Superficially they seem to be particularly relevant for benchmarking HRD.

- *Leadership . . .* how managers take positive steps to:
  - communicate with staff;
  - give and receive training;
  - assess the awareness of Total Quality;
  - establish and participate in joint problem-solving teams with customers and suppliers,

■ *People management* . . . how the organisation realises the full potential of its people by:
  – integrating corporate and HR strategy;
  – assessing the match between people's skills and organisational needs;
  – achieving effective top-down and bottom-up communication.

However these criteria are very open ended for comparison purposes and for establishing best practice approaches. The questions are no more than triggers to initiate more in-depth questioning.

Benchmarking management development

An example of benchmarking management development is afforded by the National Health Service Training Division (EDB54). The original objective was to provide HR and line managers with the means to conduct their own evaluation and analysis of the state of management development in their own organisations. The benchmarks, which were intended to reflect best practice in the National Health Service and elsewhere, identified five facets that made up management development activity in an organisation. The five facets are:

■ the link between management development and business strategy;

■ the formulation of a management development plan;

■ the assessment of skills and the identification of skills gaps;

■ the delivery of appropriate and effective training and development;

■ evaluation methods to ensure cost effectiveness.

Each of these facets is broken down into four levels of performance:

■ commitment to management development;

■ reviewing the current position of management development;

■ making progress in management development;

■ excellence in management development.

The site visit

Ulrich *et al.* (1989) state that the most common form of HR benchmarking is to identify five to ten companies who appear to have or are known to have good HR practices, and then visit them to see what they do. A visit provides richer information than the cold data generated from questionnaires and surveys. One reason for this is that it is almost impossible to word a questionnaire so that it has the same meaning for all respondents. Furthermore there is no guarantee that the person completing the questionnaire has access to all the correct data or has interpreted the questions in the same way as the designer intended. The site visit provides a marvellous opportunity to deal with any misunderstandings. It is also beneficial in two other ways. The questions asked can generate insights for the host. They can indicate what is important to the questioner and can raise issues that the host is unable to answer.

Where a visit is less effective is in providing detailed statistical information. It can, however, provide an opportunity to ask about any statistical data that have previously been provided; for example, whether they were valid and met the expectations of the questionnaire designer. An example of a potential misunderstanding could be to do with something as simple as the investment per employee in training and development. It is always worth checking who are included as employees and who excluded. Are part-time staff included, for instance? It is also worth establishing whether both organisations use the same criteria to describe 'investment in training and development'. For example, is off-the-job coaching included as well as costs associated with attendance on formal training programmes?

The Civil Service HR benchmarking project (Clulow, 1997) emphasised the importance of advance preparation for a site visit. In particular it drew attention to the value of gaining detailed knowledge of one's own internal HR processes and current performance levels. This proved to be a valuable exercise, most enlightening to the project team members, albeit hard and at times frustrating work, revealing new information and insights on how the internal processes actually worked and what internal customer expectations were.

The site visit can be revealing in another way. It is easy to be impressed by reported accounts of success in so-called best practice organisations. The site visit provides an opportunity to see how well founded these claims are. Storey (1992) comments on the difference often experienced during site visits between the rhetoric and the reality, so called breakthroughs turning out to be no more than peripheral trials, hardly recognisable to the participants on the ground, sometimes abandoned altogether. 'Such experiences on research visits soon induce caution, not to say scepticism, in one's approach' (Storey, op. cit., p. 17). To gain real insights of this sort, one's diagnostic antennae need to be astutely attuned. Whom one sees, the questions one asks, where one goes, how open the hosts are, determine what one finds. It must also be remembered that for the purposes of benchmarking one visits as a guest, not, like Storey, as a critical researcher. One's purpose in undertaking the visit is to gain insights that will benefit practice in one's *own* organisation, not to criticise the practice of others.

Figure 12.5 provides an example of topic-based benchmarking.

Figure 12.5 | Benchmarking of empowerment and self-directed work teams

At the ASTD conference at Anaheim, USA, in 1994, Finnigan and Nichols of the Xerox corporation addressed the issue of benchmarking the implementation of self-directed work teams. They undertook a detailed literature search as well as identifying companies that purported to have successfully introduced self-managed work teams. Their conclusions were as follows.

1 Organisational reinforcement is necessary to sustain empowerment and self-directed work teams.

2 Managers and supervisors are fearful of relinquishing control at the beginning.

3 Employees are hesitant to take the initiative and accountability at the outset.

4 Most self-directed teams begin in manufacturing operations with industrial staff.

5 Self-directed work teams lead to significant gains in employee morale.

▶▶

▶▶ Figure 12.5 continued

> For the purposes of this chapter their conclusions are less significant than their perception of the sort of HRD activities that could be subject to a benchmarking exercise. They looked at organisational processes; something active that was being conducted in certain organisations. They conducted what in many ways was a conventional research/data-gathering exercise about what constitutes organisational practice and experience.
>
> They had moved away from the notion of benchmarking as a continuous activity. Rather, they focused on an area of particular interest and concern, and used benchmarking techniques to gain information.

BENCHMARKING AND ORGANISATIONAL LEARNING

In its broadest sense, benchmarking is an HRD strategy that contributes to organisational learning. As Drew (1997) points out, it contributes to the import and absorption of knowledge across organisational frontiers. He quotes Texas Instruments as a firm which encourages benchmarking throughout the organisation as part of a drive to achieve a culture of learning and responsiveness to change. To encourage this, the firm links skills in benchmarking to the job evaluation and associated reward system. McGill and Slocum (1994) go so far as to contend that it is a practical approach towards operationalising the idea of a learning organisation, in the sense of triggering 'unlearning', questioning of assumptions and the revision of mental models.

Human resource development practitioners should as a matter of course encourage and support benchmarking in organisations. If an organisation is to grow and survive, it needs information from the environment. Benchmarking can be seen as a basic constituent of organisational learning. The process of carrying out benchmarking is as important for learning and development as the outcomes. Ellis and Williams (1995) believe that the overall purpose of the approach is to expose managers to new and superior ways about how to design and order their own processes. They see a relationship between the conduct of benchmarking, the concept of double-loop learning, the creation of a learning organisation and change management. Benchmarking, with its outward-looking perspective and constant challenge to established processes and practices, contributes to an organisational climate where striving for excellence is the norm, and where change is expected and rewarded. However, for HRD practitioners to be able to contribute to a learning climate where benchmarking and shared learning is encouraged, they need to be able to demonstrate that they possess the skills and awareness to benchmark their own activities.

GLOBAL BENCHMARKING AND HUMAN RESOURCE DEVELOPMENT

Global benchmarking is no more than domestic benchmarking conducted on a world-wide scale. One of the questions raised in this book is whether there is a convergence or divergence of HRD practices across national boundaries.

Benchmarking one's organisation against 'best in class' world players is an interesting development, and increasingly likely as organisations operate globally. The issue becomes how such an exercise is to be conducted. The development of comparative statistics based on metrics is so difficult as not to inspire confidence in the results, even when confined within national boundaries. With HRD practices the problems include cost, time, effort, language and the difficulty of identifying and then accessing partners. The European Foundation Quality Award is one attempt to develop qualitative measurement criteria valid across national boundaries.

Drew (1997) reports on a cross-sectoral study of benchmarking practices in North American organisations. One of the questions asked related to the frequency and the success of benchmarking against firms in other countries. On a 1–7 frequency scale of 1–7, ranging from 1 (never) to 7 (very frequent) the mean response was 2.95. In terms of success, on a 1–7 scale ranging from 1 (unsuccessful) to 7 (very successful) the mean response was 3.45. Drew does not report whether the international partners were primarily English speaking.

Despite cost implications, some organisations operating globally provide international benchmarking visits. Motorola regularly sends employees at all levels around the globe to make first-hand observations on business practices and techniques being carried out elsewhere. Wiggenhorn of Motorola, commenting upon the practice from a corporate learning perspective, argued:

> In the early 1980s, the only people who travelled outside the United States were primarily senior managers. So they had a personal view of what was going on. Today teams of all kinds – middle managers, front line etc – go to other parts of the world to see how things are done . . . Part of the reward is: one, being able to do that travelling, number two, being able to see how other people do something that they thought was impossible; number three, coming back as the teachers to their own associates . . . It's not the boss coming back and telling them: it is really their peers coming back and sharing the knowledge with them (W. Wiggenhorn, Senior Vice President of Motorola, quoted in Garfield, 1992).

There are sometimes some unexpected dangers associated with such visits. In the summer of 1987, Unipart Industries sent a group of operators to Japan for six weeks to learn how to operate some new machinery before the same equipment was installed in its Oxford factory. The team discovered that the Japanese had a completely different approach to their work, emphasising quality and waste reduction in contrast to a predominant concern with output. When the team returned to the UK and tried to enthusiastically present their discoveries, they were ostracised by their colleagues and accused of being 'management lackeys'. Some even had their tyres slashed in the company car-park (Slack *et al.*, 1995).

Some university programmes for HRD practitioners provide opportunities for international benchmarking of practices. An international visit is a feature of programmes run by partners in EURESFORM, a European network of universities running professionally oriented postgraduate HRD qualifications. In offering structured HRD exchanges they have moved away from a model based on 'industrial tourism' which is typical of many programmes incorporating an overseas visit. Individual delegates from the sending institution travel to the other country in small groups to visit the workplace of their comparators, to gain insights on current and emerging practice. To facilitate this the partners have developed a number of evaluation criteria for structured exchanges which include *discovery* and *transfer*.

321

In relation to discovery, aspects considered include:

- What are the striking points noticed by the visitors?
- What are the surprises emerging from the observation of theory in use and practices?

In relation to transfer, the criteria include:

- What methodologies did the hosts bring to their visiting colleagues?
- What methodologies did the visitors bring to their hosting colleagues?
- What kinds of partnerships could be formulated as a result of the exchanges?

My experience at London Guildhall University of participating in such exchanges is that benchmarking does not have to be against 'best in class' organisations for one to obtain real and valuable insights. The discovery of different ways of doing things, wherever they are found, can, if one is open-minded, generate new and creative ways of thinking about one's own sphere of operations. Table 12.2 presents the distinctive features of benchmarking HRD.

Table 12.2 Benchmarking human resource development: distinctive features

Competitor	*Best practice*
HRD seen in product/market terms	
Particularly relevant to competitively conscious training providers and HRD consultants	Relevant to all organisations
Commercial overtones	Comparisons of resource allocations across sectors
Intellectual capital seen as source of competitive advantage	Seeking out leading edge exemplars Quality driven
Interest in threats to and market opportunities for HRD provision	Openness in terms of providing and seeking information
Barriers to information exchange	

CONCLUSION

Benchmarking one's practices against those considered to be 'best in class' can make a significant contribution to organisation-wide information gathering and decision making. Of its very nature it is a learning process and thus of interest to the HRD profession. This chapter argues that individuals and groups in organisations should be equipped with the range of skills to conduct a benchmarking exercise. The HRD profession should contain practitioners who have the facilitation skills necessary to equip people with these competences.

However, benchmarking should equally apply to the practices of the HRD function itself, and to the range of learning support processes that underpin the HRD effort.

The chapter differentiates between different types of benchmarking, and emphasises the importance of identifying suitable partners with whom to undertake comparisons. The use of metrics in benchmarking is discussed and contrasted with the additional value that can be gained by undertaking a site visit.

Finally issues associated with conducting benchmarking across national boundaries are addressed and reference is made to the possible convergence of practices that might result in the HRD world.

REFERENCES

Camp, R. C. (1989) *Benchmarking: The Search for Best Practices that Lead to Superior Performance*. ASQC Quality Press.

Clulow, C. (1997) 'Processing Power', *People Management*, 25 September, pp. 32–4.

Department of Trade and Industry (1994) 'Best practice benchmarking – an executive guide', URN 94/617.

Drew, S A W (1997) 'From Knowledge to Action: the Impact of Benchmarking on Organisational Performance', *Long Range Planning*, 30(3), June.

Ellis, J. and Williams, D. (1995) *International Business Strategy*. London: Pitman.

Fitz-ens, J. (1993a) *Benchmarking for best performance*. San Francisco: Jossey-Bass.

Fitz-ens, J. (1993b) 'How to make benchmarking work for you', *HR Magazine*, December, pp 40–6.

Ford, D. J. (1993) *Benchmarking HRD*. ASTO.

Fowler, A. (1997) 'How to use benchmarking', *People Management*, 12 June.

Garfield, C. (1992) *Second to None – The Productive Power of Putting People First*. Chicago: Business One Irwin.

Glanz, E. and Daily, L. (1992) 'Benchmarking', *Human Resource Management*, 31.

Hiltrop, J. M. and Despres, C. (1994) 'Benchmarking the Performance of Human Resource Management', *Long Range Planning*, 27(6), December.

Holton, E. F. III, Redmann, D. H., Edwards, M. A. and Fairchild, M. E. (1998) 'Planning for the Transition to Performance Consulting in Municipal Government', *Human Resource Development*, 1(1), Spring.

IBM/London Business School (1994–5) *Made in Britain*.

Kearns, D.T. (1990) 'Leadership through quality', *Academy of Management Executive*, 4.

McGill, M. E. and Slocum, J. W. (1994) *The Smarter Organisation*. New York: Wiley.

Main, J. (1992) 'How to steal the best ideas around', *Fortune*, 19 October, pp. 102–6.

Saratoga (Europe) (1995) 'UK Human Resource Effectiveness Report', Survey Documentation for quantitative/productivity data.

Shetty, Y. K. (1993) 'Aiming high: Competitive Benchmarking for Superior Performance', *Long Range Planning*, 26, February.

Slack, N., Chambers, C., Harland, C., Harrison, A., Johnston, R. (1995) *Operations Management*. London: Pitman.

Spendolini, M. J. (1992) 'The Benchmarking Process', *Compensation and Benefits Review*, September–October, pp. 21–39.

Storey, J. (1992) *Developments in the Management of Human Resources*. Oxford: Blackwell.

Tichy, N. M. and Charan, R. (1995) 'The CEO as Coach: An Interview with Allied Signal's Lawrence A. Bossidy', *Harvard Business Review*, March–April.

Ulrich, D., Brockbank, W. and Yeung, A. (1989) 'Beyond belief – a benchmark for Human Resources', *Human Resource Management*, 28, pp. 311–25.

Zairi, M. (1994) 'Leadership in TQM Implementation', *TQM Magazine*, 6(6).

Chapter 13

SMALL AND MEDIUM-SIZED ENTERPRISES AND HUMAN RESOURCE DEVELOPMENT

OBJECTIVES

By the end of this chapter you should be able to:

■ differentiate between different categories of small and medium-sized enterprises (SMEs);

■ establish their strategic importance for the economy;

■ identify specific issues associated with providing learning opportunities for staff in SMEs;

■ demonstrate current perspectives in SMEs as to what constitutes learning, and show how a broader HRD perspective provides a richer and more promising framework;

■ describe challenges and opportunities for addressing how learning, both individual and organisational, can be orchestrated in SMEs;

■ identify some possible solutions for enhancing the SME skill base;

■ establish the extent to which it is possible to develop a strategic approach to HRD in an SME context;

■ evaluate the role of larger corporations and the state in facilitating a strategic approach to learning in SMEs.

INTRODUCTION

Small and medium-sized enterprises (SMEs) have always played a significant part in the national and global economy. With 500 employees being the upper limit of an SME, the term encompasses virtually all firms and the vast bulk of employment and output in countries such as Greece, Spain, Ireland and Portugal (Storey, 1994). How learning is orchestrated and how skills and knowledge are acquired and developed in such organisations are matters of major interest. Yet until comparatively recently there has been little attempt in the HRD literature to differentiate between larger and smaller organisations and to address the impact that size and associated resource constraints might have upon both actual and desired approaches to learning. Most of the mainstream literature seems to have assumed that HRD activities take place in organisations where training, development and learning issues are addressed by specialist staff operating within a dedicated functional unit. The majority of SMEs have no such specialist function or department, and not even a dedicated member of staff.

Such attention as has been given to SMEs has on the whole focused on the provision or absence of 'training' as the measure of 'learning'. This has given a particular slant to interpreting what is taking place 'out there' and what might be done differently. As we shall see, the concern with 'training' gives a narrow and distorted view of the realities both of what is being learned and of how it is being learned. A broader HRD perspective would help to create greater insights.

Strategic HRD as a concept has, as we have noted in earlier chapters, invariably been treated as a planned process, in which specific attempts are undertaken to establish a clear relationship between learning initiatives and the imperatives of business planning or strategy management. This creates something of a problem in developing holistic approaches to HRD within SMEs, where it seems that little formal training is undertaken and much learning is 'accidental' and entails the acquisition of so-called tacit skills. A formal, structured, planned process also seems to be out of keeping with the relatively informal, flexible approach that a number of researchers hold to be the preferred way of operating in many SMEs (e.g. Lane, 1994).

As long ago as 1970, Nadler noted that 'one of the challenges presented *today* [emphasis added] is how to assist small organisations in developing their human resources' (Nadler, 1970). There is no globally agreed definition that differentiates between 'small', 'medium' and 'large' and Nadler's notion of 'small' can be taken to include what in the UK and mainland Europe are considered to be 'medium'-sized enterprises. How well has the challenge been met? According to the evidence from a UK government survey quoted in 'How to Create a Winning Company', one of the pamphlets that comprised the information pack for the 1996 campaign entitled, 'Competitiveness – Creating the enterprise culture of Europe' the answer is not very well. Two out of five medium-sized businesses believe people development and training is their weakest discipline, and one out of five admit to doing a poor job of it. This chapter provides an overview of the situation.

One of the features of recent years has been the development by large organisations of closer partnerships with their suppliers and distributors. As Hendry *et al.* (1991) point out, many SMEs are dependent on one major customer. From an HRD perspective there are attractions in seeing SMEs establish closer learning links with larger 'upstream' or 'downstream' organisations which are their major clients/ customers. This chapter addresses a number of possibilities whereby greater 'interpenetration' might be accomplished. It also considers the role of the state as an external agent with an interest in 'levering' skills development in SMEs. This has emerged as governments have become aware of the ever increasing proportion of the working population operating in SMEs and the associated implications for national prosperity and competitiveness.

SETTING THE CONTEXT

Problems of definition

The term 'small and medium enterprise' was first used by the European Commission and disaggregated into three components based on number of employees (Storey, 1994):

■ micro-enterprises: those with between 0 and 9 employees;

■ small enterprises: those with 10 to 99 employees;

■ medium enterprises: those with 100 to 499 employees.

The Commission has subsequently (1996) redefined its original categorisation as follows:

■ micro-enterprises: those with between 0 and 9 employees;

■ small enterprises: those with 10 to 49 employees;

■ medium enterprises: those with 50 to 249 employees.

(Official Journal of the European Communities, 1996).

Other sources have used different numerical classification systems, often dependent on the focus of their research interest and availability of data for analysis. A number of the writers on the subject treat small organisations as having an upper limit of 25 employees. Hendry *et al*. (op. cit.), on the other hand, restricted their study of SMEs to organisations employing between 25 and 500 staff, adopting for analytical purposes four broad employment subdivisions: 25–50; 51–100; 101–200; 201–500. This inconsistency of definition leads to considerable confusion when one is trying to compare research findings.

For the purposes of this chapter we will consider an SME to be an organisation not exceeding 500 employees. The numerical subdivision used by Henry *et al*. (op. cit.) seems appropriate for comparative analysis of organisations between 25 and 500 employees. For those proposing to undertake studies into HRD practices in smaller organisations I would recommend, as a minimum, differentiating between those employing 2–10 staff and those with 11–24 staff. It is a moot point as to whether sole traders should be incorporated.

It is forecast that SMEs will play an increasingly important part in developed economies if the trend of the 1980s and first half of the 1990s, for larger firms to pare down their operations and engage in outsourcing strategies, continues into the next millennium. It has been estimated that 95 per cent of all UK businesses employ fewer than 20 people, and that, excluding central and local government, these account for over one-third of all employment (Daly and McCann, 1992). In 1989, the Small Business Research Trust estimated that in the UK, some 13 million people (including the self-employed), or half of all UK employees, were working for organisations employing less than 200 people (Bannock and Gray, 1989).

According to a 1994 Henley Management Centre forecast, by the year 2000, one in two of all non-governmental jobs in the UK will be in organisations of less than 50 people.

In the USA, 98 per cent of all businesses are classified as small businesses, defined as those employing 100 people or fewer (Dumaine, 1992), and it has been held that small businesses are responsible for 82 per cent of the jobs created in the United States (Megginson *et al.*, 1988). Enterprises employing up to 500 employees comprise more than 90 per cent of all businesses in the EU and provide over 60 per cent of its employment and around 50 per cent of its exports.

In the UK it is held to be of vital national importance that the 'training' needs of SMEs are met, if Britain is not to slip down the international competitiveness 'league table'. At a 1995 Management Charter Initiative (MCI) conference on SMEs the spokesman from the Department of Trade and Industry (DTI) argued – as many have done before and since – that in the global marketplace the only sustainable source of competitive advantage is the national skills base. The core theme of his presentation was that this skills base is increasingly being vested in SMEs and needs to be effectively upgraded. He also implied a change in focus from the 'operative' to the 'manager', a switch from pumping resources into basic skills training to an increasing emphasis on supporting programmes for manager development.

Figure 13.1 **UK Government White Paper on Competitiveness (1996)**

The White Paper highlighted five key areas contributing to competitiveness:

1 Workforce skills

2 Management development

3 Innovation

4 International trade

5 Investment.

In the international competitiveness tables in terms of gross domestic product per head of population, the UK held the following rank in the year indicated:

■ 1991: tenth

■ 1992: twelfth

■ 1993: sixteenth

■ 1994: fourteenth

■ 1995: sixteenth.

The survival rate of newly started SMEs is not very high. Many fail very quickly. In the USA, for example, of 600 000 small businesses started each year, 80–85 per cent fail in the first five years. Yet many SMEs have been in operation for decades and have experienced continual success.

FORMAL TRAINING IN SMALL AND MEDIUM-SIZED ENTERPRISES

Much of the past emphasis on HRD for SMEs has been on the provision of formal staff training and identifying what mechanisms and resources can be established to support this. Indeed a number of studies deliberately exclude 'experience'-style programmes from their analysis. Thus Elias and Healey (1994) contend that 'if the training activity is not structured [i.e. if it was known as informal training, consisting of learning by doing or as a period of time spent watching others] then it is not considered as job-related training'. Yet it is by no means clear that formal training is the most suitable course for SMEs.

The conventional argument for formal training in SMEs seems to run roughly along the following lines.

1 'Our' country is losing its competitive position in global league tables.

2 The future of the country in terms of enhancing its competitive capacity lies in the creation of a reservoir of highly skilled, knowledge-based workers.

3 An increasing number of organisations are SMEs and an increasing percentage of the labour force is in SMEs.

4 There is therefore a need to upgrade the capacity of SMEs to develop creative, proactive knowledge workers if 'we' are to sustain competitiveness.

5 The solution is training, especially formal, planned instruction in the skills needed to achieve the organisation's business plan.

6 The problem is that SMEs do not send people on formal training programmes, whether external or internal.

7 How therefore do we 'lever' SMEs into providing skills development given the above constraints?

UK Government initiatives have, over the years, focused on approaches to increase the level of, and investment in, formal training. Ventures include the Skills Challenge, announced in the 1995 Competitiveness White Paper. By the summer of 1996, funding had been awarded to 74 projects; over 1000 small firms are targeted to meet training needs through networking and shared resources. Similarly, 'Skills for Small Businesses', available through the national network of Training and Enterprise Councils (TECs), helps companies employing fewer than 50 staff with training so long as it is linked to business objectives. A feature is that key workers will lead the development and implementation of company training plans. Encouragement is also given to SMEs offering NVQs and seeking Investors in People (IiP) status. The national target is for 35 per cent of organisations employing more than 50 people to have achieved IiP recognition by the year 2000. This is undoubtedly unrealistic, given that the 1996 figure was 3.5 per cent.

The view that SMEs are less likely to engage in formal training provision than larger concerns is a well-rehearsed position. For example, at a management research seminar in October 1995 co-ordinated by MCI, David Storey of the Warwick University Business School Small Business Unit treated it as a given that small firms trained less than large. He suggested five explanatory hypotheses in terms of demand:

1 Training provides long-term rather than short-term benefits, and failure rates (i.e. organisational survival) are higher in small firms.

2 Poaching of staff is greater from small firms, partly because wage rates are lower.

3 Managerial aspirations are different. The rationale, he suggested, for much management development is providing training for promotion to the next level. There is no career development in small firms.

4 Training cost per employee is greater for small businesses.

5 There is no evidence that training works in small firms – if measured in terms of business survival. He referred to a Midland Bank report which suggested that if individuals from small companies go on a training course, the firm is three times less likely to fail. The Midland Bank claimed that their findings were based on Department of Trade and Industry (DTI) data but on closer examination the DTI findings proved to be mythical. The claimed connection between training and small business success does not exist.

He also presented some reasons in terms of supply:

1 Filling courses is expensive for small firms. The development costs per individual are high.

2 The content of courses needs to be customised, but this is expensive for small firms.

3 Linked to the above is the fact that small firms are in different stages of development (pre-start up; start-up; growth, etc.) and accordingly require different types of training at each stage, so adding to the expense.

Stahl *et al.* (1993) adopt a similar position. They identify a recurrent set of problems which make it difficult for SMEs to establish adequate training measures:

1 Small and medium-sized enterprises lack the capacity to define their real training needs in the context of enterprise modernisation.

2 They normally lack the capacity within themselves to plan, organise and implement training. For many SMEs it would be almost impossible to develop that capacity.

3 The external training market, provided by training institutions (such as colleges and universities), does not meet the specific demands of SMEs. The training provided is of a general nature which requires too much time in a classroom situation away from the job. To produce customised courses for a few employees is simply too expensive. Hence the justified complaint by SMEs that the delivery of training by training institutions is of little or no use for their training needs.

4 The tight financial margins within which SMEs operate, and the small number of employees, make it very difficult to release employees to attend off-site training programmes.

Stahl *et al.* (ibid.) go on to say that despite political efforts at the level of member states and at European Community level, there has been little real change in SME behaviour in relation to training and development. Research into the activities of SMEs shows very little activity and very little financial investment in training, by comparison to large firms.

Reasons include the lack of SME management competence in training and development matters. Until recently SMEs turned to the labour market for their supply of qualified staff.

The focus on training has diverted attention from broader developmental issues. On the whole there has been an assumption that career development and opportunities for promotion do not exist in SMEs. This view has been examined by Metcalf *et al.* (1994) who found in their survey that about one-quarter of the organisations which employed between 10 and 20 staff did offer some form of career path. At the same time they identified a tendency to promote people who already had what were considered to be the requisite skills, thus removing the need for subsequent training on promotion.

Nevertheless, personal development in SMEs is very much the responsibility of the individual. Support for the establishment of personal development goals, deciding how to attain them, creating opportunities for learning and development and developing career plans, is rarely orchestrated from within the organisation.

INFORMAL AND ACCIDENTAL HRD PROCESSES IN SMALL AND MEDIUM-SIZED ENTERPRISES AND THE DEVELOPMENT OF TACIT SKILLS

Thus, on the whole, HRD is equated with 'training' by those looking at learning within and for SMEs. But even given this concern with 'training' there are different perceptions of what approaches should be valued and what skills are needed.

Curran *et al.* (1996) see the need for a wider definition of training than is afforded by a focus on its formal elements. They prefer to consider training within SMEs as entailing 'any process, formal or informal, by which employees acquire knowledge and skills relevant to their performance at work. These may be initiated by the employer or employee, take place on or off the job, lead or not lead to a qualification and be self-directed or directed by another'.

In this context the 'Continuous Learning Continuum' developed by Watkins and Marsick (1993) provides a helpful insight into the range of possibilities that can be encountered (*see* Fig. 13.2).

Abbott (1993/4) makes the point that informal on-the-job training is not valued by its recipients as much as the formal planned approaches that are held to be adopted in larger firms. He is critical of the language adopted in classification systems such as that developed by Jones and Goss (1991). The terminology used, by differentiating between so-called high training and low training when assessing approaches adopted by small firms, reinforces negative perceptions of informal approaches.

According to Jones and Goss 'high training' refers to approaches which embrace a strategic and planned approach to training, whereas 'low training' refers to more *ad hoc*, fragmented and responsive approaches. The implication is that informal, 'low' training is inferior to the more structured, 'high' approach. This value orientation seems to be shared by a number of government-based initiatives to encourage investment by SMEs in HRD. In some ways this is surprising, given the move in many larger organisations away from a reliance on formal training to a consideration of broader, learning-based perspectives for skills development.

Figure 13.2	The continuous learning continuum

More formal →

- Formal qualification programme.

- Formal extensive training programme.

- Just-in-time courses.

- Structured mentoring and/or coaching, or on-the-job training.

- Combination of structured opportunities with less organised experiences. This may be facilitated by means of, say, action learning sets.

- Planning of a framework for learning, often associated with staff appraisal, career plans, training and development plans.

- Participation in Total Quality groups or other vehicles designed to promote continuous learning.

- Self-initaited and self-planned experiences – including seeking a tutor, coach or mentor or attending conferences, etc.

- New job assignments and participation in teams, or other job-related challenges that contribute to learning and self-development.

- Unanticipated experiences and encounters – at work or in one's personal life – that result in learning as an incidental or 'accidental' by-product and that may not be consciously recognisd or acknowledged.

← Less formal

Source: Based on Watkins and Marsick (1993).

The view also seems to be shared by people in SMEs themselves, although, as Hendry *et al.* (1991) found, they tend to favour practical in-house training as opposed to attendance on external courses. Partly this is in order to acquire basic skills on work systems which may be unique to that organisation, partly because of problems associated with time off for external courses.

Yet informal training and 'accidental' learning can be extremely effective in meeting the needs of a particular occupational group. Abbott (op. cit.) emphasises the value of accidental learning for the free (i.e. public) house, restaurant and wine bar category of the service sector where one learns primarily by experience the skills needed, for example, for handling difficult customers. He makes a connection with the acquisition, by such accidental and non-planned means, of 'tacit skills' which are often based on experience on the job, and informally learned. He contends that because they are acquired through learning as opposed to training they are taken for granted and accordingly devalued.

The concept of tacit skills is particularly useful for understanding training in small firms. The idea that the knowledge to perform routine tasks is acquired through experience is particularly relevant . . . Also relevant is the notion that tacit skills encompass the ability to deal with unexpected or unusual situations for which there is no prior frame of reference . . . The third dimension of tacit skills refers to the emphasis upon co-operativeness and good inter-personal skills. This is vital in a small firm. The small number of people employed, the confinement of the workplace and the wide range of tasks performed make it essential that employees 'get on' and are able to 'fit in' (ibid.).

Figure 13.3 examines 'tacit skills'.

Figure 13.3	Tacit skills – a note

A number of writers have suggested that 'tacit skills' are a key source of competitive advantage. Unlike a formally developed skill, they pertain to 'practical knowledge' and insights, acquired through daily experience. The term was coined by Polanyi (1966) who distinguished between two necessary and, for him, inseparable, components in the practical application of knowledge and skill – the explicit and the implicit (tacit).

According to Myers and Davids (1992) the practical knowledge gained is typically:

■ untaught;

■ increased by experience on the job;

■ on the whole, context dependent;

■ understood in the form of simple 'if – then' rules, such as 'if the telephone rings, then pick up the receiver';

■ an automatic, often unconscious, action in response to specific conditions.

Tacit skills are rarely listed in person specifications for jobs, but are essential to effective working. Newcomers can sometimes learn some of the 'ways of doing it around here' by listening to stories and anecdotes from experienced colleagues. Such acculturation is an important aspect of tacit skill acquisition.

Although the acquisition of tacit skills through learning is undoubtedly important, there is a risk that accidental learning can be seen as a substitute for other forms of knowledge and skill acquisition. For managers of SMEs in particular, a number of studies have shown that management skills are often perceived to be exclusively developed in the course of managing the business not through the aid of any external management development support.

ARE MORE HRD ACTIVITIES BEING UNDERTAKEN THAN WAS HITHERTO RECOGNISED?

Despite the acquisition of 'tacit skills' being an important source of learning in SMEs, it would be inappropriate to think of it as an intentional HRD strategy. It does however draw attention to the importance for learning of the work environment and the nature of the tasks being undertaken. An interesting 1995 study from the USA has challenged the notion that little in the way of HRD is done in successful SMEs. What it did establish was that people in the three organisations investigated (all in the manufacturing sector) felt that HRD activities were not being undertaken, mainly because of their rather narrow concept of HRD (Rowden, 1995). In contrast to the respondents, the researcher saw HRD as 'a multifaceted discipline' that included in its purview initiatives such as 'job enrichment' and autonomous team working which he felt contributed to individual and collective learning processes. Analysis of the participants' responses to field interviews revealed that they did not share this holistic perspective:

> For the people in these companies, HRD means a planned learning situation where participants sit in a classroom and are taught something. They simply do not view all the coaching, mentoring, on the job training (OJT), informal learning, and development they do as forms of HRD (ibid.).

Yet the field-based investigation revealed that although none labelled it as such, each organisation studied did a considerable amount of HRD, both formal and informal.

Using HRD to acculturate employees, by integrating employees into the company's work practices and helping develop tacit skills, also contributed to the success of these organisations. Indeed the existence of very strong cultural norms is a feature of many well-established relatively small organisations, and it is often not recognised how powerful the learning from informal acculturation can be! Beginning with selection, through orientation and initial job training, and periodically throughout their employment, workers are taught through the use of a variety of formal and informal methods, including OJT, assumptions about how the organisation 'works around here'.

Rowden's study emphasised the significance of going into organisations and obtaining information on the basis of observation and direct questioning, rather than relying on postal questionnaires. Had such quantitative techniques been relied upon, it is likely that the responses would have reinforced the prevailing opinion that little was being done in the way of HRD:

> Given that most scholars and researchers in HRD assume that little or no training – as they define it – takes place in small to mid-sized companies, one might speculate that this investigation was able to turn up incidents of HRD in large part because of the methodology employed, primarily because case study research is able to account for context. In addition, the participants had the opportunity to articulate their experiences in their own words, to explain what previous researchers may have seen but not fully understood (ibid.).

A number of annual and other questionnaire-based surveys are conducted into training-related issues as they concern SMEs. Typical is the annual European Business Survey by business advisers, Grant Thornton and the UK economic consultancy group, Business Strategies, which in 1996 questioned respondents on job creation and training in addition to obtaining opinions about business trends. Data obtained from surveys such as these could, of course, fall into the trap identified by Rowden. Quantitative studies need to be checked and validated by case study analysis conducted by knowledgeable and experienced practitioners.

DIFFERENTIATING BETWEEN SMALL AND MEDIUM-SIZED ENTERPRISES FOR HRD PURPOSES

It can be tempting to group SMEs together as an undifferentiated set of like organisations requiring common HRD solutions. However, this totally distorts the situation. They can be differentiated in a variety of ways and the classification system adopted tends to throw up a range of context-specific learning needs and resource issues at individual, team and organisational level. The classification system used to support the following analysis (shown diagrammatically in Fig. 13.4) is a variant of that used by Hendry *et al.* (op. cit.) for their 1991 published survey of SMEs employing between 25 and 500 people:

- size
- sector or product and service
- ownership and control
- age and stages of development
- customer base.

Figure 13.4   Influences on human resource development interventions

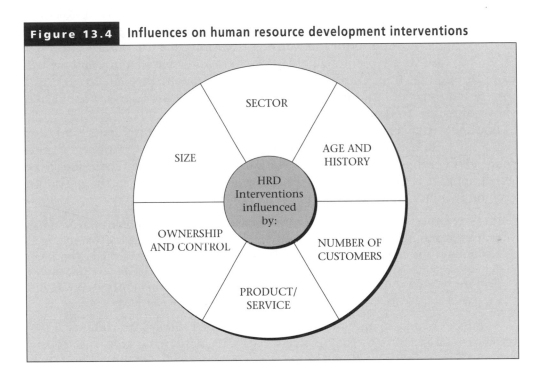

They further differentiated between enterprises showing a high level of concern for HRD which they entitled 'progressives' and those showing low concern/activity which they entitled 'laggards'. Given the more recent findings quoted in the 1996 Competitiveness White Paper, the majority of SMEs are defining themselves as 'laggards'.

Size

There is a tendency in some of the literature, and in government-sponsored initiatives, to treat SMEs as though they face similar problems irrespective of size. Yet it is a reasonable assumption that organisations with staffing levels of 250 will face different learning issues and consider alternative solutions, to those with fewer than 25. Even for small organisations with fewer than 25, differences in size could be a key factor in approaches to HRD. To make a very trivial point: if one employee in a firm of four goes on an external training course, 25 per cent of the labour force is absent; if one employee in a firm of 25 goes on a similar course, then the absence level is 4 per cent. According to the DTI (1996) over a fifth of all UK businesses had 1–4 employees at the end of 1994.

At the level of the small enterprise, one would not expect to see dedicated staff with a specific remit for HRD. Vickerstaff and Parker (1995) note that 'case-study-based work has revealed a high degree of unplanned, reactive and informal training activity in small firms, where there is typically unlikely to be a dedicated personnel manager or training officer'. This is not to say that there is no one responsible for HRD. Curran *et al.* (1996) report findings from a national (UK) telephone survey of owner-managers in enterprises ranging from 1–2 workers at the bottom end of the scale to those with 100–199 employees at the top. Of the firms questioned, 72 per cent claimed to have a person with specific responsibility for work-force training or learning. On further enquiry it turned out that in two-thirds of the cases (i.e. in 48 per cent of the firms) this person was the owner-manager, often taking on the role by default.

This statistic is a matter of great significance, emphasising the degree of dependence for the HRD effort on the attitude of the person running or owning the organisation.

Once organisations get larger then this responsibility is relatively easy to delegate. In my experience, a number of organisations employ an administrative officer/manager when they reach a certain size, and this individual takes on an HRD role. In the larger category of medium-sized enterprises the situation is likely to be substantially different, organisations at this level being more able to resource a full-time personnel and, in some instances, a dedicated training and development officer. Where a sole administrative or personnel officer has responsibility for HRD in addition to other duties, there is a risk of role overload, with the consequence that HRD will not be treated proactively.

As we shall see later, there is some evidence that growth rate is more significant than size in determining the likelihood of there being a dedicated HRD staff member in an organisation.

Sector

Small organisations employing fewer than 25 people tend to be located in the service sector. One 1988 estimate was that nine out of ten of all businesses employing between one and 24 employees were in services and construction (Gurran and Burrows, 1988). Even in the service sector, comparisons merely on the basis of size would encompass an exceptionally heterogeneous array of concerns with little in common, a point made by Curran, Blackburn and Woods (1991), who further differentiated between:

1 Free houses (i.e. public houses), wine bars and restaurants.

2 Video hire and leisure services.

3 Vehicle repair and servicing.

4 Market research, advertising and design.

5 Employment, secretarial and training agencies.

6 Computer services.

7 Plant, skip, equipment and vehicle hire.

Abbott (1993/4), as part of his research in the early 1990s into training provision in different business categories in the service sector, contrasted the learning needs of staff in free (i.e. public) houses, wine bars and restaurants with those in service sector areas such as advertising, marketing and design. In this latter arena there is a preponderance of small organisations, all of which depend upon individuals engaging in a high level of creativity, and sustaining close relations with clients. The staff relationship in such sectors is not always based on employer–employee contracts and can often entail individuals operating as partners or freelance consultants. Employees in such sectors tend to possess high-level skills before joining the firms, and a number belong to professional networks, which they access for professional updating (ibid.). It may well be a condition of their continuing professional membership that they keep an ongoing record of continuing professional development.

Curran *et al.* (1996) found that construction firms were less likely to have a written training plan or policy and much less likely to have a dedicated training budget than firms in manufacturing or services. They also found that despite manufacturing's tradition of craft training, manufactureres in turn, were less likely to have a training plan or policy and a dedicated training budget than firms in services, especially new knowledge-based and professional services. Figure 13.5 looks at creativity and innovation.

Figure 13.5   Creativity and innovation

Majaro (1988) contends that high levels of success can only be achieved in organisations if they are able to develop 'creativity' and 'innovation'. Creativity he defines as 'the thinking process that helps us to generate ideas'. Innovation he holds to entail 'the practical application of such ideas towards meeting the organisation's objectives in a more effective way'.

He identifies the following three key conditions which organisations must achieve in order to be creative, stressing that all three conditions must coexist in 'a comfortable harmony' and that whoever is in charge of the organisation must be 'wholeheartedly and relentlessly committed' to establishing and maintaining them:

■ a climate conducive to creating thinking;

■ an effective system for communicating ideas;

■ procedures for managing innovation in order to screen and evaluate ideas and identify the relatively few which are worth exploiting.

Ekvall (1996) has developed a model which can be used to evaluate the creativity of an organisation's climate on ten key dimensions.

▶▶ Figure 13.5 continued

1 *Challenge*: the level of emotional involvement with the organisation's operations and goals.

2 *Freedom*: the degree of independence exhibited by members in sharing information, discussing problems, taking initiatives and making decisions.

3 *Idea support*: the way new ideas are received.

4 *Trust/openness*: the emotional safety in working relationships.

5 *Dynamism/liveliness*: the eventfulness of life in the organisation.

6 *Playfulness/humour*: the degree of spontaneity and ease which is evident.

7 *Debates*: the frequency of encounters and clashes between members' different viewpoints, ideas, experiences and knowledge.

8 *Conflicts*: the presence of tensions – which are personal and emotional, as opposed to conflicts between ideas.

9 *Risk taking*: the organisation's response to, and tolerance of, uncertainty.

10 *Idea time*: the amount of time members devote to developing and elaborating new ideas, with the feeling that this is a proper part of their roles.

These constructs are clearly of enormous significance for the small organisations employing skilled knowledge workers that dominate the marketing communications sector. Some confirmation for this comes from a pilot study undertaken during 1997 and early 1998 for his Masters Dissertation in Human Resource Strategies at London Guildhall University by David Roberts, an independent consultant from this sector. For the organisations studied he demonstrated a clear connection between creative climate and business growth. An implication of his findings is that the HRD effort in such organisations should concentrate on the attainment of a learning climate that contributes to creativity and innovation.

Ownership and control

Differentiation in terms of ownership and control could include:

- partnerships;
- owner-managed private limited companies (the archetypal small family firm);
- quoted plc;
- joint venture;
- co-operatives;
- small consultancies;
- outsourced specialist units.

Unlike Hendry *et al.* (op. cit.) I have not included in my classification a wholly owned subsidiary or a single establishment of a larger entity. For me these constitute a separate category within a larger entity, and are not genuine SMEs.

Many SMEs are very entrepreneurial, and influenced by the management style and drive of the chief executive. This person is often the founder (or a descendant of the founder) who is also the owner. Many SMEs are likely to be family concerns, or owned by a specific individual or group of individuals. Ward (1987) argued that a family firm was any firm in which the owners could transfer ownership and control to subsequent generations of their own families. The Rowden study (op. cit.) looked at organisations that were all family owned. Whatever the ownership characteristics, as Hendry *et al.* (1991) point out it is a truism that the key figure in the early development of the small firm is the 'entrepreneur'. It is this individual (or group of individuals) who is intimately involved in the development of the firm's position in its particular niche market, its relations with key customers and its network relations more generally. How the entrepreneur perceives HRD issues is a central platform in the establishment or otherwise of a supportive learning climate.

Even for more established concerns, it is a reasonable hypothesis that issues of personal control and the value orientation of the chief executive will exert a far stronger influence in smaller enterprises than in larger ones. The personal exercise of power, as reflected in the management style adopted, is a major influencing factor on what takes place, and how it takes place. Especially in family concerns, it would not be unexpected for a number of key players to be there because of their family connections and not necessarily because of their distinctive competences. However it is undertaken, HRD as a proactive manifestation can be dependent on educating these power brokers, who are so influential in determining the current and future success of the concern. How does one gain and maintain their attention?

In total contrast to the above, there is a particular category of SMEs that came into existence on the basis of the governing principle of 'direct democracy'. Under this principle, all members have an equal right to rule and be involved in strategic decision making. Worker co-operatives are an obvious example of this form of organisation. On the whole, they tend to be small, some people considering 20 to be an optimum size. They function as a form of partnership. Many co-operatives follow the guidelines of the Rochdale principles which were laid down in the mid-nineteenth century:

1 One person, one vote.
2 Each person has equal member rights.
3 All members have equal shares in the profits.

In such organisations, members expect to be involved in all decisions affecting the enterprise and this can make management of the enterprise (as distinct from ownership of the organisation) problematic. Managers, if they exist at all, can be in an ambivalent situation, since they are in a position of directing and instructing the owners. For some such organisations, success, if measured in terms of growth, can lead to much soul-searching. Members have often bought into operations such as these because of the possibility of close-knit networking with like-minded colleagues, who all know each other and share similar aspirations and values. Often, in such organisations, individuals bring with them pre-existing high-level skills. Where energy needs to be focused is on team learning to ensure harmony and effective collaborative decision making. External facilitation can be of tremendous value, to help take organisation members 'out of themselves' should any difficulties in co-working arise.

Age and stage of development

A large number of small enterprises do not survive the first year of their establishment. However, many are well established and have been in existence for a long period of time. The Rowden study (op. cit.) restricted itself to 'successful' SMEs, which they defined as having been in existence for at least ten years. Similarly, the Hendry *et al.* study (op. cit.) represented 'survivors' rather than organisations in the early stages of formation.

Organisational life cycle theory

The Hendry *et al.* (op. cit.) classification of 'stages of development' is based on a simple 'organisational life cycle' model consisting of the stages of 'growth', 'maturity' and 'decline'/'retrenchment'. One of the most pervasive themes in the organisational literature is the notion that corporations go through some form of predetermined life cycle. Rather like individuals, they have periods of birth, growth, maturity, decay and death. The proposition is rather simplistic and is best treated as a generalised explanatory metaphor that might have some meaning in some organisational situations.

One of the most well-known organisational life cycle models in the strategy literature is that developed by Greiner (1972). Given the above caveats, it is a working assumption that many SMEs are at an early, pre-growth stage of their life cycle. Many do not progress beyond 'infancy'. Greiner's model provides a tentative explanation for this in terms other than market/product collapse. Note the implicit relationship he postulates between management style and organisation success (*see* Fig. 13.6).

Figure 13.6 Evolution and revolution as organisations grow

Larry Greiner (1972) argues that organisations typically go through five stages of evolution and revolution, the speed of which is determined by factors such as growth rate of the industry. Note that his model assumes that successful organisations, just like infants, will grow in size and level of activity and will not stay still. This is by no means indicated by the evidence from SMEs, some of which have remained small and successful over quite extended periods of time. His argument suggests that irrespective of the value 'out there' of the product or service offered, there is a potential *self-destruct* element in any organisation that has to be confronted at different, albeit relatively predictable, times during an organisation's history; and worked through in different ways. If it is not worked through, the organisation will cease to exist.

PHASE 1: CREATIVITY

In the birth stage of an organisation, the emphasis is on creating both a product and a market. Typical characteristics are:

■ the organisation's founders are usually technically or entrepreneurially oriented and they disdain management activities;

■ communication among employees is frequent and informal;

▶▶

▶▶ Figure 13.6 continued

■ control of activities comes from immediate marketplace feedback; the management acts as the customers react.

The leadership crisis

At some point, there is a crisis of leadership. As the company increases in size, it can no longer be managed in highly personal, informal ways. For the organisation to survive there is a need for a revolutionary shift to Phase 2.

PHASE 2: DIRECTION

In the direction phase the emphasis is on 'professionalising' the management and the structures and systems. Typical characteristics are:

■ increased specialisation of functions;

■ establishment of formal control systems;

■ centralised direction;

■ separation of role of CEO from that of chairman.

The crisis of autonomy

This leads to the crisis of autonomy. As the organisation expands, employees feel restricted by the hierarchy and associated control and command structures, and the top finds it increasingly difficult to maintain detailed control. To grow, the organisation needs to change formal structures and decentralise.

PHASE 3: DELEGATION

In the delegation phase the emphasis is on establishing mechanisms to facilitate autonomy of decentralised business units. Typical mechanisms are:

■ local autonomy;

■ devolved budgetary responsibility;

■ divisionalisation.

The crisis of control

The top feels it is losing control, and parochial attitudes develop in the divisions of the company.

PHASE 4: CO-ORDINATION

In the co-ordination phase systems are installed to bring about greater co-ordination and control, to ensure the continuing growth of the organisation.

The crisis of red tape

Increasingly, as the organisation grows larger and more complex, bureaucratic controls create sharp divisions between head office staffs and operating divisions.

PHASE 5: COLLABORATION

In this (final?) stage, the preceding crisis will be resolved through strong interpersonal collaboration and control, by virtue of the establishment of common cultures – as opposed to the exercise of formal controls. This could, according to Greiner, lead to a crisis of psychological saturation, in which all become exhausted by teamwork.

Hendry *et al.* (op. cit.) argue that HRD interventions and activities in SMEs are strongly influenced by where the SME is on the life cycle. As they put it:

> The pattern emerges of an initial effort at systematic training petering out after one or two years. Sometimes the firm's resources for conducting on-the-job training (through supervisors) are swamped by a large cohort intake. Other times the company believes it has completed its training having established its core workforce.

Initial training is very important when an organisation first starts up and needs to ensure that staff have the basic skills to develop and operate work systems which may be unique to the enterprise. The emphasis is also on 'hands-on' training in the workplace. Pre-start-up training is also been raised as an important issue in determining the early success of many new ventures.

When a company has been in operation for some five to seven years, however, there may be a shift in the attitude to training. This could be because it becomes apparent that people's skills have stood still in a changing and challenging competitive environment. It could be that, as the numbers of staff grow, the previously *ad hoc* approach to development is no longer appropriate. 'There may thus be a natural life-cycle of training which matches the cohort progression of employees' (Hendry *et al.*, op. cit.).

They also found evidence that the stage of growth on the organisational life cycle has more influence on the need for a specialist personnel/training officer than does size. They found that the fast-growing firms of their sample typically reached a point (after about five to seven years from being established) at which they needed to standardise their training through a specialist service to support measured progression through grades.

Nevertheless, only six firms in their sample had a dedicated training function, and of these only two recruited an individual qualified by way of credentials and prior experience. This contrasted with 15 firms which relied on a specified line manager to organise T&D-related activities.

Customer base

Many SMEs rely heavily on one large customer. In business terms such reliance can create conditions of external uncertainty and ongoing vulnerability, potentially placing the organisation at the mercy of its customer. Lyons and Bailey (1993) have coined the term *subcontractor vulnerability*, the features of which include dependence on dominant customers, the provision of outputs which are specific to particular customers, and tailoring investment decisions to meet the needs of a narrow customer base. In HRD terms this tends to make training specific and geared to meeting the needs of that customer's product/service (Hendry *et al.*, 1991).

There is another aspect of dependence on a single customer. Increasingly, large organisations are trying to establish long-term partnerships with their suppliers. This is a move away from the essentially temporary, hands-off and short-term associations that buying departments have traditionally had with their suppliers. One of the effects of partnership arrangements has been to draw suppliers into the downstream 'learning' chain of the customer organisation. In a sense, the customer takes over a substantial responsibility for the learning needs of its associate, without formally integrating it into its value chain. This development is to be expected as organisations slough off what are no longer held to be core activities, yet still wish to maintain a strong association with their service providers.

DEVELOPING STRUCTURED HRD INITIATIVES IN AND FOR SMALL AND MEDIUM-SIZED ENTERPRISES

Given the above analysis, what possibilities exist for developing a more coherent, rounded approach to HRD and learning for SMEs? A number of suggestions follow. They are not sector specific and would need to be interpreted in the context of a given organisation.

Part-time human resource development support

Unless they are at the top of the size range, SMEs are unlikely to be able to resource a full-time HRD professional. Commonly, HRD issues are incorporated into the role specification of an owner-manager, an administrative manager, or more exceptionally, a personnel officer. The absence of a dedicated professional means that often, insufficient attention is given to the contribution that learning and development can make to the organisation. One solution which is worth contemplating for mid-size SMEs is to have a part-time HRD consultant attached, who services a number of organisations. This seemed to be quite common practice in The Netherlands and was observed working effectively in a number of SMEs on a 1996 visit undertaken by a group of Masters students from London Guildhall University.

Drawing on external providers

Very few SMEs have their own training capacity (in terms of facilities etc.). Few possess much insight into learning processes. Many authorities believe that if SMEs are to move towards an integration of learning and work they will require a high level of external professional assistance. The evidence is that external training institutions have enormous problems in selling their services and products to SMEs because it is claimed that the training delivered by external training institutions does not meet their real needs.

Thus SMEs represent a potential market for T&D activities which is largely untapped. If this market is to be accessed it will require radical changes in the relationship between the training provider and the SME (*see* Stahl *et al.*, 1993).

If one thinks merely in terms of the provision of training, however, this affords a limited perspective of the range of services that external providers can offer. Many SMEs, for example, would find consultancy advice and support on team development and networking and guidance on approaches to organisation development extremely helpful.

There is concern about the cost of the services of external providers. This can, however, be far less than might be imagined and in the UK external funding support, may be available to SMEs.

Forging business links through sector-specific networks

There is a strong tradition in many countries for SMEs to participate in sector-specific networks and to develop mutual support systems. In Italy, where in many regions SMEs predominate, such networks have a long history, and are closely associated with particular external training providers.

The UK Government has invested in a support service for SMEs called Business Links, co-ordinated through the DTI and initiated in 1992. These links are a series of regional and national networks, of which some 240 were in place in 1996. Additionally, more than 350 Personal Business Advisers (PBAs) have been appointed across the country to support SMEs, although these are not necessarily sector specific. These advisers are supposed to understand the nature of business problems; know what services are available; be able to assemble a package of assistance that meets the needs of the individual customer; and establish long-term relationships. Nearly two-thirds of PBAs see their role as one of facilitator (Sear and Agar, 1996).

According to a spokesman from the DTI at a 1994 Association of Business Schools (ABS) conference, it is intended to offer 'virtual teaching' through Business Links by exploiting IT/Communications Highway opportunities.

There is also a push to create via Business Links a set of self-sufficient and mutually supporting SME networks, each of which will in turn become an enabling mechanism to empower constituent SMEs to learn and develop for themselves. This view is linked to an OECD recommendation that a move to clusters of SMEs will facilitate the 'Competitive Advantage of Regions'. By 1995 some 80 'new organisations' (SME networks) had been developed.

One challenge is get university business schools to work more collaboratively with Business Links. If this move is successful, Business Links might constitute a high percentage of business schools' target markets. An example of such a development is at Wolverhampton: Business Links Wolverhampton is physically located in Wolverhampton University Science Park.

One of the measures the European Commission proposed in its report on SMEs to the Madrid Summit in December 1995 was that its Euro-Info-Centres (EICs) should become first-stop shops for information on how smaller companies can gain access to EU programmes. There are over two hundred EICs located throughout the member states and, although individually they tend to be all-rounders, they are also organised into sector-specific groups. These develop software such as Tender Electronic Daily (TED) which carries details of invitations to tender for public works, supply and service contracts; another assists companies looking for business partners in the EU through the Business Co-operation Network (BC-Net). There are EICs in all major cities. However, one of the problems reported from field surveys into SMEs is the difficulty they have in accessing such networks.

The development of self-sufficient and mutually supporting small enterprise networks is by no means uncommon. A fascinating example from Africa is reported by Jean Lawrence. In Tanzania, small enterprises can be very small. In what is known as the 'informal' sector, business men and women set themselves up on the verges of roads and on patches of wasteland. There they run market stalls, carve wooden figures, collect, kill and sell chickens, do welding and so on. Some of these groups form themselves into Self-Help Organisations (SHOs) of, say, 20–100 entrepreneurs, and provide services for themselves as group members – such as holding funds for emergencies. Most of the members have no understanding of managerial processes in organisations, although many have survived individually in very hazardous circumstances for many years. A German government project has been providing support for the SHOs in Dar es Salaam, trying to develop staff through action learning. Learning sets have been established, external set facilitators have been provided. Work with the SHOs has been conducted on the side of the road, with flip charts pinned to cardboard shelters (Lawrence, 1996).

Providing support through external mentors

Langridge (1998) reports on a mentoring scheme run just north of London through the auspices of Hertfordshire Training and Enterprise Council (TEC) and Hertfordshire Voluntary Enterprise and Skills Training (Harvest) for voluntary agencies in the area.

The ten mentees were self selected and came from a range of voluntary organisations in the Harvest network. The ten mentors were external to the organisations and comprised individuals who responded to an advertisement in a local paper which invited 'highly motivated business people – either in employment or retired – to mentor key individuals in local Voluntary organisations' and in return 'for giving your time and commitment' each mentor would receive full training in the skills and processes of mentoring and they would have the opportunity to 'learn about their own preferred communication and learning styles, as well as core coaching and counselling skills'. The scheme also provided for a mentors forum to provide ongoing support for mentors.

Mentors and mentees were matched on a number of criteria measured by means of a variety of techniques. For example, mentees were asked to identify on a scale of 1 to 5 their development needs in terms of:

■ career management;
■ general support;
■ learning and development;
■ self-reliance;
■ specific skills.

The results of the detailed questionnaire were then compared to perceived areas of strengths against which mentors had assessed themselves, in order to identify areas of similarity.

Seven mentoring relationships survived the first six months of the scheme and a high number have proved to be of great benefit to mentees and mentors. Langridge quotes one of the mentees as saying: 'It is brilliant. For the first time in my life there is someone whose time is just for me.'

Secondments and small and medium-sized enterprises

A number of organisations use secondments to SMEs operating in the voluntary sector as a method of development for their staff. At the moment the process seems to be primarily one-way – that is, from the larger organisation to the smaller voluntary organisation. There is no reason in principle why it could not take the form of a structured exchange.

Secondments to SMEs at PriceWaterhouseCoopers are part of a structured mid-career development programme, co-ordinated by a Principal for Community Affairs, for people who have been with the firm for several years. Many of the young professionals recruited by the firm come from a comparatively sheltered educational and academic background. The belief is that working in a small community-based organisation dealing with inner city problems like homelessness and drug addiction broadens their outlook on life. In return, the SME gains access to resources from a larger organisation which could help its problem-solving capacity and contribute to organisational learning.

Standard Life, the insurance group, which runs its SME secondment scheme from the personnel department, sees the scheme as an important part of the organisation's contribution to the local community. Voluntary organisations are selected for development assignments which match the company's policy of helping in the areas of health, homelessness and education.

The company strives to match an individual's development needs to a specific project which will use his or her skills for the benefit of the voluntary organisation. Those seconded need to be very clear about what is required of them and are given time to get to know the organisation and the people in it. A 'settling-in' period is an important feature of the process when they return to Standard Life. Often they feel that they are taking a step backwards, and it is important that a new job opportunity or career move is built in as part of the programme.

Marks & Spencer, which spends £2 million each year on its secondment programme, has a policy of continuing relationships with voluntary organisations, maintaining support through cash contributions, or encouraging the person seconded to stay on in an advisory capacity (Finn, 1995).

As an alternative to secondments, learning support for SMEs could be provided through universities. One approach which is well worth exploring is to encourage mature students on MBA and other post-experience Masters courses to carry out investigative projects in SMEs. Many students are looking for such projects which will give them experience at first hand within a context other than their conventional work environment.

The European-funded PLATO scheme adopts a modified version of secondments. It has managers from multinationals operating as 'team leaders' on a voluntary basis for SME networks. In fact, much of the emphasis on learning for SMEs has been on developing sector-specific regional support networks.

Organisational interpenetration

As we have noted, many SMEs are dependent on a single customer, often a far larger organisation, for providing their distinctive product or service. Many of these larger organisations already provide training and development opportunities for their suppliers and distributors as a key strategic initiative and the trend seems set to continue. This theme is developed in greater detail in Chapters 10 (on learning support for non-employees) and 16 (on the corporate university).

Note that the idea of organisational interpenetration should not be confused with the practice of relying on suppliers to provide the bulk of an SME's training. Curran *et al.* (1996) in their survey identified suppliers as the second-most important source (after owner-managers and other employees) of in-house continuing training. They went on to observe that the training currently provided tends to be specific to the equipment and/or products supplied and does not support employees' more generic learning needs.

Investors in people as a strategic HRD initiative for small and medium-sized enterprises

Figure 13.7 presents the Investors in People (IiP) criteria.

The UK Government sees IiP as a key plank in its strategy to embed issues about training and learning into the fabric of organisations. How realistic is this, in respect of SMEs?

Figure 13.7 Investors in People

There are four broad criteria to achieving an Investors in People (IiP) award:

1 *An Investor in People makes a public commitment from the top to develop all employees to achieve its business objectives.*

- Every employee should have a written but flexible plan which sets out business goals and targets, considers how employees will contribute to achieving the plan and specifies how development needs in particular will be assessed and met.

- Management should develop and communicate to all employees a vision of where the organisation is going and the contribution employees will make to its success, involving employee representatives as appropriate.

2 *An Investor in People regularly reviews the training and development needs of all its employees.*

- The resources for training and developing employees should be early identified in the business plan.

- Managers should be responsible for regularly agreeing training and development needs with each employee in the context of business objectives, setting targets and standards linked, where appropriate, to the achievement of NVQs (or relevant units).

3 *An Investor in People takes action to train and develop individuals on recruitment and throughout their employment.*

- Action should focus on the training needs of all new recruits and continually developing and improving the skills of existing employees.

- All employees should be encouraged to contribute to identifying and meeting their own job-related development needs.

▶▶

▶▶ Figure 13.7 continued

4 *An Investor in People evaluates the investment in training and development to assess achievement and improve future effectiveness.*

■ The investment, the competence and commitment of employees, and the use made of skills learned should be reviewed at all levels against business goals and targets.

■ The effectiveness of training and development should be reviewed at the top level and lead to renewed commitment and target setting.

For relatively well-established SMEs, the learning strategy can be tied to IiP. The achievement of IiP status can also be seen as a useful marketing tool, an addition to its product portfolio which it can present to customers. The IiP rubric does not require the existence of a specifically constituted HRD unit, a requirement which would create problems for many SMEs. Instead the onus is firmly placed upon management at all levels to ensure its criteria are met.

In practice, the achievement of IiP status is not easy, and involves an investment in time and commitment that many organisations, irrespective of size, find difficult to sustain. A key requirement entails evidence of 'allocating resources' to training and development. For SMEs the question arises as to how far that is realistic. As Curran, *et al.* (1996) point out, only 10 per cent of the 751 organisations contributing to their telephone survey had a specific budget for work-force training or learning. Indeed, how far does it matter, in terms of business performance which drives the IiP initiative, whether individuals have a personal development plan that incorporates, for example, the tacit skills they need to acquire?

Another key issue confronting the exponents of IiP is that there can often be an incongruence between the relatively informal structures that owners and managers may prefer, and the formality imposed by the assessment rubric.

Nevertheless, IiP remains a promising initiative for orchestrating learning, especially for established SMEs. Thatcher (1996) quotes 1996 statistics from Investors in People (UK) which reveal that 43 per cent of organisations that had attained the standard employed fewer than 50 staff.

CONCLUSION

This chapter has demonstrated that in some established SMEs, HRD may be very much part of the management philosophy and be implemented in various ways, including job enrichment, advising or coaching and so forth. Hendry *et al.* (1991) entitle such establishments 'progressives' as opposed to 'laggards'. Much can be learned by looking at the role of HRD in successful SMEs through investigative, field-based, benchmarking studies. Some very informative studies – but not many – have been undertaken (e.g. Abbott, 1993/4, Hendry, *et al.* 1991, Rowden, 1995). One of the messages of studies that have been undertaken is how important it is to have a broad grasp of HRD and not focus on formal course-driven, off-the-job training activities. Another central message has been that key stakeholders in the organisations researched tend to see HRD in narrow course-based, off-the-job training terms, and do not always recognise the range of learning activities undertaken in their own organisation.

This is not to deny that formal planned training can be important for some SMEs. Certainly, pre-start-up and start-up training can be of great significance, but not always. A key consideration in setting learning needs is to establish the distinctive characteristics of a given SME in terms of such factors as size, product/service offered, origins and history, ownership and control.

One can infer the attitude towards HRD in a given SME from the resources consciously invested in learning at different stages in its development. The attitude of the person running the enterprise is particularly important in determining whether and how such resources are allocated, and the general HRD direction to be followed.

External advice and support are particularly important for shaping the HRD activities of SMEs. The focus of such advice in the past has been on formal training provision. This has provided a somewhat narrow perspective on ways forward, although this chapter has presented evidence of a range of alternative approaches that are being practised.

| Figure 13.8 | Human resource development consultancy case study – Glenfinnan Ltd |

The following case study demonstrates the interplay of forces that can have an impact on the approach adopted to HRD in an SME. Interventions in relation to HRD cannot be realistically undertaken without an awareness of what is taking place in the rest of the business. 'Glenfinnan' is not the name of an actual organisation.

Field notes on initial visit

Nichola, the Administration Manager of Glenfinnan Ltd invited me to the company's offices near Oxford Circus in London to see whether I could assist with a problem the organisation was facing. I had no prior knowledge of the company nor indeed any understanding of what business it was in.

In a one-hour conversation with her I discovered that its core business was selling barrels of whisky – specifically by telemarketing and direct mailing overseas. The trade term for a barrel of whisky was a 'hogshead'. Each hogshead was sold at £1000. The typical first buy was five hogs heads for £5000. Clients were predominantly from the Far East, especially Singapore. The whisky was stored in a bonded warehouse in Scotland. So far as I could establish that was where it stayed after purchase. Clients seemed to treat it as an investment which they could subsequently sell on – to other purchasers who would similarly leave it in the warehouse! Annual storage fees were £25 per barrel. However Glenfinnan's telemarketers were not allowed to refer to the investment aspect to their clients. This seemed to be for legal reasons.

The annual turnover was in the region of £1 000 000. Of this approximately 80 per cent was new business and 20 per cent repeat business with existing clients. All repeat business was handled by the two directors who were also the owners of

▶▶

▶▶ Figure 13.8 continued

the company. The phone bill was £52 000 a quarter and clearly a major cost item. The two directors had recently made a decision to move into new target markets. They had identified mainland Europe and the USA.

The sales function structure consisted of three 'telesellers' who functioned as 'warmers'. They went through trade directories to identify likely clients who would have the income to purchase the barrels. They then made initial contact with the client. Once the client expressed interest he/she was passed on to one of the six 'account executives' who completed the contract negotiations. The contract terms were drawn up by one of the three administrative staff.

The 'telesellers' were seen as trainee account executives. They were given minimal training on joining. The training constituted a brief information pack on the business and a form of words to follow when contacting potential clients.

The organisation had started in spring 1995. Since then there had been four changes to the payment system for the sales staff. Currently the 'telesellers' were on a £12 000 p.a. salary, no commission. The 'account executives' were on a £6000 basic salary, rising in £6 000 bands to a maximum of £36 000 dependent on sales. In practice no one was achieving anything like £36 000, and £12 000 seemed to be closer to the norm.

The hours varied. This was because of the time difference between the Far East and the UK. Many of the staff were in for part of the night. Direct mailing activities were undertaken at more conventional times.

A year ago the total staff complement had been 30. In recent months there had been a substantial downsizing and it was now 15. This seemed to be because of a sluggishness in sales. I was shown tables on reasons for leaving and a high percentage were for 'poor performance'. Three were for 'gross misconduct' which in two cases related to persistent drinking on the premises. One was because of 'doctoring' sales to enhance the bonus.

Recently an HR manager had been appointed. Her role seemed to be recruiting and selecting telesellers, who were predominantly unemployed graduates aged between 22 and 28. The two directors were also interested in getting Investors in People status and she had been given the job of developing an appropriate infrastructure. A management consultant was also being used to give advice on steps to be undertaken. To show their commitment to IiP the two directors had spent some £30 000 on training in recent months.

As Administration Manager Nichola seemed to have line management responsibility for all the administrative staff plus the telemarketeers plus the HR manager.

The problem presented to me was that the organisation had a particularly high labour turnover rate and I was asked whether training could help with this. In particular a high percentage of starters left in the first week. I also spotted a group of four who collectively left on the first morning. There were also examples of appointees who failed to turn up. I was asked for my advice on improving induction procedures to reduce the wastage rate.

I asked Nichola why she felt people were leaving. She felt that one explanation was that the jobs as advertised were oversold. They emphasised the possibility of quickly making £36 000 p.a. and even earning a company car. This scenario had apparently been reinforced at previous interviews conducted by the sales director

▶▶

▶▶ Figure 13.8 continued

(one of the two owners). People had then walked out when they discovered the reality was so different. Nichola was not clear how the job was being described to current candidates by the new HR manager but felt that inaccurately raising people's expectations during the recruitment process was counter-productive.

I then asked her how many of the original accounts executives/tellesellers were still with the company. She thought that there was perhaps still one, but she would need to check.

I mentioned to her the Tavistock Institute classification system of phases of decision making that individuals go through when deciding to stay with an organisation. The first phase is the 'Induction Crisis' which people experience when they first start. This was particularly marked at Glenfinnan, as reflected by the number of leavers in the first week. The second phase is the 'Period of Differential Transit' when people decide whether they wish to make a long-term commitment to the organisation. The third phase is the 'Period of Settled Connection' when individuals no longer start thinking of moving on. I told her that in my opinion the evidence indicated that no one on the sales side had got beyond the 'Period of Differential Transit'. She accepted this and asked me why this might be and what solutions might be possible.

What explanation(s) spring to mind? How would you feed this back to Nichola? What further support would you like to offer her? In HRD terms, what might be undertaken? How realistic is the attempt to achieve IiP status?

REFERENCES

Abbott, B. (1993/4) 'Training Strategies in Small Sector Firms: Employer and Employee Perspectives', *Human Resource Management Journal*, 4(2), Winter, pp. 70–87.

Bannock, G. and Grey, C. (1989) 'Small Business Statistics', A Feasibility Study Prepared for the Department of Employment. Graham Bannock and Partners.

Curran, J., Blackburn, R. and Woods, A. (1991) 'Profiles of the Small Enterprise in the Service Sector', paper presented at University of Warwick, 18 April and quoted in Storey (1994).

Curran, J., Blackburn, R., Kitching, J. and North, J. (1996) 'Small Firms and Workforce Training', 19th National Small Firms Policy and Research Conference *Proceedings*, University of Central England, pp. 499–522.

Daly, M. and McCann, A. (1992) 'How many small firms', *Employment Gazette*, 100, February, pp. 47–51.

DTI (1996) 'Small and Medium Sized Enterprise (SME) Statistics for the United Kingdom 1994', Department of Trade and Industry Small Firms Statistics Unit.

Dumaine, B. (1992) 'Is big still good?', *Fortune*, 20 April, pp. 50–60.

Ekvall, G. (1996) 'Organisation Climate for Creativity and Innovation', *European Journal of Work and Organisational Psychology*, 5(1), March, pp. 105–23.

Elias, P. and Healey, M. J. (1994) 'The Provision and Impact of Job-Related Formal Training in a Local Labour Market', *Regional Studies*, 28, pp. 577–90.

Finn, W. (1995) 'Born again secondment', *Human Resources*, March/April.

Greiner, L. E. (1972) 'Evolution and revolution as organisations grow', *Harvard Business Review*, July–August.

Gurran, J. and Burrows, R. (1988) 'Enterprise in Britain: A National Profile of Small Business Owners & the Self-Employed', Small Business Research Trust.

Hendry, C., Jones, A., Arthur, M. and Pettigrew, A. (1991) 'HRD in Small to Medium Sized Enterprises', *Employment Department Research Paper*, No. 88.

Jones, R. A. and Goss, D. M. (1991) 'The Role of Training Strategy in Reducing Skills Shortages: Some Evidence from a Survey of Small Firms', *Personnel Review*, 20(2), pp. 24–30.

Lane, A. D. (ed.) (1994) *Issues in People Management No 8: People Management in Small and Medium Enterprises*. London: IPD.

Langridge, K. (1998) 'Harvest Mentoring Scheme: Research into how a mentor scheme can benefit individuals and their organisations'. Unpublished MA HR Strategies Dissertation, London Guildhall University.

Lawrence, J. (1996) 'Action Learning at the Roadside', *Action Learning News*, 15(2), May.

Lyons, B. R. and Bailey, S. (1993) 'Small Sub-Contractors in UK Engineering: Competitiveness, Dependence and Problems', *Small Business Economics*, 5(2), June, pp, 101–10.

Majaro, S. (1988) *The Creative Gap – Managing Ideas for Profit*. Harlow: Longman.

Megginson, L., Scott, C., Trueblood, L. and Megginson, W. (1988) *Successful Small Business Management*. Business Publications.

Metcalf, H., Walling, A. and Fogarty, M. (1994) 'Individual Commitment to Learning Employers' Attitudes', Policy Studies Institute, Employment Department, Research Series No. 40.

Myers, C. and Davids, K. (1992) 'Knowing and doing: tacit skill at work', *Personnel Management* February, pp. 45–7.

Nadler, L. (1970) *Developing Human Resources*. Gulf.

Polanyi, M. (1966) *The Tacit Dimension*. London: Routledge & Kegan Paul.

Rowden, R. (1995) 'The Role of Human Resource Development in Successful Small to Mid-Sized Manufacturing Businesses: A Comparative Case Study', *Human Resource Development Quarterly*, 6(4), Winter.

Sear, L. and Agar, J. (1996) 'Business Links and Personal Business Advisers: Selling Services Irrespective of Client's Needs?', 19th National Small Firms Policy and Research Conference, *Proceedings*, University of Central England, pp. 546–66.

Stahl, T., NyHan, B. and D'Aloja, P. (1993) *The Learning Organisation – A Vision for Human Resource Development*. EUROTECNET.

Storey, D. L. (1994) *Understanding the Small Business Sector*. London: Thomson Business Press.

Thatcher, M. (1996) 'The big challenge facing small firms', *People Management*, 2(15), pp. 20–5.

Vickerstaff, S. and Parker, K. T. (1995) 'Helping Small Firms: The Contribution of TECs and LECs', *International Small Business Journal*, 13(4), pp. 56–72.

Ward, J. L. (1987) *Keeping the Family Businesses Healthy*. San Francisco: Jossey-Bass.

Watkins, K. E. and Marsick, V. J. (1993) *Sculpting the Learning Organisation – Lessons in the Art and Science of Systemic Change*. San Francisco: Jossey-Bass.

Part 3

ORGANISATION-WIDE LEARNING ISSUES

TOTAL QUALITY MANAGEMENT AND HUMAN RESOURCE DEVELOPMENT

OBJECTIVES

By the end of this chapter you should be able to:

■ describe the basic principles of Total Quality Management (TQM);

■ describe the origins of TQM;

■ demonstrate the seminal effect that TQM has had on learning within organisations;

■ indicate the contribution that HRD professionals have made in the past and can make in the future to furthering TQM initiatives.

INTRODUCTION

The HRD arena has been totally transformed over the last twenty years. When one compares the duties and responsibilities and job titles of those responsible today for learning in leading edge companies with those prevalent some twenty years ago it is difficult sometimes to think that we are talking about the same profession. Take but one example, ICL, where the head of HRD is today called the 'Programme Director for Knowledge Management'. Such a term was unheard of in the 1970s.

Throughout this book it has been argued that it is no longer appropriate to treat HRD as a synonym for Training and Development. Such changes in nomenclature serve as confirmatory indicators that those responsible for learning are being expected to reconfigure their mental set (or paradigm) and move away from thinking of themselves as 'trainers' or 'training managers'. Perhaps more than anything else, what epitomises this transformation has been the development, starting in the 1980s, of Total Quality Management (TQM) initiatives in large organisations, often linked to cultural change programmes.

This chapter provides a general background to the origins of TQM. It explores specific applications of theoretical principles, making particular reference to the role of HR practitioners in the process. It then addresses its strategic significance for HRD.

Total Quality Management has caused people to reflect on the real skills required to maintain a responsive and customer-oriented service. But it also provided a need for facilitators of such activities as quality circles and quality improvement teams which led to a regeneration of the HRD role. It also engendered an organisational climate more likely to be receptive to the learning and development needs of both employees and non-employees. In that sense it is a precursor to the 'Learning Organisation' (discussed in Chapter 15). Where did the TQM push emanate from?

There has been much criticism of the effectiveness of TQM. Nevertheless, the implementation of TQM in organisations continues to be strong. It is still the single most important change initiative in the USA. The annual report of employee training and development by the editors of the US magazine *Training* lists TQM as the top initiative in the USA in 1995–6, with 49 per cent of all organisations with 100 or more employees initiating TQM (Trends, 1996). Large organisations involved in TQM initiatives include Federal Express, Ford Motor Company, Coca Cola and Motorola.

Tom Peters (1994) lists TQM as one of the six most important concepts transforming organisations today. (The other five are reengineering, leveraging knowledge, trust, the curious or adventurous organisation and the virtual organisation.)

The TQM initiative is not without its critics. Zemke (1992) identified five reasons why TQM is being increasingly criticised.

1 There is a lack of focus on the goals and purpose of TQM.

2 There is rigid zealotry and adherence to TQM even when it is not being accepted.

3 TQM emphasises form over function.

4 There is more awareness of TQM than of implementation of TQM.

5 TQM is being viewed as the fad or flavour of the month, before being replaced with the next fad – say, reengineering.

The largest volume of criticism comes from observers of organisational performance, who note that organisations which have invested heavily in quality initiatives and have been successful in attaining prestigious quality awards have not always been successful in the marketplace. However, this chapter is concerned less with the intrinsic merits of TQM as a source of competitive advantage to an organisation than with the opportunities that implementation strategies for TQM have created for a furthering of HRD. The benefits to HRD can be seen from a number of perspectives. One aim of TQM is the enhancement of individual skills across the workplace. This is also a key aim of HRD. This skill enhancement needs to be orchestrated by accomplished facilitators of learning processes. There is thus a recognition of the contribution that HRD professionals can play in the process, so long as they can demonstrate these facilitation skills.

At the 1994 conference of the American Society for Training and Development (ASTD) at Anaheim, Los Angeles, Stephen Rhinesmith, an independent consultant and one of the keynote speakers, contended that quality now has to be perceived as akin to a product, a starting-point, not something to aim for. The challenge is getting quality to the customers to meet first world expectations. This way of thinking has filtered across to the UK. For example, Post Office Counters now claim to be moving from a 'quality driven' aim to an 'excellence driven' aim. A logical consequence of his argument is that the facilitation skills associated with TQM should be an automatic part of the HRD practitioner's toolkit.

For more than a decade, the pursuit of TQM principles has led to probably the single most significant investment in training and learning activities that many organisations have engaged in. Given the significance of TQM for so many organisations one would expect the HRD and HRM literature to have addressed the matter and its HR implications in some depth. Yet this has not been the case.

An exception is Storey (1992), who in his review of HR practices based on a number of case studies of organisations in the UK found the frequent admission from personnel managers that TQM initiatives had 'regrettably' originated outside the profession. He did, however, detect a tendency for the routine administration of TQM to be delegated to the personnel function. As a personnel director from an unnamed manufacturing company disclosed:

> I have to admit that TQM and the Top Management Workshops represent two of the major thrusts in our management development strategy and, to be perfectly honest with you, they are now the major planks in our human resource strategy as a whole. You are correct in saying that neither of them was launched by us. We sort of inherited them (quoted in Storey, 1992).

It is unclear from reading Storey where the initiatives did originate. He also does not address the relationship between HRM and HRD in either theoretical or functional terms, so it is uncertain whether HRD professionals were involved at an earlier stage than their personnel counterparts, or even whether 'personnel' is being used as a generic term to incorporate the training and development function.

BACKGROUND TO TOTAL QUALITY MANAGEMENT

Feigenbaum (1957) provided the first definition of TQM, seeing it as:

> an effective system for integrating the quality development, quality maintenance and quality improvement efforts of the various groups in an organisation so as to enable production and service at the most economical levels which allow for full customer satisfaction.

This definition focuses on TQM from the perspective of operational management and performance improvement, trying to establish a relationship between customer requirements and expectations, efficiency and service provision.

Since then definitions have abounded. Without losing the focus on customer orientation and performance improvement, the emphasis has switched increasingly over the years to people considerations, and the management of change and culture. Whatever definition is adopted, there is a consensus that investment in training and concern with employee and non-employee development and other HRD-related issues are vital elements.

DEMING

It is generally accepted that the quality revolution began in earnest in Japan during the 1950s and that its first protagonist was the American statistician, Dr W. Edwards Deming. He provided much of the intellectual drive behind Japan's post-war reconstruction, persuading the Japanese to bring the customer into the organisation, develop closer links between the worker and supplier and work for continuous improvement. He developed his famous 14 principles of quality management during the Second World War, and tried to convince people in the USA involved in the war effort about their value. He gained some minor success, but was confronted with the prevailing belief that improving quality added to costs. After the war, General Douglas MacArthur asked Deming to join him on two trips to help advise the Japanese on how to reconstruct their country. The contacts he made while on these trips led to his fame in Japan. It was not until 1980 that Deming, in his eightieth year, had any impact in the West. He was 'introduced' to America in a documentary called, *If Japan can, Why can't We?* Following the success of the documentary, Deming toured the USA, converting such organisations as Ford to his methods.

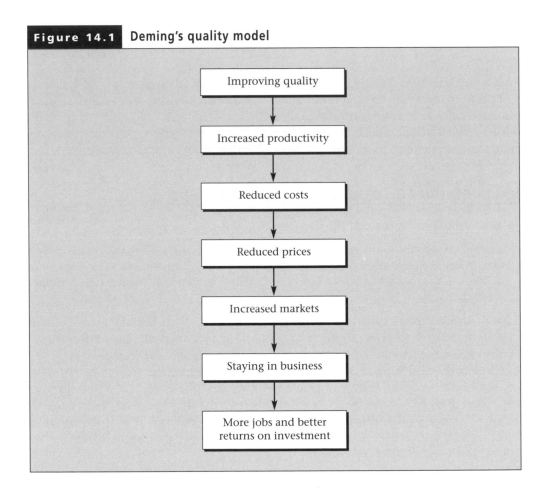

Figure 14.1 Deming's quality model

Deming contended that:

- management was responsible for 94 per cent of quality problems;
- employee participation in the quality process is essential;
- people need to work smarter not harder;
- doing one's best is not of itself sufficient – one needs to know what to do.

Deming laid down 14 points for management to abide by:

1 Create constancy of purpose towards improvement of product and service with the aim to become competitive, to stay in business, and to provide jobs.

2 Adopt a new philosophy. We can no longer live with commonly accepted levels of delays, mistakes, defective workmanship.

3 Cease dependency on mass inspection. Require, instead, statistical evidence that quality is built in.

4 End the practice of awarding business on the basis of price tag.

5 Find problems. It is management's job to work continually on the system.

6 Institute modern methods of training on the job.

7 Institute modern methods of supervision of production workers. The responsibility of foremen must be changed from numbers to quality.

8 Drive out fear, so that everyone may work effectively for the company.

9 Break down barriers between departments.

10 Eliminate numerical goals, posters and slogans for the work-force asking for new levels of productivity without providing methods.

11 Eliminate work standards that prescribe numerical quotas.

12 Remove barriers that stand between the hourly worker and his right of pride of workmanship.

13 Institute a vigorous programme of education and retraining.

14 Create a structure in top management that will push every day on the above 13 points.

From an HRD perspective it is important to note the emphasis that Deming gives to education and retraining. He is less clear on how the overall process is to be orchestrated.

JURAN

Joseph Juran, another American, worked closely with Deming in the 1940s. Like Deming he was influential in Japan, and subsequently in the USA in the 1980s as the quality movement developed. He contended that at least 85 per cent of the failures in any organisation originate in systems controlled by management. Fewer than 20 per cent of the problems are worker related. Management, and management only, have the responsibility for improving the performance of organisations. He also coined the term 'fitness for use' which he saw as a more user- based concept than 'conformance to specification' as used by Crosby (*see* below). Just because a product conforms to engineering specifications does not mean that it meets user requirements.

In developing the concept of 'managerial breakthrough' he moved away from more traditional approaches such as 'control inspection' and 'breakthrough/prevention'. In a control situation, the prevailing management attitude is that the present level of performance is not good enough and that something needs to be done about it. The managerial objective is one of achieving a better performance and the management plan is to identify and eliminate chronic obstacles to this. 'Management breakthrough' is more focused on continuous improvement. Juran argued that changing the prevailing management 'attitude' was the key to achieving this.

As a prerequisite to changing management's attitudes, a sense of 'quality awareness' must be instilled. Juran contends that training has a key part to play in this.

Juran identified the following ten steps to quality improvement:

1 Build awareness of the need and opportunity for improvement – this requires leadership.

2 Set specific goals for the continuous improvement of quality in all activities.

3 Organise to reach the goals (establish a quality council, identify problems, select projects, appoint teams, designate facilitators).

4 Provide training to ensure that all employees understand their role in quality improvement – this must include senior management since they are the cause of most of the quality problems.

5 Set up problem-solving project teams to solve problems which prevent quality improvement from happening.

6 Report and monitor progress.

7 Give recognition to outstanding contributions to quality improvement.

8 Communicate and publicise results.

9 Keep score.

10 Maintain momentum by making annual improvement part of the regular systems and processes of the organisation.

One of Juran's explanatory metaphors is the 'quality-planning road map', which has nine junctions:

1 Identify the customers (internal and external).

2 Determine the needs of these customers.

3 Translate those needs into our language.

4 Develop a product that can respond to those needs.

5 Optimise the product features to help meet our needs as well as the customers' needs.

6 Develop a process that is able to produce the product.

7 Optimise the process.

8 Prove that the process can produce the product under operating conditions.

9 Transfer the process to operations.

The Juran insights are a very formative guide to subsequent process-driven models. They have helped provide an underpinning framework for quality improvement teams operating both within and across functional boundaries. The differentiation between internal and external customers has proved to be very influential. Another feature has been his strong criticism of the 'hype' and slogan-ridden posturing that has been associated with a number of approaches to TQM.

CROSBY

Philip Crosby's model incorporates elements of both Deming and Juran. He developed a Quality Improvement Programme (QIP) which is quite a sophisticated educational system in which consideration is given to both the content and process of change. It is based on his belief that the culture of a company is going to change only when all employees absorb the common language of quality and begin to understand their individual role in making quality happen (Crosby, 1979). In putting the emphasis on employee responsibility (as opposed to managerial responsibility) he differs from both Deming and Juran.

One of the key principles espoused by Crosby was that 'in discussing quality we are dealing with a people situation'. He also summed up quality in one word – 'prevention' – as opposed to inspection. One of Crosby's inventions was a quality management maturity grid based on the concept that there are five stages in quality management maturity. Table 14.1 presents his five stages.

Table 14.1 Five stages of quality management maturity

Stage	*Characteristics*
Uncertainty	When management has no knowledge of quality as a management tool
Awakening	When management is beginning to recognise that quality management can help but will not commit resources to it
Enlightenment	When management decides to introduce a formal quality programme
Wisdom	When management and organisation reach the stage when permanent changes can be made
Certainty	When quality management is a vital part of organisational management

Crosby also identified five factors which he considered the 'absolutes' of quality management:

1 Quality means conformance to requirements not 'elegance' or 'goodness'.
2 There is no such thing as a quality problem.
3 There is no such thing as the economics of quality – it is always cheaper to do the job right first time.
4 The only performance measure is the cost of quality.
5 The only performance standard is Zero Defects.

Crosby coined the term 'Quality Vaccine' which companies may use to prevent non-conformance. Vaccine preparation comprises five ingredients:

1 *Integrity*: throughout the organisation everyone is dedicated to ensuring the customer receives what has been promised.

2 *Systems*: key systems such as quality education, performance measurement, etc. must be in place.

3 *Communications*: sustain a continual supply of information that help to identify error, waste and missed opportunities.

4 *Operations*: educate suppliers, provide routine training, continuously examine procedures, etc.

5 *Policies*: ensure that policies are clear and unambiguous.

The vaccine is administered by means of:

■ *determination*: a recognition that action is the only way forward;

■ *education*: the development of a common quality language and an understanding of each other's role;

■ *implementation*: guiding the flow of improvement.

He points out that quality improvement is a process, not a programme, since nothing permanent will arise from a programme. Nevertheless the quality improvement process in many organisations is initiated by a management development programme.

Crosby, like Deming before him, identifies 14 steps to quality improvement. However they are substantially different in many respects.

1 Make it clear that management is committed to quality.

2 Form quality improvement teams with representatives from each department.

3 Determine where current and potential quality problems lie.

4 Evaluate the cost of quality and explain its use as a management tool.

5 Raise the quality awareness and personal concern of all employees. This can be done through training supervisors, and communicating through films, booklets and posters.

6 Take actions to correct problems identified through previous steps.

7 Establish a committee for the zero defects (ZD) programme to investigate the ZD concept and ways to implement the programme.

8 Train supervisors to actively carry out their part in the quality improvement programme.

9 Hold a 'zero defects day' to let all employees realise that there has been a change.

10 Encourage individuals to establish improvement goals for themselves and their groups. Employee goal setting should take place usually on a 30-, 60-, 90-day basis.

11 Encourage employees to communicate to management the obstacles they face in attaining their improvement goals. Error-cause removal should follow the identification of problems that prevent error-free work from being achieved.

12 Recognise and appreciate those who participate by (non-financial) award programmes.

13 Establish quality councils to communicate on a regular basis.

14 Do it all over again to emphasise that the quality improvement programme never ends.

A more or less standard Crosby QIP was started in Johnson Matthey in May 1986. The new chief executive officer had been involved with QIP in his previous company. The new personnel director was charged with getting it off the ground and he attended the Crosby Executive College for two months. During 1986, 150 senior and 50 key middle managers were sent on a one-week course at the Crosby Quality College. The course content covered the Absolutes of Quality Management, the strategy of quality improvement, the 14-step Quality Improvement Process, the education system and corrective action. Quality Improvement Teams were then set up in each of the four divisions headed by senior line managers. The purpose of the teams was to take on the task of 'improving things round here' by developing a strategy with the help of a Crosby consultant. From within the four divisions, 55 instructors were identified and they attended the two-week Crosby Instructors Course. They then ran a Quality Education Course for all the 3500 employees up to the level of supervisor and a modified four-hour programme for the remaining members of the work-force.

Juran, as we have seen, also emphasises the importance of quality councils and these have become a common feature in many quality-oriented organisations. For example, they were established in BT in the 1980s as part of its TQM drive. According to the in-house BT publication entitled 'TQM – Leaders Guide to Making it Happen', the Quality Councils' responsibilities were:

- give leadership by championing quality improvement;
- agree policy and plans necessary to ensure quality improvement;
- monitor identified issues or inhibitors to ensure they are correctly managed;
- monitor unit and council members' plans and progress;
- ensure measurements are in place;
- undertake appropriate training;
- share successes and lessons;
- ensure recognition of success;
- link to other quality councils.

QUALITY CIRCLES

One of the features of many TQM programmes in the 1980s was the establishment of quality circles. They are Japanese in origin and their invention is credited to Kaoru Ishikawa (1985), who also introduced creative problem-solving techniques such as cause and effect fishbone diagrams. The first quality circle was registered in Japan in 1963 within the Nippon Telegraph and Telephone public corporation. They typically operate as follows.

1 Six to eight employees from a factory workshop or department meet regularly to examine work problems that affect the quality of output, and to recommend solutions to these problems. The meetings are often under the leadership of a supervisor or section head though sometimes they can be externally facilitated.

2 Each quality circle is based on a self-directing, bottom-up approach, drawing directly on the knowledge and skills of the participants.

3 Each quality circle is an entirely voluntary body. Nobody is paid to join, nobody is forced to join and nobody is penalised for not participating. The motivation is solely the sense of achievement in collectively finding performance improvements.

4 Each circle, once formed, sets its own terms of reference; selects for itself the problems it wishes to tackle; and in due course presents its recommendations for their solution.

5 Problems for possible solution by the circle may be identified by anyone in the organisation. They may arise, for example, from customer complaints, quality control feedback, management information. Circles often identify issues of which management may be unaware.

6 Actual selection of a problem for consideration is entirely up to the circle. To ensure that the problems have a high practical value, a Pareto analysis may be carried out as a first step (based on the rule of thumb assumption that 80 per cent of the problems arise from 20 per cent of the work). Alternatively, the circles may be based on a *Kaizen* principle, that is, the notion that a series of 0.0001 per cent improvements, which individually amount to little, collectively can make a significant contribution.

7 Groups meet regularly. By scheduling meetings during working hours the organisation is already showing a commitment to the scheme. Meetings vary in frequency, but once a month is probably too infrequent if momentum is to be maintained.

8 Effective circles need training in problem-solving techniques such as brainstorming. They also benefit from training in group working and methods of data collection. The leader also needs training in her or his specific role. Some quality circles have facilitators attached to them to deal with process issues.

9 Middle and senior managers need to understand the goals of quality circles and be committed to the process, otherwise the whole initiative will fail.

10 One of the reasons organisations are prepared to invest in the training, apart from cost savings to be achieved, is that it is a form of developing employees that has implications far beyond quality circles themselves. For example, the increased confidence, group-working skills, approach to problem solving and so on can have a positive benefit on many areas of a person's work.

Collard (1981) describes a visit he made to the Nissan Zama plant in Japan. Quality circles were introduced to the plant in 1966. At the time of his visit 500 quality circles operated at the factory which consisted of 4000 employees. In the main they comprised seven to ten members, with the leader being chosen from the group and supervisors only being co-opted as necessary. Although membership was voluntary, it was the group norm to participate, even though the meetings took place entirely in employees' own time. No formal training was provided, although informally some was provided by technical assistants. The circles were made up of blue collar workers, with white collar staff relying on the suggestion scheme to generate ideas. The focus of the circles was on problem identification and solution generation. Ideas were referred to departmental supervision or management before implementation. No payment was forthcoming, on the ground that activities in employees' own time were entirely voluntary.

Collard (op. cit.) contrasted the Nissan model with that at Nippon Steel's Kimitsu works. He found about 900 circles in existence at a plant of some 7500 employees. They had been introduced in about 1970. Members wore specially designed CAP (cost and productivity) badges. Each circle comprised five to ten members, and the team leader was usually the immediate supervisor. Participation was entirely voluntary, although the majority of blue collar workers got involved. Meetings took place in company time as well as in employees' time. When they took place in employees' time a special payment was made, on the ground that the activities were designed to improve performance and therefore profit and thus employees should receive some extrinsic reward.

One of the early exponents of quality circles in the UK was Rolls-Royce's Aero Division in Derby, which introduced them in the late 1970s. By 1981 there were some 70 groups operating. A key motivation was the opportunity afforded for cost reductions and operational savings. It has been claimed that over the 30-month period up to the end of 1980, savings of over £500 000 were achieved (Hutchins, 1981). A stated objective was to raise the general level of 'quality consciousness' in the hope that by 'harnessing the energies of the shop floor there would be a return of the pride in performing skilled work which had been partly lost through recent technological changes (Lewis and Rooney, 1981).

A training package was designed in conjunction with the local college, which provided special training sessions for the foremen and work group members who had volunteered. Presentations about quality circles were made to managers, foremen and shop stewards to allay any anxieties about why they were being introduced. As in Japan, membership was entirely voluntary.

After the first circles had been established, the training was modified to enable the foremen more scope in coaching their own group. The foremen attended a two-day, on-site course of circle leadership training led by the college tutor. They then led the training of their own groups, each period of instruction lasting for one and a half hours at weekly intervals for four weeks. The training consisted of instruction in problem-solving techniques such as Pareto and fishbone diagramming. The focus was on applying these to work-related problems.

Circles normally met formally for about an hour every fortnight in work time. Informal sessions often occurred towards the end of a shift, taking place either in the foreman's office or even round a work bench. Unlike in Japan, the teams consisted of a cross-section of staff. A typical group consisted of a production foreman (as circle leader), a production engineer, an inspector, two production operatives, a setter and a quality engineer.

It is not clear to what extent quality circles extended to other areas of the Rolls-Royce Group. Storey (1992) found no evidence of them at the Industrial and Marine Division, near Coventry, in his survey in the late 1980s.

Jaguar introduced 82 circles between 1982 and 1987. However, over this period, there were no circles involving their factory floor workers at their main production site. This was because of union opposition (Storey, 1992).

Quality improvement teams are similar in purpose to quality circles, but often are broader in scope and cut across departmental and functional boundaries.

LABELLING THE TOTAL QUALITY MANAGEMENT EFFORT

Organisations that have introduced some form of TQM invariably give it a name, using an overall umbrella slogan. British Rail used the slogan 'Quality Through Teamwork', IBM that of 'Market Driven Quality, and Xerox, that of 'Leadership through Quality'. This concern with providing a marketing-style slogan has extended beyond TQM. Virtually every major change effort introduced over recent years has had its accompanying rallying cry.

THE TOTAL QUALITY PRINCIPLES IN THE 1990s

Drawing upon TQM practices in the field Binney (1992) developed the following total quality principles. In his three-part classification system he saw 'unlocking people potential' as a significant part of managerial activity in this area. He stated:

In order to improve continuously and delight customers, organisations need to:

Focus on customers
- Listen carefully to customers
- Measure the things that are important to them
- Maintain personal contact with them

Improve processes
See businesses as sets of processes, not hierarchies:
- Consider systems as a whole, not blame individuals
- Break down barriers between functions
- Think of departments to whom goods/services are supplied as internal customers
- Set up long term partnerships with suppliers

Establish fact-based management:
- Open people's eyes to the opportunity for improvement
- Prevent errors and re-working
- Speak with data
- Seek out root causes of problems
- Set standards

Unlock people potential
- Foster continuous learning
- Manage by values, not controls
- Encourage team working
- Continuously develop the self-confidence and sense of responsibility of staff.

According to Smith and Lewis (1997) the literature identifies four fundamental principles or pillars that form the basis of application of TQM within an organisation:

■ Customer satisfaction;

■ Continuous improvement;

■ Speaking with facts;

■ Respect for people.

Customer satisfaction

The core purpose of any quality improvement process is to ensure that the needs and reasonable expectations of the customer are identified and satisfied. Serving the customer addresses three important questions:

■ Who are our customers?

■ What do they want/need?

■ What must we do to meet or even anticipate their needs?

■ Once the customer's required needs are identified, work processes can be designed or modified to ensure these requirements are met.

Continuous improvement

Continuous improvement is both a commitment and a process. As stated by Gallagher and Smith (1997):

> the commitment to quality is initiated with a statement of dedication to a shared mission and vision and the empowerment of everyone to incrementally move towards the vision. The process of improvement occurs through the initiation of small, short-term projects and tasks that collectively are driven by the achievement of the long term vision and mission.

Speaking with facts

Speaking with facts, a phrase coined by Deming, is based on two functions. First, data are collected so valid conclusions can be drawn; and second, decisions are based on the data.

Respect for people

Respect for people is the acknowledgement that, while people work in an organisation, they still work for themselves in trying to create a meaningful and satisfying life. Accordingly they are entitled to be kept informed and to be involved in the wider scheme of things within a given organisation. Smith and Lewis believe that it is this recognition which is crucially missing from unsuccessful TQM programmes.

Chang (1993) in a detailed review of the literature on TQM success stories and various quality award criteria and certification guidelines around the world, identified 10 'core threads' that are evident in successful TQM initiatives.

1 An intense customer focus.

2 Hands-on involvement of senior management.

3 Deployment of strategic objectives.

4   Continuous process improvement.

5 Long-term orientation.

6 Targeted measurement data.

7 Market responsiveness.

8 Empowered involvement of satisfied employees.

9 Continuous learning and development.

10 Internal and external partnerships.

It is the last three that reflect a respect for people. These are the three that are most often not implemented. They are also the three that are the most difficult to implement.

EXAMPLES OF ORGANISATIONAL PRACTICE

There are innumerable case examples of organisations engaging in total quality initiatives. Although there are a number of common features they do not all have the same emphasis. This is apparent in on an ongoing audit trail into approaches adopted by large privatised organisations in the UK being undertaken by Bobby Basra as part of her Doctorate at London Guildhall University. Although 'quality improvement' and 'continuous improvement' and 'customer focus' are common features, two distinct emphases seem to emerge. Manufacturing organisations such as British Steel, which do not have direct contact with the consumer, have over the years put more effort into 'zero defects', 'statistical process control' and 'teamworking' as part of a process of continuous improvement. Organisations such as BT and BA which have direct dealings with very large numbers of individual customers have put more emphasis on the customer relationships side of quality. 'The Customer is King' was a slogan of BT in 1991, 'Putting Customers First' was the slogan for a BA programme launched even earlier – in 1983.

The cases presented in Figs 14.2 to 14.7 are taken from organisational practice over the last two decades. The first concerns Xerox.

Figure 14.2   Xerox

Xerox has always been seen as one of the prime movers in the drive for quality. In 1983 it established its 'Leadership Through Quality' philosophy and programme, based upon competitive benchmarking, employee involvement and a total commitment to meeting customer requirements. The programme had as its role model Fuji Xerox, which in 1976 launched a total quality process effort entitled the 'New Xerox Movement' and in 1980 won the Japanese Deming Prize. The 'Leadership Through Quality' initiative was intended to be the spearhead of a complete cultural change based on the policy statement that:

▶▶

▶▶ Figure 14.2 continued

Xerox is a quality company. Quality is the basic business principle for Xerox. Quality means providing our external and internal customers with innovative products and services that fully satisfy their requirements. Quality improvement is the job of every Xerox employee (Walker, 1992).

The company's priorities were recalibrated to reflect the culture shift and quality orientation. The four key priorities were restated as:

No. 1 Customer satisfaction.
No. 2 Employee satisfaction.
No. 3 Return on assets.
No. 4 Market share.

The strategy to address those priorities was based on six principles:

1 Customers define our business. We must continue to identify and define critical market segments and fully understand customers' problems, requirements and needs.
2 Success depends on the involvement and empowerment of trained and highly motivated people. We look to become the benchmark for employee motivation and satisfaction.
3 Quality is 'on the line by the line'. Line management is responsible for leading quality improvement.
4 Management develops, articulates and deploys clear direction and objectives.
5 Strategic quality challenges are identified and met.
6 Business is managed and improved by using facts. We must enhance our use of quality tools through a more rigorous application of management by fact.

There has always been a reliance on hard data in the organisation and it is not surprising that measurable performance criteria were used to assess the effectiveness of its Leadership Through Quality (LTQ) programme. At a 1989 conference, John Welch, Manager Quality gave the following statistical improvements:

– improved customer satisfaction – survey results show 35 per cent improvement;
– product development cycle down by between 25 and 50 per cent;
– inventory levels cut from six months of production to less than one month;
– improved return on assets;
– market share being regained from the Japanese.

As with any complex business it is difficult to establish a precise cause and effect relationship between these outcomes and LTQ.

Outcomes of LTQ, measured on a project basis, also showed very positive results. For example, a quality improvement team in India identified that high attrition rates were being caused by poor staff selection. Training in interview skills was introduced and the turnover rate reduced from 40 per cent to 15 per cent.

An important measure of quality at Xerox is 'cost of quality', that is, 'the balance between the costs we incur when we ensure that we satisfy customer requirements, and those costs we incur when we do not satisfy their requirements'. Following the guidance of Philip Crosby, Xerox concluded that the costs of doing things wrong first time could amount to about 20 per cent of revenue.

▶▶

▶▶ Figure 14.2 continued

> Companies tend to spend insufficient sums on conforming to customer require-
> ments – costs such as prevention, inspection, training, recruiting the right people,
> working with suppliers to prevent faulty parts and developing good processes. Yet by
> focusing attention on conformance, non-conformance costs, such as the cost of
> scrap, rework, unnecessary effort and lost opportunities can be cut drastically
> (Welch, quoted in Giles, 1989).
>
> In other words, Xerox hoped to substantially reduce the costs of lack of quality.

Figure 14.3 looks at the case of British Rail.

Figure 14.3 British Rail

In the pre-privatised British Rail, 'Quality through Teamwork' (QTT) workshops started in early 1990 as part of a national training initiative, the biggest in Europe, that was intended to eventually encompass all 130 000 members of staff. These workshops were originally designed for middle management.

Four key values underpinned the whole of British Rail's approach to TQM. These were:

1 The customer is number one.

2 Value people at the workplace.

3 Recognition and reward.

4 Encourage enterprise, innovation and initiative.

As the training programme was part of a national initiative, the general course objectives were set by the then British Railways Board. These were:

> That every one will leave the workshop with a basic understanding of, and the abil-
> ity to practise, participate in or use . . . Total Quality Management, Quality Tools,
> Effective Teamwork, Quality Improvement Teams, and Team Action Plans.

Soon after these objectives and key values were set the organisational structure of BR changed radically, giving greater autonomy to the operational businesses and to newly created profit centres inside those businesses. One of the businesses was Network SouthEast; here the profit centres were known as divisions, of which there were nine. Each division formulated its own policies on total quality inside the guidelines laid down by the Board.

The policy of the Great Eastern Division was to have 'Local Area Quality Management Groups' (LAQMGs) consisting of approximately six local managers representing all the railway functions. Their role was to support and push any local quality-related drives and initiatives. As a result of training carried out by consultants from the Kaizen Institute, they identified and prioritised service gaps, differences between what is produced and what is perceived by the customer. From this prioritising, lists were drawn up of projects in which they wanted local staff to be involved and on which they would work as teams.

▶▶

▶▶ Figure 14.3 continued

> The three-day 'Quality Through Teamwork' workshops were aimed to build those teams, which were all multifunctional, and to enable them to start work on the projects away from the distractions of the workplace. They were facilitated in the beginnings of teamwork and the first steps of problem solving by staff from within the business, who themselves were specially selected and trained for this purpose.
>
> The basic topics covered at the workshops were:
>
> ∎ an introduction to TQM;
> ∎ quality-related costs;
> ∎ teamworking;
> ∎ quality improvement teams;
> ∎ quality improvement process;
> ∎ quality systems and procedures;
> ∎ customer focus;
> ∎ brainstorming;
> ∎ structured problem solving;
> ∎ action planning.

Figure 14.4 presents the case of IBM.

Figure 14.4 IBM

> IBM has adopted a number of approaches to TQM over the years, each underpinned by IBM's published 'basic beliefs' of 'the best customer service in the world'; 'the pursuit of excellence'; and 'respect for the individual'. In the 1980s a TQM programme based on the Crosby approach was implemented in IBM United Kingdom Ltd. Employees were given the opportunity to develop statistical process control skills and problem-solving skills. Many quality circles started.
>
> Within the IBM Industrial Sector, which in 1991 employed approximately 1000 people and was responsible for about 25 per cent of IBM's business in the UK, a new TQM programme was launched in 1990, which focused on customer satisfaction rather than internal quality measures.
>
> The resultant Customer Satisfaction Project (CUSP) entailed the formation of voluntary improvement project teams which focused on the results and customer comments contained in the twice-yearly customer satisfaction survey. This process was strengthened by the introduction of a more systematic approach to improving customer satisfaction based on the US Baldrige criteria. The overall slogan was Market Driven Quality (MDQ).
>
> Cultural change was seen as a core outcome of the process, and to facilitate this a two-day MDQ Blueprint workshop was introduced MDQ improvement techniques include using a set of Baldrige-inspired assessment or diagnostic techniques which enable groups of employees to compare the group's behaviour with that of IBM's 'World Class' vision (Hobson, 1992).

Figure 14.5 presents the case of Nissan.

Figure 14.5 **Nissan**

Wickens (1991) provides an interesting insight into the application of TQM princi-ples at Nissan UK. The key business principles have been defined as:

- *Quality*: Build profitably the highest quality car sold in Europe.
- *Customers*: Achieve target of No. 1 in customer satisfaction in Europe.
- *Volume*: Always achieve required volume.
- *New products*: Deliver on time, at required quality, within cost.
- *Suppliers*: Establish long-term relationship with single source-suppliers. Aim for zero defects and just-in-time delivery. Apply Nissan principles to suppliers.
- *Production*: Use 'most appropriate' technology. Develop predictable 'best method' of doing job. Build in quality.
- *Engineering*: Design 'quality' and 'ease of working' into the product and facilities. Establish 'simultaneous engineering' to reduce development time.

To support the business principles are a number of 'people principles', the absence of which Smith and Lewis (op. cit.) felt led to the collapse of many TQM initiatives. They include:

- *Responsibility*: maximise the responsibility of all staff by devolving decision making.
- *Teamwork*: recognise and encourage individual contributions with everyone working to the same objectives.
- *Flexibility*: expand the role of the individual – multiskilling, no job descriptions, generic job titles.
- *Communications*: every day, face to face.
- *Single status*: treat everyone as first class citizens. Eliminate all illogical differences.

Included in the 'people principles' is *Kaizen*, defined as 'continuously seek the hundreds of 0.01 per cent improvements. Give ownership of change'.

Nissan has developed a company core training curriculum. This includes topics which everyone needs to know such as basic induction material and an understand-ing of the role of other departments. It also covers an introduction to concepts of *Kaizen*, TQM and problem-solving techniques, for everyone at every level.

Figure 14.6 looks at TQM in a food-processing plant in Central Florida.

Figure 14.6 **Food processing plant in Central Florida**

Smith and Lewis (op. cit.) described a recent initiative to promulgate TQM by emphasising the people dimension in developing support for the process. They identified 23 descriptors that collectively reflected the increasing mutual respect by managers and workers in evolving an effective TQM process.

▶▶

▶▶ Figure 14.6 continued

1   The valuing of individual differences and worth.

2   The attempt to enhance individual self-esteem.

3   The attempt to provide necessary but not excessive direction.

4   Provide adequate resources to do the job.

5   Communicate with people on a timely basis.

6   Delegate appropriate responsibility with authority.

7   Respect people's time.

8   Respect other people's authority.

9   Look for ways to make jobs better, easier and interesting.

10 Provide environments for people to express views and feelings.

11 Listen and respond to people.

12 Provide appropriate feedback.

13 Recognise people's needs.

14 Stand up for people.

15 Respect individual privacy.

16 Respect personal obligations.

17 Acknowledge individual hardships.

18 Recognise accomplishments.

19 Provide opportunities for job skill development.

20 Provide opportunities for self-development.

21 Provide models for standards of excellence.

22 Provide an environment of trust with permission to fail.

23 Emphasise relationships, respect and reconciliation.

In many respects, the dimensions listed in Fig. 14.6 are not specific to TQM. They can be seen as a set of criteria, drawing on the insights of motivational theory, which could be applicable in any change scenario which is attempting to increase the commitment and involvement of staff.

The concern with developing a more customer-oriented process has not been restricted to large commercial concerns. It has had an impact in all areas of service provision. A typical set of guidelines were developed by the UK Department of Health in 1989 (*see* Fig. 14.7).

Figure 14.7   Total Quality Management in the Health Service

TQM aims at harnessing the efforts of management and all staff in ensuring that every aspect of their work is directed towards the attainment of high quality. It puts the need of the patient at the centre of health service provision.

  Its main elements are:

▶▶

▶▶ Figure 14.7 continued

> 1 It is a corporate approach, involving all staff, and led from the top.
> 2 It focuses on customer needs.
> 3 It aims to prevent errors and promote excellence rather than to correct matters after the event.
> 4 It requires the organisation to 'review continually its processes to develop the strategy of never-ending improvement'.
> 5 It conceptualises the necessary processes as one of managing 'quality chains' (each link being a supplier/customer exchange) which runs right through every department of the organisation and then out to external customers and suppliers.
> 6 It emphasises the need for both teamwork and a continual flow of systematic quality information. Quality is not a one-off effort.

Source: Department of Health (1989).

QUALITY AWARDS

One of the features of the quality movement has been the growth of national and international quality awards and annual competitions. Organisational policy makers are prepared to subject themselves to critical scrutiny, wishing to show that they are 'leading edge' and 'best in class' in the quality world, capable of being benchmarked against any externally imposed standards.

The Deming Prize

The Deming Prize was established in Japan in 1962 to recognise companies that have excelled in TQM. It is based on achievement against the following criteria:

- policies and objectives
- operation of the organisation
- education
- information management
- analysis
- standardisation
- control
- quality assurance
- results
- future plans.

Under the 'Education' heading, which is of particular interest to HRD practitioners, the following sub-criteria are found:

- educational plans and accomplishments;
- consciousness about quality and control; understanding of quality control;
- education concerning statistical concepts and methods, and degree of permeation;
- education for subcontractors and outside organisations;

■ quality circle activities;

■ suggestion system and its implementation.

The concern with statistical techniques reinforces the influence that Deming himself has had upon the Japanese approach. The concern with education for sub-contractors and outside organisations demonstrates the attention that the Japanese have given to non-employee development issues.

Baldrige

The Malcolm Baldrige National Quality Award, originated in 1987, is the premier US quality award. It aims to codify the principles of quality management in clear and accessible language, and to provide organisations with a comprehensive framework for assessing their progress towards goals such as customer satisfaction and increased employee involvement. But winning it incurs a price. Both Xerox, a 1989 winner, and Corning, a 1989 finalist, admit to having spent, respectively, $800 000 and 14 000 person hours preparing applications and briefing employees in advance of site visits by Baldrige examiners (Garvin, 1991).

The award originated from the Malcolm Baldrige National Quality Improvement Act, signed in 1987 by President Reagan. Awards were to be given in three categories – manufacturing, service and small business – with no more than two awards per category per year.

By 1992 a 1000-point scoring system had evolved, and application forms of up to 75 pages (50 pages for small businesses) describing their quality practices in each of seven required areas – Leadership, Information and Analysis, Strategic Quality Planning, Human Resource Development and Management, Management of Process Quality, Quality and Operational Results and Customer Focus and Satisfaction. Figure 14.8 indicates how the total score is built up. Figure 14.9 presents the assessment criteria for two areas, Human Resource Development and Management and Customer Focus and Satisfaction.

The HRD implications clearly go far beyond a mere concern with 'Employee Education and Training' (Category 4.3). But it is interesting to note some of the areas under this heading that are expected to be addressed by candidates for the award. These include:

■ percentage of employees receiving education and training annually;

■ average hours of education and training annually per employee;

■ percentage of employees who have received education and training in statistical and other problem-solving techniques;

■ key methods and indicators the company uses to evaluate and improve the effectiveness of its education and training.

Such measures are pursued in more detail in Chapter 12.

European Quality Award

The European Quality Award was launched in 1992 under the auspices of the European Foundation for Quality Management (EFQM) which in turn was launched in 1988 by 14 leading Western European companies.

Figure 14.8 Malcolm Baldrige National Quality Award:
Examination Categories and Points, 1992

1992 Examination Categories/Items	Point Values
1.0 Leadership	**90**
1.1 Senior Executive Leadership	45
1.2 Management for Quality	25
1.3 Public Responsibility	20
2.0 Information and Analysis	**80**
2.1 Scope and Management of Quality and Performance Data and Information	15
2.2 Competitive Comparisons and Benchmarks	25
2.3 Analysis and Uses of Company-Level Data	40
3.0 Strategic Quality Planning	**60**
3.1 Strategic Quality and Company Performance Planning Process	35
3.2 Quality and Performance Plans	25
4.0 Human Resource Development and Management	**150**
4.1 Human Resource Management	20
4.2 Employee Involvement	40
4.3 Employee Education and Training	40
4.4 Employee Performance and Recognition	25
4.5 Employee Well-Being and Morale	25
5.0 Management of Process Quality	**140**
5.1 Design and Introduction of Quality Products and Services	40
5.2 Process Management – Product and Service Production and Delivery Processes	35
5.3 Process Management – Business Processes and Support Services	30
5.4 Supplier Quality	20
5.5 Quality Assessment	15
6.0 Quality and Operational Results	**180**
6.1 Product and Services Quality Results	75
6.2 Company Operational Results	45
6.3 Business Process and Support Service Results	25
6.4 Supplier Quality Results	35
7.0 Customer Focus and Satisfaction	**300**
7.1 Customer Relationship Management	65
7.2 Commitment to Customers	15
7.3 Customer Satisfaction Determination	35
7.4 Customer Satisfaction Results	75
7.5 Customer Satisfaction Comparison	75
7.6 Future Requirements and Expectations of Customers	35
TOTAL POINTS	1000

Source: National Institute of Standards and Technology.

| Figure 14.9 | Malcolm Baldrige National Quality Award: Extracts from Assessment Criteria, 1992 |

4.5 Employee Well-Being and Morale *(25pts.)*
Describe how the company maintains a work environment conducive to the well-being and growth of all employees; summarize trends and levels in key indicators of well-being and morale.

Areas to address

a How well-being and morale factors such as health, safety, satisfaction, and ergonomics are included in quality improvement activities. Summarize principal improvement goals, methods, and indicators for each factor relevant and important to the company's work environment. For accidents and work-related health problems, describe how root causes are determined and how adverse conditions are prevented.

b Mobility, flexibility, and retraining in job assignments to support employee development and/or to accommodate changes in technology, improved productivity, changes in work processes, or company restructuring.

c Special services, facilities, and opportunities the company makes available to employees. These might include one or more of the following; counseling, assistance, recreational or cultural, non-work-related education, and outplacement.

d How and how often employee satisfaction is determined.

e Trends in key indicators of well-being and morale. This should address, as appropriate: satisfaction, safety, absenteeism, turnover, attrition rate for customer-contact personnel, grievances, strikes, and worker compensation. Explain important adverse results, if any. For such adverse results, describe how root causes were determined and corrected, or give current status. Compare results on the most significant indicators with those of industry averages, industry leaders, and other key benchmarks.

7.1 Customer Relationship Management *(65pts.)*
Describe how the company provides effective management of its relationships with its customer and uses information gained from customers to improve customer relationship management strategies and practices.

Areas to address

a How the company determines the most important factors in maintaining and building relationships with customers and develops strategies and plans to address them. Describe these factors and how the strategies take into account: fulfillment of basic customer needs in the relationship; opportunities to enhance the relationships; provision of information to customers to ensure the proper setting of expectations regarding products, services, and relationships; and roles of all customer-contact employees, their technology needs, and their logistics support.

b How the company provides information and easy access to enable customers to seek assistance, to comment, and to complain. Describe types of contact and how easy access is maintained for each type.

c Follow-up with customers on products, services, and recent transactions to help build relationships and to seek feedback for improvement.

d How service standards that define reliability, responsiveness, and effectiveness of customer-contact employees' interactions with customers are set. Describe how standards requirements are deployed to other company units that support customer-contact employees, how the overall performance of the service standards system is monitored, and how it is improved using customer information.

e How the company ensures that formal and informal complaints and feedback received by all company units are aggregated for overall evaluation and use throughout the company. Describe how the company ensures that complaints and problems are resolved promptly and effectively.

f How the following are addressed for customer-contact employees: (1) selection factors; (2) career path; (3) special training to include: knowledge of products and services; listening to customers; soliciting comments from customers; how to anticipate and handle problems or failures ("recovery"); skills in customer retention; and how to manage expectations; (4) empowerment and decision-making; (5) attitude and morale determination; (6) recognition and reward, and (7) attrition.

g How the company evaluates and improves its customer relationship management practices. Describe key indicators used in evaluations and how evaluations lead to improvements, such as in strategy, training, technology, and service standards.

Source: National Institute of Standards and Technology.

377

The nine elements of the EQA (Business Excellence) model are defined as follows.

1 *Leadership*: how the executive team and all other managers inspire and drive total quality as the company's fundamental process for continuous improvement.

2 *Policy and strategy*: how the company's policy and strategy reflects the concept of total quality and how the principles of total quality are used in the determination, deployment, review and improvement of policy and strategy.

3 *People management*: how the company releases the full potential of its people to improve its business continuously.

4 *Resources*: how the company's resources are effectively deployed in support of policy and strategy.

5 *Processes*: how processes are identified, reviewed and, if necessary, revised to ensure continuous improvement of the company's business.

6 *Customer satisfaction*: the perception by the company's external customers of its products and services.

7 *People satisfaction*: what the company's employees feel about the company.

8 *Impact on society*: how the company is perceived among the community at large. This includes views of the company's approach to quality of life, the environment and the preservation of global resources.

9 *Business results*: what the company is achieving in relation to its planned business performance.

The overall scheme has been summarised as shown in Fig. 14.10.

Figure 14.10 European Quality Award (Business Excellence) Model

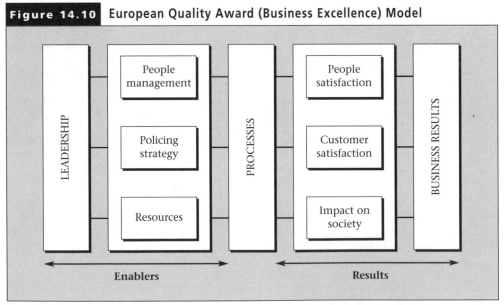

Source: European Quality Award Foundation. Reproduced with permission. © 1999 European Foundation for Quality Management.

CONCLUSION

The area of TQM is of enormous significance to the enhancement of HRD because it pushes learning issues to the forefront of the organisational agenda. Concepts such as continuous improvement and continuous learning, which have featured so strongly in the learning organisation literature, emanated from the quality management ideology. As we shall see in Chapter 16, there was a strong undercurrent of quality thinking running through the establishment of corporate universities at companies such as Motorola and Unipart – indeed, Jeanne Meister's original book on the subject was entitled *Corporate Quality Universities* (Meister, 1994). Quality issues featured strongly in many of the corporate transformation programmes that have been so evident throughout the 1990s. Consistent messages reflect a perceived need to generate a more customer-responsive, quality-oriented, flexible work-force. Developing team-building skills, customer communications, problem-solving skills, empowerment and management style assumes great importance and enormous resources have been spent on investing in development of such skills.

Professionals in the HRD area can have a catalytic role in the whole TQM process – helping to ensure that individuals have the necessary skills and insights to engage in the type of problem-solving and solution-seeking activities that are associated with so-called continuous improvements. Through facilitating their development HRD specialists are presented with an opportunity to raise their profile and influence organisational direction.

The HRD agenda arising out of TQM should include the following:

- seizing the opportunity to become better informed about TQM and acquiring the necessary TQM-speak and know-how;
- appropriate positioning of the HRD function to play an active role in the development of TQM initiatives;
- acquiring the consultancy and internal change agent skills required to contribute to the TQM process;
- developing a detailed understanding of facilitation skills for both team-building and problem-solving activities;
- providing managers with the education and training they need to engineer a fundamental shift in the 'way things are done';
- identifying and developing the organisational competences needed to sustain a customer-responsive, quality-oriented service.

The strategic implications for HRD are vast. If TQM is to be seen as a way of organisational life, which entails continuous development of staff at all levels, then HRD practitioners should aim to be involved at every level of strategic and organisational planning, to guide organisational members in an ongoing creative process of discovery.

However, there is a counter-message, in that there is strong evidence to indicate that those involved in facilitating the TQM learning process are not 'career professionals'. They are often drawn from the line, and may not be formally or even indirectly attached to an HRD function. Human resource development personnel may not even be aware of their existence, as demonstrated in an in-house survey conducted by British Rail prior to privatisation. At one level it is extremely encouraging to see so many people being directly involved in HRD issues. At another level, it should perhaps be worrying for the HR function that the quality function seems to be driving the strategic learning process.

REFERENCES

Binney, G. (1992) *Making Quality Work: Lessons from Europe's Leading Companies*, Special Report No. P655, Economist Intelligence Unit.

Chang, R. (1993) 'Ten core threads: weaving through successful TQM initiatives', *ASTD Total Quality Management Newsletter*, Spring.

Collard, R. (1981) 'The Quality Circle in Context', *Personnel Management*, September.

Crosby, P. H. (1979) 'Quality is Free'. New York: McGraw-Hill.

Department of Health (1989) 'Total Quality Management Guidelines'. Internal publication.

Feigenbaum, A. V. (1957) *Total Quality Control*. New York: McGraw-Hill.

Gallagher, J. and Smith, D. (1997) 'Building training on the pillars: applying total quality to education and training in the US', *International Journal for Training and Development*, 1(1).

Garvin, D. (1991) 'How the Baldrige Award really works', *Harvard Business Review*, November–December.

Giles, E. (1989) 'Is Xerox's Human Resource Management Worth Copying?'. Paper presented to the British Acadamy of Management Annual Conference.

Hobson, C. (1992). Proceedings of Euroqual Conference, Amsterdam.

Hutchins, D. (1981) 'How quality goes round in circles', *Management Today*, January.

Ishikawa, K. (1985) *What is Total Quality Control?: The Japanese Way*. Englewood Cliffs, NJ: Prentice Hall.

Juran, J. M., Gryna, F. M. and Bingham, R. S. (eds) (1988) *Quality Control Handbook* (4th edn) New York: McGraw-Hill.

Lewis, C. and Rooney, J. (1981) 'Quality Circles in Situ', *Personnel Management*, October.

Meister, J. (1994) *Corporate Quality Universities: Lessons in Building a World Class Work Force*. Irwin Professional Publishing.

Peters, T. (1994) 'Looking to the Future', *Creative Training Techniques*, 7(11), November.

Smith, D. H. and Lewis, R. G. (1997) 'The Effectiveness of Total Quality Management: A Response to the Critics'. AHRD Conference Proceedings.

Storey, J. (1992) *Developments in the Management of Human Resources*. Oxford: Blackwell.

'Trends in Employee Training and Development', *Training*, October 1996.

Walker, R. (1992) 'Rank Xerox – Management Revolution', *Long Range Planning*, 25(1), pp. 9–21.

Wickens, P. (1991) 'Innovation in Training creates a competitive edge', quoted in J. Stevens and R. Mackay, (eds) *Training & Competitiveness*. London: Kogan Page.

Zemke, R. (1992) 'TQM: fatally flawed or simply unfocused', *Training*, 29(10), October.

Chapter 15

THE LEARNING ORGANISATION

INTRODUCTION

For many practitioners the ultimate goal of organisationally based HRD has become the achievement of a 'learning organisation'. Senior executives of a number of high profile organisations such as ICL and Rover in the UK and Motorola in the USA have made public pronouncements that they are, or intend to become, one. They have been impressed by claims that it provides a framework, methodology and way of thinking for integrating learning with business imperatives at individual, group and organisational level. Perhaps more than anything else it has helped to put HRD on the strategic agenda. It is seen as the key to unlock the learning potential of individuals and groups which will, above all else, contribute to the sustainable competitive advantage of a given organisation or even to sustainability itself. It is held to provide an overarching framework for shaping processes and generating a culture that will enhance an organisation's readiness and capacity for change. How well do such claims hold up? What in practice does this mean? In particular, what does it mean for people in such organisations? What do they experience that is different from what they would experience in organisations that do not claim to be learning organisations?

Dibella and Nevis (1998) point out the difference between *normative* and *developmental* perspectives towards the treatment of the topic in the literature.

The essence of a normative perspective is that organisational effectiveness will be enhanced by the realisation of a set of characteristics which together represent 'the learning organisation'. Furthermore, these features will not emerge by chance, as if by some process like osmosis. It is only through disciplined action and planned interventions that the many forces that constrain learning can be overcome (Dibella and Nevis, op. cit.). In the chapter we analyse a number of formula-driven approaches based on expert prescriptions on how to achieve the overall learning goal.

The developmental perspective treats the learning organisation as a particular phase reached in an organisation's life cycle or evolution. Thus for some it is the final stage on an HRD journey of discovery originating some years ago in menu-driven provision of training courses and resulting in an environment where learning is more self managed, continuous and broad based (*see* Fig. 15.1).

Figure 15.1	Human resource development migration path to 'world class'

Class 5	Class 4	Class 3	Class 2	Class 1	World class
Menu of courses	Objective setting	Skill matrices	Competence-based training	Open learning	Learning company
	Functional development routes	Delegated responsibility	Team briefing	Investors in People	Personal development plans
		Performance appraisal		Multi-functional teams	Upward appraisal
		Secondments		Career counselling	Empowered multidisciplinary teams
				Lateral development routes	Shared values
					Continuous learning

Source: Based on Proctor (1995).

Dibella and Nevis (op. cit.) propose a third position, which they call a *capability* perspective. By this they mean that within all organisations there are intrinsic learning capabilities, but that how these are manifested will vary from institution to institution through distinctive styles or patterns of learning. The underpinning assumptions are that there is no one best way for organisations to learn and that learning processes are embedded in an organisation's own culture and structure and need to be brought to the surface. The key task before any interventions take place is to diagnose what those processes are – how, where and what gets learned.

A variant of the capability perspective can be derived from the work of Illich (1971), who emphasises the importance of tacit as opposed to explicit or intentional learning. He has remarked that 'learning is the human activity which least needs manipulation by others. Most learning is not the result of instruction. It is rather the result of unhampered participation in a meaningful setting.' For those who wish their organisation to become a learning organisation the task, it could be contended, is to find and create more 'meaningful settings' in which people can participate in more meaningful ways.

'The learning organisation' is an extremely fashionable term. However its meaning can seem very abstract, particularly when it is linked to concepts currently in vogue such as deutero-learning, and it is difficult to translate into practical terms. As a senior manager of a learning team from Andersen Consulting said: 'The concept is still quite fluffy' (Prothero, 1997). Another senior consultant from the same organisation expressed it in this way: 'How do you communicate to others what is essentially an *experiential* concept. That is, you can't see or feel or touch a Learning organisation or get a 'Certification' but you can *experience* it' (Prothero, op. cit.). It can impose not inconsiderable demands on organisational members at all levels. Furthermore, a number of organisations are understandably sceptical about what they fear may be no more than another 'flavour of the month' notion (Jeris, 1997). Its exponents contend that only learning organisations have the capacity to be truly sustainable. Others suggest that such an assertion is no more than an idealistic hypothesis that remains to be tested.

This chapter looks at attempts to put the concept into operation.

The achievement of a learning organisation is usually held to be a manifestation of 'organisational learning'. This connection has led some to argue that the very notion of a 'learning organisation' is fundamentally flawed. Individuals can learn, they contend, but not organisations. An organisation is not an entity. The concept of a learning organisation is at best a helpful metaphor, trying to establish some sort of parallels with individual learning processes. But it should not be stretched too far.

> Organisations only exist through individuals who are their members, while at the same time we use an individual human being as a metaphor for the organisation as a whole (Doving, 1994).

Learning can take place in organisations, and systems and processes can be designed to support individual learning. But is the outcome 'organisational learning'? Doving (op. cit.) argues that we cannot conclude that 'organisational knowledge' – which would be an outcome of organisational learning – exists just because we recognise that individuals have knowledge, and that organisations are composed of individuals. This core concern will be pursued in this chapter.

One of the challenges facing those who see the learning organisation as being in some way akin to individual learning, is to understand the notion of 'continuous transformation' which permeates the literature on the subject. It brings to mind the aphorism of the ancient Greek philosopher Heraclitus: 'All changeth, nought remaineth'. It implies that everything and everyone is in a state of flux. I know of no individuals who can 'continuously transform' themselves. Is it realistic to expect that organisations can? It is also counter-intuitive. Without any stability, there is no sense of continuity or order, no time to enjoy and build on what has been achieved. It is the obverse of the mechanistic, closed-systems explanatory models adopted by the early organisational theorists who in equally counter-intuitive vein saw the outside environment as a constant. It is also the antithesis of the implicit meaning contained in the word 'organisation'. This chapter explores and evaluates the various features and properties that learning organisations are held to possess.

Given such perspectives, what is the place of HRD practitioners in a learning organisation? Who will be the learning architects of the future? Will those who manage learning adopt the same career path as those who in the past have managed training? One of the consequences in HRD terms of espousing the learning organisation ideology is to reduce the traditional emphasis on formal training provision. Does it also mean that such provision is being replaced? What effect is it having on the HRD profession?

CAN ORGANISATIONS LEARN?

According to Kim (1993), 'All organisations learn whether they consciously choose to or not.' Is this a viable assertion? It takes us to the heart of a debate about what an organisation actually is. Can it exist apart from its individual members? Can it consciously choose? Over the years many have advised caution about reifying organisations, and seeing them as some form of living entity which can be imbued with some sort of primitive vitalism. Organisations do not 'do' anything, they do not 'act' or possess a 'business brain' that enables them to choose. They are no more than frameworks, contrivances, which enable numbers of people to do things and achieve outcomes which individually would not have been possible.

Katz and Kahn (1965) contend that segmental involvement of individuals is the basis of organisational functioning. By this they mean that in general terms, only part of an individual's life space is occupied by a given organisation. We are not like bees or ants. Unless we are in total institutions such as monasteries we 'go home' for some of the time. Furthermore, not only are many people in membership of a number of organisations at any one moment, but during a lifetime they can move into and out of a range of organisational contexts. These authors also consider that an organisation is, in essence, no more than a contrivance to enable people to function together, and certainly not a sentient entity. However, they say, this 'central fact that organisations consist of segments of people rather than an integration of their whole personalities has been consistently ignored both in popular thinking and in scientific theory'. One consequence has been that organisations somehow become endowed with 'purposes and with many of the qualities of human agency as if this pattern were capable of feeling, thinking and acting. This misconception persists because we are trapped by language habits which make it difficult to communicate about organisations in any other fashion'. They go on to say that even in their own writings it has not been possible to entirely avoid anthropomorphic language in writing about organisations. They are strongly influenced in their thinking by Allport (1933) who felt that this tendency to anthropomorphise organisations was in large part due to an over-utilisation of the language of metaphor in the social sciences.

Kumra (1996) takes a different perspective. She contends that 'the use of anthropomorphisms in organisational theory will not simply stop – we will continue to think of organisations as human entities'. What is important is that we become skilled in knowing how and when to apply the human metaphor. If we accept this view of the reality of the situation, then it is crucial, in terms of describing learning in organisations, that we recognise that we are using a metaphor and that it is no more than a metaphor. Otherwise we are liable to assume that there is an organisational entity, x, that can learn and remember and act independently of the actions of its members.

An example of anthropomorphic language is provided by the UK Information Technology Service Agency (ITSA) which was formed in 1990 as an Executive Agency of the Department of Social Service. According to published policy statements:

ITSA will *live by* three core values:

■ to delight the customer, by providing the right advice and information on all IS/IT issues, and by ensuring the provision of high quality products and services;

■ to focus on people, by supporting and developing staff to enable their contribution to ITSA's success to be tangible and recognised;

■ to provide value for money by reducing costs and maintaining high quality provision.

For Kumra a model of organisation learning needs to see the organisation as a 'behavioural system'. For learning to serve any purpose requires the ability to act on the experience, that is, to alter behaviour in the light of experience. She further contends that an organisation is not just a behavioural system but an interpretation system:

In order to act on the lessons of the past (i.e. alter behaviour) the organisation must be capable of interpreting the consequences of previous actions and experiences of individuals appropriately. Thus the organisation must also be viewed as an 'interpretation system'.

She draws upon the work of Daft and Weick (1984) to indicate where 'interpretation' fits into an organisation's learning process. They developed a three-stage model of:

SCANNING which leads to INTERPRETATION which leads to LEARNING.

One risk of adopting this anthropomorphic perspective is that it does not address who, within the behavioural and interpretation system, will orchestrate and oversee the learning process. What systems need to be in place? Will it run itself? Another consequence is that individual learning seems to be bypassed in favour of something grander and more holistic. This is not to say that holistic thinking about organisational processes should be eschewed. It is clearly significant to develop an appropriate set of diagnostic tools which will enable one to make sense of what is happening in and to the system.

Dixon (1994) has developed a modified version of the Daft and Weick three-stage model, presented as a virtuous cycle or organisational learning cycle which more effectively recognises the contribution of individuals, who either singly or collectively generate, integrate, interpret and act upon information. Where continuous learning is part of corporate philosophy, three simplified processes are evident for any given learning cycle:

- *Scanning*, in order to gather ideas and insights and bring them into the organisation;

- *Interpretive* activities to make sense of them through problem solving, experimentation, shared understandings, etc.;

- *Acting*, or actions as a result of interpretations, which include the transfer of knowledge and how it is ultimately used.

In the final analysis, the only resource capable of learning within an organisation is the people who comprise it. The very diversity of the experience of these people is a valuable asset, if one can only learn to harness the experience and use it.

Organisation memory

The notion that organisations learn has led to questions being asked about whether organisations have memories. If organisations can learn, does such learning depend on 'organisation memory'? Argyris and Schon (1978) argue that organisation memory is only a metaphor and that 'organisations do not literally remember'.

Organisation memory has been defined as:

> Stored information from an organisation's history that can be brought to bear on present decisions. This information is stored as a consequence of implementing decisions to which they refer, by individual recollections and through shared interpretations (Walsh and Ungson, 1991).

For them, constituents of organisation memory include:

- *acquisition*: through interpretations about organisation decisions and their subsequent consequences;

- *retention*: of information which is useful. That which has served little purpose is discarded;

- *individuals*: they share their organisation memory in their ability to recall and take action based on experience to effect organisation decisions;

- *storage*: to aid memory, individuals and organisations keep records and files, which constitute the physical, tangible aspects of an organisation's memory;

- *culture*: this embodies past experience;

- *transformations*: these include practices such as work design, selection and socialisation.

None of the above needs to be seen in anthropomorphic terms. Most can be viewed as components of an information system. Information systems can be designed whereby data can be stored. But this is not the same as memory. Indeed it is individuals who have to remember where the information which they need to access is stored.

The above definition and accompanying features emphasise the storage aspects. Equally important are the retrieval systems and means of access. For many individuals, the key issue of memory is being able to bring to the surface or recall. User-friendly systems need to be designed which facilitate interrogation. What tend to get lost in organisational information systems are the fables, tales, informal practices, short-cuts, events and their interpretation that provide vibrancy and colour.

Roger Schank (1996) has attempted to address this in his organisation-specific, multimedia interactive training packages. His approach incorporates experienced members of staff providing accounts on video of what happened to them when they undertook a particular and, in retrospect, ill-advised course of action. Trainees would then be presented with these stories if, as they navigated through the video software package, they suggested a similar course of action. The stories operate as scripts, post-mortem examinations of past events which become raw material for an apprentice worker structuring his or her behaviour until the apprentice can be self-structuring (Demarest, 1997).

Claims of loss of organisational memory resulting in organisational amnesia have become increasingly common in the literature. The claims are associated with anxieties concerning organisational downsizing which has been a consistent response in the 1990s to competitive pressures in the private sector, funding pressures in the public sector, and perceived opportunities for doing more with fewer through exploiting IT breakthroughs. It is one of the strands behind the current interest in knowledge management. The argument is that much learning about key activities is held in the experiences of individuals, and that this is lost when too many key people leave. The Schank approach to learning would be impossible if there did not exist within the organisation sufficient people in a position to relate significant experiences.

THREE LEVELS OF LEARNING IN ORGANISATIONS

The defining concepts developed by Argyris and Schon (1978) have been extremely influential in helping to frame subsequent models of organisational learning. For them:

> Organisational learning occurs when members of the organisation act as learning agents of the organisation, responding to changes in the internal and external environments of the organisation by detecting and correcting errors in organisational theory-in-use, and embedding the results of their enquiry in private images and shared maps of organisation.

There are a number of points that are worth drawing out of this definition.

1 'Organisational theory-in-use' refers to what actually takes place in an organisational setting. This can be contrasted with 'espoused theory', the term they use to describe what is claimed to happen in organisations. An example of an espoused theory is a claim made within an organisation that it is an equal opportunity employer. The organisational theory-in-use may or may not support that claim.

2 They place heavy emphasis on the role of individuals in the learning process. One criterion of the success of this learning process, implied by the map metaphor, is the extent to which there is a shared understanding among individuals in respect of where the organisation is going to and where it is coming from.

3 Organisational learning involves the detection and correction of error, a process that emanates from the cybernetic tradition. In essence, cybernetics, as applied to organisations, focuses on showing how complex systems can be controlled and managed through feedback mechanisms based on a process of regulation.

Following Bateson (1973) they go on to differentiate between three levels of organisational learning. Level one learning is derived from the idea of what Stacey (1993), drawing upon Ashby (1956), calls 'error-controlled regulation' – in that feedback is provided, enabling action to be taken, after an error or performance deviation has been detected. Level two is more akin to 'anticipatory regulation' – the regulatory system senses potential disturbances before they occur and enables preventative action to be taken. In each instance the assumption is made that the system wishes to return as close as possible to a state of equilibrium. That is the purpose of the regulatory process. Both of these can be contrasted to Level three, which is broader in scope.

Level one

Single-loop learning occurs when error detection and correction enables the organisation to continue with current policies and objectives. This, they contend, is a sort of lower-level, reactive learning that is inadequate in itself to confront the challenges that organisations now have to face. Nevertheless, such 'operational learning' is important. 'Operational learning forms the foundation of any work organisation. [It] springs from an organisation's efforts to improve its basic work processes' (Broersma, 1995). Broersma considers that the attempt by Motorola, the USA-based electronics manufacturer, to achieve 'six sigma' – a quality standard of less than 3.4 defects per million opportunities for error – is an example of operational or single-loop learning.

Burgoyne (1995) calls this level of learning 'habitual' learning and argues that habits, once learned, can be hard to unlearn. He feels that an emphasis on single-loop learning can inhibit future learning.

Level two

Double-loop learning is generated by detection and correction activities which modify and change the organisation's fundamental norms and aims, often through challenging traditional norms and values and resolving subsequent conflict. Thus Argyris and Schon (op. cit.) argue that while many organisations can and do achieve single-loop learning, the more valuable and insightful learning which occurs through the double-loop process is rather more difficult. It is clearly more problematic to challenge, or even to think about challenging, accepted orthodoxies and strategies, than to engage in crisis management – which is essentially a time-serving process leading to cure rather than prevention.

Broersma (op. cit.) refers to this as 'systemic learning' because the learning not only addresses the work itself but focuses on evaluating the complex of interacting systems and activities that constitute the entire organisation. People are encouraged to think holistically and to challenge fundamental assumptions that underpin the organisation's systems and procedures. Error detection and connection goes beyond modifying work procedures and practices and encompasses values, policies and objectives. Redefining organisation mission and core values could be an outcome of systemic or double-loop learning.

Burgoyne (op. cit.) suggests that 'level two learning' equates to the position of an 'adaptive' organisation which has discovered how to adjust to, and take advantage of, contextual changes. It is dynamic and customer driven. It is the level at which issues concerning corporate strategy and the management of change are located. In many people's minds it represents the sort of learning the 'learning organisation' engages in.

Level three

'Level three learning' Argyris and Schon (op. cit.) call 'deutero-learning', a term borrowed from Bateson (1973). It is a form of higher level 'learning to learn' activity, as can be seen from the following description.

> When an organisation engages in deutero-learning, its members . . . reflect on and inquire into previous episodes of organisational learning, or failure to learn. They discover what they did that facilitated or inhibited learning, they invent new strategies for learning, they produce these strategies, and they evaluate and generalise what they have produced. The results become encoded in individual images and maps and are reflected in organisational learning practice (Argyris and Schon, op. cit.).

This learning is involved with reviewing and reflecting on previous learning experiences and using such experiences as a basis for the formation of new learning activities and insights.

Broersma calls such learning 'transformative learning', which he sees as the process of continuous development of the whole organisation. Transformative learning incorporates operational and systemic learning into an ongoing process of evolutionary change.

Burgoyne suggests that level three learning represents the position of a 'sustainable' organisation, which has discovered the art of creating its environment as much as adapting to it, being able to maintain core values as opposed to being swept away by change. There is a paradox entailed in this. Some of the most long-established organisations are notoriously conservative in their practices – take, for example, the Catholic Church.

A key argument of Argyris and Schon's work is that organisations learn through the agency of individuals working therein. However, in anthropomorphic vein, they contend that individual learning is an insufficient condition for organisational learning, since the learning experienced by the individual may not become transferred or encoded into the memory of the organisation; there are many cases where the organisation knows less than its members.

Argyris and Schon argue that very few organisations are involved in either double-loop or deutero-learning, although it is possible for an organisation to move towards this state if it is able to do a number of things:

■ to show greater tolerance for perceived error, enabling members to acknowledge jointly and publicly the mismatch of outcome to expectation, and to identify and be aware of events which are not or are no longer relevant to the organisation's theory-in-use;

■ to disseminate more widely the aims and objectives of the organisation and make clear the logic which governs its existence so that members know their own organisation and encourage members to share rather than internalise experiences of conflict and resolution;

■ to increase internal challenges to the organisation's theory-in-use by the use of collaborative review, enquiry and reflection, that is, to encourage double-loop learning;

■ to share awareness of the learning which the organisation has already experienced and encourage further enquiry and reflection.

LEARNING ORGANISATION FRAMEWORKS

A number of frameworks have been developed since the late 1980s in an attempt to encapsulate the essence of a learning organisation. More recent ones tend to be derivatives and composites of earlier versions. The frameworks tend to be very general. The more specific they are, the greater the risk that they will be regarded as providing practical solutions to a problem. This reflects a tension in the field. The more abstract and conceptual the models, the more one gains a sense of dynamism and excitement, and intellectual challenge. At the same time, one detects an element of idealism and associated 'fluffiness' in the explanations provided by some of their proponents. The more pragmatic the models, the more one can get to grips with practical guidelines, but the more there is a sense of being recipe driven and of following predetermined prescriptions. We examine four models, spanning a period of ten years. Each can be classified as having a *normative* orientation (Dibella and Nevis, op. cit.).

Senge's five disciplines

The seminal work of Peter Senge at the Centre for Organisational Learning at the Sloan School of Management, Massachusetts Institute of Technology, has had an enormous impact, both in the USA and overseas. His original ideas were presented in *The Fifth Discipline*, first published in 1990, and extended with examples from organisation practice in The *Fifth Discipline Fieldbook* which came out four years later.

'Learning organisations', according to Senge (1990), are organisations where people continually expand their capacity to create the results they truly desire, where new and expansive patterns of thinking are nurtured, where collective aspiration is set free, and where people are continually learning how to learn together.

He is concerned with achieving excellence in organisations, without specifically providing measurable success criteria. For him organisations that will truly excel in the future will be those that discover how to tap people's commitment and capacity to learn at all levels in an organisation.

A learning organisation is not something of the past, but an innovation, based on the gradual convergence of five new 'component technologies' which, when incorporated into organisational functioning, will become the model for the future. The absence of any one of these 'component technologies' would prove critical to success, just as the absence of any key engineering element in a product would prevent its effective functioning.

I find the term 'component technologies' to be somewhat misleading as an analogy. With the exception of 'systems thinking', the disciplines do not reflect structural or design imperatives, but are more akin to value orientations. It would be clearer to suggest that 'enabling structures' should be in place which would permit and encourage the exercise of those 'disciplines' which really reflect ways of behaving and seeing the world. If we accept Senge's approach, then HRD practitioners have a key responsibility in developing and sustaining the processes that support the exercise of the disciplines, as well as facilitating individual and group learning activities and opportunities to develop 'mastery' in them. Figure 15.2 presents Senge's Five Disciplines diagrammatically, and Fig. 15.3 examines the components of each discipline.

Figure 15.2	Senge's Five Disciplines

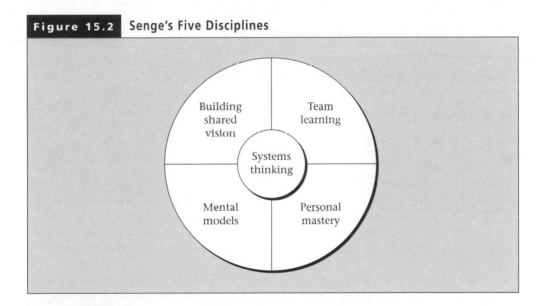

Figure 15.3	Analysis of Senge's Five Disciplines

Systems thinking

Businesses and other human endeavours are systems. They are bound by invisible fabrics of interrelated actions, which often take years to fully play out their effects on each other. Systems thinking is the fifth discipline. It is the discipline that

▶▶

▶▶ Figure 15.3 continued

integrates the following disciplines, fusing them into a coherent body of theory and practice. By enhancing each of the other disciplines, it continually reminds us that the whole can exceed the sum of its parts. Perhaps more than anything else, one needs to understand one's particular relationship and contribution to and impact on the system.

Personal mastery

Personal mastery is the discipline of continually clarifying and deepening our personal vision, of focusing our energies, of developing patience and of seeing reality objectively. It is the learning organisation's spiritual foundation. People with a high degree of personal mastery are able to consistently realise the results that matter most deeply to them. They do that by becoming committed to their own lifelong learning.

Mental models

'Mental models' are deeply ingrained assumptions, generalisations or even pictures or images that influence how we understand the world and how we take action. The discipline of working with mental models starts with learning to unearth our internal pictures of the world, to bring them to the surface and hold them up rigorously to scrutiny. It also includes the ability to carry on 'learningful' conversations where people expose their own thinking effectively and make that thinking open to the influence of others. There is an implication that previously ingrained ways of thinking are capable of being unlearned.

Building shared vision

The practice of shared vision involves the skills of developing shared 'pictures of the future' that foster genuine commitment and enrolment rather than compliance.

Team learning

How can a team of committed managers with individual IQs above 120 have a collective IQ of 65? When teams are truly learning, not only are they producing extraordinary results, but the individual members are growing more rapidly than they could otherwise have done.

The discipline of team learning starts with 'dialogue', the capacity of members of a team to suspend assumptions and enter into a genuine 'thinking together'. The discipline of dialogue also involves learning how to recognise the patterns of interaction in teams that undermine learning. The patterns of defensiveness are often deeply ingrained in how a team operates.

Team learning, according to Senge, is vital because teams, not individuals, are the fundamental learning unit in modern organisations; unless teams can learn, the organisation cannot learn.

To practise a discipline is to be a lifelong learner. You never arrive, you spend your life mastering disciplines. You can never say 'We are a learning organisation' any more than you can say 'I am an enlightened person'. The more you learn, the more acutely you become aware of your ignorance. Thus a corporation cannot be 'excellent' in the sense of having arrived at a permanent excellence.

Source: Based on Senge (1990).

According to Senge there are seven common organisational disabilities which act as blockages to the creation of the learning organisation and which the interaction of the five disciplines is designed to overcome.

1 *I am my position.* By focusing only on one's organisation position, one has little sense of responsibility for results when all positions interact.

2 *'The enemy is out there'.* There is in each of us a propensity to find someone or something outside ourselves to blame when things go wrong.

3 *The illusion of taking charge.* All too often 'proactiveness' is reactiveness in disguise. True proactiveness comes from seeing how we contribute to our own problems.

4 *The fixation on events.* The primary threats to our survival come not from sudden events but from slow, gradual processes.

5 *The parable of the boiled frog.* If you place a frog in a pot of water at room temperature and gradually increase the heat the frog will do nothing to get out. Why? Because the frog's internal apparatus for sensing threats to survival is geared to sudden, not gradual, environmental changes.

6 *The delusion of learning from experience.* We learn best from experience but we never directly experience the consequences of many of our most important decisions.

7 *The myth of the management team.* All too often there is a pretence that everyone is behind the team's collective strategy – maintaining the appearance of cohesiveness.

Commentary

Note that Senge's 'personal mastery' and 'mental models' reflect individual competences and predispositions. The implication is that one cannot engineer a 'learning organisation' unless one harnesses such individual 'forces'. In HRD terms the question then arises as to whether the 'system' needs to have in place mechanisms that can 'induce' 'personal mastery'.

Senge's emphasis on building a shared vision seems to indicate a potential contradiction in his thinking. The 'shared visions' that are created for the future can lead to new 'mental models' that become as fixed as those that were previously held. We may take the argument even further: given the importance of achieving 'personal mastery', is there not a conflict with being attached to a 'shared vision'?

It seems to me that Senge eschews the idea of an 'organisation' as some independent force. The emphasis throughout his approach is on the individual, operating within teams within organisations. He emphasises that the five learning disciplines are 'personal' disciplines: 'Each has to do with how we think, what we truly want, and how we interact with one another.' He does contend that 'teams, not individuals, are the fundamental learning unit in modern organisation'. But teams, of course, consist of individuals. His linking mechanism is the notion of a 'system' – but even here he emphasises design elements as opposed to some 'living' system. And it is individuals who must engage in 'systems thinking'. His organisational disabilities also are based more on individual perceptions than on intrinsic 'mysterious' forces. Nevertheless he believes that the whole can be greater than the sum of its parts – in the same way that a finished product exhibits qualities that could not be predicted from the components that constitute it.

The learning company

In an influential book – one of the few management books written by UK authors which I have seen on sale in the USA – Pedler, Burgoyne and Boydell (1991) develop the notion of the learning company. They prefer 'learning company' to 'learning organisation' because of the somewhat abstract and lifeless connotations that they associate with the word 'organisation'. 'Company', they feel, is rather more accessible as a term. In everyday parlance we often talk about being 'in company' and 'accompanying' others and it is such associations of working and being with others that they are trying to capture.

They define a learning company as 'an organisation that facilitates the learning of all its members and continuously transforms itself'. 'Members' should be taken to encompass all key stakeholders – including customers, suppliers and representatives of the local community.

The notion of continuous transformation has been challenged as a necessary condition by many who are sympathetic to the idea of a learning company. Whereas it is recognised that such organisations need to be responsive to environmental pressures that both influence, and are influenced by, what is 'out there', continuous transformation can be seen as a barrier to learning and a source of instability, a vicious as opposed to a virtuous circle. Some writers have preferred 'continuous improvement', taken from the ideology of Total Quality Management (TQM), to 'continuous transformation'.

Let us return to an image used in an earlier chapter. Imagine that you are on the boundary of an organisation. What would help you to identify whether it is a 'learning company'? You are looking outwards. Would there be any distinctive activities taking place? How might you learn from what is happening out there? You are looking inwards. Would there be features, practices or happenings that would enable you to differentiate between a 'learning organisation' and a 'not-learning' organisation? Pedler *et al.* (op. cit.) adopted a similar perspective in one of their attempts to model the learning company.

Their review of the literature and of emergent organisational practice led them to identify a list of 11 dimensions or features of a learning company. These, they felt, could be grouped under the five headings of 'strategy', 'looking in', 'structures', 'looking out' and 'learning opportunities'. The primary dimensions are as follows:

1 *Learning approach to strategy*. Policy and strategy formulation, implementation and evaluation are consciously structured as a learning process.

2 *Participative policy making*. All key stakeholders of the organisation have a chance to contribute to major policy decisions, including customers, suppliers and representatives of community and environmental groups.

3 *Informating*. Information is made as widely available as possible through IT in order to inform and empower people.

4 *Formative accounting and control*. Systems of accounting, budgeting and reporting are structured to assist learning and hence delight internal customers.

5 *Internal exchange*. All internal units and departments see themselves as customers and suppliers, engaging in constant dialogue with each other. The requirement is collaboration rather than competition.

6 *Reward flexibility*. The assumptions underlying reward systems need to be brought out into the open, and alternatives explored.

7 *Enabling structures*. The aim is to create an organisational architecture that gives space and headroom for meeting current needs and responding to future changes.

8 *Boundary workers as environmental scanners*. All members who have contact with external customers, clients, representatives of the community and so on should systematically collect and carry back information that is then collated and disseminated.

9 *Inter-company working*. In seeking to please customers, there will be attempts to engage in mutually advantageous learning activities such as joint training, job exchanges and strategic alliances.

10 *Learning climate*. Recognition is given to the fact that we need to try out new ideas and new ways of doing things and to accept that mistakes might be made.

11 *Self-development for all*. Resources and facilities for self-development are made available to all members of the organisation.

English Nature, the government's adviser on nature and conservation, has attempted to establish its status as a learning organisation against the above checklist. Table 15.1 indicates how they diagnosed their situation in 1995.

One of the features of the approach of Pedler *et al.* (op. cit.) is the integration of structural and HRM features into the model. This model of a learning organisation is very different from that presented by Senge. It is much more structural and recipe driven, much more focused on processes and practices. This comes across in particular in some of the visual means for conveying the message, such as seeing each element as part of an 11-piece jigsaw. The temptation is to think that if you have put the pieces together, you have solved the puzzle. If we accept Senge's construct of 'systems thinking' as the integrative discipline, then the 11 dimensions can be viewed as ways of putting bones on to 'systems thinking'. We do not know from the model where the authors stand specifically on the dimensions 'mental models', 'personal mastery' or 'building shared visions'. We can only infer from 'self development for all' that personal learning and therefore personal mastery has salience. The authors were very conscious in their writings that the presentation of the 11 dimensions could lose the sense of energy and dynamism which they associated with a true learning organisation. They generated an 'energy flow' model as an alternative representation (Pedler *et al.*, p. 32). This operates on two dimensions: the horizontal axis moved from 'vision' to 'action'; the vertical axis moved from 'individual' to 'collective' (*see* Fig. 15.4).

Tom Boydell, one of the authors, once described to me how he represented the energy flow model on the floor of a large training area, and had delegates walking round on the flow lines, stopping where they felt comfortable, and engaging in conversation with other delegates who had halted at the same spot. Although this image is quite evocative, I have nevertheless found that in practice people have turned to the 11-dimension framework for guidance.

Table 15.1 English Nature: status as a learning organisation

Feature	Progress so far
Learning approach to strategy	Strategy is reviewed and refined but it is not always seen as easy to change direction.
Participative policy making	Everyone has an opportunity to influence policy; there are tensions between bottom-up and top-down management.
Open information systems	Information is not always readily accessible: a project aims to improve information flow and use.
Formative accounting and control	Government accounting procedures require some control, although the finance team does help other teams to control their own resources.
Internal exchange	Variable. The internal customer ethos is still not fully accepted. Some teams have made considerable progress. Networking is crude.
Flexibility of rewards	Government rules restrict options. Performance-related pay, small special bonuses and flexible working are all possible.
Enabling structures	Individuals do move and flexibility is encouraged, but boundaries are seen as fixed in the short to medium term.
Boundary workers act as environmental scanners	Local teams and national partner teams have access to considerable information but to date have not always taken opportunities to influence their environmental scanners.
Inter-company learning	Although there is liaison with nature conservation groups, both in Britain and abroad, meetings with organisations not involved in nature issues are rare.
Learning climate	There is a history of knowledge-based learning and expectations are high. Process reviews for continual improvement are less common.
Self-development opportunities for all	There are many opportunities to learn and and develop, but time and money often limit such activity to key areas of the job.

Source: Dolan (1995).

The INVEST model

Pearn *et al.* (1995) have developed a model for conceptualising learning organisations which they contend incorporates all the key features emanating out of a detailed review of the published literature to that date. Their six-factor INVEST model is:

- **I**nspired learners
- **N**urturing culture
- **V**ision for the future
- **E**nhanced learning
- **S**upportive management
- **T**ransforming structures.

Figure 15.4 Energy flow model

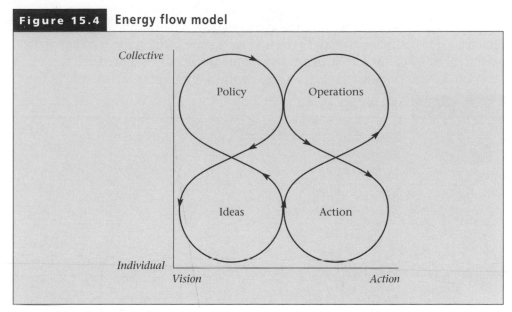

Source: Pedler et al (1991, p 35)

They develop the model as follows. The measure of 'inspired learners' is where all employees learn continuously, are excited by learning and understand the sig nificance of individual, group and organisational learning for the current and future viability of the organisation.

The measure of 'nurturing culture' is where there is universal support for continuous examination of established ways of thinking and doing at all levels in the organisation, and processes for achieving learning at all levels are highly regarded by everyone.

The measure of 'vision for learning' is where the vision is shared, fully articulated, communicated and understood by all members of the organisation who are committed to it. The vision should reflect the organisation's capacity to identify, respond to, and benefit from future possibilities. Part of the vision should specify the importance of learning at individual, group and system level to enable the organisation to transform itself continuously and thus survive and thrive in an increasingly unpredictable world.

The measure of 'enhanced learning' is where all employees benefit from practices and techniques to enhance and enrich learning, for example, learning contracts, shadowing, networks, mentoring, personal development plans, systems thinking and learning laboratories.

The measure of 'supportive management' is the extent to which managers in all parts of the organisation actively support and encourage their own and other people's continuous learning.

The measure of 'transforming culture' is the extent to which the organisation is designed to facilitate and encourage continuous learning. For example, there is great emphasis on sustained business partnership encouraged by a high degree of autonomy. The organisation is as flat as possible.

The approach of Pearn *et al.* differs from those of Senge and Pedler *et al.*, but one recognises elements from both of the above sources. Their framework with its six dimensions is both directive and prescriptive. A true learning organisation would need to be moving towards 'high' on each of the six dimensions (*see* Fig. 15.5).

Figure 15.5 The INVEST model

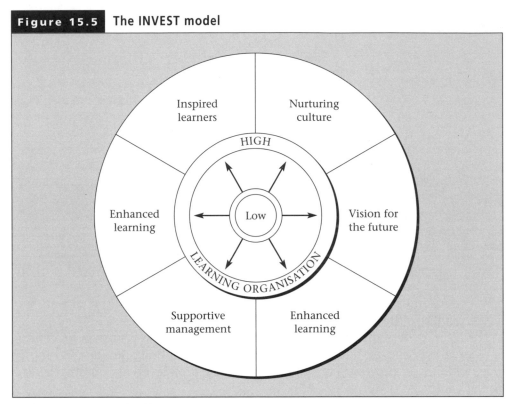

Source: Based on Pearn *et al.* (1994).

Other composite dimensions of the learning organisation

Watkins and Marsick (1993, 1996) identified seven dimensions of the learning organisation:

- create continuous learning opportunities;
- promote dialogue and enquiry;
- promote collaboration and team learning;
- empower people towards a collective vision;
- establish systems to capture and share learning;
- connect the organisation to its environment;
- provide strategic leadership for learning.

This list is heavily influenced by Senge's five disciplines and also contains elements from Pedler *et al.* (op. cit.). There is no mention of 'transformation' in their dimensions. 'Continuous learning' is their closest equivalent. It is noteworthy that they see continuous learning in individual terms: how the continuous learner can be supported is a particular theme of their work. Their model was influential in informing the ASTD studies reported in Fig. 15.6.

Figure 15.6 Learning lenses of leading organisations – best practices review

The Learning Organisation Network, a special interest group of the American Society for Training and Development (ASTD) conducted, over the period 1993–7, a survey of eight organisations across several industries. The group's remit was to investigate current practices and behaviours in implementing the kinds of systemic changes involved in becoming a learning organisation, that is, how, through learning, organisations are better equipped to meet the challenges posed by 'permanent white water', a metaphor first used by Vaill (1989) to capture the notion of continuous environmental turbulence. The study reported here takes the position that given the different contingencies that organisations are subject to, it is too simplistic to suggest that there will be one archetypal manifestation of a learning organisation. Instead, the likelihood is that the core learning dimensions will be given different weightings and will be subjected to different interpretations in practice. The metaphor used to explain this is that of a lens. In other words, the meaning attached to the principles of a learning organisation will be filtered, and interpreted differently, depending upon the lens used to view them through. Early work conducted by Marsick *et al.* (1994) identified four such lenses to explain differences in the learning processes of organisations which described themselves as learning organisations.

The proposed lenses are:

■ cultural

■ experiential

■ informational

■ structural.

Cultural

Typical behaviours are:

■ vision driven with minimal bureaucracy;

■ practices replaced when usefulness is outlived;

■ heavy emphasis on valuing differences to become truly transcultural.

Experiential

Typical behaviours are:

■ lots of JIT training;

■ people involved in their own development;

■ people understand their role in the organisation;

■ people report: 'This is fun';

■ people actively seek to learn from each other in the course of their work;

■ leaders model of calculated risk taking and experimentation;

■ learning is supported with plentiful resources.

▶▶

▶▶ Figure 15.6 continued

Informational

Typical behaviours are:

- useful information from the customer, supplier and community is fed back into the organisation;
- systems are in active use for people to express their ideas;
- extensive use of IT for environmental scanning and all types of internal communication;
- systems in place to capture and store learning.

Structural

Typical behaviours are:

- heavy emphasis on measurement of performance;
- structure promotes dialogue, creativity and information sharing;
- structure adapts easily to new tasks.

Marsick and colleagues presented the hypothesis that any given organisation uses a single lens out of the four for shaping initiatives and that, while an organisation may have a distinct preference for a single lens, that preference has certain shortcomings which may inhibit the effectiveness of the learning organisation initiative.

A subsequent study of eight organisations was undertaken to provide preliminary conclusions.

As reported by Jeris (1997), seven of the eight organisations displayed both a primary lens preference and a back-up lens preference. The back-up lens preference tended to counteract the potential drawbacks of the most preferred lens.

Thus one company studied demonstrated a preference for the experiential lens. Although this lens may be the most desirable way to deeply analyse organisational issues, challenge framing assumptions, and alter existing behaviours and practices, the degree to which a company is able to support these learning opportunities may be inhibited by a functional structure that severely restricts the free flow of information. However in the company studied the back-up lens was structural, with behaviours that would support collaboration and dialogue with all organisational stakeholders through structural interventions and configurations.

This study emphasises very clearly that whatever 'dimensions' are proposed in theory, they represent highly complex, composited constructs that need to be 'unpacked' and 'unravelled' in practice. In the unpacking they will inevitably lose some of the meaning intended by the original proponents. Skilled HRD practitioners can provide help in the unpacking process, but only if they are sufficiently knowledgable about the dimensions and supporting criteria on the one hand; and the realities of the organisation and its readiness and capacity for change on the other.

Table 15.2 compares the learning organization features of the four models discussed below.

Table 15.2 Comparison of learning organisation features

Pedler et al.	INVEST	Senge	Marsick
Learning approach to strategy	Vision for the future		Provide strategic leadership for learning
Participative policy making		Systems thinking	Create continuous learning opportunities
Informating	Supportive management		
Formative accounting and control		Personal mastery	Promote dialogue and enquiry
Internal exchange	Enhanced learning		
Reward flexibility		Mental models	Promote collaboration and team learning
Enabling structures	Transforming structures	Building shared vision	
Boundary workers as environmental scanners			Empower people towards a collective vision
		Team learning	
Inter-company working			Establish systems to capture and share learning
Learning climate	Nurturing cultures		
			Connect the organisation to its environment
Self-development for all	Inspired learners		

Figure 15.7 (on p. 402) presents diagrammatically the evolution of the learning organisation.

COMPANY EXAMPLES

In a survey in the 1980s of 15 large UK organisations going through organisational change and transition, Storey (1992) makes no mention of the term 'learning organisation'. A decade later a number of organisations claim to be learning organisations, and it is unlikely that a similar survey conducted today would make no reference to the term. We look next at two claimants from the UK (*see* Figs 15.8 and 15.9).

Figure 15.7 The evolution of the learning organisation – from theory to practice

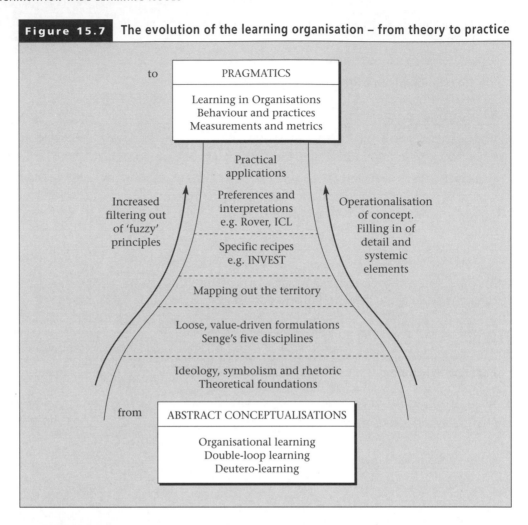

to

PRAGMATICS

Learning in Organisations
Behaviour and practices
Measurements and metrics

Practical
applications

Increased
filtering out
of 'fuzzy'
principles

Preferences and
interpretations
e.g. Rover, ICL

Operationalisation
of concept.
Filling in of
detail and
systemic
elements

Specific recipes
e.g. INVEST

Mapping out the territory

Loose, value-driven formulations
Senge's five disciplines

Ideology, symbolism and rhetoric
Theoretical foundations

from

ABSTRACT CONCEPTUALISATIONS

Organisational learning
Double-loop learning
Deutero-learning

Figure 15.8 Rover

In the late 1980s the senior management team of Rover saw the need to transform the organisation into an agile, fast-learning, dynamic 'success through people' company as a key platform in its strategy to handle global competition and satisfy customer demands for quality. One of its critical success factors was to be featured in the media as a learning organisation. The Rover model of a learning organisation was closely linked to Total Quality Management (TQM) precepts, the principles of corporate learning being clearly aligned with those of total quality improvement. Thus every learning process was to be tested against a set of quality standards.

The total quality culture was built on seven fundamental beliefs about organisational learning. These were:

1 Learning is the most natural human instinct.

2 Creativity, involvement and contribution are fuelled by learning and development.

3 Everyone has two jobs – the present job and improving that job.

▶▶

▶▶ Figure 15.8 continued

4 People own what they have created.

5 People need to be valued.

6 Creativity and ingenuity are under-distributed and grossly under-used.

7 Management does not have all the answers.

To facilitate and sustain the process a business unit known as the Rover Learning Business (RLB) was established. The key objectives of the RLB were:

1 *Associate encouragement and contribution.* To stimulate, encourage and provide ease of access for all associates to 'climb the learning ladder' in order to develop themselves and enhance their contribution to team objectives. (All staff are known as 'associates'.)

2 *Learning process.* To provide leading-edge learning processes, supported by innovative tools, techniques and materials for achieving major business changes.

3 *Corporate learning.* To lead and facilitate the design, sharing and deployment of best-practice corporate learning based on internal and external benchmarking.

4 *Extended learning.* To support the business objectives of dealers and suppliers with learning support and collaboration to facilitate world-class activities.

5 *World-class image.* To achieve 'world-best-in-class learning company' by the end of 1995, RLB must lead in the creation and support of this perception through internal and external communications and public relations.

At Rover, every employee or associate is responsible for her or his own learning. The old way of thinking was that training and learning were something that you had done to you – almost like taking medicine or as punishment for having done something wrong.

Managers have a key role to play in the process, being encouraged to actively transfer their own experience to other colleagues. They take full responsibility for creating a learning environment in their area, and for coaching employees/associates in all aspects of their learning. They are seen as facilitators, coaches, mentors and motivators empowering the real experts who are the associates. This philosophy and practice is called 'copy plus'.

Initially Rover identified 20 internal and external targets for critical success. These included:

■ £2m in cost savings through better learning;

■ abundant materials and programmes to guide the company's learning process;

■ 1000 employees with their own self-development programmes;

■ 500 managers qualified and acting as coaches;

■ to receive national training awards.

Rover claims that it has grown and benefited immensely in its journey as an emerging learning organisation. There has been a continuous flow of improvements initiated and generated by empowered employees or associates. The process has resulted in a better bottom line, happier employees and a superior global reputation. It is interesting to consider which, if any, of the four lenses proposed by Marsick *et al.* (op. cit.) is dominant.

Figure 15.9 ICL

ICL is a member of the Fujitsu family of companies, which had global revenues in 1995 of $4 billion, and 23 000 employees in over 70 countries. The holding company hopes that ICL will develop its IT exposure across Europe. To facilitate this it is believed that the 'rate of learning' at all levels is the key to meeting organisation goals and to achieving consistent improvements.

ICL's approach to a learning organisation is based on the following definition:

A learning organisation harnesses the full brainpower, knowledge and experience available to it, in order to evolve continually for the benefit of all its shareholders (Mayo and Lank, 1994).

ICL has developed the following explanatory diagram to describe its approach to the learning organisation. It is based on the European Quality Award model.

The ICL Model

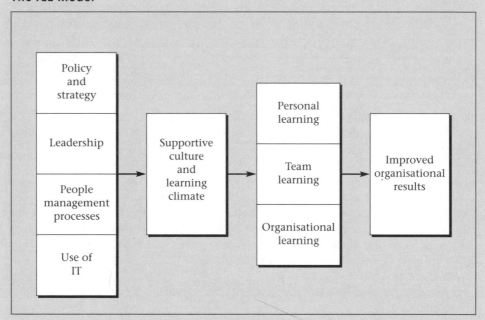

ICL claims to operate what has historically been a supportive learning culture. Mayo and Lank (1995) reveal some tensions in the system. They make the point that ICL has a declared intention 'to be a learning organisation', but contend that to build strategy around this declared intention makes many senior executives uncomfortable. They also emphasise the lack of overall consensus, due to the devolved nature of ICL, which does not operate as one homogeneous company but as a group of several businesses each of which is encouraged to develop its own way ahead.

ICL emphasises the importance of IT, as might be expected in an IT-driven firm. The effect of electronic communication on the exchange of information has perhaps done more than anything else to break down the structural divisions that restrict knowledge transfer and learning.

▶▶

▶▶ Figure 15.9 continued

More recently, knowledge management and the development of 'intellectual capital' have become central to the ICL way of thinking and are fundamental objectives
of becoming a learning organisation.

ICL's definition of knowledge management is:

> In order to maximise value to customers, we must have an outstanding capability to
> create, enhance and share intellectual capital across ICL's global organisation. 'Knowledge
> management' is a shorthand term covering all the things that must be put in place, e.g.
> processes, systems, culture and roles – to build and enhance this capability (Lank, 1997).

Indeed the ICL approach can be seen as a stepping-stone from TQM to a strategically oriented 'knowledge management' approach to HRD.

The focus on knowledge management puts a particular slant on the ICL concept
of a learning organisation. It runs the risk, perversely, of turning 'resourceful

Knowledge creation and transmission

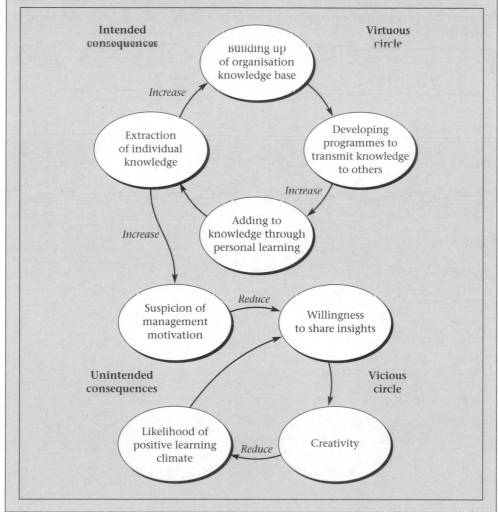

▶▶ Figure 15.9 continued

humans' into human resources. As we have seen, one of its basic tenets is to translate tacit knowledge which is locked into the discrete experiences of individuals into publicly accessible explicit knowledge which becomes part of the corporate memory. The individual is seen as a source of knowledge which the organisation wants. Skandia, the Swedish company that differentiated between 'human capital' and 'structural capital' as the component parts of 'intellectual capital', refers to the joint imperatives of value creation and value extraction in the process. Extraction, as of teeth, can be a painful experience.

Lank (1997) recognises this. She says that one of the key problems is to get individuals to share their knowledge. 'If part of employability is the knowledge and experience you hold, what motivation do you have to share that knowledge with someone else from your organisation?' It can lead to the tension between a vicious and virtuous circle shown diagrammatically on p. 405.

Framework to establish where a given organisation stands as a learning organisation

Simple questionnaires can be designed to indicate where a given organisation fits on a learning organisation scale. A good example is based on Prothero (1997) – *see* Table 15.3.

Table 15.3 Learning organisation scale: framework for measuring

Stage	Key descriptors	Category
Not even started	No sharing of vision; no supportive learning climate; no participative policy making; no encouragement of creativity; no encouragement of risk taking; no empowerment of individuals; no enabling structure; no systems thinking.	0
Quarter of the way there	Organisation at foundation stage of learning organisation, with current characteristics and state of development clearly much nearer to 'zero' stage of category 0 than 'learning organisation' stage of category 5.	1
Half-way there	Organisation at formation stage, currently displaying a balance of characteristics between the 'zero' stage of category 1 and the 'learning organisation' stage of category 5.	2
Three-quarters	Organisation at continuation stage and clearly nearer to 'learning organisation' stage of category 5 than to 'zero' stage of category 1.	3
Already a learning organisation	Organisation at transformation stage, shared vision built, openness, stimulating learning environment; all managers facilitate learning of others; self-discovery learning; creativity and risk taking encouraged; all managers as coaches and facilitators; learning is recognised as key to behavioural change and increased performance.	4

Any such framework as that presented in Table 15.3 is dependent on the dimensions that the originator thinks are important.

THE DEVELOPMENT PERSPECTIVE TOWARDS BECOMING A LEARNING ORGANISATION

Dibella and Nevis (op. cit.) contrast a normative approach to creating a learning organisation with a developmental orientation. This involves a sequence of stages through which an organisation needs to pass before achieving the desired goal. A version of this approach, based on the thinking of Sumantra Ghoshal from INSEAD in France, is presented by Jaap Germaans to students attending the Masters programme in Management Learning run from the University of Tilburg in the Netherlands. He refers to the existence of first-, second- and third-generation organisations, each with their distinctive structures, management ideologies and learning philosophies. His contention is that you cannot build a third-generation learning organisation with structures, strategies and management ideologies based on first- and second-generation archetypes. As he puts it, 'You cannot strive for a third generation learning organisation with a first- or second-generation mindset. The learning challenge is to change the whole network of mindsets.'

IMPLICATIONS FOR HUMAN RESOURCE DEVELOPMENT PRACTITIONERS

At one level, everyone in a learning organisation is an HRD practitioner. In the pure form of learning organisation, it is expected that we will all take responsibility for supporting our own learning and that of others. We become part of a network of self-supporting and other-supporting learning communities.

Nevertheless it is excessively-idealistic to assume that the learning effort will become totally self-managed and self-sustaining. There is still a role for individuals who are familiar with the theoretical principles and conceptual underpinnings and practical applications of learning and development, who have made it their business to become immersed in and to achieve personal mastery of the subject, who have the credibility and know-how to drive and direct the learning effort. They may not emerge exclusively, or even primarily, from training and development, or even HR backgrounds. As pointed out earlier in this text we may be seeing the emergence of new career paths for line managers and others (*see* Chapter 8).

For HRD practitioners to play a major role in the development and sustaining of the learning organisation philosophy, they need to be credible in a number of areas.

1 They need to become designers of systems and processes for learning across the whole organisation, as opposed to being purveyors of training. They need to be able to develop and sustain an overall framework, with supporting rationale, for the learning effort. It is not just a matter of designing systems for the conduct of learning activities. According to Garratt (1997), systems are required to 'move' the learning to where it is needed.

2 They need to demonstrate sophisticated diagnostic and intervention skills in respect of areas such as learning climate, corporate culture, performance management and reward systems. Garratt (op. cit.) contends that even if the systems are there the emotional climate is often not right to ensure that they are used at the appropriate place.

3 They need to oversee the overall process, and to develop 'nudging' strategies if facilities or opportunities are not being utilised and energy levels seem to be flagging.

4 They need to ensure an appropriate balance between directed and self-managed learning.

5 They need to be very clear about their relationship with other stakeholders in the learning process. What role, for example, should line management and individual employees play in the learning effort? How can they be supported?

6 They need to adopt organisational titles that properly reflect the nature of their role as sponsors and stewards of learning.

7 They need to be credible at top management level and able to influence the particular approach to learning that is adopted.

8 By their actions and the language they use, they need to be able to create a sense of meaning across the organisation for the learning effort.

9 They need to avoid relying on prescriptive recipes which might block ideas for the future.

10 They need to develop structured learning activities which will make individuals in the organisation familiar with the systemic qualities of the operating procedures, structures and processes.

Figure 15.10 Building an organisation's capacity to learn

13 Action steps

1 Transform the individual and organisational image of learning.
2 Create knowledge-based partnerships.
3 Develop and expand team-learning activities.
4 Change the role of managers.
5 Encourage experiments and risk taking.
6 Create structures, systems and time to extract learning.
7 Build opportunities and mechanisms to disseminate learning.
8 Empower people.
9 Push information throughout the organisation and to external associates (customers, vendors, suppliers and so forth).
10 Develop the discipline of systems thinking.
11 Create a culture of continuous improvement.
12 Develop a powerful vision for organisational excellence and individual fulfilment.
13 Root out bureaucracy.

Source: Marquardt and Reynolds (1994).

CONCLUSION

Despite some concerns about the term 'learning organisation' and potential anthropomorphic connotations, it has become very fashionable, and is a convenient shorthand term for describing an overall philosophy for sustaining learning in organisations.

Some of the prevailing definitions, however, make claims for a philosophy of learning which are not supportable. In particular, the notion of continuous transformation seems to be counter-intuitive in terms of how organisations function and how individuals learn. Continuous improvement would seem to be a safer term.

For HRD practitioners the current interest in learning organisations constitutes both a threat and an opportunity. It has strategic connotations, with learning being seen as one of the key driving forces of the organisation. Few HRD practitioners have traditionally had any strategic exposure, and to survive and be credible they will have to reconfigure their knowledge and skill base. Otherwise responsibility for the process will be taken out of their hands. There will also be a general raising of the level of competition for jobs, with more and more people wishing to take on HRD roles because of the career opportunities afforded.

On the other hand, assuming that individuals can demonstrate a strategic awareness, it provides them with an entry into organisational strategic thinking that would have been unheard of in the past. Almost certainly, one will see a general shift in HRD job roles.

One of the consequences of some of the thinking about learning organisations, and the emphasis on self-development and empowerment, is the risk that resources allocated to formal training events will be cut back to the detriment of the profession. The role that formal training events should play in the overall learning philosophy will need careful attention.

The current interest in learning organisations should also be seen in the context of individuals increasingly being expected to take responsibility for their own career development – as opposed to there being an organisational culture that will support career development in an institution.

The advocates of learning organisations claim substantial benefits can occur (or have occurred). These include:

- creative thinking resulting in new responses to environmental turbulence;
- greater commitment and energy levels of staff;
- sustained flow of innovations and improvements;
- superior global reputation;
- a means for enhancing the organisation's intellectual capital.

The term 'learning organisation' has proved to be a most powerful and inspirational catch-all phrase for bringing together a set of ideas and initiatives centred around notions such as 'the productive power of putting people first'. One detects a snowball effect as those early in the field become a benchmark for later followers. However it still needs to be demonstrated that basic concepts such as 'deutero-learning', which underpin so-called organisational learning, have anything more than symbolic and ritualistic significance.

One of the problems associated with the construct of the 'learning organisation' is establishing appropriate tests for its existence, and the benefits conferred. The problem is not helped by the view often expressed that one can never 'become' a learning organisation; the notions of continuous learning and development and flux mean that one is always in a state of 'becoming', and never of arrival – a sort of never-ending journey. Given this caveat, an obvious test is continued organisational functioning over an extended period of time. This creates two major difficulties. The first is that those organisations that have sustained a long historical presence do not manifest the sort of features which the advocates of the learning organisation are looking for; indeed the reverse is often the case. Most exponents argue that the approach entails an innovative way of thinking, a coming together, as Senge puts it, of newly designed 'component technologies'. That being the case, practical applications of the 'design' are of insufficient duration for any realistic longitudinal studies to be carried out in which one could have confidence.

REFERENCES

Allport, F. H. (1933) *Institutional Behaviour*. Raleigh, NC: University of North Carolina Press.

Argyris, C. and Schon, D. (1978) *Organisational Learning: A Theory of Action Perspective*. Reading, MA: Addison-Wesley.

Ashby, R. (1956) *Introduction to Cybernetics*. New York: Wiley.

Bateson, G. (1973) *Steps to an Ecology of Mind*. London: Paladin.

Broersma, T. (1995) 'In search of the future', *Training and Development*, January.

Burgoyne, J. (1995) 'Feeding minds to grow the business', *People Management*, 21 September, pp. 22–5.

Daft, R. L. and Weick, K. E. (1984) 'Towards a model of organisations as interpretation systems', *Academy of Management Review*, 9.

Dibella A. J. and Nevis, E. C. (1998) *How Organisations Learn – An Integrated Strategy for Building Learning Capability*. San Francisco: Jossey-Bass.

Dixon, N. (1994) *The Organisational Learning Cycle*. New York: McGraw-Hill.

Dolan, S. (1995) 'A different use of natural resources', *People Management*, 5 October, pp. 36–9.

Doving, E. (1994) 'Using anthropomorphistic metaphors: organisation action, knowledge and learning'. Conference proceedings, *Metaphors in Organisational Theory and Behaviour*, Kings College, London.

Garratt, B. (1997) 'Learning Organisation'. BBC Radio 4, 16 March.

Illich, I. (1971) *Deschooling Society*. Colder and Boyars.

Jeris, L. S. (1997) 'Learning Lenses of Leading Organisations: Best Practices Survey'. AHRD 1997 Conference Proceedings, Atlanta, Georgia.

Katz, D. and Kahn, R. L. (1965) *The Social Psychology of Organisations*. New York: Wiley.

Kim, D. H. (1993) 'The link between individual and organisational learning', *Sloan Management Review*, Fall.

Kumra, S. (1996) 'The organisation as a social entity', in C. Oswick and D. Grant (eds) *Organisation Development, Metaphorical Explorations*. London: Pitman.

Lank, E. (1997) 'Leveraging Invisible Assets: the Human Factor', *Long Range Planning*, 30(3), June, pp. 406–12.

Marquandt, M. and Reynolds, A. (1994) *The Global Learning Organisation*. Homewood, IL: Irwin.

Marsick, V. J., Watkins, K. E., O'Neil, J., Dixon, N. and Catanello, R. (1994) 'Portrait of a Learning Organisation: Stories from early adopters'. Proceedings of the Adult Education Research Conference, Knoxville, Tennessee.

Mayo, A. and Lank E. (1994) *The Power of Learning: A Guide to Gaining Competitive Advantage*. London: IPD.

Mayo, A. and Lank, E. (1995) 'Changing the soil spurs new growth', *People Management*, 16, November.

Pearn, M., Roderick, C. and Mulrooney, C. (1995) *Learning Organizations in Practice*. McGraw-Hill.

Pedler, M., Burgoyne, J. and Boydell, T. (1991) *'The Learning Company'*: *A Strategy for Sustainable Development*. New York: McGraw-Hill.

Proctor, J. D. (1995) 'Getting teams off the ground', *People Management*, 4, May.

Prothero, J. (1997) 'Investors in People – a true measure of the Learning Organisation'. Unpublished MSc HRD dissertation, Liverpool John Moores University.

Schank, R. (1995). ASTD Conference proceedings, Plenary presentation, Dallas.

Senge, P. (1990) *The Fifth Discipline – the Art and Practice of the Learning Organisation*. New York: Doubleday.

Senge, P. (1994) *The Fifth Discipline Fieldbook*. London: Nicholas Brealey.

Stacey, R. D. (1993) *Strategic Management and Organisational Dynamics*. London: Pitman.

Storey, J. (1992) *Developments in the Management of Human Resources*, Oxford: Blackwell.

Vaill, P. (1989) *Managing as a Performing Art*. San Francisco: Jossey-Bass.

Walsh, J. P. and Ungson, G. R. (1991) 'Organisation Memory', *Academy of Management Review*, 16(1).

Watkins, K. E. and Marsick, V. J. (1993) *Sculpting the Learning Organisation: Lessons in the art and science of systemic change*. San Francisco: Jossey-Bass.

Watkins, K. E. and Marsick, V. J. (1996) *In Action: Creating the Learning Organisation*. ASTD.

Chapter 16

HUMAN RESOURCE DEVELOPMENT AND THE CORPORATE UNIVERSITY

OBJECTIVES

By the end of this chapter you should be able to:

■ define the basic characteristics of a corporate university;

■ describe the origins of the concept;

■ distinguish between a number of approaches to operating a corporate university;

■ establish the similarities with and differences from a conventional university;

■ evaluate the benefits of having a corporate university;

■ locate corporate universities within an overall SHRD framework.

INTRODUCTION

Over the years organisations have imported a variety of terms from the academic arena to denote their in-house training and development provision. The terms 'training school' and 'management college' have often been preferred to 'training centre'. The Rover Group has an 'Academy of Learning'. IBM Rochester in the USA for some years had a 'Management College' which in the late 1980s was recast as IBM's Leadership College. In the UK IBM has a management business school.

However, inspired by an original idea generated at the Walt Disney Company, the notion of a corporate university is becoming increasingly fashionable as an overarching designation for formal learning and knowledge-creating activities and processes in an organisation. At the time of writing there are said to be some 1200 in existence, a 20 per cent increase from 1997 and a 300 per cent increase from 1990. (This figure, based on Meister (1998), is misleading in that not all of the so-called corporate universities actually use the term 'university' to encompass their activities. For example the Bank of Montreal which is featured in Meister's writings prefers the term 'Institute of Learning'. Of the 50 corporate universities listed by Meister, 27 (54 per cent) do not have the word 'university' in their title.) In North America they are particularly common and the evolution of some, such as the Motorola University, is well documented. Others from the USA include Air University, the arm of the US Air Force responsible for providing professional military education, and the National Defense University. General Motors Corporation announced the launch of General Motors University in 1997. In the UK they are an emergent phenomenon, with Unipart University well established, Anglian Water having recently developed a University of Water and British Aerospace having launched the British Aerospace 'Virtual' University in 1997. Elsewhere in Europe, examples include Cap Gemini University in France and Volvo University in Sweden. Many use the tag 'U', to signify that the overall framework for their training and development activities is known as a 'university'. Thus we have Motorola 'U', Sun 'U', AXA 'U', Unipart 'U' and so on.

In this chapter we shall explore a number of practical case studies from those organisations which have created corporate universities, and seek to identify core strands in their composition. Perhaps the most significant issue addressed is why corporations should feel the need to import the label 'university' as a designation for their structured learning activities. What is the underlying motive for its usage? Is it merely, as suggested in one debate on the subject, a dissatisfaction with the curricula of traditional universities, a desire to control what is taught and frustration over academics' misunderstanding of the 'real world' (Meister and King, 1996). This implied motive is detected in the following definition offered by one of the leading American exponents of the concept and a contributer to the above debate:

> Corporate universities are essentially the 'in-house' training facilities that have sprung up because of the frustration of businesses with the quality and content of post-secondary education on the one hand; and the need for life-long learning on the other. They have evolved at many organisations into strategic umbrellas for educating not only employees, but also customers and suppliers (Meister, 1998).

This definition raises a number of interesting subsidiary points. What if anything do corporate universities offer that is distinctive from previous in-house training provision? If it is no more than a relabelling of an organisation's training and development provision why should it be felt that a corporation's training and development function can truly be deemed a 'university'? It is not as if in-house training provision is new!

Who are the students? How are they selected? What do they study? Do the universities award degrees and if so on what basis? How is research perceived? How do they see their relationship with existing academic universities? How do they define their educational (as opposed to training) objectives? In other words what does the notion mean in practice?

It also reflects an emerging dichotomy in the attitude towards learning in organisations. The very ethos of a 'corporate university' can imply a centralist and structured model emphasising formal, off-the-job training and development activities at a seat of learning. This contrasts strongly with those organisations which are moving towards an approach where individuals are responsible for their own personal learning, with the emphasis being directed towards on-the-job or work-related experiential activities. Is this a genuine dichotomy, or are organisations such as Motorola able to balance centralist-taught and local-experiential learning patterns within the overall corporate university framework?

Some of my respondents in the UK have spoken with considerable fervour about the newness of approach which they feel is represented in their corporate universities and how it puts them at the forefront of SHRD practice. In the USA their longer history and more extensive usage has led to a greater diversity of perspectives. This chapter differentiates between so-called universities which seem to use the term to badge or re-badge their training departments and those who see it as a central plank of their attempt to become a knowledge-creating learning organisation.

Given the theme of this chapter it is useful to define the term 'university' as conventionally understood. The *Concise Oxford Dictionary* refers to 'an educational institution designed for instruction, examination, or both, of students in many branches of advanced learning, conferring degrees in various faculties, and often embodying colleges and similar institutions'. Faculties are groups of university departments concerned with a major division of knowledge and, especially in the business area, are often termed 'schools'. Universities are usually associated with providing an environment in which independence of thought and scholarly activity, including research, can be undertaken. Is this independence apparent, or even possible, in a corporate environment?

FROM TRAINING SCHOOLS TO CORPORATE UNIVERSITIES

One of the first historical surveys of corporate training mentions the introduction of a corporate training school at the National Cash Register Company in the United States in 1894. This focused on sales training and broad aspects of business administration (Spates, 1960). Eurich (1985) traces the 'individual corporation school, the predecessor of the modern corporate classroom' to an even earlier date, 1872. Over the years 'school' became a commonplace term to refer to the location where in-house off-the-job training was conducted. In the UK 'training schools' are particularly associated with apprentice training in the engineering industry. Bob Hamlin, who is currently responsible for HRD programmes at the University of Wolverhampton, recalls the early 1970s at Alfred Herbert Ltd, a specialist machine tools manufacturing company. Some 120 apprentices a year were recruited, and they spent 12 months in the training school before being allowed on to the factory floor for the remaining four years of their apprenticeship. The training school was on the same site as the factory, and constituted one-half of one of the factory production 'shops'. It consisted of a massive workshop where some 100 apprentices seated in rows were given instruction on milling machines and drilling machines. Annexed to the workshop were 'classrooms' where theoretical work instruction was provided. There were also 'commercial apprentices' who were given clerical and administration training. The apprentices were also expected to attend the local state-funded Further Education College as part of their studies.

On the whole 'training schools' were (and where they exist still are) in close proximity to the place of work. Some organisations went one step further with the introduction of 'colleges', often at a separate location, where some residential accommodation and a range of courses would be provided. These include, in the UK, the Civil Service Staff College, the Fire Service College and the Police Staff College. IBM UK and BT are amongst a number of commercial organisations which have a management college. The earliest of these colleges would seem to be of military origin. For example, the Britannia Royal Naval College was opened at Dartmouth in 1905 to provide a training base for naval officers. Previously training had been undertaken on vessels moored in the river estuary. In Japan, all large companies have their own education and training colleges, some of which – such as at Nippon Telegraph and Telephone, and Hitachi – have received much international benchmarking attention.

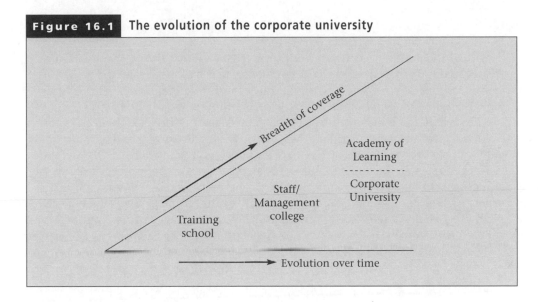

Figure 16.1 The evolution of the corporate university

The trend towards corporate *universities* emanated in the USA with the Walt Disney Company being the forerunner (*see* Fig. 16.2).

Figure 16.2 Disney University

World-wide, the Walt Disney company has some 33 000 employees, who are called 'cast members'. 'Cast members' need to be indoctrinated into the values of Disney before they go 'on stage'. Installing the Disney philosophy and 'keeping the juices flowing' for hourly paid and salaried 'cast members' is seen as an important and continuous process. Much of the training is done through classes at the so-called Disney University. Disney University is that aspect of the corporate structure that teaches 'Disney courtesy', and interprets company policy into training programmes.

The concept of the Disney University was first mooted in 1955, when Walt Disney decided that the new theme park at Anaheim in Los Angeles needed a training facility to introduce new employees to the business of entertainment. What started as a one-hour programme entitled 'You Create Happiness' grew until in the 1960s the Disney University was officially established. Today, each Disney facility has its own Disney University, responsible for training and development and employee communications. Successful candidates emerge with a Mousters Degree or a Ducktorate Degree. The Mousters Degree is in essence an attendance certificate. To achieve the award all students are required to complete 30 educational contact hours. These consist of 20 contact hours derived from participation in five core business classes, together with ten additional contact hours acquired

▶▶

▶▶ Figure 16.2 continued

through elective seminars and self-directed study. To gain the Ducktorate Degree, candidates must also present a portfolio of their learning for assessment.

The Walt Disney Company contends that its product is happiness. Irrespective of the role a cast member has been assigned, the most important part of training is how to attain the goal of happiness. The whole approach is designed to immerse the work-force into a 'corporate way' culture.

Part of the culture is associated with the 'Disney look'. Before the creation of Disneyland California in the early 1960s amusement parks had earned a bad reputation for lack of cleanliness, safety hazards, and rude employees. The 'Disney look' is wholesome entertainment, sparkling cleanliness and friendly employees.

The Disney orientation course for new employees, to prepare them to go on stage is part of the core curriculum held at the Disney University and lasts for one day. Called 'Traditions' it teaches new employees the language of Disney and aspects of the four Disney disciplines of safety, courtesy, show and efficiency. It also covers components of the organisation's corporate culture under the headings of Past (traditions), Present (operations) and Future (visions). Issues such as the strict dress code are reinforced – no moustaches or dangling earrings. 'Walt's cast should blend in with the show.' 'It's not my job' is a forbidden phrase.

The other four curriculum subjects in 1997 were:

■ *Maximising People Potential Through Leadership Flexibility*. Based on Hersey and Blanchard's Situational Leadership model (Hersey and Blanchard, 1969), it covers what are held to be core leadership behaviours such as co-operation, influence, integration, problem solving and quality improvement.

■ *Communicating with Style*. Participants will identify their predominant personality/communication style and learn how to better appreciate and communicate with others whose style is different from their own.

■ *The Ever-Changing World of Business*. Participants are provided with an opportunity to explore current business issues through headlines in newspapers and business journals. Topics addressed include rightsizing, empowerment and self-directed work teams. The session also addresses ways in which one can model Disney values and beliefs in the workplace.

■ *Understanding Differences and Coping with Cultural Change*. Participants are introduced to the many facets of diversity management through the cultural adjustment cycle. They explore the many ways in which people are grouped by cultural differences that extend beyond race, gender, birthplace and social status.

There is a manager of 'casting and training services' at the University. However Traditions is taught on a rotating basis by various cast members who initially volunteered and then successfully completed a screening and training programme. The process is called 'cross-utilisation training'. The cast members who conduct this 'cross-utilisation training' are called University Leaders and their assignment lasts for one year.

Other programmes at the University are open to outsiders and include 'People Management' and 'Quality Management' seminars (Martinez, 1992 and Disney documents).

FIRST-GENERATION CORPORATE UNIVERSITIES

The Disney approach has directly or indirectly influenced many of the subsequent wave of corporate universities up to the present. Typical features include a range, often quite narrow, of organisation-specific training modules requiring classroom attendance; an emphasis in the programme units on the acquisition of corporate values; reference to the creation of a 'world class' work-force; and in many cases careful attention given to providing extrinsic manifestations of achievement to programme participants.

The first three criteria are manifested in the recently established Reynolds University, formed in 1995 as a service to the 9000-strong Reynolds and Reynolds Company with its headquarters in Dayton, Ohio, and whose businesses include selling computer systems to healthcare organisations. Prior to that date there was no training function. According to a statement made by the CEO in 1996, 'Since people are the company's most important asset we launched Reynolds University and made major investments in new training programmes at all levels to drive people's skills to world class.'

Reynolds University is basically a building with classrooms offering a taught curriculum in the following areas.

- *Common Culture*: orientation to the culture, organisation and business of Reynolds and to how things work.
- *Team Behaviours*: establishing and building skills necessary to function successfully in a team-based environment.
- *Core Expertise*: providing core competences for individual effectiveness and effective participation in responding to customer needs.
- *Functional Expertise*: provision of specialised skills in designated functional areas.

For the first three years of its existence, the Reynolds University was run by two full-time members of staff and it continues to be heavily reliant on external partners for its programme delivery. In many ways its approach has marked similarities to that of any newly formed training department. Key activities involved:

- proposal of a university vision, mission and a business plan. The mission adopted by Reynolds 'U' emphasises *targeted* learning and development;
- establishment of an advisory board consisting of internal and external representatives;
- creation of a curriculum framework;
- revision and validation of vision and plan;
- obtaining staff;
- seeking external suppliers (partners) to deliver programmes;
- seeking internal support from, and creating partnerships with, the businesses;
- creation of a 'university' brochure, marketing image and a brand;
- evaluation of programmes, including demonstration of benefits to the business; and testimonials (from Luckenbach and Wade, 1998).

The value-oriented connotations are also exemplified by the Manco University, which is particularly interesting because of its overt inspiration from Disney, the hands-on involvement of the chief executive and its use as a public debating chamber (*see* Fig. 16.3).

Figure 16.3 Manco University

Manco Inc. is a $60 million company, based in Ohio, which markets tapes, weather stripping and mailing supplies. Walt Disney provided inspiration to its Chief Executive Officer in terms of its approach to marketing and packaging, and the Manco 'Duck' is a corporate symbol. The in-house staff magazine, which is called 'Duck Tales', includes a section which philosophises about business in general. One extract written by the CEO stated:

> We've recommitted our organisation to a major investment in time and money to improve the educational level of all Manco partners. One of the most difficult obstacles to cultural change in any organisation is the reluctance of senior managers to admit that they don't know everything . . . Today's leaders must be students of change first before they become teachers of change to others.

In order to ensure that learning is translated into new organisational behaviour, forums are held at the 'Manco University', which is a corporate conference room in which a variety of courses are offered. Senior executives meet there every Thursday afternoon. In the evening a debate on ideas about the business and the industry takes place, orchestrated by the CEO and to which all members of the company are invited.

Source: Garfield, 1992.

Corporate University change (1998) reveals that 16 per cent of corporate universities report to a Chief Executive Officer and Meister (1998) emphasises the importance of the CEO's backing at the launch stage. Mention of the corporate university in the annual report is also seen as a desirable demonstration of ongoing commitment. A typical example is provided by the following quotation from J. Arthur Gensler of the USA-based Gensler Group, a multinational architectural/ design corporation:

> In order to help each individual to become the best that he or she can be, we invest about one million dollars annually in firm-wide education programmes. Learning can be formal (our long-standing Gensler University programmes) or informal (in-house workshops, seminars and task force meetings) (J. Arthur Gensler, Annual Report, 1996).

In this example (as with Reynolds 'U') the 'university' is specifically associated with formal in-house training and development courses as opposed to more experiential and *ad hoc* learning activities. Helping 'each individual to be the best that he or she can be' has a self-consciously inspirational ring about it, and is undoubtedly heart-felt. It is nevertheless unclear what this means as a practical proposition, beyond helping to equip individuals with the skills and knowledge that are needed within the confines of the employing organisation.

Another much publicised first-generation corporate university is McDonald's. A particularly noteworthy feature of the McDonald's model is its exclusivity. Most corporate universities are open to all employees. Access to the McDonald's campus is very restricted. Conventional universities of course do not provide unrestricted access to the public at large, but at the same time entry is not reserved to individuals just because of their occupancy of a specific job role (*see* Fig. 16.4).

| **Figure 16.4** | McDonald's Hamburger University |

McDonald's is the largest fast-food chain in the world, with some 12 000 stores. In the USA it is the country's largest employer of young people, with about half of the 500 000+ employees being under the age of 20. In terms of training it claims to be larger even than the US Army for the size and scope of its classes. The restaurants are operated by the company, or, under the terms of franchise arrangements, by franchisees who are independent third parties. There are also examples of joint venture agreements between the company and local business people. The corporate university at McDonald's opened in 1963, is called 'Hamburger University' and is located at an 80-acre campus outside Chicago, Illinois. All the company's restaurant managers and franchise holders must attend a development programme there. On campus there are simultaneous translation facilities for 18 languages. Each year more than 3000 franchise holders and managers graduate with a degree in hamburgerology. Topics covered in a formal classroom-based management development programme include management skills, market evaluation, financial budgets and the reinforcement of the corporate philosophy. This latter is the brainchild of Ray Kroc, who bought the company from the founders in 1961, and is based on the slogan of Q.S.C.&V. (Quality food; fast, friendly Service; restaurant Cleanliness; and a menu that provides Value) in the context of a family-oriented image. The training programme at Hamburger U is designed to reinforce the uniform global standards the company lays down for quality, service, cleanliness and value. Attendance for franchise holders is part of the two-year period which they must spend in training before being allowed to open their restaurant. There is an additional expectation that during these two years they work for about 2000 uncompensated hours in a McDonald's restaurant.

Ordinary employees do not attend the Hamburger U campus. According to the 1990 McDonald's annual report their training begins with in-store videotapes and one-to-one instruction 'even before the crew member cooks their first french fry'. McDonald's was founded on a principle of uniformity and the company's 600-page policies and procedures manual spells out the precise operational details for each station at the restaurant to ensure consistency and quality of products served. In recent years there has been more flexibility allowed at restaurants because of changing customer expectations. McDonald's has adopted more of a 'do whatever it takes to make a customer happy' strategy (Therrien, 1991).

A number of other HRD initiatives exist independently of the Hamburger U. For example McDonald's provides training into employment programmes for both the elderly and people with disabilities – known respectively as McMasters and McJobs.

Source: Orsin *et al.*, 1993.

In the UK, the retail chain Asda has created a university with a different kind of exclusivity. The Asda Academy is described as a 'university' for butchers, bakers, greengrocers and vintners. There are four 'faculties' within the Asda Academy to reflect the various training schemes – the bakery craft and meat craft schemes being launched in 1995, the greengrocer scheme in 1997 and the beer, wine and spirit scheme at the beginning of 1998. At the time of writing there are plans to extend the academy to include fishmongers and, for the delicatessen counter, cooked meat and dairy skills. However, managers will be excluded – the focus is on traditional produce skills. The programmes are recognised by industry bodies such as the Meat and Livestock Commission and are linked to occupation-specific NVQs.

Graduates from the academy are rewarded with a celebratory night out, a certificate and in-store display which brings their achievement to the attention of customers and colleagues. In a major departure for Asda, members of the academy also wear a special name badge, a black and gold badge which marks them as skilled craftsmen.

It is remarkable how many US training and development departments have over the last two decades designated or rebadged themselves as universities. Kanter (1989) refers without comment or surprise to monthly 'leadership experience' events run in 1985 for groups of middle managers at a seaside location in California by Apple University, which she defines as the training and development arm of Apple Computer Inc. This has not just been a US phenomenon. The Thomson University is the training and development arm of the Thomson Corporation which is a Canadian-based multinational group specialising in financial services and professional publishing. The university mission is 'to increase the speed that employees learn required skills and knowledge and apply those skills and knowledge to the success of the business'. Underpinning this mission is the belief that in today's business environment, the speed of learning is a competitive advantage, necessary to serve customers both internal and external. To achieve this goal, Thomson University focuses upon four strategies for delivering educational programmes and information. These are:

- *Performance consulting*: providing customised training and facilitation designed to meet specific business needs;
- *Open Enrolment Courses*: regularly scheduled training courses, which are offered through their course catalogue. These were 263 courses scheduled for 1997, offered at a variety of locations, primarily in North America. Broad subject areas covered include: Leadership and Management Development; Change Management; Marketing/Sales; Customer Service; Team Building; Personal Productivity; Human Resources Management'; Self Study;
- *Self-paced learning*: a variety of self-based learning media such as books and computer programs which are designed to facilitate individual learning;
- *Information sharing*: information gained through conferences, symposia and learning networks which is made available to Thomson employees.

Figure 16.5 provides one further example of a first-generation corporate university.

Figure 16.5 AXA University

The AXA Group is a multinational corporation, the world's second-largest insurer and its number one asset manager. It has more than 100 000 employees and agents working in more than 60 countries. AXA University plays a crucial role in creating the shared values and common corporate culture that define the AXA Group. The University's role is to design and offer customised training programmes to Group employees. The seeds of the University were sown in 1986 in the Sahara desert during an international management retreat.

There are three kinds of programmes:

■ the 'confirmation programmes' that transmit the theoretical foundation which helps to develop attitudes that are compatible with the Group's values and corporate mission;

■ the 'open-ended' programmes that address the needs of a different audience. Their aim is to encourage participants to engage in open-ended reflection and strategic thinking, in part by providing key concepts for understanding the world around them;

■ 'customised programmes', which are offered in response to Group or company needs.

Every year more than 2000 Group managers participate in the AXA Manager programme at the Management Training Centre near Bordeaux. Some 80 senior manager instructors lead week-long training sessions that bring together 40 managers of different nationalities.

The notion of a 'confirmation programme' sits uneasily with the idea of a conventional university. The terminology adopted is redolent of cultural conditioning, which may be seen to be very important in terms of trying to develop a set of core values consistently applied across five continents. However it does not seem to encourage challenge or independent thinking which one would normally see as key ingredients of a university ethos and which to some extent are reflected in the 'open-ended' programmes.

SECOND-GENERATION CORPORATE UNIVERSITIES: THE MOTOROLA UNIVERSITY

Second-generation corporate universities can be defined as those which go beyond a dependence on a relatively narrow, and heavily value-driven, culturally specific curriculum. They often tend to emanate from a desire to embed learning from TQM initiatives into the fabric of the organisation. The overall HRD framework is in turn broader and more encompassing. The most detailed exposition to date of how a large corporation has developed and implemented the idea of a more broad-based corporate university was provided in a seminal 1990 *Harvard Business Review* article on Motorola (Wiggenhorn, 1990) a summary of which is given below. The article provides a real flavour of the values and associated practices which Motorola attach to the concept. As described, it is still culturally specific in terms of programmes delivered and approaches to delivery and it causes one to reflect whether that is unavoidable in any institution for which learning is not the primary object but can be no more than a means to an end.

The article claims that the original suggestion of a corporate university was mooted in the USA in 1979 by Robert W. Galvin, the Motorola CEO at that time. William Wiggenhorn, subsequently to become the first president of Motorola University, interviewed 22 senior Motorola executives to get their reaction, which at the time was not favourable. Concern was expressed that a university, so called, would drain resources from the business instead of adding value. Wiggenhorn himself was anxious that the term 'university' was too pretentious for what would be no more than a forum for training and education for the work-force and its managers, and not a seat of free and open enquiry. Instead, what was established in 1980 was the Motorola Training and Education Service (MTEC), with objectives of expanding participative management processes in the corporation and helping improve product quality tenfold in five years. As originally constituted, MTEC had its own board of directors, which included the CEO, two of his top executives and senior managers from each of the operating units.

Like many organisations in the 1980s, Motorola gave a significant amount of attention to quality-oriented training. A five-part curriculum was developed for the factory-floor work-force. This consisted of:

- statistical process control;
- basic industrial problem solving;
- how to present conceptual material. This could entail an hourly paid worker, say, presenting a technical solution to a problem to an engineer;
- a course on effective meetings that emphasised the contribution of both participant and chairperson;
- goal setting, that is, how to define objectives, how to describe them in writing; how to measure progress.

By the early 1980s, at a typical Motorola plant with 2500 employees, the quality programme was taking up some 50 000 hours of employees' time per year on off-the-job training. However, it was not proving particularly effective. Workers who had learned how to keep a Pareto chart and make an Ishikawa fishbone diagram found they were rarely asked to reproduce these at the factory floor. This was diagnosed as being in large part because senior and middle managers had not adjusted their behavioural patterns, which in turn was partly because they had not attended an equivalent programme. By 1984 it was decided to offer to senior managers the same course that the line workers were experiencing. The quality training message was reinforced by CEO stating that quality should be given even more attention than financial results.

Senior executive training events were added to over the period 1985–7, during which time the top 200 executives spent 17 days each in the classroom. The curriculum entailed:

- ten days on manufacturing;
- five days on global competition;
- two days on cycle-time management.

A shortened version of the programme was then offered throughout the organisation. Thus the ten days for a senior executive were reduced to eight hours for a production worker.

Motorola then had a major surprise. Since 1980, when MTEC had been initiated, it had been assumed that the work-force had the basic skills for the jobs they were doing. MTEC had seen itself as an agent for change, a vocational instructor in the new quality skills and measurements that would place Motorola at the forefront of the global electronics industry. However, there was discovered a high degree of illiteracy and an absence of basic maths amongst the work-force, for a high percentage of whom English was a second language. To meet its business needs, Motorola suddenly discovered that it had to add remedial elementary education to its core curriculum. It was in the education business!

Remedial education was not an area in which Motorola professed to have skills, so it turned to local community colleges and other institutions for support. At the same time, the shock of discovering that so many of its work-force lacked basic numeracy and literacy skills led to an investigation of whether schools and colleges equipped their pupils and students with elementary technical and business skills such as accounting and computer operations and basic electronics. When it was discovered that they did not, Motorola turned to the community colleges which were providing remedial English and maths training. However the courses on offer and the facilities provided were not up to modern industrial standards. These discoveries collectively led to the building of educational partnerships and dialogues which led to the formation of Motorola University in 1989.

All teachers at Motorola University are certificated at the end of a 160-hour course of tuition. One key difference from a conventional university is in the treatment of the subject-matter of courses. Teachers are talked through each course they might have to deliver. Take a course such as Effective Meetings. Motorola does not want each teacher to impart his or her version of the topic; it must be taught the Motorola way. Academics, contends Wiggenhorn, have difficulty with this. They may produce a fascinating course but Motorola cannot have 3000 people learning 35 different versions of how to conduct and participate in effective meetings.

Some 1200 people were involved in training and education at Motorola in 1990, of which 410 were at the University. Of these 110 were full-time and 300 part-time. Three groups have been found to make effective teachers. One group is recently retired Motorola employees who believe in what they are teaching, know how to apply it and are full of work-related stories and anecdotes. A second group are married women with college degrees whose children have left home. A third group are individuals who have taken early retirement from other companies. The process of finding teachers operates on a reciprocal network basis. Other companies, such as AT&T or IBM, provide a list of 100 potential instructors who have just left their employ, and Motorola provides a list in return.

Involved in co-ordinating the whole effort are 23 product design engineers who function, using the university analogy, like departmental Chairs. The senior product manager is like a Dean. The faculty are the actual course writers, audiovisual specialists and instructors.

In 1990 there were three elements to the curriculum:

1 *The functional curriculum*. Each functional area (engineering, manufacturing, sales and marketing) is divided into relational skills, technical skills and business skills. Relational skills, which consist of topics such as customer satisfaction, effective meetings, effective negotiations and effective presentations, are the responsibility of Motorola U. Technical and business skills are delivered in co-operation with community colleges and technical schools.

2 *Culture*. This includes team-building activities, and the iteration of stories from Motorola's history.

3 *Remedial reading and maths*.

The overall investment in these three areas was in the order of $120 million per annum in 1990. The investment to correct the literacy problem was $35 million.

The model of the university is evolving. There is an attempt to make the education relevant to the corporation, the job and the individual. There is no intention to grant degrees, but to design courses that accrediting boards will certify and that the universities that give degrees will count as providing credits. There is a desire to establish sustainable partnerships with established universities, both in the USA and globally.

The word 'university' is seen as being ambitious but is designed to arouse curiosity and to raise the expectations of both the work-force and the training and education staff. It could have been termed an 'educational resource facility', but that would not have animated anyone (Wiggenhorn, 1990).

By 1998 Motorola's strategic planning process had identified five issues critical for the business that the university must tackle:

■ leadership and management development in a global market;

■ systems for the customer;

■ business growth through organisational renewal;

■ global brand equity management;

■ knowledge management.

Serritella (1998), the Head of Motorola University, argues that it is essential that the university builds processes to establish and maintain aligned systems in order to support these critical business issues.

For me, the key points that emerge are the following:

1 The idea of 'university' at Motorola is designed to be a metaphor, an analogy. There is no suggestion that it is a similar entity to conventional universities.

2 Nevertheless, it is presenting very specific challenges to the education sector in terms of the vocational relevance of courses offered and standards attained.

3 The term 'university' is chosen for its symbolic connotations. It is designed to have an inspirational effect on its contributors and customers, to generate energy and make people feel they want to be associated with it and to attend.

4 It has caused Motorola to think in terms of providing an educational facility instead of a training activity. In some ways this is rather misleading. Many of the activities undertaken seem to be more developmental than educational. However its involvement in remedial learning has provided a significant lever to extending its remit into a broader educational arena.

5 The original prescriptive nature of its approach to the curriculum and materials to be presented would be unacceptable in a genuine university context, as Wiggenhorn recognises. There is also no sense of the spirit of enquiry and freedom of thought that he himself provided as a caveat to the notion of 'university' when it was first voiced. It does seem rather pretentious that he could suggest that the term 'university' is being used instead of 'educational resource facility'.

6 In strictly HRD terms this is a most exciting development. It provides a real focus for the HRD effort, and a real sense of purpose for what is being undertaken. It is providing learning which is of broader social relevance than merely benefiting the organisation itself – although the learning that is being provided relates to basic skills, and is of an order that one would not expect a higher education institution to be undertaking.

7 The initial driving force was around the search for 'quality' and this reinforces the perception that so many of the major initiatives in the field of HRD have been inspired by the TQM movement. In this instance, it was encouraging – from an HRD perspective – to see the key involvement of HRD as a functional area from the outset.

8 The general impression gained from Wiggenhorn's article is that the whole initiative was subject to central control, co-ordination and direction. The CEO was strongly committed to it. He drove it through by dint of his own personal energy and commitment to quality. For him the link between HRD and quality seemed clear. As with other US organisations, the impetus for the development of a corporate university came from the CEO or Chairman.

9 Motorola emphasises the importance of developing partnerships with external educational bodies, recognising that it is not realistic to expect the corporation to possess the range of in-house skills to encompass all of the learning needs of individuals in today's highly technical environment. The establishment of partnerships with external academic institutions including universities is another distinctive feature of a second-generation corporate university.

10 An emerging issue has to do with funding implications. Are broad-ranging second-generation corporate universities only applicable to resource-rich institutions such as Motorola which can justify pumping $120 million each year into sustaining education-oriented activities?

VISION AND MISSION STATEMENTS OF CORPORATE UNIVERSITIES

It is not unusual for corporate universities to produce their own discrete vision and mission statements, in the same way that a number of training and development departments, and a number of conventional universities, have done.

The Iams Company was founded in 1946 and has a quarter share of the $3 billion premium dog and cat food business in the USA. The founder had a vision providing a comprehensive educational programme for employees and partners, who included external contributors such as vets. This led to the formation of the Iams University where the overarching values are articulated as follows:

- *Vision*: To be among the best educational organisations in the food industry.
- *Mission*: To provide Iams employees and our business partners with the knowledge and skills to achieve the Iams vision.

Recognising the element of wish-fulfilment embodied in such statements, we do nevertheless gain an insight into how the concept of university is perceived in those organisations that have produced them. The Iams University mission statement is clearly instrumental and utilitarian in its orientation. It is concerned with skills and knowledge in a restricted sense – that is, those which will be of value to the parent organisation. There is nothing unexceptional in this; it is unrealistic to think that organisational training and development departments are going to see their vocation as educating society at large. This, however, is the remit of conventional universities!

THE RELATIONSHIP BETWEEN EDUCATION AND TRAINING

Whereas the Motorola University does seem to have given some thought to the relationship between education and training and is operating on a reasonably large scale, this is not the case for the majority of so-called universities in the USA. A typical example is offered by Mervyn's University (*see* Fig. 16.6).

Figure 16.6	Mervyn's University

Mervyn's is a $4.5 billion retail chain, selling clothing and housewares. In 1995 it had 265 stores across the United States. It is half-way between a discount store and a department store.

Rapid expansion in the 1980s more than tripled the number of stores, changing Mervyn's from a small, family-owned department store into a national retailer. By the early 1990s, the company's distribution and buying systems were struggling to keep up with the growth. At the same time, California, where 45 per cent of Mervyn's stores were located, was deep in recession. One of the problems identified was a lack of managerial skills, and high labour turnover, amongst the departmental store managers. To help resolve these difficulties, the regional managers, in conjunction with the training department, created Mervyn's University (MU).

MU claims to have a number of trappings associated with a conventional university. It has a campus, a faculty and alumni. It even has sweatshirts. But there is no resemblance to a university in other respects. This is partly a matter of scale. There are three well-equipped classrooms, customised videos, five course designers, seven full-time trainers and several administrative support staff.

The manager of programme development for MU sees it as a place for ongoing dialogue, as an ever-evolving forum in which ideas are exchanged through an experiential learning environment focused on continuous improvement. There is a reliance on a threefold model of training:

1 Training must originate from a perceived need, identified by line managers.

2 Training delivery should involve line managers, to increase credibility and to draw on their practical experience.

3 The training ethos should be experiential, drawing on practical exercises.

▶▶

▶▶ Figure 16.6 continued

> The core business is accordingly to provide experience-based training programmes, the corner-stone of which is the 'Area Manager in Training'. This is a ten-week programme for new area managers, involving an initial five weeks on-the-job training, followed by one week's classroom instruction, and concluding with four weeks of supervised practice. The classroom modules cover performance management, leadership and the presentation and management of merchandise. At the end of the week, trainees present a sales plan, a shortage-reduction plan, and a merchandise-presentation plan to a team of store managers. They must also pass short answer and essay questions. They are provided with detailed feedback about their performance over the week.

Source: Downs, 1995.

Corporate universities at business unit level

Some organisations have developed corporate universities at business unit level. An example is that of the Ford Heavy Truck University, which was set up over the period 1985–7 following a training needs analysis carried out by an external consultant and which initially offered training programmes for the sales force and dealer principals. It was the first example of a corporate university in the Ford Group and also unique in the heavy truck industry. Speakers from the company at the 1994 conference of the American Society for Training and Development in Anaheim, California, stated that before 1988 training was static, reactive, forced and unenthusiastic. In particular it was unrelated to the corporate vision and goals, and dealers were dissatisfied. By 1994 the corporate university had established a backcloth for an approach that was held to be dynamic, proactive and highly successful, credible with both dealers and employees, now known as associates.

Programmes are linked to a three-level certification process. Successful completion of five courses results in one becoming a 'Certified Associate', ten courses a 'Senior Associate' and 15 courses a 'Master Associate'. Associates who successfully attend and complete all three stages get a plaque entitled 'Ultimate Achievement Masters Associate'. The course content is customised and delivery formats vary to include seminars, self-study and satellite delivery.

In many respects, the example follows a fairly conventional path for corporate universities in the USA, and the focus on dealers as well as employees reflects the influence of Meister (op. cit.). However, the most interesting feature is the fact that the 'university' has started at business unit level. If this trend continues, we could well witness each of the various subsidiary companies in a large holding group having its own corporate university. That, of course, is quite a feasible consequence of divisionalisation and local autonomy.

The course-based non-campus corporate university

A number of corporate universities seem to be based on the courses they offer, as opposed to functioning out of a distinctive campus, or even a suite of training rooms. An example is the Dexter University which, inaugurated in the 1970s, operates as an annual event. It can be described as a concentrated week-long experience in Connecticut for executives covering a series of programme objectives. In 1997 these were as follows:

■ to provide a learning opportunity linking contemporary knowledge and training in creativity, process improvement, marketing, finance and communications to the current business activities in Dexter;

■ to create a common developmental experience among key Dexter individuals that will encourage and enhance understanding between facilities and disciplines and enable participants to address business challenges, both now and in the future;

■ to offer a unique setting where senior management and course participants can come together to share experiences, learn more about each other's businesses and appreciate the strengths of Dexter as a diversified speciality materials company.

The programme is delivered by a mixture of consultants, graduate school faculty staff and internal executives.

The non-campus virtual university

A feature of more recent thinking on corporate universities has been the notion of 'virtuality'. Meister (op. cit.) contends that while corporate universities tended in the past to operate out of a campus or physical location, today the emphasis has shifted from place 'to developing a learning process where networking the entire organisation's knowledge becomes the priority'.

The relationship of corporate universities to conventional universities

In 1998 the results of a survey of 100 deans of corporate universities was published. The survey was sponsored by AACSB, the accrediting body for US business schools and carried out by Corporate University Xchange (1998), a New York-based consultancy led by Jeanne Meister. The sample consisted of 90 deans from the USA, and a further ten representing institutions in South Africa, France, Germany, The Netherlands and Venezuela.

One of the conclusions of the survey was that conventional universities should treat the rise of corporate universities as an opportunity rather than a threat.

Some corporate universities are attempting to develop degree-awarding powers themselves. But the survey suggests a decisive shift in corporate universities' thinking towards developing joint degree programmes with institutions of higher education, mostly in business administration, computer science, engineering and finance.

Almost two-thirds of corporate universities have an alliance with an undergraduate college offering three or four year courses. By the end of 1999 this number is planned to rise to 78 per cent.

Also notable was the fact that half of the deans questioned have alliances with distance learning vendors, a trend that was set to increase to 78 per cent. Only 16 per cent have links with Internet-based universities, but this figure is set to rise to 62 per cent.

Meister comments on the likely effects of a requirement to become a profit centre that has surfaced among a growing number of corporate universities. The resultant need to operate on a self-funded basis means they are more likely to explore new ventures with outsiders to supplement their corporate education and training budget, than to embark on the much more expensive route of gaining degree-awarding powers in their own right.

This need to demonstrate profitability has influenced the criteria sought from potential partners. High on the corporate deans' list of priorities was a desire that their partner should 'share risks'. Other important criteria listed in the survey responses were 'flexibility and responsiveness', 'technology for learning' and 'performance measures'.

CORPORATE UNIVERSITIES IN THE UK – TOWARDS THE THIRD-GENERATION VIRTUAL UNIVERSITY

Given the proliferation of corporate universities in the USA, and the tendency for US management initiatives to be imported into UK practice, it is surprising that until recently they have not attracted more attention in the UK. This situation is now changing. Following a pioneer initiative by Unipart in 1993 (*see* Fig. 16.7) a select but growing number of large corporations have now introduced them.

Figure 16.7 Unipart University

Unipart, until 1987 a subsidiary and not particularly profitable business of the UK motor manufacturing group BL, was subject to a management buyout in that year. A proportion of the shares were made available for employees to buy.

In the late 1980s, following the buyout, it turned its attention to quality management and customer-care issues, running 'Putting people first' courses akin to those offered by British Airways. These developed into a more sophisticated quality management programme known as 'My contribution counts', and an approach to quality circles, known as 'Our contribution counts'.

By 1992 Unipart senior management had established a steering group to review the whole training package, believing that the existence of a sounder skills base among employees was a key route to competitive advantage. As part of its research the group looked at various examples of both 'company universities' and 'learning organisations', including the corporate universities at Motorola and McDonald's.

Opened in the autumn of 1993, the Unipart University ('U') was not intended to be additional to the company's training but to be seen as *the* training. One of the themes was to educate factory floor employees in the principles of lean production, continuous improvement and related issues, such as managing new technology.

In 1994 the company developed a mission to become 'the world's best lean enterprise'. The 'university' was seen an integral mechanism for achieving this and for becoming a learning organisation. In-house documents state that the 'U' exists to foster a climate of learning and a continuous reskilling culture with a focus on quality and customer service.

▶▶

▶▶ Figure 16.7 continued

Don Jones, professor of motor industry management at Cardiff Business School, was appointed as the first 'principal' of the 'U', chairing the deans' group. This consisted of the managing directors from all nine of the group's businesses, each of which is designated a 'faculty'. The support staff – both trainers and personnel professionals – make up the 'core' faculty.

All in-house courses are now run by and from the 'U'. In addition, many managers, including all of the managing directors, are involved in developing and delivering training. A major role of the 'U' has been to train these managers, together with some supervisors and even a few production workers, to be trainers.

The activities of the 'U' are not restricted to employee training. Learning about continuous improvement and lean production is also being shared among all stakeholders, including customers, suppliers and the community. The supplier development programme is called the 'Ten to Zero' programme, shortened to TTZ and so called because it teaches people to measure the effectiveness of any customer-supplier relationship (internal or external) on a scale of zero to ten against ten principles, such as sharing information, time delays, number of defects, etc.

The Head of Training at Unipart in 1996 saw the 'U' as a catalyst for getting training on to the strategic agenda because it provided 'a highly visible infrastructure for discussion on training with management involvement . . . it gets more exposure . . . it has been a focus and almost a laboratory in which to conduct experiments'.

The whole offering is based in a plush new suite on the ground floor of the group HQ building in Cowley, Oxford. It includes a state of the art lecture theatre, four training rooms and two small meeting rooms.

Sources: Pickard (1995); Campbell (1996).

Like Motorola, Unipart 'U' derives its impetus from the quality management movement. It clearly is strongly supported by the top management team, who are maintaining a hands-on approach. One particular feature of note is the importance that is being afforded to incorporating suppliers and customers in the overall equation. Unipart pride themselves on the fact that the university is not just one aspect of training provision as at Motorola, but encompasses all training. Nevertheless the emphasis on course-delivered training, supporting a 'lean enterprise' mission, gives the impression of a somewhat restricted and particular focus to its range of activities. Despite its claims to be a central plank in the learning organisation, there seems to be a limit to the range of learning and development concerns included in its ambit, with experiential learning, career development and other personal development activities apparently excluded from its sphere of operations. In that sense it echoes a number of the US prototypes we have referred to.

Figure 16.8 looks at a more recent corporate university, Anglian Water's University of Water.

Figure 16.8   University of Water

In 1995 Anglian Water Ltd, one of the privatised water companies, formally accepted the term 'University of Water' as a key plank in its attempt to become a 'Learning Organisation', which the business had previously committed to. The idea originated from Peter Matthews, who was one of the first Directors of Innovation to be appointed in a British company, and was developed in partnership with the Director of HR. The *Aqua Universitas* aims to create work environments that promote learning, encourage knowledge creation and enable collaboration with external partners, especially higher education. According to Matthews: 'The learning organisation is a logical progression towards the knowledge creating company and our university provides the opportunities for this process to take place.'

It was felt that the 14 businesses could be organised into four key areas, or 'knowledge grounds', which would form the basis for learning and development:

■ Humanities and Social Science

■ Finance and Information Technology

■ Environmental Planning

■ Technology and Engineering.

Each of these became a faculty of the new university. All business activities were held to fall into one of these areas.

The university has no Vice Chancellor or Rector or Provost, but each faculty has a dean, who is a member of the Board of Directors. Current role holders include the Managing Director, the General Manager, and the Managing Director of Anglian Water Ltd International.

There is currently a debate taking place as to whether it should be a campus university or a virtual university. Arguments in favour of the latter include the opportunities the Intranet offers for provision of knowledge. Thus, although there is no university library, there is an Encyclopaedia of Water on the Intranet. So, if any student wished to obtain information on, say, the benchmarking of customer service, there is, as my respondent put it, a reservoir of knowledge.

Each of the faculties is divided into a number of colleges, ranging from one to four depending on the size of the faculty. The colleges have partnership arrangements with conventional universities for the delivery of programmes and qualifications. For example, the customised MSc in Customer Service is accredited and delivered by an external university. The intention is that internal staff will increasingly be involved in the delivery of courses.

Programmes for the university are divided into modules with credit points attached to them. Some managers may not wish to undertake a fully fledged Masters degree, but will take some of the units contributing to it. On successful completion they would then be provided with internal certificates.

One of the roles that has been created in the HR directorate is that of 'Facilitator of the University of Water'. Facilitators tend to come from an operational background, and have the responsibility of acting as internal consultants to the 14 business units, helping the people in the businesses to say what they need. In addition each business unit has its own 'learning champion'.

▶▶

▶▶ Figure 16.8 continued

The underpinning philosophy of learning is that there is a need for educational provision to be job specific and to have a clear vocational orientation. It is important to give people the tools to do the job. Additionally, there should be personal ownership of one's own development.

One of the significant features of the Anglian Water model is the relationships that they are developing with conventional universities. In common with many organisations, it has developed relationships with universities whereby in-house programmes can be offered which lead to the award of a university qualification. They can be wholly or partly delivered by either partner, but the university is responsible for quality assurance arrangements. Anglian Water is not competing as an awarding body.

The university incorporates a number of open-learning centres which provide a focal point for obtaining advice and sharing ideas. They are particularly important because employees are scattered around a number of counties.

Compared to the earlier Unipart 'U', the University of Water seems to be more broad ranging in scope, and in many respects more advanced in concept. The links with what is held to be a 'learning organisation' are more clearly drawn out, and there is a sense that knowledge creation and generation, as opposed to skills acquisition, is important.

The perspective adopted by British Aerospace, whose corporate university is of even more recent origin, is that it is not a campus but a process (*see* Fig. 16.9).

Figure 16.9 British Aerospace Virtual University

In May 1997, British Aerospace announced the launch of its new corporate university and the appointment of its first vice chancellor/managing director. The expectation was that it would take one and a half years to become fully operational. There are three faculties.

1 *Faculty of Engineering and Manufacturing Technology*. This covers traditional R&D-type activities and has developed links with mainstream universities in order to keep at the forefront of technology development. The faculty programme is intended to be more than a reordering of what is currently being undertaken. It is hoped that it will seek new directions in the interdisciplinary development of engineering research and technology relevant to the future policy and competitive position of the company. At first sight this faculty seems to be quite 'concrete' as opposed to 'virtual', since it is based on existing, location-specific, functional activities.

2 *Faculty of Learning*. This is intended to 'reach out' to, to encourage, facilitate and support the learning of, all of the 44 000 employees, most of whom do not have degrees and for whom the notion of 'going to university' might be seen as elitist. It is seen as a major component in the overall driving concept of a 'learning corporation'.

▶▶

▶▶ Figure 16.9 continued

3 *Business School.* This is intended to provide a focus on the rapidly evolving business climate for executive and management development, corporate learning, business process improvement, benchmarking and best practice, as well as to undertake strategic studies in support of marketing and strategic planning. This would incorporate developing advanced management techniques such as scenario planning. Within the Business School is a corporate learning unit, with staff operating as 'knowledge brokers' for purposes such as benchmarking.

The overall philosophy sees the new university as the future 'intellectual engine' of British Aerospace. Additionally, it will provide educational opportunities for partner companies, customers and suppliers. There are tensions associated with this. For example British Aerospace is in partnership with Aerospatiale, the French company based in Toulouse, on the Airbus project. However, it would be reluctant to allow Aerospatiale full access to the corporate university because of commercially sensitive research-based activities in areas not associated with the Airbus collaboration.

It is not to be a campus university, but a 'virtual' university, in which the 39 sites both in the UK and abroad are connected via the Intranet.

The virtual university provides accredited courses, ranging from NVQs to Ph.Ds. It will not be awarding its own degrees, but partnering leading edge conventional universities and colleges. Each faculty can be expected to find its own university partners, recognising the fact that expertise across the range is not contained in one particular university environment. Currently there is no intention to have their own in-house professors, but that will not exclude the notion of visiting professorships.

The university is intended to be an integral part of the business, governed by a Strategy Board made up of senior directors from across the company along with respected figures from the academic and business world. Each faculty will have a dean, appointed from within the company, and a Faculty Advisory Board. Each business will also have its own nominated 'champion' of learning.

At the time of writing, discussions were still taking place on the nature of the university library. The impression gained is that there will be the equivalent of open-learning drop-in centres at specific locations.

The incoming vice chancellor contended that:

British Aerospace wants to develop people across the organisation – this is seen as the key to the future. This Virtual University will increase the company's ability to offer educational opportunities relevant to the business and to as wide a cross section of the work-force as possible.

Whilst other companies in Britain and abroad have set up their own Training institutes to address their individual needs, the British Aerospace Virtual University is unique. It combines continuous learning with research and technology acquisition: with strategic development focused directly on the local and global needs of the business and our employees.

Alumni associations

Other university-based terms are coming into vogue, even where the notion of university is not drawn upon. For example, there is increasing reference to the 'alumni' of programmes attended and the creation of 'alumni associations'. One example is the Willis Corroon Management Development Consortium (Anfield, 1997). This is a consortium consisting of eight of the UK's best-known companies, including Rolls-Royce, Standard Chartered Bank, Tesco, Willis Corroon Group and the Halifax. Since 1990, more than 120 managers have completed a 12-day management development programme that has taken them into different consortium companies. More than 50 modules (of two or three days in length) have been designed and delivered by the participants themselves. The consortium has now introduced alumni seminars on selected business themes which are intended to run twice a year.

WHERE DO CORPORATE UNIVERSITIES FIT INTO THE OVERALL STRATEGIC HRD PICTURE?

Students on the MA in Human Resource Strategies programme at London Guildhall University in 1998 generated the step diagram model shown in Fig. 16.10 to evaluate corporate universities on two dimensions. One dimension looks at the extent to which corporate universities contributed to the strategic direction of the organisation. The second dimension looks at the extent to which they demonstrated a strategic HRD approach – in terms of embedding learning into the fabric of the organisation's processes.

The conclusions were informative. Most of the universities analysed seemed to support the overall strategic direction of the organisation concerned. However, in terms of learning philosophy and a mature approach to SHRD, substantial differences were identified, with a growing level of sophistication in some more recent examples. Key phrases to be looked for that represent the growing level of maturity include 'learning organisation', 'intellectual capital', 'knowledge creation', 'continuous learning', 'strategic learning partnerships'. There is a strong sense of their being influenced by the concept that people and learning processes are the only true source of competitive advantage in a world where products can so easily be replicated. It is also remarkable how many have emanated from the TQM tradition.

CONCLUSION

What is likely to be the future of corporate universities? A number of possibilities present themselves.

1 They could disappear, being seen as a fad of a particular time or an expensive overhead. American Express in the early 1990s had a thriving 'Quality University' but this was disbanded in the middle of the decade. The determining factor as to whether they disappear could well be the extent to which notions such as 'people are the only true source of sustainable competitive advantage' stay current.

Figure 16.10 The step model: alignment with strategic human resource development and with strategic goals

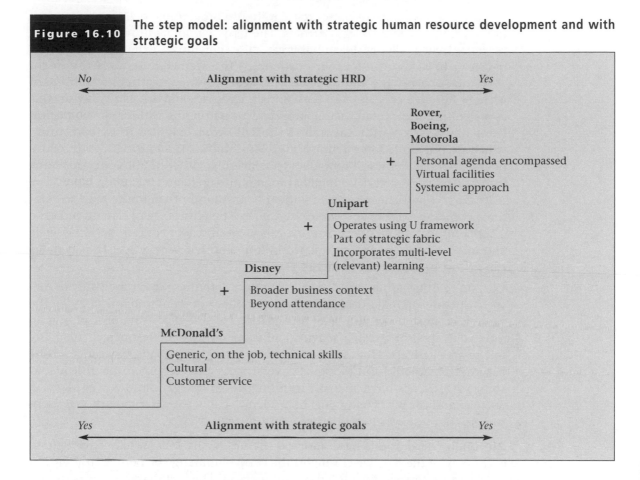

2 We could be seeing an unstoppable trend in which training and development departments, so named, will become a thing of the past. Organisations could relabel their course-based training provision as 'university', without there being any change in practice. Old wine in new bottles.

3 Linked to the above the term could be used as a symbolic device to gain line management commitment to HRD and learning. Elsewhere in the book we have commented on a fashion in organisations where learning is taken seriously, for departmental heads to take on the role of 'champions of learning' (*see* Chapter 7). Alternatively, to be designated 'Departmental Dean' could be attractive.

4 Will the corporate universities of the future be third-generation non-campus 'virtual entities', with all employees being attached to location-independent faculties, and learning support being provided on a distance learning basis through the Intranet?

5 The new universities could provide a real focus for developing and sustaining long-term partnerships with conventional universities. Many organisations already provide in-house programmes leading to qualifications accredited externally and delivered jointly with academic providers. For global organisations, the partnerships could well be with a range of overseas providers.

Note the possibility of outsourcing in-house programme delivery to conventional university and college partners. The term 'corporate university' might be no more than a rallying slogan but it can raise individuals' expectations in terms of credits to be awarded for courses attended. This seemed to be a key feature for Motorola – identifying and working with 'real' university partners which might accredit in-house programmes. Both British Aerospace and Anglian Water see this as a significant feature in their approach. This partnering with academic institutions has been a significant trend in recent years, even for those companies which do not aspire to be a 'university'. Most universities in the UK with a business school or faculty will nowadays be delivering, either in full or in part, some in-house management development programmes up to and including MBAs.

There is a problem associated with this. In-house programmes tend to reinforce corporate culture and corporate values. The advantage of having access to a conventional university is that one can have a broader educational experience and meet people who will see the world from another perspective. Thus benefits can be lost in in-company provision.

6 Corporate universities could start to support activities which are still the preserve of conventional universities. Research does not seem to figure large on the agenda of most of the corporate universities. Nevertheless, a number of organisations do sponsor research activity, and some sponsor professorships, including in the area of HRD. Thus, in the UK, there is the Littlewoods professor in HRD based at Liverpool John Moores University. As a development of this, just as some art galleries have an artist in residence, and organisations like Marks & Spencer and the BBC have a poet in residence, could we see organisational sponsorship for professors in residence?

Although corporations have adopted the university label it is not realistic to expect many of them will ever support the curriculum range of a university, with its research commitments an additional consideration. The best that most corporations can aspire to is to function as a 'monotech'. There is also always going to be the inevitable tension between the performance-driven learning imperative for corporations and the independence of thought required of a true academic community.

If nothing else, the fashion for corporate universities does demonstrate the importance of how the training and development effort is labelled. But focusing so much on formal learning activities can also divert attention from the breadth of HRD.

REFERENCES

Anfield, J. (1997) 'Joint development', *People Management*, 6 February.
Campbell, G. (1996) *Unipart Review 1996*, p. 8.
Corporate University Xchange (1998) 'The 1998 Survey of Corporate University Future Directions', *Corporate Universities International*, 4(1), January–February.
Downs, A. (1995) 'Mervyn's U to the Rescue', *Training and Development*, June, pp. 59–62.
Eurich, N. P. (1985) *Corporate Classrooms: The Learning Business*. Princeton: Princeton University Press.
Garfield, C. (1992) *Second to None – The Productive Power of Putting People First*. Chicago: Business One Irwin.

Hersey, P. and Blanchard, K. H. (1969) *Management of Organisation Behaviour: Utilising Human Resources*. Englewood Cliffs, NJ: Prentice Hall.

Kanter, R. M. (1989) *When Giants Learn to Dance – Mastering the Challenges of Strategy, Management and Careers in the 1990s*. New York: Simon & Schuster.

Luckenbach, M. and Wade, P. (1998) 'Building a World-Class Learning Organisation'. Presentation at ASTD International Conference and Exposition, San Francisco.

Martinez, M. N. (1992) 'Disney Training Works Magic', *HR Magazine*, May.

Meister J. C. (1998) *Corporate Universities – Lessons in Building a World-Class Work Force*. New York: ASTD/McGraw-Hill.

Meister, J. C. and King, W. (1996) 'Corporate Universities: opposing schools of thought', *Computerworld*, 30(29), pp. 98–9.

Orsin, A., Martin, M., Nielson, K. and Graves R. (1993) 'McDonald's Corporation', in W. P. Anthony, P. L. Perrewe and K. M. Kacmar (eds) *Strategic Human Resource Development*. New York: Dryden Press.

Pickard, J. (1995) 'Learning that is far from academic', *People Management*, 9 March, pp. 32–4.

Serritella, V. (1998) 'Motorola University strategy for business success'. Presentation at Motorola University, March.

Spates, T. G. (1960) *Human Values where People Work*. New York: Harper & Bros.

Therrien, L. (1991) 'McRisky', *Business Week*, 19 October, p. 117.

Wiggenhorn, W. (1990) 'Motorola U: When Training becomes an Education', *Harvard Business Review*, July–August.

Chapter 17

MANAGING TRANSFORMATIONAL CHANGE FROM A HUMAN RESOURCE DEVELOPMENT PERSPECTIVE

OBJECTIVES

By the end of this chapter you should be able to:

- define transformational change and contrast it with first order organisational change;
- differentiate between transformational change and transactional change;
- establish the individual and organisation dynamics which need to be addressed in a programmatic transformational change effort;
- clarify the relationship between external and internal HRD expertise in the process;
- diagnose the hrd capability of an organisation intending to undertake a programmatic transformational change effort;
- describe the various HRD processes entailed in managing a transformational change effort;
- explain the difficulties in evaluating large-scale change;
- indicate the contribution of HRD practitioners to the various stages of a transformational change effort.

INTRODUCTION

Much has been written in recent years on the management – and mismanagement – of large-scale organisational change. The field has been characterised by injunctions, exhortations, recipes and prescriptions, from academics, consultants and business executives alike, on how the change can best be handled and on why so many previous attempts were unsuccessful. With competitive positioning and even survival sometimes at risk, the stakes are high. As we saw in Chapter 1 the need for such change has particularly come about because of the effect of environmental forces. Throughout the global economy, organisations have merged, demerged and been reinvented to cope with the demands of intense competition, governmental pressures for efficiency and privatisation in the public sector, and greater expectations of customers in terms of service delivery and responsiveness and equality of treatment.

Some situations can be extreme. Augustine (1997) refers to restructuring a complex commercial organisation during a period of profound decline when 50 per cent of the market disappeared overnight. At the time of writing a number of state-owned corporations in mainland European countries such as France and the Netherlands are wrestling with the implications of impending privatisation as a result of governmental policy. For example, the Netherlands Railway is being subjected to an incremental annual reduction in governmental grants to zero by the year 2000, when it will have to function according to free market conditions.

The triggers for change do not always occur in response to dramatic environmental turbulence. In a number of instances the driving force has been a CEO who, in almost visionary vein, has tried to create something new in an endeavour to put an organisation, whose members are perceived to be reliant on traditional ways of operating, at the forefront of progressive strategic thinking.

These major organisational shifts often result in what is termed transformational change, the management of which is the subject of this chapter (*see* Fig. 17.1).

Figure 17.1	**Factors leading to transformational change**

The factors leading to transformational change include:

1 *External environment*: the impact of external factors such as world financial conditions, changes in marketplaces, political interventions and so on.

2 *Mission and strategy*: a reconfiguration of the central purpose of the organisation and how the organisation intends to achieve that purpose over time.

3 *Leadership*: new forms of executive behaviour that provide changes in direction and encouragement for others to take action.

4 *Culture*: a felt need to reposition core values and 'the way we do things around here'.

Source: Burke (1992).

Transformational change is not necessarily reserved for large organisations. Small organisations such as worker co-operatives which are experiencing a sudden upsurge in demand may have to confront issues of size, ownership and control. Voluntary organisations may have to respond to changed expectations of members and external sponsors alike.

This chapter first provides a definition of terms and develops a classification system for thinking about transformational change, and then addresses how HRD interventions and HRD practitioners can contribute to the process. A distinction is made between those approaches to transformational change that lend themselves to managed HRD interventions, and those crisis-driven and coercive situations which do not. In the latter case, learning may take place but it will be *incidental* to the process and *accidental* as to whether its effects are perceived beneficially.

The overall shaping of transformational change, as a professional HRD discipline, has in the past been the preserve of organisation development (OD) consultants, operating mostly in an external advisory capacity, whose services have been drawn upon by organisational clients to inform the process. Many of the large consultancies such as McKinsey and PriceWaterhouseCoopers have specialist staff in this area.

However, external consultants cannot sustain the process over time, nor can they oversee on a day-to-day basis how it maps out in practice. And at some stage they need to withdraw! Responsibility for the short-term operational aspects of learning transition, and for the long-term continuation of learning processes needs to be in the hands of in-house staff with appropriate expertise and awareness. This chapter addresses the relationship between internal and external HRD involvement.

This facilitation of transformational change by external OD consultants and internal staff with appropriate HRD expertise should not be confused with the activities of those HRD specialists who previously focused on designing and delivering training events and are now being redesignated as performance consultants in organisations. Their sphere of operations is much narrower, in that it focuses on facilitating systems and performance improvement changes for operational departments. This chapter is concerned with a broader and more holistic level of organisational involvement.

Transformational change leads to a whole series of fundamental questions about where HRD fits in. It also sets a whole series of challenges for HRD practitioners. These include:

■ What is the relationship between transformational change and learning? How is learning facilitated? What sort of learning is entailed?

■ Are some forms of transformational change more susceptible to learning interventions than others?

■ What diagnostic skills does an HRD practitioner need to possess about the organisation being subjected to transformational change?

■ How far can learning about and during the change process be managed in a contained programmatic way?

TYPES OF CHANGE: DEVELOPING A VOCABULARY

The organisational system

To understand and contribute to organisational change, one needs a sense of how the organisation operates as a system. Later in this chapter we shall make reference to a range of diagnostic models, each of which provides different insights into the organisational arena. However, a simple and overarching way of conceptualising organisations is to think of them as consisting of a series of levels or layers, moving from the tangible and identifiable to the interpretive.

Physical entities and *assets* can be seen as the most tangible layer. These incorporate physical and visible organisational elements such as buildings, people, machines, raw materials and products, and include measurable resources such as money. Viewed out of context and in isolation they would have no meaning to an external observer.

| Figure 17.2 | Transformational change: four layers of organisation |

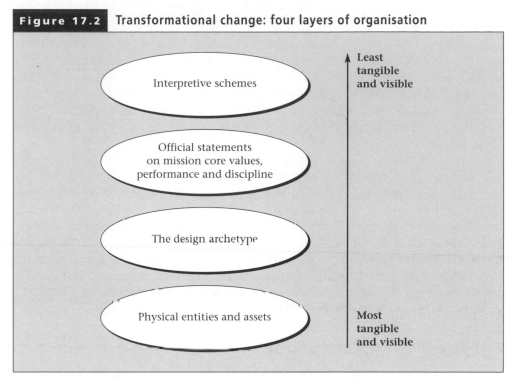

Source: Based on Laughlin (1991).

The design archetype is less tangible and consists of formal organisation structures, reporting relationships, roles, procedures, plans, decision processes and communication systems which provide a rationale and *modus operandi* for the the visible and tangible features. It provides an integrative framework to an external observer for understanding how the organisation functions as a system, and perceiving how and why the different elements link together.

Official statements on mission, core values, performance and discipline guide members' actions by providing a set of espoused values about purpose and direction, together with an indication of what behaviours will be rewarded and what less so, what is permissible and not permissible.

Interpretive schemes are the most intangible. They govern the actual meaning which those within the system attach to the formal elements and the stated purpose and values, and thereby influence the nature of the contribution which is afforded by participants. They include culture (the underlying set of norms, values and beliefs), power relationships and 'meta-rules' (underpinning processes, strategies, leadership behaviours and pronouncements).

TRANSFORMATIONAL CHANGE

Transformational change can be defined as change which results in entirely new behaviour sets on the part of organisational members (Burke, 1992). It entails a reorientation of the intangible interpretive schemes underpinning operations.

441

Bolman and Deal (1991) emphasise that change alters power relationships, undermines existing agreements and intrudes on 'deeply rooted symbolic agreements and ritual behaviour'. Transformational change in particular challenges these embedded behavioural norms. Indicators could be trade unions working in partnership with management to redefine work roles, whereas previously there had been an ongoing history of confrontation and industrial unrest. Another instance could be a public sector organisation positively reaching out to the public it serves – and the public in all its diversity – as opposed to operating within a 'we know what is best for you' ethos.

Gioia *et al.* (1994) adopt a similar position in making the connection between transformational change and strategic change. They contend that the effect of simultaneous shifts of strategy, structures and processes can constitute a pronounced discontinuity in the life of the organisation, rarely brought about by mandate, and requiring a process of negotiated social reconstruction to be effective. The onus is thus placed on top management to develop a vision of the intended reorientation, and disseminate an 'abstract' of the transformed organisation to key stakeholders. This perspective suggests that to understand and manage strategic change, it is necessary to examine symbolism, sensemaking and influence processes that serve to create and legitimate the meaning of the change.

First-order and second-order change

Strategic change is often described as second-order or (drawing on terminology from biology and cybernetics) morphogenetic change. It can be contrasted with first-order or morphostatic change (Smith, 1982; Laughlin, 1991).

First-order, morphostatic changes 'are those which arise from the workings of the organisation within the framework of its received wisdom and view of its existence, within the current definitions of its objectives and of the processes which are appropriate to achieving them' (Robb, 1988, quoted in Laughlin, 1991). They are associated with ongoing adjustments on an established path of development and only accidentally reach the interpretive layer.

Second-order, morphogenetic changes will permeate and alter the intangible as well as the tangible elements of the organisation by penetrating 'so deeply into the "genetic code" that all future generations acquire and reflect these changes' (Smith, 1982). The distinction made has affinities with that made between single-loop and double-loop learning by Argyris and Schon (1978) in their analysis of organisational learning.

Many transformational change efforts do not achieve their objectives. Watzlawick *et al.* (1974) refer to the phenomenon of 'underachievement' where second-order ambitions end up with only limited first-order consequences. A way of measuring whether transformational change has actually occurred is to imagine that you leave an organisation for which you have worked over a period of time, and return at some point in the future. Do you still recognise it as the same organisation? Have things happened that you would not have believed were possible?

The approach to such change can take many forms, but for it to be transformational there should be an intention to create a new underlying ethos which, in turn, reshapes the design archetype and the subsystems to be in line with the new chosen interpretive scheme. Although the changes may take many years to complete, the important point is that the interpretive scheme shifts in a major way (Laughlin, op. cit.).

This is not to say that less ambitious intentions cannot have transformational outcomes. Mabey and Mallory (1995) draw attention to a change programme at IBC Vehicles Ltd over the period 1987–90 which focused on transactional and reengineering elements. These consisted of drawing up and implementing a totally new employment agreement, introducing a radically revised production inventory system and reconfiguring the whole work-force into multiskilled teams, supported by comprehensive skills training – in an endeavour to modify individual and group behaviour at a time of organisational crisis. IBC was created in 1987 as a joint venture between the Bedford Commercial Vehicle part of General Motors Vauxhall plant in Luton, England, and Japan's Isuzu which took a 40 per cent stake in the new business. The main lever for change was the threat of massive redundancies and even plant closure resulting from losses totalling £500 000 per week. The unexpected outcome of a successful turnaround was a wholesale transformation in workplace norms and beliefs which, for the researchers, was represented in terms of a totally new culture at the core of the enterprise. This was achieved with virtually no reference to vision, mission and core values in company documentation or managerial vocabulary.

TRANSFORMATIONAL CHANGE VERSUS TRANSACTIONAL CHANGE

Transactional change refers to modifications in and redesign of systems, procedures, processes, tasks and activities that take place between individuals and groups both within and outside the organisation. It is a change in the design archetype. Business process reengineering focuses primarily on transactional change. As seen in the above example the outcome of transactional change could well be transformational if it results in fundamentally new ways of perceiving roles, responsibilities and relationships. It is also unlikely that a major transformational change effort will succeed without some significant changes in transactions.

The distinction between transformational and transactional change has not always been clearly made, even by some of the most well-known authorities on the subject. Richard Beckhard has written copiously on the subject of change for over thirty years. His position in 1989 was that the types of organisational change that can be called transformational include moving from low-technology to high-technology manufacturing systems, implementing computers and telecommunications processes and redesigning the customer interface (e.g. providing salespeople with laptop computers so that they can interact directly with both customers and suppliers) (Beckhard, 1989). These examples would seem to be more akin to transactional change.

TRANSITIONAL CHANGE

Transitional change relates to the process of moving from one state to another, of getting from here to there. All changes involve a transition – the bigger and more ambitious the change the greater the transitional element. Much of thinking on transformational change has focused on how to *manage* the transition, addressing both the systemic elements of change and the psychological effects on the individuals concerned. This concern with managing the transition is partly because large-scale change takes place over a wide arena and often involves a considerable timescale in getting from A to B, from here to there; and partly because the greater the scale of change, the greater the potential for individuals to resist and experience difficulties in adjusting. Sir Ian Marshall, who was the architect of British Airways' reconfiguration towards a customer-focused service business commencing in the 1980s, believes that it takes 'a business generation' twenty years to forget the lingering memories of an old culture (Kennedy, 1998).

The underpinning thinking behind managing the transition originates from the work of Kurt Lewin (1952) and was further elaborated by Schein (1987). Both emphasise the individual and interpersonal aspects of the process as opposed to the *systemic* characteristics.

Lewin's three-step procedure for change entailed:

■ *unfreezing* the current behavioural patterns;

■ *movement* through taking action that will convert current behavioural patterns within the organisational system to new and desired patterns;

■ *refreezing* of new patterns so that they become relatively secure against change and in particular against reverting to previous forms of behaviour.

For Schein:

■ *unfreezing* entails creating a motivation and readiness to change through:
  - disconfirmation or lack of confirmation that what is happening currently is appropriate;
  - creation of guilt or anxiety about current behaviour and performance;
  - the provision of psychological safety in the face of disconfirming evidence so that people do not lose self-esteem;

■ *movement* entails changing through cognitive restructuring. This means seeing things, judging things, feeling things and reacting to things differently, supported by:
  - identifying with new role models or mentors who possess and can project a new point of view;
  - scanning the environment for new relevant information;

■ *refreezing* entails integrating the new point of view into:
  - the total personality and self-concept;
  - significant relationships.

Schein believes that none of these stages is susceptible to self-management but needs the intervention of various 'change agents'.

Beckhard and Harris (1987) define managing the transition in these terms:

> It may be stating the obvious to say that any major organisational change involves three distinct conditions: the *future state*, where the leadership wants the organisation to get to; the *present state,* where the organisation currently is; and the *transition state*, the set of conditions and activities that the organisation must go through to move from the present to the future.
>
> Thinking about the change process as involving these three states helps clarify the work to be done in managing major change – *defining* the future state, *assessing* the present, and *managing* the transition.

Managing the transition entails identifying the activities and commitments required to reach the future state, and developing strategies and supporting action plans:

Nadler (1983) argues that organisational change is effectively managed when:

■ the organisation is moved from the current state to the desired future state;

■ the functioning of the organisation in the future state meets expectations; that is, it works as intended;

■ the transition is accomplished without undue cost to the organisation;

■ the transition is accomplished without undue cost to the individual members.

He proposes a number of action steps to manage the transition.

1 *Develop and communicate a clear image of the future.* As clear an image as possible of the future state should be developed to serve as a guideline, target or goal. In particular a written statement or description of the future state may be of value. It is important to communicate information to those involved in the change, including why the change is necessary and how individuals will be affected. Methods include briefing groups.

2 *Use multiple and consistent leverage points.* Structural change, task change, change in the social environment, as well as behavioural changes in individuals themselves, are all needed to bring about significant and lasting changes in the patterns of organisational behaviour. The changes should be so constructed that they are consistent; the training of individuals, for example, should dovetail with new job descriptions, reward systems and reporting relationships.

3 *Develop organisational arrangements for the transition.* The following organisational arrangements are important for managing the transition:

   ■ a transition manager;

   ■ resources for the transition;

   ■ a transition plan;

   ■ transition management structures.

INCREMENTAL CHANGE

The notion of managing the transition implies that one does not move overnight from 'here' to 'there'. As in much of strategic thinking, there may be an overall sense of direction, but precisely what happens on route depends upon circumstances and adjusting to them. As we saw in Chapter 2 on the strategic backcloth, Quinn (1980) has developed the concept of 'logical incrementalism' as a discrete philosophy whereby decision makers engage in a step-by-step movement towards ends which initially are broadly conceived, but become more and more refined and reshaped over time. His elaborated position is that an incremental approach within an overarching direction-seeking framework allows one to:

■ improve the quality of information utilised in the decision-making process;

■ cope with the varying lead times, pacing parameters and sequencing needs of the subsystems through which the change will be enacted;

- cope with personal resistance and political pressures the change process encounters;
- build organisational awareness, understanding and psychological commitment needed for effective implementation;
- decrease the uncertainty surrounding the change by allowing for interactive learning between the enterprise and its various impinging environments;
- improve the quality of the change process itself by:
  - systematically involving those with most knowledge;
  - obtaining the participation of those who must carry it out;
  - avoiding premature closure which could lead the change process in improper directions.

METAPHORS FOR CHANGE

One of the most significant determinants of whether a change is transformational has to do with the ambitions of those driving it. This can often be indicated by the rhetoric used to support it.

Marshak (1993) identifies four underpinning metaphors for judging how ambitious a proposed organisational change is in reality. The metaphors are often reinforced by the language used by protagonists to describe their aspirations and intentions. Marshak also suggests that there can be an incongruity between aspirations and language, which unless addressed can lead to blockages and disappointments.

Fix and maintain

The fix and maintain metaphor implies that there is nothing seriously wrong with the system that a little fine-tuning and adjustment cannot resolve. The change agents are in effect seen as repairers and maintenance workers.

Build and develop

The build and develop metaphor implies that movement is desirable but in a relatively predictable direction.

Move and relocate

The move and relocate metaphor recognises that quite substantial change is necessary and that there is a requirement for a change of direction. In extreme form it could be the consequence of a crisis situation.

Liberate and re-create

The liberate and re-create metaphor is most effective in capturing the connotations associated with transformational change. Marshak argues that the imagery of the expression is more radical and extreme than in other change scenarios where 'the organisation doesn't abandon its foundation, roots, or essential being'. In this situation he feels there is a need for a figurehead or transformational leader who is seen as a visionary, liberator or creator possessing the ability to help give birth to a new organisation.

PLOTTING THE SCALE, EXTENT AND STYLE OF PROPOSED CHANGES

Stace and Dunphy (1991), in reporting on how change was managed in 13 Australian organisations, also use metaphorical terminology to plot its scope and extent. Their four-point scale moves from *fine-tuning* through *incremental adjustment* and *modular transformation* to *corporate transformation*. There are obvious parallels with Marshak (op. cit.), the exception being that their explanation of *corporate transformation* focuses more on how to reconfigure transactional and structural elements as opposed to visionary and path-finding approaches.

Stace and Dunphy extend their model by identifying different styles of change management, ranging from *collaborative* to *consultative* to *directive* to *coercive* and cross-mapping these against the four points on their scale-of-change axis. Their empirical research data indicated that many corporate transformations are based upon a directive and coercive strategy as opposed to the more participative and collaborative approaches recommended in much of the literature. This would seem to be because the lever for change in the organisations they studied was often an organisational crisis necessitating a turnaround solution, typical features of which were downsizing, retrenchment and radical work process and job restructuring. The consequence would seem to be a lack of attention to or concern in the organisation with the psychological aspects of managing the transition.

Young (1991a) recognises this by differentiating between *crisis* and *transformation* in his fourfold classification of change presented in Fig. 17.3. He puts crisis at one end of the change continuum and transformation at the other, being influenced by the degree of urgency associated with a crisis situation. In terms of transformational consequences, he recognises that crisis, for possibly the wrong reasons, has the potential to drastically change people's attitudes and behaviours far more than fine-tuning and building. The key aspects that differentiate it from the more visionary model of transformational change is that it is an imposed change situation, requiring solutions over a short timescale, drastic measures and the tendency to adopt prescriptive and coercive methods.

Table 17.1 compares the terminology used by Marshak, Dunphy and Stace and Young.

Table 17.1 Comparative table of terminology

Marshak	Dunphy and Stace	Young
Fix and maintain	Fine-tuning	Fine-tuning
Build and develop	Incremental adjustment	Building
	Modular transformation	
Move and relocate	Corporate transformation	Crisis
Liberate and re-create		Transformation

Figure 17.3 Young's classification of change

TYPES OF CHANGE

SCOPE
OF
CHANGE

Incremental change

1 *Fine-tuning*	2 *Building*
• introduction of involvement techniques such as quality circles • detailed organisation and methods analysis • training for performance improvement and skills upgrading	• longer-term planning and strategic systems • longer-term incentive plans focusing on market share • extensive development and training

Fundamental change

3 *Crisis*	4 *Transformation*
• selling parts of the business • major restructuring of control and accountability processes • removing/replacing people quickly • rewards tailored to short-term results • communicating simple messages about targets and consequences	• developing extensive networks of change agents • incentives and competitions • Visible backing by key people of transformation themes • extensive and intensive training or indoctrination involving a mass of people

Short time-frame　　　　*Long time-frame*

TIME-FRAME

Source: Based on Young (1991a).

The visionary perspective versus transformation through crisis

The above analysis indicates that transformational change can be approached either from a long-term visionary perspective with a conscious desire to 'liberate and re-create' resulting in a desired future state; or from an externally imposed crisis situation.

One of the best known writers on transformational change from a visionary (desired future state) perspective is Richard Beckhard (mentioned earlier). He has described it in the following terms:

> There is no question that there is an increasing need for a complex organisation in today's world to change its shape . . . in terms of both size and complexity, that will allow it to function effectively in the dynamic world in which it operates.
>
> However, an in-depth assessment of shape, structure, character or nature, and environment – difficult and essential as that task may be – is insufficient of itself. Undertaking transformational change also necessitates re-examining the organisation's mission and creating a vision or desired future state as well as the strategies by which the organisation can move towards that vision (Beckhard, 1989).

He sees this approach as requiring an organisation development (OD) approach. The criteria which he associates with a successful OD programme are:

1 It is planned and involves all of the organisation.

2 It does not improve the managerial process in isolation.

3 Senior management commitment to the programme goals must be gained.

4 It is a long-term effort; at least two–three years will be needed to see the benefits.

5 It is action oriented, designed from the outset to generate action.

6 The emphasis is on changing perceptions, attitudes and behaviour, not solely achieving structural change.

7 It relies on experience-based learning, through which people can examine the present situation, define new goals and explore ways of achieving them.

8 Groups or teams from the organisation form the basis of programmes.

9 It is practical, simple, easy to understand and implement (ibid.).

It is that ethos which has underpinned much of the ideology of OD consultants who have seen the need to manage a transformation and have developed a repertoire of approaches to support decision makers in doing this.

The externally imposed crisis situation may be far more common but it is less likely that HRD practitioners will be in a position to take a proactive role in the process, or indeed that HRD issues will be in the foreground.

Like all either/or situations, the visionary versus crisis dichotomy is too simplistic. In practice transformational change can be plotted on a scale ranging between these two extremes. There is also a danger in adopting a visionary perspective of thinking that the whole of the old order needs to be overturned. Many OD consultants are aware of this and try to ensure that stability is built into the process. Thus Nadler (1983) states that:

> Organisations and individuals can only withstand so much instability and turbulence. One way of dealing with this is to provide some sources of stability (structures, people, physical locations that stay the same), that serve as anchors for people to hold onto and provide a means for definition of the self in the midst of turbulence.

DIFFERENTIATING BETWEEN ORGANISATIONAL AND INDIVIDUAL DYNAMICS IN THE CHANGE PROCESS

A number of writers (e.g. Nadler, 1983, Tichy and Devanna, 1986) have drawn attention to the importance of recognising, and simultaneously managing, the individual and organisational dynamics associated with change. This is not always reflected in theoretical frameworks and practical suggestions, where either element comes to the fore.

Handling the organisational dynamics, such as those reflected in the set of incremental steps proposed by Kotter (1995) (*see* Fig. 17.4), is important, since they govern the managerial and political processes associated with changing the system.

Figure 17.4	Eight incremental steps to transforming your organisation

1 **Establishing a sense of urgency**
   - Examining market and competitive realities.
   - Identifying and discussing crises, potential crises or major opportunities.

2 **Forming a powerful guiding coalition**
   - Assembling a group with enough power to lead the change effort.
   - Encouraging the group to work together as a team.

3 **Creating a vision**
   - Creating a vision to help direct the change effort.
   - Developing strategies for achieving that vision.

4 **Communicating the vision**
   - Using every new vehicle possible to communicate the new vision and strategies.
   - Teaching new behaviours by the example of the guiding coalition.

5 **Empowering others to act on the vision**
   - Getting rid of obstacles to change.
   - Changing systems or structures that seriously undermine the vision.
   - Encouraging risk taking and non-traditional ideas, activities and actions.

6 **Planning for and creating short-term wins**
   - Planning for visible performance improvements.
   - Creating those improvements.
   - Recognising and rewarding employees involved in the improvements.

7 **Consolidating improvements and producing still more change**
   - Using increased credibility to change systems, structures and policies that do not fit the vision.
   - Hiring, promoting and developing employees who can implement the vision.
   - Reinvigorating the process with new projects, themes and change agents.

8 **Institutionalising new approaches**
   - Articulating the connections between the new behaviours and corporate success.
   - Developing the means to ensure leadership development/succession.

Source: Kotter (1995).

The individual dynamics are important since they address how people feel at different stages of the process and how these feelings might be managed. Most authorities who have considered the individual element have been influenced by the Kubler-Ross (1969) stages of:

■ *Denial*: psychologically protecting oneself from the reality of loss by stating to oneself: 'It hasn't really happened.'

- *Anger*: asking, 'Why has this happened to me (us)? How could the person have done this to me (us)?'
- *Depression*: waves of anguish and depression occur as the reality of the loss begins to take hold.
- *Bargaining*: struggling within oneself to restore the lost state or object.
- *Acceptance*: taking on board the reality of the loss and moving forward in response to traumatic personal loss.

Tichy and Devanna (op. cit.) have drawn on this schema in likening transformational change to a three-act drama in which individuals play out endings, transitions and new beginnings while experiencing the substantive and cumulative impact of the changes upon their roles and organisational relationships.

The notion of loss has operated as a consistent analogy for why people resist the early stages of the change process. Mabey and Salaman (1995) have identified from their literature review three predominant sources of loss that people experience – perceived loss of control over what is happening; loss of face in terms of being identified with the previous situation; and loss of security in terms of what the future might hold for them personally.

Weiss (1996) proposes a five-stage sequence that individuals need to work through as part of a resistance, adjustment and assimilation process (*see* Fig. 17.5).

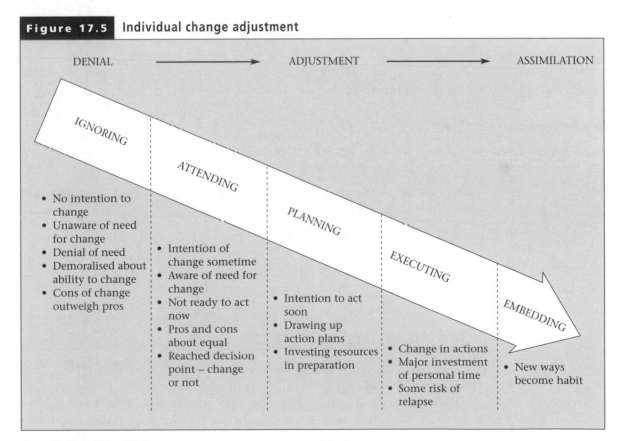

Figure 17.5 Individual change adjustment

Source: Based on Weiss (1996).

For many writers – and practitioners – on the subject, the individual goal is not just achieving a state of acceptance, but demonstrating commitment to the changed state. The consultancy group Coopers & Lybrand (as it then was), in contrasting 'commitment' to 'compliance', have expressed it this way:

> Whilst building commitment is usually the goal of change management effort, it is an expensive, many staged process. However, if the nature of any required change is likely to be behavioural within an unconstrained environment, the only implementation option is via commitment (Coopers & Lybrand, 1997).

By 'unconstrained environment' they are referring to situations where the change process is not imposed by the pressure of external events or forces. They go on to propose a a staged approach in which individuals move from *awareness* to *commitment* (*see* Fig. 17.6).

Figure 17.6	Two ways in which individuals respond to transformational change

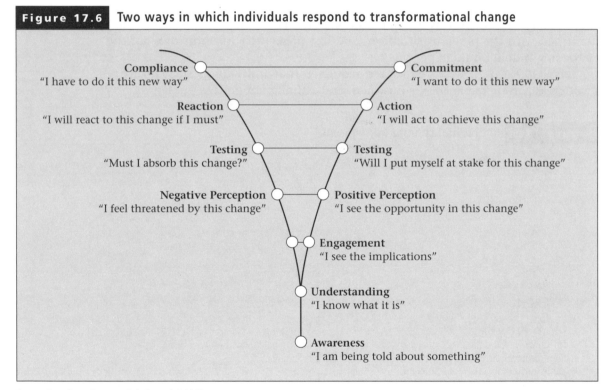

Source: Based on Coopers & Lybrand (1997).

HANDLING THE INTERPLAY OF FORCES

Orgland and Von Krogh (1998) suggest that many large-scale change efforts have failed to achieve their objectives because insufficient attention has been given to the interplay of forces and factors impinging upon the change. They go on to propose three principles which need to be attended to if a managed change effort is to be successful.

Principle 1

Principle 1 requires the simultaneous exercise of three distinct 'forces for change'. These are:

■ top-down direction setting;

■ horizontal process redesign;

■ bottom-up performance improvement.

They suggest that attempts to orchestrate transformational change in the past have failed because of a failure to integrate these three forces. Thus bottom-up performance improvement techniques such as quality circles failed because they were applied piecemeal without a clear direction from the top.

Principle 2

Principle 2 relates to an understanding of three phases of change based on the insights of Kurt Lewin (op. cit.):

■ initiating change;

■ managing the transition;

■ sustaining momentum.

Principle 3

Principle 3 relates to simultaneously applying the soft and hard facets of change, the Yin and the Yang.

The Yin in Confucian philosophy is the 'dark side of the mountain' and symbolises the soft and behavioural side of change. It is fundamentally right brain. It relates to handling people's anxieties before and during the change process.

The Yang is 'the light side of the mountain' and symbolises the hard, analytical and technical side of change such as making x people redundant, introducing y new systems and relocating z members of staff. It is fundamentally left brain.

THE PARADOXES OF TRANSFORMATIONAL CHANGE

The then Price Waterhouse Change Integration Team (1996) have come up with an alternative set of change principles or propositions which influence and guide their practice, based upon their experiences in intervening in large corporate systems. They have expressed them in terms of paradoxes or apparent contradictions, in order to capture the messy complexity associated with the overall process.

1 **The first paradox principle is:** *Positive Change Requires Significant Stability*. Change in the absence of sources of stability and continuity from the past leads to turmoil and loss of direction. Beacons of stability are needed as one maps through the turbulence of change.

2 **The second paradox principle is**: *To Build an Enterprise, Focus on the Individual.* To create an organisation capable of operating in a global arena, it must be recognised that the fundamental building block is each individual member.

3 **The third paradox principle is**: *Focus Directly on Culture, Indirectly.* Culture change does not result from a focus on culture itself, nor does it emanate from training programmes, wish lists of values and beliefs, or exhortations to care about the customer. Such initiatives do not work. To change culture, focus on the 'levers' that create and shape culture, of which the most important are leadership actions; vision, purpose and strategy; performance measures; structure; people practices; and competitive context.

4 **The fourth paradox principle is**: *True Empowerment Requires Forceful Leadership.* Those who advocate that employees should run the workplace are mistaken. Empowerment will not happen in the absence of strong and purposeful leaders who set direction and determine the business focus. The outcome is an emergent interactive model of leadership, relying more on the power of influence than on command and control.

5 **The fifth paradox principle is**: *In Order to Build, You Must Tear Down.* We should not be seduced into thinking that what we have built in the past will be sustainable in the future. Forces for change are so dramatic that the solutions and business models of the past will not support competitiveness in the decades ahead.

The notion of paradox is a powerful way of expressing countervailing forces and is a useful approach to understanding the conflicting dynamics and tensions experienced when trying to orchestrate large-scale change. One can of course accept the notion of paradox without assuming that there is a set of universal paradox principles. The above 'principles' incorporate a number of underpinning assumptions and prescriptions for which a universal validity is claimed, and which for many would be contentious.

THE TRIGGERS FOR CHANGE

The assumption behind transformational change is that it does not just happen, but is in some way 'triggered'. In the broadest sense one can differentiate between triggers emanating from the external environment and those driven by internal forces.

Laughlin (op. cit.) is just one of a number of writers who contend that change does not happen naturally within established organisational settings because of an inherent tendency of people to become accustomed to and comfortable with familiar and learned patterns of behaviour. In his world-view therefore the prevailing force in established organisations is 'inertia' around a dominant corporate perspective.

In his opinion shifts in the inert characteristics of organisational life are only triggered by disturbances in the external environment. When that happens the tendency will always be to return to some other balanced state around which a new level of inertia can set in. The nature of those triggers and the power of the environmental 'kick' determine the type of response. He identifies situations leading to second-order changes which are not chosen but which are seemingly forced on the organisation. Thus 'there could be a financial crisis (an initial kick) which feeds into the design archetype calling for major changes to manage such threats which in turn, through complex processes, colonises the guiding interpretive schemes of the organisation' (Laughlin, op. cit.).

He contrasts this with situations where the initial environmental disturbance causes such reverberation in the organisation that it generates a felt need for major transformational change among key decision makers and a conscious attempt to reconfigure the interpretive layers. An example could be a series of incidents in which a police force or local authority is accused of bias and institutional racist practices in respect of its dealings with the public.

Although the case for an exclusively external cause is convincingly presented, not everyone accepts this position. Dawson (1994) contrasts it with a more proactive, inner-generated approach which could be based on a belief that change will help anticipate future competitive demands. This situation often hinges upon the appointment of a new CEO, with new strategic intent and a desire to keep ahead of the field.

There is evidence in some organisations of the reverse of 'inertia' as organisational decision makers introduce wave after wave of initiatives. One of my correspondents, a manager from BT which was one of the UK corporations which was privatised in the 1980s, refers to being bombarded with so many of these that it feels as though one is 'always chasing oneself up a moving staircase'.

THE LEVERS OF CHANGE

Those involved in initiating or facilitating change should be aware of what leverage they can draw on to help the change process. The following list based on an array generated by Young (1991b) gives an insight into what has been thought to be appropriate in various previous change situations, and includes a number of specific HRD-oriented interventions.

Analytical levers

The use of analytical levers involves drawing on complex and convincing analysis, clearly presented, of the need for change. The analysis may draw comparisons with benchmarked organisations, use performance indicators from within the organisation, incorporate feedback data from diagnostic surveys. What is imperative is that people can understand and be persuaded by the results presented.

Systems as a means of leverage

The use of systems as a means of leverage entails overhauling, redesigning or introducing particular systems, procedures or processes, on the basis that any changing transactions that people are engaged in can have a transforming effect on what they do.

Reward systems and processes

Careful thought given to reward-related procedures could be undertaken against the question, 'What would we like people to do that is different and how can that be reflected in how we reward them?' Note that the emphasis is on rewards and not punishments or sanctions which would be featured in a coercion-driven ideology. Rewards do not have to be individually oriented. They can occur through achievement of externally valued kitemarks such as quality awards. The question then becomes, 'What can we do that is different and how would our achievement be recognised by others?'

Communication and leadership

How top management communicates the change process and the 'themes' chosen can be a significant source of leverage. However, experience shows that people are likely to respond most strongly to other people and not to videos or newspapers. Most sustainable change processes have involved large numbers of people at all levels in initiating, guiding and implementing the changes.

Developing change networks

The use of existing informal and formal networks can be a valuable way of communicating the message. The introduction of training facilitators such as are used in many TQM initiatives, and 'apostles' of change who sponsor the approach at key decision-making points in the organisation, is of great importance.

The attainment and use of power

If there is the likelihood of significant resistance, the securing of a power base can be extremely useful. A number of CEOs have brought in what can euphemistically be called 'strategic replacements' to occupy key positions if they assume there is insufficient support in the system to drive the change process.

Developmental levers

HRD-related interventions are seen as one of the most important levers in transformational change efforts. Young believes that changes, especially those initiated from the top of an organisation, will not have deep sustained effects unless many people are persuaded that change is necessary, and are encouraged to learn new ways of doing things. 'In many organisations it is often seemingly expensive investments in training and development which will have the greatest long term payoffs – provided always that the *means of delivery* of the learning is such that people can actually practice what they learn' (Young, 1991b). However, when used inappropriately they can be counter-productive. He goes on to argue that 'training or learning levers which are used out of synchronisation with, or separate to, other interventions for change can be worse than useless' (ibid.).

Bolman and Deal (op. cit.) make a similar point in acknowledging that restructuring and retraining can be powerful levers for change, 'But they must be done in concert . . . Managers who anticipate that new roles require new skills and vice versa have much greater likelihood of success.'

Aitken and Saunders (1995) refer to a questionnaire-based survey they conducted into the change management process, resulting in 152 responses from 63 different organisations. When asked what helped and what hindered successful change, all managers named education and training as the most important helpful factor. One organisation said it had invested five days for each of the 2000 people involved in the first year of the change programme. Another had used a cascade method, training a group of people from each depot as trainers, who then trained everyone else for three to four days using real-life simulation. Training was used to build commitment, to give people an understanding of the whole picture, to encourage change in working practices and to sustain the change and nurture 'survivors' after a period of redundancies.

STAGES IN THE MANAGEMENT OF TRANSFORMATIONAL CHANGE FROM A HUMAN RESOURCE DEVELOPMENT PERSPECTIVE

Most writers on managed, large-scale change have concluded that there is a logical and sequential set of stages which need to be followed to get from 'here to there'. Burack (1991) introduces an additional element. Reporting on a US culture change programme with which he was familiar and which extended over four years, he concludes that there are a series of generic HRD strategies which can be undertaken at each stage of the change process. The organisation he described had a long series of adversarial relations between employees and management. Severe competition necessitated a major retrenchment effort which included structural streamlining and new approaches to performance management. Although business matters received much attention in order to re-establish a profitable competitive edge, HRD personnel were involved in helping to launch a 'determined culture strengthening effort'. Expected behaviours for organisation members were reinforced through hard HRM changes such as extensive job redesign, developing comprehensive and behaviourally oriented job descriptions and the introduction of various performance pay schemes.

Central to the communication of the programme was the use of a cascade technique. This entailed focusing initially on top officials, who then operated as coaches and guides for subordinates, who in turn were responsible for facilitating change among those who reported directly to them.

The Burack approach provides some interesting insights into how HRD practitioners might become involved in a 'culture at the core' (Mabey and Mallory, op. cit.) change process and these are incorporated in the forthcoming analysis. There are a few crucial areas on which he is silent. He does not provide any details on the HRD function and where it was positioned in the organisation at the outset of the process. How the function is seen within the organisation, and, equally important, how HRD practitioners themselves see their role, can be the determining factors in determining the contribution to a change programme. Nor is the relationship between internal and external HRD players made clear. He indicates that HR planners and OD people correctly diagnosed the need for corporate-wide change, and that T&D and HR were *delegated* (my italics) key and leading roles for internal change. Did external OD consultants initiate the process, and then slowly – or indeed suddenly – withdraw? Or was the whole process orchestrated in house?

Figure 17.7 builds on Burack and takes the form of a five-stage model depicting how the management of transformational change might be conducted from an HRD perspective. By positioning HRD as a linchpin between the individual and organisation dynamics of the process it draws attention to the central role that HRD can play, by contributing to and mediating between those two elements at each stage. It is presented as a version of logical incrementalism. The steps follow each other in logical sequence, but the precise details of specific interventions emerge, as opposed to being planned at the outset.

We now look in detail at how HRD can contribute to each stage of the process.

Recognising the need for change – the human resource development contribution

Recognising the need for change – *see* Fig. 17.8 – depends upon there being someone in the organisation able both to pick up the relevant signals and then to act on them. It is important for HRD practitioners to evaluate potential triggers for change since they will determine the prevailing attitude towards learning in general and the appropriateness of specific HRD interventions in particular during the subsequent process. The more salient practical issue is whether they act on their insights and operate as harbingers of change.

Crisis-driven change is contrasted in the model with change arising out of a felt need. Although as we have seen crisis-driven change can be highly transformational, it is held to be not susceptible to HRD solutions and thus is excluded from the rest of the analysis. The analogy with organisational health, a concept which permeated the early OD literature, can be made. Human resource development cannot help make a sick organisation in terminal decline recover – it is there to make a healthy organisation more healthy.

Within his overall model of logical incrementalism referred to earlier in this chapter, Quinn (op. cit.) emphasises the importance of 'need sensing' as a precursor to anticipatory and proactive change that is not crisis driven. Need sensing relies on:

- using people who see the world very differently to those in the dominating culture (i.e. those who can break out of the 'paradigm' or the 'box');
- consciously seeking out options and threat signals that go beyond the status quo.

Using people who see the world differently

There is a case for arguing that by virtue of being in HRD one will see the world through a learning perspective and will be constantly challenging assumptions and looking for new ways of doing things. Such studies as have been done into the value sets of HRD practitioners indicate independence of thought and a tendency

Figure 17.7 Effective transformational change from a human resource development perspective: the integrated package

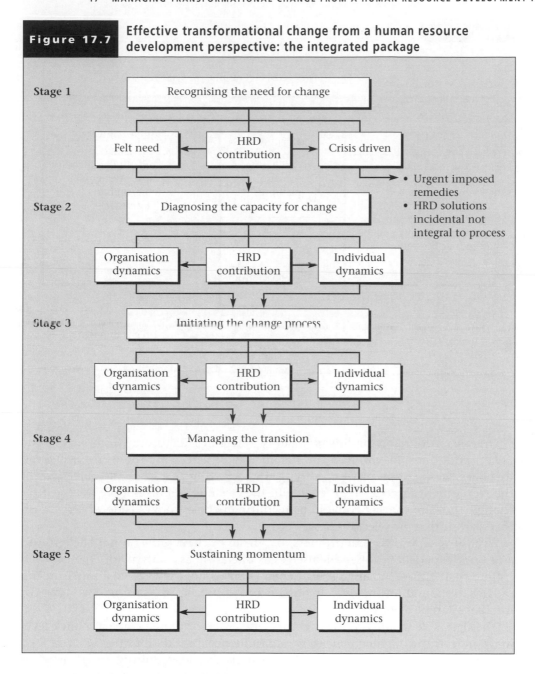

to look within themselves for direction and validation as opposed to an imposed authority (e.g. Rains, 1997).

However, this hypothesis is not necessarily borne out in reality. Traditional trainers often operate as passive providers in a very narrowly defined and circumscribed brief. At one of the sessions at the 1998 ASTD conference in San Francisco, it was asked where the greatest resistance to extending the HRD role lay. The spontaneous answer from those present was, 'The trainers themselves'.

Figure 17.8 Recognising the need for change

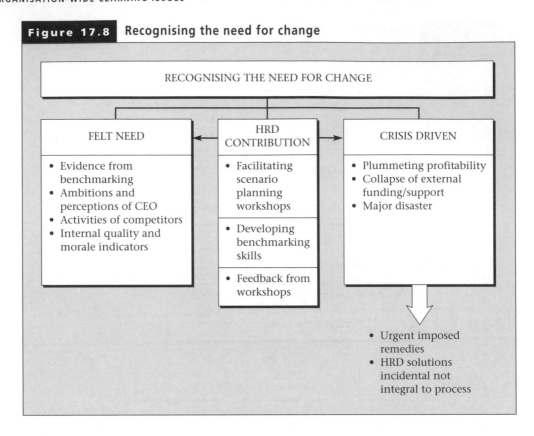

One means of resolving this problem is to recruit HRD people from outside the organisation, people who have a different way of perceiving the world. However, this begs the question of who is doing the recruiting and what the objectives of the recruitment exercise are. If people in the organisation do not see the need for change, they are scarcely going to be recruiting people from outside who focus on this issue during the selection process!

Assuming that HRD practitioners, by virtue of their professional background and prior experience, do see themselves as operating as catalysts for change, their influence at this pre-change stage depends on where they are positioned in the organisation, and on the overall climate and approach to learning. Two types of influence can be identified.

The first is *direct influence*. This occurs where one or more people at policy level draw on learning-oriented perspectives to influence decision making.

The second is *indirect influence*. This is more subtle, requiring a high level of sophistication. It entails asking questions of people when the opportunity is presented such as:

■ 'What can we learn from this?'

■ 'What are we learning from what is taking place out there?'

■ 'Are we listening to the messages that are coming from our customers?'

■ 'What is our current preferred way of operating and is it appropriate for the future?'

- 'Do we need help to take us out of the box?'
- 'Do we have the competences to take us into the future?'
- 'What does the future hold for us if we continue as we are?'

Indirect influence is the more uncertain, and can be very risky if one is working against the grain and not operating in an environment where a reflective mode is valued. On the whole it depends on HRD practitioners using opportunities in workshops and formal learning settings to bring to the surface dissatisfaction with the present state and anxieties about the future direction.

The influence of HRD practitioners is more likely to be *indirect* than *direct* unless they have the backing and support of the CEO. At this stage of the process, it could be that the key HRD protagonist exercising direct influence on learning is the CEO.

Processes for seeking options and threat signals

There are a number of HRD actions and processes that could help people break out of the box by challenging the status quo and generating a genuine spirit of enquiry. Symbolically, this could be signalled by a change in the nomenclature of the HRD effort. 'Learning and Development' as a title for the functional HRD unit in a large organisation gives stronger messages than 'Training and Development'. 'We are seeking to become a learning organisation' could be even more powerful. Teaching the techniques of benchmarking in staff development programmes and supporting these with actual site visits, facilitating scenario-planning workshops – both have the potential to generate recognition of the need for change. However, the messages could still be interpreted in terms of the old story. It is at the interpretive layer that the greatest resistance is encountered.

Burack (op. cit.) makes the point that today's managers generally possess excellent knowledge about relatively tangible aspects of an organisation concerning planning, budgets, structures and strategies. Where they are often less at ease is in understanding and reflecting on the more intangible elements surrounding behaviour and culture. If the dominating approach in organisational discussions has been to focus on operational, short-term issues, it can be very difficult to create a climate in which people both recognise this and simultaneously see the value of adopting a more reflective and long-term stance. Moves towards becoming a 'learning organisation' can provide a context in which people can be encouraged to constantly reflect on internal processes and on exchanges with the environment.

We have noted that it may be an unwarranted assumption to think that internal HRD practitioners will be the harbingers of change; and that there is not a great deal of evidence to support such a proposition. As a result internal HRD practitioners can be vulnerable to a change process. They might be identified with old ways of working and perceiving the world. Kono (1994) suggests that the culture of a company can be changed by measures including 'changing of the corporate creed and training staff'.

It is like sailing between Scylla and Charybdis, the two monsters guarding either side of the narrow strait that Ulysses had to pass through on his epic journey. Too close to the rocks on one side and you run the risk of becoming identified with the traditions of the old organisation by the new order: too close to the whirlpool on the other side and you are seen as a revolutionary before the need for change has actually been accepted by others.

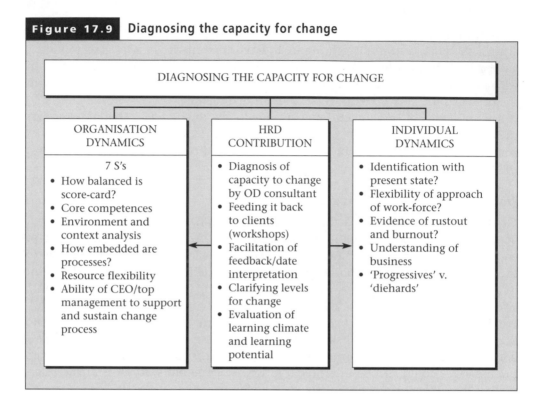

Figure 17.9 Diagnosing the capacity for change

DIAGNOSING THE CAPACITY FOR CHANGE

ORGANISATION DYNAMICS	HRD CONTRIBUTION	INDIVIDUAL DYNAMICS
7 S's	• Diagnosis of capacity to change by OD consultant	• Identification with present state?
• How balanced is score-card?	• Feeding it back to clients (workshops)	• Flexibility of approach of work-force?
• Core competences	• Facilitation of feedback/date interpretation	• Evidence of rustout and burnout?
• Environment and context analysis	• Clarifying levels for change	• Understanding of business
• How embedded are processes?	• Evaluation of learning climate and learning potential	• 'Progressives' v. 'diehards'
• Resource flexibility		
• Ability of CEO/top management to support and sustain change process		

Diagnosing the capacity for change – the human resource development contribution

We now turn to the second stage of the process presented in Fig. 17.7 – diagnosing the capacity for change. The details of this stage are set out in Fig. 17.9.

French and Bell (1978) emphasise the significance of the diagnostic element as a precursor to any large-scale managed change programme. The conduct of this diagnostic exercise is held to be a key part of the toolkit of an OD consultant – who is often specifically contracted to provide an outside perspective for helping the organisation through the change process.

For French and Bell the diagnostic component represents a collection of data which focuses on and provides meaning about the total system, its subsystems and system processes. Much of this will be descriptive information based on a rational interpretation of the design archetype.

The diagnostic element should include an evaluation of the capacity and readiness of the organisation to sustain a large-scale change process. This is more interpretative, based on perceptions provided by individuals within the system mediated through the consultant's own depth and breadth of experience. How the situation is read could govern what change scenario would be deemed appropriate.

Beckhard (1989) provides the following criteria for assessing the capacity and readiness for embarking on a major transformational change effort. He suggests one should ask whether there is evidence of:

■ committed top leaders;

■ written description of the changed organisation;

■ conditions that preclude maintenance of the status quo;

■ the likelihood of a critical mass of support;

■ a medium- to long-term perspective;

■ awareness of resistance and the need to honour it;

■ awareness of the need for education;

■ the conviction that change must be tried;

■ willingness to use resources;

■ commitment to maintaining the flow of information.

Harrison (1987) takes into account also assessment of the technological, structural and resource capabilities.

Questions that would be asked of senior managers to guide the interpretation could include:

■ How do you feel about the structure?

■ What do you think about the systems?

■ How do you experience the management style?

■ What do you think are the key features of the communication process?

■ What do you consider to be the main elements of the prevailing culture?

There are a number of diagnostic models in existence. A useful summary can be found in Burke (1992). Many of them adopt a systems perspective which takes into account the relationship of the organisation with its environment.

In general terms a good diagnostic model should contain the following key features:

1 It captures the complexities of the system in simple form.

2 It is presentable in a form that is meaningful to the target audience and yet challenges their way of thinking.

3 It is capable of generating insights for the person who is using it.

4 It possesses the potential to generate working hypotheses for taking things forward.

From an HRD perspective, the diagnostic model should pay attention to the distinctive contribution and concerns of the people in the system. It should see them not just as a task-accomplishing resource but as individuals undergoing (and gaining satisfactions from undergoing) learning and developmental experiences. The organisation is thus seen as a socio-technical system (*see* Fig. 17.10).

Figure 17.10 The socio-technical framework

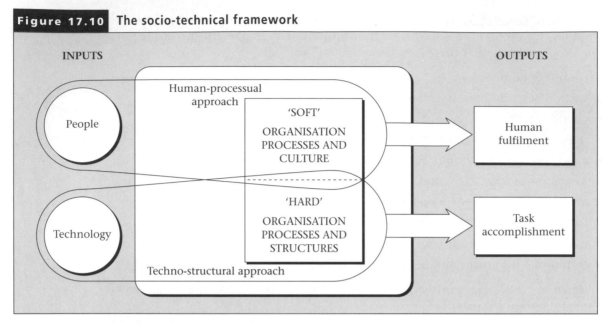

Source: Derived from Friedlander and Brown (1974).

Internal HRD staff members may play no active role in this diagnostic process. The external consultant will however assess their own capacity and readiness for change, and make judgements about how they can help in subsequent stages. The outcome of the diagnosis may be a much higher profile for HRD than was previously the case.

Figure 17.11 Initiating the change process

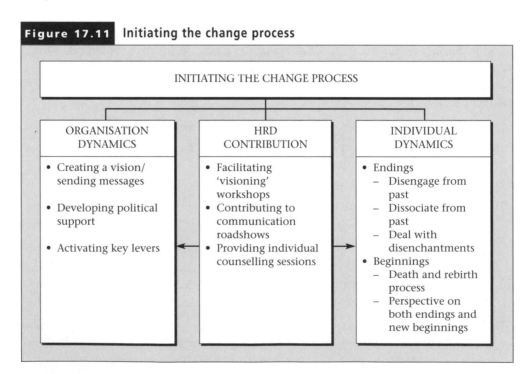

Initiating the change process – the human resource development contribution

Figure 17.11 shows in detail the third stage of the process set out in Fig. 17.7. The change process is often initiated by means of a grand launch, in which the CEO acts as figurehead and principal change agent. A major City of London based insurance company has adopted this strategy (*see* Fig. 17.12).

Figure 17.12	Initiating change at Royal and Sun Alliance

In July 1998 a conference was held in Barcelona for 375 senior staff of the global business network of the Royal and Sun Alliance Group. Delegates wore different-coloured 'Winning Team' T-shirts to indicate the different regions of the world they came from. This style of dress was a major culture shift, formal business wear having been the norm at gatherings in the past.

The conference was opened by the new American CEO, Bob Mendelssohn, who reinforced the new way of thinking by starting the conference in full business dress, and then changing to casual wear while the music from the Beatles song 'Revolution' blared across the auditorium to flashing lights (check spelling). He greeted the audience with the words, 'Well folks, it's not the same old insurance company any more. Welcome to the twenty-first century.'

Each member of staff in the Group was informed of what took place at the conference and the new way of thinking by means of a videotape.

The messages contained included:

■ The winning team for the twenty-first century.

■ We must listen to our customers.

■ We must adopt a more listening style of management.

■ Make decisions as far down the organisation as we can.

■ We come to work saying, 'We trust our employees to do a good job'.

■ There should be an element of fun in this.

Mendelssohn emphasised that the change was revolutionary not evolutionary, but that its impact was not intended to affect the day-to-day working operations, nor would it result in job losses. 'Basically we are here to change attitudes, not jobs'. . . 'We are going to look and act differently than before.'

To support and sustain the new ideology, a culture change director has been appointed. It is too early to say how the change will take effect.

At the outset when change is initiated, much confusion can be expected regarding expected behaviours for 'such and such' circumstances. Questions can be expected as to how to handle a wide array of novel situations for which there may be no ready answers. There will be a widespread sense of pressure and stress if the design archetype is affected and job losses are forecast. There will be evidence of a raising of corporate consciousness with people talking about 'it' or what to do. There is a likelihood of passive communications in meetings and workshops communicating the change, with some people hanging back and not being forthcoming.

Activities to be undertaken by HRD agents include:

- assisting top management to present its agenda and the need for change in a graphic and understandable way;

- anticipating value conflicts with subcultures and preparing to deal with these slowly and selectively;

- identifying ways in which change can be incorporated into basic processes such as decision making – to serve eventually as identifiable features of the new culture.

A collaborative arrangement between the external consultants and internal staff who will be responsible for the HRD function and communicating the message is usually established at this point. The external consultants may train internal staff to function as facilitators, not all of whom need come from the existing in-house HRD function.

Figure 17.13 **Managing the transition**

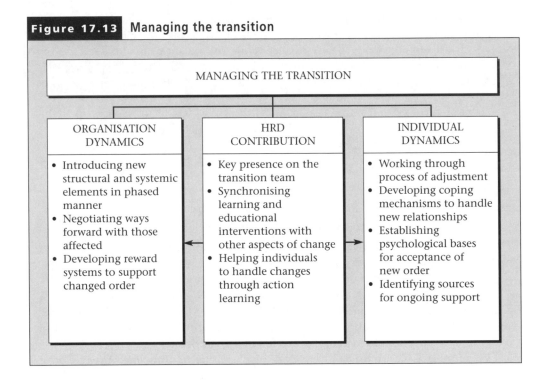

Managing the transition – the human resource development contribution

The fourth stage – managing the transition – is shown in Fig. 17.13. At this stage one can expect continuing evidence of stress, with a mixture of positive and negative results. People will begin to take positive unsolicited actions. There may be evidence of more active communications in meetings – even to the extent of an expression of (constructive) agreement. Conversations will begin to occur amongst key constituencies regarding the organisation's newer ways of doing things. Much greater conformity occurs in terms of people's sense of expected behaviours.

Activities to be undertaken by HRD agents include:

- HRD presentations covering new staffing, career paths, development and implications for individual change;
- enactment of climate change which reinforces item by item newer values and beliefs and expected behaviours;
- facilitation of group problem-solving activities;
- provision of internal education and training programmes.

The HRD contribution is of a different order to that at the diagnostic or launch stage. It is during the transition that internal members of staff come into their own, people who are trusted and known, and who have the facilitation skills to handle the communication and educational processes.

The relationship between internal and external change agents needs to be very clearly established. Is there a handover stage? The external consultants should increasingly be withdrawing from the process.

Nadler (op. cit.), in discussing organisational arrangements for managing the transition, emphasises the importance of a transition team. This is akin to what Kotter (1995) terms a powerful guiding coalition with enough power to lead the change effort. An HRD presence is most important on such a team in order to ensure that the educational process is properly thought through and accomplished.

The transition is not just a matter of communicating to people that new ways of operating and thinking are expected. New transactions will need new skills and attitudes and in turn specific training events (*see* Fig. 17.14).

Figure 17.14 **Breaking with the past**

William Bridges has provided a carefully considered argument for examing the psychological aspects of large-scale change. He contends that when one is having trouble implementing a change that looked easy on paper, the possibility should be considered that the problem isn't with the change but with the transition. 'A *change* is situational and defined by outcome. A *transition* is psychological and defined by process.' The difference between the two concepts can be illustrated by means of a physical relocation metaphor. The change involves selling ones home, finding somewhere new, packing and physically moving. The transition involves all the confusion, distress and excitement that families go through.

'Whereas changes are always unique to the situation in which they take place, transitions show a remarkable similarity, one to another.'

a Transitions always start with an ending. Although change can be initiated by something new, the internal, psychological process that accompanies it always starts by separating from, getting closure on, or bidding farewell to the old reality, and the identity that went with it. Even in a 'good' change, like starting a family, one has to let go of the old life. A new beginning cannot be made without making an end first.

b After the ending a beginning is possible – but it does not occur immediately. One must go through an in-between state that there is no accepted name for – a

▶▶

▶▶ Figure 17.14 continued

time when the old reality and the old identity are gone, but the new ones have not yet taken root in your mind or heart. This can be called the 'neutral zone', to capture the in-betweenness and the neither-this-nor-that quality.

c   The ending disengages us and the neutral zone is a kind of fallow time when old habits are extinguished and new possibilities are born. It is out of the neutral zone that the third and final phase of the transition – the beginning – emerges. This beginning is not to be confused with the 'start' of the new situation, which may have happened on day one. The beginning is when people really 'buy in', 'get on board' and feel at home with the new.

Those affected by change need to go through all three of these psychological phases as they come to terms with the new situation. Whenever people do not go through them, the change simply fails to 'take'. It is paper change; the new strategy is written down, the new organisation chart is circulated, the new policy is announced. But inside people, nothing is any different.

Now think back to some organisational change that did not work as it was supposed to and ask the following:

■ Whatever the details, was the reason because people failed to let go of the old way, or got lost in the neutral zone, or were unable to make the new beginning that was expected of them?

■ Was the assumption that if the change was well planned and executed, the transition would take care of itself?

What was needed was a transition management plan – a way to manage the endings, the neutral zone and the new beginnings. Ask yourself the following further questions about that change situation:

1   Was all the emphasis on the new things that people were supposed to start doing as opposed to classifying what old things they could stop doing?

2   Was there any symbolic recognition (ranging from a memorable incident to a full-scale ceremony) to mark the endings being made and the losses being experienced?

3   Did the organisation's leadership analyse and acknowledge who was actually doing what, or did they focus on expressions of anxiety, dismissing them as 'negative', 'unconstructive' or 'opening Pandora's box'?

4   In the confusing time when the old way was gone and the new had not yet taken full shape, was communication continued regularly or was the approach adopted: 'We'll get back to you as soon as we have something to tell you'?

5   During this in-between time, were new, temporary solutions found to resolve emergent problems or did people try to bend old ways to fit the new problems?

6   Were conscious efforts made to provide people with temporary sources of control and support, or were people simply told that they'd have to manage as best they could?

▶▶

▶▶ Figure 17.14 continued

> 7 How was it ensured that further, unrelated changes were not disrupting the attention that needed to be paid to this one?
>
> 8 Was there constant feedback on how the transition was going from a transition monitoring team (created just for that purpose), or were people told that the situation was in hand?
>
> 9 Were efforts focused on a few areas that were most likely to work, and achieve quick successes there as a way of building credibility, or was the emphasis on trying to bring off the whole change in one piece?
>
> 10 Was the reward system in the organisation redesigned to reinforce the behaviour and attitudes appropriate to the change, or were people expected to act in new ways and yet rewarded for acting in old ways?
>
> A total of 10 points for each question you answered Yes to. *What's your transition-management quotient?*

Source: Based on Bridges (1995).

Sustaining momentum – the contribution of human resources development

At the fifth stage – sustaining momentum – the key organisational concern is usually (though not always) with embedding new processes and reinforcing new behaviours. A number of organisations have tried to sustain momentum by

Figure 17.15 Sustaining momentum

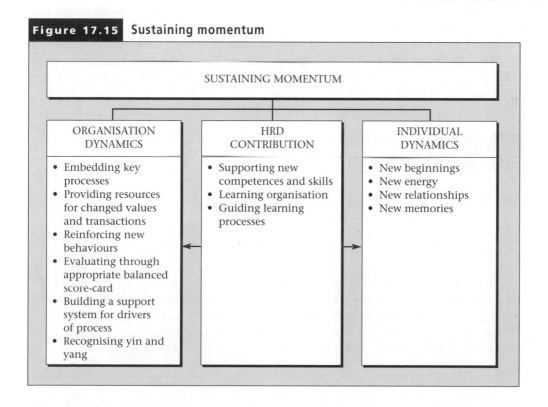

introducing a stream of new initiatives, sometimes before the earlier ones are embedded. Over the years BT has introduced a number of initiatives such as Project Sovereign (1991), Project Breakthrough (1993) and Project Breakout (1994). One manager in BT told me that, in her experience, each initiative tended to be communicated by means of a cascade process, with a new one coming in before one reached the end of the last. 'Sometimes it feels like it's done just to keep people on their toes.' She talked rather wearily of a sense of 'initiative overload'.

In terms of the individual dynamics there should by now be diminishing consciousness regarding the organisation's new way of doing things. New practices and behaviours are becoming part of the day-to-day reality. There should be positive stress – as opposed to distress – directed towards performance, creativity, objectives and competition.

Approaches by HRD agents to facilitate this include according to Burack (1991):

- 'institutionalise' internal education and training programmes;
- reinforce new directions, processes and relationships through new recognition meetings, programmes and communications;
- strengthen employee sufficiency skills through career counselling;
- provide counsel and serve as a sounding-board for change leaders (problems could be at unit, group or individual level).

During the stage of sustaining momentum, and assuming that a new initiative has not been launched, the external consultancy role will now be at an end. The responsibility for driving the learning processes will now be in the hands of internal staff.

In respect of the organisational dynamics new competences and skills will need to be supported and enabled through a range of HRD interventions, and incorporated into the performance-management process.

Momentum can be reinforced through learning processes that sustain a sense of energy as opposed to inertia. It is for reasons such as these that executives have been drawn to the idea of a learning organisation, with its power to support ongoing change.

Figure 17.16 | **Case study of a transformational change initiative: 'Transforming Hackney'**

The London Borough of Hackney, which was formed in 1965 from the amalgamation of a number of smaller boroughs in East London, has a population of just under 100 000, and in 1997 had the highest unemployment rate of any London borough. It has often been in the news for the wrong reasons, such as having one of the highest council tax rates in London and provision of poor and failing services. Indeed there has been a prevailing mindset of 'Poor Services for Poor People'. There was also political complacency which led to the strongly held (and misfounded) belief that, regardless of the service provided or the rate of council tax, the Labour Party would remain in control and that poor services could be blamed on cuts in central government grants. It employs more than 10 000 staff across a range of directorates and occupational groups.

▶▶

▶▶ Figure 17.16 continued

'Transforming Hackney' was launched in 1995 by the recently appointed Chief Executive Tony Elliston. The launch was followed by extensive discussion and consultation at all levels of the organisation. This resulted in the publication in the same year of the 'Transforming Hackney' defining statement which was circulated to all staff and elected members and formed the Transforming Agenda. The statement explained the council's values and beliefs and set out an overall strategy for transformation. The programme was adopted by the council and in 1998 was the central force behind everything the council did.

It is an ambitious change programme, at one level being an action plan to make significant and measurable improvements in the quality of the services that the council provides to its customers. It is also a programme of organisational and cultural change to transform the way the council operates.

After much discussion and brainstorming Hackney agreed its core values to be:

- Public Service
- Quality
- Equality
- Empowerment.

These principles are intended to underpin the way that Hackney works.

Again after considerable debate these values were translated into ten organisational beliefs, which define Hackney's values and operate as a framework for the transformational programme.

Organisational beliefs

- Strong and committed leadership;
- Maximum involvement and ownership;
- Developing and valuing staff;
- Valuing diversity and challenging discrimination;
- Belief and pride in Hackney;
- Customer focus;
- Commitment to quality;
- Devolving and empowering centre;
- Encouraging innovation and creativity;
- Simple direct communication.

Transforming Hackney was seen as requiring radical cultural change solutions. They entailed:

- closing the gap between Hackney's self-perception and the reality others see. Hackney needs to move from defensive reasoning and self-justification towards taking the necessary action to transform services;
- accepting the need to be creative and innovative, to research best practice and improve on it, then implement;

▶▶ Figure 17.16 continued

- adopting a performance culture, to achieve measurable improvement targets;
- the need to become customer driven rather than provider focused;
- the need to strip away unnecessary and bureaucratic procedures which reduce performance rather than improve it;
- the need to remove the 'fear factor' and adopt a style which was open, involving and empowering;
- to support and value staff who were on board.

Strategic choice – Hackney's vision

Before strategic options were discussed it was necessary for Hackney to establish a vision of the organisation the council will become. To achieve this it was agreed that elected members and staff must be committed to making the vision a reality.

Hackney Council will be an organisation which:

1 Represents citizens and acts as an advocate on their behalf.
2 Consistently delivers services of the highest quality.
3 Is at the leading edge of innovation and best practice.
4 Is an organisation staff, the community and partners have pride in.

What is not stated but has a major impact on the strategic choice is the need to reduce the council tax. The strategies must be in place to achieve the vision but at a lower cost. This is not contradictory; if the vision is achieved savings will be made.

McKinsey's 7-S

The 7-S model was originally developed in the late 1970s by McKinsey and Company in conjunction with Richard Pascale of Stanford University and Anthony Athos of Harvard University (Pascale and Athos, 1981). This model was used to identify, evaluate and select strategic options for Hackney. It enabled an analysis to be made of if and what changes were needed for:

- *Strategy.* It was felt that if 'Transforming Hackney' was to succeed, each S would need to be reviewed and changed, and the strategy must assist the change. To do this it must be developed in conjunction with the other S's.
- *Structure.* This was judged as being too centralised, with decisions being made too far from the service providers. The centre was not adding value to the organisation but rather making their jobs more difficult by the introduction of more and more procedures which were pushed down without consultation. Compulsory Competitive Tendering had forced structural change on blue collar and some white collar services but this had not been replicated at the centre. They were judged as not living in the real world. Each directorate had two centres, one for their own directorate and one at the council centre. Each seemed removed from the daily provisions of services.
- *Systems.* At Hackney there was a proliferation of procedures, rules and regulations which were used as reasons not to do something. They had developed as a way of dealing with the 'Fear Factor': you could not be wrong if you followed procedures

▶▶

▶▶ Figure 17.16 continued

even if the procedures were wrong. Again staff at the frontline found that the many procedures hindered them in their jobs rather than assisted them.

■ *Staff.* Staff were demoralised and often unhappy to admit that they worked for Hackney. There were high absence rates and a culture of getting your rights. This included the right to dependency leave and the right to work hours that suited the employee rather than the service.

■ *Shared values.* Hackney was there for the benefit of staff not of customers. It was believed that because Hackney was difficult you could not make a difference and therefore there was no point in bothering. There was always reasons for not achieving.

■ *Styles.* Examples of styles were: to not achieve targets, to not arrive on time for meetings, to not return calls, to normally fail.

■ *Skills.* Training had been non-existent and staff felt undervalued. Although modern IT was in place staff were not trained to use it. General skills were poor. Appraisals did not take place and the lack of capability of staff was not identified or followed through.

Selecting a strategy and implementing it – changing the structure

After much consultation and collaboration with other local authorities it was decided that a radical reorganisation of the management structure was necessary. The new structure would include:

■ an executive board comprising the chief executive and a small team of executive directors who will be responsible for areas of major corporate importance, the strategic co-ordination of major service areas and the performance management of service directors and the head of core and trading units. Executive directors will have no budgets and no staff; they will be accountable to the policy board which will comprise leading members and the executive board;

■ service directors will be responsible for service strategy, development and commissioning a number of services based on local customer groupings. Service directors will be supported by small strategy and commissioning teams and will be accountable to service committees;

■ service managers will be responsible for service delivery, operating on a fully devolved basis accountable to service directors;

■ core units will be responsible for corporate strategic, service and regulatory functions;

■ trading units.

This structure will provide an effective commissioning/provider split, far-reaching devolution and clarity of roles and accountabilities based on a comprehensive performance-management role.

All existing senior management had to compete with external applicants for these jobs. In the great majority of cases they were not successful and left the organisation. The first barrier had been cleared.

▶▶

▶▶ Figure 17.16 continued

> All support services in all directorates were deleted. Staff had to complete forms outlining their skills to allow them to be matched with the new but reduced jobs in the service, core and trading units.
>
> Voluntary redundancy was not initially available. A particular problem in previous local government reorganisations is that the best staff wish to take voluntary redundancy, confident that they will be able to get another job if they so wish. The chief executive did not wish to affect service delivery by risking losing these staff. Therefore initially nobody was allowed to take redundancy until their skills had been matched to jobs and a surplus of skills identified. At the time of writing some staff are now being allowed to leave.
>
> What recognition do you find, in this diagnosis and action plan, of the distinctive contribution of HRD?

EVALUATION OF TRANSFORMATIONAL CHANGE

Sashkin and Burke (1987) comment that a long-standing problem has centred on the question of what really changes as a result of transformational change interventions which are designed to modify behaviour. There are innumerable examples of OD consultants having completed a project that to all appearances was quite successful and yet the clients report that the situation is worse, not better.

Golembiewski *et al.* (1976) sought to explain this puzzling paradox. They defined three types of change:

1 ALPHA change is 'true' change, a change in measured attitudes and behaviour that can be shown to result from an OD intervention.

2 BETA change occurs when measurement scales themselves change, in the minds of organisation members. For example, what had before the OD intervention seemed a pretty good climate might afterwards be viewed as rather poor in comparison with a newly recognised ideal. And this might be the case even though the OD intervention actually improved the situation! Thus the outcome might appear to be little or no change, or even to be negative, although the 'true' result is a positive change. This true result is, however, detectable only if the shift in organisation members' internal measurement scales can be identified and taken into account.

3 GAMMA change makes quantitative OD effects almost impossible to demonstrate because the basic dimensions, the very ways in which organisation members see the organisation, have been changed as a result of OD activities.

This is compounded by the fact that many transformational change exercises are not initiated by the 'populace' but by the senior management, often by the CEO alone. As we have observed, the timescale for forgetting old ways can also be substantial.

Perhaps the only true way to evaluate the change is not to ask the question 'Is it better?' but 'Is it different?' That is much easier to establish, and also much more revealing.

CONCLUSION

At the start of this chapter a number of questions were asked. How much further on are we to answering them?

What is the relationship between transformational change and learning? How is learning facilitated? What sort of learning is entailed?

This whole area of macro-organisational change and its management has been shown to be of particular significance to HRD professionals because of its implications for individual and collective learning. It is of course a defining characteristic of HRD that by virtue of being concerned with learning it is concerned with change. Even the most elementary definition of learning at the individual level suggests that it should have the potential to result in some form of change (be it considered in behavioural or performance terms) The reverse is also true. Just as learning entails change, so too does the achievement of change imply that learning has taken place. 'Change is about learning' (Beer *et al.*, 1990). In both situations HRD practitioners, as part of their professional repertoire, should be able to make some contribution towards helping learners through the learning transition process, and facilitating learning transference.

Perhaps the most significant implication for HRD practitioners is to be in a position to influence the change and learning process. On the whole this tends to be done by external organisational development consultants at the outset. The transfer of responsibility from the external to the internal consultant is an important part of the overall process.

What diagnostic skills does an HRD practitioner need to possess about the organisation being subjected to transformational change?

This chapter has argued that a deep diagnostic understanding of the organisation, in terms of its capacity and readiness to change, is needed, mediated by an understanding of the external forces affecting it. The understanding should not be so deep that one is too enmeshed in its cultural norms and mores to be able to escape from the existing mores and preferred ways of operating.

This in turn links to the range of skills and capabilities that HRD staff bring to the task. Ulrich (1998) argues that the hardest thing senior managers can do to drive a new mandate for HR is to improve the quality of HR staff itself. Organisations 'need people who know the business, understand the theory and practice of HR, can manage culture and make change happen, and have personal credibility'.

Are some forms of transformational change more susceptible to learning interventions than others?

This chapter has argued that HRD interventions are less suited to coping with crisis-driven situations which require instant, imposed solutions. Much of the methodology on HRD involvement has focused on the behavioural aspects of a transformation, balancing the individual and organisational dynamics of the situation through an organisational development perspective.

At the same time transformational change should not be seen as a synonym for organisational development. In many instances, especially those arising out of a crisis situation, the organisation is not developed, it is uprooted. Nor should organisation development be seen as the only approach entailing a legitimate HRD role. A number of transformations have been achieved through a focus on transactional elements affecting the design archetype. In such situations people need to acquire the skills associated with new job roles and responsibilities.

How far can learning about and during the change process be managed in a contained programmatic way?

A five-stage framework has been presented for looking at a programmatic approach to managing transformational change. It is presented in the context of logical incrementalism, as opposed to being a sequence of predetermined interventions.

Additional questions arising out of transformational change emerge as a result of the foregoing analysis. They include:

■ What is the relationship between transformational change and organisational learning?

■ Is transformational change more readily accomplished in an organisation that purports to be a learning organisation?

■ Are new forms of learning – such as the learning organisation a desired outcome of the change process?

■ Is transformational change possible in a multidivisional global organisation?

Such questions will be addressed at various stages in the remaining chapters of this book.

REFERENCES

Aitken, A. and Saunders, I. (1995) 'Vision only works if communicated', *People Management,* 21 December, pp. 28–30.

Argyris, C. and Schon, D. (1978) *Organisational Learning: A Theory of Action Perspective.* Reading, MA: Addison-Wesley.

Augustine, N. R. (1997) 'Reshaping an Industry – Lockheed Martin's Survival Story', *Harvard Business Review,* May–June.

Beckhard, R. (1989), in J. William Pheiffer (ed.) *The 1989 Annual Handbook for Group Facilitators: Developing Human Resources.* Pfeiffer and Company.

Beckhard, R. and Harris, R. T. (1987) *Organisation Transitions – Managing Complex Change,* (2nd edn). Reading, MA: Addison-Wesley.

Beer, M., Eisenstat, R.A. and Spector, B. (1990) 'Why Change Programmes don't Produce' Change', *Harvard Business Review,* November–December, pp. 158–66.

Bolman, L. G. and Deal, T. E. (1991) *Reframing Organisations – Artistry, Choice and Leadership.* San Francisco: Jossey-Bass.

Bridges, W. (1995) 'Breaking with the Past ', *Human Resources,* September–October.

Burack, E. H. (1991) 'Changing the Company Culture – the Role of Human Resource Development', *Long Range Planning,* 24(1), pp. 88–95.

Burke, W. W. (1992) *Organisation Development – A Process of Learning and Changing* (2nd edn). Reading, MA: Addison-Wesley.

Coopers & Lybrand (1997). Internal publication.

Dawson, P. (1994) *Organisation Change – A Processual Approach.* London: Chapman.

French, W. L. and Bell, C. H. (1978) *Organisation Development.* Englewood Cliffs, NJ: Prentice Hall.

Friedlander, F. and Brown, L. D. (1974) 'Organisation Development', *Annual Review of Psychology,* 25, pp. 313–41.

Gioia, D. A., Thomas, J. B., Clark, S. M. and Chittipendi, K. (1994) 'Symbolism and Strategic Change in Academia', *Organisation Science,* 5(3), August.

Golembiewski, R. T., Billingsley, K. and Yeager, S. (1976) 'Measuring Change and Persistence in Human Affairs: Types of Change Generated by OD Designs', *Journal of Applied Behavioural Science,* 12, pp. 133–57.

Harrison, M. (1987) *Diagnosing Organisations: Methods, Models and Practices'.* Beverly Hills: Sage.

Kennedy, C. (1998) 'The Roadmap to Success: How Gerhard Schulmeyer Changed the Culture at Siemens Nixdorf', *Long Range Planning,* 31(2), April, pp. 262–71.

Kono, T. (1994) 'Changing a Company's Strategy and Culture', *Long Range Planning,* 27(5), pp. 85–97.

Kotter, J. (1995) 'Leading Change – Why Transformation Efforts Fail', *Harvard Business Review,* March–April.

Kubler-Ross, E. (1969) *On Death and Dying.* New York: Macmillan.

Laughlin, R. C. (1991) 'Environmental Disturbances and Organisational Transitions and Transformations: Some Alternative Models', *Organisation Studies,* 12(2), pp. 209–32.

Lewin, K. (1952) 'Group Decision and Social Change', in G. E. Swanson, T. M. Newcomb and E. L. Hartley (eds) *Readings in Social Psychology* (rev. edn). New York: Holt.

Mabey, C. and Mallory, G. (1995) 'Structure and culture change in two UK organisations: A comparison of assumptions, approaches and outcomes', *Human Resource Management Journal,* 5(2), pp. 1–18.

Mabey, C. and Salamon, G. (1995) *Strategic Human Resource Management.* Oxford: Blackwell.

Marshak, R. J. (1993) 'Managing the Metaphors of Change', *Organisation Dynamics,* Summer.

Nadler, D. A. (1983) 'Concepts for the Management of Organisational Change' (Delta Consulting Group Inc.), reproduced in M. L. Tushman and W. L. Moore (eds) (1988) *Readings in the Management of Innovation.* New York: Ballinger.

Orgland, M. and Von Krogh, G. (1998) 'Initiating, Managing and Sustaining Corporate Transformation – A Case Study', *European Management Journal,* 16(1), February.

Pascale, R. T. and Athos, A. G. (1981) *The Art of Japanese Management.* New York: Simon & Schuster.

Price Waterhouse Change Integration Team (1996) *The Paradox Principles – How High Performance Companies Manage Chaos, Complexity and Contradiction to Achieve Superior Results.* Homewood, IL: Irwin.

Quinn, J. B. (1980) *Strategies for Change: Logical Incrementalism.* Homewood, IL: Irwin.

Rains, J. (1997) 'The Values of HRD Practitioners'. AHRD Conference Proceedings, Atlanta.

Robb, F. F. (1988) 'Morphostasis and morphogenesis: contexts of participative design inquiry in the design of systems of learning and human development'. Unpublished discussion paper, University of Edinburgh.

Sashkin, M. and Burke, W. W. (1987) 'Organisation Development in the 1980s', *Journal of Management,* 13, pp. 393–417.

Schein, E. H. (1987) *Process Consultation Volume 2, Lessons for Managers and Consultants.* Reading, MA: Addison-Wesley.

Smith, K. K. (1982) 'Philosophical problems in thinking about organisational change', in P. S. Goodman and L. B. Kurke (eds) *Change in Organisations*. San Francisco: Jossey-Bass.

Stace, D. and Dunphy, D. (1991) 'Beyond traditional paternalistic and developmental approaches to change and human resource strategies', *International Journal of Human Resource Management*, 2(3), December, pp. 263–83.

Tichy, N. M. and Devanna, M. A. (1986) *The Transformational Leader*. New York: Wiley.

Ulrich, D. (1998) 'A New Mandate for Human Resources', *Harvard Business Review*, January–February, pp. 125–34.

Watzlawick, P., Weakland, J. H. and Fisch, R. (1974) *Change: Principles of Problem Formation and Problem Resolution*. New York: Norton.

Weiss, J. W. (1996) *Organisational Behaviour and Change – Managing Diversity, Cross-Cultural Dynamics, and Ethics*. West.

Young, D. (1991a) 'Managing for a change – the strategic route to making organisational change sustainable', *Multinational Business*, 2.

Young, D. (1991b) 'Organisation and change – developing an understanding of an organisation and its constituent elements in order to implement change', *Multinational Business*, 3.

Chapter 18

THE ROLE OF HUMAN RESOURCE DEVELOPMENT IN CREATING SYNERGY AMONG BUSINESS UNITS AND SUB-UNITS

OBJECTIVES

By the end of this chapter you should be able to:

- define synergy in an organisational context;

- identify factors which restrict the synergistic potential in organisations;

- establish the bases of a horizontal strategy for organisations;

- differentiate between HRD approaches to developing synergy in existing organisations and those which might be appropriate in the context of mergers, acquisitions and strategic alliances.

INTRODUCTION

As an organisational concept, synergy originated in the social psychology literature to help explain the dynamics of groups and manifestations of team cohesiveness. In an early formulation Cattell (1951) defined synergy as the sum total of the energy which a group can command. The concept was subsequently refined by group and organisation behaviour theorists, imported into the strategy management literature by Ansoff (1969), and is typically defined as relating to 'situations where two or more activities or processes complement each other to the extent that their combined effort is greater than the "sum of the parts"' (Johnson and Scholes, 1993). It is making connections for the benefit of the whole where previously none existed. It is often expressed in mathematical terms as the $2 + 2 = 5$ effect. In HRD terms the creation of synergies can be construed as how to enable collective learning and knowledge about processes and operations that contribute to people working together for the benefit of the whole (*see* Fig. 18.1).

Synergies can be sought both within and between organisations. Within an organisation the manifestation of 'synergy' is sometimes seen as the outcome of successful organisational design. The constituent parts have fitted together in such a way that outcomes have been achieved which are dependent upon the

| Figure 18.1 | Human resource development at the heart of synergy seeking |

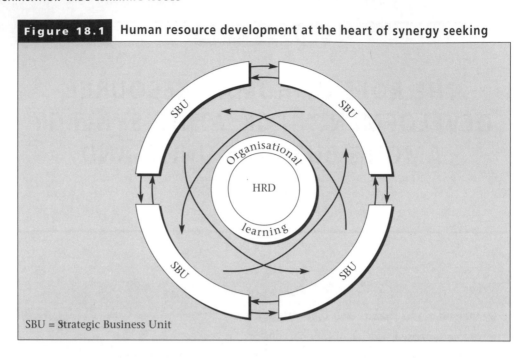

SBU = Strategic Business Unit

interaction of individual components but that could not have been predicted from knowledge of those individual components. In its most extreme expression talk of synergy sometimes leads to associations with organisational reification. In other words, because one cannot predict the behaviour of the whole from the characteristics of the constituent parts of the whole, it is inferred that the whole has a life force independent of the constituent parts. This intriguing avenue of thought is discussed more thoroughly in Chapter 15. In the present context, the issue is how HRD insights can facilitate the co-ordination of the constituent functional areas of an organisation, and the people who work in them, in such a fashion that one can truly say, 'this is an organisation'; the parts are working together for the benefit of the whole.

The development of synergies is not a once and for all process, but can be an ongoing act of seeking out and learning about linkages and resultant benefits between activities which have been previously unconnected or where the connection has been of a different type (Johnson and Scholes, op. cit.).

Trends in recent years towards the establishment of autonomous business units and devolution of authority to line managers, together with the decentralisation that goes with this, have challenged the notion that synergy is something universally to be aimed for. Synergy by definition is concerned with co-ordination, establishing linkages and 'fit'. Business unit autonomy and exhortations to exercise local discretion in decision making have led to an emphasis on 'split'. This move away from seeking synergies within organisations confronts head-on conventional ideas as to what constitutes an organisation and the purpose of organising. The idea of synergy assumes that there is some organisational rationale that supports the pulling together in the same direction.

Kanter (1989) tries to find a way around the apparent contradictions embodied in decentralisation. She defines synergies as 'interactions of businesses that . . . provide benefits above and beyond what the units could do separately'. For her the search for synergies is fundamentally different to those linkages sought by the large bureaucratic monoliths that dominated most of the twentieth century. She refers to an era of 'post-entrepreneurial corporations' that have applied 'entrepreneurial principles to the traditional corporation, creating a marriage between entrepreneurial creativity and corporate discipline, co-operation and teamwork'. Such organisations have been initiating a fundamental reconfiguration of their operations and *modus operandi* through such mechanisms as downsizing, delayering and strategic partnerships. In their new restructured, decentralised world she feels they need to make the search for synergies a central plank of their strategies. She goes on to say:

> Whether reorganisations occur because of internal drives to increase effectiveness or because of mergers and acquisitions, whether acquisitions are in related or unrelated businesses, whether the company is adding activities or divesting them, the management task is similar: to manage the process so that value is at least retained. That provides the minimum foundation on which real synergies – value added and multiplied – can be built (ibid.).

Synergy has thus, with the trend towards strategic alliances, mergers and acquisitions, come to the fore as an issue between as well as within organisations.

Mergers, acquisitions, joint ventures and strategic alliances differ from other processes of organisational change in terms of:

■ the speed of change;

■ the scale of change;

■ the existence of a critical mass of unknowns that are presented to both parties.

A high percentage of mergers and acquisitions have failed. Many argue that this is because of the absence of synergistic potential between the partners. Often this is not because the products or markets do not complement each other. Rather it has to do with the fact that the 'critical mass of unknowns' represent fundamental and impenetrable 'cultural' differences. The partners see the world in such a different light that the coming together was misconceived from the outset.

In an existing, established organisation HRD has a key role in trying to orchestrate learning processes that will facilitate greater understanding and enhanced competences between units that have drifted apart. Between previously separate organisations the situation is rendered more or less complex dependent on the context and prior understanding in which the initial coming together was conceived. In many respects the basic HRD principles and approaches will remain constant, although the likelihood of success is clearly constrained by the situation.

Note that even the HR field is not exempt from allegations of lack of synergy and the need to act together more effectively. In many organisations the division of labour has led to HRD and HRM functional activities becoming distant in location and distinct in terms of who undertakes them. This chapter emphasises the importance of working together on a common agenda if HR is to make a significant contribution to achieving greater synergies.

CREATING SYNERGIES IN EXISTING ORGANISATIONS

The effective operation of any organisation can be seen as an act of synergy – the grouping together and co-ordination of a set of previously unrelated parts into a set of structures, systems and processes that provide goods or services or other desired outcomes that would have not been possible without co-operative effort. Indeed, the simplest definition of synergy is 'co-operative effort'.

An organisation, by definition, consists of two or more (often many more) people working together in co-operative effort to try to achieve some desired result. A central design feature is how the work is divided between the individual contributors. Rather than all organisational members doing identical tasks in parallel, there will be some degree of specialisation. Functional differentiation occurs in order that individuals can concentrate on, develop skills in and give attention to a specific area of activity.

However, as organisations get larger, the problems of co-ordination and co-operation become greater. Different functional areas tend to get absorbed into handling and resolving the specific issues facing them, often without reference to other parts of the organisation, certainly on a day-to-day basis. Boundaries are established between departments, reinforced by separate physical locations and reporting relationships. Over time boundaries can become barriers as individual groups tend to see others as being the source of their problems.

Over time also, many organisations tend to develop new ranges of products and services, or operate over a larger geographical area, which enlarges the structural arena and compounds the problems of co-ordination. Some writers have suggested that growth is an inevitable consequence for organisations operating over extensive time spans and is a manifestation of an organisation working through a predetermined life cycle.

Some of the functional subdivisions can lead to the emergence of distinctive structures and cultures which are at odds with those elsewhere in an organisation. Lawrence and Lorsch (1969), for example, compared the research and production sub-units of complex manufacturing concerns on a number of dimensions and identified substantial structural and cultural differences which they contended were accounted for by the nature of the environmental exchanges undertaken. They went on to generalise that the type of work entailed in a research unit would lead to the appointment of highly qualified independently minded scientists who would not respond readily to structural controls. The nature of the work, and of the scientists' expectations, would lead to irregular working hours, and to the maintenance of closer links with the academic scientific community than with other units in the organisation. In other words, the structure would be conditioned by a departmental culture based on an overriding scientific 'ethos'. Sales and marketing departments similarly developed distinctive sub-cultures based on the organisational environment with which they were associated.

Lawrence and Lorsch recognised the potentially negative impact of the emergence of separate cultures and structures in the same organisation. They contended that there are two major and potentially contradictory tensions confronting organisational designers – 'differentiation' and 'integration'. The balance between them operates as a sort of ongoing dialectic.

Differentiation went beyond a simple structural connotation. They viewed it as encompassing 'the difference in cognitive and emotional orientation among managers in different functional departments' in respect of dimensions such as:

■ their goal orientation – for example, how far is attention focused on the particular goals of the department as opposed to a broader organisational perspective?

■ their time orientation – for example, how far is attention focused on short-term horizons rather than longer-term perspectives?

■ their interpersonal relations with staff – for example, is the predominant management style task or person focused?

Integration they defined as 'the quality of the state of collaboration that exists among departments that are required to achieve unity of effort by the demands of the environment'.

If the move towards differentiation got out of balance then new integrative solutions needed to be found. They noted a number of solutions adopted in their sample organisations, such as introducing link departments to facilitate co-ordination and communication between mainstream functional units. They also saw the benefits of undertaking HRD strategies such as the provision of cross-departmental communication programmes during which members of the different departments were exposed to the problems and issues facing the other.

The divisionalised form

Mintzberg (1979) argues that there are five basic parts in any organisation. Although the balance between them will vary there are a limited number of resultant structural configurations. The five basic parts are as follows.

1 The *operating core* relates to the employees who carry out the various tasks involved in the primary activities of the value chain.

2 The *strategic apex* relates to the strategic leadership of the organisation who are responsible for developing the overall corporate strategy, handling the environmental interface and allocating resources.

3 The *middle management* connects the strategic apex to the operating core by translating strategy and policy into practice. It is this group which have been heavily affected by the delayering strategy of recent years.

4 The *support staff*, often grouped together in functional departments such as marketing and HR, carry out support activities to both middle managers and the operating core.

5 The *technostructure*. This includes IT systems.

One structural solution adopted by many large organisations to handle the complexities resulting from size and scale has been to create separate businesses operating on a geographical or territorial basis or on a discrete product-oriented basis or in some instances both. Mintzberg (op. cit.) captures the essence of this structural approach when he refers to the 'divisionalised form' of many diversified or multiproduct organisations as one of his structural configurations. As the product divisions become larger they can be further subdivided into smaller 'divisions', replicas of the larger, rather like a nest of Russian dolls (*see* Fig. 18.2).

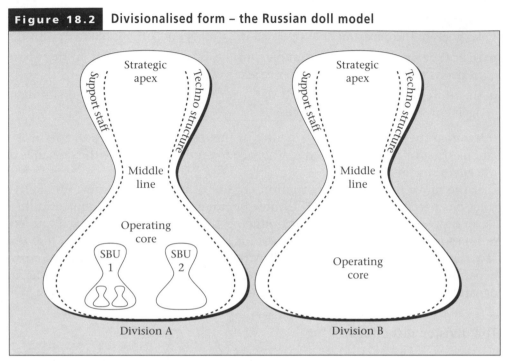

Figure 18.2 Divisionalised form – the Russian doll model

Source: Derived from Mintzberg (1979).

Porter (1985) has also drawn attention to the idea of an organisational value chain, consisting of primary operational and secondary support activities. Drawing upon Porter's original formulation, organisation designers nowadays tend to differentiate between customer-facing operational units and back-office support units (*see* Fig. 18.3). Where synergy does not exist, especially between support services and operational units, the greater is the risk of functions being outsourced. There is a need to develop new synergistic ways of working together in partnership to demonstrate added value.

In many instances each division or directorate has its own set of support staff represented by functional activities on the support value chain – resulting in separate marketing departments, finance departments, training departments, personnel departments and so on. Sometimes there has been cross-communication and cross-fertilisation of ideas between divisions, but this has by no means been a universal norm. The divisionalised form has also often resulted in tensions between centralised 'parent' functions operating out of a corporate HQ and decentralised equivalent functions located in the businesses.

This is often because the decentralised nature of the divisionalised form has led to a tendency to develop local practices. The HR function has been particularly caught up in this in recent years. Hirsh and Jackson (1996) refer to a trend in large organisations with devolved business units to design and implement local, as

Figure 18.3

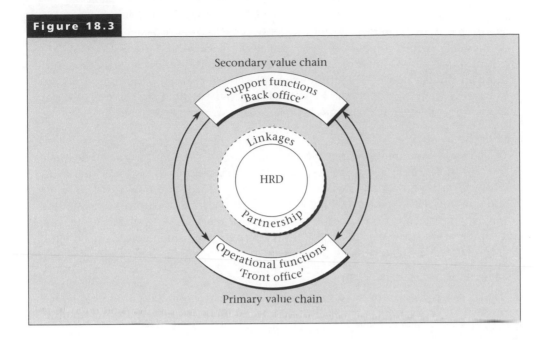

opposed to central, career development approaches and pay and grading structures. They also mention criticisms made at the local level that small, fragmented HR functions do not sustain their support to the line.

Richard Pascale (1991) provides a thought-provoking framework relating to the structural tensions that affect large organisations. His view is that our current managerial mindset (or paradigm) is inadequate for the organisational problems faced. We have no basis whatsoever for our confidence that we know how to manage a corporation in a fashion that sustains its vitality and that engenders adaptation. He suggests that a good place to start is by identifying the factors that drive stagnation and renewal in organisations. Four factors can be identified, termed *fit*, *split*, *contend* and *transcend* (*see* Fig. 18.4).

Figure 18.4 Fit, split, contend, transcend

Fit

'Fit' refers to the consistencies and coherence of an organisation. When fit is absent, organisational life can be confusing. For example, a new strategic thrust may direct us to improve customer service, yet the organisational chart relegates customer service to a weak and undermanned staff function, the reward systems drive exclusively for profitability and cost containment and the personnel department regularly provides this function with cast-offs from other departments, and so on. This is an example of poor fit. When the gears engage and all of these elements mesh, fit is attained.

Split

'Split' pertains to a variety of techniques used to sustain autonomy and diversity, such as decentralised profit centres and stand-alone subsidiaries. Typically, these

▶▶

▶▶ Figure 18.4 continued

entities are assigned responsibility for specialised products and markets outside the parent organisation's mainstream. Other types of split rely less on structure, and more on human networks. Multifunctional task forces and new venture teams are examples. Many corporations today utilise a variety of such approaches to build special capabilities that a customer or a particular technology demands.

Contend

The concept of contention draws attention to the presence and value of constructive conflict. There are some tensions in organisations that should *never* be resolved once and for all (such as between cost control and quality). The functional disciplines that advocate different points of view rub up against one another and generate debate. Contention across these boundaries is inescapable. Moreover, it can be productive. We are almost always better served when conflict is brought to the surface and channelled, not suppressed.

Transcend

Transcend' is an approach to management that can cope with the complexity entailed in orchestrating fit, split and contend. This is not just an incremental increase in the difficulty of the management task. It requires a different mindset. It looks to the tension (or dynamic synthesis) between contradictory opposites as the engine of self-renewal. It is predicated on the notion that disequilibrium is a better strategy for adaptation or survival than order and equilibrium.

Source: Pascale (1991).

It is in this context that the search for intra-organisational synergies that transcend the fit-split-contend dynamics has taken root in the 1990s.

THE 'EVERYTHING BUT' RULE

One attempt at regulating relations between the strategic apex and the operating core has been through the application of an 'everything but' rule. The global AXA insurance group, which purchased in the UK during the 1990s both the previously independent Sun Life Assurance Society and 'Equity and Law', operates on a 'think global, act local' basis, but with local decentralised decision making mediated by the application of such a rule.

Thus the AXA Group has chosen a decentralised structure to foster autonomous decision making among its operational units – for *everything but* a few central functions that include:

- Executive Career Management Policy
- HR Philosophy
- Use of the AXA tardemark and Group image
- Information Systems Policy
- Capital Management structure and strategy: resource allocation.

HORIZONTAL STRATEGY

One of the most well-known approaches to creating synergies in large organisations is by means of what is known as a *horizontal strategy*. A horizontal strategy reflects a series of policies which seek to maximise the interrelationships between existing operational business units for the benefit of the overall business. It is known as a horizontal strategy to differentiate it from so-called *vertical integration strategies* which seek to incorporate within an organisation's boundaries activities which are 'upstream' or 'downstream' of its existing sphere of operations. It should not be confused with a *horizontal diversification strategy,* which refers to an extension into activities or businesses which are directly complementary to an organisation's current sphere of operations.

Porter (1985) believes that there is constant pressure from business units to increase their sense of autonomy which in consequence results in a reduction in the degree of synergy. He identifies two reasons why there seems to be an inability to exploit potential interrelationships between business units:

1 *Different values*. Individual business units in an organisation hold different viewpoints on the significance of establishing interrelationships with other business units.

2 *Strategic freedom*. Business units tend to develop plans that optimise their own commercial development, given a free hand. They can also can resist attempts to achieve synergistic relationships because of fear of political or competitive interference from other units.

These lead to a number of negative consequences for the organisation as a whole:

1 *Pricing and investment decisions*. Left to their own devices, business units tend to develop uncoordinated pricing and investment decisions.

2 *Formation of outside alliances*. External relationships may be developed at the expense of more appropriate internal alliances.

3 *Ignoring key potential competitors*. Each business unit may conduct its own competitor analysis, not comparing results with or picking up signals identified by other units.

4 *Technology transfer*. Local isolation can result in individual business units not learning from the experiences of other units with new technology.

Without an explicit horizontal strategy, Porter argues, there will be no systematic mechanism to identify, reinforce and extend relationships. Business units acting independently simply do not have the same incentives to propose and advocate strategies based on interrelationships as do higher-level managers with a broader perspective.

The issue for HRD is what contribution can be made to facilitate relationship building, given such an explicit strategy and recognising the ongoing counter-tendency towards split. Figure 18.5 examines the creation of synergy in multi-business corporations.

Figure 18.5 Creating synergy in multibusiness corporations

According to Rosabeth Moss Kanter (1989) the only real justification for a multi-business corporation is the achievement of synergy – that magical mix of business activities that are stronger and more profitable together than they would be separately. The 'portfolio' or 'holding company' approach – in which each part stands alone and needs to be different in order to compensate for the weakness of other parts – has been increasingly discredited.

What differentiates winners from losers is co-operation between the heads of the different business units. One especially comprehensive and successful case of a concerted effort to build 'value multipliers' or synergies is American Express. In 1986 roughly 10 per cent of American Express's net income came from cross-selling between SBUs and other synergies. The CEO made achieving synergies a priority in 1982, emphasising that American Express was 'one enterprise' united by overall common goals and asking senior executives to identify two or three promising 'One Enterprise' synergy projects in their annual plans. A manager of corporate strategy watched over this, issuing a One Enterprise report to 100 executives, giving visibility to those involved in collaboration.

Evaluations and incentives were tied to this programme. The Chairman of American Express Bank received one of two bonuses for efforts such as selling travellers cheques for the card division and introducing overseas brokerage services to its overseas clients. And by 1987 the company had sifted through about 260 ideas for collaboration between businesses, about 70 per cent of which worked. Among these ideas were sharing of office space, data-processing capabilities and marketing expertise among departments, and also cross-marketing of products.

Two forms of synergy seem most common at American Express, one externally oriented (marketing leads) and one internally oriented (efficiencies from using another company's 'back-office' information-processing capacity).

American Express's search for synergies rests on an entrepreneurial foundation – a set of rather autonomous and focused business units are each trying to maximise their profits and if their leaders can see that help from someone else is going to aid them, they will seek it out and try to convince the others that it is in their best interests also.

SYNERGY AND DIVERSIFICATION

Mergers and acquisitions

The 1960s and the 1970s saw the beginning of a trend for organisations to look for growth through diversification, often through mergers and acquisitions.

A merger is defined as the joining or gradual blending of two previously discrete entities. Many mergers represent co-operative agreements between organisations closely matched in size.

An acquisition is defined as an outright gain of something (especially useful). It can be 'friendly' or hostile. The distinction between a friendly or hostile acquisition tends to reflect the attitude of senior management and other power brokers rather than that of the work-force, although work-force support can be drummed up in an endeavour to resist the incursions of predators.

Mergers or acquisitions can reflect an attempt at extending the degree of vertical or horizontal integration that previously existed between the players. Where there is a combination of two similar organisations in the same industry, it is a form of related diversification contributing to horizontal integration in the industry. Where the outcome is a coming together of two organisations from completely unrelated fields of business activity, this is a conglomerate. Where the resultant grouping is from two organisations operating in related but previously unfamiliar fields, there is concentric diversification.

A variety of competitive forces continue to contribute to national and global mergers and acquisitions across a range of industries. Grocery retailing was an extremely fragmented industry 25 years ago. However there has been an increasing tendency towards mergers and acquisitions in order both to respond to major changes in consumer behaviour and to achieve economies of scale. In global terms, many developed countries have strict restrictions on opening large new stores or lack prime locations of adequate size (e.g. Switzerland), leaving mergers and acquisitions the only domestic expansion strategy available (Kumar, 1997).

The achievement of synergy between the resultant businesses has been one of the major justifications of such a strategy. Porter (1980) used the concept of *relatedness* as a precondition for synergy to occur. He identified two types of synergistic relationship which could emerge between the value chains of business units:

- the sharing of a resource across businesses (same manufacturing equipment, same distribution channels, etc.);
- the transfer of a skill across businesses (transfer of product or process technology, transfer of marketing techniques, etc.).

Implementing relatedness means that the organisation shares a resource or transfers a skill in order to improve its competitive advantage in at least one of the linked businesses. The creation or the reinforcement of the advantage (lowering costs and/or increasing differentiation from the competition) leads to a better competitive position. When an organisation adds to its portfolio according to this logic, managers can create a new set of businesses with a value superior to the sum of the intrinsic values of these businesses.

Compatible managerial perspectives and skills are also important in the context of diversification strategies. Bettis and Prahalad (1986) refer to the dominant logic of general management, defined as 'the way in which managers conceptualise the business and make critical resource allocation decisions', to explain the success of diversified organisations.

Thus in situations where the top managers want to manage a new business themselves they should acquire businesses which can share the same dominant logic as themselves. In situations where managers prefer to enter businesses which operate under a different logic they should also recognise that they need to acquire new management skills. In the latter case, the managers must assess whether they can quickly learn a new logic of management or whether they have to recruit a skilled manager or new management team to run the new business (Verey, 1993).

Michael Porter's longitudinal analysis of a set of Fortune 500 companies in the USA showed that most could not digest acquisitions unrelated to their core business; over 70 per cent of the firms divested such unrelated units after about five years (Porter, 1987).

Mergers and acquisitions lead to very different synergistic implications than when one is trying to extend the network of relationships and connections in existing organisations. One is facing the attempt to create one new organisation out of two. People will be facing a sense of loss and anxiety will be high. Mirvis (1985) suggests that the psychological response to merger and acquisition can be understood within the framework of the Kubler-Ross (1969) model of personal bereavement referred to in Chapter 17. According to Mirvis, one can expect employee reactions to pass through four stages:

- *Stage 1: Disbelief and denial.* Typically the individual's first reaction is extreme shock. He or she may deny that the merger or acquisition will ever happen despite circulating rumours or a bid announcement. Even when the deal is actually signed, the individual may strive to convince herself or himself that nothing will change. Often an existing organisational leader is identified as a champion of the status quo who will successfully fight to preserve the established identity and culture of the organisation.

- *Stage 2: Anger through rage and resentment.* As the reality of the situation becomes more obvious, feelings of shock and disbelief are replaced by anger and resentment towards those considered responsible, such as the old management or the new merger partner.

- *Stage 3: Emotional bargaining, beginning in anger and ending in depression.* As fear and uncertainty about the individual job future develops, this anger often turns inwards. The individual becomes angry with himself or herself for not anticipating the event and may come to resent the commitment and loyalty invested in the organisation. Often the individual becomes increasingly nostalgic for what is past and may worry that existing skills or areas of expertise are not transferable to the new organisation. These feelings may subsequently subside, to be replaced by depression.

- *Stage 4: Acceptance.* Finally the individual comes to recognise that what is past is gone forever, and accepts that the new situation must be faced up to.

Hunsaker and Coombs (1988) provide a similar but expanded version of the same theme (*see* Table 18.1).

They do not propose that the later stages inevitably occur, but that these are stages to be aimed at as part of the adjustment and integration process. Until these later states are achieved, it is difficult to visualise effective synergies taking place between the merged or acquired organisations. Cartwright and Cooper (1992) make the point that those responsible for merger management have been invariably over-confident in their estimation of the speed and ease with which integration can be achieved. For a while at least there is an increase in internal cohesiveness, with each merger partner engaging in a knee-jerk reaction to close

Table 18.1 Stages in the response to merger and acquisition

Stage		Characteristic response
1	Denial	'It won't happen.'
2	Fear	'What will happen to me?'
3	Anger	'We've been sold out.'
4	Sadness	Mourning for the past.
5	Acceptance	'Let's make the best of it.'
6	Relief	'It's better than I feared.'
7	Interest	Increasing feelings of security.
8	Liking	Recognition of new opportunities.
9	Enjoyment	'It is really working out well.'

ranks as part of a temporarily shared sense of loss. They go on to state that:

> Managerial relationships are a well recognised source of merger problems, but the successful integration of senior management alone is insufficient if the line managers and the rest of the workforce are fractious. Employees need not be directly involved in the negotiation or execution of an acquisition to feel its impact, in that it produces a psychological ripple felt throughout the organisation. Mergers and acquisitions are about power, differing perceptions, cultures and definitions of the situation and so are potentially conflictual, the social and cultural ramifications of which extend beyond the boardroom.

Assimilation issues relating to mergers

True mergers are the exception rather than the rule. Invariably there is a dominant partner, or one partner is seen to be dominant. Feelings and anxieties can run high, as people jockey for key posts, and await the inevitable downsizing.

Culture differences can be quite substantial, and there is a heightened awareness of symbolic actions. When the Westminster Bank merged with the National Provincial Bank in the early 1970s, it mattered where the new boating club would be located on the River Thames, both of the previous institutions having had their own, with their own colours and rituals. It matters what happens to the old war memorials that one finds in the foyers of well-established long standing organisations.

Opportunities need to be provided at an early stage for people to learn from each other – although this can be troublesome where there is uncertainty over the residual jobs and one is awaiting decisions on macro reorganisation.

It is generally assumed, and this is demonstrated by experience, that postmerger integration can take some three to five years. Initially both parties usually function as separate partners before there is actual physical or cultural integration. Figure 18.6 looks at one way of creating synergy from a merger.

In my opinion the Halifax and Leeds adopted an HRD approach which contributes to organisational learning and gets staff members involved in the shaping of the new organisation. It also contributes to developing a closer partnership between various stakeholder groupings.

| Figure 18.6 | Suggestion schemes as a human resource development approach contributing to organisational synergy |

The creation of new learning and synergistic relationships from a merger is not a simple matter of reorganisation or of putting people on to a team-building course. The merger of the Halifax and the Leeds building societies in August 1995 posed many challenges, not the least of which was how to build on the best ideas and working practices of both organisations. One approach adopted was the use of an employee suggestion scheme.

The idea of a suggestion scheme was not new. Indeed, one had operated at the Halifax for some time, generating around 3500 suggestions a year, from 26 000 staff. But this had been set up primarily to find ways of cutting costs and improving customer service and profitability. Since the need was for a scheme to assist in integrating the societies and encouraging a two-way flow of ideas between staff and managers, the decision was made to start again.

The new approach was entitled 'The Why Don't We' programme and was launched by the CEO. Its features included:

■ a maximum turnaround time of eight weeks, from entering idea into the system to sending out letter of response;

■ people being encouraged with small awards for every idea, rather than being asked to devise the perfect solution. Even duplicate ideas are rewarded with a small token prize. Ideas worthy of further consideration, and ideas likely to be implemented, merit awards worth £15 and £25 respectively, with quarterly awards for the top three ideas;

■ the total involvement, presence and backing of the CEO, who signs letters to prize winners, attends quarterly prize-winner lunches and supports the scheme through *Halifax TV* and other communication channels;

■ provision of personal packs to all 34 500 employees, containing guidelines and forms inviting them to 'find something that we don't do and should be doing, or something we could be doing better'.

Staff are encouraged to make suggestions relating to areas such as improving customer service, increasing revenue, enhancing the product range, cutting red tape and improving the way people are developed. Suggestions are currently running at 34 000 per annum. Although the original rationale of the scheme was to improve communications rather than to save money, it is clear that substantial savings have been made. For example, a change to the credit-scoring system, suggested by a cashier in the Midlands, is expected to generate up to £10 million of new business.

One executive committee member suggested using the scheme to reduce bureaucracy across the whole group. This led to a special campaign over the summer of 1996 entitled 'Why Don't We Stop?' in which employees were asked to suggest ways of reducing red tape. In one month, more than 2500 ideas were generated.

Source: 'Ideas for building a better society', *People Management*, 12 September 1996.

Assimilation issues relating to acquisitions

With acquisitions, relevant issues include whether there was a hostile takeover and the objective of the acquisition – was it a related or non-related diversification?

Assimilation is normally expected to take less time than a merger. Over a period of 12–18 months the acquirer is anxious to impose its own control systems on the acquired organisation. As a result the employees of the acquired organisation feel that they have lost out. In such an atmosphere the new control systems may be imposed but the hoped-for synergies are unlikely to result. There is unlikely to be a positive atmosphere towards learning, without which it is difficult to see how HRD can make a significant contribution (*see* Fig. 18.7).

Figure 18.7 Coping with organisation restructuring

Rosabeth Moss Kanter (1989) quotes examples from an American case she observed at first hand – Delta Airlines' 1986/7 acquisition of Western Airlines – to show some of the sensitivities arising out of takeovers and how they might be handled in HRD terms. Note that the actual intervention conducted by the HRD consultant has culturally specific overtones and may not be appropriate for groups outside the USA.

Managing the past – mourning the losses

Issue number one in managing a difficult transition smoothly is to allow employees to mourn the past, to grieve over their losses. Employees make major emotional investments in their organisations and in their jobs. Employees of Western regarded their firm with great affection. Several remarked that the reality of the merger had not fully set in until they watched the company logo being removed from the aircraft. And one special employee group was affected in a particularly jarring way: those who had retired from Western were issued with Delta retiree travel passes; they became retirees of Delta, on paper at least, although they had never worked one day for that company.

The sense of personal loss was accentuated by the state of upheaval experienced by approximately 2000 Western employees – those who had been employed at the company headquarters in Los Angeles but now had to transfer to Atlanta, Georgia. Many of Western's middle managers were demoted as a result of Delta's efforts to integrate the new work-force without creating redundant positions. Leaving behind families, friends and memories, and pulling up deep roots, is traumatic enough. When one loses a job, a life style and one's company as well, the sadness is magnified. Western executives not only allowed but encouraged a period of mourning, to help people bury the past. A testimonial distributed to all employees by a Western vice-president and employee of 18 years standing stated, 'A final wish for the lives of us who mourn is to go on with joyful memories.'

Managing the future – positive visions

The second key to building commitment during the restructuring process is getting the survivors excited about the future – offering a positive vision to compensate for the loss. For example, a consultant to Western during the merger process brought

▶▶

493

▶▶ Figure 18.7 continued

to the merger an awareness of the power of formal ceremonies to bridge the gap between loss and vision:

> Each of the eighty attending managers was asked to write down the three worst things that could happen to them personally as a result of the merger. Then the managers were given sheets of their former letterhead and business cards. The group was led outside and assembled around a wooden casket. A band was playing a funeral march. One by one, the managers were asked to crumple up their statements, cards and letterheads and toss them into the coffin. Suddenly, a hundred-ton paver emerged from around the corner. As it approached the coffin, the band broke into a rendition of 'On Wisconsin', and the group cheered wildly as the paver flattened the coffin and its contents. Next, the group was whisked back inside where they were given academic caps and gowns to put on. They marched into an auditorium. There the boss gave a graduation speech, resembling any college ceremony: 'You are the architects of our future; our destiny lies in your generation's hands.' After the speech, the name of each manager was called. They walked across the stage, shaking hands with the regional manager and receiving a 'Doctorate in Merger Management' and a share of company stock as a graduation gift.

Delta stressed its version of a great future immediately by creating a slogan for the merger that made Western people feel valued: 'The Best Get Better'.

Managing the present – reducing uncertainty

The third issue involves the transition period itself. Transitions engender uncertainty not only with regard to employees' careers and daily work but also in terms of bills, mortgages, families and life styles. Delta reduced uncertainty by its methodical, open, and, with few exceptions, concise style in communicating about the merger process. Delta's style was first shown in a memo sent by Telex to each Western work location and shortly after to each employee's home just after the merger was approved. That letter outlined Delta's plans for managing the details of integrating the two companies and their respective employee groups. For example, it stated, 'During the week of February 16, 1987, a bulletin will be distributed containing the following information'. Thus even when workers did not have facts and details at a certain time, they knew when the information would be forthcoming and that it would be reliable and certain.

At the same time, Western executives minimised discontinuity and disorder by stressing 'business as usual', making sure they came into the office for regular workdays to create a reassuring presence. During the transition period, Western continued its established pattern of openness and communication. The airline's regular newsletter, called *Update*, was renamed *The Best Get Better* – Delta's slogan for the merger – two weeks after the first merger announcement. Regular features included articles describing Delta's plans for the merger process and comments by Delta and Western officials.

Finally, Western used the structure and services of its health services programme (HSP) to deal with employee stress and anxiety caused by the merger. The programme used counsellors, pamphlets and other educational aids to help employees work out their emotional difficulties. After the merger announcement, HSP personnel began to develop programmes, including seminars and videotapes, to address employee anxieties about the merger.

STRATEGIC ALLIANCES

A strategic alliance is a co-operative partnership between two or more organisations to create competitive opportunities for their mutual advantage. Frequently it is manifested through a *joint venture* whereby a third commercial entity is formed by virtue of the investment and shared ownership of the holding partners. It often happens when the individual partners wish to reduce their exposure to the financial risks associated with the development of new products or technologies which are notoriously susceptible to failure. Joint ventures can be between large multinational corporations in which each party has strengths that seem to offset areas where others are less strong. They can also be common between large corporations and small businesses whose entrepreneurial flair is not backed up with the financial strength to produce goods in highly capital-intensive industries. Some large corporations are involved in an array of joint ventures. IBM has been quoted as being involved in more than 400 joint ventures with firms ranging from Sears to Apple (Miller and Dess, 1996).

Between 1988 and 1992 it is reported that more than 20 000 business alliances were formed in the USA alone, part of a trend that has seen a 25 per cent annual rate of increase since 1985 (Pekar and Allio, 1994). Joint ventures have mixed chances of success.

Perhaps the most serious problem that faces companies participating in strategic alliances and joint ventures is that of achieving appropriate co-ordination when goals, strategies, procedures and cultures will be different if not incompatible. It has been suggested that nearly half of all joint ventures that failed have experienced conflict between partners (Scanlon, 1990). This may be because the primary motive for the alliance is a response to a market opportunity between partners who would normally be in a competitive situation, resulting in a volatile state of 'competitive collaboration' (Doz *et al.*, 1986). Medcof (1997) emphasises the importance of careful preselection of partners. As he puts it, 'a poorly chosen partner can make co-operation very difficult, and in the worst case, doom an alliance from its inception, eating up enormous resources in salvage activities before finally bringing it down. In contrast, a well-chosen partner allows a synergy which blossoms into outcomes far beyond expectations.'

Medcof identifies the following traditional criteria for helping to pre-diagnose likely success:

■ Does the alliance have a good business strategy rationale?

■ Is the prospective partner a good strategic fit?

■ Is the prospectic partner *capable* of carrying out its role in the alliance?

■ Is the prospective partner *compatible* operationally?

■ Is the prospective partner *committed* to the alliance and the strategic aims?

■ Are the *control* arrangements for the co-ordination of the alliance appropriate?

He draws attention to the importance of HRD-related issues such as business and managerial skills and compatibility of organisational culture. The issues are the same as with mergers and acquisitions except that shared learning opportunities are more difficult to orchestrate.

He goes on to argue that there are two forms of learning that can result from a strategic alliance:

1 The partners can obtain from each other technical knowledge about processes relating to commercially valuable technology.

2 The partners can learn from each other management and business skills that individually they were lacking.

The learning does not, however, happen by itself, as if by some form of osmosis. There need to be in place mechanisms which will allow for the sharing of information and ideas. People need to possess the skills whereby they can learn to learn about and from each other.

HUMAN RESOURCE DEVELOPMENT STRATEGIES TO ENHANCE SYNERGY

From the armoury of HRD strategies that can be drawn on to enhance learning in organisations, a number have specific value in trying to integrate more effectively the various business sub-units. A generic sequence of steps is offered for where one is starting from scratch. Differences of approach are then suggested which could apply to established organisations, and for dealing with the immediate challenges offered by new mergers and acquisitions.

Strategies for business sub-units in all contexts

A possible sequence of steps is as follows:

1 Make contact with HRD counterparts in other units.
2 Establish an organisation-wide HRD learning support network.
3 Measure and compare the learning climate in different units.
4 Facilitate cross-functional quality improvement working groups.
5 Develop regular cross-divisional best practice benchmarking visits.
6 Set up a centre for cross-divisional communication on synergy-related issues.
7 Create structured learning events relating to synergy.
8 Encourage the formation of cross-divisional action learning sets.
9 Reward and publish successes.

Make contact with HRD counterparts in other units

In large diversified organisations it can be remarkable how many people have a formal or semi-formal HRD role. It is important to establish who these people are and the precise details of their role. Some may operate from functional support units attached to a given division or directorate. Others may facilitate quality improvement teams, yet others may be line managers and may have been designated official champions of learning. Even in existing organisations the attempt to generate an HRD staff inventory can generate real surprises. British Rail undertook such an exercise a few years before privatisation and discovered over 1500 staff members with a specific HRD-oriented role in its various businesses, most of whom were operating independently of, and unbeknown to, each other.

Establish an organisation-wide learning support network

Learning support networks need to be established drawing on these established resources. The National Westminster Bank's 'Heythrop Learning Network' operates as an umbrella term to co-ordinate the HRD effort. This step is a vital precursor to considering the nature of synergistic relationships and how horizontal strategies across businesses might be effected.

Measure and compare the learning climate in different units

The more devolved the locus of authority, the more geographically dispersed the organisation and the larger the spread of businesses, the more likely it will be that the business sub-units will have developed their own particular culture of learning. This should be tested out by means of a learning climate questionnaire, the elements of which are covered in Chapter 4. Additional questions relating to synergy would be:

- Does the unit in question have a tradition of welcoming and contributing to collaborative efforts with other units?
- Do staff positively seek out new and creative partnerships?
- Does the unit support cross-divisional exchanges and secondments?
- Does the unit draw on resources provided by the centre or seek out its own way of doing things?
- Do staff feel threatened by changing relationships between businesses or treat them as an opportunity?

Comparison of answers from questions such as these will indicate the synergistic potential for the organisation as a whole.

Facilitate cross-functional quality improvement working groups

The use of cross-functional quality improvement teams who have a specific remit to identify new ways of working together can be a most effective way of generating ideas which contribute to new synergies. Many such teams have been established in organisations over the years as part of the Total Quality Management (TQM) drive. As explained in Chapter 14, HRD-oriented staff can have an influential role in facilitating these teams – especially through the use of idea-generating and process-analysis techniques.

Develop regular cross-divisional best practice benchmarking visits

Benchmarking has traditionally been seen as a source of information gathering from external organisations which are deemed to be 'best in class' in carrying out a particular activity. It can be equally effective within organisations in improving understanding between businesses and functional areas. Benchmarking should be pushed as an important source of organisational learning and HRD practitioners should be involved in providing skills in benchmarking practices.

Set up a centre for cross-divisional communication on synergy-related issues

Kanter (1989) argues that attendance at training centres and educational events is a potent way for increasing communications and facilitating networking. She draws attention to General Electric's facility at Crotonville, New York, which is much more than a corporate college. It is, in effect, a synergy centre that helps people identify shared interests across businesses and tackle common problems together.

Create structured learning events relating to synergy

Shared understanding and trust are vital preconditions for creating synergies; they do not arise from virtual interactions. Human resource development professionals should be in the vanguard of attempts to extend face-to-face communication as a way of generating shared understanding. For this reason Digital Equipment Corporation runs a helicopter service to and from major New England facilities to permit people to get together to transmit information and pursue joint projects (Kanter, op. cit.).

Events which provide opportunities for greater shared awareness are an effective starting-point for better communication. Thompson (1997) refers to an attempt, which commenced in 1992 with the arrival of a new CEO, to more effectively integrate the diverse retail businesses which constituted the 'sprawling and unwieldy' Sears Group. Training events were used as a strategy to bring together both functional and store managers from the various chains and ideas were shared and 'stolen'. Additionally cross-functional project teams were established to seek out opportunities for intergroup savings in buying, merchandising and marketing, resulting in some £8 million being found in a matter of months.

Encourage the formation of cross-divisional action learning sets

Action learning sets provide an excellent focus for managers across business and functional sub-units to draw on each other's experience and insights to resolve problems. Hendry (1990) makes reference to the strategy employed by Pilkington (the world's market leader in flat glass production), of assigning people to 'task-centred action learning teams outside their normal area of operation to help knowledge transfer, promote an organisational perspective and assist cohesion'. This was part of an attempt 'to offset the incipient fragmentation of decentralisation' arising out of divisionalised business units. Action learning sets do not necessarily need to be introduced with a particular theme of developing synergistic relationships. The very act of a number of managers from diverse backgrounds coming together and sharing problems can facilitate a common understanding.

Reward and publish successes

Where horizontal strategies need to be developed, there should be some sense of accomplishment in their achievement. Examples from American Express and from the Halifax Bank have shown in different ways how rewarding and publicising can be effected. In both instances the overall strategy has been strongly endorsed by top-level management.

Strategies for business sub-units in existing organisations

In addition to the generic HRD strategies suggested above, the following are worthy of consideration in established organisations.

Transfers as part of career and management development

Understanding of the operations and imperatives facing different functional areas and businesses is always more effective if people have actually worked in these areas. A structured approach to inter-divisional or departmental exchanges and managerial tours of duty in different business areas can achieve this.

The establishment of a structured exchange programme as part of an integrated career and management development system takes a long time to set up and would be inappropriate in the aftermath of most mergers and acquisitions.

Incorporating synergistic thinking into the management competence framework

Many large organisations have developed their own discrete set of management competences which inform their performance-management system. Creating and gaining agreement on a generic set of competences that are relevant for all business units would be a significant achievement. When British Airways attempted to do this in 1987 as part of its Topflight Academy strategy, it anticipated conflict between corporate and departmental needs and interests. The organisation at the time was strongly departmentalised, leading to organisational 'smokestacking' and parochial thinking. In the event few managers took issue with the Topflight Academy's aim to create talent pools as a primary source of future leaders based on predetermined generic competences (O'Neill, 1990). The ability to handle synergistic relationships and engage in the lateral thinking that building new linkages entails could be seen as a distinctive strategic management competence that adds competitive advantage.

Strategies for business sub-units arising out of mergers and acquisitions

Creating synergy between human resource development and human resource management

In many large multidivisional organisations there is a functional separation between HRD and HRM. In a number of instances the HRD function is physically distant from HRM – for example if HRD staff operate from a management training centre or staff college. Resultant feelings of separateness can be reinforced by the different routes whereby people have accessed the profession. Many HRM people tend to be career professionals who have been in HR for much of their working lives. Staff in HRD, particularly direct trainers, are often imported in mid-career from other areas of the organisation. In merger and acquisition situations it is essential that the HRD and HRM staff groups work together and indeed reflect synergistic practices.

Human resource development issues versus human resource management issues

The area of HRM is conventionally seen as providing 'hard' bottom-line solutions to problems of integration. In acquisitions, the dominant party will normally seek to impose its own terms and conditions, whereas in mergers and strategic alliances it is often as if a clean sheet of paper has been handed to the HR professional to create a new 'package' of benefits and behavioural rules within a new cultural framework.

Experience shows that to achieve successful integration and synergy can take between three and five years. Given the pressure to speedily achieve harmonisation of pay structures, terms and conditions of employment, performance-management systems and indeed staff numbers and structures, the HRM specialist will find difficulty in balancing and setting priorities for the immediate post-merger period. Issues relating to creating a positive learning climate will not necessarily feature at the top of the agenda. Issues that will require specific attention include those in the areas of strategy formulation and employment legislation.

In the area of strategy formulation, there are the following considerations:

■ design and implementation of change in the management decision-making process;

■ design of new organisational structures;

■ design and implementation of job-evaluation systems and associated grading systems;

■ creation or modification of pay and benefits packages;

■ review of employee relations procedures and making recommendations for change.

As regards employment legislation, the following issues need to be taken into account:

■ ensuring redundancy policies and initiatives to harmonise terms and conditions etc. comply with legislation designed to protect the rights of the individual and, where appropriate, meet particular requirements for consultation with recognised trade unions;

■ being aware of appropriate transnational legislation in the case of international alliances and its potential impact on negotiations and subsequent staff-related changes.

Whereas the results of HRM activities will provide the framework, the 'hearts and minds' can only really be captured and locked in through the use of HRD strategies and practices. Typical areas of HRD influence and activity include:

■ evaluation and integration of management styles and practices through facilitating joint working parties, training courses, etc.;

■ ensuring personal development needs are adequately identified and supported;

■ helping to identify the skills and competences required to perform specific job functions;

■ formulating an overall training and development strategy to ensure appropriate skills are developed and in place to meet the future corporate objectives of the newly acquired or merged organisation;

■ designing and delivering in-house training programmes, 'roadshows' and educational events to communicate the rationale behind, the progress towards and the values of the new organisation;

■ developing learning support activities relating to anxiety and stress handling in a time of uncertainty.

CONCLUSION

The thrust of this chapter has been to see the development of synergies and horizontal strategies between business sub-units as resulting in organisational learning and therefore worthy of the attention of HRD practitioners. When strategists talk of the development of horizontal strategies they are concerned with co-operative processes in multidivisional enterprises whereby greater organisational cost effectiveness and market penetration is engineered. Human resource development practitioners are concerned with contributing to this through the establishment of an organisation-wide learning climate where people see the benefit of learning from others and engaging in co-operative partnerships where previously none existed. This chapter differentiates between creating synergies in organisations that have been in existence for some time and creating synergies for organisations that come together through mergers and acquisitions. In these latter situations, the pressure for integration is particularly forceful, and synergistic working relationships need to be demonstrated across the whole of the HR arena.

REFERENCES

Ansoff, H. I. (ed.) (1969) *Business Strategy*. Harmondsworth: Penguin.

Bettis, R. and Prahalad, C. K. (1986) 'The dominant logic of general management', *Strategic Management Journal*, 7.

Cartwright, S. and Cooper, C. L. (1992) *Managing Mergers, Acquisitions and Strategic Alliances: Integrating People and Cultures*. Oxford: Butterworth-Heinemann.

Cattell, R. B. (1951) 'New concepts for measuring leadership, in terms of group syntality', *Human Relations*, 4, pp. 161–84.

Doz, Y., Prahalad, C. K. and Hamel, G. (1986) 'Strategic Partnerships: Success or Surrender?'. Paper presented at Conference on Co-operative Strategies in International Business, Wharton School/Rutgers University, October.

Hendry, C. (1990) 'The corporate management of human resources under conditions of decentralisation', *British Journal of Management*, 1, pp. 91–103.

Hirsh, W. and Jackson, C. (1996) 'Ticket to ride or no place to go', *People Management*, 27 June.

Hunsaker, P. L. and Coombs, M. W. (1988) 'Mergers and acquisitions: Managing the emotional issues', *Personnel Journal*, 65, pp. 58–63.

Johnson, G. and Scholes, J. (1993) *Exploring Corporate Strategy* (3rd edn). Englewood Cliffs, NJ: Prentice Hall.

Kanter, R. M. (1989) *When Giants Learn to Dance – Mastering the Challenges of Strategy, Management and Careers in the 1990s*. New York: Simon & Schuster.

Kubler–Ross, E. (1969) *On Death and Dying*. New York: Macmillan.

Kumar, N. (1997) 'The Revolution in Retailing: from Market Driven to Market Driving', *Long Range Planning*, 30(6), December.

Lawrence, P. R. and Lorsch, J. W. (1969) *Organisation and Environment*. Homewood, IL: Irwin.

Medcof, J. W. (1997) 'Why too many Alliances end in Divorce', *Long Range Planning*, 30(5), pp. 718–32.

Miller, A. and Dess, G. G. (1996) *Strategic Management* (2nd edn). New York: McGraw-Hill.

Mintzberg, H. (1979) *The Structuring of Organisations*. Englewood Cliffs, NJ: Prentice Hall.

Mirvis, P. H. (1985) 'Negotiations after the sale: The roots and ramifications of conflict in an acquisition', *Journal of Occupational Behaviour*, 6.

O'Neill, B. (1990) 'Developing future leaders at British Airways', in M. Devine (ed.) *The Photofit Manager: Building a Picture of Management in the 1990s*. Ashridge Management Research Group.

Pascale, R. (1991) *Managing on the Edge*. Harmondsworth: Penguin.

Pekar, P. Jr and Allio, R. (1994) 'Making Alliances Work – Guidelines for Success', *Long Range Planning*, 27(4), pp. 54–65.

Porter, M. (1980) *Competitive Strategy: Techniques for Analysing Industries and Competitors*. New York: Free Press.

Porter, M. (1985) *Competitive Advantage: Creating and Sustaining Superior Performance*. New York: Free Press.

Porter, M. (1987) 'From Competitive Advantage to Corporate Strategy', *Harvard Business Review*, 65(3), May–June, pp. 43–59.

Scanlon, P. R. (1990) 'Collaborative Ventures', *Journal of Business Strategy*, July–August, pp. 81–3.

Verey, P. (1993) 'Success in Diversification: Building on Core Competences', *Long Range Planning*, 26(5).

Chapter 19

OPERATING IN A GLOBAL ENVIRONMENT

INTRODUCTION

For the lone practitioner trying to develop an HRD policy and practices in a small or medium-sized enterprise, it is not easy to visualise the scale and scope of the HRD activities in some larger organisations. In turn, a person working in a large organisation with developed HRD practices – perhaps in the public sector – may be equally mystified by the scale and scope of operations of so-called global corporations. And even for some of the HRD staff working in global organisations it can be quite difficult to appreciate what being 'global' actually means.

For example, I recently interviewed a person who told me that he worked as a director with HRD responsibilities for a small insurance company employing some 35 people. On further investigation it turned out that the business was risk insurance for large insurance companies which could face massive claims arising out of major disasters such as earthquakes. The 'small insurance company' was a wholly owned subsidiary of a large Japanese company which provided the capital base. Handling 'the Japanese connection' was not an issue he had thought about.

Yet globalisation and its implications has been one of the key strategic themes of the last twenty years. Kenichi Ohmae talks about it in the context of managing in a borderless world. 'On a political map, the boundaries between countries are as clear as ever. But on a competitive map, a map showing the real flows of financial and industrial activity, these boundaries have largely disappeared' (Ohmae, 1989). The consequence is the growth of the global corporation that is not tied to a single country or geographic region. Thus the Mazda sports car, the MX-5 Miata, was designed in California, financed from Tokyo and New York, its prototype was created at Worthing on the south coast of England, and it was assembled in Michigan and Mexico using advanced components invented in New Jersey and fabricated in Japan (Reich, 1991).

Another effect is the ability to move resources from one country to another as economic circumstances or government policies dictate. Thus tariff cuts in South American and Asian countries strongly contributed to many of the 30 plant closures carried out by Procter & Gamble since 1993 as part of its 'Strengthening Global Effectiveness' programme. It was announced in August 1998 that the £1 billion Siemens semi-conductor factory in the north-east of England was to close, reportedly due to a combination of a 95 per cent fall in microchip prices because of dumping from the Far East, the strength of the pound compared to other currencies, and the existence of four comparable factories in Taiwan, the USA, Germany and France.

Rhinesmith (1995) defines a global company as follows:

> To be global, a company not only must do business internationally but also must have a corporate culture and value system that allow it to move its resources anywhere in the world to achieve the greatest competitive advantage. This is far more than exporting, licensing and distribution agreements or foreign sourcing of technology, capital, facilities, labour and material. Being global requires a mindset and skills that extend far beyond the current scope of most organisations.

He goes on to argue that global organisations require very adaptable managers and a value structure that allows companies such as Unilever, Coca-Cola and Sony to shed their original national origins. He quotes P. Barnevik, the CEO of ABB, the global corporation formed from the merger of Asea of Sweden and Brown-Boveri of Switzerland as saying: 'You optimise globally, you call the shots globally and you have no national allegiances.' This can mean companies relocating their headquarters or other core operations to a 'neutral' venue. Thus Siemens, the German electronics giant referred to above, relocated its medical electronics division headquarters from Germany to Chicago in the early 1990s. Such developments are supranational and can supersede decisions taken by politicians on behalf of nation-states.

Practitioners accustomed to the domestic sphere need to totally rethink what HRD entails if they are involved with organisations operating on a global stage. It is not just doing more of the same on a larger scale or having a learning strategy about the culture and languages of other countries, although this helps. Mayo (1994) hints at the complexity of what might be entailed when he states that 'the requirement to think through the level of international capability needed in an organisation increases all the time as the business becomes global in more and more sectors'. It is associated with developing a mindset that equips you to look outwards at the big picture and inwards at how each particular bit fits in.

This chapter is concerned with establishing the organisational context for globalisation and identifying and evaluating HRD approaches and practices connected with a global mindset. In so doing it makes the point that developing a *global* mindset is not the same as developing an *international* mindset. An international mindset tends to be more one-directional, ethnocentric, outward looking from the country in which one is based, as opposed to a multidimensional,

360-degree perspective. A one-directional international mindset focuses attention on issues associated with travelling and staying abroad, and how to prepare individuals for short or longer-term overseas assignments.

Developing a global mindset entails thinking about the HRD implications of people working for, or having some dependence on, an organisation which originated in a country other than one's own. This in turn extends beyond merely translating global thinking into local outcomes by means of establishing a common corporate culture, which is a recurring theme in the literature. If a factory, for example, can be closed down in a developing country because it is more efficient and cost effective to centralise production in a first world economy, what does this say about attempts to create a shared corporate culture that all employees can buy into? In global terms there is little evidence that generating a shared culture significantly adds genuine *sustainable* value at local level, unless one is in, say, the hotel or airline industry, where there are certain expectations of common service standards.

The assumptions underpinning many of the HRD approaches to the subject revolve round a perceived need for greater shared understanding between the various countries and companies that make up a global corporation. This can be assisted through learning interventions that increase intercultural awareness, strengthen the corporate glue and enhance language sophistication. There is little reference to how processes, systems and skills can be levered up in a given country to create sufficient distinctiveness to stave off closure when the parent body is reviewing its strategic options. The message from the strategy world is clear: if you cannot demonstrate that your part of the whole has a distinctive competence that is difficult to replicate elsewhere, then you are vulnerable – a sophisticated cash crop.

WHAT IS A 'GLOBAL COMPANY'?

What does being a 'global company' actually mean? Many companies trade internationally, but that does not make them global. Many organisations, operate across national and continental boundaries, but in no more than an import-export capacity. Are there some characteristics which we would expect of a global organisation that are absent in other types of corporation?

There have been a number of attempts in the literature to differentiate between types of multinational organisations, the typology generated by Bartlett and Ghoshal (1989) being the most publicised. It is both descriptive and normative. It is descriptive in terms of trying to capture how multinational organisations emanating from different parts of the globe have tackled the problem of co-ordinating and controlling their activities in various types of industries. It is normative in the sense that the authors imply that the transnational model is the way forward. The terminology they use, especially in differentiating between 'international', 'global' and 'transnational', is somewhat confusing. This chapter therefore adopts a modified system for labelling their original headings.

FOUR APPROACHES TO OPERATING INTERNATIONALLY

Model A

Model A (the multi-domestic organisational model) refers to a configuration that is organised on a country-by-country basis in order to be responsive to differences between national markets. It can be described as a *decentralised federation* and also as 'multi-domestic' on the grounds that each national operation is independent of what is happening elsewhere. It has echoes of the British colonial model of indirect rule which was particularly associated with Lord Lugard during his term of office in Nigeria. Bartlett and Ghoshal (op. cit.) contend that this kind of structure was particularly compatible with the management norms of the mainly European companies that sought international presence in the period between the two world wars. Family ownership had been the dominant tradition and therefore organisational processes were built on personal relationships and informal contacts rather than formal structures and systems.

Some industries seem to fit the 'multi-domestic' classification, with international strategy consisting of a 'nuclear' aggregation of domestic strategies. Competition in one country is essentially independent of competition in other countries. Typical industry characteristics are determined by cultural, social and political differences between countries. A classic example of a multi-domestic industry is the branded packaged products industry, items such as detergents and food.

Model B

Model B (the international organisational model) describes a formalised *co-ordinated federation*, often structured according to function. This model was prevalent in the early post-war decades when US companies were dominant. The culture is based on a professional management philosophy which is willing to tolerate a certain measure of local autonomy, especially in developed economies, but overall co-ordination and control by headquarters is maintained through sophisticated management systems and specialist corporate staff. Subsidiaries are largely dependent on the parent company for new products, processes or ideas, but are given some measure of discretion in how to use them. Transferring knowledge and expertise to countries that are less advanced in either technology or market development is the key task for these organisations. It is a process of sequential diffusion of innovations that were originally developed in the home market. A classic example of an industry that meets these characteristics is telecommunications switching.

Model C

Model C (the global organisational model) describes a configuration in which assets, resources and responsibilities are centralised. The role of subsidiaries is often limited to sales, service and screwdriver assembly and their freedom of action is very limited compared with their counterparts in Model A or Model B organisations. The structural configuration of this organisation is called a *centralised hub*.

This model was the basis of the world-wide competition of many Japanese companies in the 1970s and early 1980s. Centralised decision making and control allowed Japanese companies to retain their complex management system requiring intensive communication and personal commitment.

The Japanese have tended to adopt this approach in industries where standardised consumer needs and opportunities for scale efficiencies make centralisation and integration profitable, and where the rivals compete against each other on a truly world-wide basis. In such industries, a corporation's competitive position in one country is significantly influenced by its position in other countries. The industry is not merely a collection of independent domestic industries, but a series of linked cross-national operations. A classic example is consumer electronics.

Model D

Model D (the transnational corporation) is an 'ideal' organisational form to describe companies which are required both to meet simultaneously the demands of local responsiveness and global efficiency, and to demonstrate learning or knowledge transfer across boundaries. In recent years a number of organisations (e.g. Unilever and BP) have claimed to be working towards a transnational model, irrespective of the type of industry in which they originated.

Transnational industries are characterised by a complex set of environmental demands. The food industry provides good examples of some of the issues facing them. At one level there is 'global fast food' (largely American), such as the hamburger, fried chicken and certain soft drinks. The hamburger has generated incredible popularity in Moscow, as has fried chicken in Tokyo. Then there is international food, common in one country but transferable to others. In the UK, for example, there has been a growth in popularity of Indian, Chinese, French and Italian foods. Third, there is national food. In the UK that would include Yorkshire pudding, steak and kidney pie and fish and chips.

Hedlund (1986) uses the term 'heterarchy' to describe what is in essence the transnational organisation as defined by Bartlett and Ghoshal. His characterisation of its most prominent features is presented in Fig. 19.1.

| Figure 19.1 | **Features of the transnational corporation of 'heterarchy'** |

1 *Many centres.* Competitive advantage is not the preserve of one country, but can originate in many different countries simultaneously in the form of new ideas and products. Expertise is therefore spread throughout the entire network of the corporation, a network consisting of locations, relationships and countries. Each subsidiary or operating company might therefore serve as a strategic centre for a particular area of attention (e.g. a certain product-market combination) and at the same time, play a much smaller role as a production or distribution centre for the rest of the range.

2 *Subsidiary managers are also given a strategic role.* As a result of the previous feature, managers of subsidiaries can also play a strategic role, not only in their own operating companies, but also in the company as a whole.

▶▶

▶▶ Figure 19.1 continued

3 *No overriding organisational dimension*. Companies organised in this fashion do not have an easily identifiable organisational structure such as, for example, organisation by country or by divisions based on product groups. Depending on the issue, a structure will be chosen that makes the best use of any competitive advantage.

4 *Different degrees (high or low) of linkage between organisational units*. There is flexibility in selecting different governing modes. Depending on the circumstances, the various sections of the company will be governed either very strictly or very loosely. The degree of freedom that each organisational section is allowed in forging alliances with other sections or with third parties, for contracting etc., will also fluctuate in time and between different topics and locations. The task is to find the institutional arrangements that appear to offer the best results, given a particular goal.

5 *Integration is achieved through normative control (culture)*. Considering the great variety of markets, activities, products, countries and organisational forms (with widely varying degrees of bureaucratic control), integration must primarily be achieved through the corporate culture and management style.

6 *Information about the whole is contained in each part*. Although it cannot be assumed that every organisational unit will be aware of every single interface with the organisation as a whole, there is a great deal of emphasis on disseminating information throughout the company, sharing common goals and viewing short-term or local interests in the context of the entire company, now and in the future.

7 *Thinking is present in the whole organisation*. Whereas one-dimensional organisations tend to separate 'thinking' from 'doing', the transnational organisation brings these two activities together at every possible level, including the periphery of the organisation.

8 *Coalitions with other companies and other actors*. In order to make optimal use of every opportunity to exploit synergetic effects and competitive advantages on a global scale, the transnational company forges multiple relationships with other companies and actors (including governments). These relationships take a wide range of different forms, leading to a multitude of governance forms and different degrees of internalisation.

9 *Radical problem orientation*. Frequently, the existing competitive advantages will not serve as the governing strategic principle. Instead, there will be an ambitious concentration on problem solving, in which context the company's global presence is seen as an important opportunity in that it provides an extensive network of available resources, people, systems, etc.

Source: Based on Hedlund (1986), summarised in Paauwe and Dewe (1995).

The term heterarchy is very suggestive and is a conscious attempt to differentiate new-style global organisations from the hierarchies of the past. The original concept of hierarchy was generated by the philosopher Denys the Pseudo Areopagite in the fifth century. He postulated that there was a celestial series of ascending levels which he termed 'hierarchy' consisting of angels, archangels and so on until one reached the supreme being who was God. This celestial hierarchy was mirrored on earth, rather like a reflection in water, by the ecclesiastical hierarchy of bishops, archbishops and so on. At the various levels of his order were hierarchs. In the new order perhaps we can substitute for 'hierarchs' the term 'heterarchs' to indicate the new global managers who are characterised by Robert Reich as cosmopolitan citizens, eschewing narrow parochial allegiance to a particular country but seeking to:

- 'exploit the opportunities created by high-powered technologies of worldwide communication and transportation and by the relaxation of national controls over cross-border flows of capital';

- 'meet the needs of customers worldwide for the highest value at the least cost';

- 'parcel activities around the world according to economic criteria, putting them wherever they can get the best return, intentionally playing no favourites to avoid setting off political alarms' (Reich, op. cit.).

A key learning issue in operating globally is to create meaning about what the organisation does, for all the people who work locally in the organisation. It is not sufficient to focus learning just on the 'heterarchs' and to enable them to communicate effectively with each other, heterarch with heterarch (*see* Fig. 19.2).

Figure 19.2   The path of *kyosei*

Wickens (1987) draws attention to the propensity of the Japanese for self-analysis, constantly attempting to explain the cultural, ethical and logical basis of their management philosophy. Ryuzaburo Kaku was president of Canon from 1977 to 1989 and Chairman from 1989 to 1997 – was he a heterarch? He describes how a five-stage process called *kyosei* that he has developed at Canon can contribute towards the achievement of a global, 'transnational' corporation. The *kyosei* journey begins by laying a sound business foundation and ends in political dialogue for global change. If he is correct in his suppositions, then his analysis provides significant messages about the role of global corporations on the political stage as they begin to flex their economic muscles.

Stage 1: Economic survival

The dominant concern at this stage is to secure a predictable stream of profits and establish strong market positions in one's industry. Canon found itself in 1975 in a loss-making situation and needed to re-establish a firm business foundation. It initiated a strategy called the Premier Company Plan that was designed to place Canon in the top ranks of global companies and move it from being a camera producer to a global high-technology manufacturer.

Stage 2: Co-operating with labour

Managers and workers begin to co-operate with each other. Each employee makes co-operation a part of her or his code of ethics. Management and labour see each other as vital to the organisation's success. Canon does not differentiate between office and factory workers. Everyone is a *sha-in* or a 'member of the company'.

▶▶

▶▶ Figure 19.2 continued

Stage 3: Co-operating outside the company

The organisation now starts to co-operate with outside groups, such as customers and suppliers. Competitors are invited into partnership agreements and joint ventures. Community groups become partners in solving local problems. Canon makes sure that the R&D department interacts with customers early on its product development process. Its engineers visit suppliers' plants to learn about production processes and help solve production problems. Suppliers are helped to improve their technical skills and the quality of their products.

Stage 4: Global activism

When a company begins large-scale business operations in foreign countries, it is ready to enter the fourth stage of *kyosei*. By co-operating with foreign companies, large corporations not only can increase their base of business but also can address global imbalances. By training local workers and introducing them to new technology, corporations can improve the standard of living of people in poor countries. And by developing and using technology that reduces or eliminates pollution, companies can help preserve the global environment.

Stage 5: The government as a *kyosei* partner

Fifth-stage companies are very rare. Using their power and wealth, they urge national governments to work towards rectifying global imbalances. Kaku argues that, because of national sectoral interests, domestic politicians are not capable of addressing global problems. In rather suspect terms – especially for those who espouse responsible representative democratic government – he argues that the mantle of leadership has fallen on the shoulders of corporations such as Canon. He talks about his intended approach to educate political leaders about the need to rectify global imbalances.

Source: Based on Kaku (1997).

WHERE DO THE MANAGERS COME FROM?

A three-part classification system devised by Perlmutter (1969) to establish the attitude of headquarters management towards their global subsidiaries is particularly helpful in understanding the underlying influences on staffing policy.

An *ethnocentric* approach is parent-country oriented. Key jobs at headquarters and abroad are filled by nationals from the country where the company originated. In other words, nationals from the parent country dominate the organisation both at home, and, in an expatriate capacity, abroad.

A *polycentric* approach is host-country oriented, treating each subsidiary as a distinct operation with local control of its activities. Each subsidiary is managed by local nationals although headquarters operations are still located in the parent country and dominated by staff from the home country.

A *regiocentric* approach is an extension of the polycentric approach, with control and staff movements being organised on a regional geographic basis. Promotion to the very top jobs continues to be dominated by managers from the parent country. (The *Regiocentric* approach is a subsequent addition to the original classification.)

A *geocentric* approach eschews the national origins of the parent company. The composition of the board and of management in general, including subsidiaries, reflects a range of nationalities. Multidirectional staff movements can be extensive, often on a rotating basis, as part of a global placement policy. It is an approach that is congruent with the transnational, heterarchical model.

THE GLOBAL MINDSET

Over the years, reference has often been made to the importance of possessing a 'global mindset'. This is a complex construct in which the mindset perspective recommended for adoption by managers is often not the same as that expected of the lower echelons. For the latter this is often presented as a much more partial picture concerning the acquisition of shared corporate values.

Rhinesmith (op. cit.), who is typical of this way of thinking and whose work has been very influential in the USA, groups the managerial characteristics and linked competences under three broad headings, listed below. He sees the characteristics as capable of being acquired, and thus accessible to HRD influences.

Mindset attributes for managing strategy and structure

The strategy/structure dimension requires the ability to manage competitiveness and complexity. Managers should:

■ strive for the bigger picture, globally scanning for information relating to the business;
■ balance the contradictions inherent in the many demands placed upon them by the competition, the marketplace, stakeholders and environment.

Mindset attributes for managing corporate culture

The corporate culture dimension requires the ability to manage alignment and change. Managers should:

■ learn to trust process over structure, and then align the two to ensure consistency of execution of global strategies;
■ flow with change and manage the organisation's ability to respond to surprise and ambiguity.

Mindset attributes for managing people

The people dimension requires the ability to manage teams and learning. Managers should:

■ value diversity and work well with multicultural teams to accomplish their professional and organisational objectives;
■ seek continuously to learn globally by rethinking boundaries.

As a global managerial ideology this system is internally consistent. If all the messages are passed down to the lower echelons, however, there is a risk of an inherent conflict of interest. Ellis and Williams (1995), for example, believe that:

> the organisational challenges of managing across boundaries need to be articulated clearly and widely shared throughout the organisation . . . This necessitates creating a system of shared values across the company's operations, enabling a collective mindset to replace more nationally focused views previously held.

The apparent conflict lies in the notion of expecting people to accept a set of shared values for an organisation that is indifferent as to where it trades. '[I]t is vital that the organisational communications and logistics network is sufficiently efficient and effective to permit business anywhere . . . the business should be managed from either where key business skills are present and/or the most strategically important country' (ibid.).

Moran and Riesenberger (1994) avoid the dilemma by suggesting a rather lengthy list of 12 global competences, and evaluating which are needed by groups ranging from the corporate CEO at one end of the spectrum to all employees at the other:

1 Possesses a global mindset.

2 Works as an equal with persons from diverse backgrounds.

3 Has long-term orientation.

4 Facilitates organisational change.

5 Creates learning systems.

6 Motivates employees to excellence.

7 Negotiates and approaches conflicts in a collaborative mode.

8 Manages skillfully the foreign deployment of expatriates.

9 Leads and participates effectively in multicultural teams.

10 Understands his or her own culture, values and assumptions.

11 Accurately profiles the organisational culture and national culture of others.

12 Avoids cultural mistakes and behaviours in a manner that demonstrates knowledge and respect for other countries.

Later in the chapter, we will look at possible ways of strengthening the local focus in the context of an HRD global mindset that is not just reliant on imparting cultural messages.

TARGET MARKET FOR HUMAN RESOURCE DEVELOPMENT INTERVENTIONS

Given these global settings, what is the market for HRD interventions? As with all forms of SHRD the customers will be employees and non-employees. For internal customers, this will depend on how global influences affect people's functional roles. Auteri and Tesio (1991) have identified four key role categories for managers in a global organisation: the categories could equally apply to people in a non-managerial role.

1 *Occupants of local positions* operate merely in the domestic context. However they may require product knowledge and corporate value training from an overseas supplier. Much investment on product familiarisation programmes has been undertaken by some organisations for overseas distributors and their mechanics. McDonald's provides an extensive acculturation programme for franchise holders.

2 *Occupants of open local positions* operate in the context of a single country, but make significant connections outside the country. They include national managers who report to someone outside their country and local managers who source from suppliers or sell to customers in other countries; it increasingly encompasses those communicating by e-mail to international colleagues.

3 *Occupants of multinational positions* operate in (and travel to) a number of countries. There may be some restrictions on geographical responsibility.

4 *Occupants of transnational positions* operate across the whole geographic area pertaining to the business, without restriction.

Applying this classification system to Fiat, the authors found that more than 40 per cent of managerial positions worked with international interaction, with HR being one of the most exposed areas. As Rhinesmith (op. cit.) points out, these figures have significant implications for HRD and global management education if they are replicated across other global concerns. He singles out the need to develop managers and others who occupy 'open local positions', as opposed to focusing the global development effort on the upper echelons and those involved in extensive overseas travel.

International versus domestic human resource development

A classification developed by Acuff (1984) identifies five basic points that have traditionally distinguished the activities of international (as opposed to globally minded) HRD managers from those of their domestic counterparts:

1 *More functions.* There are functions to perform in international HRD that do not occur in domestic HRD. They include: orchestrating reciprocal international secondments as part of an acculturation and knowledge-exchange process; cross-culture awareness training; international orientation (including pre-departure training); product familiarisation for overseas customers.

2 *More heterogeneous functions.* Even where the same functions have to be performed, they become more diverse and complex, because they have to be administered to a more extensive group of employees and non-employees, namely parent-country nationals, host-country nationals and third-country nationals.

3 *More involvement in non-work-related situations.* The training and development of expatriates often entails helping people learn how to handle themselves in situations outside the work environment. This does not generally arise in domestic settings.

4 *Different emphasis.* As foreign operations grow more established, the initial heavy reliance on expatriates is often replaced by a focus on host-country nationals. This development brings yet another broadening of traditional HRD activities, such as career development and diversity training, as these areas are likely to be different in different cultures.

5 *More external influences.* Government, unions, consumer organisations and other interest groups can all influence international HRD practices. Of course, these groups also exist in the home country, but their influence is familiar, which is not the case in the foreign country. Furthermore, these groups often put more pressure on foreign than on local companies.

How much training is given to employees involved in international operations? An answer to this question was sought in a survey conducted by the ASTD in 1994 and for which 79 responses were received from Fortune 500 companies with sales turnover of $500 million or more. All of the responding companies offered some training to some of their international employees. However most (59 per cent) of respondents characterised their firms' international training efforts as a small percentage of their total training activity. Most of the international training goes to employees in the executive and middle-management ranks. Each of these two groups receive 23 per cent of the international training done in the responding companies.

Almost a third of the companies also provided training for the families of employees who are posted abroad. Of those firms, 37 per cent train family members in language skills, 30 per cent train them in the customs and cultures of their host countries and another 30 per cent provide them with general orientation training.

The international training function is much more likely to be decentralised than centralised in the responding firms. Almost three-quarters of the companies have decentralised international training, with authority usually divided by country or division.

CROSS-CULTURAL ISSUES

One of the implications of operating in a global environment, highlighted in all the lists of management competences, is to develop the ability to engage in effective cross-cultural communication. The HRD function has invariably been seen as having an instrumental part to play in this.

> Cross-cultural communication occurs when a person from one culture sends a message to a person from another culture. Cross-cultural miscommunication occurs when the person from the second culture does not receive the sender's intended message. The greater the differences between the sender's and the receiver's cultures, the greater the chances for cross-cultural miscommunication (Adler, 1991).

Weiss (1996) argues that to communicate effectively with culturally diverse individuals and groups, you must have an understanding first of your own culture and then of the other culture's assumptions and differences. Answering the following questions can assist you in preparing to communicate more effectively in multi-cultural environments.

1 What must I know about the social and business customs of country X?

2 What skills do I need to be effective as a negotiator in country Y?

3 What prejudices and stereotypes do I have about the people in country Z?

4 How will these influence my interactions? (Weiss, 1996).

Perspectives on culture

One of the most interesting approaches to culture was developed by Hall (1976). He argues that cultures have a 'silent language' which includes the language of time, of space, of things and of contracts.

The language of *time* is related to present, past and future orientations. Past-oriented cultures evaluate new policies, change and innovation in terms of their fit with customs and tradition. China and the Middle East he holds to be examples of past-oriented cultures. British culture is generally present and future oriented. Relating to people with past-oriented time perspectives requires a knowledge of their historical beliefs and values and of how to properly demonstrate respect for these beliefs and values. Of course, not all people in a given culture share the same time orientations and as a visitor one should always beware of undue stereotyping.

The language of space and how its meaning and use is interpreted is the subject of *proxemics*. Proxemics, which is the study of the nature and effect of the spacial separation individuals naturally maintain, is an integral part of non-verbal communication. Cultures value and treat public and private space differently. Thus Latin Americans and Middle Easterners generally tolerate smaller space separations in public spaces, both with acquaintances and strangers, than do, say, Americans, who value privacy and therefore larger space separations.

The silent language of things can speak loudly. Status symbols like business cards, one's clothing, watch and shoes are very important and can signal credibility for a person doing business in Japan, China, Singapore and other Asian countries. When I visited Singapore in 1994 everyone exchanged business cards, almost on first meeting.

The approach adopted to contracts is also important in business communications. In the UK, written contracts are final agreements that are long-standing and legally binding. This is not so, for example, in China, where a contract may simply be the beginning of negotiations and it is expected that the contract will be changed and modified.

Hall (1976) also distinguishes between high- and low-context cultures (*see* Fig. 19.3). High-context cultures, which for him include China, Japan, Korea, Greece and Spain:

■ establish social trust first;

■ value personal relations and goodwill;

■ reach agreement by general trust;

■ engage in slow and ritualistic negotiations.

Low-context cultures, which include Germany, Switzerland, the UK and North American countries:

- get down to business first;
- value expertise and performance;
- reach agreement by specific, legalistic contract;
- engage in negotiations that are as efficient as possible.

| Figure 19.3 | The 'Dutch School' on national culture |

The most comprehensive empirical study on culture to date has been conducted by Hofstede (1967–73) who used a huge data base embracing 53 countries or regions to identify the following four dimensions which differentiated between the value orientations of staff of IBM with different national origins.

1 *Power distance.* One area in which societies differ and to which they have found different solutions is that of social equality between their members. Hofstede defines power distance as 'the extent to which members of a society accept that power in institutions and organisations is distributed unequally'. Inequality in power in organisations is usually formalised in hierarchical superior-subordinate relationships. Hofstede found large power distance values for Latin countries (both Latin and Latin American countries) and for Asian and African countries. Northern Europe and the Anglophone countries scored low on this dimension.

2 *Uncertainty avoidance.* The dimension of uncertainty avoidance involves the fundamental issue of how a society deals with uncertainty and conflicts. This dimension reflects a society's tolerance for situations of uncertainty and ambiguity and the extent to which it tries to manage these situations by providing explicit and formal rules and regulations, by rejecting deviant ideas and behaviour, by accepting the possibility of absolute truths and the attainment of expertise. High scores on this dimension occur for the Latin American, Latin European and Mediterranean countries, as well as for Japan and South Korea. In these countries the inclination to avoid situations of uncertainty is strong. The scores of the German-speaking countries in Europe – Austria, Switzerland and Germany – are medium-high. Asian countries, African countries and the Anglophone Northern European countries score medium to low.

3 *Individualism versus collectivism.* Individualism describes the relationship between the individual and the group or society at large. It reflects the degree to which people in a country learn to act as individuals rather than as members of cohesive groups. In countries where collectivism predominates, the emphasis is on social ties or bonds between individuals, whereas in individualistic societies, the ties between individuals are loose and people are supposed to look after their own interests. In general, wealthy countries score high on individualism, whereas poor countries score low. One notable exception is Japan, which, in comparison to most Western countries, shows relatively strong collectivist features.

▶▶

▶▶ Figure 19.3 continued

4 *Masculinity versus feminity*. This dimension refers to the extent that dominant values in a society emphasise masculine social values like a work ethic expressed in terms of money, achievement and recognition, as opposed to feminine social values, which show more concern for people and quality of life. Masculine societies define male and female roles more rigidly than do female societies. Japan and Austria are highly masculine; the Scandinavian countries and The Netherlands are highly feminine.

Another Dutch writer, Trompenaars (1993, Hampden-Turner and Trompenaars, 1994), has explored the relationship between national cultural differences and workplace behaviour and identified seven key ingredients.

1 *Universal* or *particular* responses in respect of rules and relationships. Universal cultures reflect relative rigidity in respect of rule interpretation. Particular cultures emphasise the importance of relationships, which may lead to flexibility in interpreting the merits of a given situation.

2 *Individual* or *collective* orientation. This reflects the conflict between what we desire as individuals and the interests of the group to which we belong. Collective societies may take a variety of different forms: the corporation in Japan, the Catholic Church in the Republic of Ireland, the family in Italy.

3 *Neutral* or *emotional* approaches to displaying feelings in public. Neutral societies favour the 'stiff upper lip' whereas emotional societies are more likely to demonstrate overt displays of feeling. Trompenaars cites a survey in which 80 employees in each of various societies were asked whether they would think it wrong to express upset openly at work. The numbers who thought it was wrong were 80 in Japan; 75 in Germany; 71 in the UK; 55 in Hong Kong; 40 in the USA; and 29 in Italy.

4 *Diffuse* or *specific* cultures. In diffuse cultures the whole person is involved in the business transaction and it takes time to build up a supportive relationship. In a specific culture, of which the USA is given as an instance, the basic relationship is limited to the contractual.

5 *Achievement-based* or *ascription-based* societies. Achievement-based societies value accomplishment or recent evidence of success, whereas ascription-oriented societies bestow status through such factors as age, gender or educational record.

6 *Time as sequence* or *time as synchronisation*. Like Hall, Trompenaar considers that how societies view time and tradition has an important impact on business transactions. The American dream, it is suggested, is the French nightmare. Working for the future is to the French the *nouveau riche* perspective as opposed to the *ancien pauvre*.

7 *Inner directed* or *outer directed*. This dimension reflects the tension between making inner-directed judgements and commitments and feeling the need to adjust to signals, demands and trends from the outside world. The resolution can be strongly conditioned by the external environment. In Western societies, individuals are typically masters of their own fate; in other parts of the globe, the world is more powerful than individuals.

Non-verbal communication and cultural differences

Harrison (1974) defines non-verbal communication as 'the exchange of information through non-linguistic signs' and redefines 'non-linguistic' as 'non-word signs'. A number of aspects of non-verbal communication, in addition to *proxemics* (already mentioned), have significance for the global arena.

1 Oculesics

This addresses the ways in which eyes are used in communication. Messages can be conveyed by using eyes to stare at another person or by looking away. These messages can be interpreted very differently between cultures.

In the USA continuous direct eye contact of between six and eight seconds is used to indicate listening and attention. A Japanese speaker will feel uncomfortable at this prolonged 'stare' and will look down or at the corner of the room (Hall and Hall, 1987). As a general rule, the American style of eye contact will be seen as invasive and insulting in many Asian cultures where Dodd (1982) noted that the meeting of the eye gaze of another is seen as invading one's privacy.

2 Haptics

This is the science of studying data obtained by means of touch. American business people are reported to engage in twice the amount of physical contact with friends than do the Japanese (Barnlund, 1989). Socially polite male–female greetings in France involve two kisses, one on each cheek. In Holland the convention is for three kisses. In all cultures the extent of touching increases with intimacy. Heslin (1974) expresses this by means of a continuum ranging from professional (level one) to social/polite (level two) to friendship (level three) to love (level four) to sexual arousal (level five). The nature of handshakes differs according to whether they are level one (professional) or level three (friendly). They will also vary across cultures. For Canadians, who use handshakes frequently, a level one handshake is a brief and perfunctory exercise, whereas a level three handshake is a firmer and more extended activity, accompanied in the main by smiling and standing closer together (Langtry and Balchin, 1994).

3 Paralanguage

This refers to every part of language other than the spoken word. It incorporates: *voice quality* – such factors as pace, intonation and rhythm; *vocalisation* – the use of noises other than words; and *voice qualifiers* – volume (soft to loud), pitch (high to low) and length (word elongation to clipped sounds). Vargass (1986) notes that an American will lower the voice when uncertain, whereas the Saudi business person lowers the voice as a sign of respect.

Pascale and Athos (1981) draw attention to the Japanese concept of *ma*. It takes the form of an unspoken word, or a pause in mid-sentence. It can be construed as an artefact of Japanese paralanguage and symptomatic of a culture 'which instructs its members not to plunge straight ahead, but to move knowingly and deftly through time'.

4 Kinesics

This refers to systematic observations of postural and gestural behaviour (Birdwhistell, 1961). In other words it is an analysis of body language. The observations can draw attention to culturally learned cues whose meaning may be clear to members of the same culture. However there is little evidence that body language has universal meaning.

What are the HRD implications of the above? What range of learning interventions might be considered to foster greater cultural understanding? What training methods might be considered? How might it influence an HRD practitioner operating as an internal consultant and trying to make contact with an overseas client?

Neuro-linguistic programming

Neuro-linguistic programming (NLP) is concerned with utilising a range of techniques to influence the behaviour of others through an awareness of verbal and non-verbal sensory messages received and sent. It has developed from insights generated in the early 1970s (Bandler and Grinder, 1975 and 1976). It draws upon four basic concepts:

- the possession of a *goal* or *desired outcome* from one's interaction with others;
- *behavioural flexibility* to achieve the desired outcome;
- sufficient *sensory acuity* to be aware of the effect of one's behaviour on others and to modify it as necessary;
- *self-maintenance* – staying resourceful and on target.

Underpinning the basic NLP techniques is a concern for *rapport,* defined as 'responsiveness or a process of contacting or being with another person or people that is buildable. This foundation skill in communication is emphasised and highlighted by calibration and sensory acuity skills' (Lyon, 1996). Rapport can be built by matching such things as body posture, facial expressions and hand gestures with those of another. It can also involve vocal and verbal mirroring as well as adjustments in auditory tone and speech tempo. It would seem that NLP provides a valuable framework for communicating across national boundaries. However the skills are not readily learned and can come across as being unduly manipulative.

National culture should be contrasted with 'corporate' cultures, the achievement of which is often seen as the object of HRD interventions in a global organisation. Can the norms of an organisation transcend national value systems? Are corporate cultures specific to the values and norms of the parent country? Can host-country or third-country nationals import the culture of the parent country? Does globalisation lead to a cultural convergence as Kerr *et al.* (1973) predicted and if so will this be at the level of haptics, proxemics and oculesics?

THE HUMAN RESOURCE DEVELOPMENT CONTRIBUTION

Rhinesmith (op. cit.) identifies a number of components which he considers contribute to an effective global HRD strategy.

- global sourcing;
- assessment and selection;
- global orientation centres;
- global mindset education;
- global business training;
- cross-cultural management training;
- cultural and language training;
- multicultural team building;
- staff exchanges and network development;
- international mentoring and re-entry planning;
- global career paths for the global management cadre;
- performance management.

Overall, this is a somewhat restricted list. At no stage does it make any reference to improving individual skills and competences at local level to avoid being vulnerable to global policy shifts.

In global terms, a broader range of HRD strategies is required to achieve a truly multidimensional outlook. Building on and extending Iles (1996), we see that there is a need to ensure that:

- learning systems are in place which encourage both global integration and local responsiveness;
- organisational cultures are fostered which value diversity and difference while acting as the 'corporate glue' that provides some sense of common identity;
- managers and staff are developed with the knowledge, skills and global mindset required to perform effectively in a world-wide business environment;
- an HRD presence is manifest in efforts to create a distinctive, valued and sustainable business contribution at local level to the global enterprise.

Figure 19.4 provides a framework for reflecting on a network of initiatives and interventions that might contribute to the above.

Intervention area 1: Developing an individual's ability to sustain working in a given overseas location

This has been the focus of the traditional international mindset model. Rhinesmith (op. cit.) considers that predeparture language and cultural training for an expatriate and accompanying family should be routine practice in a global corporation. Ronen (1989) has suggested that interventions fall into the following range, each being suited to a particular target group or meeting a particular set of needs. They can be viewed as pre-arrival development activities.

Didactic-information training

This form of training is basically concerned with tutor-initiated approaches to transferring information by lectures, handouts, videos, films, etc. Information provided would include basic background about the host country environment.

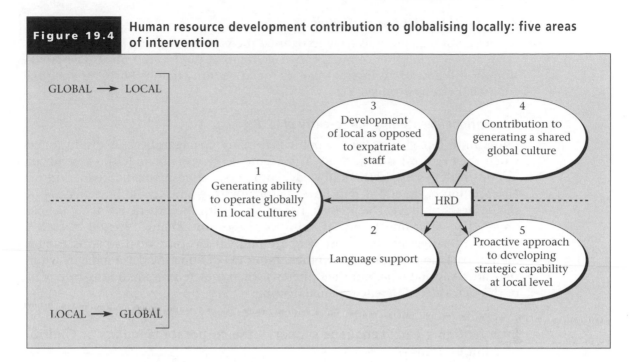

Figure 19.4 Human resource development contribution to globalising locally: five areas of intervention

Information would also be provided about the parent country and its institutions in order that participants will be able to represent their organisation and society in an informed and credible manner.

Intercultural experiential workshops

Through methods such as simulations and roleplay, attempts are made to provide experiential involvement and to engage the participant at affective, cognitive and behavioural levels. The aim is to examine the impact of one's own cultural values on personal attitudes and behaviour improve specific cultural awareness through targeted country experiences and to enhance general cultural awareness.

Sensitivity training

Such training can enable participants to explore underlying values and personal styles through exploring behaviour in direct confrontations with people. Its general applicability can be challenged.

Field experiences

Preparatory visits, if well prepared, are very useful. Field experiences can also be used for groups of staff to observe practices in overseas companies and to compare them against one's own.

Language and communication skills

Fundamental language skills will of course make daily encounters easier and more fulfilling.

Ronen's list can be extended to cover other areas as follows.

Post-arrival development activities

A number of organisations have recognised the value of ongoing learning support upon arrival in another country. Language training can be continued. The provision by the host of an internal 'buddy' or in certain circumstances an external counsellor can be invaluable.

International mentoring and re-entry planning

Rhinesmith (op. cit.) makes the point that many managers become disillusioned when they return from an overseas placement. Reasons include the absence of opportunities to apply the knowledge and perspectives gained abroad, and no appreciation being afforded of how the foreign experience could be beneficial in the domestic context. The problem has parallels with the experience many people have when returning from a training course or an extended period of study. Rhinesmith suggests that those who are on overseas placements be assigned a mentor back home who will keep them informed of domestic developments while they are away and represent their interests when they return. Mentoring by e-mail or through videoconferencing could develop.

Intervention area 2: Language support – the corporate language or English as a lingua franca?

Much of the focus on operating globally has been in respect of language training. This has often been in the context of an individual and their family undertaking an overseas placement for a period of time. However, in a global organisation, there is a strong likelihood that one will be engaged in making connections with individuals from a range of national backgrounds. There are simply too many languages for one to know them all well.

Organisations have tackled the issue of language in different ways. Some organisations see fluency in the parent company language as a prerequisite for potential managers. Gillette has over 30 000 employees world-wide and 57 manufacturing plants in 28 countries. Since 1983 it has operated a fairly conventional fast-track graduate training programme for young people from outside the USA. Each trainee works in their own country for six months, then spends 18 months in Boston, London or Singapore, Gillette's three international headquarters. While on these assignments, they are appointed to real jobs and their performance is assessed to determine their next move. However the trainees are very carefully selected. They need to be university graduates, with a business background, good social skills, adaptable, younger than 30, mobile, single and fluent in English (reported in Rhinesmith, 1996, pp. 213–14).

Some observers have noted a shift in perceptions on language, and identified an increasing tendency to accept English as the language of international communication on the grounds that a global mindset necessitates a lingua franca. Shell has, for some years, have used English as the common language of the group despite its Anglo-Dutch origins. Ohmae (1989) refers to the different reception over a ten-year period afforded to a session he gave in English to students at an Italian university. In 1978, most listened through a translator. In 1988 students listened to him directly, and even asked questions in English. Holden (1994) notes that many Japanese companies see English language learning as one of the keys to global success and cites NEC, one of the world's largest manufacturing companies, as a particular example.

Reich (1991) refers to the emergence of the cosmopolitan management team, with different nationalities represented at the top echelons of a number of the world's leading companies. He draws attention to the six-person management committee of Whirlpool International, a US-Dutch global joint venture in the white goods business, being made up of representatives from Belgium, Holland, Sweden, Germany, Italy and the USA. He points out that IBM has five different nationalities represented amongst its highest ranking officers. Unilever in 1992 had members from six different countries on its board, as well as an Italian managing its large company in Brazil, a Dutch national in Taiwan, an Englishman in Malaysia and an American in Mexico. A key issue, of course, is how many of these come from third world countries, and for how many English is a second language.

Communication is far more problematic among the lower echelons. Here it is unlikely that people from the non-English-speaking world will have the skills to converse fluently in English (*see* Fig. 19.5).

Figure 19.5   The language issue in the aerospace industry

Language is a crucial issue for all industries operating globally, none more so than the aerospace industry. Planes from a manufacturer operating in an English-speaking country, say, can be delivered to airlines for which English is only a second language. A key requirement of the International Air Transport Association's specification for training programmes is the use of a simplified English standard, developed by the Association européenne des Constructeurs de Matériel Aérospatial (AECMA). This standard imposes a limited list of words, which generally are assigned single meanings that are familiar to all aviation personnel.

In most cases, the words included in the AECMA standard can function only as specific parts of speech. For example, a person can use the word 'centre' as a noun, but not as a verb. The standard also favours the use of active voice and short sentences, without hard-to-read clusters of nouns (Cox, 1994).

The call centre

About one-third of all jobs created by inward investment in Scotland in recent years have been in call centres, which in 1998 employed some 16 000 people. For example IBM employs 250 operators at its call centre at Greenock which was launched in 1995. It runs 24 hours a day and offers technical support to PC buyers and dealers in 16 European countries speaking 11 languages. Allison Whittaker, the help centre training co-ordinator, argues that languages as well as IT skills are needed, and it is very difficult to find people with both: 'Sometimes we go abroad but even then it is hard to persuade people to relocate.' Companies such as IBM are now recruiting graduates with the language skills and teaching them the IT skills as opposed to the conventional way of recruiting which has focused on the IT knowledge.

Call centres represent another feature of globalisation: IT breakthroughs have created the opportunity for working at a location independent to that of a client in high-tech knowledge-based industries. American Express has centralised the back office of its European Card division in Brighton on the south coast of England. Relocated members of staff work in discrete national groups in the same building responding to calls from across Europe. Operating in a global arena in this field does not necessarily mean having a physical presence in a given country. This is fundamentally different from the position in manufacturing industries.

Language and corporate culture

A key corporate objective at ICI has been the attempt, through its Core Development Programme, to lay down world-wide standards of knowledge, skills and attainment for its subsidiary businesses. Generic culture development programmes such as 'Understanding ICI' are also provided. National companies like ICI Brazil are responsible for translating the standards and documentation into their own language. At corporate level, ICI is proactive in encouraging these approaches as part of a need to get total employee involvement and learning across boundaries from one country or company to another (Wille, 1990).

Price Waterhouse, prior to its merger with Coopers & Lybrand, endeavoured to present its core cultural message by means of an induction video for new staff members world-wide. This contained no words, no written or spoken language, only symbols and pictures to reflect the multinational, global and diverse nature of the organisation that people had joined. I remember being deeply impressed by its creativity, when showed it in 1997 by Naomi Stanford, a former student of mine who had had a key role in its production – entailing a period of secondment from the UK to the USA.

Language and e-mail

Developments in technology have given people far more opportunities to communicate across national boundaries without having to engage in face-to-face contact. Multinational teams can operate virtually through e-mail and the intranet. More and more *local positions* are becoming *open local positions* (to use the Auteri and Tesio (op. cit.) classification system). However, the language skills required are written, not spoken. The point was made at the 1998 ASTD conference in San Francisco that communicating by e-mail can often be more threatening than communicating face to face as people find their written skills inadequate for the task. It is also unrealistic to assume that each communication will be in the mother tongue of the person sending the message. It can be anticipated that the development of written skills will constitute a significant development in global language training.

Intervention area 3: Development of local as opposed to expatriate staff

Hailey (1996) notes that expatriates continue to hold key positions in many of the dynamic Asian economies, including senior management jobs in Hong Kong, Malaysia and Singapore. A survey conducted by the International Development Centre at Cranfield School of Management, however, suggests that the traditional respect shown by local staff towards expatriates is also waning and that they are increasingly seen as a legacy of an old colonial tradition. In particular there is resentment at the perks and privileges enjoyed by many expatriate managers as well as a perception that expatriates create a 'glass ceiling' for local managers that blocks career ambitions and restricts promotion opportunities.

According to Hailey expatriates have in the past been justified by the following arguments:

■ they have specialist expertise and knowledge not available locally;

■ they have a grasp of the wider international environment;

■ they have a greater understanding of the internal workings of the organisation;

■ they are an essential element in the internationalisation process as they can facilitate the transfer of skills and values, and help to reinforce international networks.

Additional functions were suggested by local respondents to the Cranfield survey in response to the question of why employers may try to justify the continued use of expatriates:

■ an expert role providing managerial and technical expertise;

■ a training role to facilitate the transfer of knowledge and skills to local staff;

■ a representative role in terms of shareholder interests;

■ a co-ordinating role to link the subsidiary with headquarters;

■ a globalising role enabling high-flyers to get international exposure;

■ an overseeing role in respect of local staff;

■ an educational role in terms of inculcating company culture and values;

■ a controlling role because they did not trust local staff.

The Cranfield study identified two key issues.

■ the increasing number of local managers who are obviously resentful and frustrated at the continued employment of expatriate managers by multinationals (with the one exception of technical specialists);

■ the potential resistance from local staff to expatriate managers that could threaten not just productivity but also corporate loyalty.

The following caveats to the use of expatriates have long been known and again surfaced in the Cranfield study:

■ they are expensive;

■ they are seen as outsiders with only a limited understanding of the local business environment;

■ rarely do they speak the vernacular language;

■ rarely do they become culturally assimilated into the local community.

The suggestion made is that companies should invest resources in developing local managers and build on their local knowledge and contacts. This approach seems to be further reinforced by the perception held by many respondents from the same study that 'Most expatriates learn on the job, and the locals end up teaching them'. One Singapore manager said that 'expatriates arrive here on the pretext of transferring skills to the locals, but they tend to learn more from the locals without transferring any skills whatsoever. The most frustrating thing is that they get paid for it from our profits.'

Clearly, surveys and findings of this sort have all sort of implications for HRD. If one adopts an ethnocentric perspective and increasing reliance is going to be made of local staff, issues that have to be considered include: how are they to be trained? How are corporate values to be inculcated? What about career opportunities for high-flyers?

It should not be thought that the issue is restricted to expatriates from the West going to Asia. It is still common for Japanese companies to send expatriates to Europe and the USA, American companies to send expatriates to Europe, European companies to send expatriates to the USA.

True transnational mobility may be the answer, with reciprocal exchanges. Reciprocal overseas secondments are becoming a feature of a number of global organisations as part of a development path and global acculturation process for individuals and a knowledge transfer method for the wider organisation. At the time of the merger with Price Waterhouse in 1998, Coopers & Lybrand had 1500 staff from the UK on overseas secondments, assignments ranging from one to three months to three years. The UK operation also received incoming personnel from across the global network of businesses. The UK company provided language training for both outgoing and incoming staff.

An interesting case study in localisation is that of Royal Brunei Airlines (*see* Fig. 19.6).

Figure 19.6 **Royal Brunei Airlines**

In 1981, all Royal Brunei Airlines' senior managers, pilots and engineers in East Asia were expatriates. Today all but one of the senior managers are locals. The only expatriates working for the company are a few pilots and engineers.

At the start of the localisation programme, the management board accepted that the training budget would have to be increased substantially, to pay for external training, in-house training and the appointment of supernumary staff. These were either nationals who were gaining work experience after training, or foreign workers who were assisting newly appointed individuals until they were capable of performing the work of the expatriate they were replacing.

The change to developing its own employees was expensive in the short term but more than paid for itself by having people who understood the local culture and were loyal because their employer was investing in them.

Management of morale was crucial. The expatriates who would be losing privileged positions (if not their jobs) had to be persuaded to train and encourage those who would be replacing them. They were given opportunities, at the company's expense, to increase their skills and so add to their value for future employers. They also had to be paid sufficient to stop them leaving before their replacements had been trained. This was managed by such inducements as education allowances and end-of-service bonus payments.

Source: Harry (1996).

Intervention area 4: Establishing a cohesive learning culture in transnational organisations

The Unilever model

Rhinesmith contends that in a diverse global organisation, there is a constant need for people from different backgrounds to be orientated to the corporate culture and its values and vision. Andersen Consulting has established its Centre for Professional Education just outside Chicago. Each partner must spend at least one week a year there while with the group. Multinational groups of managers are given the latest information about the corporation and have an opportunity to network with one another about global trends and future needs. This concern with networking has long been a feature of what can be called 'the Unilever model' (*see* Fig. 19.7).

| Figure 19.7 | Unilever |

Maljers (1992) describes Unilever, the Anglo-Dutch consumer goods group, as an archetypal transnational corporation that in the most basic sense thinks globally as well as acts locally, and strives for unity in diversity. Before the onset of the Second World War, local operations were almost exclusively managed by Dutch and British expatriates, but at a very early stage in its history the company started developing local managers through a management process that insiders termed '-isation' . In 1942, 'Indianisation' was the outcome of filling executive and technical positions in the Indian subsidiary with local managers – to be followed by 'Australianisation', 'Brazilianisation' and so on. At the same time the co-ordinating headquarters recognised the need for a common culture and set up formal training programmes aimed at the 'Unileverisation' of all its managers.

In 1955 Unilever opened Four Acres, its international management training college near London. Every year some 300–400 managers from all over the world attend training there. This in done in conjunction with programmes arranged on a local basis in the various subsidiaries.

Managerial trainees, all university graduates, undertake courses at Four Acres in parallel with on-the-job experiences. Courses include the 'International Management Seminar' as well as on specific subjects such as 'Developments in the Retail Trade'. Each trainee becomes part of a group of 25–30 people recruited for similar managerial positions. This shared experience creates an informal network of equals who know each other well and often continue to meet in future years on other events. The activities reinforce the need for people who can work in teams and understand the value of co-operation and consensus, qualities which are tested for at the time of initial selection.

Unilever supports its formal training initiatives with an extensive system of global attachments. A manager can be placed for a short or long period (typically 6–12 months) in a head office department or a subsidiary. Exposure to another environment not only gives them more know-how but also improves their 'know-who'.

▶▶

▶▶ Figure 19.7 continued

Cross-postings between companies are another very important mechanism for developing a global awareness and an understanding of different national cultures and attitudes and for establishing a sense of unity.

Unilever has in place a top-level 'Special Committee' which tracks as many as 200 managers moving over development assignments all over the world as an essential part of its succession planning procedures.

One of the features of the Unilever approach is the development of what can be called a 'transnational network'. Informal exchanges between managers as much as the formal structure are seen as key ingredients in the corporate glue that holds the organisation together. The network facilitates the transfer of ideas between companies. Through the network, international working parties, committees and similar groups form to work on common problems.

The network is sustained through HRD interventions such as running major conferences. Once a year, each of the two chairmen of the group addresses a meeting of 350–500 senior managers from all over the world, one conference taking place in Rotterdam, the other in London. It is a mechanism to communicate new initiatives as well as reconfirming old friendships.

Hendry (1994) provides interesting insights into the changing business needs and accompanying HRD responses of BP as it tries to make the transition towards becoming a global transnational corporation, swinging from a historically rooted ethnocentric perspective to a more geocentric approach (*see* Fig. 19.8).

| Figure 19.8 | Making the transition towards becoming a transnational corporation: human resource development messages from BP |

Between 1940 and 1970 there was a need to transfer job skills from the UK to new plants being opened up in the Middle East. Plants were managed as though they were an extension of domestic operations. A pattern developed of experienced operations staff (plant managers, craftsmen, engineers and plant operators) being sent abroad on permanent, long-term assignments, typically lasting for around twenty years. The result was a population of expatriate Britons, rising to a peak of around 1400. For some time BP engaged in cultural training to prepare such people for assignments abroad.

During the 1970s and 1980s BP engaged in a policy of related and unrelated diversification through acquisition. Of particular significance was the acquisition of Standard Oil of Ohio, which gave it access to the North American market and an outlet for its Alaskan oilfields. In the 1980s, BP began to make much greater use of shorter secondments (two to three years) from the UK to newly acquired overseas companies. Following the acquisition of Standard Oil, in any given year there were likely to be some 300 in the USA, including senior managers, marketing and IT staff. This had a dual objective: from an individual learning perspective it was linked to a career development path and from an organisational learning

▶▶

▶▶ Figure 19.8 continued

perspective it was seen as a way of inculcating a universal British-driven corporate culture.

More recently, the group has encouraged two-way secondments, with many more non-British managers coming to the UK on two to three year assignments. This is designed to contribute to a multinational team culture that recognises that 'the Brits do not have all the answers'. The creation of the team culture has been supported by a new set of corporate values that emphasise teamwork, openness and networking. To reinforce the new way of thinking, most headquarters staff have moved out of the old head office building with its imperial-colonial ambience. Educational programmes have been run to raise awareness of different cultures within the group and get everyone 'facing the same way'.

The compressed transformational change approach

Hendry (op. cit.) suggests that HRD interventions are unlikely to take place simultaneously and that there is a need to take into account how long a given organisation has been operating globally. He suggests that influenced by the changes implemented in organisations such as BP, companies can be expected to shift the emphasis of their interventions from:

> training in preparation for assignments and their management through a formal career system with personal development in mind, including the extension of this system to an increasingly diverse and dispersed population; to, eventually a broader educational effort to internationalise the organisation at large.

However there is increasing evidence that organisations competing globally are not prepared to follow the extended evolutionary model and the rather leisurely pace of change of corporations that were early on the global stage.

The Unilever model and the BP example have emerged over a long time period. A more compressed OD-based approach to developing teams and organisations in a global context was reported by Tichy (1994) (*see* Fig. 19.9).

Figure 19.9 GEMS

GEMS, a large US-based engineering concern, experienced rapid globalisation in the 1980s as a consequence of European acquisitions and Asian strategic alliances. Top management felt that its US-based, engineering-dominated culture required an organisation transformation programme for the globalisation to be successful. A new global structure was introduced with European, Asian and American centres each being given product line responsibilities. To support the structural changes, a set of integrated HRD initiatives were introduced to facilitate the development of global mindsets for senior management, together with associated leadership, change agent, team-working and networking skills. A global leadership development programme was introduced in 1988, using diverse teams working together on common issues and starting at top management level. Common features were team building, future planning, feedback on skills and action planning.

▶▶

▶▶ Figure 19.9 continued

> The top 55 people in the company worked on a variety of issues in small multi-cultural teams, coached by a senior manager. Both hard and soft 'real' problems were addressed in workshops on team and project work and in outdoor development activities. Project completion required continued networking and the presentation of the projects to a senior 'top team' to enhance dialogue and gain commitment. Additional approaches entailed secondments, transfers, new programmes, networking and the involvement of other managers in similar programmes.
>
> The features of this initiative are:
>
> ■ managerial focus;
>
> ■ learning about how to change 'hard' *yang* areas (e.g. competitiveness) and 'soft' *yin* areas (e.g. leadership style, interpersonal skills) simultaneously;
>
> ■ extensive use of experiential methods;
>
> ■ development of multicultural, multifunctional teams;
>
> ■ work on 'real' global problems;
>
> ■ continuance of learning through secondments and networking;
>
> ■ transfer of learning directly to the workplace;
>
> ■ support provided by a multicultural, multilingual training team.
>
> Tichy terms this approach 'compressed action learning' because of the need to use shorter cycle times than is normally associated with organisational development, given the strategic imperative.

Approaches from Daimler-Benz

Sattelberger (1994) cites an approach adopted by Deutsche Aerospace (DASA), part of the larger Daimler-Benz group, to develop its transnational capabilities. Features of both of the two approaches outlined above are evident.

Figure 19.10 Daimler-Benz

> Daimler-Benz views crosscultural learning as a core skill to be aimed for, but does not see this being achieved merely through crosscultural training. Its favoured approach is to tie learning to corporate strategy and integrate it into ongoing business activities, drawing on a crosscultural team of facilitators. Individual development takes place through a variety of transnational initiatives which include recruiting and developing staff with high potential, networking by means of exchange programmes, conferences and meetings, preparation for overseas assignments through cultural awareness and intercultural skills programmes.
>
> In another separate initiative in the Daimler-Benz group, efforts are being made to expand the global vision of its management at a faster rate than in the past. Managers are felt to need exposure to a way of learning that differs from the tradi-

▶▶

▶▶ Figure 19.10 continued

tional passive didactic style prevalent in Germany. As a means towards achieving this, in 1995 the University of Southern California's (USC) Marshall School of Business was chosen as a 'learning partner' to deliver an intensive executive development programme targeted at senior managers, along with another programme for high-potential middle managers. Daimler-Benz went beyond Germany's borders to find a learning partner because the company felt it could benefit from the American approach to participatory learning to advance its business goals. The programme designed for the middle management lasts 40 weeks and uses distance learning – teleconferencing and the internet – as the primary vehicle for delivery. Its choice was influenced by the fact that USC was capable of providing training in the most up-to-date technology available.

This example reflects a trend for organisations with global aspirations to develop strategic partnerships with universities outside their country of origin to increase their awareness of what is happening on the global stage. To give another example, LG (Lucky Goldstar Company), the South Korean based conglomerate with over 125 000 employees world-wide, has forged a strategic partnership with Indiana University in the USA as part of its drive for performance improvement.

Intervention area 5: Leveraging up distinctive competences at local level

In a study into the ability of a number of UK firms to manage strategic change, Pettigrew and Whipp (1991) noted that 'if in the wake of globalisation, marketing, financial and manufacturing techniques become ever more capable of imitation, then their competitive advantage is correspondingly diminished . . . in this sort of world the ability to learn faster than competitors may be the substantial advantage'. In a global company, the competitors may well include other units within the overall group.

Matsushita, whose brands include Panasonic, National and Technics, is the world's largest consumer electronics company. JVC is a subsidiary business. The product range includes video and audio products, electronic components, batteries, home appliances and kitchen equipment.

In the early 1990s Matsushita operated 150 plants in 38 countries, including Brazil, the USA, Austria, Tanzania, Malaysia and China. It has been said that 'the sun never sets on its holdings'. Schlender (1994) offers a number of lessons from the international experience of Matsushita, of which the following have direct HRD significance and have been influential in the development of this chapter.

1 Be a good corporate citizen in every country; respect local cultures, customs and languages.

2 Minimise the number of expatriate managers and groom local talent to take over.

3 Allow plants to establish their own rules and procedures, fine-tuning the manufacturing processes to match the skills of the local work-force.

It is this third area to which attention is now drawn. For an individual working in a global corporation at one of its local centres, it is worth reflecting on this contribution that this centre's operations make to the whole, and why it should be located where it is. The following classification, which provides useful insights, is a modification of Ferdows (1997). Each instance described could be a result of acquisition or arise out of a greenfield investment.

- A *beach-head* operation is one established primarily to gain access to markets and distribution channels that the company needs.

- An *outpost* operation is one established primarily to gain access to knowledge or skills that the company needs.

- An *off-shore* operation is established to gain access to low wages or other factors integral to low-cost service provision.

- A *server* operation supplies specific national or regional markets.

- A *source* operation is established to develop, produce and distribute products or parts of products for the company's global markets.

- A *contributor* operation both serves a local market, and also assumes responsibility for product customisation, process improvements, product modifications or product development.

- A *lead* operation has the ability and knowledge to innovate and create new processes, products and technologies for the whole.

Today, when every activity is constantly subjected to critical scrutiny, and questions are asked about distinctive competences, strategic capabilities and what value is added, long-term security of provision is best established by demonstrating that one offers something distinctive that cannot be offered more readily elsewhere. Distinctiveness is not based on offering a supply of labour that is cheaper than elsewhere, but on providing a centre of expertise for the entire organisation.

Ferdows (op. cit.) contends that the Sony factory in Bridgend, Wales, has effectively made the transition from a *server* to a *contributor* operation . It was originally built in 1973 as part of Sony's strategy of 'global localisation' (thinking globally when making local decisions), with a remit to produce television sets and components for the European market. Many sub-assemblies were bought from Sony in Japan which led critics to refer to it as a typical Japanese 'screwdriver assembly factory', established in a foreign country to overcome trade barriers.

Over the years management worked hard to reduce its dependence on Japanese components by producing more parts in the factory and purchasing more from European suppliers. By 1990 nearly 90 per cent of the content of its products either was manufactured in house or came from European suppliers.

Product design was also customised for the European market and in 1984 a local engineering and development facility was established. By 1988 there were 185 engineers in the plant out of a total headcount of 1500, working with other employees to learn how to manufacture new models. Since 1988, the plant has designed and developed most of the products it has produced, exporting more than three-quarters.

Learning processes played a key part in the transition, led in particular by TQM ideology. By the early 1980s the plant management had invested in quality management and education programmes as part of a process of improvement that led to a zero-defect campaign. By 1986 it had extended its zero-defect programme to suppliers, co-operating extensively with over 140 in order to institute a 'no incoming inspection' regime.

Ferdows (op. cit.) believes that the acid survival test for the managers of a factory owned by a global corporation is:

How can a factory located outside a company's home country be used as a competitive weapon not only in the market that it directly serves but also in *every* market served by the company?

The question can be broadened to:

How can operations located in each country served by a global corporation be used as a competitive weapon not only in the market that it directly serves but also in *every* market served by the company?

The HRD challenge is: 'How can HRD practices contribute to operations in a given country being seen as a sustainable source of competitive advantage for the whole?'

CONCLUSION

This chapter has provided an overview of key issues facing global organisations and members working in them. It has demonstrated that there is considerable interest in organisations becoming transnational corporations that eschew narrow parochial national considerations in determining policy directions and resource allocations. From an HRD perspective the chapter has argued that there is a difference between possessing an international mindset, which tends to be one dimensional, and possessing a more multidimensional global mindset. The chapter has summarised and examined the rationale underlying a range of HRD initiatives and interventions that various organisations have attempted as they have tried to become transnational in their outlook.

A key message of this chapter is the vulnerability of local centres to global policy shifts that result in closures and relocations. It has addressed the role of HRD in providing local support to a subsidiary of a global undertaking, a feature which has not been covered in the literature on the subject to date.

The overall messages for HRD are stark. Generating career development programmes incorporating overseas secondments might be part of the global equation and might benefit a select group of relatively mobile individuals; at grass-roots level helping to transmit messages about a new corporate culture might provide some sort of feel-good factor but does not provide much in the way of transferable skills if the business itself is not seen as adding sustainable value. An important area of focus must be on generating a mindset that can enable a significant local contribution to the global package.

REFERENCES

Acuff, F. (1984) *International and Domestic Human Resources Function: Innovations in International Compensation.* Organisation Resources Counsellors.

Adler, N. (1991) *International Dimensions of Organisational Behaviour* (2nd edn). Boston: PWS-Kent Publishing.

Auteri, E. and Tesio, V. (1991) 'The Internationalisation of Management at Fiat', *Journal of Management Development,* February, pp. 26–7.

Bandler, R. and Grinder, J. (1975) *The Structure of Magic I.* Science of Behaviour Books.

Bandler, R. and Grinder, J. (1976) *The Structure of Magic II.* Science of Behaviour Books.

Barnlund, D. C. (1989) 'Public and Private Self in Communicating with Japan', *Business Horizons,* March–April, p. 35.

Bartlett, C. A. and Ghoshal, S. (1989) *Managing across Borders – The Transnational Solution.* Cambridge, MA: Harvard Business School Press.

Birdwhistell, R. L. (1961) 'Paralanguage: Twenty-Five Years After Sapir', in H. Brosin (ed.) *Lectures on Experimental Psychiatry.* Pittsburgh: University of Pittsburgh Press.

Cox, C. R. (1994) 'Customer Training takes off at Boeing', *Training and Development* (US), December, pp. 39–42.

Dodd, C. H. (1982) *Dynamics of Intercultural Communications.* William C. Brown.

Ellis, J. and Williams, D. (1995) International Business Strategy. London: Pitman.

Ferdows, K. (1997) 'Making the most of foreign factories', *Harvard Business Review,* March–April.

Hailey, J. (1996) 'Breaking through the glass ceiling', *People Management,* 11 July, pp. 32–4.

Hall, E. T. (1976) *Beyond Culture.* New York: Doubleday.

Hall, E. T. and Hall, M. R. (1987) *Hidden Differences: Doing Business with the Japanese.* New York: Doubleday Anchor.

Hampden-Turner C. and Trompenaars, F. (1994) *The Seven Cultures of Capitalism.* London: Piatkus.

Harrison, R. P. (1974) *Beyond words. An introduction to non verbal communication.* Englewood Cliffs, NJ: Prentice Hall.

Harry, W. (1996) 'Lessons in High Flying for Nationals', *People Management,* 11 July, p. 37.

Hedlund, G. (1986) 'The modern MNC – a heterarchy?', *Human Resource Management,* 25.

Hendry, C. (1994) *Human Resource Strategies for International Growth.* London: Routledge.

Holden, L. (1994) 'International Human Resource Management', in I. Beardwell, and L. Holden (eds) *Human Resource Management: A Contemporary Approach.* London: Financial Times Pitman Publishing.

Iles, P. (1996) 'International HRD', in J. Stewart and J. McGoldrick (eds) *Human Resource Development – Perspectives, Strategies and Practice.* London: Pitman.

Kaku, R. (1997) 'The path of *Kyosei*', *Harvard Business Review,* July–August, pp. 55–63.

Kerr, C., Dunlop, J. T., Harbison, F. and Myers, C. A. (1973) *Industrialism and Industrial Man.* Harmondsworth: Penguin.

Langtry, R. and Balchin, A. (1994) 'The International Context', Module 6 of Diploma in Training and Development', Centre for Labour Market Studies, University of Leicester.

Lyon, U. (1996) 'Influence, Communication and Neuro-linguistic Programming in Practice', in J. Stewart and J. McGoldrick (eds) *Human Resource Development – Perspectives, Strategies and Practice.* London: Pitman.

Maljers, F. A. (1992) 'Inside Unilever – The Evolving Transnational Company', *Harvard Business Review,* September–October, pp. 46–51.

Mayo, A. (1994) 'Business Strategy and International People Development in ICL', in *Handbook of Management Development.* Aldershot: Gower.

Moran, R. T. and Riesenberger, J. (1994) *The Global Challenge: Building the New Worldwide Enterprise*. New York: McGraw-Hill.

Ohmae, K. (1989) 'Managing in a Borderless World', *Harvard Business Review,* May–June.

Paauwe, J. and Dewe, P. (1995) 'Organisational structure of multinational corporations: theories and models', in A.-W. Harzing and J. Van Ruysseveldt (eds) *International Human Resource Management*. Beverly Hills, CA: Sage.

Pascale, R. T. and Athos, A. G. (1981) *The Art of Japanese Management*. New York: Simon & Schuster.

Perlmutter, H. V. (1969) 'The tortuous evolution of the multinational corporation', *Columbia Journal of World Business,* January–February, pp. 9–18.

Pettigrew, A. and Whipp, R. (1991) *Managing Change for Competitive Success*. Oxford: Blackwell.

Reich, R. B. (1991) 'Who is them?', *Harvard Business Review,* March–April.

Rhinesmith, S. H. (1996) *A Manager's Guide to Globalisation – Six Skills for Success in a Changing World* (2nd edn). Homewood, IL: Irwin.

Ronen, S. (1989) 'Training the International Assignee', in I. Goldstein (ed.) *Training and Development*. San Francisco: Jossey-Bass.

Sattelberger, T. (1994) 'Building transnational capabilities'. ASTD Annual Conference, Anaheim, May.

Schlender, B. R. (1994) 'Matsushita shows how to go global', *Fortune,* 11 July.

Tichy, N. M.(1994) 'Global Development', in V. Pucik, N. M. Tichy and C. K. Barrett (eds) *Globalising Management*. New York: Wiley.

Trompenaars, F. (1993) *Riding the Waves of Culture*. London: Nicholas Brealey.

Vargass, M. F. (1986) *Louder than words: An Introduction to Non Verbal Communication*. Des Moines: Iowa State University Press.

Weiss, J. W. (1996) *Organisation Behaviour and Change, Managing Diversity, Cross-Cultural Dynamics and Ethics*. West Publishing Co.

Wickens, P. (1987) *The Road to Nissan – Flexibility, Quality, Teamwork*. London: Macmillan.

Wille, E. (1990) 'Should management development just be for managers?', *Personnel Management,* August, pp. 34–7.

Chapter 20

WORKING IN THE VIRTUAL ORGANISATION

OBJECTIVES

By the end of this chapter you should be able to:

- differentiate between different approaches towards understanding a virtual organisation;

- establish the implications of IT breakthroughs for virtual forms of communicating;

- describe HRD contributions to working in a virtual world.

INTRODUCTION

In September 1996 Bob Ayling, CEO of British Airways talked of the 'Virtual Airline'. He saw this as a new streamlined set-up to meet the challenges of the new millennium. To achieve his 'virtual airline' he intended shedding 5000 staff through the outsourcing of non-core functions such as accounts, check-in and baggage handling.

Why did Ayling hit upon the term 'virtual'? How does his concept fit into how others see the 'virtual organisation'. Is 'virtual' just a trendy term for the end of the millennium or does it entail something distinctive and new in organisational practice? This chapter is intended first to help you to unravel various connotations of the word 'virtual' and establish what this means for organisational practice. It then addresses implications for HRD.

The idea of a 'virtual organisation' seems to have two broad connotations in the literature and in the way people talk about it in practice. In general terms, one approach is to see it as a network of independent, autonomous business units, linked together, often on a global scale, to achieve a mutually beneficial set of product or service objectives – a sort of macro-business partnership. Alexander (1997) refers to this as a virtual ownership organisation. The second approach emphasises the importance of new communications-based technology such as e-mail and the Internet in supporting new organisational forms. In emphasising the lack of physical proximity, it concentrates on the opportunities this affords for home working, 'telecommuting' and other forms of 'location-independent working' as an alternative to individuals commuting to and working together in a central location.

Both approaches emphasise the different range of operational skills and competences required, compared to more conventional structures. Each approach also imposes major challenges for HRD practitioners. Various HRD issues emerge, such as:

■ How does one create and sustain 'virtual teams'?

■ How does one generate a corporate culture with a shared set of values if there is no central location or focus?

■ How does one counter feelings of isolation and even loneliness if there is no face-to-face contact?

■ Can a virtual organisation become a 'learning organisation'?

But the challenge extends beyond such issues. More so than for any other organisational form, the central question becomes:

■ Where should the responsibility for learning be located?

THE VIRTUAL ORGANISATION AS A NETWORK

What is a network organisation?

According to Joseph Weiss (1996) networks are organisational structures that attempt either to circumvent the problems of previous forms or to re-create organisations in order to take better competitive advantage of markets. He differentiates between internal networks, stable networks, and dynamic networks.

Internal networks are designed to capture entrepreneurial and market benefits without causing the organisation to outsource.

Stable networks inject flexibility into the overall value chain of a company. Assets are usually owned by more than one firm: the assets are dedicated to one particular business. It often entails a set of vendors nestled around one large 'core' firm, either providing inputs to the firm or distributing its outputs. BMW, for example, outsources between 55 and 75 per cent of total production costs using a stable network structure.

Dynamic networks work in faster-paced or discontinuous competitive environments. A lead firm may, for example, outsource core skills like manufacturing, R&D and design or editing.

Depending on one's perspective on the airline business, Bob Ayling's concept of a 'virtual airline' entails the establishment of either a stable or a dynamic network.

Carlos Jarillo (1993), in introducing the notion of 'strategic networks', contends that enterprises face two kinds of costs or sources of value: *doing* the things, that is, the different activities needed to deliver a finished product or service; and *co-ordinating* those activities. The second type of cost is especially affected by the choice of organisational form. He identifies two conventional ways of organising:

1 The vertically integrated organisation is one where the ownership and control of the various activities leading to a product or service reaching an end-user is in the hands of a given 'proprietor' organisation. This he sees as the dominant

organisational form of the twentieth century. He instances banks, most of which take care of the whole business cycle from taking deposits in branches which they own, by staff they employ, to recycling them into loans to individuals and companies, while keeping track of all transactions through their own IT systems, looked after by their own systems employees.

2 Subcontracting is where the various activities which lead to a finished product or service are divested in the hands of self-managed, independently owned sub-units. This is a market-based organisation form; when an organisation needs an input, it goes to the market, and has it provided by, and delivered by, a third party. He instances Nike Shoes, where – in contrast to a conventional bureaucracy – there is a constellation of companies, from large chemical manufacturers making the soles, to smaller operations in the Far East, where the different parts are sewn.

Both organisational forms have their attendant problems. Vertical integration can lead to suffocating bureaucracy; subcontracting can entail losing the basic technological know-how on which the business is based. Furthermore, co-ordinating a large number of outsiders creates its own problems and can result in an increase in long-term costs due to, say, lack of time responsiveness.

'Strategic networks', Jarillo believes, provide organisations with the advantages of the two old organisational forms. In a 'strategic network' one company takes the role of 'central controller' and organises the flow of goods and information among many other independent companies, making sure that the final client gets exactly what he or she is supposed to get in an efficient way. It is an arrangement by which companies set up a web of close relationships that form a veritable system geared to providing products or services in a co-ordinated way. He instances Benetton which in 1992, for sales of US$2 billion, only employed directly about 1000 people. At Benetton, more than 80 per cent of manufacturing is done outside the company, by 350 subcontractors, which employ more than 10000 people.

Weiss (1996) establishes four characteristics of such 'strategic networks':

1 Independent organisations within a network perform such business functions as marketing, product design and manufacturing. This *vertical disaggregation* saves overhead costs while gathering expertise from different areas.

2 *Brokers* pull together and align business groups through targeting and subcontracting for targeted services.

3 *Market mechanisms* (not contracts, plans, supervisors or control systems) link and align the networked components.

4 *Full-disclosure information systems* align the networked groups.

A number of writers who refer to the virtual organisation are in fact talking about a network of more or less independent yet co-ordinated sub-units similar to what Jarillo had in mind. Stephen McIntosh (1995) contends that its defining characteristic is: 'various companies temporarily pool[ing] their strengths to exploit fleeting but lucrative opportunities'. Teams are created and dismantled in response to business needs. In specifying the temporary nature of the relationship he differs from Jarillo who sees the network as operating relatively permanently.

He coincides with Jarillo in seeing the network as an alternative to a centralised vertically integrated operation. Chesbrough and Teece (1996) argue that a virtual company goes beyond a strategic alliance, which they consider occupies a sort of organisational middle-ground between a virtual company and an integrated corporation. As they put it:

> virtual companies can harness the power of market forces to develop, manufacture, market, distribute, and support their offerings in ways that fully integrated companies can't duplicate (ibid., p. 46).

According to the American consultancy company, the Gorge Group (1994), network organisations are 'information age organisations designed to adapt quickly, effectively and efficiently to rapid and discontinuous change in market conditions'. They have come into existence because the organisational scene has changed. Hierarchical forms evolved to serve the needs of machine age companies. Networks are better suited to information age requirements of speed, adaptability, innovation and globalisation. They believe there are two possibilities for organisational networking. One entails informal cross-organisational teams that exist within the framework of a hierarchical model. This is akin to Weiss's 'internal network'. The other entails a myriad of formal, internal and external partnerships and alliances linked together through shared goals and values. It is this latter situation that is for them the virtual organisation.

They identify seven distinguishing characteristics of the network:

- flat, disaggregated structures;
- employees who see themselves as suppliers and customers to one another, within a complex web of relationships;
- dynamic, self-organising teams which are fully integrated into the fabric of the organisation;
- fully developed partnership arrangements with suppliers and customers;
- communication flows across the organisation and with external partners;
- fast adaptation to changing conditions;
- widespread adoption of IT.

In such networks power is distributed; everyone owns their own situation; those who can make continuous adaptations to discontinuous change survive and flourish; teams are the norm.

Their model seems to incorporate features of the 'internal network' as well as of the 'strategic network'. It is also significant that they emphasise the importance of IT in getting to grips with the 'virtual' aspect of the network. In rather visionary vein, they believe that networks provide an overarching organising logic – the right system – fundamental to achieving results in today's tumultuous environments. They create new shared meaning; they legitimise new ways of behaving; they provide systemic (as opposed to programmatic) solutions; and they provide a framework in which focused improvement efforts can be launched.

The concern for competitive advantage which underpins much of the above is understandable in commercial undertakings. However, it is possible to visualise network-type organisations operating in the voluntary or public sector.

Implications of network organisations for human resource development practitioners

Identification of skills and competences to operate in network organisations

The Gorge Group (1994) has been conducting an extremely interesting research project to 'identify the real skills being used by real people on the front lines, so others can learn to succeed as network style companies emerge amidst a backdrop of chaotic conditions'.

The steps in the process entailed:

1 Development of an *a priori* skills classification model through extensive literature search.

2 Conduct of 'critical behaviour interviewing', that is, two-hour interviews with 100 people deemed both 'highly successful' and 'average' performers in ten target companies.

3 Identification of themes arising from the interviews.

4 Development of a skills profile instrument.

5 Validation of instrument with 500 additional people.

'Critical behaviour interviewing' seeks information on behaviours that have been actually demonstrated in the recent past. It is more reliable than asking for intentions or opinions, and more comprehensive than observing behaviour. It focuses on key situations where the interviewer probes to uncover what a person was thinking, feeling and doing.

The findings reported were that hierarchies still exist in the chosen organisations but their purpose seems to be different. They focus resources as opposed to controlling; coach and develop as opposed to commanding; and influence partners as opposed to maintaining 'silos'. Beliefs, methodologies and strong cultures are at the fore. There are a strong project management methodology, a strong quality improvement focus and a passion for doing things right.

In the skills overview, an overwhelming number of examples cited had to do with team skills. These examples came mostly from average performers who also emphasised tools and techniques. The excellent performers were more focused on stretching the limits.

The themes emerging from the skills categories were; team problem solving; selling and persuading; spanning structural boundaries; making transitions; communicating; problem solving; project management; power relationships. In each of these it was possible to differentiate between the 'excellent' and the 'average' performer. Skills categories where the themes are not yet clear were: dealing with ambiguity; clarifying roles and expectations; vision/goal alignment; conflict management.

In *team problem solving*, the excellent performer focused on creating synergy involving team members, on building commitment to a common goal, on fostering independence, on constructive debates and on concerns for others/mutual respect. The average performer focused on using tools such as stakeholder analysis, followed a step-by-step process and used a facilitator. She/he also had a hierarchical framework and told the team what to do and engaged in voting rather than consensus.

In relation to *selling and persuading*, the excellent performer had a driving purpose – let the customer be successful. He/she also facilitated agreements and understood customer needs; there was lots of upfront dialogue; he/she undertook iterative activities, was interactive and enlisted support. The excellent performer worked from strong convictions. The average performer tended to get people to 'buy in' to a predetermined solution, told them, used personal appeals and had strong convictions.

In *spanning structural boundaries*, the excellent performer did not honour the hierarchy, he/she had broad networks and worked them directly, making opportunistic use of chance meetings. The average performer also did not honour the hierarchy; he/she was aware of a broad network but worked networks through others.

In *making transitions*, the excellent performer was afraid but maintained positive attitudes and forward momentum; he/she used transitions as opportunities to learn new skills, looked for alternatives/role models, tended to dive in and enter quickly; stayed focused on needs being served; and facilitated major change through lots of communication, setting new expectations and building trust. The average performer demonstrated much more fear, resisted changes; his/her ego was involved and he/she felt forced to change.

In relation to *communication skills*, the excellent performer proactively engaged in building shared understanding; he/she focused on the needs of others and anticipated questions; the real communication tended to go on outside meetings. The average performer executed communication transactions by listening, answering and asking questions at scheduled times.

In relation to *problem solving*, the excellent performer used 'right brain' processes – out of boundary or lateral thinking, looking at the whole situation or the 'big picture' and coaching others. The average performer used 'left brain' processes – parallel processing, exploring alternatives, anticipating problems, and was customer focused.

On *project management*, the excellent performer worked on projects with vigorous goals, did whatever it took to get things done (ethically) and cut across boundaries quickly and directly. The average performer followed disciplined processes, adhered to timelines and used tools/resources.

In terms of *power relationships*, the excellent performer talked about bosses as coaches or mentors, as supporters or as people who could add value to an idea; he/she took on leadership roles without real authority. The average performer talked about a boss as the person to whom ideas would be taken for permission to proceed and as the person with whom he/she shared frustrations.

In terms of overall attitudes, the excellent performer expected to succeed, admired other people, understanding the added value they bring, and was committed to the organisation. The average performer engaged in blaming – seeing a client as someone who does not understand and others as not seeing him/her for what he/she was. The average performer also was committed to the organisation.

These findings are very suggestive in HRD terms. They could help to dictate the criteria and themes underpinning assessment and development centres of the future. Indeed, if valid, they could provide a governing logic for the whole array of organisational initiatives governing performance management and self-development in a network structure.

What might the human resource development function look like?

McIntosh (1995) compares the characteristics of what he considers to be a virtual training organisation and a traditional department (*see* Table 20.1).

Table 20.1 Comparison between traditional and virtual HRD function

A traditional training department	*A virtual training organisation*
Strategic direction	
■ Organises its offerings by courses	■ Provides customised solutions to its clients' needs
Product design	
■ Views suppliers as warehouses of materials	■ Involves suppliers strategically
Structural versatility	
■ Relies solely on training staff to determine the department's offerings	■ Involves line managers in determining direction and content
Product delivery	
■ Distributes a list of courses	■ Offers a menu of learning options
Accountability for results	
■ Believes that the corporation manages employee development	■ Believes individual employees must take responsibility for their personal growth

Source: Based on McIntosh (1995).

McIntosh's list seems to equate less to a virtual organisation than to any set-up that is trying to be responsive to the needs of its customers and which incorporates line managers as key players in the process. The assumption is also made that there will be a training and development function operating in the organisation. There could be such a function if the organisation's philosophy is to focus on internal networks. But there is an increasing tendency for organisations to outsource much of the delivery of training. In the spirit of Jarillo's 'strategic networks', this could result in one designated HRD locus which takes on the role of 'central controller', and organises the flow of services and information about learning, the provision of which originates from a number of devolved sources. Such a locus could also provide a focal point for articulating and orchestrating the network's overall philosophy of learning and development.

Fit or split – should there be an integrated approach to learning?

One of the recurrent themes of this book is whether there should be an integrated and coherent approach to HRD in an organisation. How does one reconcile the need for the autonomy of devolved and independent business sub-units; provide an overall philosophy and logic for learning; and establish a sense of organisational coherence and identity? In a network structure it is likely that each business unit will wish to set up its own approach to the provision of learning and will be reluctant to submit to central decree. The question becomes whether there should be an overall policy umbrella which establishes a set of core values and principles for learning, to which each sub-unit is expected to subscribe. If there is an overall policy umbrella, what should be included in it, and how should it be communicated? These are decisions which each organisation should undertake. They are addressed elsewhere in this book; possible answers to the mode of communication for network organisations will become clearer as we explore the second connotation of the word 'virtual'.

THE VIRTUAL ORGANISATION AND ELECTRONIC TECHNOLOGY

The second approach to the virtual organisation emphasises electronic technology, and explores the opportunities it affords for home working and global communications.

Individuals can today send information around a global organisation cheaply and almost instantaneously. The real cost (as opposed to the price paid) of a phone call to the USA, for example, is no more than of that to a local neighbour.

Regardless of the form an organisation takes, electronic networking is a fact. Benefits of 'wired companies' are held to include the savings in time and money that accrue across geographic locations; easy access routes and 'short-circuits' that cut through functional boundaries and integrate operations; and the potential to identify and penetrate markets that otherwise would have been unknown and unreachable.

It is forecast that high-tech informational exchanges will continue to increase in the twenty-first century. It will be commonplace to use e-mail, voicemail, cellular phones, the Internet, group software, fax, teleconferencing and other wireless systems not yet invented. These electronic forms of communication will speed up the rate at which information is transmitted and will connect users up, down, across, inside and outside organisational boundaries in ways never before possible. The rate at which companies such as Hewlett Packard generate information today will probably be the norm for the organisation of tomorrow. 'Every month Hewlett Packard's 97,000 employees exchange 20 million e-mail messages (and 70,000 more outside the company); nearly 3 trillion characters of data, such as engineering specifications; and execute more than a quarter of a million electronic transactions with customers and suppliers' (Stewart, 1994).

Such telecommunications and IT advances, it is suggested, are allowing organisations to compete in both a domestic and a global competitive environment by 'virtualising' the nature of their business. It has led to remote back-office activities whereby US airlines process ticket stubs in Bermuda and a New York insurance company processes claims in Ireland. The place of business, so the argument runs, is in electronic media, not in a physical location. Thus disparate parts of the organisation can be linked without the need for hierarchy or conventional management control mechanisms. It can be expected that such 'virtualisation' will become more and more common as organisations seek to improve their competitiveness and become more responsive to market situations and customer demands while reducing overhead costs.

Ken Benns from London Transport, a 1996–7 student on my Masters programme in Human Resource Strategies at London Guildhall University, has suggested the following definitions for such a virtual organisation:

1 'An organisation that has minimum infrastructure with maximum geographical distribution and a flexible workforce that communicates information by electronic means.'

2 'An organisation that has no visible physical infrastructure but provides knowledge work by transference of information in a virtual manner.'

An organisation can take many forms, depending on the service or product being supplied. But some distinctive features may be expected.

Organisations that are 'wired' through a host of technologies will resemble a dispersed electronic all-channel configuration.

> Businesses around the world will spend three and a quarter billion dollars this year to buy 'intelligent hubs'; hardware and software devices that sit at the centre of computer networks . . . Networks connect people-to-people and people-to-data. They allow information that once flowed through hierarchies – from me up to my boss and then hers, then down to your boss and to you – to pass directly between us . . . In a wired world, fundamental management jobs such as planning, budgeting, and supervising must be done differently. Tools like e-mail, teleconferencing, and groupware let people work together despite distance and time, almost regardless of departmental or corporate boundaries, which networks fuzz up or even obliterate (Stewart, 1994).

Electronic communications in organisations are thus disrupting old ways of managing business. Formerly closed bureaucracies and command and control systems are being pressed to open up. Importance is given to the role of all staff in achieving the aim of all corporate communication: co-ordinated action that achieves the organisation's goals and mission.

Another consequence is the impact on the individual, as work becomes more 'abstract' and information intensive. With ever-larger volumes of information transmitted electronically, it becomes increasingly important for employees to be able to differentiate the types of information they receive and to correctly decide the appropriateness of the communication form, with whom the message should be shared, and for what purpose it should be transmitted. Being able to manage the flow, the appropriateness and the quantity and cost of information is a necessary part of the communication structure in and between organisations.

Weiss (1996) provides the following guidelines to those either entering or already participating in the wired environments of organisations today:

1 'Don't fight the net.' Information networks are here. Avoiding or escaping the use of increased speed in information exchange causes reactions and more delays.

2 'Create a climate of trust.' Networks open up information and force the sharing of resources across functions. Trust becomes a key ingredient for doing business inside organisations.

3 'Manage people, not work.' With information networks, less focus is needed on work content, and more attention can be given to overall performance and careers. Professionalism and commitment on the part of employees replaces direct supervisory controls.

4 'Press the flesh.' Paradoxically, people need more, not less face-to-face interaction in electronic communication environments.

5 'Build and support teams.' Teams do more of the 'real work' of the entire enterprise in integrated wired organisations. Teams must, therefore, be trained, rewarded and supported in their work.

6 'Do the things leaders do.' Work in wired organisations also emphasises the need for leadership – at all levels. A 1994 study, reported in *Fortune* magazine, of over 170 teams of knowledge workers, found that teams 'are most successful in an environment where decisions spring from rigorous evaluation of costs and benefits, corporate strategy is firmly laid out, and the company has a clear view of its market. All [of this] depends on leaders' (Stewart, 1994).

Effect on the work environment

New ways of working are inevitably going to influence the work environment (*see* Fig. 20.1). A widely heralded aspect of flexible working is that it opens the way for non-territorial offices. Out goes the concept of one person, one workstation, incurring running costs of between £1500 and £3000 a head in the UK. In come terms such as 'team spaces', 'hotelling' and 'satellite offices'. IBM has reckoned to achieve floor space savings of 25–30 per cent at its European sales centre in Staines as a result of shared space. Digital reduced the size of its UK Newmarket office by 90 per cent, moving from a multi-storey building to a wood cabin which serves as a pit stop cum drop-in centre for a dispersed sales force.

Figure 20.1 BT's 'Workstyle 2000'

A major initiative underway at BT is 'Workstyle 2000'. This aims to radically change the way that office-based people work. Westside, BT's first Workstyle 2000 building, is now home for approximately 1500 people. Of these, 1100 use permanent desks, 200 use hot desks and 200 use the building as a base with e-mail and voicemail accounts, but no right to use a desk except Touchdown desks.

Every desk is identical, even for the directors in offices, and so accommodation has been de-politicised. The standard desk means that BT is able to move people and not furniture. The approach is based on 'multi-setting workplaces', that is, where a workplace provides a different setting for different tasks. Thus there is quiet space, social space, meeting space, etc.

The following are the key features:

■ *Touchdown centres* – desks equipped with pre-configured PCs or laptop connections for people just popping in for a short time. Touchdown desks are booked by the hour.

▶▶

▶▶ Figure 20.1 continued

■ *Hot desks* – for a variety of skills and functions, where occupancy of desks is substantially less than 100 per cent. Sales representatives, computing specialists, finance and marketing staff are some of the functions sharing desks. Typically a team of 12 people would share nine desks. A pedestal park provides space for each to have their own storage on site. The accommodation is managed by the team.

■ *Project rooms* – these are large meeting rooms equipped with six desks and a full IT infrastructure. Project teams can book these rooms for three months at a time and move people in instantly. The composition of the teams tends to be very fluid. Once a room is allocated, the project team is given the keys.

■ *Quiet rooms* – these are located away from the main office area and contain just a desk and in some cases a PC, but no telephone. They are booked on a needs basis for people who need to get away from the constant interruptions of the office. Interestingly, they have proved to be the least successful element of the Westside concept.

Source: McLocklin *et al.* (1996).

Virtual organisational forms have specific advantages for small and medium-sized enterprises (SMEs) in terms of telecottages and neighbourhood (third party managed and operated) business telecentres. Large organisations can use their own local satellite offices.

In September 1996 Surrey County Council unveiled a new teleworking centre in Epsom, just south of London, with phones, computers and faxes for around 15 people who do not need to travel to regional offices in order to carry out their work. The intention is that social workers, highway engineers and specialist teachers, who are always on the move, will drop in and send their work via the Internet. This was an extension to existing arrangements elsewhere within the council for hotdesking and homeworking (Littlefield, 1996).

Internal and external networks

The Internet is an example of an external network and has received huge publicity. However, for many organisations the first tangible benefit of the Internet has come from improved internal communications that result when Internet technology is reapplied to form an intranet or internal network. An intranet is merely a private version of the World Wide Web, a network of information published in multimedia form, which is available only to staff and members of a given organisation. Companies such as Mobil, Ford, Olivetti and McDonnell Douglas have already installed, encouraged or in some cases simply allowed both official and unofficial intranets to be set up, as have – in the UK – such organisations as SmithKline Beecham, Ford, the BBC and BP.

One of the key outcomes of the development of intended networks could be facilitation of the shift to teleworking or telecommuting. Currently one of the main obstacles to efficient teleworking is that information is frequently in the wrong place. In the office you may store files on the hard disk that you find you need at home and vice versa. Intranet technology allows files to be made available over the network; and future teleworkers will be able to store all of their work in progress and archive material on a security-protected web server which they can then access from their home, their office, or indeed, anywhere in the world.

What is telecommuting?

Prior to the Industrial Revolution most people worked at home, or adjacent to their homes. The Industrial Revolution, with its concentration on mechanised machinery and the building of factories, made such working from home relatively inefficient. This was extended into office work where the nature of technology and work processes required large groups of people working together in the same place. This process was facilitated with the growth of the transport infrastructure which enabled people to access relatively distant work locations relatively easily. This became linked to the growth of suburbs and commuters.

Telecommuting represents a reversal of this separation of workplace from the home. It entails working at a location away from the 'parent' office on either a full-time or part-time basis, communicating with it electronically, rather than commuting to it physically. This can be done from the telecommuter's home or from a neighbourhood office.

It is not known how many teleworkers there are in the UK; estimates vary, depending on one's definition, from 2.4 per cent to 12 per cent of the work-force in 1996. Generally, teleworkers are held to be people who operate from home at least one day a week and use telecommunications and computer equipment to link up with their employer. Using this definition, the National Association of Teleworkers estimates that 4.7 per cent of the work-force are teleworkers. In the USA, according to IDC/Link, a research firm that tracks telecommuters, the annual work-at-home number rose 7.6 per cent to 39 million households in 1995. The Federal Administration aimed to increase the 1996 figure of between 3000 and 4000 US government officials covered by teleworking arrangements to 60 000 by the end of 1998. There is a suggestion that the figure could increase to 160 000 by the end of 2002.

Further evidence of the trend towards flexible working

At a 1995 London conference entitled 'Initiating location-independent working in the virtual organisation' the impact of 'virtualisation' on work styles was addressed. Speakers from organisations as diverse as BP, Reuters, Mercury and Rank Xerox talked about facing new choices and possibilities by roughing up their once sharp organisational boundaries and breaking free of the constraints of time and geography through use of advanced office technology. It was interesting that a number of the organisations represented had created a 'flexible working' function. Based on experiences reported at the conference Sheena Wilson (1995) identified ten ways in which organisations could profit from flexible working.

Enhanced individual productivity

1 *Taking work home – fewer interruptions, catching up time.*
The head of flexible working at Digital commented: 'Home is perceived as a quality environment; it is where people feel they are at their most productive'. 'Everyone sees home working as an ideal,' said the programme manager for flexible working at Rank Xerox. Feedback surveys by these companies show that being able to spend a proportion of time at home, with portable kit so as to stay in touch with the office, is considered immensely beneficial. Not that entrepreneurial knowledge workers want to be in seclusion every day. 'We reckon two days a week is enough,' said the Mercury representative, 'more than that can become sterile.'

2 *Optimising travel – work on the move, fewer journeys.*
For Sheena Wilson (ibid.) the ultimate image of the virtual worker is the busy executive talking into her mobile phone instead of waiting a listless hour in the airport lounge. The last decade has seen increases in travel times, in the form of business trips or tiresome journeys to and from work. Digital calculates that, on average, the equivalent of five working weeks a year are spent, per head, travelling. If this time can be used productively, or cut down, all the better.

3 *Greater personal control over time.*
People have greater freedom to work where and when they like, planning their day around travel schedules, domestic requirements and personal proclivities.

Enhanced organisational effectiveness

4 *Outside skills acquired, as needed, resulting in lower long-term employment costs.*
When Reuters launched a project to test the usability of their products, the project manager was given an assistant and told to get on with it. This led to a five-year project with a shifting team of contractors drawn from some six different consultancies. The emphasis was on 'picking the best brains' while keeping the headcount down.

5 *Supporting flexible, market-focused project teams.*
Flexible office layouts, combined with remote technologies, provide valuable support to companies which are making the shift from hierarchical, departmental structures to molecular structures organised around flexible, market-focused project teams.

6 *Keeping staff who have conflicting domestic obligations (curbing recruitment costs).*
Anderson Consulting keep experienced support staff by allowing them to set up a fully equipped home office. Solicitors Nabarro Nathanson help women lawyers balance child-rearing and work through flexible hours. Both are thus able to keep expensively trained staff and curb recruitment costs.

7 *Reducing relocation costs – short-term overseas assignments in place of full-scale relocation.*
BP, as part of its restructuring, has revised its policy on overseas assignments. Where possible, staff go abroad on short assignments, to assist projects at key stages and support locally recruited teams, rather than move abroad for several years. This cuts down on relocation costs and is less disruptive to families.

Enhanced productivity of office premises

8 *Non-territorial layouts reduce per capita fitting out and running costs.*

9 *Process of handling changes in headcount is liberated.*
During the early 1990s the number of employees of Mercury Communications grew from 2000 to 11 000. This would have been impossible if the company had worked to a fixed ratio of space per head.

10 *Morale boosting – more emphasis on teams, less on status.*
Offices become an instrument of organisational change. Many organisations, like Mobil Oil, which has a world-wide programme of reducing facility costs, have been taken by surprise by how well employees have responded, in part because of fewer signs of hierarchy.

Mercury is an example of a partial virtual organisation that has implemented location independent working that requires each employee to submit a business case for their working pattern. Currently over 3000 of its employees regularly use their laptop PCs and remote access software to work:

- at home (typically for one or two days a week);
- from home (perhaps going to a customer's or supplier's site);
- while on the move (e.g. from a hotel bedroom or even from their car).

Mercury provides 'Touch Down' shared, managed offices (located strategically around the country), with 'team' desks at the main office.

HUMAN RESOURCE DEVELOPMENT IMPLICATIONS

Skills retention

Rank Xerox found that one of the benefits of its own telecommuting experiment was the retention of skills. In particular, by offering those of 'early retirement' age a 'networking' contract the company had access to skills which might otherwise have been lost through abrupt retirement.

Training of teleworkers

Huws (1996) suggests that there will increasingly become a need to develop entirely new approaches to the training of remote workers which will retain the advantages of flexibility while encouraging the 'learning organisation' principles of mutual trust, team working and commitment, and sharing in decision making. She also considers that there will be a growing number of teleworkers who have never experienced working in an office environment.

Currently, she contends, employers of remote workers are 'making do' with a similar approach to training to that they have adopted in relation to their on-site staff. The results of a 1992 'Teleworking in Britain' survey which her consultancy, Analytica, conducted for the Employment Department showed that only 3 per cent of the 65 British employers surveyed who train their teleworkers have developed methods for providing remote training. The majority include teleworkers in their in-house training schemes or rely on self-training from manuals or conventional courses run by outside training suppliers.

However the survey did reveal some innovative schemes which had been specially created to prepare staff for the transition to independent working. These included:

- one-day workshops for new teleworkers;
- a scheme for new teleworkers to 'shadow' more experienced colleagues;
- a scheme whereby personnel officers act as mentors for new teleworkers;
- the inclusion of modules on psychological and self-management issues in induction programmes for new teleworkers;
- time management courses.

She also found that many managers would not consider teleworking for existing staff, unless they were deemed 'self-sufficient, mature, productive and trustworthy'. As she then points out, once these staff cease to be employed full-time in the office, knock-on problems occur:

1 They are not available to train new entrants.

2 As their own skills became out of date, how could one devise means both of identifying their training needs, and then subsequently retraining them?

It was revealing that only 16 per cent of the employers surveyed had individual training plans for their teleworkers, and only 3 per cent had conducted a skills audit.

There is one point that she only touches upon, but which is very significant. How do teleworkers learn the corporate culture?

To induct an 'on-site' employee into becoming a telecommuter working from home, it is recommended that a version of the traditional approach, 'sitting next to Nellie', be employed. The new homeworker should be given the name and telephone number of a mentor – someone who has already been working from home for some months and who can share experience and be a support to the new homeworker.

Because telecommuters work from home it will be tempting to train them using distance learning methods. *Indeed, open learning may become the training and development method.*

Virtual teams

Superficially it might seem that, thanks to IT, building a team has never been simpler. By using e-mail, videoconferencing and satellite links, employees on different sides of the world can communicate with each other and possibly never meet face to face. But can teams really exist without face-to-face contact? How can one satisfy the need for social contact, the need to affiliate and belong, which for many years have been seen as powerful motivating forces governing organisational membership?

Virtual teams are most likely to exist in multinational companies that need to overcome large geographical barriers. But UK organisations whose employees work from home or who are regularly away from the office are also searching for solutions to team-building problems.

Arco Chemical Europe, according to a 1996 report, make regular use of videoconferencing. Yet, according to their HR Development adviser, Christine Debougnoux, employees still miss the opportunity of face-to-face contact. 'You lose the physical vibrations. Sometimes during a videoconference, you feel that people are acting.'

The British Council, which has responsibility for a range of cultural exchange programmes and employs 6000 people in 109 countries, uses e-mail to maintain contact with its various outposts because videoconferencing is not available ouside the UK. A key issue for them is to ensure that staff are working towards corporate goals even though they are based all over the world. 'The problem is, how do you weld together people who have been fiercely independent, and who had a degree of latitude, so that they develop activities in line with the corporate agenda?' (Edmund Marsden, Assistant Director-General, quoted in *People Management*, 26 September 1996, p. 41).

The British Council found that the opportunity to develop ten technology-based virtual teams in designated overseas regions only came about after a series of face-to-face week-long workshops based in the UK. These were supplemented by two-day roadshows for employees in each country.

Once initial contact has been established, the objective is to maintain momentum, given that many employees will not meet again in the flesh for up to two years – if at all. This has led to a series of virtual teams being set up across national boundaries to look at issues such as sexual equality, management training and the overseas sale of NVQs. The feeling in Digital, which is experimenting with personal desktop videoconferencing facilities, is that technology can only ever support team-building and cannot replace human contact.

Virtual induction

The *Independent,* on 5 August 1996, reported an example of virtual induction (*see* Fig. 20.2).

Figure 20.2   Virtual induction

After the paperless office and the golden hello, a firm of accountants has dreamed up the next stage in technology: the virtual welcome.

New recruits to Morton Thornton, based in St Albans, Hertfordshire, will in future be shown around the three-floor building without leaving their desks – and without taking up the valuable fee-paying time of other members of staff.

The new virtual-reality tour, which will replace the day-long induction programme that the firm used to offer to its recruits, will also include a guide to the town's cathedral and pubs.

▶▶

▶▶ Figure 20.2 continued

'It gives you a guided tour in which you can start outside the front door of the practice and "walk" through the front door and all over the building,' said Christopher Lowe, a partner in the 70-strong firm.

The guided tour takes the form of movies in which the user can control the speed and direction of travel. The pictures were collected from digitised camera and video films made on the premises.

But the program's usefulness extends much further. 'It can show you pictures of key people in the organisation, and explain procedures such as how to handle clients on the phone, or how to claim expenses.'

The pressure for replacing the personal touch with the personal computer did not come from previous recruits, Mr Lowe said. Instead, it was the drive for profitability.

'We were looking at cost structures, and training is expensive, costing up to £70 per hour,' he said. 'We wanted to get the best value from it. There is a cost-saving in doing it this way.'

Rather than tying up a senior partner – who might have to use valuable chargeable time on telling a recruit where the photocopier is – the CD-ROM based product will be able to point the way and save the firm thousands of pounds annually.

Source: Arthur (1996).

Interactive training

The interactive training approach can, in my opinion, be linked to the interactive training/learning sessions referred to by Roger Schank in his plenary session at the Annual ASTD Conference in Dallas in 1996. Schank specialises in multimedia interactive training and artificial intelligence. He recommends that, for interactive exchanges, things should never be explicitly taught. He argues that one needs to adopt goal-based scenarios. The approach entails:

- find stories of incidents that have happened in the company;
- find when incidents come up;
- create simulations of those situations;
- index stories to likely mistakes.

He contends that learning is facilitated if one:

- lets people explore through the medium of a case study or case incident;
- puts people in the most realistic simulations;
- breaks down the simulation into discrete chronological tasks to be undertaken by the individual, with yes/no responses on choices made so that errors can be detected and feedback provided;
- makes use of experts in the organisation to relate stories (via video navigation systems) of what happened if a particular path of action was chosen;
- makes it as much fun as the buyer of the package will allow.

The Schank system has been introduced as a training aid at North West Water.

Checklist for telecommuters

A number of organisations have emphasised some of the pitfalls of telecommuting. The following is a typical checklist for intending telecommuters:

1 Establish a routine and follow it.

2 Pace yourself. If you don't take breaks, you may find yourself burnt out by 2.30 p.m.

3 Become self-sufficient. It's not impossible to toss something on another person's desk, figuratively, when you're telecommuting, but it's harder.

4 Be consistent with children and other family members. Office hours should be office hours.

5 Stay visible. Phone people. E-mail them.

6 Make sure you bring home more than enough work. Telecommuters tend to work faster at home than at the office.

7 Establish a buddy relationship with somebody at the office to do 'legwork' for you when you can't be there.

8 Get a second phone line. It's not worth fighting with family members and fielding telemarketers' calls.

9 Make sure you have access to a fax machine (from Hequet, 1996).

The advice in the above list is fine while one is actually working at home. But all the evidence indicates that it is important to ensure that some of a telecommuter's weekly time is devoted to making face-to-face contact with others. If this is not via regular visits to the corporate 'office', then linking to a local drop-in centre is an alternative possibility.

Some telecommuters work at sites near to their home to help resolve these problems. Thus some organisations in Southern California provide satellite offices, where office space is leased near neighbourhoods where many of its employees live. Another possibility is neighbourhood work centres, which resemble satellite offices, and where several companies join forces to equip and share office space near a residential area.

The strategic implications of open learning

In HRD terms, it is a reasonable hypothesis that the evolution of the virtual organisation will lead to considerable emphasis on open learning as a way of providing development opportunities. Open learning is usually seen as an approach to facilitate learning at a time, pace and place suited to the personal needs of the individual. It acknowledges that we all learn at different speeds and bring with us varying levels of experience derived from work and non-work situations. It emphasises the use of a variety of media to support learning. Such media might be provided directly to the individual in the form of support packages, or might be available at specially designated support centres, or both. The support centres, operating in some ways like libraries, should be open at times convenient to the target users. It is broader in scope than distance learning, which on the whole relies primarily on materials delivered to the individual's home.

Open learning for the virtual organisation can take a number of forms:

■ provision of drop-in centres, either owned or run by the host organisation, or operated, under franchise, on behalf of a number of contributing institutions;

■ development of interactive video packages for use at the drop-in centre;

■ provision of networking opportunities via the Internet/e-mail. These can include open dialogue sessions on specific themes; pen pal arrangements; and so on;

■ greater reliance on high-tech distance learning materials;

■ use of learning need questionnaires sent via the Internet.

One does not have to rely on one's employing organisation to take advantage of some of the open learning opportunities available. For example, many dialogues on specific themes can be accessed through the World Wide Web. Thus for HRD practitioners there is now the opportunity of accessing the IPD Training and Development network, launched in autumn 1996 and contributing to a range of discussions. This is what is known as a moderated network – some control is exercised over the dialogues that are permitted.

The virtual course

A related initiative is the 'virtual course', seen as an extension of the distance learning methodology. Advantages claimed by erstwhile distance learning providers typically include that it:

■ creates opportunities for global networking of students/tutors;

■ reduces isolation and demotivation;

■ supplements distance learning material;

■ sustains interest between workshops;

■ enables faster turnaround of course work;

■ facilitates easier administration of programme;

■ gives access to wider information sources;

■ affords opportunity to learn about new technology.

Henley operate their distance learning MBA programmes on a global scale through an international network of support organisations – for example they have a partner in Australia. They use a software package called Lotus Notes to provide support for conventional distance learning materials. In 1996 they had 2000 note users in 80 countries. They have one central 'server' in Henley and have been introducing servers into each of their support organisations.

The following are some of the facilities available on 'notes':

■ e-mail;

■ general and topical discussions;

■ submission of course work;

■ workshop and examination booking;

■ access to research findings, working papers, journal articles.

Henley supply the software, a comprehensive users manual, and other support services. Students are responsible for obtaining their own personal computer and modem.

The drop-in centre

In recent years organisations have given increasing attention to providing open learning drop-in centres. Many employers contend that staff who undertake open learning in work-based centres are more likely to remember what has been covered than if they attend traditional off-the-job courses. A typical example is the Body Shop, which in 1996 had three open learning centres in operation. Their head of learning and development alleged that in setting them up they were trying to move away from a 'package holiday' approach to training where people are used to having everything done for them to the concept of 'independent travel' (Merrick, 1996). However training at drop-in centres should not consist solely of leaving someone alone with a computer and a set of self-study aids. A drop-in centre has strong affinities with the ethos of the virtual organisation. Of course, it is possible that many drop-in centres will be owned and/or managed by independent training organisations, providing services for a range of client organisations.

Nevertheless, there is evidence that open learning centres are underutilised. The Woolwich Building Society used to have a number of learning resource centres at different sites but by 1996 they were abandoned because of lack of use, with the exception of one located at its head office. At the 1996 'World Open Learning for Business Conference and Exhibition' the business development manager from the Open College stated that some 40 per cent of organisations have some form of open learning centre. However they generally suffer from under-use and limited access.

At the conference many promoted the idea of the virtual learning resource centre, a resource 'centre' accessible via linked computers. Several organisations were in the process of developing the idea and putting it into practice. A number of UK Civil Service Departments are in the vanguard of developments. The Inland Revenue in particular is using this approach to meet its needs as a large national, multi-sited organisation, going through major changes and downsizing.

Fit versus split

Earlier in this chapter, it was asked how an overall learning philosophy could be orchestrated and communicated in a network organisation. For the IT-intensive virtual organisation, the issue becomes less of a problem as one draws on the technological possibilities of the intranet. Thus in the early 1990s BP abolished the central HR and training function, devolving responsibility to line managers or to local HR and training specialists. BP is now using its intranet to provide a company-wide perspective, which the decentralised units find it hard to do. The intranet also enables its 55 000 staff to share ideas across the globe.

In May 1996, BP launched its 'Einstein' project, which provides details on the intranet of training courses, networks, shadowing schemes and all forms of learning taking place in the company. The intention is to get the benefits of a central function without going back to central control (Thatcher, 1996).

CONCLUSION

In conclusion, is it possible for a virtual organisation to be a 'learning organisa-tion'? As we saw in Chapter 15 there are a number of perspectives on what constitutes a learning organisation, and, in some quarters, a challenge posited to the very notion. Whatever position one adopts, the virtual organisation causes a transformation of many conventional notions about organisational learning. This is in large part because of the somewhat amorphous nature of what constitutes 'the organisation'. Where are the boundaries? What is in and what is out? Who is in and who is out?

Nevertheless, there is a correlation between some of the features usually associ-ated with a 'learning organisation' and those of a 'virtual organisation'.

Take, for example, the following often quoted definition of a learning organisa-tion: 'an organisation which facilitates the learning of all its members and continuously transforms itself' (Pedler *et al.*, 1991). The 'continuous transforma-tion' of a virtual organisation is possible to conceive. More problematic is the facilitation of the learning of all its members.

Take also the perspective that 'the core idea behind the "learning organisation" is that organisations of all kinds will not survive, let alone thrive, if they do not acquire an ability to adapt continuously to an increasingly unpredictable future' (Pearn *et al.*, 1994). There is no doubting that the new emergent organisation forms associated with 'virtuality' demonstrate corporate adaptability of a very high order. And yet, with people scattered in their 'location independent environ-ments', where is the corporate memory? How are norms and values and indeed learning itself to be transmitted? That is the real challenge for the 'learning archi-tects' of the overall system.

REFERENCES

Alexander, M. (1997) 'Getting to grips with the virtual organisation', *Long Range Planning*, February, pp. 122–4.

Arthur, C. (1996) *Independent*, 5 August 1996.

Chesbrough, H. W. and Teece, D. J. (1996) 'When is virtual virtuous? Organising for Innovation', *Harvard Business Review*, January–February, pp. 65–73.

Gorge Group (1994) 'Getting results in network organisations'. Unpublished paper presented at ASTD annual conference, Anaheim.

Hequet, M. (1996) 'Virtually working', *Training*, August, pp. 29–35.

Huws, U. (1996) 'Training and flexible work', *Flexible working*, 1(2), February, pp. 7–9.

Jarillo, J. C. (1993) *Strategic Networks: Creating the Borderless Organisation*. Oxford: Butterworth-Heinemann.

Littlefield, D. (1996) 'Council asks workers to log into PC centre', *People Management*, 29 August, p. 9.

McIntosh, S. S. (1995) 'Envisioning the Virtual Training Organisation', *Training and Development*, May, pp. 45–9

McLocklin, N., Maternaghan, M., Lowe, S. and Bevan, M. (1996) 'Workstyle 2000 – a new flexibility', *Flexible Working*, 1(2), February, pp. 28–32.

Merrick, N. (1996) 'Well remembered, but not that dear', *People Management*, 12 September, pp. 45–6.

Pearn, M., Roderick, C. and Mulrooney, C. (1995) *Learning Organisations in Practice*. McGraw-Hill.

Pedler, M., Burgoyne, J. and Boydell, T. (1991) *The Learning Company*. New York: McGraw-Hill.

Stewart, T. A. (1994) 'Managing in a Wired Company', *Fortune*, 11 July.

Thatcher, M. (1996) 'A platform for sharing', *People Management*, 30 May, p. 27.

Weiss, J. W. (1996) *Organisational Behavior and Change: Managing Diversity, Cross-cultural Dynamics and Ethics*. West Publishing.

Wilson S. (1995) 'Beyond Space and Time', *Human Resources*, September/October.

Part 4

ORGANISATIONAL VALUES

THE CONTRIBUTION OF HUMAN RESOURCE DEVELOPMENT TO THE DEVELOPMENT OF AN ORGANISATIONAL VALUE BASE
Commitment, business ethics, managing diversity and environmentalism

---

OBJECTIVES

By the end of this chapter you should be able to:

- establish the role that shared values play in today's corporations and the impact of this on HRD practitioners;

- describe potential inconsistencies between the values of HRD practitioners and those of the organisations with which they are associated;

- describe different connotations relating to the value of achieving commitment in an organisational context;

- differentiate between ethics and values;

- differentiate between values contributing to society at large (societal values) and the specific value orientation of an individual organisation;

- identify the contribution that HRD can make to a strategic response towards managing diversity, business ethics and environmentalism.

INTRODUCTION

Human resource development exponents have conventionally been described as having a responsibility for achieving relatively permanent changes in individual and team behaviour resulting in new knowledge, skills and attitudes at the workplace. The following 1981 definition of training is a typical instance of this perspective. Training is seen as:

> A planned process to modify attitude, knowledge or skill behaviour through learning experience to achieve effective performance in an activity or range of activities. Its purpose, in the work situation, is to develop the abilities of the individual and to satisfy the current and future needs of the organisation (Manpower Services Commission, 1981).

Some anxiety has been expressed by practitioners over the years about being involved in attitude modification activities that go beyond encouraging task-specific behaviours, such as attitude towards safety, and which entail trying to convince individuals of the appropriateness of taking on a set of broad-based, culturally specific organisational values. Yet in today's organisational climate, this is what many HRD practitioners are expected to do. An extreme historical version of this was represented by a large electrical goods company in the USA in the early 1950s where a two-year training programme was established 'to combat antidemocratic propaganda by presenting an accurate description of modern industrial practices and selling the American way of life' (Galagan and Carnevale, 1994). Values are linked to attitudes in that a value serves as a way of organising attitudes (Gibson *et al.*, 1993).

This chapter is about the role of HRD in putting across an organisational value set as part of a strategic thrust. To what extent do and should HRD practitioners be the exponents and propagators of organisational values? Is HRD about changing attitudes or about changing behaviour? Is this a realistic dichotomy?

For me, a central question is: 'If we are attempting to change people's behaviour, and yet accepting that their attitudes and underpinning values remain unchanged, are we not then recognising that people are being encouraged to act "dishonestly"?'

The chapter looks in general terms at how HRD practitioners can contribute to gaining commitment to an overarching set of organisational values. It addresses inconsistencies that may emerge in the relationship between organisational values and those of individuals given the task of disseminating them. It then looks specifically at HRD approaches adopted to inculcate perspectives on business ethics, managing diversity and addressing environmental issues. It builds upon earlier chapters which addressed issues such as the role of HRD in managing transformational change and in globalisation.

OBJECTIVES VERSUS VALUES

Until the 1980s the dominating ideology for commercial and public sector organisations in the West was to manage by 'hard' objectives not 'soft' values. Commercial success was measured in terms of return on capital, market share, control of costs and effectiveness of investment decisions, not in terms of environmentally friendly policies. Operational success was measured principally in terms of economically, efficiently and effectively providing products and services to customer specifications, not in terms of the provision of rewarding and enriching jobs. The performance of managers was likewise measured in terms of the achievement of predetermined efficiency and effectiveness targets such as those based on the SMART acronym (Specific; Measurable; Achievable; Realistic; Measurable; Time bound). With some noticeable exceptions, equal opportunity and ecological considerations were seen as external context factors operating as constraints on action, not as imperatives to be aimed for. This is reflected in models such as the stakeholder theory of objectives (*see* Fig. 21.1, based on Cyert and March, 1963), in which the dominant decision-making coalition establishes and attempts to contain possible sources of resistance to proposed courses of action, leading to operational effectiveness. The outer circle represents the groups influencing the decision-making process, the inner circle represents the interplay of goals and constraints affecting their choices.

| Figure 21.1 | Stakeholder theory of objectives |

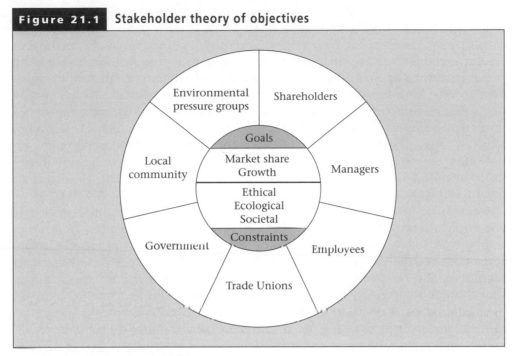

Source: Based on Cyert and March (1963).

Blau and Scott (1966) are representative of supporting theoretical modelling relating to organisational purpose. They developed a classification system for differentiating between types of organisations based on who is the prime beneficiary (*see* Table 21.1).

Each type of organisation, they contended, generates its own distinctive problems. For business concerns, they felt that the central problem was that of maximising operational efficiency in a competitive environment. In contrast, for service organisations the problem was reconciling conflict between providing a

Table 21.1 Blau and Scott's organisation classification

Organisation type	Prime beneficiary	Examples
Mutual-benefit associations	Members or rank and file participants	Trade unions Political parties Professional bodies
Business concerns	Owners or shareholders	Industry Commerce
Service organisations	Clients or public-in-contact	Schools Social Services Hospitals
Commonwealth organisations	Public at large	Police Armed Services

professional service to the public-in-contact and maintaining administrative systems and regulations that govern relations with the public. Although the classification system is suggestive that different types of organisations might propound different values, the authors do not pursue this line of enquiry. By implication their approach supports the maxim of Friedman (1970) that 'the business of business is business'. Friedman goes on to say that 'there is one and only one social responsibility of business – to use its resources and engage in activities designed to increase its profits so long as it stays within the rules of the game, which is to say, engages in open and free competition without deception or fraud'.

Contractual obligations for employees in the UK have similarly not been overtly value laden in terms of expecting individuals to adopt a set of explicitly articulated organisational beliefs.

Individuals have been expected to comply with a set of rules and regulations governing attendance, performance-in-task requirements, obedience to authority, honesty, reliability and general conduct. Historically managers of large organisations have on the whole felt most comfortable assuming that people have an instrumental orientation to work and prefer operating under a behavioural code that restricts itself to rational-legal contractual obligations and implied terms of 'faithful service'. This is not to say that employees do not become 'accultured' by virtue of membership of a given organisation and often, almost subconsciously, get accustomed to operating under a set of implicit codes of behaviour that can be distinctly value laden.

Motivational theory has provided a conceptual underpinning for how people behave at the workplace and how they might behave differently. It has focused more on circumstances influencing one's attitude towards one's job as opposed to attitude towards what an organisation stands for.

However, we are now moving into an organisational world where adherence to a set of published core values and governing principles is being propagated as a condition of organisational membership (*see* Fig. 21.2).

Figure 21.2   **Core values**

The 1994 IPD position statement, 'People Make The Difference', has a section devoted to the issue of values. The following points are made:

- people management policies will have an impact upon values;
- such values, whether implicit or explicit, must be apparent to everyone;
- they need to be relevant, understandable and linked to mission and/or vision statements;
- inappropriate alternative values could emerge if there is incompatibility between stated, espoused values and actual management behaviour;
- commitment to values is associated with trust, which is easier to achieve with staff working on full-time contracts;
- top-team training is necessary to ensure that senior managers understand both the values of the organisation and the importance of acting in ways which are consistent with them.

▶▶

▶▶ Figure 21.2 continued

A number of challenges are set for policy makers. These include:

1 Is the value set, within which business strategy is developed, articulated, owned by the top-team and widely understood in the organisation?

2 Does the top team understand the development and implementation of values in terms of:
- their own responsibility as role models;
- behaviour which positively undermines the values and what sanctions might be imposed to discourage non-compliance;
- what constitutes 'supportive behaviour' and how this might be rewarded.

3 What specific actions – statements, training procedures and awareness training – does the organisation need to reinforce the required values? Are these actions visibly championed by top management?

4 If the organisation operates in the international arena, has it considered the extent to which the values should be applied consistently across national boundaries? If not, what should be undertaken?

'Value-talk'

'Value-talk' was introduced into the mainstream of Western organisational thinking by the commercial success of Japanese organisations and by the popular success of books such as *In Search of Excellence*. In it Peters and Waterman (1982) advocated a search for shared values in the workplace. As they put it: 'Every excellent company takes the process of value shaping seriously, either buy into the company's values or get out'. Peters and Waterman were not specifically thinking about diversity management or environmental-value-oriented issues.

A number of broad types of values-management philosophy can be identified. These include:

- buy values versus make values;
- re-create values versus maintain values;
- social responsibility based values versus organisation-specific values.

Buy values and *make values*. A buy-value management style assumes that one's values are not changeable and looks to hire people who already share the organisation's basic values. A make-value management philosophy, in contrast, assumes that employees are malleable and, assuming basic intellectual abilities and motivational readiness, capable of being socialised to the corporate values. It is in facilitating this socialisation process that HRD practitioners are liable to be drawn in. This in turn leads to a need for practitioners to evaluate their own value position on what they are undertaking. To what extent has the search for core values and guiding principles to underpin organisation vision and mission statements brought in its train a re-educative process akin to cultural conditioning?

On another dimension, there is the issue of how appropriate or clearly articulated the organisation's values are. Is the philosophy to *re-create values* or to *maintain values*?

On yet another dimension there is the question of how strongly articulated people wish the organisation's values to be. It has led to the association of strong values with strong cultures (*see* Fig. 21.3).

| Figure 21.3 | Strong cultures |

As defined by Deal and Kennedy (1988) a strong culture is one where everyone knows the goals of the organisation and is working towards them. They go on to argue that a strong culture is a powerful lever for guiding behaviour; it helps employees to do their jobs a little better, especially in two ways.

1 *A strong culture is a system of informal rules that spells out how people are to behave most of the time.* By knowing exactly what is expected of them, employees waste little time in deciding how to act in a given situation. Deal and Kennedy estimate that a company can gain as much as one or two hours of productive work per employee per day.

2 *A strong culture enables people to feel better about what they do, so that they are more likely to work harder.* Strong cultures remove a great deal of uncertainty because they provide structure and standards and a value system in which to operate.

Deal and Kennedy identify the following influences on and constituent parts of corporate culture.

Business environment

Each organisation faces a different reality in the marketplace depending on its products, competitors, customers, technologies, government influences and so on. This business environment in which an organisation operates determines what it must do to be a success and is the single greatest influence in shaping a corporate culture.

Values

Values are the basic concepts and beliefs of an organisation; as such they form the heart of the corporate culture. Values define 'success' in concrete terms for employees – 'if you do this you too will be a success' – and establish standards of achievement within the system.

Heroes

Heroes personify the culture's values and thereby provide tangible role models for employees to follow. Smart companies take a direct hand in choosing people to play these heroic roles, knowing full well that others will try to emulate their behaviour.

The rites and rituals

The rites and rituals are the systematic and programmed routines of day-to-day life in the organisation. In their mundane manifestations (rituals) they show employees the kind of behaviour that is expected of them. In their more extravagant form (ceremonies) they provide visible and potent examples of what the organisation stands for.

▶▶

▶▶ Figure 21.3 continued

The cultural network

The cultural network is the 'carrier' of the corporate values and heroic mythology. Storytellers, spies, priests, cabals and whisperers form a hidden hierarchy of power within the organisation. Working the network effectively is the only way to get things done.

DEFINITIONS OF ORGANISATIONAL VALUES

The prevailing metaphor for describing organisation values seems to be that just as a human being has a central belief system which incorporates values, so too does an organisation. Thus *organisation values* can be defined in exactly the same way as one defines *individual values*.

Individual values can be defined as 'the constellation of likes, dislikes, viewpoints, shoulds, inner inclinations, rational and irrational judgments, prejudices and association patterns that determine a person's view of the world' (Spranger, 1928). This is too subject oriented a definition to satisfy organisational requirements of rationality. A perspective affording a more acceptable analogy is that provided by Rokeach (1972) who defined individual values as 'a type of belief, centrally located within one's total belief system, about how one ought or ought not to behave, or about some end-state of existence worth or not worth attaining'. Rokeach went on to address the nature of the value-action link:

> Once a value is internalised it becomes, consciously or unconsciously, a standard or criterion for guiding action, for developing and maintaining attitudes towards relevant objects and situations, for justifying one's own and others' actions and attitudes, for morally judging self and others and for comparing self with others.

Rains (1997) makes the point that the concept of values is frequently (and mistakenly) used interchangeably with the concepts of ethics, attitudes, morals and beliefs. Such confusion is exemplified in many of the pronouncements made on the subject by senior organisational executives. Typical is the statement made in 1990 by Robert Haas, the Chairman and Chief Executive of Levi Strauss: 'A company's values – what it stands for, what its people believe in (i.e. its ethics) – are crucial to its competitive success. Indeed values drive the business' (quoted in Howard, 1990).

TYPES OF ORGANISATIONAL VALUES

Internal values and external values

As we have seen throughout this book, organisations in the West are becoming more value oriented, and articulating core values and supporting principles in their published documentation. In parallel, senior management is increasingly looking for more than compliance from staff and other stakeholders to those values. Individuals are being expected to import new sets of values into their behaviour.

Value statements tend to be a mixture of propositions relating to how transactions in an organisation should be conducted and how individuals in the organisation can hope to be treated; and statements governing external relations with the outside world, including an articulation of societal values such as the contribution that the organisation as a whole will have upon society at large.

Words that keep popping up are 'commitment' and 'shared'. The connotations associated with both need to be understood by the HRD practitioner. 'Shared' has connotations of 'mutuality'; 'commitment' has connotations of reciprocity. That is, underpinning the value is a form of bargain: we will commit ourselves to X and in return you will demonstrate your personal commitment to Y.

Keep (1989) uses the term commitment in his definition of HRD:

One of the primary objectives of HRD is the creation of conditions whereby the latent potential of employees will be realised and their commitment to the course of the organisation secured. This latent potential is taken to include not merely the capacity to acquire new skills and knowledge but also a hitherto untapped wealth of ideas about how the organisation's operations might be better ordered.

Note that this statement contains no indication of reciprocity.

Examples of 'commitment' statements

There follow some examples of 'commitment' statements.

Within the bounds of commercial confidentiality we will encourage open channels of communication. We would like everyone to know what is happening in our company, how we are performing and what we plan.

. . . our aim is to build a company with which people can identify and to which we all feel commitment.

We want information and views to flow freely upward, downward and across the company (Nissan Communication Philosophy).

At SmithKline Beecham, healthcare – prevention, diagnosis, treatment and cure – is our purpose. Through scientific excellence and commercial expertise we provide products and services throughout the world which promote health and well being.

The source of our competitive advantage is the energy and ideas of our people. Our strength lies in what we value: customers, innovation, integrity, people and performance.

At SmithKline Beecham we are people with purpose, working together to make the lives of people everywhere healthier, striving in everything we do to become The 'Simply Better' Healthcare Company as judged by all those we serve: customers, shareholders, employees and the global community. (SmithKline Beecham plc).

Figure 21.4 Allied Domecq Spirits and Wines (UK)

Allied Domecq Spirits and Wines (UK) (ADS&W (UK)) is part of the Allied Domecq group. It markets and sells premium spirits and fortified wines in the UK, and has in its portfolio brands such as Teacher's whisky, Tia Maria liqueur, Courvoisier cognac, Harveys sherry and Cockburn's port. Its headquarters are in Bristol; there are a sales, marketing and administration unit at Horsham in West Sussex and a depot in Leicester. In 1995 Allied Domecq brought in the external consultancy group McKinsey to orchestrate changes in business practices across the range of its

▶▶ Figure 21.4 continued

European operations as part of a survival strategy. The overall objectives of this initiative are to increase both short-term and long-term profit, to build on Allied Domecq's sales and marketing expertise and to share best practice and learning across the various Allied Domecq companies.

In 1996, ADS&W (UK) working with consultants called Breakthrough International also initiated a culture change programme, designed to encourage creativity, innovation, improved relationships and self-belief. The hoped-for outcomes are changes in attitudes and values, resulting ultimately in new behaviour. To support the culture change, a new vision and mission were developed by the senior management team guided by Breakthrough.

The new vision is to be: '*The greatest UK Drinks company famous for our energy, creativity and daring deeds.*'

The mission is: '*To create magic with our brands and customers, inspire passion in our people and deliver outrageously good results.*'

In order to harness the energy and motivation which it was expected the resultant culture change programme would generate, and focus it into practical terms, five key 'destinations' were established. Each incorporated comprehensive one- and three-year plans. The five destinations are Brands, People, Customers, Finance and New Business Development. Employees were then encouraged to look at the changes that needed to be made at individual and team level in order to achieve the vision, mission and supporting 'destinations'. A group of six internal staff were appointed to 'create energy' as dictated by the new vision and mission. The group of six were called 'Adventure'. A specific initiative to train people in the new value-driven approach was called 'Transfusion' and delivered by the Adventure team. Delegates constituted groups of 30 people at a time, from each of the business units making up ADS&W (UK), voluntarily attending a two-day programme, supported by two one-day follow-ups some months later to act as refreshers and re-energisers. The programmes were held at conveniently sited hotels.

The programme emphasised the importance of creativity, fun and teamwork at the workplace. It encouraged people to look at themselves and be able to move out of their comfort zones and work towards being stretched without being stressed. Supporting training methods involved use of videos and extracts from films such as *The Dead Poets Society* (seize the moment – *carpe diem*). The idea-generating work of Edward de Bono was drawn upon. The 'destinations' developed from the vision were discussed and worked through. Each participant was encouraged to 'open up' and go on stage to express their feelings – resulting in clapping and applause. My correspondent, Ruth Hartley, who was HR manager at the Horsham Division at the time, found it to be a powerful experience and enabled her to focus on what was 'important to you'. However, she felt that the articulation of what behaviour change was expected at the workplace was unclear, and the energy levels created at the end of the two days were difficult to sustain in a work environment where little seemed to have changed in terms of day-to-day transactions. She felt that clearer links could be made between the programme and the existing performance management system. She also pointed out that the energising programme was done at a time of organisational downsizing and restructuring resulting from the McKinsey intervention. At the time I spoke to her (December 1997) she had just been made redundant. During the year, the Managing Director had also left, creating additional uncertainty.

Security of employment

Sometimes, but not always, commitment statements promise security of employment. Japanese companies such as Toyota, for example, have been associated with this approach:

> Highly competent, motivated people will show great commitment to the fulfilment of the company's objectives. Fundamental to the people philosophy is a determination to provide to the individual both growth opportunity and stable employment (Toyota).

Other organisations have not been prepared to give such a guarantee:

> Whilst it is impossible to argue emotionally against the appeal of employment security as a desirable framework for improving employee involvement, it is simply so out of phase with present reality that I do not believe it is credible (Director of Merchant Bank, quoted in IPA, 1997).

Spelling out the reciprocal nature of the commitment

Brent Council

Brent Council, one of the local authorities serving London, has developed a Staff Charter. This is intended to reflect the espoused internal values the council holds in respect of its staff and to incorporate its view of the reciprocal nature of the relationship (*see* Fig. 21.5).

Figure 21.5   Brent Council's Staff Charter

Brent Council has adopted four core values. One of the most important of these is the Council's commitment to valuing and empowering our staff. The Staff Charter is a statement of intent by Brent Council to support this commitment.

The Council Commitment	Your Commitment
Brent Council is committed to:	*In return Brent Council expects your commitment to:*
Treating you with respect, courtesy and consideration	Taking pride in your work and ensuring the principles of total quality are reflected in all your work
Being as open and honest as possible in its dealings with you	Ensuring that the Council's Mission and Core Values are reflected in all your work
Identifying and encouraging your training and personal development	Developing and maintaining high quality services to meet the Council's commitments in its Customer Charters
Encouraging your creativity initiative and new ideas	Complying with all reasonable management instructions
Providing you with a clear statement of your responsibilities and expected performance standards and providing you with regular feedback on your performance	Treating customers and work colleagues with respect, courtesy and consideration

▶▶

▶▶ Figure 21.5 continued

The Council Commitment	Your Commitment
Brent Council is committed to:	*In return Brent Council expects your commitment to:*
Treating you fairly and equitably on the basis of your skills, abilities and performance	Taking responsibility for your own work and ensuring that you meet the performance standards set for you
Informing, consulting and communicating with you on significant matters that affect you and your work	Maintaining public confidence in your integrity and honesty
Providing you with the best quality terms and conditions to motivate you and reward your contribution to the Council	Avoiding conflicts between private interests and your Council duties
Providing you with a safe and healthy work environment	
Promoting and protecting your health	

We have in a previous chapter referred to Neville Russell Chartered Accountants and their mission statement entitled 'Going the extra mile' (*see* Fig. 21.6).

Figure 21.6 | **Neville Russell mission statement**

Going the extra mile

■ by exceeding our clients' expectations through content, quality and integrity of our service delivered in a personal and professional manner

■ by developing the potential of our people through individual recognition, tailored training and constructive appraisal, leading to personal fulfilment, proper reward and enjoyment

■ by being a successful firm hallmarked through its national and international outlook, high ethical and technical standards, profitability, growth and corporate pride.

They too have developed a reciprocal staff charter influenced by the approach adopted at Brent.

Neville Russell's Commitment	Your Commitment
We will:	*In return we expect you to:*
Share our plans for the firm with you	Ensure that the firm's mission and values are reflected in your work
Let you know regularly, how your office and the firm are performing financially	Treat colleagues and clients with consideration and respect
Treat you with consideration and respect	Take pride in all aspects of your work
Be honest and open with you, and give you regular feedback on your performance	Be honest and open with us

▶▶

▶▶ Figure 21.6 continued

Neville Russell's Commitment	Your Commitment
We will:	*In return we expect you to:*
Consult and communicate with you on matters which affect you and your work	Ensure you gain the most out of the training and development opportunities provided
Encourage you to use your initiative and develop new ideas	Take ownership of your work and ensure that you meet your required performance standards
Treat you fairly, based on your performance, skills and attitude	Maintain others' confidence in your honesty and integrity
Help you identify your personal development and training needs	Ensure that you treat sensitive information confidentially
Provide means to meeting those needs, which also meet the firm's business needs	Develop innovative ways of improving the way we do things
Provide you with a safe and healthy work environment	Communicate in a friendly manner with colleagues and clients avoiding unnecessary conflict
Keep future employees informed during the recruitment process	Develop appropriate skills in order to carry out your job effectively
Provide you with details of your responsibilities and expected performance standards	Be well presented and professional at all times
Provide you with pay and benefits to reward your contribution to the firm	Take care of your environment and any equipment which the firm provides for you
Make sure that you have the appropriate accommodation and equipment necessary for you to carry out your job	Help to make your office a place where people enjoy working
Make sure that each office is an enjoyable and fun place to work	

Taken in its entirety, the level of commitment is very demanding for both parties to the bargain.

WHOSE VALUES?

When we talk about organisational values, we face the same dilemma as that faced when we talk about organisational learning. Can values emerge independently of the people who constitute the organisation? Harrington (1987) takes the position that what drives an organisation is the values of top management.

> An organisation takes on the personality of its top management . . . The process starts with top management, will progress at a rate reflecting management's demonstrated commitment, and will stop soon after managers lose interest in the process.

This perspective is sometimes known as 'the upper echelon perspective' (Hambrick and Mason, 1984) and is an extension of the view developed by Cyert and March (1963) arguing for the primacy of the 'dominant coalition' in decision making. It can probably be narrowed down even further in some instances to the values, personality and drive of the Chief Executive or owner or founder. Sometimes the values get built into the fabric of the organisation. It is hard to visualise The Body Shop moving away from the espoused values of its founder.

The increasing impact and success of Japanese companies in Western market places in the 1970s led to a number of attempts by Western writers to identify the source of their success. One of the most influential contributions was *The Art of Japanese Management* by Pascale and Athos (1981). They emphasised the role of 'shared values' in the philosophy and approach of successful companies such as Matsushita, and contrasted this unfavourably with the approach adopted by American counterparts (*see* Fig. 21.7).

Figure 21.7 Japanese influences

Matsushita Electric Company, at the time they were writing, was one of the top 50 largest corporations in the world. The founder, Konosuke Matsushita, launched the company in 1918 and was still a dominant force in 1980 despite his retirement in 1973. Matsushita was the first Japanese company to have a song and a code of values. A planning executive in 1980 said, 'It seems silly to Westerners but every morning at 8.00 a.m., all across Japan, there are 87 000 people reciting the code of values and singing together. It's like we are all a community.'

The founder believed that the experience one gains through extended work exposure in an organisation has a major influence on shaping one's character and one's relationship to society at large; furthermore the corporation has a social responsibility to participate positively in the shaping process. Accordingly management should serve as trainers and developers of character not just as exploiters of human resources.

The basic principles, creed and 'spiritual values' of the corporation are as follows.

Basic Business Principles

To recognise our responsibilities as industrialists, to foster progress, to promote the general welfare of society, and to devote ourselves to the further development of world culture.

Employees Creed

Progress and development can be realised only through the combined efforts and co-operation of each member of our company. Each of us, therefore, shall keep this idea constantly in mind as we devote ourselves to the continuous improvement of our Company.

The Seven 'Spiritual' Values

1 National Service through Industry
2 Fairness
3 Harmony and Co-operation

▶▶

▶▶ Figure 21.7 continued

4 Struggle for Betterment

5 Courtesy and Humility

6 Adjustment and Assimilation

7 Gratitude.

The founder is notorious for the following statement spelling out the significance of these values for the company.

If you make an honest mistake, the company will be very forgiving. Treat it as a training expense and learn from it. You will be severely criticised [a euphemism for dismissal] however if you deviate from the company's basic principles.

Given this focus on corporate values it is no surprise to learn that Matsushita's approach to HRD emphasised the importance of inculcating and reinforcing values. In addition to training in them, each person is asked to give a ten-minute talk at least once every other month on them and how they relate to society.

Source: Based on Pascale and Athos (1981).

It would be a mistake to assume that the search for shared values in organisations emanated solely from Japan. Pascale and Athos draw our attention to:

the widespread acceptance of the use in [US] business of explicit, usually Christian religious metaphors [in the 1930s] . . . The development of 'creeds' which employees were expected to hold, of 'cults' of membership differentiating employees from outsiders and identifying them with insiders, and of 'codes' of behaviour that reduced uncertainty and prescribed right action and attitudes was an important part of the early years of some companies.

At IBM in this period, all of the following were apparent:

the use of company songs, dress codes . . . ubiquitous displays of 'the leader' in photographs, oils and bronze statues, slogans presented in expensive and long-lasting materials, an often referred to book of the leader's speeches and essays . . . and a house organ to reinforce values and educate.

IBM is often referred to as a values model firm. IBM employees are expected to embed into their practice three tenets: commitment to excellence; respect for the individual; service for the customer. These are supported by long-standing principles such as:

■ to enlarge the capabilities of our people through job development and give them the opportunity to find satisfaction in their tasks;

■ to accept our responsibilities as a corporate citizen of the USA and in all the countries in which we operate throughout the world.

The son of the founder of IBM said, in a McKinsey Foundation Lecture in 1962:

> I firmly believe that any organisation, in order to survive and achieve success, must have a sound set of beliefs on which it premises all its policies and actions. Next I believe that the most important factor in corporate success is faithful adherence to those beliefs. And finally I believe that if an organisation is to meet the challenges of a changing world, it must be prepared to change everything about itself except those beliefs as it moves through corporate life (T. Watson Jr, quoted in Pascale and Athos, op. cit.).

'Shared values' was incorporated into the notion of 'superordinate goals', one of the components of the 7-S framework which Pascale and Athos used to diagnose organisational functioning. In later formulations Pascale reverted to 'shared values' in preference to 'superordinate goals' (e.g. Pascale, 1991). The position of Pascale and Athos was that 'generally speaking people want to identify with their organisation; they want to trust and depend on those they work with and invest through their labour in the organisation's success'.

Organisational seduction

Karen Legge, in her 1996 Alec Rodger memorial lecture at Birkbeck College, London, criticised cultural management programmes such as those used at British Airways that are designed to secure the commitment of employees to the values espoused in corporate mission statements and the like. She suggested that in the context of high unemployment they might generate what has been termed 'resigned behavioural compliance'. In other words people will profess to espouse them in order to hang on to jobs. Others will internalise them and act as advocates both in word and deed.

Gibson *et al.* (1993) refer to a particular manifestation of an organisational socialisation process that they hold amounts to 'organisation seduction'. They isolate four key elements.

1　The organisation induces initial commitment to corporate values through its reward strategy.

2　Employees are influenced to remain loyal by enticement not force.

3　The abundance of opportunities and rewards draws individuals away from their own values and goals towards the organisation's values and goals.

4　The organisation creates the illusion of free choice being exercised by those individuals who join and subsequently remain in the job.

They go on to contend that an organisation implements this form of socialisation by only hiring those individuals who have apparent inclinations to accept the organisation's values and goals. Once hired the individual is provided, by the organisation, with opportunities to work in high-status, challenging, responsible, enriched jobs. With their ego massaged through the ongoing reward structure, individuals feel obliged to be loyal to such a benevolent organisation.

However people respond to such initiatives, there is no doubting that these practices are becoming endemic. We have referred to a number of them in previous chapters. Take, for example, the AXA Group which provides 'confirmation programmes' at the AXA University to develop attitudes which are compatible with the

Group's values and corporate mission. Disney tries to immerse individuals into their 'Corporate Way' culture. In both of these instances there is a strong presence from HRD practitioners in terms of both designing and delivering the programmes.

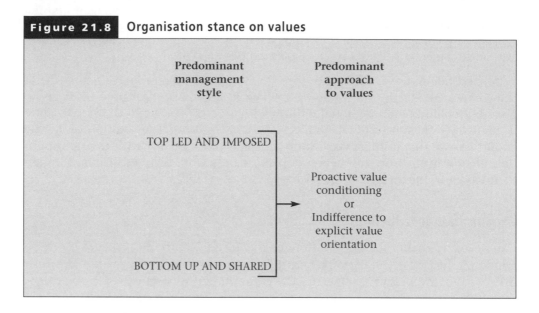

Figure 21.8 Organisation stance on values

Whatever the stance, HRD professionals often have a key role in interpreting and transmitting organisational standards and values to others.

THE VALUE OF 'COMMITMENT' IN THE LITERATURE

Argyris (1964), in addressing how an individual might relate to the organisation in which he or she works, emphasised the importance of avoiding the extremes of an overpowering manipulative organisation on the one hand, and an organisation that will 'keep people happy' on the other. He argued that happiness, morale and satisfaction were less important than an individual's competence, self-responsibility and commitment. What should be aimed for are fully functioning, committed individuals in active, viable, vibrant organisations. This, he believed, could not be achieved without an ongoing tension. He hypothesised that 'the incongruence between the individual and the organisation can provide the basis for a continued challenge which, as it is fulfilled, will tend to help man to enhance his own growth and to develop organisations that will tend to be viable and effective'.

'Commitment' he saw as an aspect of self-esteem and associated it with the nature of goal-seeking behaviour which individuals manifest towards their work. Following earlier work by Kurt Lewin he believed that the probability for enhancing self-esteem (and hence commitment) increase if individuals:

■ are able to define their own goals;

■ can relate the goals to their central needs and values;

■ are able to define the paths to these goals;

■ feel that the achievement of these goals represents a realistic level of aspiration; involving new challenges and an element of risk.

He predicted that the organisation of the future (that is, of today!) will: 'give much more thought to its basic values' in order to overcome the levels of individual apathy, psychological ill-health and absence of commitment he found to be present at the time when he was writing. He forecast that 'the organisation will require people who are not threatened by, but actually value, psychological success, self-esteem, self-responsibility, and internal commitment' (op. cit., p. 274).

Katz and Kahn (1965) refer to the presence of an 'adult socialisation process' in an organisation which 'can build upon the the personal values of its members and integrate them around an attractive organisational mission. If the task of the organisation has emotional significance, the organisation enjoys an advantage in the creation of an attractive image'. In speaking of emotional significance, they are referring to organisations whose basic objectives are likely to create other than an instrumental orientation to work. An example would be offering services to humanity by working in a cancer research unit. Other organisations are not so fortunate as to have such 'emotional significance'. They suggest that an imaginative leader can, however, help in the development of an attractive image of an organisation by means of a reconceptualisation of its mission. In motivational terms, they refer to an idealised situation where an individual is activated towards the goals of the organisation because these goals represent his or her own personal values. 'People so motivated are usually described as having a sense of mission, direction or commitment' (p. 346).

In Chapter 5, where the relationship between HRD and HRM was discussed, we referred to the philosophy underpinning the work of the Harvard school in the early 1980s. This emphasised that work relations should be organised around the value of commitment. The Harvard notion of commitment has strong echoes of Argyris, but goes beyond his focus on the individual's attitude to his/her work. Beer and Spector (1985) saw commitment as being of people to both their work and their organisation. The intended outcome would be more loyalty and better performance for the organisation, and greater self-worth, dignity, psychological involvement and identity for the individual. Such commitment entailed the creation of high trust relations between all sectors of the work-force, which in turn meant employees being able to exercise influence and in some way be 'empowered'. Thus commitment is dependent upon 'mutuality' – mutual goals, mutual respect, mutual rewards and mutual responsibility (Walton, 1985).

Guest (1989), among others, has commented on the *unitary* perspective that seems to be implicit in the Harvard philosophy and the implications it has for relations between management and trade unions. Unitarism is usually taken to relate to a belief system implying commonality of interest between parties, and a belief that any conflict other than personality clashes is the result of mismanagement. Building on the work of Fox (1974) the key components of a unitarist frame of reference are as follows:

1 There is no fundamental conflict of interest between management and the work-force. Both are equally concerned with the survival and success of the whole and can work in partnership towards its attainment.

2 Harmony and goodwill are the essential components for efficiency and growth. Conflict is an unnecessary evil.

3 Trade unions, and the associated risk of adversarial industrial relations, are unnecessary since good management can be trusted to act in employees' best interests.

4 Industrial disputes will only occur when management makes a mess of things.

5 Management will fairly and honourably act in the best interests of the various stakeholders who have a claim on organisational resources and might be affected by organisational decisions.

That view can be contrasted to a pluralist frame of reference where the key components of the prevailing belief system are as summarised below:

1 There is inevitable conflict of interest between management and the work-force. In particular, the work-force is concerned with maximising the benefits from its association with the organisation, whereas the management is, at best, concerned with balancing conflicting and competing demands on resources.

2 Some conflict between management and work-force is a perennial possibility: arrangements should be made for containing it before it gets out of hand. Grievance procedures, disputes procedures and negotiating apparatus should be established for discussions between management and work-force representation.

3 Work-force representation is typically by means of some form of trade union. Full rights should be given to trade union officials.

Many organisations endeavouring to achieve shared values have adopted a unitarist perspective. In recent years, Japanese and American companies, as a condition of offering employment opportunities in the UK, have endeavoured to exclude trade unions or absorb them into a partnership relationship with the enterprise.

Commitment to shared values should not be confused with shared purpose or shared objectives. It has long been contended that one of the measures of an effective team is the identification of, and commitment to, a common set of objectives, which defines the overall task and its operational context. Thus Alexander (1985) includes the achievement of shared goals and objectives as the first of the nine components of his Team Effectiveness Critique. He argues that in order for a team to operate effectively, it must have stated goals and objectives. These goals go beyond a simple understanding of the immediate task, to incorporate an overall understanding of the role of the group in the total organisation, its responsibilities and the things the team wants to accomplish. In addition, the members of the team must be committed to the goals. Such commitment comes from involving all team members in defining the goals and relating the goals to specific problems that are relevant to team members. The time spent on goal definition in the initial stages of a team's life results in less time needed later to resolve problems and misunderstandings.

The agents of such value 'conditioning' are often HRD staff. It is seen as a legitimate part of their activities to engage in what Chin and Benne (1976) termed normative-educative strategies, based on the assumptions that norms form the basis for behaviour and that change can be achieved by means of a re-educative process in which old norms are replaced by new ones.

Organisations such as The Body Shop have made very public commitments to ethical and environmental values. A recent Body Shop advertisement in *People Management* for a 'Strategic Leadership Development Consultant' included the following clause:

A word of caution: it would be unwise to write to us if you are not passionate about changing the world of business into an ethical, inclusive, socially active and environmentally responsible place to be. You would probably find it hard to stick the pace of the chaotic agenda arising from these aspirations.

Figure 21.9 looks at the 'vision strategy' espoused by Mercury.

| Figure 21.9 | 'Imagine 1997' |

In the early 1990s Mercury, a subsidiary of Cable and Wireless invested millions of pounds in a 'vision' strategy to 'change the culture' of the telephone company for the late 1990s. It was a transformational change approach to strategy. Employees were invited to visualise how things would be in 1997 and then stand in the 'gap' – the unknown – and determine how to bridge it. Employees were encouraged to declare a breakdown on all processes that did not further the strategic intent. Central to 'Imagine 1997' were 50 'value coaches' – employees who acted as confessors or referees to others who felt they could not conform or who had concerns about their role. They helped employees talk about their 'value breakdowns' in order to solve problems and embrace the company vision.

Perret Roche, the American consultants who masterminded the programme, explained: 'Everyone needs to be able to create the vision for themselves if it is to succeed.'

Some participants did not enjoy the 11-hour training events at specially designed halls at the National Exhibition Centre in Birmingham, where all the seats had microphones to encourage contributions. One female employee who attended with 150 others said that experiencing the hyped-up applause and prolonged 'whooping' after speeches was both intimidating and disturbing. The company accordingly provided a helpline for problems with 'Imagine'. Of the 10 000 employees, 8500 volunteered to take part in the programme which started with an 'ignition' period and was followed with a 'take-off' period. When interviewed about 'Imagine' and its apparent Orwellian overtones of '1984' the then Chief Executive Officer, Mike Harris said: 'There is a strong swell of support for it in the company.' He insisted that individuals who did not volunteer were not being sidelined.

THE VALUES OF HUMAN RESOURCE DEVELOPMENT PRACTITIONERS

An American study (Rains, 1997) of the values of HRD practitioners was based on a stratified random sample from the membership lists of three professional organisations in the USA with an HRD focus – the American Society for Training and Development; the National Society for Performance and Instruction; and the Organisation Development Network. Two instruments were used to determine the predominant value sets. The *Study of Values* (Allport *et al.*, 1970) differentiates between aesthetic, economic, religious, social, theoretical and political values. Rains' interpretation of his data from this instrument was that they described a group which support an appreciation of individualism. The *Values Scale* (Nevill and Super, 1989) is a 21-scale instrument designed to establish values underpinning vocational choice. The cluster of values on this scale intimated that HRD practitioners are self-sufficient, independent people who look inward for validation and direction, as expressed by the high ranking of achievement and autonomy. One of Rains' observations was that the study only looked at the values of the individual practitioner. He considered that there could be a clash between the values of the organisation and those of the HRD practitioner, but that hypothesis remained to be tested.

The strong focus on individualism would indicate that practitioners would be emotionally equipped to challenge overarching organisational values if they felt uncomfortable with them. Walton (1973) touched on this when he identified the following five 'inconsistencies' that could lead to a mismatch between an HRD practitioner's values and beliefs, and received wisdom on how the organisation should function. These inconsistencies are those between:

- the goals and strategies of the organisation and the HRD practitioner's norms and values;
- the managerial actions with which the HRD practitioner's actions are associated and his/her concept of justice;
- the consequences of the HRD practitioner's actions and his or her personal value system;
- the actual behaviour and actions of the practitioner and the professional standards which normally cover his or her relationship with the organisation;
- the consequences of interventions and the values which are attributed to HRD.

He went on to suggest that the practitioner has a number of roles which he or she can adopt in response to these inconsistencies. He gave no indication of how frequently these roles were adopted in practice.

1 The practitioner as *voyeur*. In this role the practitioner does not believe that any personal action taken can really effect change. Therefore, the practitioner is happy to observe and evaluate any situation in an organisation, irrespective of how abhorrent its aims and values. In effect, the practitioner becomes a covert observer.

2 The practitioner as *conscientious objector*. Here the practitioner handles any inconsistency by refusing to have a role involving any situation where there might be a major conflict of values. No problem exists where the practitioner has the power in terms of authority and autonomy to be able to refuse to participate.

3 The practitioner as *therapist*. In this role, the practitioner attempts to deal with the individuals in any situation who, as 'victims' of the system, are capable of growth and development. In order to resolve any inconsistency the practitioner will view the individual as having needs over and above those of any organisation or situation.

580

4 The practitioner as *catalyst*. In this role, which is often seen as the traditional role for those engaged in OD, the practitioner believes that there exists the capability for change and that he or she can play an important part in getting an organisation to look at its current method of operating.

5 The practitioner as *skilled craftsperson*. In this role the practitioner is more concerned about the excellence and intellectual challenge of her or his work. Organisations or situations are perceived as opportunities to try out new training techniques and novel approaches. Inconsistencies are only a problem where the organisation's objectives are seen to interfere with the successful outcome of the exercise of his or her craft.

6 The practitioner as *missionary*. In this role the practitioner has a set of strongly held values or ideas which he or she considers to be the answer to any situation. Inconsistencies pose no problem as eventually others will come round to the practitioner's way of thinking. Spoor and Bennett (1984) substituted the term 'evangelist' for 'missionary'. However, there has always been a conflict between an articulation of personal values in training sessions, and elsewhere, and the performance-in-task requirement to present an official viewpoint.

7 The practitioner as *entrepreneur*. In this role the practitioner is unconcerned about the process of problem diagnosis. It is up to the 'client' to decide what the problems are. Inconsistencies pose no problem as in this role the practitioner becomes completely absorbed and integrated into the organisation or situation.

Both Rains and Walton seem to be thinking in terms of HRD through the eyes of a career professional. However, as we have seen, all managers have a responsibility for HRD.

The above categorisation of 'inconsistencies' and practitioner roles suggests that practitioners might hold the following views on values:

- believe implicitly in them;
- feel that they do not go far enough;
- feel that they are very worthy but that the organisation cannot deliver them;
- believe that they are espoused values which are for public consumption and that the organisation has no intention of delivering.

MANIFESTATION OF VALUES IN SPECIFIC AREAS

Given the possible interpretive roles which the practitioner might undertake in response to projecting organisational values, let us now look briefly at three specific areas – business ethics, managing diversity and environmentalism. For all three some common themes emerge.

1 Competitive advantage or adding customer value has often been used as the basis of selling the advantages to organisational members. In other words, there is an element of instrumentality. This is often done as a promotion campaign by 'missionaries' trying to get others on board.

2 In practice, HRD interventions tend to fit into two broad categories:

■ awareness training, sometimes leading to specific attempts to change attitudes;

■ coaching in policies and what one needs to do in terms of changing practices and behaviour to meet the requirements of the organisation.

Whatever intervention is undertaken needs to be supported with ongoing manifestations of good practice at the workplace, evidence of commitment from the top, appropriate publicity, etc.

BUSINESS ETHICS

Figure 21.10 looks at some examples of business ethics.

| Figure 21.10 | Ethical leadership and training |

In August 1994, the merger of Lockheed and Martin Marietta was announced, thus creating the world's biggest defence company.

Ethics is not a word normally associated with arms makers. Lockheed, of course, has been in the news in the past on matters such as offering bribes and backhanders to gain contracts. However the chief executives of the two former companies have created an ethics office, a code of ethics, compulsory ethical training courses and an ethical helpline for troubled staff. Some of their sales representatives complain that, because they have to be squeaky-clean, they are losing contracts to European firms which offer *pots de vin*. It is all part of an attempt to define a common culture of ethics and engineering for the new corporation.

Lucas Aerospace is taking steps to raise employee awareness of the ethics programme it launched in the UK early in 1995 after two of the company's North American divisions were found to have falsified tests on components supplied to the US navy.

All 3000 UK employees have received a booklet entitled *The Lucas Ethics Programme Depends On You* explaining the company's new code of conduct. This states that when conducting business, all employees must comply with its letter and spirit. By October 1995, over 90 per cent of staff had attended ethical awareness presentations. Introduced by general managers and led by 'site ethics officers', most of whom are HR professionals, the presentations give employees the opportunity to ask questions about the ethics policy, which encourages them to report suspected breaches of the code, either directly to their managers or through an anonymous hotline.

Concern with business ethics is not new. When I was working for Boots the Chemists in the 1960s a whole section of its range was referred to as 'ethical products'. There were also products which it classified as 'unethical' and which it was not prepared to sell. At the time these included condoms. It would probably now consider it unethical not to sell condoms!

One of the features of recent years has been for organisations to reveal their approach to business ethics, and make a deliberate attempt to engage in so-called ethical behaviour. Pickard (1995) considers 'ethics' to be the latest business buzz-word and cites survey evidence from the Institute of Business Ethics that in 1995 more than one-third of major organisations had ethics codes, compared to 18 per cent in 1987. There is a tendency in the literature on business ethics to argue that it is in an organisation's self-interest to be ethical, because it can give it a competitive advantage over so-called unethical organisations. Johns (1995) contends that if the rationale for ethical leadership were nothing more than a concern with competitive advantage, then the case for it would itself be unethical.

Business ethics can at one level be perceived merely in terms of individual behaviour. Some of the most frequently mentioned examples of actions which managers in the West generally regard as dubious – or worse – include:

- giving gifts or gratuities to buyers in the hope of influencing them;
- receiving gifts or gratuities from customers;
- misrepresentation of product features to customers and clients;
- misrepresentation of personal qualifications to employers and clients;
- putting one's own name to a report someone else has written;
- dismissing someone without a full, impartial investigation;
- giving rewards to certain individuals and withholding rewards from; others for reasons unconnected with performance;
- victimisation;
- nepotism.

Factors encouraging unethical behaviour include:

- the presence of a 'blame culture': where staff perceive that making criticisms will be perceived as a 'career limiting move', they may be tempted to keep their heads down and allow unethical practices to persist;
- the presence of a close-knit culture based on loyalty, custom and practice, where individuals are implicitly expected to collude with ongoing practices;
- pressures associated with performance management, especially where job reductions and other cost-cutting initiatives dominate the agenda.

But the scale of concern has extended beyond these areas and has broader global connotations. Should organisations import goods from countries which seem weak on civil rights or where workers are being exploited? What about multinational corporations transferring production to emerging economies just because labour there is cheap? What about global corporations closing down factories in emerging economies because the governments of such countries remove tariff barriers, thus making it more attractive to import from plants elsewhere?

Johns (1995) develops the notion of corporate 'ethical values', which he considers embrace an organisation's ethically inspired vision, its core values and its operational code of conduct. If these expressed ethical values are vague, or appear to be in conflict with the perceived behaviour of senior personnel then any attempt to spell them out will be unproductive. He takes the position that the articulation of such 'ethical values' is something new, a precursor to a behavioural change within the organisation, and that there is an intention to do something differently from how it was done before:

> As with any other change, developing and implementing ethical values has to be managed. Publishing some high-sounding statements and an associated code of conduct without doing anything else usually means that, after a short period of uncertainty, things will carry on as before.

He goes on to provide the following ten-point action plan for embedding a new ethical orientation in an organisation. This he bases on a conventional change framework for managing the transition, that is, for moving the organisation from where it currently is, to a desired future state.

1 *Establish a sound and preferably positive foundation for change.* The driving force for the articulation of ethical values has to come from somewhere. It could be a new chief executive officer (CEO) or it could be stimulated by adverse publicity resulting from a commercial mistake or fraud.

2 *Solicit employee input and involvement in developing ethical values.* Evidence from companies such as Phillips Petroleum, Philips Electronics and SmithKline Beecham shows that design and 'roll-out' for corporate values and associated leadership practices can take many months of discussion, revision and updating.

3 *Allow time for adjustment to the ethical values.* People may need time to disengage from the traditional way of doing things and be convinced that top management is serious.

4 *Make one person accountable for driving the ethical leadership programme.* This may be the CEO or someone who has direct access to the CEO. Conventionally, ethical leadership implementation may fit the profile of the HR Director, but much depends on whether HR is perceived as a key strategic contributor. The credibility attached to the whole exercise is greater if high-level ownership is accepted by some senior figure in a direct line role – especially in organisations where HR has been marginalised.

5 *Conduct 'market research' during the launch and dissemination phases.* Managers responsible for embedding ethical values across the organisation need feedback about the effectiveness of the programme.

6 *Involve corporate members in the implementation process.* The initiative can be enhanced by the allegiance and public support of politically powerful groups and credible individuals in the organisation. The incorporation of symbols, stories and company-specific language into the presentation of ethical values enables them to be woven into the organisation's operating fabric more easily.

7 *Define appropriate reward and sanction systems.* As with any initiative, for ethical leadership to be effective, people need to be rewarded for operating within its guidelines and punished for non-compliance.

8 *Establish effective education and training linked to ethical leadership.* A 'top-down' sequence of cascade interventions is preferable, starting with the top management team and then working through the organisation. It is important to use

credible trainers and realistic realistic, relevant material. Case studies focusing largely on the ethical dilemmas confronted by top management when making strategic choices, or relying on notorious cases, should be avoided, since the likelihood is that key staff handling day-to-day operational issues will not relate to these.

9 *Remove the need for whistle-blowing.* Concerns by individuals about others' non-compliance with the stated ethical values should be effectively dealt with through laid-down communication channels. Whistle-blowing is usually evidence of the failure of ethical leadership to supply communication channels that enable employees to voice their concerns without being victimised, and to take such concerns seriously when they are expressed. There is a history of many organisations regarding whistle-blowers as disloyal villains. Soeken (1987) found that of 233 whistle-blowers in his study, 84 per cent had been fired as a result of their actions.

10 *Create systems to measure the effectiveness and progress of the ethical leadership programme.* This could be accomplished through the appointment of an ombudsman, and/or a business conduct committee (appropriately chaired). Some organisations have requested written assurances of commitment by employees, others have drawn upon surveys, questionnaires and periodic audits to monitor adherence to ethical prescriptions.

Pickard (1995) suggests that there are three ways in which HR professionals can enhance an awareness of ethical issues:

■ helping to develop and communicate an ethics policy, including holding training sessions to help people think through the issues;

■ contributing to the formation of that part of organisational strategy that touches on mission and core values;

■ setting an example to others through one's own conduct in areas such as fairness, equal treatment and confidentiality.

Pickard was thinking in terms of employees within an organisation. The ethical dimensions might, however, need to be transmitted to a range of external stakeholders. Strategies would have to be considered for the following:

1 *Non-employee training.* This would focus on groups such as suppliers, distributors and external contractors who might be invited to attend in-house training-related activities. Issues to be considered include: What standards of behaviour does the organisation expect of them, in terms of policies and practices if it is going to do business with them? What is acceptable? What is not?

2 *Non-employee education.* Interventions could extend to offering advice and information to representatives of other organisations through networking or as part of a benchmarking exercise. Mechanisms could also include disseminating information to the wider community through school visits, and to members of the public during site visits.

MANAGING DIVERSITY

The equal opportunity background

The equal opportunity background is examined in Fig. 21.11.

| Figure 21.11 | Equal opportunity legislative background |

The USA

Much of the original legislative concern for equal opportunity and equal rights issues in the USA became embodied in Title VII of the Civil Rights Act 1964. This prohibits discrimination against any individual on the basis of race, colour, religion, sex or national origin in any employment condition (for example hiring or training). In the previous year, 1963, the Equal Pay Act was passed, which requires that men and women who work for the same organisation be paid the same for work that is equal in skill, effort, responsibility and working conditions. There have been a number of subsequent pieces of legislation. For example, under the Pregnancy Discrimination Act 1978 a female employee or job applicant cannot be treated differently from a male because of the female's pregnancy or capacity to become pregnant. The Age Discrimination in Employment Act 1967 protects employees who are 40 years or older from discrimination based on their age. One feature is that in general terms an employer cannot refuse to hire or promote an individual because he or she is 70 or over. The Equal Employment Opportunities Commission has a responsibility for enforcing compliance with these and associated laws.

The UK

The UK anti-discrimination legislation has been strongly influenced by that in the USA, although the groups specifically protected by legislation are not so comprehensive. The key Acts of Parliament include the Equal Pay Act 1970, the Sex Discrimination Act 1975, the Race Relations Act 1976 and the Disability Act 1996.

The Sex Discrimination Act made it unlawful to discriminate either directly or indirectly on the basis of sex or marital status. The Race Relations Act used similar terminology in prohibiting discrimination on the basis of race, colour, ethnic or national origins.

Direct discrimination occurs when a person has been dealt with less favourably than others, and thereby disadvantaged, because of his/her personal circumstances and/or membership of a particular group, where these are not relevant to the job being applied for or undertaken. Unlawful direct discrimination applies specifically to categories/groups covered by legislation such as sex, colour, race, national or ethnic origins.

Indirect discrimination occurs when a condition or requirement is applied which, whether intentionally or not, adversely affects representatives of a particular group considerably more than others, and which cannot be justified. For example, certain types of technical qualifications may be demanded which few women and ethnic minorities may possess and which are *not* necessary for the job.

▶▶

▶▶ Figure 21.11 continued

> Organisations are obliged to meet the requirements of legislation in the countries in which they operate. They can also provide protection for groups and categories not covered by legislation, so long as such protection is not itself unlawful. Such protection is not meaningful if it is not reinforced by associated provisions, including sanctions for non-compliance, in the disciplinary code and in appropriate disciplinary action when breaches occur.
>
> The implications of legislation led to many organisations developing equal opportunities policies and generating supporting training programmes.

Equal opportunities training in the 1980s

In the 1980s in the UK there were a number of training courses, primarily run by local authorities, which were designed to support on the equal opportunity policy statements that were being developed to articulate organisations' value structures. Local authorities were at the forefront of the EO movement because of the felt need that a local authority has a particular responsibility to represent the whole community it serves. On the whole, Labour-controlled authorities were more proactive than their Conservative counterparts. The courses fitted into two broad categories.

Awareness training

Awareness training is specifically concerned with addressing prejudices which surround certain groups in society and which has led to their being overtly or covertly excluded from opportunities available to others or oppressed. Examples from the London Borough of Islington included Heterosexism Awareness Training (known as 'HAT'), Racism Awareness Training ('RAT') and Sexism Awareness Training ('SAT'). The aim of the training is to raise awareness of the nature of the oppression, how it operates in society, how it is perpetuated and how participants themselves collude in its continuation. The philosophy behind it is that if people responsible for the collusion can be made to realise and own their part in the continuation of the oppression, then they will be motivated to change and discontinue the collusion.

Such training programmes were designed to try to change people's attitudes and, often, to tackle prejudices head-on. They frequently became very confrontational, and very stressful for the trainers responsible for delivering them. Activities involved here-and-now experiential elements to bring feelings to the surface; these were often supported by role-play exercises designed to put people into role-reversal situations.

There has been much debate about the relevance and effectiveness of this sort of training. As with all forms of off-the-job training there is the problem of transference, or how to provide follow-up mechanisms, so that once the worker is back in the workplace, learning from the course can be confirmed, and changes in behaviour be sustained. Trainers need to be totally committed to the values associated with the training and can often come from the group held to be oppressed. This in turn can create an emotional and stressful involvement, which requires considerable self-control and interpersonal skills to contain. There is also a risk that trainers from these groups may be stereotyped and marginalised, in the sense that equal opportunities training is seen as their sole preserve and they accordingly do not get involved in other operational areas that affect the organisation.

An American example from the early 1980s is provided by the Digital Equipment Corporation, which developed a five-step approach to educating employees to value work-force diversity and in so doing to revisit and revise inappropriate attitudes.

- *Step one*. Get people to look directly at their stereotypes and have conversations – in some cases confrontations – about whether a particularly held belief about race and gender is a stereotype. The purpose of these conversations was to afford people the opportunity to refine their views.

- *Step two*. Learn how to listen to and flow with the differences in the assumptions of others. Even if one could get rid of every stereotype that one possessed, there will still be different assumptions, values and ways of seeing the world. Learning how to value differences means that even if we absolutely disagree with another's position we will slow down and listen.

- *Step three*. Proactively, deliberately go out of one's way to build authentic and significant relationships with people one regards as different.

- *Step four*. Learn how to deepen or enhance one's sense of empowerment by *talking* about differences, especially talking about the way in which we feel victimised by differences.

- *Step five*. Try to identify and explore the differences amongst groups of people. At Digital this was discouraged until individuals had at least learned what a stereotype was, had at least one white or black or Asian friend, and/or friend of the opposite gender.

The outcome of this approach was that Digital ended up with more minority men and women in the most prestigious operational posts in the company (Barbara Walker, Manager of International Diversity at Digital Equipment Corporation, reported in Garfield, 1992).

Policy and practice training

During the 1980s the emphasis in equal opportunities training in the UK turned from changing attitudes to changing behaviour. The implicit argument is that 'the organisation' is not interested in your real position on a topic; what it needs to ensure is that you behave in a way which is congruent with policy guidelines. Nevertheless, this is a fall-back position. It is difficult to conduct a training programme on such matters as equal opportunities recruitment and selection without having a value predisposition towards fairness of treatment.

In practice, training courses were introduced to help employees develop their understanding of equal opportunity policy and what action they needed to undertake to contribute to its effective operation. Courses had to be introduced where the organisation had already made a specific commitment to equal opportunities. They usually contain some or all of the following elements:

- checking the assumptions behind the organisation's commitment to equal opportunities to make sure staff are at the same level of understanding;
- an introduction to the legal requirements of equal opportunities in employment and recruitment;
- presenting the contents of a basic statement of intent or policy;
- discussion of the service the organisation provides to its various stakeholders and how this may be improved;
- drawing up of departmental and individual action plans.

This type of training assumes at the very least a basic acceptance of issues and focuses on spelling out and developing appropriate behaviour within the organisation to support policy. Courses of this type usually last two or three days, may include a follow-up day some months later and are often specifically tailored for the organisation. Commitment to the programme is enhanced if training sessions are started off or concluded by remarks from either the Chief Executive Officer or a senior spokesperson. Practical issues relating to the application of the policy should be addressed, and at the end of the programme these can be presented to the organisational representative responsible for overall implementation, for comment and action.

The difference between equal opportunities and managing diversity

A number of writers have differentiated between equal opportunities (EO) and managing diversity (MD). The latter started to become popular in the early 1990s. Ross and Schneider (1992) contend that, unlike EO approaches, an initiative to manage diversity will:

- be internally driven, not externally imposed;
- be focused on individuals, not groups;
- be concerned with diversity, rather than equality;
- address the total culture, not just the systems;
- be the responsibility of all, not just a personnel/HR function.

The core of the argument is that the objective of managing diversity is for its value constructs to become internalised by individuals and embedded in the culture of the organisation; whereas the provision of equal opportunities is an add-on to the individual and organisational value system, not something integrated into it. The distinction has echoes of that between 'personnel' and HRM. The latter is seen as more strategic and integrated into the decision-making processes of the organisation, whereas 'personnel' is more operational.

Some writers have suggested that an EO paradigm perceives difference as a liability which somehow has to be managed, whereas MD sees difference as an asset. This seems a faulty dichotomy. Although it is quite possible that some individuals and management teams pay lip-service to EO issues, the overwhelming experience of EO in the 1980s was that the underlying value judgements of its exponents were 'asset oriented'.

Key tenets of diversity management

Kandola and Fullerton (1994) suggest that definitions of MD share the following key tenets:

1 Differences between people and diversity in the round should be seen as a source of real value to the organisation if managed effectively.

2 The scope of MD goes beyond visible and tangible differences associated with gender, ethnicity and disability and encompasses virtually all the ways in which people can differ.

3 Diversity has as its primary concern the creation of an enriched organisational culture and working environment. Rather like a mosaic, the differences create a whole organisation in which each piece is acknowledged and has a positive and valued place.

They use the the word 'mosaic' both as a metaphor to show how individual parts can be fitted together to make a greater whole, and as an acronym to indicate core features of their philosophy:

- *Mission and values*. Entails the presence of a strong positive mission and core values making MD a necessary long-term business objective of the organisation.

- *Objectives and fair processes*. Entails a regular audit of all key people-management processes to ensure objectivity and fairness.

- *Skilled work-force, aware and fair*. Entails having a work-force which is aware of, and guided by principles of diversity.

- *Active flexibility*. Creation of flexible practices in terms of working patterns, and a 'cafeteria' of benefits such as child-care assistance from which employees select those most suitable to their needs.

- *Individual focus*. The potential of all employees should be enhanced.

- *Culture that empowers*. The diversity-oriented organisation must ensure that the organisation culture is consistent with, and complementary to, MD.

Considerations managing diversity in creating a positive organisational climate

It has been a basic theme of this book that effective SHRD depends on the creation of a positive learning climate both at the workplace and on courses. That is not possible for all in the absence of a clearly delineated EO approach to learning. Many of the barriers to learning come from practices that, often unintentionally, preclude access by individuals or groups. For example, weekend or residential management development programmes are more difficult for people with domestic responsibilities to attend. Outdoor management development activities have implications for, among others, people with disabilities and pregnant women.

Barriers to learning resulting from ineffectual diversity management practices

1 *Training level*

- in-house course programmes start/finish hours do not take into account domestic arrangements;
- course materials use gender-specific language (e.g. 'he' all the time);
- examples or role models used in literature and diagrams do not reflect the diverse range of society.

2 *Work-group level*

- work teams engage in behaviour and activities which unintentionally or otherwise are not inclusive of all members and can sometimes actually exclude (e.g. a group norm that everyone should participate in after-hours drinking).

3 *Organisation level*

- people from disadvantaged groups do not feel the need to learn – because of a 'glass ceiling' and because of the absence of career development opportunities;
- organisation policies create blockages, whether intentionally or not to career development (e.g. the existence of mobility clauses).

In terms of their strategic response to managing diversity, organisations can be either proactive or reactive.

Proactive and reactive responses

At one extreme, organisational decision makers can be merely reactive and do no more than ensure they comply with the law. An organisation where this is the case will restrict its protective coverage as expressed in its published statements to only those groups referred to in the legislation. The culture of such an organisation would not encourage open discussion of diversity-related issues. Any HRD interventions would focus on basic training to alert managers and staff of their legal obligations and what to do to avoid falling foul of the law. In such a situation HRD practitioners who wish to be more interventionist can function as no more than covert ambassadors for EO-related issues, seeking to influence through the examples and words they use in their professional practice.

At the other extreme organisations can seek to be proactive and move EO issues 'from the margins to the mainstream' – the slogan for the policy drive at the London Borough of Haringey. In such a situation, significant resources are allocated to issues of diversity, and in the final regard, diversity drives the learning agenda.

Global diversity training

Diversity training has extended beyond national boundaries as corporations have become increasingly global, and individuals are working in very diverse multinational team situations. One interesting approach to handling this has been developed by the USA-based Amoco Corporation (*see* Fig. 21.12).

> ### Figure 21.12 Global diversity training in Amoco Corporation
>
> Amoco Corporation employs more than 40 000 people and operates in 35 countries. It is the seventh-largest privately owned international energy company involved in the exploration and production of oil and gas. It has established a series of 40 Diversity Advisory Councils, known as Dacs, across the globe, working in locations such as Egypt, Trinidad and the UK. It uses a tool known as 'Teamwork – Valuing Individual Differences' (T-Vid) to facilitate diversity training. The approach begins with all members of a team completing an anonymous questionnaire, which is returned to a department in Chicago where results world-wide are monitored. The analysed data are then forwarded to a facilitator, who may be a member of the local HR Department, chosen by the team. The facilitator will then review the results with team members, and help them to develop an action plan to address any issues that might have arisen.
>
> The T-Vid questionnaire asks respondents to agree or disagree, on a sliding scale, with a range of statements. For example:
>
> Generally other people within my work group . . .
>
> ■ encourage others to express opinions that are different from the group norm;
>
> ■ use suggestions given by individuals who are at a lower grade;
>
> ■ value opinions and perspectives from individuals outside of their discipline or job function.
>
> It also seeks opinions on a series of statements focusing on the more traditional aspects of diversity, such as race, sex and religion. The facilitator will encourage an open discussion between team members on specific issues or points of difference emerging from the completed questionnaire returns. The philosophy is that only when contentious issues are aired can tensions in a team be eased and greater harmony achieved (Watson, 1997).

ENVIRONMENTAL MANAGEMENT

The current strategic rhetoric goes beyond talking about competitive advantage. Reference is made to sustainable competitive advantage. The notion of 'sustainability' has two connotations. It can refer to strategic initiatives which are designed to maintain a dominant position in the marketplace for a long time. Increasingly however, it is having 'ecological' connotations referring to strategies that are environmentally friendly. For example the Woolworths note pad I am currently using states: 'This paper is produced from material derived from sustainable forests. For each tree felled at least one more is planted.' Similar statements were not made on previous pads I obtained from the same supplier.

It is this second connotation which is the focus of this section. As initiatives in this regard strengthen, it is important that HRD practitioners are aware of the contribution they can play. This might be at the level of the organisational consultant endeavouring to orchestrate transformational change. It might also be at the level of a training and development or learning unit involved in educating the work-force about the part they can play. Or it might be at the level of the individual manager who has the responsibility of interpreting environmental messages for her or his staff.

Business Charter for Sustainable Development

In 1991 the International Chamber of Commerce based in Paris published a set of 16 'Principles for Environmental Management' as part of a Business Charter for Sustainable Development. Companies were encouraged to endorse the following aims:

1 *Corporate priority*. To recognise environmental management as among the highest corporate priorities and as a key determinant to sustainable development; to establish policies, programmes and practices for conducting operations in an environmentally sound manner.

2 *Integrated management*. To integrate these policies, programmes and practices fully into each business as an essential element of management in all its functions.

3 *Process of Improvement*. To continue to improve corporate policies, programmes and environmental performance, taking into account technical expectations, with legal regulations as a starting-point; and to apply the same environmental criteria internationally.

4 *Employee education*. To educate, train and motivate employees to conduct their activities in an environmentally responsible manner.

5 *Prior assessment*. To assess environmental impacts before starting a new activity or project and before decommissioning a facility or leaving a site.

6 *Products and services*. To develop and provide products and services that have no undue environmental impact and are safe in their intended use, that are efficient in their consumption of energy and natural resources, and that can be recycled, reused, or disposed of safely.

7 *Customer advice*. To advise, and where relevant educate, customers, distributors and the public in the safe use, transportation, storage and disposal of products provided; and to apply similar considerations to the provision of services.

8 *Facilities and operations*. To develop, design and operate facilities and conduct activities taking into consideration the efficient use of energy and raw materials, the sustainable use of renewable resources, the minimisation of adverse environmental impact and waste generation, and the safe and responsible disposal of residual wastes.

9 *Research*. To conduct or support research on the environmental impacts of raw materials, products, processes, emissions and wastes associated with the enterprise and on the means of minimising such adverse impacts.

10 *Precautionary approach*. To modify the manufacture, marketing or use of products or services to the conduct of activities, consistent with scientific and technical understanding, to prevent serious or irreversible environmental degradation.

11 *Contractors and suppliers.* To promote the adoption of these principles by con-tractors acting on behalf of the enterprise, encouraging and, where appropriate, requiring improvements in their practices to make them consis-tent with those of the enterprise; and to encourage the wider adoption of these principles by suppliers.

12 *Emergency preparedness.* To develop and maintain, where appropriate hazards exist, emergency preparedness plans in conjunction with the emergency ser-vices, relevant authorities and the local community, recognising potential cross-boundary impacts.

13 *Transfer of technology.* To contribute to the transfer of environmentally sound technology and management methods throughout the industrial and public sectors.

14 *Contributing to the common effort.* To contribute to the development of public policy and to business, governmental and intergovernmental programmes and educational initiatives that will enhance environmental awareness and protection.

15 *Openness to concerns.* To foster openness and dialogue with employees and the public, anticipating and responding to their concerns about the potential haz-ards and impacts of operations, products, wastes or services, including those of transboundary or global significance.

16 *Compliance and reporting.* To measure environmental performance; to conduct regular environmental audits and assessments of compliance with company requirements and these principles; and periodically to provide appropriate information to the Board of Directors, shareholders, employees, the authorities and the public (International Chamber of Commerce, 1991).

To what extent is the educational responsibility being translated into HRD thinking? The following are some examples of organisational practice.

Volkswagen

VW has instigated a company-wide environmental protection training pro-gramme, as part of an attempt to develop the attitudes which VW recognises as a crucial component of efficient environmental protection. According to Welford (1994) VW views its training programme as a more efficient strategy for environ-mental protection than the application of new technologies.

The VW learning strategy goes beyond the provision of training courses for staff. For example it has established a framework for the assessment of the environmen-tal performance of its dealers in Germany through the VW Audi Environmental Consultancy Service.

British Telecom

BT formally recognises in its environmental policy the importance of staff train-ing if environmental awareness is going to be raised and environmental programmes are going to be effectively implemented. It completed a full review of its environmental training requirements by 1993. It developed a special course on broad environmental strategies for key personnel from each of the functional units, and other courses which address specific issues such as waste disposal and energy management. Its intention to focus on environmental performance as a quality issue has led to the incorporation of training programmes associated with environmental issues in the company's TQM training programme entitled 'Involving Everyone', attendance on which is mandatory for all non-managerial staff. Learning is cemented through articles in the company's internal newspaper, and campaigns aimed at specific issues such as waste disposal and energy conservation.

IBM

IBM UK conducted a comprehensive internal review of its environmental activities, the results of which, together with a list of future objectives and targets, were published in 1992 in a document entitled 'Environmental Programmes for the 90s'. Staff consulted as part of the review felt that training in this area was still insufficient, particularly with regard to the middle management who were responsible for implementation of environmental strategies. IBM at the time considered that the numbers and grades of staff which the company enrolled on its environmental training programmes would serve both as an indicator of the further commitment of the company to environmental improvement, and as a conduit for translating corporate environmental policies into realisable benefits.

Monsanto

Monsanto, a global chemical company based in St Louis, Missouri (and much in the news in recent years over its involvement in genetically modified crops), has, in an attempt to move 'beyond greening', created seven sustainability teams. These include a *global hunger team* which is studying how Monsanto might develop and deliver technologies to alleviate world hunger. The final team is called the *communications and education team* whose specific contribution is to develop the training that gives Monsanto's employees a common perspective. Its features include providing a framework for understanding what sustainablity means, how employees can play a role, and how they can transmit this knowledge to key audiences outside the company (Magretta, 1997).

Gaining support for environmental policies

The recommended process for gaining support in an organisation for environmental policies is remarkably similar to that for other issues which one wishes to support:

■ instil environmental values of *reducing*, *reusing* and *recycling* throughout the organisation;

■ build support from top management;

■ engage in corporate sponsorships of environmental causes;

- appoint environmental advocates to executive boards;

- establish visible executive positions responsible for corporate ecology;

- dramatise external threats, detrimental legislation, litigation or hostile media attention;

- implement corporation-wide environmental education programmes;

- encourage voluntary 'green teams' of employees to identify ecological problems in corporate operations and to make recommendations;

- reward successful cost-saving ecological ideas and programmes;

- conduct internal environmental audits;

- issue environmental policy statements (Hartman and Stafford, 1997).

Learning alliances with environmental pressure groups

Hartman and Stafford (1997) draw attention to the emergence of alliances of environmentally conscious organisations with environmental pressure groups. For example Body Shop International have forged an alliance with Friends of the Earth; McDonald's are associated with the Environmental Defence Fund (EDF) with the specific aim of improving ecological soundness of operations to enhance environmental image and lower costs. They see it as part of a process called 'Market-Based Environmentalism'. It involves environmental groups specifically seeking to help businesses solve ecological problems and become environmentally responsible. The objective is to 'create market incentives that make ecology strategically attractive to businesses' (ibid.) It recognises that most organisations do not possess the expertise or, indeed, public trust, to adequately invest in responding to environmental issues. It also takes the position that environmentally responsible solutions can be found which add to the commercial competitiveness of a given organisation. McDonald's, for example, has implemented over 90 environmental initiatives as a result of its partnership with EDF. Outcomes include waste reduction, the use of fixtures and furniture made in part from recycled materials and lower disposal, packaging and building costs.

The alliances can take a number of forms. On the one hand, a firm can contribute to the environmental group through various forms of corporate sponsorship. In turn, the environmental group can endorse a firm's products as being environmentally sound. Task forces can be established which take the form of collaborative partnerships between an environmental group and one or more companies to develop economically feasible solutions for the 'greening' of business practices.

Careful attention needs to be given to the choice of environmental partner and the nature of the resulting relationship. Tensions are always likely to exist where the external partner uses both confrontational public protest style tactics and co-operative tactics to get green messages across. There is also a need for both parties to maintain an arm's length relationship. Environmental groups often include among their roles that of acting as corporate watchdog: they may have difficulties maintaining their public credibility and perceived objectivity if they become too closely attached to particular businesses. It is unlikely, too, that a given corporate organisation can develop an exclusive relationship with a given external group.

'Environmental groups tend to be opportunistic, willing to ally with many businesses to further broad ecological goals' (Hartman and Stafford, op. cit.).

Such alliances have enormous implications for HRD, both in terms of providing developmental opportunities for individuals, and in facilitating new mindsets across culturally disparate organisations. For example, staff from the EDF worked in McDonald's restaurants for a time to get to grips with the operational realities faced by the company. They increase opportunities for secondments across two very diverse organisational types. Learning can arise from association with specific projects.

CONCLUSION

This chapter has presented an analysis which indicates that organisations are becoming more value oriented and expect a range of very specific behaviours from individuals demonstrating 'commitment' to these values. A challenge is posed to HRD practitioners who are seen as front-line 'normative-educators'. The assumption is that they have 'bought into' the values they are being expected to project. A number of interpretive roles have been introduced to reflect how HRD professionals 'play it out' and balance their own personal value orientation against that of the corporation.

The second half of the chapter has looked at three specific areas in which organisations are conscious of particular values and touches upon some of the interventions that might be made from an HRD perspective to translate the intent into practice.

REFERENCES

Alexander, M. (1985) 'Team Effectiveness Critique', *Annual Handbook of Developing Human Resources*. Pfeiffer & Jones.

Allport, G. W., Vernon, P. E. and Lindzey, G. (1970) *Study of Values*. New York: Houghton Mifflin.

Argyris, C. (1964) *Integrating the Individual and the Organisation*. New York: Wiley.

Beer, M. and Spector, B. (1985) 'Corporate transformations in human resource management', in R. E. Walton and P. R. Lawrence (eds) *HRM Trends and Challenges*. Cambridge, MA: Harvard Business School Press.

Blau, P. M. and Scott, W. R. (1966) *Formal Organisations*. London: Routledge & Kegan Paul.

Chin, R. and Benne, K. (1976) 'General strategies for effecting changes in human systems', in W. G. Bennis, K. D. Benne, R. Chin and K. E. Corey (eds) *The Planning of Change*. New York: Holt, Rinehart & Winston.

Cyert, R. and March, J. G. (1963) *A Behavioural Theory of the Firm*. Englewood Cliffs, NJ: Prentice-Hall.

Deal, T. E. and Kennedy, A. (1988) *Corporate Cultures*. Harmondsworth: Penguin.

Fox, A. (1974) *Beyond Contract: Work, Power and Trust Relations*. London: Faber & Faber.

Friedman, M. (1970) 'The social responsibility of business is to increase its profits', *New York Times Magazine*, 13 September.

Galagan, P. A. and Carnevale, E. S. (1994) 'The Coming of Age of Workplace Learning: A Time Line', *Training and Development* (US), May.

Garfield, C. (1992) *Second to None – The Productive Power of Putting People First*. Chicago: Business One Irwin.

Gibson, J. L., Ivancevich, J. M. and Donnelly J. H. (1993) *Organisations – Behaviour, Structure, Processes* (8th edn). Homewood, IL: Irwin.

Guest, D. E. (1989) 'HRM: Implications for industrial relations', in J. Storey (ed.) *New Perspectives on Human Resource Management*. London: Routledge.

Hambrick, D. C. and Mason, P. A. (1984) 'Upper echelons: the organisation as a reflection of its top managers', *Academy of Management Review*, 9, pp. 193–206.

Harrington, H. J. (1987) *The Improvement Process*. McGraw-Hill.

Hartman, C. L. and Stafford, E. R. (1997) 'Green Alliances: Building New Business with Environmental Groups', *Long Range Planning*, 30(2).

Howard, R. (1990) 'Values make the Company: an Interview with Robert Haas', *Harvard Business Review*, September–October.

International Chamber of Commerce (1991) *Prnciples for Environmental Management*. Paris: The Chamber.

Involvement and Participation Association (IPA) (1997) *Towards Industrial Partnership – New Ways of Working in British Companies*. London: IPA.

Johns, T. (1995) 'Don't be afraid of the moral maze', *Personnel Management*, 5 October.

Kandola, R. and Fullerton, J. (1994) *Managing the Mosaic*. London: IPD.

Kanter, R. B. (1978) 'Work in a New America', *Daedalus, Journal of the American Academy of Arts and Sciences*, pp. 47–8.

Katz, D. and Kahn, R. L. (1965) *The Social Psychology of Organisations*. New York: Wiley.

Keep, E. (1989) 'Corporate training strategies', in J. Storey (ed.) *New Perspectives on Human Resource Management*. London: Routledge.

Magretta, J. (1997) 'Growth through Global Sustainability – An Interview with Monsanto's CEO, Robert B. Shapiro', *Harvard Business Review*, January–February.

Manpower Services Commission (1981) *Glossary of Training Terms*. London: HMSO.

Nevill, D. D. and Super, D. E. (1989) *The Values Scale* (2nd edn). Consulting Psychologists Press Inc.

Pascale, R. T. (1991) *Managing on the Edge*. Harmondsworth: Penguin.

Pascale, R. T. and Athos, A. G. (1981) *The Art of Japanese Management*. New York: Simon & Schuster.

Peters T. J. and Waterman, R. H. (1982) *In Search of Excellence: Lessons from America's Best-Run Companies*. New York: Harper & Row.

Pickard, J. (1995) 'Prepare to make a moral judgment', *People Management*, 4 May, pp. 22–5.

Rains, J. (1997) 'The Values of HRD Practitioners'. AHRD Conference Proceedings, Atlanta.

Rokeach, M. (1972) *Beliefs, Attitudes and Values*. San Francisco: Jossey-Bass.

Ross, R. and Schneider, R. (1992) *From Equality to Diversity – A Business Case for Equal Opportunities*. London: Pitman.

Soeken, D. (1987) 'Whistle-blowers face retaliation, dismissal, study shows', *Ethikos*, September–October.

Spoor, J. and Bennett, R. (1984) *Guide to Trainer Effectiveness*. London: Manpower Services Commission.

Spranger, E. (1928) *Types of Men*. Max Niemayer Verlag.

Walton, R. E. (1973) 'Ethical issues in the practice of organisational development', *Harvard Graduate School of Business Administration Working Paper*, No. 1840, May.

Walton, R. E. (1985) 'Towards a strategy of eliciting employee commitment based on policies of mutuality', in R. E. Walton and P. R. Lawrence (eds) *HRM Trends and Challenges*. Cambridge, MA: Harvard Business School Press.

Watson, P. (1997) 'Diversity Challenge', *People Management*, 1, May, pp. 30–2.

Welford, R. (1994) *Cases in Environmental Management and Business Strategy*. London: Pitman.

Welford, R. and Gouldson, A. (1993) *Environmental Management and Business Strategy*. London: Pitman.

AUTHOR INDEX

Abbott, B. 330, 331, 336, 347
Abernathy, W.J. 42
Ackerman, K-F. 132
Acuff, F. 513
Adler, N. 514
Agar, J. 343
Aitken, A. 457
Alexander, M. 288, 298, 536, 578
Allio, R. 495
Allport, F.H. 385
Allport, G.W. 580
American Society for Training and Development 156, 171
Anfield, J. 434
Ansoff, H.I. 255, 479
Ansoff, I. 46
Argenti, J. 15, 34
Argyris, C. 1, 35, 179, 386, 387, 388, 389, 390, 442, 576, 577
Arkin, A. 295
Armstrong, M. 147
Arnold, D.E. 2, 134, 137
Arthur, C. 552
Arthur, M. 230, 325, 326, 331, 334, 337, 338, 339, 341, 347
Asch, D. 16, 17
Ashby, R. 388
Ashton, D. 85
Athos, A.G. 72, 518, 573, 574, 575
Atkinson, J. 280
Atkinson, J.S. 273
Augustine, N.R. 439
Auteri, E. 512, 524

Bailey, S. 341
Balchin, A. 518
Bandler, R. 519
Banfield, J. 183, 186, 188, 193
Bannock, G. 326
Barham, K. 275
Barney, J. 24, 289
Barnlund, D.C. 518
Barrington, H. 205
Bartlett, C.A. 505, 506, 507
Bartram, D. 115
Bateson, G. 388, 389
Beaumont, P. 137
Beckhard, R. 443, 444, 448, 463
Beer, M. 7, 127, 128, 135, 187, 248, 475, 577
Bell, C. 246, 247
Bell, C.H. 462
Benne, K. 578
Bennett, R. 159, 581
Bennis, W. 190
Bettis, R. 489
Bevan, M. 546
Bevan, S. 183
Billingsley, K. 474
Binney, G. 366
Birdwhistell, R.L. 519
Blackburn, R. 330, 335, 336, 346, 347
Blanchard, K.H. 416
Blau, P.M. 563
Bolman, L.G. 147, 442, 457
Boschetti, C. 168
Boston Consulting Group 239
Bowman, C. 16, 17

Boydell, T. 196, 204, 394, 395, 398, 556
Boyle, S.K. 194, 195
Bradley, P. 199
Bridges, W. 467, 469
Brockbank, W. 316, 317, 318
Broersma, T. 388, 389
Brown, A.J. 115
Brown, L.D. 464
Buchholz, S. 223
Buell, V. 231
Burack, E.H. 457, 458, 461, 470
Burgess, S. 221
Burgoyne, J. 87, 89, 90, 204, 388, 389, 394, 395, 398, 556
Burke, W.W. 169, 170, 439, 441, 463, 474
Burnes, B. 17
Burrows, R. 335
Butler, A. 245

Cabinet Office, Office of Public Service and Science 146, 192
Camp, R.C. 302
Campbell, A. 26, 27
Campbell, G. 430
Carnevale, E.S. 562
Cartwright, S. 490
Catanello, R. 399, 400, 403
Cattell, R.B. 479
Chambers, C. 321
Chang, R. 367
Charan, R. 191, 303

Chesbrough, H.W. 539
Chin, R. 578
Clark, K.B. 42
Cleland, D.I. 33
Clulow, C. 310, 319
Clutterbuck, D. 196
Collard, B.A. 219
Collard, R. 364, 365
Collins, A. 193
Coombs, M.W. 490
Cooper, C.L. 490
Coopers & Lybrand 72, 452, 526
Corporate Leadership Council 289
Corporate University Xchange 418, 428
Costello, M. 162
Cox, C.R. 270, 523
Crosby, P.H. 361, 369
Curran, J. 330, 335, 336, 346, 347
Cyert, R. 562, 563, 573

Daft, R.L. 385, 386
Daily, L. 312
D'Aloja, P. 329, 342
Daly, M. 326
David, F. 33
Davids, K. 332
Davidson, J.H. 250
Dawson, P. 455
Deal, T.E. 147, 442, 457, 566
Department of Health 373
Department of Trade and Industry 309, 327, 335
Despres, C. 312
Dess, G.G. 15, 495
Devanna, M.A. 123, 130, 449, 451
Dibella, A.J. 201, 381, 383, 390, 407
Dixon, N. 386, 399, 400, 403
Dodd, C.H. 518
Dolan, S. 100, 396

Donnelly, J.H. 562, 575
Dore, R. 35
Doving, E. 383
Downs, A. 427
Doz, Y. 495
Drew, S.A. 303, 304, 307, 308, 320, 321
Drewett, T. 295
Drewitt, T. 95
DTI 309, 327, 335
Dumaine, B. 327
Dunlop, J.T. 519
Dunphy, D. 447

Easterby-Smith, M. 185
Edvinsson, L. 119
Edwards, M.A. 310
Eggland, S.A. 251, 255, 256, 257
Eisenstat, R.A. 475
Ekvall, G. 336
El-Namaki 30, 31
Elias, P. 328
Ellis, J. 302, 303, 306, 320, 512
Eurich, N.P. 414

Fahey, L. 36
Fairchild, M.E. 310
Feigenbaum, A.V. 357
Fell, A. 177
Ferdows, K. 532, 533
Finn, W. 92, 345
Fisch, R. 442
Fitz-ens, J. 308, 309, 311, 316
Fogarty, M. 330
Fombrun, C.J. 123, 130
Ford, D.J. 313, 314
Foster, J. 115
Fowler, A. 301, 307
Fox, A. 577
French, W.L. 462
Friedlander, F. 464
Friedman, M. 564
Fullerton, J. 590

Galagan, P.A. 96, 298, 562
Gallagher, J. 367
Garavan, T.N. 84
Garfield, C. 3, 4, 5, 167, 178, 191, 201, 204, 257, 321, 418, 588
Garratt, B. 407, 408
Garvin, D. 375
Geiger–Dumond, A.H. 194, 195
Ghoshal, S. 505, 506, 507
Gibson, G. 225
Gibson, J.L. 562, 575
Giles, E. 371
Giles, W.D. 27
Gilley, J.W. 178, 242, 243, 251, 255, 256, 257
Gilligan, C. 236, 237, 251, 252
Gioia, D. 45, 442
Glanz, E. 312
Golembiewski, R.T. 474
Goold, M. 26, 27
Gorge Group 539, 540
Goss, D.M. 330
Gouldner, A.W. 227
Gouldson, A. 594
Grant, R.M. 174
Graves, R. 419
Gray, C. 326
Greiner, L.E. 339, 340
Grinder, J. 519
Grundy, T. 109
Guest, D.E. 577
Gurran, J. 335

Hailey, J. 524, 525
Hall, D.T. 216
Hall, E.T. 515, 517, 518
Hall, M.R. 518
Hambrick, D.C. 573
Hamel, G. 15, 16, 17, 23, 41, 495
Hamel, K. 24
Hammer, M. 43
Hampden-Turner, C. 517

Hansen, D. 221
Harbison, F. 519
Harland, C. 321
Harrington, H.J. 192, 572
Harris, R.T. 444, 448
Harrison, A. 321
Harrison, M. 463
Harrison, R. 84, 85, 121, 153, 182, 185, 224, 225
Harrison, R.P. 518
Harry, W. 526
Hartley, R. 192
Hartman, C.L. 596, 597
Hawes, D. 279
Hayday, S. 183
Healey, M.J. 328
Hedlund, G. 507, 508
Hendry, C. 126, 129, 135, 137, 143, 199, 230, 325, 326, 331, 334, 337, 338, 339, 341, 347, 498, 528, 529
Hequet, M. 553
Herriot, P. 225
Hersey, P. 416
Hiltrop, J.M. 312
Hinterhuber, H.H. 14
Hirsch, W. 202
Hirsh, W. 222, 223, 484
Hofer, C.W. 28
Holden, L. 522
Hollinshead, G. 129
Holton, E.F. III 310
Honey, P. 114
Hood, G. 274
Howard, R. 567
Hunsaker, P.L. 175, 176, 490
Hutchins, D. 365
Huws, U. 549

IBM/London Business School 310
Idenburg, P.J. 18, 28
Iles, P. 520
Illich, I. 383
Institute of Manpower Studies 273

Institute of Personnel and Development (IPD) 124, 133, 134, 137, 201, 205
Institute of Personnel Management (IPM) 124, 125, 126
International Chamber of Commerce 593, 594
IPD (Institute of Personnel and Development) 124, 133, 134, 137, 201, 205
Irvine, C. 185
Ishikawa, K. 363
Ivancevich, J.M. 562, 575
Ives, W. 168

Jackson, C. 202, 222, 223, 484
Jarillo, J.C. 273
Jarillo, J.S. 537, 538, 539, 542
Jay, A. 298
Jeris, L.S. 383, 400
Johns, T. 583
Johnson, G. 41, 264, 479, 480
Johnston, R. 321
Jolles, R. 244
Jones, A. 230, 325, 326, 331, 334, 337, 338, 339, 341, 347
Jones, G.R. 160, 161
Jones, R.A. 330
Joy-Matthews, J. 183, 186, 188, 193
Juran, J.M. 359-60

Kahn, R.L. 384, 577
Kaku, R. 221, 510
Kandola, R. 590
Kanter, R.B. 598
Kanter, R.M. 113, 267, 268, 270, 420, 481, 488, 493, 498
Kaplan, R.S. 46, 47, 185, 186
Katz, D. 384, 577
Kazanas, H.C. 85, 107, 215, 216, 232, 233, 234, 235, 253, 254

Kazanes, H.C. 143
Kearns, D.T. 302
Keep, E. 568
Keith, J. 94
Kennedy, A. 566
Kennedy, C. 444
Kenney, J. 91, 92, 93, 205
Kerr, C. 519
Kim, D.H. 384
King, W. 413, 427
King, W.R. 33
King, Z. 224, 225
Kitching, J. 330, 335, 336, 346
Kono, T. 461
Kotler, P. 37, 238
Kotter, J. 449, 450, 467
KPMG consultancy group 284
Kram, K.E. 195
Kubler-Ross, E. 450, 490
Kuei, C. 269
Kuhn, T.S. 3
Kumar, N. 489
Kumra, S. 385

Lane, A.D. 325
Langley, A. 29
Langridge, K. 344
Langtry, R. 518
Lank, E. 82, 174, 404, 405, 406
Laughlin, R.C. 441, 442, 443, 454, 455
Lawrence, J. 344
Lawrence, P.R. 127, 128, 135, 187, 248, 482
Leat, M. 129
Lee, C. 212
Legge, K. 123
Leibowitz, Z.B. 195
Leider, R. 223
Letza, S.R. 245
Lewin, K. 444, 453
Lewis, C. 365
Lewis, R.G. 267, 372
Lindley, P.A. 115
Lindzey, G. 580

Lippitt, G. 167, 170, 171
Lippitt, R. 167, 170, 171
Littlefield, D. 546
Lorsch, J.W. 482
Lowe, S. 546
Luckenbach, M. 417
Lyon, U. 1, 519
Lyons, B.R. 341

Mabey, C. 97, 121, 144, 145,
    182, 185, 443, 457
Macdonald, M. 239
Macmillan, I. C. 267, 268
MacNulty, W.K. 219
Madu, C. 269
Magretta, J. 595
Main, J. 303, 312
Majaro, S. 336
Maljers, F.A. 527
Mallory, G. 443, 451, 457
Manpower Services
    Commission 561
March, J.G. 562, 563, 573
Marquendt, M. 408
Marshak, R.J. 446, 447
Marsick, V.J. 166, 205, 330,
    331, 398, 399, 400, 403
Martin, M. 419
Martinez, M.N. 416
Mason, P.A. 573
Maternaghan, M. 546
Mayo, A. 82, 113, 114,
    404, 504
McCann, A. 326
McGill, M.E. 320
McGoldrick, J. 79, 144
McIntosh, S.S. 538, 542
McLagan, P. 145, 146, 210
McLagen, P. 169
McLocklin, N. 546
Medcof, J.W. 495
Megginson, D. 183, 186, 188,
    193, 196
Megginson, L. 327
Megginson, W. 327

Meister, J.C. 379, 412, 413,
    418, 427, 428, 429
Merrick, N. 555
Metcalf, H. 330
Miles, R.E. 25
Miller, A. 15, 495
Miller, E.J. 213
Mills, Q.N. 127, 128, 135, 187,
    248
Millward, N. 279
Mintzberg, H. 18, 25, 119,
    154, 155, 483, 484
Mirvis, P.H. 490
Mole, G. 252, 253
Moran, R.T. 512
Morgan, G. 147
Morgan, K.M. 162
Morris, J. 137
Mulrooney, C. 396, 398, 556
Mumford, A. 114, 196
Myers, C. 332
Myers, C.A. 519

Nadler, D.A. 445, 449, 467
Nadler, L. 155, 233, 325
Nagle, T. 248
Nanus, B. 190
Narayanan, V.K. 36
Neale, B. 245
Nevill, D.D. 580
Nevis, E.C. 201
Nevis, E.E. 381, 383, 390, 407
Newmark, D. 221
Next Steps Review 273
Nielson, K. 419
Nixon, S. 115
Nonaka, L. 83
North, J. 330, 335, 336, 346
Norton, D.P. 185, 186
Norton, D.R. 46, 47
NyHan, B. 329, 342

Oates, D. 275
Ohmae, K. 231, 503, 522
O'Neil, J. 399, 400, 403
O'Neill, B. 499

Open Business School 16
Orgland, M. 452
Orsin, A. 419
Ouchi, W.G. 133

Pacelli, L. 221
Parker, K.T. 335
Pascale, R. 485, 486
Pascale, R.T. 4, 39, 472, 518,
    573, 574, 575
Pearn, M. 396, 398, 556
Pearson, D.J. 236, 237, 251,
    252
Peattie, K. 46
Pedler, M. 204, 394, 395, 397,
    398, 556
Pekar, P. Jr 495
Pemberton, C. 225
Perkins, S. 199
Perlmutter, H.V. 510
Peters, T. 356
Peters, T.J. 565
Pettigrew, A. 230, 325, 326,
    331, 334, 337, 338, 339,
    341, 347, 531
Pettigrew, A.M. 160, 161
Petts, N. 289, 290
Phillips, K. 161
Pickard, J. 430, 583, 585
Pinchot, G. III 178
Pinder, R. 225
Polanyi, M. 332
Polsky, D. 221
Popp, W. 14
Porter, M. 266, 281, 484, 487,
    489, 490
Porter, M.E. 20, 38, 39, 114
Poulteney, J. 294
Prahalad, C.K. 15, 16, 17, 23,
    24, 41, 489, 495
Prete, M. 168
Price Waterhouse Change
    Integration Team 453
Proctor, J.D. 382
Prothero, J. 383, 406

Quinn, J.B. 18, 445, 458

Rains, J. 459, 567, 579, 580, 581
Ranson, S. 17
Reason, P.W. 160, 161
Redmann, D.H. 310
Rees, H. 221
Reich, R.B. 211, 504, 509, 523
Reid, M.A. 91, 92, 93, 205
Reynolds, A. 408
Rhinesmith, S.H. 275, 504, 511, 513, 519, 520, 522, 527
Rice, A.K. 213
Riesenberger, J. 512
Robb, F.F. 442
Robinson, D.G. 168
Robinson, J.C. 168
Roderick, C. 396, 398, 556
Rokeach, M. 567
Ronen, S. 520, 521
Rooney, J. 365
Rosenbaum, R.E. 213
Ross, R. 589
Rothwell, W. 215, 216, 232, 233, 234, 235, 245, 253, 254, 262, 263, 274, 275
Rothwell, W.J. 85, 107, 143
Rowden, R. 332, 339, 347
Ryan, J. 225

Sadler, T. 135
Salaman, G. 97, 121, 182, 185
Salamon, G. 451
Sambrook, S. 141, 147
Saratoga (Europe) 315
Sashkin, M. 474
Sattelberger, T. 530
Saunders, I. 457
Scanlon, P.R. 495
Schank, R. 387
Schein, E.H. 173, 212, 444
Schendel, D. 28
Schlender, B.R. 531

Schlossberg, N.K. 195
Schneider, R. 589
Scholes, J. 264, 479, 480
Scholes, K. 41
Schon, D. 35, 179, 386, 387, 388, 389, 390, 442
Schuler, R.S. 267, 268
Scott, C. 327
Scott, W.R. 563
Sear, L. 343
Senge, P. 31, 32, 390, 391, 392, 393, 395, 398
Senge, P.M. 175
Serritella, V. 424
Shaw, P. 161
Shetty, Y.K. 303
Singh, R. 137
Sisson, K. 114
Slack, N. 321
Slocum, J.W. 320
Sloman, M. 161, 178, 179
Smart, D. 279
Smith, D. 221, 225, 367
Smith, D.H. 267, 372
Smith, K.K. 442
Smith, P.A. 105
Smith Payton, E. 94
Snow, C.C. 25
Soeken 585
Spates, T.G. 414
Spector, B. 7, 127, 128, 135, 187, 248, 475, 577
Spendolini, M.J. 305
Spoor, J. 159, 581
Spranger, E. 567
Stace, D. 447
Stacey, R.D. 21, 411
Stafford, E.R. 596, 597
Stahl, T. 329, 342
State of Illinois 245
Steeples, Marion, M. 268
Steinburg, C. 177
Stevens, M. 279
Stevenson, H.H. 40
Stewart, J. 17, 79, 141, 144, 147

Stewart, T.A. 71, 222, 227, 543, 544, 545
Storey, D.L. 324, 326, 328
Storey, J. 135, 287, 311, 319, 357, 366, 401
Super, D.E. 580
Swanson, R.A. 2, 134, 137

Takeuchi, H. 83
Talwar, R. 44
Tame, J. 218
Taylor, S. 111, 112
Teese, D.J. 539
Tesio, V. 512, 524
Thatcher, M. 555
Therrien, L. 419
Thomson, R. 144, 145
Tichy, N.M. 123, 130, 191, 303, 449, 451, 529, 530
Torrey, B. 168
Trompenaars, F. 517
Trueblood, L. 327
Tunis, C.J. 96
Tuppen, C. 267
Tyson, S. 54, 123, 125, 132, 133, 140, 141, 142, 143, 177

Ulrich, D. 7, 316, 317, 318, 475
Ungson, G.R. 386
Unipart (UGC) 265, 321, 429–30

Vaill, P. 399
Vargass, M.F. 518
Verey, P. 489
Vernon, P.E. 580
Vickerstaff, S. 335
Von Krogh, G. 452

Wade, P. 417
Walker, J.W. 101, 129, 132, 138, 214, 215, 217, 223, 285

Walker, R. 184, 369

Walling, A. 330

Walsh, J.P. 386

Walton, J. 233, 300

Walton, R.E. 127, 128, 135, 156, 187, 248, 577, 580, 581

Ward, J.L. 338

Waterman, J.A. 219

Waterman, R.H. 3, 80, 219, 565

Waters, J.A. 18

Watkins, K.E. 166, 205, 330, 331, 398, 399, 400, 403

Watson, P. 592

Watzlawick, P. 442

Weakland, J.H. 442

Weick, K.E. 385, 386

Weiss, J.W. 451, 514, 515, 537, 539, 544

Welch, J. 2, 169, 296

Welford, R. 594

Wellins, R.S. 118

Whipp, R. 531

Wickens, P. 15, 113, 372, 509

Wiggenhorn, W. 246, 288, 421, 422, 423, 424, 425

Wille, E. 524

Williams, D. 302, 303, 306, 320, 512

Williamson, O.E. 133

Willis, V.J. 144

Wilson, Richard M.S. 236, 237, 251, 252

Wilson, S. 547, 548

Wood, S. 205

Woods, A. 335, 347

Yeager, S. 474

Yeung, A. 316, 317, 318

Young, D. 288, 298, 447, 448, 455, 456

Zairi, M. 305

Zemke, R. 85, 197, 230, 356

GENERAL INDEX

Note: The index does not cover preliminaries, introductions, conclusions, or figures

accidental learning 60, 331, 332
acculturation 333, 526, 564
acquisitions 488–91, 493–4, 499–501
administrators 155, 156, 157
advertising 139–40, 244–8
advisor 196
advisory committees 245–6
advocacy 196, 201
agreements, formal 194, 515
alliances 495–6, 500, 596–7
alumni associations 434
America *see* USA
analysers 25–6
analysis
  see also diagnostics
  career path 215–16
  cash flow 239
  competitor 304
  customer 236–7
  industry 38
  portfolio 239–41
  qualitative 310, 315
  quality 304
  quantitative 315, 333
  stakeholder 40, 263–5
  strategic model 28–30
  value chain 281–2
Andersen Consulting 73, 168, 298, 527, 548
Anglian Water Ltd 430–2
annual report 418
anthropomorphism 385, 387, 389

appraisal 36–40, 198–201
apprenticeship 60–1, 63, 414
assessment *see* appraisal
asset controller 174
asset value of people 135, 137
assimilation 491–4
Australia 447, 554
autonomy 487, 542
awareness 3, 515, 519, 585
  training 582, 587–8
AXA Insurance Group 197, 486, 575

back-office support units 484
backward vertical integration 22, 266, 282
balanced score card 46, 185
barriers to entry 289
benchmarking 40, 165, 303–4
  see also competitive advantage
  aspects of 305–7
  code of practice 310
  frameworks 317
  of human resource development 312–20
  origins 304–5
  process 308–12
best in class 304, 321, 322, 374
best practice 40, 114, 142
  benchmarking 306, 309, 311
Blake-Mouton managerial grid 54–5
body language 519

Body Shop 52, 166, 555, 573, 596
  environmental values 579
Boston Matrix 239–41
boundaries 540, 541
BP 202, 222, 528–9, 546, 548
  training 555
British Airways 368, 444, 499, 575
British Rail 147, 366, 370–1
British Telecom 47, 267, 414, 470, 594–5
  outsourcing example 291–2
  quality 363, 368
brokers 196, 538
bureaucracy 64, 212
Burgoyne typology on management development 87–9
business ethics 3, 581, 582–5
business excellence model 378
business process reengineering 3
business strategy 67–8
business units 427, 484–5, 487
buy-value management style 565

call centres 523–4
Canada 420
career anchors 212–13
career development 64, 71–2, 202, 211–27, 234
  and employee development 225

career enhancement 201
career paths 2, 214, 227, 330, 407
  analysis 215–16
  for knowledge workers 225–7
  tournament notion of 213
  traditional notion of 213–16
career plateau 223
career resiliency 219–20
career workshops 222
caretaker 159
cascade method of change 457
cash cows 240–1
cash flow analysis 239
catalysts 156, 581
cavaliers 27
cellular telephones 543
centralised hub 506
change 192, 440–1, 452–3, 529
  demographic 138
  diagnostic models 440, 457–74
  dynamics of 449–52
  evaluating 474–5
  incremental 445–6
  and leverage 455–7
  metaphors for 446–7
  terminology 447–9
  transformational 441–3, 448–9, 453–4, 457–74
  transitional 443–5
  triggers for 454–5
change agent 175–7
change facilitator 177
change role manager 207
China 515
co-learner 175
co-operatives 337, 338
co-ordinated federation 506
coaching 196–7, 582
code of practice, benchmarking 310
commercial success 562

commitment 127, 568–72, 576–9
communication 195, 456, 527, 540, 541
  cross-cultural 514
  as mentor role 195
  non-verbal 518–19
  telecommunication 543
competence 24–5, 116, 129, 289–90, 499
  identifying 540
competitive advantage 20, 73, 539, 592
  see also benchmarking
competitive benchmarking 306, 309
competitive environment 37–8
competitiveness 327
competitor analysis 304
component technologies 391
compulsory competitive tendering 272, 281
concentric diversification 22, 489
conglomerate 22, 489
congruence 129, 576
conscientious objector 156, 580
construction firms 336
consultancy/consultants 155, 156, 169–74, 249, 337
  external 273, 295
  internal 72, 167–8
  trainers as 168–9
consumer behaviour 489
contingency 130–4
continuing professional development (CPD) 205–6
continuous improvement 367
continuous learning 330, 398, 399, 434
contract managers 166–7, 293
contracts, written 194, 287–8, 515

control 26–7, 29, 174, 267–8, 270
  control models 267
core activities 280–1, 288
core competence 24–5, 116, 289–90
core values 34–5, 564–5, 567
Corning 206, 284, 289, 292–3
corporate culture 519, 527–31
corporate ethical values 583–5
corporate restructuring 22
corporate strategy 22, 67
corporate turnaround 22
corporate universities 3, 116, 246, 414–16, 427–8
  curriculum 417, 421, 422, 423–4, 425
  degree programmes 428
  facilitator at 167
  first-generation 417–21
  second-generation 421–5
  and senior managers 197
  step diagram model 434, 435
  in UK 429–34
  vision and mission statements 425–6
corporate vision 30–2
costs 22, 129, 232, 288, 289
counselling 156, 195
course-based corporate universities 427–8
courses see corporate universities; learning; training
CPD (continuing professional development) 205–6
craft workers 63, 156, 581
Cranfield study on HR practices 142–3
creative swiping 303
creativity 336–7, 339
crisis 447, 448–9, 458
critical behaviour interviewing 540

Crosby, Philip 361–3
cross careering 225
cross-culture 275, 514–19
culture 397, 491, 514–19, 566, 575
  corporate 519, 527–31
curriculum, corporate
    universities 417, 421, 422, 423–4, 425
customers 102, 103, 231–2, 269–70, 484
  customer analysis 236–7
  customer needs 232, 254, 257
  customer satisfaction 367
  single customers 341–2, 345
customised marketing 255

data 305, 310
decentralisation 484, 486, 506, 514
decision makers 562
defenders 25
demand 328–9, 339
Deming, Dr W. Edwards 357–9
demographic change 138
Department of Health 373–4
deutero-learning 389, 390
development centres 222
development, individual 58, 143, 198–9, 234
development and training see training
diagnostics 440, 457–74, 495–6
  see also analysis
didactic-information training 520–1
differentiation 58, 286, 482, 483
Digital Equipment
  Corporation 268, 545, 548, 588
direct democracy 338
direction and control 29

distance learning 428, 554
distancing strategies 281
distributors 268–9
diversification 22, 256–7, 487, 488–94
diversity 581, 586–92
divestment strategy 22
divisionalised structure 483, 484
dogs 240, 241
domestic versus international human resource development 513–14
double-loop learning 388–9, 390, 442
downsizing 2, 216, 217, 221, 387
drop-in centres 515, 516, 554, 555
dynamic networks 537

e-mail 524, 543
ecology 3, 39, 562, 592
education and training 58, 69, 75–6, 263, 426–9
educator 159
elasticity 248–9
electronic technology 543–9
embedded outsourcing 287–8
emergent strategy 18
emotional significance 577
employee development 143, 225, 234, 263, 514
  own learning 201, 202, 217
  targeted development 214–15
employees 189, 212, 274, 490–1, 577
employment legislation 500
employment market 272
employment, security of 570
empowerment 577
enabling structures 391
energy flow model 395, 397
English Nature 98–9, 395

enhanced learning 397
enterprise strategy 22–3
entrepreneurs 156, 338, 581
environment management 592–7
environmental appraisal 36–9
environmentalism 581
equal opportunities 562, 586–9
ethics, business 3, 581, 582–5
ethnocentric management 510
European Quality Award 375–8
European Vocational Education and Training (EVET) 76
evaluation 46–8, 474–5
evaluator 156
evangelist 159
EVET (European Vocational Education and Training) 76
expatriates 520, 524–6
external consultants 273, 295
external contractors 299
external grand strategy 20, 21–2
external groups 263
external market 235–6
external mentors 344
external networks 546–7
external providers 342
external stakeholders 264, 274
external values 567–8

facilitators 167
family ownership 338, 506
Feigenbaum, A.V. 357
financial-control organisations 26
first-generation corporate universities 417–21
first-order change 442–3
fit or split learning 542–3, 555

flexibility 271, 280–1, 545, 547–9
Ford Motor Company 2, 271, 311, 358, 546
  mass marketing 252
  mission statement 33–4
forecasting 37
formal agreements 194, 515
formal benchmarking 307
formal planning model 107–8, 109
formal training 328–30
forward vertical integration 22, 266, 267, 282, 283
frames of reference 147–8
frameworks, learning 390–401, 406–7
France 76, 428
friendly acquisition 488
functional flexibility 281
functional roles 72, 154–5, 156–9, 165, 166–74
functional strategies 23–4

general benchmarking 307, 308, 316
general managers 127, 128
Germany 76, 344, 428, 516
glass ceiling 2
global benchmarking 320–2
global companies 116, 303, 591–2
  defined 505–10
  management in 510–11, 513, 533
  staff 524–6
global language training 522–4
global marketplace 303
global mindset 511–12, 520
goals 310–11, 578
grand strategy 19–22, 42
Greece 515
group facilitator 156, 157
group therapy strategy 29

growth 239, 335, 339
guiding principles 35–6, 544–5

haptics 518
hard contracting 132–3
Harvard model 133–4, 135, 187
heterarchy 507–8, 509
hierarchy 508–9, 539
high training 330
high-context culture 515–16
high-tech training 294–6
horizontal diversification 487
horizontal integration 489
horizontal strategy 23, 114, 487–8
hostile acquisition 488, 493
HRD (human resource development) see human resource development
HRM (human resource management) see human resource management
human capital 58, 59, 135, 137
human resource development 1, 2, 6–8, 56–74
  and benchmarking 312–20
  definitions 1, 52–6, 58, 60
  and human resource management 141–7, 499–501
  as leverage 456–7
  marketing strategies 252–3
  scope 74–8
  and small and medium-sized enterprises 342–7
  target markets 512–14
  terminology 56, 57, 143
human resource development roles 155–64, 576
  practitioner 407–8, 540–3, 578, 579–81, 585
human resource development strategies 87–9, 113–14, 496–501, 519–33

human resource management 122–3, 126–35, 137–9
  definitions 122–3, 132
  and human resource development 141–7, 499–501
  and personnel management 124–6, 135, 138–41
human resource wheel 70, 71, 144–6

IBM 269, 270, 495, 545, 574
  call centres 523
  environmental programme 595
  management colleges 414
  outsourcing 289, 290–1
  quality 371–2
  slogans 366
ICL 73, 174, 404–6
IiP (Investors in People) 100–1, 200, 346–7
in-house training 197, 331
incrementalisation 18–19, 445–6
individual development 58, 143, 198–9, 234
individual development counsellor 156
individual dynamics 449–52
individual values 567
individualism 1, 520–2, 580
induction programmes, virtual 551–2
Industrial Revolution 547
Industrial Training Act (1964) 65
industry analysis 38
informal benchmarking 307
informal training 330–2
information 3, 29, 520–1
innovation 22, 336–7
innovator 159
insourcing 282–4, 286–8, 297
inspired learners 397

Institute of Personnel and Development (IPD) 124, 133–4, 137, 201, 205

Institute of Personnel Management (IPM) 124, 125, 126

instructional writer 156

instructor 156

intasking 286, 287

integrated package learning model 116–17

integration 482, 483, 489, 491
see also vertical integration

intellectual capital 72–3, 211, 434

intentional learning 60

interactive training 552

internal appraisal 39–40

internal consultant 72, 167–8

internal grand strategy 20, 22, 42

internal networks 537, 539, 546–7

internal stakeholders 264

internal values 567–8, 570

international benchmarking 321

international organisational models 506–8

international training function 514

international versus domestic human resource development 513–14

Internet 428, 543, 546

interpenetration, organisational 345–6

interpretive roles 154–5, 156, 165, 175–9

intervention 59–60, 512–14, 520–33, 582

interviews, critical behaviour 540

intranet 546, 547, 555

intrapreneur 178

INVEST model 396–8

Investors in People (IiP) 100–1, 200, 346–7

IPD (Institute of Personnel and Development) 124, 133–4, 137, 201, 205

IPM (Institute of Personnel Management) 124, 125, 126

Italy 221

Japan 321, 415, 507, 515, 573
quality management 357, 358, 359, 363

job advertisements 139–40

job market 233–4

job tenure 221

jobs for life 221–2

joint ventures 22, 337, 495

Juran, Joseph 359–60

Kaizen 274, 364

'Kansei engineering' 304

kinesics 519

knowledge creation 434

knowledge management 72–3, 174, 387, 461

knowledge workers 2, 3, 6, 211, 328
careers 216, 225–7
retaining 276

Korea 515

labour market segregation 74–5

language 515, 518, 519, 522–4

leadership 27–8, 317, 456

learners 232–6

learning 59–60, 390–401, 406–7, 496–8, 527–31
barriers to 590–1
benefits from 68–9
continuous 330, 398, 399, 434
deutero-learning 389, 390

distance 428, 554

double-loop 388–9, 390, 442

fit or split 542–3, 555

integrated package 116–17

lifelong 205, 221

marketing 258

for non-employees 235, 275–6

open 95, 553–4, 555

self-managed 69, 71, 201, 202, 205

and small and medium enterprises 342

team 69–70

terminology 166

through benchmarking 312–13

virtual course 554–5

learning architects 6, 177, 276

learning climate 114–16

learning company 394–6

learning cycles 386

learning and development manager 166

learning needs 235–6, 271–2

learning orchestrator 177–8

learning organisations 3, 116, 166, 401–7, 434
concept of 72
frameworks 390–401

learning philosophy 555

learning resource centres 222

learning specialist 155

learning support 261–78, 294–6, 345

LEONARDO da Vinci training programme 76–7

leverage 443, 447, 455–7

Levi Strauss and Co. 72, 101, 167, 204, 567

life cycle theory 339–41

life planning models 217–19

lifelong job 221–2

lifelong learning 205, 221

lifespan development 217–19

line management 124, 183–4, 192, 282
  roles 184–8, 192–3
line managers 164, 188, 189, 198, 407
  roles 197, 201
lingua franca 522–4
liquidation 22
literacy and numeracy skills 423, 424, 524
logistics 14, 250, 251
looking in/out strategy 104
loss, psychology of 490–1
low training 330
low-context culture 516
loyalty patterns 236–7

macro environment 39
make or buy 282, 565
Malcolm Baldrige National Quality Award 304, 314, 375
management 222, 358, 359, 452–3, 510–11
  skills 332, 489
management breakthrough 359, 360
management competence 499
management development 64, 87–9, 234, 318, 499
managers 207, 338, 511–12, 533, 562
  contract 166–7, 293
  general 127, 128
  of learning and development 166
  managerial grid 54–5
  personnel 335
  roles 129, 154–5, 513
  senior 188, 197, 489
  of training and development 156
manual workers 216, 223–4
manufacturers 296, 336
mapping 107

market driven quality 270
market extension 21, 255
market growth 239
market intervention 512–14
market penetration 21, 255
market segmentation 231–2, 263
market share 239
marketer 156
marketing costs 232
marketing mix 237–8
marketing plan 251, 257
marketing problems 257–8
marketing strategy 251, 252–7
Marks & Spencer 138, 185, 345
mass marketing 252, 253
media specialist 157
mental models 393, 395
mentoring 193–6, 344
mergers 488–92, 499–501
metaphors 385, 446–7
metrics (quantitative) 305, 313–15
mid-career rustout 223
mission, as object of intention 15
mission statement 32–4, 101, 102–3, 206, 571
  of corporate universities 425–6
missionaries 27, 156, 581
monitoring 36
Monsanto, environmental programme 595
morphogenetic change 442
morphostatic change 442
motivational theory 564
Motorola 69, 191, 201, 321
  corporate university 246, 421–5, 426, 430
multi-domestic organisational models 506
multi-skilled operatives 216
multibusiness corporations 487

multidimensional strategies 520–33
multinational organisation 505

national culture 519
National Vocational Education and Training (NVET) 75, 78
National Vocational Qualifications (NVQs) 56, 76, 420
needs analyst 157
Netherlands 76, 342, 428
network organisation 456, 527, 537–9, 540–3, 555
neuro-linguistics 519
Nissan 112–13, 311, 364, 373, 568
non-campus corporate university 427–8
non-core activities 288
non-employees 69, 262–3, 271–2, 274, 275–6
  ethical training 585
  learning needs 235
non-verbal communication 518–19
North American 516
Nuclear Electric 293–4
numerical flexibility 280
nurturing culture 397
NVET (National Vocational Education and Training) 75, 78
NVQs (National Vocational Qualifications) 56, 76, 420

oculesics 518
office environments 545, 547, 548, 549
on-the-job training 330
open learning 95, 553–4, 555
operational benchmarking 307

operational learning 388
operational success 562
organisation 70–1, 143,
    482, 483
  memory 386–7
organisational amnesia 387
organisational change 445,
    450, 451
organisational consultant
    169–74
organisational disabilities 393
organisational dynamics
    449–52
organisational
    interpenetration 345–6
organisational learning 72,
    320, 384–7
  models 387–90
organisational mission 577
organisational models,
    international 506–8
organisational seduction
    575–6
organisational strategic types
    25–8
organisational strategy 16–17
organisational structure 391,
    483, 484
organisational system 28–30,
    58–9, 114, 389, 440–1
organisational values 567, 572
organisations, classifications of
    563–4
out-tasking 284–6, 290–4
outside providers 95
outsourced units 337
outsourcing 95, 271–2,
    282–98, 542
overseas relocation 520–2
own career development 203,
    204, 222
owner managed plc 337
ownership 337–8

PAL (pooling/allying/linking)
    271, 276

paradigm 3–4, 5, 123, 148
paradox, of change 453–4, 474
paralanguage 518
'Partners in development'
    model 189, 190, 192, 193
partnerships 5, 188–90, 201,
    268, 337
  and outsourcing 289
  and shared learning 271
  with universities 531
pay flexibility 281
people management 187, 317,
    318, 551, 579
  people as assets 135, 137
  respect for people 367–8
performance 2, 168–9,
    198–201, 303
peripheral activities 280–1
personal development 199,
    202, 203, 222
personal mastery 393, 395
personal selling 243–4
personnel management
    124–6, 135, 138–41, 142,
    143
  terminology 122
PESTLE (macro environment
    acronym) 39
piecemeal strategies 89–90
place 237, 250–1, 303
planning strategies 18, 26,
    28–30, 107–8, 109
plc (public liability company)
    337
pluralism 578
polycentric management 510
Porter, Michael 19–20
portfolio analysis 239–41
positioning 249
post-industrial era 3
post-merger integration 491
post-merger period 500
power 456, 540, 541, 577
practices and human resource
    development 316–20

pressure groups 596–7
price 237, 248–50
Price Waterhouse 72, 345, 524
primary value chain 272
problem children 240, 241
problem solving 70, 363, 540
process benchmarking 307
process-orientated roles see
    interpretive roles
product 237, 238–43,
    255, 257–8
product costs 232
product development 22, 255
product diversification 22
product life cycle 239, 241–3
product-market strategy 255–7
programme administrator 157
programme designer 157
project management 540, 541
promotion 237, 243–8
prospectors 25
protégé–mentor relationships
    193–5
proxemics 515
psychological response to
    mergers 490–1
public environment 38–9
public relations 29
public sector 17–18
pundits 27

qualitative analysis 310, 315
qualitative data 305
quality analysis 304
quality awards 374–8
quality circles 363–6
quality enhancement 22
quality improvement 361–3
quality management 3, 269,
    357–63, 533
quality vaccine 361–2
quality-orientated training
    422, 425
quality-planning road map
    360

quantitative analysis 315, 333
quantitative data 305, 313–15
questionnaires 333, 406, 457

Rank Xerox 15, 28, 184,
    268, 548
  benchmarking 304, 315
  outsourcing 285
  quality 368–70
  slogans 366
rapport 519
reactors 26
reciprocity 568, 570–1
recruitment 460
redundancy 443
reengineering 42–4
referral agent 196
regiocentric management
    510–11
relatedness 489
remedial education 423, 424
representative democracies 40
resegmenting the market 232
respect for people 367–8
retrenchment 22
reward 2, 456
roles 72, 154–5, 184–8,
    201–6, 576
  mentoring 195–6
  new and emergent 165–6
  practitioner 407–8, 540–3,
    578, 579–81, 585
  role players 164–5
  trainer 159–64
Rolls Royce 201, 222, 434
Rover 201, 202, 203, 204, 269
  learning organisation 402–3
Russian doll divisions 484
rustout, mid-career 223

scanning 36, 386
scientific management 62–3
second-generation corporate
    universities 421–5
second-order change 442–3

secondment 344–5
sectors 335–7, 343–4
seduction, organisational
    575–6
segmentation 231–2, 252–5,
    263
selective benchmarking 307
self-development 204, 205,
    222
self-employed 202, 272, 273
self-esteem 576–7
self-managed learning 69, 71,
    201, 202, 205
self-report questionnaires 186
selling 540, 541
semi-skilled workers 62–3,
    212, 216, 223–4
senior management 70, 188,
    190–2, 489, 572–3
service sector 335, 336, 563
shared objectives 578
shared purpose 578
shared values 574, 575, 578
shared visions 393, 395
SHRPD (strategic human
    resource planning and
    development) 109
silent language 515
single customers 341–2, 345
single-loop learning 388, 442
site visits 310–11, 318–20, 321
skills 156, 540, 549, 581
  literacy and numeracy 423,
    424, 524
  management 332, 489
  multi-skills 216
  semi-skill s 62–3, 212, 216,
    223–4
  tacit 331, 332
  transferable 68
slogans 360, 366
small and medium-sized
    enterprises (SMEs) 326–7,
    342–7, 546
  career paths 330

differentiating between
    333–42
SmithKline Beecham 294, 546,
    568, 584
societal development 74–5
socio-technical systems 59
soft contracting 132–3
sole traders 326
South Africa 75, 428
Spain 515
speaking with facts 367
speed of response 22
split models 132, 486
stable networks 537
staff 165, 201–6, 282, 524–6
  staff charters 570–1
stagnation 485
stakeholders 40–1, 188–9,
    263–5, 274, 562
stars 240, 241
strategic alliances 495–6, 500
strategic benchmarking 307
strategic business units 22–3
strategic capability 25
strategic change 442
strategic context, setting the
    30–6
strategic diversification 22
strategic facilitator 78–9
strategic human resource
    development 85–6,
    113–14, 434
  examples 109–13
strategic human resource
    planning and
    development (SHRPD) 109
strategic learning partnership
    434
strategic networks 268, 537,
    538, 539, 542
strategic partnering 287–8
strategic planning 18, 26,
    28–30, 107–8, 109
strategic sophistication 87–9,
    90

strategic types 25–8
strategic-control organisations 26–7
strategic-planning organisations 26
strategist 157
strategy, definitions 14–17
strategy documents of firms 140–1
strategy evaluation 46–8
strategy formulation 41–4, 500
strategy implementation 44–6
strategy management 17–28, 42, 116, 289–90
    horizontal strategy 23, 114, 487–8
    incrementalisation 18–19, 445–6
strong cultures 566
sub-units 482, 496–501
subcontracting 341, 538
succession planning 214
suppliers 267–8
supply of training 329
support services 343, 344, 484
support value chain 273
supportive management 397
sustainable development 593–4
sustainable organisations 389
Switzerland 489, 516
synergy 482–6, 489, 540
systematic strategic analysis model 28–30
systemic learning 389
systems divergence 114

tacit skills 331, 332
tactics 14
Tanzania 343
target market 253–5, 512–14
targeted development 214–15
task environment 37
task roles 154–5, 157

see also functional roles
teams 69–70, 234–5, 338, 578
    problem solving 540
    virtual 550–1
technical system model 58–9
technical training 294–6
technology 137, 543–9
telecommuting 546, 547, 553
teleconferencing 543
teleworking 546, 547, 549–50
terminology
    of change 447–9
    of human resource development 56, 57, 143
    of learning 166
    market segmentation 233
    of personnel management 122
texts on human resource development 143–4
theoretician 157
therapist 156, 580
time, language of 515
top management see senior management
topic-based benchmarking 308, 316
total quality management (TQM) 3, 269, 357–63
total quality organisational practice examples 368–74
total quality principles 366–8
tournament notion 213
TQM (total quality management) 3, 269, 357–63
trade unions 137, 138, 578
trade-off 232
traditional career paths 213–16
traditional training 141–2, 542
trainers 159–64, 168–9, 206, 243–4
training 58, 97, 166, 330
    see also learning; NVQs

attitudes to 341
awareness 582
decentralised 514
demand and supply 328–9
and education 426–9
in equal opportunities 588–9
external providers 342
formal 328–30
in-house 197, 331
informal 330–2
interactive 552
international 514
language 522–4
life cycle 341
national 75–6
non-employee 585
and outsourcing 294–6
packages 387
strategies 91–101
technical 294–6
traditional 141–2, 542
training cycle 179
versus human resource development 61–2
virtual organisation 542
work-role 60–1
training and development see training
training officer 335
training packages 387
training schools 414–16
training specialists 189
transactional change 443
transfer agent 157
transferable skills 68
transformational change 441–3, 448–9, 453–4, 457–74
transformative learning 389
transforming culture 397
transilience 42
transition 443–5, 540, 541
transnational organisation 76–8, 507, 526, 527–31

triggers for change 454–5
Trustee Savings Bank 110–12, 202

UK 70, 75–6, 221, 343
   corporate universities in 65–6, 73–4, 159–64, 327, 429–34
unemployed, learning needs 235
unions 137, 138, 578
Unipart Group 265, 321, 429–30
unitarism 577–8
United Kingdom *see* UK
universities 345, 428–9
   see also corporate universities
upper echelon perspective 573
USA 65–6, 71, 155–9, 327, 332
   advertising 245
   and alliances 495
   company and supplier links 267–8
   corporate universities 420
   and internal consultancy 72

labour market 221
   quality management 359
   self-managed teams 70
   training 298–9

value chain 39, 265–71, 283, 484, 489
   analysis 281–2
   and non-employee learning 274–5
   and synergy 484, 489
value, and outsourcing 288
values 562–76
   value conditioning 578
   values scale 580
Venezuela 428
vertical integration 265–71, 487, 489, 537–8
   backward 22, 266, 282
   forward 22, 266, 267, 282, 283
virtual courses 554–5
virtual induction 551–2
virtual organisation 3, 537–43
virtual university 428

vision 15, 30–2, 397, 448–9, 579
vision and mission statements 101, 425–6
voicemail 543
Volkswagen 594
voluntary organisations 272, 345
voyeurs 156, 580

Walt Disney company 415–16, 575
whistle-blowing 585
white collar workers 137
win-win relationship 69
wired companies 543, 544
   guidelines 544–5
work environment 545–6
work groups 234–5
work-force 1
world class benchmarking 303, 310
World Wide Web 546, 554